Kate M. Herring
Mrs. J. Henry Highsmith

Collected Writings

edited by
D. Kern Holoman

AU VIEUX LOGIS
Méricourt — Raleigh — Davis
2020

Produced by: EditPros LLC, 423 F Street, Suite 206, Davis, CA 95616
www.editpros.com

ISBN: 978-1-7356907-0-4

AU VIEUX LOGIS
sites.google.com/view/dkholoman

*Dedicated to the memory of
the Misses Herring:*

Vara Louise
Kate Maude
Lucy Cunninggim
Pauline
Pherobe Eugenia
Mary Belle

*... and for the grandchildren of
Kate Herring Highsmith:*

John Lewis Highsmith
Lula Marion Highsmith
Dallas Kern Holoman
Richard Highsmith Holoman
Louise Highsmith Wilkerson
Henry Highsmith Rich
Carol Farthing Wilkerson
Louis Reams Wilkerson, Jr.
Christopher Louis Holoman
Martha Herring Wilkerson
David William Holoman

... and all their issue.

CONTENTS

CHRONOLOGY

Kate Herring Highsmith's Principal Positions

1900–02
Student at Littleton College, Littleton, NC

1904–06
Student at Trinity College, Durham NC

1906–07, 1907–08
Teacher of English, Kinston High School

1908–09 and Fall 1909 (three semesters)
Teacher of English and German, Louisburg College

1911–14
Associate Editor, *The Orphans' Friend*
Oxford Orphan Asylum

June 1914 – December 1917
Director of Publications
North Carolina State Board of Health
Editor, *The Health Bulletin*

1 February 1918 – 1 January 1919
Publicity Director, North Carolina War Savings
Winston-Salem

January 1919
Assistant Secretary, North Carolina State Board of Health

February–December 1919
Publicity Officer and Director of War Savings Societies
War Loan Organization
United States Treasury
Fifth Federal Reserve District, Richmond

January–December 1920
Director of Publicity / Educational Secretary
Maryland Social Hygiene Society, Baltimore

January–May 1921
Director of Publicity
American Social Hygiene Association
New York City

1923–35
Chairman, Press and Publicity
Founding Editor, *North Carolina Clubwoman*
North Carolina Federation of Women's Clubs

1927–29
President, Hugh Morson High School PTA

1929–30, 1931–32, 1933–34, 1934–35
Executive Secretary
Legislative Council of North Carolina Women

1929–35
President, Wake County League of Women Voters

1930–35
Executive Secretary, State Headquarters
North Carolina Federation of Women's Clubs

1932–35
Division Chairman, editorials, state federation magazines
Department of Press and Publicity
General Federation of Women's Clubs

1935–36, 1936–37, 1937–38
Chair of Press and Publicity
General Federation of Women's Clubs

February 1936 – December 1938
Assistant Director of Health Education
North Carolina State Board of Health

1939–41, 1941–43
President, North Carolina State Legislative Council

1941–42, 1942–43
President, Raleigh Woman's Club

1943–44, 1944–45
President, North Carolina Federation of Women's Clubs

1945–50
Founding Chair, Youth Conservation Committee
North Carolina Federation of Women's Clubs

The chronology that introduces each chapter below, based largely on items in the Society pages, is necessarily selective. Not every Tuesday meeting of the Twentieth-Century Book Club, for instance, nor all the regular meetings of the Woman's Club of Raleigh make sense to include. Mrs. Highsmith was said to have attended every single Duke University commencement after her own graduation from Trinity in 1906. She organized the Wake County Duke Alumnae Association, which often met at her home. Doubtless she was present at, often speaking to, many dozens more PTA and church meetings than cited here, and I imagine she tried to be present when Dr. Highsmith gave major orations, which was often. I note social events and vacations, for their insights into her rich social life and into her devotion, in the midst of everything else, to her sisters and her children.

Abbreviations in the Chronology

832 = the Highsmith home at 832 Wake Forest Road, Raleigh

AAUW = American Association of University Women

B&PWC = Business and Professional Women's Club

Edenton Street = Edenton Street Methodist Church, Raleigh

GFWC = General Federation of Women's Clubs, Washington, D. C.

NCFWC = North Carolina Federation of Women's Clubs

RWC = Raleigh Woman's Club

SACW = Southern Association of College Women

WCTU = Woman's Christian Temperance Union

A NOTE ON SOURCES
ACKNOWLEDGMENTS

There are nearly 2,000 matches with "Mrs. J. Henry Highsmith" in the *Raleigh News and Observer* alone, and to search "Kate M. Herring" yields many more. Most of what is here came from searches on newspapers.com and related engines. These searches remind us, incidentally, of what a marvelous thing the great newspapers of old had become in the twentieth century: a dozen or more large-format, eight-column pages every single day, fifty on Sunday—pages of endless fascination, both factual and cultural.

The collection here of just over 250 entries represents only a portion of Mrs. Highsmith's published work. For one thing, it's impossible to establish who wrote what pieces in such publications as *The Health Bulletin* and the *North Carolina Clubwoman*. And any number of unsigned Sunday-paper Woman's Club pieces might well be by her. I hope sometime soon to have the opportunity of finding and consulting other journals in which her work appeared prior to her marriage, notably the Methodist magazines and daily press from Sampson County.

So far as I know, typescripts of her hundreds of public addresses have not been preserved.

The bulk of her work is in the form of typescript press releases, duplicated and provided by mail to the North Carolina press. The three papers in which her Sunday columns reliably appeared are the Raleigh *News and Observer,* the *Charlotte Sunday Observer,* and in some periods the Asheville *Sunday Citizen.* House styles varied widely among these, and I have tried to reconcile their approaches as unobtrusively as possible. I've also corrected obvious typographical errors and a few factual ones.

Other important manuscripts transcribed here include short memoirs by both Mrs. Highsmith (chapter 1914–1917) and her husband (chapter 1921). I have not included the several biographical articles by other writers that appeared during her lifetime, but these are accessible from my website.

This material is, we believe, in the public domain, and Mrs. Highsmith's own claim to copyright has expired. The State Library of North Carolina has determined *The Health Bulletin* to be in the public domain. I am grateful to the North Carolina Federation of Women's Clubs (now GFWC-NC), Jill Dedene, executive director, for authorization to reproduce Kate Herring Highsmith's work in this manner.

The wonderful photograph from the NCFWC Pinehurst convention of 1925, "No Hats," is from *Sallie Southall Cotten's History of the North Carolina Federation of Women's Clubs, 1901–1925* (Raleigh, 1925), and is used by permission. The other photographs are from the family collection, presently in my own custody.

I thank Elizabeth R. Holoman for her usual eagle-eyed reading and proofreading of a manuscript we never imagined would reach 644 pages. The extended family has seen and heard an awful lot over the last months about their grandmother and great-grandmother, and I appreciate their willing ears. My brother David joined us for a pleasing journey through Sampson County by motor (as our Grandmother would have said) during the summer of 2020. The Wilkerson branch weighed in via my first cousin, Martha Wilkerson Roberts.

Production was by EditPros LLC of Davis, that is, two old friends Jeff March and Marti Childs, with whom it was my pleasure to work, years ago, on the *UC Davis Magazine* and related publications. It was good to renew the acquaintance, despite the masks.

Recognizing the difference in concept and appearance between the book and e-book versions of this text, I've endeavored to limit it to the simplest typographical elements. Where warranted, editorial commentary is in-text, before the newspaper or journal citation. Annotations to my Introduction, along with additions as they are found, corrections, amplifications, and hyperlinks to related literature, appear on my website:

sites.google.com/view/dkholoman

— DKH

Kate M. Herring
(center front)

with her sisters
Pauline, Eugenia, Mary Belle, Lucy, Vara
c. 1915

INTRODUCTION
D. Kern Holoman

THE MISSES HERRING

My maternal grandmother, known to her readers as Miss Kate M. Herring and, from 1921, Mrs. J. Henry Highsmith, was one right accomplished lady. She espoused Progressive Era values on front pages, in corridors of power, and polite-lady teas for half a century. The health and welfare of every North Carolinian—farmer, factory worker, waitress, domestic employee, inmate, clubwoman, businessman—were the paramount concerns of her life. After, she insisted, her family.

She was the second of nine children, three brothers and six sisters—"the Misses Herring"—born to Rufus King Herring and his wife Paulina Ann Westbrook Herring on a farm in Sampson County near Newton Grove, North Carolina. It was a lovely tract at Beman's Crossroads on the post route, now US 421: the main north–south axis in the county. Before that the same spot was called Herring, NC, at Herring's Crossroads. Herring Township exists still, there between Dunn and Clinton, past Spivey's Corner. Westbrook Township, named after another branch of the family, is adjacent. Here Rufus Herring, direct descendant of the Colonial planter John Herring, successfully farmed his crops, doubtless employing laborers who remembered slavery as well as members of the Coharie Indian population. The household was largely self-sufficient: the mail and papers arrived on site, and the Hopewell Methodist Church was a few miles north on Church Road, at Vann's Crossroads, perhaps an hour by horse and buggy. Pa and Ma rest in the graveyard there.

Of her long Sampson County lineage, Kate liked to cite Isaiah Warren, Sr., who had lived in the county since 1793 and fought in the American Revolution. Her father, Rufus King Herring, was likely named for William Rufus King, a Sampsonian and 13th vice president of the United States and reputed paramour of President Buchanan.

In 1962, toward the end of her life, Kate fondly recalled Christmases at the Herring house:

> We had a large family: nine children plus ma and pa, ... church people,
> the Sunday School type. ... On Christmas day around 11 or 12 o'clock, our
> Clinton cousins and other kin from over the county would gather at our
> home. We were so excited. We lived in a big house in the midst of a large
> grove of oak trees. We had lovely, warm days then, so we'd play outside.
> Why I can remember picking violets, jonquils and narcissi on Christmas
> day. [She goes on to describe the dinner with turkey, yams, ambrosia, and
> custard], the linen napkins folded and twisted and stuck in the fine, thin
> glasses to help decorate the table.
>
> We knew all the carols and we'd sing and recite Bible verses and poems on
> Christmas Day. It usually fell to me to direct the program. ... It'd be a poor
> Christmas without the gathering of kin and guests coming in and out.

The girls got China dolls, some of which were still in her attic in 1962, and on one occasion she still remembered, a treasured wax doll.

Nine children plus pa and ma. Plus, it turns out, a grandmother: pa's mother, Elizabeth Ann McPhail, Mrs. Joseph Herring, who was born in 1812 and lived to be 102. In one of a series of articles on old age—indicating, I think, that the topic was on her mind, Kate devotes four paragraphs to her grandmother:

> My grandmother, who lived to be one hundred and two years old and had
> remarkable use of all her faculties to the day of her death—she could
> read without glasses, hear well, and remember easily names and faces—
> was frequently asked by what rules she had lived to such a good old age.
> Her usual modest reply was: "Live right, my son." Her life was altogether
> exemplary of this brief but comprehensive bit of advice.
>
> We who lived with her and knew her daily habits and commonsense way of
> meeting life, observed that there were certain practices to which many of
> her happy years could have been attributed. Temperance could be said to
> be her chief virtue. She more than any other person I have ever known was
> temperate in all things—work, rest, play, food and fun. She worked hard, but
> she knew when to rest. She enjoyed a good meal, but she never overate. When
> she was fifty years old, she found she suffered with indigestion if she ate a
> regular evening meal. Forthwith, she decided to eat nothing at night except
> fruit occasionally, a glass of milk or something light, and it was often said
> of her that for fifty-two years she did without supper. She found time for all
> things without hurry and hustle. She never worried excessively, and yet her
> interests were varied and extensive. Young people were her joy and delight.
>
> Furthermore, God was real to her. Religion was vital. She attended services
> at her church regularly, even on the Sunday a week before her death.
>
> Needless to say, that the commonsense practices and wholesome philosophy
> of this centenarian which enabled her to live far more than the usual

allotment of years and meanwhile retain an uncommon use of body and mind—at no time helpless or an invalid, but enjoying life to the end—can be recommended to all who would live long and enjoy life to the end.

The editor added the remark that "Mrs. Highsmith has omitted the most important item in Longevity—Ancestors."

Pa died at home in May 1898 at age 50. The Clinton *Democrat* tells us that he had suffered for years and "for the past several months had declined rapidly in strength." Paulina, sometimes called Lina, was left with the nine children: Vara, Kate, Troy, Joe, Pauline, Eugenia, Lucy, Rufus, and Mary Belle. And, presumably, responsibility for the farm.

At least through June 1904, they kept the family home, as we know from 12-year-old Lucy's letters in the *North Carolina Christian Advocate,* which give "Herring, NC" for a return address.

> My mamma takes your paper, and I like to read the little folks' letters. My papa is dead. I have five sisters and three brothers. I have two sisters at Littleton Female College—one goes to school [Pauline] and the other teaches [Vara]. I have a brother at the A. and M. College [Troy, at NC State] and one sister at Newton Grove teaching [Kate].

(It seems that Lucy's middle name was not, by the way, Cunningham, but rather Cunninggim, after the prominent family of Methodist preachers. Dr. Jesse A. Cunninggim was Presiding Elder of the Methodist churches in the area at the time, and his wife was named Lucy.)

Sometime thereafter, perhaps in 1908, Paulina moved herself and her family the twenty-five or so miles northwest to Dunn, possibly sojourning for a time in Clinton as well. The house in Dunn was on Harnett Street, more or less in the center of the railroad town, and there the sisters maintained their permanent address until moving to Raleigh in 1917.

Her obituary suggests that Paulina moved to town in order for the children to have better access to schools and colleges, but by that time Vara, Kate, and Pauline had graduated from Littleton College and Kate had her BA from Trinity in Durham. Troy was finishing at NC State College, and Eugenia was at Woman's College in Greensboro, now UNCG. But certainly she had long had in mind that all the children would go to college, and they did.

Another prominent Sampson County family, besides the Herrings and the Westbrooks, was the Highsmiths. J. Henry Highsmith, born 1877, was the son of Lewis Whitfield Highsmith of McDaniels Township, also a planter. But that branch of the family is soon centered in Durham, which is where our narrative will next encounter them.

To jump to the end of Ma's story, Paulina Westbrook Herring died in January 1912 after "great and long time" suffering. She was 57. Fulsome notices appeared in the Clinton *News Dispatch* and the Greensboro *Christian*

Advocate. We read that her "spacious and beautiful home [at Herring's Crossroads], which she vacated three years ago," was "one of culture and refinement, and of devotion between mother and children who surrounded her with every comfort and ministered to her every need; a home in which Christ was the supreme thought." The nine children all survived her. "Miss Katie Herring," we read, "is Editor of the Orphans Friend published at Oxford, Miss Vara has for some time until recently been Secretary of Littleton Female College, at Littleton, Lucy and Eugenia have positions in Dunn [school teachers, presumably], Mary Belle is in school there, and Messrs. Troy and Rufus are in the lumber business at Roseboro and Joseph in Clinton."

"She leaves," the obituary noted, "a family of bright children who promise to make their marks in the world in the calling that they have chosen." A "great throng" of people traveled to the burial in Herring Township.

It's worthwhile to consider what life in Sampson County was like for the six girls bound so strongly together that they never separated for long and spent most of their adult lives living, if not in the same house, then only a couple of blocks from one other. Of the homestead we know about the big Christmas gatherings of kith and kin, that they were "the Sunday School type," and that they subscribed to the *Christian Advocate* and were devoted members of the Hopewell Methodist Church down the road. The children were "bright," their environment cultured and refined. Ambition was a common trait; so, too, for the girls, an abiding commitment to the notion that the state owed all people health, education, upward social mobility, and a degree of happiness—the very definition of public welfare.

The three boys succeeded, after military service in World War I, in the lumber and dry goods trades. Troy and his cousin Robert built the grand and almost identical mansions that still stand in Roseboro and Clinton. Troy's son Rufus Geddie Herring ("Cousin Geddie") was a World War II hero, awarded the Congressional Medal of Honor for his actions at Iwo Jima.

Of the sisters Vara, the eldest, was the first to seek independence. Prior to her return to Littleton College to join the administrative and teaching staff, we find her searching for work as a secretary, typist, or stenographer, by way of a week of classified ads in one of the Raleigh papers. More than all the rest, she practiced a stern Christianity, with a life revolving around the Woman's Christian Temperance Union (the Raleigh chapter carries her name), the church and Sunday school, and various service leagues for Methodist women. Pauline and Eugenia, our Aunt Jean, cut merry figures in Dunn society and were, I think, the closest pair of the six. (Kate and Lucy were very close, but Lucy died young of breast cancer; we always sensed a sadness when Grandmother talked about her.) All the Misses Herring spent at least a portion of their careers teaching school. Only Kate and Pauline married.

Jean, properly Pherobe Eugenia, graduated from the NC College for Women in Greensboro (now UNC-Greensboro), and in 1928 passed and was admitted to the North Carolina bar. She enjoyed a long career as secretary to the state Supreme Court—notably to Sam Ervin, later Senator Sam of Watergate hearings fame—and to the biennial sessions of the Legislature. She was an organizer and leading member of the Business and Professional Women's Club of Raleigh.

We catch one or two other glimpses of the Misses Herring during their time in Dunn. They were active in the Epworth League, an organization for young adult Methodists, and in other church activities. They belonged to the Thursday Evening Book Club and organized a Dunn Social Club. There was music all about: they sang and played piano and organ, not just for church but to entertain at house parties and later in college concerts and revues. Jean played collegiate tennis in Greensboro. Now and then we find one or more of the Misses Herring at a mixed-gender, chaperoned, house party or country picnic. We grandchildren and grand nephews and nieces often heard that Aunt Mary Belle had been something of a coquette in her prime, with plenty of beaux. Our mother Katherine remembered sitting in the back seat while Aunt Mary Belle charmed her latest gentleman friend up front.

Of a "delightful barge party" for 50 in August 1908 on the Perquimans River, near Winfall NC and the Albemarle Sound, the Raleigh paper noted, poetically:

> Such a scene of beauty aided by the choice enchantment of soft breezes and gliding waters failed not to stir the gentle courses of both old and young affections, and until the late hours the affair was one of rapturous praise and ecstatic merriment.

They made up parlor games and played a lot of cards, including the latest fads like Flinch, Progressive Rook and Progressive 42 (dominoes), and Up-Jinks. For instance:

MISSES HERRING AT HOME

Dunn, July 11 [1913].—In honor of their house guests, Misses Annie V. Crews of Oxford and Ellen McPhail of Mt. Olive, Misses Kate and Pauline Herring entertained at their attractive home on Harnett street, Tuesday evening, 8:30 to 11. The guests were received at the door by Miss Gene [Jean] Herring and were shown to a leafy bower on the porch where Miss Lucy Herring served punch. The porch was brilliantly lighted with Japanese lanterns and electric lights and there the guests found tables arranged for progressive rook. After a series of spirited games in which Mr. Gentry won honors, delicious refreshments were served. Music and readings were also entertaining features of the evening.

You have the impression from the Society pages that, as mature ladies, the Misses Herring sat down for bridge a dozen times a month. But never, never on Sunday. My brother Dick and I loved playing cards with our grandmother—Old Maid and Go Fish—primarily because she always giggled when she drew the Old Maid, so there was never much of a secret about it. The only board games she would play with us were Parcheesi and Chinese Checkers. Once, at White Lake, we watched in amazement as she played Mah Jongg with her sisters and old-lady friends. Who'd have known?

Officially she was Katherine Maude, but this is a name encountered only on formal documents like her college diploma. At home and into her 20s she was Katie and Katie Maude, and early mentions in the Society pages are to Miss Katie Herring. At college she published twice as Katie M. Herring and once as Katherine. From then on out she was Kate M. Herring and then Mrs. J. Henry Highsmith. Her husband and sisters called her Kate, her children called her Mother, and we grandchildren called her Grandmother and were in fact forbidden from trying anything less formal, like our friends did with their grandmas and grannies. She, in turn, would not call my mother by her preferred name, Kaye, but always used the more formal Katherine.

Toward the end, my mother often called her Katie Maude to her face, as though it gave them both comfort.

Kate Herring graduated with honors from Littleton College in Halifax County, not far from Roanoke Rapids, class of 1902. So did her sisters Vara, Lucy, and Pauline. Littleton, with perhaps 200 students, was among the more prestigious of the dozens of colleges and seminaries and preparatory schools that dotted Eastern North Carolina in those decades, offering a significant curriculum in the liberal arts—there was even an orchestra—but also courses in the basic business skills. Among its many prominent graduates were her lifelong friends and fellow crusaders Mrs. Charles Doak, *née* Frances Blount Renfrow, and her '02 classmate Miss Mary Graves Shotwell. (To us these ladies were only mildly distinguishable one from another, as among the countless *grandes dames* to be encountered in Grandmother's living room. Miz Doak exuded a whiff of notoriety as her husband, Chick, was the famous baseball coach at NC State.)

Aunt Vara became Treasurer of Littleton College and Principal of Business Courses, until it burned down in 1919 and was never rebuilt. Kate and her sisters took care to attend meetings of the Littleton College Memorial Association, organized and led, until her death, by Aunt Vara. The Raleigh picnics were splendid potluck affairs in the rotunda at Pullen Park. The last of these was July 15, 1961, and, as a photograph shows, Kate was there with her sisters Jean and Pauline. (Aunt Vara died shortly after that, and the activities of the association, and its archive, were transferred to the new North Carolina Wesleyan College in Rocky Mount.)

Between her graduation in spring 1902 and the fall of 1904 Kate Herring lived with her sisters in the house on Harnett Street in Dunn. In April 1903, she was a bridesmaid at the wedding of family friends.

For at least the school year 1903–04 she was the assistant principal at Newton Grove Preparatory School. On May 5, 1904, the noted orator Plato Tracy Durham, of Trinity College (later Dean of Divinity at Emory), gave the commencement address before 2,500 people, a hortatory affair urging his young audience to aspire to the higher life and not to stop until their goals have been achieved and great things accomplished. As Miss Kate Herring is cited in the press as having helped secure the speaker and for her outstanding community service that year, it's easy to imagine that, one way or another, Prof. Durham's visit to Sampson County solidified her desire to seek higher ground herself.

She matriculated as a junior at Trinity College in Durham, predecessor of Duke University, in 1904, from which she graduated after two academic years, in the class of 1906. (Her future husband, J. Henry Highsmith, had graduated in the class of 1900, so they would not have known each other there.) The yearbook entry says she was president of the YWCA, as she had been at Littleton. Her graduation photograph pictures her, like the rest of the women, in a high-necked white blouse and a mildly Pompadour coiffure, parted at the center—the overall effect being one of no-nonsense.

For President Theodore Roosevelt's visit to Trinity on 19 October 1905, she wrote and may have read aloud "A Welcome to the President," printed the next month in the campus student literary magazine, *The Trinity College Archive*. In December she published an epistolary short story, "The Heart Interprets for the Eye," a tale of anguish and misunderstanding on the part of a young couple separated at Thanksgiving and Christmas—heavy, as in much youthful fiction, with hints of autobiography. Hers was the valedictory poem published in the *Archive* the next April, "No Letting Down."

She graduated from Trinity College, *cum laude,* in a class of 46, of whom 11 were women. Of these, Mary Shotwell had graduated in her class at Littleton, and their subsequent careers overlapped strikingly in education, War Loans, and public welfare. Mary Reamey Thomas, a Virginian, married the dean, William Preston Few, who became the first president of Duke. Mrs. Few and Mrs. Highsmith stood together in dozens of receiving lines over four decades. Grandmother was not a boastful person, but she was mighty proud of her Duke pedigree and, yet to come, her Phi Beta Kappa key.

Kate M. Herring, c. 1921

WRITING FOR HEALTH
WORKING FOR VICTORY

After her graduation from Trinity, Kate Herring taught English at Kinston High School during the academic year and returned to Dunn for the vacations. (Mary Belle followed much the same plan for her entire career, teaching mostly in Rockingham, but returning to live with her sisters for holidays and vacations.) We encounter Kate from time to time in the Society sections, once as a bridesmaid for her first cousin Donnie Mae Royal in Clinton ("one of the State's most highly cultured and accomplished young ladies")—a family affair, where Troy was an usher and Pauline escorted the happy couple to Niagara. Then, for three semesters, she taught English and German at Louisburg College, the venerable Methodist two-year college northeast of Raleigh and Wake Forest, founded in 1787.

There she was faculty editor of the newspaper, *Louisburg Echoes,* which reported when she left:

> During her year and a half association with the College Miss Herring infused new life and spirit into certain lines of work. As head of the English Department, she became the director of the Societies and placed them on a higher scale. She was also Superintendent of the College Sunday-school, and one of the Faculty Editors of *Echoes.* Her ability is evidenced in their success.

One of these societies was a literary group called The Younger Set, where one evening there was a Japanese party with formal papers read but also an eating-rice-with-chopsticks contest.

Her separation from Louisburg at the end of the Fall term 1909 was unexpected and regretted. Louisburg *Echoes* suggests that it had something to do with her eyesight, and this explanation is plausible. She had thick bifocal glasses when I knew her, and drama over their loss or breakage was common. At one point there's a forlorn classified ad seeking to recover the glasses she had left at the Olivia Raney Public Library in Raleigh.

By the time of her year "off" in Dunn, 1910, it's clear she has identified journalism as her chosen profession. She must have been writing one-off articles for lots of publications, including the *Christian Advocate* and Methodist publications for home and family. In a short item carried by the Wilmington paper in July 1913, we find her attending the 41st annual meeting of the North Carolina Press Association in Asheville, one of the very few women among the 125 present. There she is said to be connected with the Dunn *Weekly Guide.*

We have few leads as to how she became involved with the press service of the Orphans' Home in Oxford, NC, a town some 30 miles northeast of

Durham, on the main road to Clarksville, Virginia. Possibly the connection was through Miss Annie V. Crews, a socially inclined young woman from a large Oxford family. We find Miss Crews being entertained by the Herring sisters at the porch party in Dunn in 1913; within a few years she's a frequent guest in Raleigh and begins to be called, in the papers, Miss Annie V. Crews of Oxford and Raleigh. Eventually she gives her address as 604 North Blount Street, that of the Misses Herring, and, sure enough, still had an apartment there fifty years later.

The Oxford Orphan Asylum, now the Masonic Home for Children, had reopened after the Civil War in 1873, publishing its bulletin, *The Orphans' Friend and Masonic Journal,* beginning two years later. The cumbersome title aptly describes the contents, with news of the orphanage in the front and of the lodge in the back. In January 1911 the Durham *Sun,* followed by other state papers, reported Miss Kate Herring's "promotion" to associate editor, suggesting that she was already working for the publication. (The senior editor was a local Mason.) The version of the story in the Wilmington paper observes that she has moved to make Oxford her home. The piece notes that "she has developed into a very bright newspaper woman, and her friends here are pleased to know of her success." The Oxford paper began to report her comings and goings: when her mother died in 1912, it called her a "popular and faithful" editor. One biographical article says that she was in Oxford for "one summer," but published accounts have her there for at least the full year between January 1911 and January 1912; probably she stayed into 1913 at least.

Her particular achievement was, apparently, the Thanksgiving 1911 edition which appeared on November 24, an institutional retrospective with newly commissioned photographs and a "History of the Orphanage Told Briefly in Facts and Figures." This was praised in a dispatch datelined Oxford, Nov. 25, which remarks that "Miss Kate M. Herring, the very talented and accomplished editor, richly deserves congratulations for the unsurpassable appropriateness of the contents of the edition, full of genuine information in regard to the history of the institution from its beginning, and the pictures of the beautiful buildings as they now stand."

Whatever else she read and wrote in Oxford, one publication, thus far unknown to her, seized her attention: *The Health Bulletin,* a monthly provided free to any citizen by the North Carolina State Board of Health. Its combination of research findings and practical, sometimes colloquial advice resonated with her dawning sense, from her origins on the farm, of mission. She began to think of herself as an agent of the public good.

Not long after their mother had died in 1912, the sisters began to migrate from Dunn. Kate moved to Raleigh in 1914, boarding at 118 North Wilmington

Street, a long-established hostelry of Miss Celeste Smith located a few steps from the historic Christ Church, Episcopal, and the State Capitol. In 1916 the other five Misses Herring "joined their sister" in Raleigh, as the paper noted, living in a house she had found for them all, and Vara had bought, at 709 Hillsboro Street. She would spend virtually all the rest of her life within a ¾-mile radius of Capitol Square.

Very soon upon arriving she joined the Raleigh branch of the Southern Association of College Women. Raleigh was an ideal place for the ladies to have landed: home of St. Mary's, Meredith, and Peace Colleges as well at State College (now NC State); of a major newspaper, *The News and Observer;* of Edenton Street Methodist Church, then and now an anchor of the South; and of course seat of the government, where the Legislature assembled in January of odd-numbered years.

You should skip ahead, now, and read her memoir on getting her first major post, as director of publications for the State Board of Health. This is the story of preventable death from flies-in-the-milk in Sampson County, and what she meant to do about it, that we heard again and again as we were growing up. Virtually all of it is verifiable. The man in the office who listened to her was Warren H. Booker, chief sanitary engineer for the state, and a specialist in . . . the modern privy—also a very good writer. The reporters from the *Raleigh Times* and *News and Observer* were Oscar Coffin, who went on to become dean of the School of Journalism at UNC, and Frank Smethurst, later the Managing Editor of the *News and Observer.*

The "Flyless Greensboro" movement, led by a public health officer named E. P. Wharton, had begun to attract attention in the papers the year before and by February 1914 was garnering ongoing public interest; by May and June "flyless town" was a statewide mantra. The chronology of Mrs. Highsmith's memoir suggests that she applied for the job in Raleigh in the spring of 1914, probably May, and was told to come to work "in two weeks." Public record has her receiving her first pay in June 1914—for three weeks, not four.

But I cannot trace a front-page article in the *News and Observer* with the heading "Greensboro to Become a Flyless Town," as she describes. What's surely her work is the press release from the State Board of Health that July 15, "Greensboro the Flyless," picked up by a dozen papers in the state. Every phrase sounds like Miss Herring.

Her monthly salary of $50, incidentally, was the same starting salary her future husband had made as a high school principal; within a few months she was making $100, about half that of Warren Booker. The workload must have been staggering, as her office distributed a press release on some form of health work every day, provided features for the Sunday papers, and published the monthly *Health Bulletin* to boot. The position duties also included, each fall, staging exhibitions on good health and hygiene at county fairs throughout the state.

Neither the Board of Health press releases nor the original articles in *The Health Bulletin* were signed, so we lack what might be as many as several hundred pieces from her typewriter. (In 1936 she returned for almost three years to the *Bulletin,* and these long monthly essays are indeed signed.) A typical issue of the *Bulletin* included departments headed Editorial Brevities, Public Health and Sanitation, Child Hygiene, Tuberculosis, Personal Hygiene—about two dozen items over the same number of pages. The cover would feature an announcement panel in display type, its verso giving the table of contents, staff of the board of Health, and list of free brochures (Sanitary Privy, Hookworm Disease, Whooping Cough, Public Health Laws) available on demand by postcard.

Any number of these many dozen pieces from 1914 to 1917 might be the work of Kate Herring herself. At the Board of Health she identifies the issues and begins to undertake the crusades that define her life of service. The flies seldom escape her attention for long. Conquering tuberculosis—a dominant theme in her life, including her long association with Christmas Seals. Personal hygiene, from dental care to foot care to the prevention of venereal disease. Nutrition. Even the weather, and the danger of transmitting disease via shared harmonica (which she calls the "French harp"). These matters, and their extensions—from proper speech to acceptable conditions of incarceration of women to a humane work week for women and children— become her life's agenda.

The two attributed pieces from 1915 begin to suggest the spectrum of her work: the long, soulful treatment of the North Carolina Sanatorium for the Treatment of Tuberculosis ("the Young Man's Scourge") that appeared in *The Farmer and Mechanic* that March, on the one hand, and the pop-psychology take on talking about the weather that bemused a columnist that July.

Increasingly she got noticed. On May 23, 1915, the *News and Observer* reported:

> Dr. and Mrs. Harold Glascock and Miss Kate M. Herring will go to Dunn today in an automobile.

(Dr. Glascock soon designed and built Mary Elizabeth Hospital, three blocks down Wake Forest Road from the Highsmiths' house, and at about the same time served as a groomsman at their wedding.)

Her routine in Raleigh seems to have consisted largely of her work, monthly meetings of the local branch of the Southern Association of College Women, and frequent holiday visits to Dunn. She addressed the College Women on her role with the Board of Health, part of a series on state agencies that also included sessions on the Historical Commission and a visit to the

Hall of History, an institution she had many opportunities to promote over the years. For her tenth college reunion in 1916 she offered one of the toasts.

A turning point in her career was the summer class she took in July and August 1917 at the Pulitzer School of Journalism at Columbia University. The school itself, one of the original journalism programs in the country, was only five years old; the first Pulitzer Prizes were awarded later that very year. We don't know much about her curriculum there, though subsequent references to her technique suggest that the focus was on selecting topics of newsworthiness and on observing the proper distinctions between *reportage* and editorial content. In fact she went on to become a grand master at mingling those very genres.

Toward the middle of August her sister Jean came to visit, then accompanied her back home to Raleigh. Her return was noted in an item that appeared across the state, to which the *Greensboro Daily News* added its own, curiously phrased, assessment:

> Miss Herring was greatly pleased with her short stay in New York and with the training that Pulitzer's school gives to its students. Before she left she had been pronounced far and away the most acceptable publicity artist in the state departments and her work in Columbia greatly assists her in finding news values and making proportions.

The names "Pulitzer" and "Columbia"—and "New York"—had real cachet in Carolinian circles, and the remark that she was a "trained" journalist became common. Littleton, Trinity, Pulitzer at Columbia was, to be sure, a pedigree not to be sniffed at. But the real admiration for her work sprang from how she was redefining the concept of health education.

Apart from the obvious, that none of the Misses Herring had married, there is little indication of how the war in Europe was so far affecting their daily lives. Little enough, I should think, until the reality of American boots on the ground began to be understood in the towns and counties of North Carolina. We do not find the ladies taking public positions on entering the war, and of course they could not yet vote. By contrast, Mrs. Highsmith later took a strongly anti-war position in the run-up to World War II, writing, speaking, and at times demonstrating against further military conflict.

Her dramatic "loan" as of 1 February 1918 from the state Board of Health to the federal War Savings Campaign, headquartered in Winston-Salem, attracted considerable press. First there was the announcement the *News and Observer* ran on 27 January, which went on to say:

> Miss Herring is a trained newspaper woman, having made her work during her service with the State Board of Health meet with the needs and the limitations of the daily and weekly newspapers of the State.

As an AB graduate of Trinity College who since her graduation took a special
course in Journalism at Columbia University, Miss Herring has put into
her work for the State Board of Health a very healthy grasp of the human
equation which, combined with a clear conception of news, has made her
material generally acceptable to the press of the State. Miss Herring has
been more than a health propagandist: she has been an unbiased reporter of
the health conditions in North Carolina and a ready conveyor of progressive
movements.

With brevity, conciseness and the news idea as the basis for her writing
policy, Miss Herring carries into her new work precisely what is needed to
put a State-wide publicity campaign of the sort across.

Highly laudatory editorials ensued from papers across the state: old
standbys like the *Charlotte Observer,* the *Christian Advocate,* and the
Wilmington *Morning Star,* on through the Siler City *Grit*[!], Morganton
News-Herald, Kings Mountain *Herald,* the Enfield *Progress,* the Lumberton
Robesonian. "A First Class 'Publicity Man'," crowed the *Star*'s headline. (I
have collected some of these raves in chapter 1918, below.) "She will write
various newspaper copy for distribution to the weeklies and dailies," said
the Winston-Salem paper, noting that the man she was relieving had been
"fairly swamped with work." The boiler-plate

Miss Kate H. Herring is publicity agent
of the War Savings campaign in North Carolina.

was picked up by the wire service and used as filler in dozens of papers, coast
to coast: El Paso, Wilkes-Barre, San Francisco, and Regina, Saskatchewan, to
name only a few. The same item was then included verbatim in a compilation
of shorts about What Women Are Doing in the war, positioned between
blurbs on women bellhops and women railway conductors in Bavaria, who
were demanding to wear trousers.

After she was already at work in Winston-Salem, a letter from Warren
H. Booker, to whom she had reported in Raleigh, made the rounds of the
newspaper editors—identifying her, as if that were necessary, as the author
of all those unsigned bulletins from the Board of Health:

Recently several very complimentary editorials have been noted in the
State papers in regard to the press service issued by the Board. I assure
you these compliments are highly appreciated by this Board, and it is only
fair that the editors of the State should know who is personally responsible
for this material. I write to say that this department is deeply indebted to
Miss Kate M. Herring for this work. In this same connection I am writing to
say that after February 4th, Miss Herring will sever her relations with the
Board for the remainder of the year in order to take up the publicity work in

connection with Col. F. H. Fries of Winston-Salem, who is State Director of the War Savings Stamp campaign.

In asking this Board for the loan of Miss Herring's services until January 1, 1919, Col. Fries made it very plain that he, together with his executive committee, had canvassed the field thoroughly and decided that Miss Herring was the person for the place.

Miss Herring and this Board view the matter as a call to a patriotic service that could be answered only in the affirmative.

In taking up her new work, the Board bespeaks for her the same full measure of splendid cooperation in this patriotic Service she is undertaking that you have shown her endeavors in the past.

Booker may also have wanted it known that her departure was amicable, and to remind readers that it was temporary. Or maybe it was simply late going out, since she was no longer around to send it.

The United States had entered World War I in April 1917, supplying mostly goods and money until the bulk of the American troops arrived in France in 1918. The Armistice was achieved that November. Among the entities created to finance the war was the War Savings Organization, with a goal (in the end unmet) of raising $2 billion in cash from ordinary citizens in the form of War Bonds and savings stamps. War Savings Stamps were available in denominations within reach of even the smallest incomes. $50 million was the goal for North Carolina.

Americans were encouraged to see their participation as patriotic, vital, a personal debt owed by the citizen to his country. The striking visuals were in the flamboyant propaganda mode—"Boys and Girls: You Can Help Your Uncle Sam Win the War," for instance. Perhaps the most stirring was the full-color representation of . . . Joan of Arc: "Joan of Arc Saved France; Women of America, Save Your Country: Buy War Savings Stamps."

(Savings stamps programs were still run out of the public schools when Dick and I were at Myrtle Underwood Elementary. Our parents opposed the scheme from a couple of different points of view, and we soon turned what little we had by way of bonds and passbooks from Wednesday sales into savings accounts where the interest rate was a little higher.)

There were multiple Liberty Loan Campaigns, in which North Carolina women, chaired by Mary Smith Reynolds, wife of the tobacco baron, took a leading role. Miss Herring was almost surely drawn to Winston-Salem, and then to Richmond, by her friend and classmate Mary Shotwell, a field director in the regional campaigns. It was Miss Shotwell's particular brief, as a public school educator, that the War Savings Campaign was an excellent opportunity for teaching thrift to school children and, thus, to their parents.

Supervisor of Misses Herring and Shotwell in Winston-Salem was Colonel Francis H. Fries. "Colonel" was not a rank but an honorary, from his time in the state government. By turns Fries had been a textile baron (blue jeans), rail magnate (builder of the Roanoke and Southern railway), and formidable financier, first president of Wachovia Bank. In his *History of* [the] *War Savings Campaign of 1918 in North Carolina,* he is fulsome in his praise of Miss Herring, describing her responsibilities as "dual": the preparation of an article on War Savings every day for the daily papers and one each week for the weeklies—"practical reading matter," they said. "The other [duty] was editing the *War Savings News,* a weekly news sheet ... sent to the War Savings committeemen, the newspapers, and to others who were interested and active in the cause." During the June and December drives she also circulated plate matter—items not set in the local composing room but rather distributed by a syndicate (like comic strips and Dorothy Dix's advice column). For instance:

Every Family a Fighting Family!
That is the war-time spirit of true-blue Americans—the spirit that will win the war.
The day of talking patriotism is passed—the time has come to practice it.

Your government has officially set—
Friday, June 28th
National War Savings Day

On June 28th every American will be summoned to enlist in the great "army that stays at home." On that day every local American should "sign the pledge" to invest a definite amount in War Savings Stamps each month during 1918.

W. S. S. Cost $4.17 in June
Worth $5.00 Jan. 1, 1923
Help the Fighters Fight — On June 28th.

Finally, as if these duties as Director of Publicity were not enough, she also held the dossier as Director of War Savings Societies.

Miss Herring became as popular in Winston-Salem as she was in Raleigh. She fed the press more than they needed: it's almost certain that she wrote most of the long stories on the War Savings Stamps that appeared in the papers, and I've attributed several to her below. She spoke in public at women's meetings. She crisscrossed the state on multiple tours to offer "War Savings Institutes" promoting the sale of savings stamps and war bonds. She advanced the idea, possibly her own, of Victory Acres and Thrift Gardens, where farmers, low on cash for most of the year, would plant an acre of high-profit crops, proceeds of which would go to War Savings at market time.

On one of those missions, to Asheville, probably in April, she encountered at breakfast in her hotel an old acquaintance, Dr. Loula Ayres Rockwell, whose son Kiffin had been the first American pilot to shoot down a German plane in World War I, and who was himself killed in an aerial battle shortly afterward. Kate was moved to write a major story on the Rockwells, one of her very best and on one of her most memorable subjects. It first appeared in the Sunday *News and Observer* on May 26, 1918, and went on to be the copiously illustrated lead article in the *Sunday Atlanta Constitution Magazine* three weeks later.

And it was as a federal employee that she published two eyebrow-raising essays to demonstrate how African American citizens of North Carolina had, in fact, borne more than their "fair" share of the War Savings effort: in November 1918, "How the Southern Negro is Supporting the Government," which appeared in *The Outlook,* a Christian weekly published in New York; then in January 1919, "The Negro and War Savings in North Carolina," in the *South Atlantic Quarterly*—pieces cited frequently in the scholarly literature ever since. The wire-service version was titled "Southern Woman on Negro Loyalty" and traveled across the country. She seems no more self-conscious about the subject matter than for any other of the dozens of nuanced topics she took up in her career, and her conclusions are striking: "The blackest counties are the richest counties. ... North Carolina recognized the Negro as an American citizen and gave him responsibilities the same as white men. ... Like the colored soldier at the front, he heard the call and responded."

By autumn 1918 it was clear that the North Carolina campaign was considerably behind its goal, and her messages became strident, her schedule punishing. In November 1918 she led institutes in 13 cities in as many days. And dangerous they were, as the influenza epidemic peaked in the state that very October and November. Her Raleigh session had to be subdivided since only a dozen were allowed to assemble at one time. Meetings for Asheville and Salisbury had to be moved to Hendersonville and Statesville, safer towns. The final canvasses, to have taken place on Thanksgiving Day, were largely rained out, and in the end this Victory Drive "was not fruitful."

Miss Herring would surely have been welcome back at the Health Department, given statewide conditions. It was later agreed that official response to the Spanish Flu had been a failure, especially in Charlotte. Health educators could and should have done better.

By the end of the calendar year 1918 a decision had been reached to close the State War Saving Headquarters in Winston-Salem, even though whether they had met their goal, after heavy holiday sales, would not be known until late January. (She probably wrote the summary sentence: "The work has been notable throughout the State, and the educational campaign conducted in thrift will have a lasting effect upon the state.") In any event her leave of absence with the Board of Health was set to expire. She was in Raleigh in time to spend Christmas with her sisters.

News of her return to Raleigh was received with satisfaction. A press release from W. S. Rankin, North Carolina's Secretary of Health, confirmed her return as publicity director and now managing editor of the *Health Bulletin,* assuring readers that she was "ready, with a wider experience as a journalist and newspaper writer, to again service the health interests of the state." The *Concord Times,* running the story, noted how "the work of Miss Herring was a conspicuous success, and much of the success of the War Savings campaign was due to her work. She is capable and highly efficient because of her ability and the fact that she is deeply interested in her work." Other papers suggested of the title Managing Editor that it was a "deserved promotion" and a "flattering" one. In fact her new title was grander still: Assistant Secretary. The Oxford paper noted her previous association with *The Orphans' Friend* and went on: "she seems to be especially talented, and we rejoice in her popularity."

But her tenure in Raleigh lasted three weeks at most. Instead, she was lured— again, I am certain, by Mary Shotwell—to Richmond, Virginia, seat of the Treasury Department's Fifth Federal Reserve District (Maryland, Virginia, West Virginia, North and South Carolina). Here, for the rest of 1919, she would continue her War Savings work as Director of War Savings Societies in North Carolina, with a particular emphasis on War Savings Stamps (WSS), essentially the same job she had had all along. Lucy, incidentally, had meanwhile taken a job at the Bureau of War Risk Insurance in Washington, having to do with insurance for the vessels and men of the merchant marine.

Under the headline "Again Under Confiscation," the *Charlotte Observer* reported this quick turnround: "she has been again conscripted, this time by the Treasury Department. ... It was Colonel Fries who first discovered the talent that had been hidden in the office of the State Board of Health and who brought it into utilization to the good of the country, and as a matter of course this talent was not to escape the eager eye of the Government."

Her arrival in Richmond was delayed by the onset of a two-week bout of unspecified illness at almost exactly the same time her move was announced, on January 22, 1919. On that very day in Raleigh, Lula Johnson Highsmith, the first Mrs. J. Henry Highsmith, succumbed in the flu epidemic, leaving her husband and two children.

But for the fact that it now originated in Richmond, Miss Herring's work was familiar. Her focus remained North Carolina. There were strategy sessions at the Federal Reserve, and considerable retooling as the war effort closed down while the raising of money to pay for it needed to carry on. One of her first major pieces from Richmond, for instance, concerned extending the deadline for redeeming 1918 pledges—that is, delivering up the cash—until the end of 1919. She returned to North Carolina often. On August 1, for instance, she was to have presented a major oration to the North Carolina Press Association meeting in Wilmington: "Financing the American Future." This was signed by the director of the office in Richmond, Albert S. Johnson, though she must have had a major hand in writing it. But the meeting derailed over a resolution, eventually passed unanimously, in support of the League of Nations, and Miss Herring and others were "crowded off the program," with their remarks to be published later. The members of the press nevertheless found time to enjoy a watermelon feast on Shell Island, a dance party at the historic Wrightsville Beach pavilion called Lumina, and some deep-sea fishing.

During fair season, her "Government Thrift Exhibit" traveled to state fairs in Maryland, Virginia, and both Carolinas, and to as many county and district events as she could manage. (She enlisted her sister Pauline to help.) The display booth, billed as "one of the first of its kind ever to be put out under the auspices of the United States Treasury," was unveiled in Elizabeth City. In addition to charts and posters, the Liberty Bond and Victory Note prices were updated directly from Washington. Rocky Mount boasted that there the exhibition would be "under the personal direction of Miss Herring." The display ad for the Greensboro NC Fair, October 14–17, 1919, counted it a main attraction:

FOUR BIG NIGHTS!
A fine Brass Band
of eighteen pieces

WAR EXHIBITS!
Navy Exhibit of One of Big Navy Guns!

GOVERNMENT THRIFT EXHIBIT
ANIMAL SHOWS
VAUDEVILLE, MERRY-GO-ROUND,
WHIP, MOTOR DROME, MANY OTHERS.
THESE ATTRACTIONS
ARE WELL WORTH GOING MILES TO SEE
REDUCED RAILROAD FARE

While she was in Raleigh for Christmas 1918 with her relatives—a veritable family reunion at the house on Hillsboro Street, with all nine siblings and Troy's wife, Gladys, and young son, Troy Marvin—news was released of her appointment as director of publicity for the Maryland Social Hygiene Association in Baltimore, beginning the first of the year 1919. This was to be a two-year experimental program in public education directed toward the eradication of venereal disease. If successful, it would mutate after two years into a United States Public Health Service program in every state. She was one of a staff of three.

The national crusade to eradicate venereal disease had begun to coalesce before the war, partly through the work of the Woman's Christian Temperance Union. Such organizations as the American Social Hygiene Association (ASHA, now American Sexual Health Association), established

1914, advanced the tenets of the Social Hygiene movement, which touched also on prostitution and sex education. An early, and generally successful, focus was on American soldiers departing for war: venereal disease acquired by U. S. forces abroad had turned out to be very low.

The Maryland organization had been formed from the fusion of several state agencies already involved. Its stated purpose was "acquiring and diffusing knowledge on societal health and in conducting a thorough and vigorous attack on vice and venereal disease in an effort to check the moral, physical, and economic ravages of these scourges." It invited the assistance of "every man and woman who is interested in the moral cleanliness, physical fitness and economic welfare of the citizens of Baltimore and the State of Maryland." Alan Johnstone, Jr., was brought from South Carolina as executive secretary.

Johnstone, a Columbia lawyer and civic leader, had been an executive of the Richmond office of the War Organization, so it was doubtless he who attracted Miss Herring to the Baltimore experiment. On his appointment, he remarked that the Maryland Social Hygiene Society proposed to conduct in Maryland "an experiment to see if the human race may be freed from the moral and physical hazard, which for time out of mind vice and venereal disease have presented. The program is similar to that which was followed by America in the war in Europe and will consist of law enforcement, rehabilitation, prevention, recreation, education and medical activities."

She surely wrote the article "Maryland Society Completes Organization" that appeared in the New York *Social Hygiene Bulletin* in February 1920, concluding:

> The business and professional men and women of Maryland are willing and anxious to give this experiment a thorough work-out, and our present plans call for a budget of $40,000. Maryland is a particularly good field for laboratory work in many respects, as it is neither North nor South, it has an equal rural and urban population; it has a large Negro population; and it is centrally located.

Almost at once she was called back to Raleigh to attend to her sisters Pauline and Eugenia, both "quite sick" with influenza. Both survived, as she had the year before.

A highlight of Grandmother's life, in more ways than one, was the installation of the Beta chapter of Phi Beta Kappa at Trinity College, soon to be Duke University, on March 29, 1920. Two of the alumni inducted as founding members that night were Kate Herring, '06, and her husband-to-be, J. Henry Highsmith, '00. Three women alumni and six women students were among the 28 inductees. There were orations and the presentation of the charter, also a banquet. Governor Thomas Bickett and Joseph G. Brown, later chairman of the Duke Board of Trustees (and namesake of Brown dormitory on Duke's East Campus, as well as a prominent leader of Edenton Street Methodist Church in Raleigh) were made honorary members. The governor addressed his audience as "sisters and brethren." He learned the secret grip from one of the sisters, I like to think Kate herself, remarking "You know I enjoyed that." After the ceremony she stood in the receiving line at the home of President and Mrs. Few, her classmate, along with the governor.

She was appropriately proud of her Phi Beta Kappa membership and is wearing her key in many of the studio portraits from then on. (At one point she loses it and offers a reward in a classified ad in the *News and Observer*.) Her husband wore his ΦBK key on a watch-chain across his waistcoat every single day, and my father would take care to show his own key to his mother-in-law whenever it was with him. She would have loved knowing that I wore that key, my dad's, whenever I conducted a concert. When I was elected to ΦBK at Duke in 1967, a newspaper headline in the Raleigh paper noted our three generations—to which another is added now, as her great-grandchildren Kate and Allie are also ΦBK.

I am increasingly certain that this event marks the beginning of J. Henry Highsmith's doubtless nuanced, and certainly rapid, courtship of Kate Herring. Grandfather was a recent widower whose much lamented wife, Lula V. Johnson, had died in Raleigh during the flu epidemic just over a year before. After graduating from Trinity in 1900 he had taken a Master of Arts and served three years as principal of North Durham School; he then attended Teachers College, Columbia, for the two academic years 1904–06. From then on he was nearly always addressed as Dr. Highsmith, though I can't demonstrate that he actually finished such a degree. (He tells the story of his career in his own memoir, below.) From 1920 he was state Inspector for high school education, eventually Director of Instructional Services for the State of North Carolina.

However they became acquainted, they would not have been serious about pursuing a friendship until a year had elapsed since Lula's passing. Miss Herring must have been uncomfortably aware of her age, 40, in the seeking of a husband. Dr. Highsmith was concerned most of all for the well-being of his children John Henry and Lula Belle. I'm guessing the stress of her career in venereal disease work, and the increasing distance from her sisters in Raleigh, played constantly on her mind. You could not gainsay the perfection of the match, in its Sampson County origin, educational achievement (Duke, Columbia), passionate commitment to education, authorial and oratorical skills. I'd like to have heard the parlor gossip in old Raleigh that Christmas.

The Trinity *Alumni Register* has her leaving Baltimore for a similar position in the New York home office of the umbrella American Social Hygiene Association, 105 W. 40th Street, beginning January 1, 1921. She took lodging near Columbia. The backers of the ASHA—Jane Addams of Hull House, John D. Rockefeller, Jr., Harvard President emeritus Charles Eliot—were certainly uppercrust (and the Treasurer was Henry Higginson, founder of the Boston Symphony Orchestra). Their message was scientific and stern, uncomfortably righteous. Again, we don't know quite what she did there, but it seems reasonable to imagine she worked primarily on the *Social Hygiene Bulletin,* vol. 8 (1922), which in editorial approach and general content directly paralleled the North Carolina *Health Bulletin* she had run for so long. Any, or even all, of the original pieces that winter might have come from her typewriter. Given her experience with fairs, for instance, she was doubtless keen to promote a joint project of the ASHA with the American Red Cross in North Carolina, where a truck, the "social hygiene field car," "fully equipped for showing motion pictures anywhere and under almost any circumstances," carried its message to 40,000 people in five counties.

New York did not last long. In the third week of May 1921, at a tea given by friends on 118th Street, the engagement of Miss Herring and Dr. Highsmith was announced—and, of course, released to the press. The wedding was set for June 30. Their already impressive careers to date were summarized. "Miss Herring and Mr. Highsmith have a wide circle of friends," the release understated, "both within and without the State. They will make their home in Raleigh."

Mrs. J. Henry Highsmith
of 832 Wake Forest Road

Kate M. Herring and J. Henry Highsmith, a widower with two children, were married on 30 June 1921 after announcing their engagement—from New York—in late May. The dispatch disseminated widely in the Carolina papers. Under the heading "Two Distinguished Sampsonians to Wed," *The Sampson Democrat* suggested its readers would take "especial interest," having "followed the brilliant careers of Dr. Highsmith and Miss Herring with pride." The wedding invitation was tendered by Vara in mid June and published in full in the Winston-Salem paper.

They were married the same week as her brother Rufus Herring married Gladys Jerome, our Aunt Gladys. The *Sampson Democrat* reported that their brother Joe (J. O.) "went away on June 15 and helped marry off Rufe, and then on the 30th he saw Miss Kate married. He still has five single sisters, he says, but he insists that he is next to the bat." Lucy was her maid of honor; Troy escorted her down the aisle. "Her dress was grey canton crepe, embroidered in crystal beads and cut roses. She wore a large grey hat, with shoes and gloves to match. She carried a shower bouquet of orchids and lilies of the valley." The groom's sister, Margaret Highsmith (our Aunt Margaret, later Mrs. Peyton Brown), sang.

The notice was carried in the Sunday papers the next weekend. The headline in the *Charlotte Observer* noted the marriage of a "Prominent Raleigh Couple"; the Asheville *Sunday Citizen* reported a "Wedding of Note is Held at Raleigh: Mr. Highsmith Claims Miss Herring as His Bride." The *Sampson Democrat* bragged "Both these distinguished people are native Sampsonians, and their many friends and relatives in their native county congratulate them upon their joining hearts, hands, and fortunes."

They honeymooned at Mountain Meadows Inn, a rustic, often photographed, establishment on the mountainside six miles from Asheville, after a drive said to be "one of the most picturesque to be found in any land." It finished with work, as they passed through Lenoir en route to Boone, where Dr. Highsmith twice addressed the summer session at the Appalachian Training School, the academy for teachers that is now Appalachian State University.

After about two years in the Highsmiths' house at 322 New Bern Avenue, doubtless because a third child, Katherine, had arrived, they established their new home at 832 Wake Forest Road—walking distance to work for Grandfather Highsmith, who did not drive, and a very short distance from the Herring sisters' house at 604 North Blount Street. There they lived for the rest of their lives.

Kate Maude Herring Highsmith
with her daughters Katherine Herring
and Louise Westbrook
Raleigh, 1925

Probably they moved in July 1923, since the newspaper reports Dr.
Highsmith's relocating to a new home "in the northern part of the city" that
July 31. There was confusion as to whether the street was North Person
Street or Wake Forest Road. The 1924 city directory lists Dr. and Mrs.
Highsmith residing at 832 Wake Forest Road, while John Henry, Jr., in
the next line, gives his address as 832 North Person. Dr. Highsmith went
on record as favoring the notion that Wake Forest Road began at the dog-
leg to the north-east (toward Wake Forest), from number 812 on—past the
A&P and pharmacy (and just later, an early Krispy Kreme). His solution
ultimately held sway.

It was a fashionable if not exclusive address, certainly *nouveau,* not far
from the outskirts of that part of the city. The Highsmiths were more or less
directly across the street from the historic Mordecai house and what was left of
the plantation there. To the right of 832, also across from the Mordecai House,
bordered by a side street named for him, was the enormous lot and house of
her neighbor Mr. Sasser, of whom she did not approve. The big mansions were
closer to Capitol Square, along Blount Street, though a little further out from
832 were the lovely house of her friend and co-worker Mrs. R. N. Simms and
the small, private Mary Elizabeth Hospital that Dr. Glascock had built. Past
the Mordecai house, to the left, came a series of "tourist homes," one with a

large neon sign that said something like "Lodge," and at the end the Circle filling station. Grandmother disapproved of these, too.

Wake Forest Road was also at the time US 1-A. It was not a little historic. Sherman's troops had camped not far away in April 1865 and had taken that route north to Richmond and Washington—after Appomattox, then Joseph Johnston's surrender at the Bennett Place, near Durham. The historical marker to that effect was one of several along the road not far from the Highsmith house.

Family distress and anguish accompanied the state's decision in the mid 1950s to claim a third of the front yard to widen Wake Forest Road by adding a lane, or maybe two. The tractor-trailer trucks thereafter rolled past her bedroom window all night long—pretty terrifying if you were sleeping over. She managed with a night mask and earplugs. Not so long after that the Downtown Boulevard became Route 1, and relative quiet returned to her much smaller lot.

The garden was to the right of the house, through a gate and down some stairs: it was tiny and formal in a Colonial sort of way, the various brick patterns serving to outline beds that we knew as great places for the annual Saturday Easter egg hunt. The garden gave, through another gate, onto a small fish pond surrounded by caladiums and other tropical plants. Just to the front of the pond was a pillar and sundial, by which the Easter family portraits were taken. We would often feed the fish—eventually the fine koi disappeared and were replaced by hobby-shop goldfish—and try to spot one of the large frogs that typically lived there. A few steps further on were a small lawn, where we would retreat to eat watermelon, the parking spot and under-house garage, then the driveway out into Sasser Street. Like many another guest, I remember Grandmother's gardens as idyllic and to be imitated.

The front porch opened into the living room or parlor to the left, the stairwell directly in front, and a narrow hall that held a coat rack and a small table on which reposed a decidedly old-fashioned telephone. (832 Wake Forest Road had a telephone number from the time they moved in.) Mrs. Highsmith was often as not on the telephone, standing. She answered it by clearing her throat into the mouthpiece, then greeting her caller with a muscular "All right?"

Behind the living room was Grandfather Highsmith's library, college professor-ly in size and content, where the books sat in glass-front cases. Both parlor and library opened onto a fine porch, with the typical Southern couple's swing, rocking chairs, and a contraption called a glider, where you risked having your fingers pinched. Between the formal dining room and the kitchen was a breakfast nook, which also served as a ready room and maid's pantry for social affairs.

Upstairs were four ample bedrooms and a big bathroom. Grandmother's room had two high-poster beds, her dressing table, and I think a walk-in dressing room with wash-stand. Grandfather, who was sometimes poorly by the time we knew him, had a room at the far end of the floor, heavy with the aroma of remedies and potions.

The downstairs rooms were in fact, as the press would observe, "gracious and hospitable." The parlor was dominated by a fireplace, and if the opening had been covered in *faux* brick, the mantelpiece and huge gilded mirror drew the eye away from that particular detail. Dick's and my eyes were on the pile of change Grandfather emptied from his pockets each day and left on the mantel; this money would go home with us on Sunday afternoon, following a little presentation ceremony he much enjoyed. There were beautiful pieces of Colonial-style furniture, heirlooms still in the family. There must once have been a piano, as all three daughters played and one, Louise, became a professional musician. But in my time "the" piano was the Steinway in the parlor at 604 North Blount Street, said to be Aunt Mary Belle's.

From the beginning the house and gardens were in use almost constantly for the civic business and pleasures of the ladies of Raleigh. The Twentieth Century Book Club, not the first but among the most established of a dozen literary societies in town, met there at least twice a year. (Miss Herring had belonged to book clubs in both Dunn and Louisburg.) In 1926 she spoke on "Huguenots and Quakers, Their Origins and Customs," part of a series that year on world religions; in 1938, *Strong Man of China: The Story of Chiang Kai-Shek,* by Robert Berkov. She was still hosting book club in 1962, at Louise's home on Dixie Trail.

Both Highsmiths, incidentally, were interested in the writings of the Chapel Hill playwright Paul Green. They were at the 100th performance of *The Lost Colony* in Manteo in July 1939, and in October 1940 joined Aunts Vara and Jean, Josephus and Addie Daniels, and a number of other Raleighites in an excursion to Fayetteville to see Green's new "symphonic play" on Flora MacDonald in the Cape Fear valley. Likewise they attended Kermit Hunter's *Unto These Hills* in Cherokee, shortly after it opened in July 1950.

Other frequent guests were the Trinity College Alumnae, later the Duke Alumnae Association of Wake County, founded at 832 Wake Forest Road in January 1922, a few months before Katherine's birth. Her connections with the Duke Alumni Association grew over the years into upper-level leadership of the organization. She was said never to have missed a Duke commencement, and very few Woman's Club conventions. She and her husband were founding members of the Duke and Duchess Club of married alumni. The *Duke Alumni Register* of March 1937 features an inset picture with the caption "Louise Westbrook Highsmith and Katherine Herring

Highsmith, daughters of Dr. and Mrs. J. Henry Highsmith, are shown above. Dr. and Mrs. Highsmith were the first couple of become members of the Duke and Duchess Club."

You might have found her parlor occupied by the Raleigh Garden Club, circles from the church, the Board of the Olivia Raney Public Library, politicians trying to get elected or citizen committees organizing to get some noble undertaking underway—the State Art Society, for instance, working toward a North Carolina Art Museum from 1926; or the State Symphony Society, leading to the North Carolina Symphony in 1930. Sometimes people borrowed her home, especially the groups that intersected with concerns and sympathies of the Woman's Club: the Business and Professional Women (including great-Aunt Jean and Aunt Lula Belle), the Woman's Christian Temperance Union (Aunt Vara), the YWCA.

One other organization to which she belonged was Beta Sigma Phi, a national literary and social sorority for young women organized in the early 1930s from the mid-West. She sponsored one of the Raleigh chapters, Rho, installed in October 1939. The chapter sponsors were quite prominent women: the other chapter in town was sponsored by Mrs. Clyde R. Hoey, the governor's wife, and her Blount Street neighbor, Mrs. Hartness, wife of the Secretary of State. (In the obituary of Mrs. Highsmith in the *News and Observer,* almost certainly written by my mother, she is listed as a member of Delta Kappa Gamma, the honorary sorority for teachers, but this must be a mistake for Beta Sigma Phi. Mother was a member of the Duke social sorority, Delta Gamma, whence the probable confusion.)

Much of what became her personal agenda required action of the North Carolina Legislature, which assembled in the Capitol beginning in January of odd-numbered years until its business was exhausted and it could adjourn *sine die.* Raleigh would swell in size, and spare rooms in the big downtown houses would be rented out to the legislators while they were in town. The Sir Walter Hotel would become the center of the political and social universe, where the legislators drank and smoked cigars and made deals while their wives visited, received, and poured tea at near-daily social events. Mrs. Highsmith thrived on this life, with fraught political meetings in her living room and, sometimes, a legislator lodging upstairs.

Often as not when we came by on a week day, there would be ladies sitting around her living room in a circle, while she sat in her upholstered rocking chair, with swan's necks for arms. When it wasn't our great aunts, it was members of her gang of conspirators—the formidable ladies you will meet below.

And she was seldom idle. In one week in 1933, for instance, she oversaw an annual convention of the North Carolina Federation of Women's Clubs, as both executive secretary and chair of press and publicity, then two days later hosted the Twentieth Century Book Club in her living room, then the next day took first place in the Raleigh Garden Club category "arrangements of flowers in two colors."

When 832 Wake Forest Road was not large or grand enough for her social purpose, she would either use the Woman's Club on Hillsboro Street or the various facilities at the church. Or co-host with a well-heeled friend, of which she had many. Take for example a reception for 500 in January 1933, co-hosted with Mrs. Hartness, *née* Annie Sloan, in the fabulous Hartness mansion on North Blount Street—three blocks due north of the Misses Herring, now the office of the Lieutenant Governor. The event was to honor the new first lady, Mrs. J. C. B. Ehringhaus, and Lily Morehead Mebane, an early female legislator, twice decorated relief worker in World War I, and granddaughter of John Motley Morehead. Invitations had been sent across the state, and hundreds showed up. The receiving line included, in addition to the honorees and hostesses, wives of a United States senator and of other senior legislators, and of the presidents of UNC and Duke. Among the assisting hostesses were Vara, Eugenia, Mary Belle, Gladys (Mrs. Troy Herring), and Margaret Highsmith (Mrs. Peyton Brown), and such inner-circle clubwomen as Annie Kizer Bost.

For Christmas the whole family would be seated in the living room at 832— the Misses Herring, aunts and uncles, cousins. Gifts would be distributed by the grandchildren old enough to read the labels, and eventually there would be cake and punch and mints. (The Christmas tree was often scraggly: she believed live trees to be an environmental affront—and wrote about it.) You can get a good sense of that room from the dozens of photographs taken there—Debutante Ball pictures and the like. The occasion I remember best is of Aunt Lula Belle's wedding to Uncle O. N. in 1951, where the pictures show the house trimmed to the nines. I'm there in a little white suit. Sadly, my grandparents kept their distance from the camera that day.

She was in her 70s, the age I am now, when Dick and I, and our cousins Louise and Carol Wilkerson and Henry Rich—the others came later—knew her. Those Christmases were our special time with her.

Dr. Highsmith's career prospered as he became essentially the senior career officer in the state public school system. On November 24, 1925, he gave the primary address, "The Function of the College," at the inauguration of Elmer Rhodes Hoke as president of the new Catawba College in Salisbury and was then awarded the honorary degree Doctor of Laws. (His speech was published in January 1926 as one of "Three Addresses" in vol. 1 of the college *Bulletin*.) He was given a second honorary doctorate, Doctor of Education, by Wake Forest in 1934. He gave easily twice as many speeches as his loquacious wife. During commencement season he would speak every night, sometimes two or three times a day.

I know almost nothing of their financial means, which must have been modest in comparison with the prominent doctors, lawyers, and bankers all around them. But of course their primary interactions were with public employees and educators, also legislators from every nook and cranny of the state, with whom they probably enjoyed economic parity. Both her positions as executive secretary—of the NCFWC and of the State Legislative Council—involved some compensation, and after Dr. Highsmith was gone she was supported by a stock portfolio capably managed by her daughters and a family friend.

Every biographical treatment of Kate Highsmith and her contributions mentions her devotion to Methodism and to Edenton Street Methodist Church, but the documentation is sparser than for her clubwork and civic involvement. She typically enumerated service to her church just after home and family in the list of her primary interests, once remarking that "no work I have ever done was so rewarding or enjoyable as this." In her youth she wrote a good deal for such Methodist publications as *The Christian Home* and *The Southern Methodist,* though accessible runs of these are rare. She belonged to women's circles and influential committees, including the Official Board and groups formed to address financial crises and needs of brick-and-mortar: in her time there were multiple remodels of both the church and its formidable Sunday School building, and a full rebuilding when the newly remodeled church was struck by lightning and burned down entirely in July 1956. She and Vara led and won the fight to keep a Shell station off the southwest corner of that block.

Edenton Street, Methodism, and her other interests often overlapped, as for example when the church and the Woman's Club co-sponsored events for armed service members during World War II, and in the many cases where she led the church into her coalitions to advance public health and welfare. Or the many times the Duke Alumni and Alumnae, or public school teachers and PTAs, met at Edenton Street. She taught and for a generation served as Assistant Superintendent of the thriving and populous Sunday School program there. She had been a Sunday School leader at Louisburg College, a Methodist school, and Dr. Highsmith was a major figure in the Baptist Sunday School movement in North Carolina and beyond.

She often already knew the pastors and their wives, not a few of them from Duke Divinity, before they were assigned to Raleigh; she welcomed each new pastor and wife at a reception at 832. She was particularly fond of T. Marvin Vick, who went on to officiate at her funeral, having first encountered him as a young man long before through a state welfare committee they jointly served. Of all the warm memories I have of my grandmother, the proudest is of both Dr. Vick and Governor Dan K. Moore pausing by her wheelchair at the close of service, as I stood behind to wheel her out, taking care to wish Mrs. Highsmith a very good day.

In about 1945 Mollie H. Harrell took a room at 832 Wake Forest Road and there resided until her death in 1957. Having lost her husband in 1927 she had relocated from eastern North Carolina to Durham to work for Hospital Care Association, a parent of Blue Cross in North Carolina and in fact first developed under the aegis of the Duke University School of Medicine. She appears to have moved from Durham to organize Hospital Care in Raleigh, about 1940, and soon emerged as a leading member and then president of the Raleigh Business and Professional Women's Club—an organization in which both great-Aunt Jean (Eugenia) and Aunt Lula Belle were also leading figures. She was a powerhouse in her own right, but increasingly an adopted member of the Highsmith clan, too. Often as not she would be listed in the Society pages as greeting or pouring at 832, along with the Herring sisters and eventually my mother and Aunt Louise. On at least one occasion she hosted the B&PW's first meeting of the year, a tea at 832. "Mollie's chair" in the parlor was the classic wooden barrel, perhaps Grandfather's Wake Forest chair. She's pictured in Christmas photographs and at the grandchildren's birthday parties. Mollie was a member of Edenton Street Church and was given her funeral there (though buried in Durham next to her husband, who had died 50 years before; there were two children and grandchildren, whom we did not know). To Dick and me she was Aunt Mollie, but when the question came up, it was made clear to us that she wasn't our *real* aunt.

After Grandfather died (it was Mollie who found him, slumped in his easy chair), she became essentially Grandmother's protecting companion— in fact she had long been—until her own demise from cardiac disease in 1957. And after she was gone it was necessary to have paid live-in companions. They were a problematic and short-lasting bunch, almost Thurber-ian. One couldn't cook after all. One was a hoarder; another was just nuts.

The upstairs rooms were occupied, as they became vacant, by renters, often nurses or nursing students at Mary Elizabeth Hospital just down Wake Forest Road. As early as January 1930, a room, presumably John Henry's, is advertised for rent to a "young man, preferred. Steam heat, adjoining bath, breakfast and dinner if desired." In 1943–44 a public school teacher new to Raleigh lived upstairs. One long-term lodger, Virginia something, was a tall no-nonsense woman in the full nurse's uniform of the era over which she wore what I thought was a swashbuckling blue cape as she strode purposefully in and out each day. (I wonder if part of the arrangement was to keep her eye on Grandmother and Mollie.) After she broke her hip, Grandmother moved downstairs to what had been Grandfather's library, but not much changed there except for wedging in the hospital bed. From there on, she got about the place, grumpily, with a walker.

832 Wake Forest Road is still there. For a time it was rented for lodging, while Katherine and Louise sought some public service agency to purchase it. Since then it's served a number of public purposes but doesn't look so different from the outside, though the gardens and fish pond have given way to off-street parking. 604 North Blount Street, the aunt-hill, also looks much the same and is now divided into private apartments.

832 Wake Forest Road said as much about Kate Highsmith as her writing did. It wore her values well. Like the big house in Sampson County it was cultured and loving. It was a good place for our families and for her loved ones of high and low estate. And it was consistently a place of good works for the people of North Carolina.

She stands in front of her home, much as I remember her at her grandest, in the photograph accompanying Blanche Brian's portrait of her in the *Raleigh Times* of January 4, 1960. The fur stole, the tight silver permanent hair-do, the glasses, the "beads" and "ear-bobs," the flowers from her garden—this was her look in my lifetime. In a photograph I like even more, she stands in her back yard between Dick and me on Easter Sunday 1956, wearing gloves, her mink stole, a brimmed black hat, and an orchid corsage. (This one, being one of the first photographs my father took with his new Argus C-3 35 mm. camera, is out-of-focus; a later frame, much better, shows my mother Katherine in *her* fur stole, standing in the same spot.) We are just getting back from Easter services at Edenton Street Methodist Church, doubtless followed by lunch at the S&W Cafeteria on Fayetteville Street, and dropping her off at home. That is how I like most to think of her.

Kate Herring Highsmith
with grandsons Dick and Kern
Easter 1956
832 Wake Forest Road

EXECUTIVE BOARD AT PINEHURST, MAY, 1925
The Superiority of Mind Over Matter
"No Hats"

Mrs. R. R. Cotten and Mrs. Palmer Jerman at center
Mrs. J. Henry Highsmith, front row left

North Carolina Federation of Women's Clubs

WRITING FOR WOMEN

She *said* she was retiring from journalism and public life in order to create, as a first priority, a happy home for her husband and children. It was indeed a happy home, notably as to the blending of the families. Before she had children of her own, we find Kate Highsmith attending and soon—as was her custom—presiding over PTA meetings at Lula Belle's schools. Both my mother, Katherine, and my Aunt Louise adored their older sister Lula Belle, never referring to her as a half sister, and in Grandmother's obituary no distinction is made between the grandchildren of the two Mrs. Highsmiths.

I know less about what passed between Kate and her stepson John Henry. He was becoming a teenager just as she became a Highsmith. In high school (class of '25) he achieved distinction in academic studies and on the debate team, while singing in the chorus and writing for the yearbook. From there he went to NC State, where at one point he was hit by a car as he crossed Hillsboro Street by the campus and remained unconscious for some time. In November 1929 John Henry married Eva Diffenderfer, our Aunt Eva, in a "secret" double wedding in Danville, Virginia—secret for a few days, perhaps, but revealed to the public with a splendid portrait of the bride in the paper a few Sundays later. The Highsmiths, Jr., ended up in Green Cove Springs, Florida, from where we received bushel baskets of Florida citrus, packed in Spanish moss, every Christmas. We only met John Henry once that I recall, and by that time he was crippled and disfigured by rheumatoid arthritis. Aunt Eva we saw every few years. I don't remember ever meeting my two cousins from Florida.

Lula Belle, too, taught in Florida for a time, then at the New Jersey School for the Deaf, before returning to Raleigh for her own distinguished career with the Health Department.

How Mrs. Highsmith managed all her roles—devoted parent in a blended family, spouse of a high-profile educator admired across the state, journalist, public speaker, tireless traveler to every corner of the state and eventually far beyond—is not easy to fathom. We know Lula Belle to have done a lot of baby-sitting for her little sisters, and that one or another of the Misses Herring, just a few blocks away, was typically standing by. There must have been cooks and housekeepers, and some sort of staff for the luncheons and teas, but the only kitchen memories I have, aside from one oldish and grumpy cook, are of the aunts and great-aunts crowded in the steamy kitchen at Thanksgiving. That, and Grandfather Highsmith hand-cranking the mayonnaise in a stoneware Wesson Oil crock. When we stayed over, Grandmother herself did the baby-sitting but didn't often cook: she was big on cheese and Town House crackers.

Public service was in her blood. In fact the only thing she could have meant by "retirement" after marriage was giving up her paid position at the Board of Health. Before the year 1921 was out she was directing the Christmas Seals campaign in town, thus returning to her largely successful crusade to eradicate tuberculosis and to assure the ongoing success of the State Sanatorium. The original Christmas Seals campaign, in 1912, had been sponsored by women's clubs; she would serve as state chair in 1944. The 1921 campaign was the 38th annual, with a statewide goal of $215,000.

We first find her involved with what was called in her era "club work," or even "clubdom," in the Raleigh Woman's Club Year Book of 1916–17; in 1917–18 she is listed, along with Vara, at the address of the Misses Herring on Hillsboro Street. Her pre-wedding "porch party" was given at the home of Mrs. Palmer Jerman, *née* Cornelia Petty, a central figure in the Woman's Club movement. After the birth of her daughter Katherine Herring Highsmith, in June 1922, she emerges dramatically and for the rest of her life as a major figure in the Woman's Club scene. The morning Mrs. Jerman was elected state president, May 5, 1923, in Winston-Salem, Mrs. Highsmith was named statewide chairman and director of publicity by the board of trustees. She was after all "well known to the newspaper fraternity of North Carolina," and her close association with Trinity College, shared with her "prominent" husband, enhanced her already impeccable credentials.

Strikingly, that same fall—just after she moved to 832 Wake Forest Road—the Raleigh Woman's Club designated her chairman of the Educational Department, under the presidency of Mrs. Josephus Daniels, *née* Addie Bagley Worth, and the papers published her aggressive agenda promoting a new high school for Raleigh, remedies for truancy, and a course, "Know Your Child," led by none other than Dr. J. Henry Highsmith. The file photograph is from the same sitting as her wedding portrait, with the over-the-elbow white gloves.

It's clear that her main mentors in the Woman's Club were Mrs. Jerman and Mrs. Daniels, both of them leading proponents of suffrage for women, just then becoming law. She must have met, early on, Sallie Southall Cotten, founding "Mother Cotten" of the Federation. Closer to her own age group were Mrs. W. T. Bost, *née* Annie Kizer, whose brilliant career included the post of state Commissioner of Public Welfare; and Mrs. Charles G. Doak, *née* Frances Renfrow, Littleton College classmate and indefatigable activist on behalf of organizations from the first Negro PTA to the League of Women Voters to the Democratic Party in all its facets. Mrs. Doak was Mrs. Highsmith's successor as chief publicist for the State Federation and its executive secretary. Mrs. Bost was succeeded at Public Welfare, at Mrs. Highsmith's suggestion, by Dr. Ellen Winston of Meredith College.

Dr. Winston liked to tell the story of getting Mrs. Bost's job, how Mrs. Highsmith put her up to it in a phone call: "Annie Bost is retiring and you might as well get that job." In a 1974 interview, Dr. Winston remembered Mrs. Highsmith as "one of the important leaders at that time." We Holoman grandchildren had another close connection with Dr. Winston, since, when she went to Washington in 1963 to accept President Kennedy's appointment as U. S. Commissioner of Welfare, her maid, Naomi Burt, came to work for us and became a beloved member of our family.

The striking list of Mrs. Highsmith's Woman's Club friends catalogues the pathfinding ventures of one after another fascinating figure in North Carolina history, women of great consequence. Kate Burr Johnson, in the 1910s and 1920s, led the State Board of Charities and Public Welfare and preceded Mrs. Bost as Commissioner, then moved to administer the New Jersey State Home for Girls. Jane Simpson McKimmon, of Blount Street, first woman graduate of NC State, led the Home Demonstration movement in rural North Carolina—"one of the world's great movements," she rightly said, "in adult education." (The NCSU Extension and Continuing Education Center is named for her.) Lily Morehead Mebane, granddaughter of Governor John Motley Morehead, was North Carolina's first woman legislator. Gertrude Dills McKee, of Sylva, formally Mrs. E. L. McKee but known to her friends as Gert, became the first woman Senator in the state. Dr. Delia Dixon-Caroll, first woman physician in Raleigh, member of the Meredith College faculty, and strident, sometimes belligerent voice of progress for women. Judge Susie Sharp, later Justice Sharp of the North Carolina Supreme Court.

Mrs. Highsmith's Wake Forest Road neighbor, Mrs. R. N. Simms, was a lifelong intimate and reliable co-producer of social events of every kind. You will read of all these remarkable women time and time again below—also, of the wonderful Mamie Latham, who ends up moving to Raleigh at her suggestion.

The Raleigh Woman's Club was a constituent of the North Carolina Federation of Women's Clubs, which ran from small rural clubs of a dozen members to book clubs and study groups to the big, multi-department clubs in Asheville, Charlotte, Greensboro, Raleigh, and Winston-Salem, where it had all begun in 1902. The NCFWC was in turn a member, and an influential one, of the Washington-based General Federation of Women's Clubs, numbering over 1,000,000 members—they said; estimated membership varied wildly—in her time. The State Federation had the usual officers and department chairs but also sixteen regional districts of clubs, each with its president. The General Federation of those years had a similar structure of officers, directors and chairs, and regions. Mrs. Highsmith would come to hold offices at all three levels: local, state, and national.

Much of the governance was accomplished at executive council and board meetings, with annual state conventions and biennial, later triennial national meetings focused on pageantry, pre-determined agendas by mission—Education, the American Home, Arts, Gardening, Public Welfare—and often ending with "Play Day" garden visits, motor tours, and the occasional beach day with fish fry.

In Raleigh the club year began in the fall with a Get-Together Dinner and shortly thereafter a round of committee meetings to map out the year's agenda and, at the state level, begin to pin down convention plans. Fall 1926, for instance, brought discussion and action on Wear-Cotton Day (a response, in part, to the vogue for silk stockings, which threatened the NC hosiery industry), the campaign for a State Art Museum, and a loan fund for college-bound women. The state president and her vice president for districts would visit every district in October. The year would reach its peak with the State Federation convention, then wind down with end-of-year celebrations including the installation of new officers, followed by a summer lull before it all began again.

It was not in her nature to decline responsibility, but you wonder if she could have foreseen the number of pages she would produce, week in and week out, on behalf of North Carolina women over the next decade. The State Federation press releases begin in late 1923 and are weekly, every Sunday, by 1926. (I can't explain her sudden absence from p. 1 of the Society section from June 1927 to January 1929.) In 1933 she wrote every single Sunday but for the summer vacation, 35 pieces in all. Incredibly, she stayed at it through the spring of 1936. There are, too, releases for the PTA and Legislative Council to be found in her ordinary spot in the Sunday paper.

And not only that. By the fall of 1924 she was able to announce a bigger project still. The Federation meant to accept the offer of the UNC Woman's College, Greensboro, to publish a monthly NCFWC *Bulletin*. It was an attractive arrangement for both the Federation and Woman's College, part of the extension mission of the state university system and, moreover, mailed for free. The press release on the appearance of vol. 1, no. 1, probably in late November, reached newspapers across the country. The *Bulletin* was published in Greensboro for ten years, 1924–34, then absorbed into *The North Carolina Clubwoman*, still produced today. She took care to assure her readers that the *Bulletin* would not replace her column in the Sunday papers.

Sallie Southall Cotten's *History of the North Carolina Federation of Women's Clubs, 1901–1925,* concludes with the statewide convention of May 1925 in Pinehurst. She holds that the most outstanding feature of that meeting was the presentation of the new *Bulletin*, and compliments Mrs. Highsmith and her associate editor for the speed with which they had turned out the first issue: "A long cherished dream of a Bulletin all our own had become a rosy reality, needing only the cooperation of the clubs to make it another shining light in the history of the Federation."

I am almost sure Mrs. Highsmith appears in the charming photograph of the executive board taken at that meeting, titled "The Superiority of Mind Over Matter: No Hats." Mrs. Cotten, nearly 80, and Mrs. Jerman sit on the front row, hands entwined. To their right, at the left of the picture, sits a younger woman who can only be our Kate.

Her upward trajectory as a clubwoman was steady. For instance in fall 1927, on the death of the Raleigh club president, all the officers advanced, and she moved from corresponding secretary to first vice president. As it happens, she was not in fact elected to the presidency of the Raleigh Club in 1941, but rather tapped by the executive board to fill an unexpected sudden vacancy. Meanwhile the Woman's Club work overlapped, often purposefully, with her work for other organizations, including the League of Women Voters of Wake County, of which she was president from 1929, local and state PTA organizations, and of course the Board of Health, with which she never lost touch.

Dr. and Mrs. Highsmith shared an abiding commitment to the parent-teacher movement, especially at Hugh Morson High School. The brand new Raleigh High School building at the corner of Person and Hargett Streets, across from Moore Square, formed its PTA in 1924—the year before John Henry, Jr., graduated—with Mrs. Simms as president. The first meeting saw the presentation of a portrait of Raleigh High principal Hugh Morson from the parents to the school, and on Morson's death shortly afterward the new school was named in his memory. Both Highsmiths were among the committee chairs in that first PTA. When the school opened for the 1927–28 academic year as Hugh Morson High School, Mrs. Highsmith was president of the PTA and Dr. Highsmith the library committee chair. All three daughters—Lula Belle, Katherine, and Louise—graduated from Morson, which was almost exactly a mile due south of their home. They were quick to remind us that they walked, every day, sometimes through ice and snow.

As Katherine and Louise, born in 1922 and 1924, grew, their mother quietly increased her public commitments, often through short-term offices with clear end dates: as publicity chair for a congress of 600 Methodist missionary folk at Edenton Street, say, and, the same week, hosting with her sisters a reception for the former president of Littleton, J. M. Rhodes and his wife, now of Florida. For that event, bushel baskets of fresh citrus fruit were sent to Raleigh from Florida—birth, perhaps, of that long Christmas tradition in the Highsmith family.

From her two terms as president of the Hugh Morson High School PTA, 1927–28 and 1928–29, she went on to hold vice-presidential office with the State Congress of Parents and Teachers. She placed PTA-specific essays in the Sunday papers, occasionally having a Federation piece and at PTA piece in the same issue. The state organization was modest in size compared to the Women's Clubs, some 20,000 members statewide, but growing in influence. Child welfare was at the top of the agenda, and she closely followed, but did not attend, the 1930 White House Conference on Child Health and Protection. It sought, she reported, "For every child, protection against labor that stunts growth, either physical or mental, that limits education, that deprives children of the right to comradeship, of play and of joy."

The local schools welcomed her addresses. At Hayes-Barton, now Myrtle Underwood PTA, she suggested in "Character Training in the Home," eleven "laws of right" for pupils: "self control, good health, kindness, sportsmanship, self-reliance, duty, reliability, truth, good workmanship, team work, and loyalty." When Depression came she presented the Wiley School PTA with "A Challenge to Parents and Teachers": "The PTA should accept the challenge to help in this chaotic state by looking after the education of the children, by emphasizing the ideals of home and family life, by enriching our leisure hours and spiritual enrichment." Later she addressed the Lewis School PTA on "Sex Education in the Home."

She was a gifted and sought-after public speaker, her schedule sometimes nearly matching that of her husband, famous for his commencement addresses, who during some parts of the academic year was at one podium or another nearly every day. Unlike Dr. Highsmith, she drove herself to engagements all over the expansive state. She became a familiar voice on the radio as the Women's Clubs sought to increase their public exposure over the air. Other pioneer women broadcasters at WPTF, Raleigh, had more air time, including Harriet Pressly, wife of the president of Peace College, and Margaret Early, editor of The Woman's Digest every morning at 10:30. But WPTF was on her route, just across the street from two of her haunts, the Sir Walter Hotel and the S&W Cafeteria, and there she was happy to present "Federation Hour," actually fifteen minutes, from the start. Her daughter Katherine was also a radio personality, as a disc jockey during the World War II and on the long-running panel show Time Out ("the program that pays you to play").

Dr. Highsmith ran afoul of the press and public fairly often, as for instance when he took a position against high school Latin for every public school. Mrs. Highsmith, admired everywhere for her tact and good will, endured a single run of notoriety in papers, in an episode that stretched from 1926 to 1929. This had to do with a survey of women in industry, an idea that began to be promoted in 1923 by the Women's Clubs, League of Women Voters, Business and Professional Women, YWCA, and others, with the strong support of the indefatigable Kate Burr Johnson, Commissioner of Public Welfare and at the time the highest-ranking woman executive in the state.

They sought reliable data on the work conditions of women in the labor force, expecting to find a direct link between working mothers and juvenile delinquency. Some 200,000 North Carolina women were working in industry in what were suspected to be deplorable hours and conditions. Twenty-six other states had already conducted such a survey.

The survey was strenuously opposed by leaders of the textile industry, men who tried to convince the governor that it would be too expensive and could not be left to women workers, even if they were "trained sociologists." They suggested that the unrest was being directed from "out of state." Not so, barked Dr. Delia Dixon-Carroll in February 1926. It could be free, she said, if conducted by the Women's Bureau of the Labor Department. The executive secretary of the Commission, E. F. Carter, was a crony of the textile bosses (and the governor was deemed to be "hand in glove" with the cotton mills) and was in any event, thought the women, in a conflict of interest, since he was charged with enforcing the women's labor laws.

A compromise, it seemed, was found when Mrs. Highsmith agreed to direct the survey, as announced in the headlines of June 10, 1926. Her title was Director of the Survey of Women in Industry by the Child Welfare Commission. (A later narrative asserted that it was understood from the beginning how she would serve "in name only," and that Mr. Carter would be in charge.) In the last week of June she found her way to Washington to discuss the project with the Women's Bureau, hoping to be done with the task by the beginning of the 1927 Legislature. Jonathan Daniels, in the Washington bureau of the *News and Observer,* reported her visit, noting that she refused comment on the issue and that the survey was bitterly opposed by state mill operators.

But on July 1, Mr. Carter announced that he himself would select eight employees to conduct the survey, pledging that five would be "trained" women. The cost would be only $12,000. The brouhaha that followed over who was leading and who was assisting gathered momentum, and on July 13, Johnson, the Commissioner, left a meeting in Chapel Hill for an emergency session of her Child Welfare Commission—herself, Dr. A. T. Allen, superintendent of public instruction, and Dr. G. M. Cooper, acting secretary of the Board of Health—in Raleigh. (All three members of the commission were professional colleagues and personal friends of the Highsmiths.) During a show-down in the office of Governor Angus McClean, they reached impasse. The governor, dead set against working with the Women's Bureau, would consent to a $25,000 price tag, but only if Mr. Carter would conduct the study. Kate Burr Johnson was unalterably opposed to Carter, and the two men would support no one else—the Commission thus breaking along gender lines. She withdrew her support of the survey, since it was "not to be carried out as she had been led to believe."

In that case, the governor ruled, the survey, so long sought by a woman's constituency numbering 30,000 or more, would be terminated. This came as a surprise in Washington, though at the Department of Labor the bureau chief, Mary Anderson, opined that "the people of North Carolina will demand it sooner or later." The Child Welfare Commission was thought in some circles to have "obliterated itself." The Federation continued to call for a survey "by competent experts," but let the matter lapse for the 1927 Legislature, meaning to put it before the body in 1929.

With that the Survey of Women in Labor effectively reached its dead end. Mrs. Highsmith tells her side of the story in a major essay of late 1929 ("Explains Why Survey of Women in State Industry was Dropped ... Gives Story of Its Collapse"). By the 1931 Legislature, existing agendas had been eclipsed by the economic situation. In the end it's no sadder a story than that of a dozen other progressive ideas she, and women in general, supported that never made it to an affirmative vote—the Child Labor Amendment, for instance; for that matter, the Equal Rights Amendment. But as late as the "25 Years Ago" feature in the *News and Observer* of June 10, 1951, the struggle was still thought worthy of historical note.

Pauline was married on August 18, 1926, to Sergeant James R. Sloo in a private ceremony at the house on North Blount Street. Though there were no attendants, Dr. Highsmith sang, and her brother Troy's wife, Gladys, played violin, both of them accompanied by Mary Belle. There had been a couple of social events in the two weeks preceding to announce and celebrate the engagement. At one of these "little Miss Katherine Highsmith" appeared with flowers from the garden at 832 to announce the bridal news. The happy couple secured the license that morning for a wedding at 9:30 p. m.

Uncle Jim is a shadowy figure in the written record. I remember him mostly for his khaki uniform, sometimes worn with knee-high riding boots. Perhaps there was a broad-brimmed military hat. When he got to know Pauline, he was, I think, recruiting officer for the ROTC at NC State. In 1929 he was transferred to San Francisco, though it appears that Pauline spent much of that time in Raleigh; then from 1930 they were in Memphis, where we find him as Secretary-Treasurer of the Memphis Chapter of the Sons of the American Revolution. In November 1941, presumably after his retirement from the military, they are reported as having moved from Roseboro back to Raleigh, where they occupied a spacious apartment on the second floor at 604 North Blount Street. They had a private entrance from Peace Street, opening onto a stairwell I recall as threateningly steep. He held a position as Veterans Service Officer in that part of North Carolina, and in that capacity in 1951 established the Department of Negro Hospitalization, based in Durham County. His principal interest in retirement was history, and together with Pauline he authored an important genealogy of the Herrings.

One reason the wedding was low-key may have been Lucy's fragile state. She died at the house on Blount Street at the end of October, and there the funeral was held with roughly the same cast as the wedding. After her War work in Washington, Lucy had taught public school in Clinton, Greensboro and North Wilkesboro before taking a post at King's Business College in Raleigh for the preceding two years.

In January 1929 Mrs. Highsmith was named executive secretary of a group originally calling itself the Legislative Council of North Carolina Women and generally referred to as the State Legislative Council. This consisted of delegates from civic organizations—the NCFWC, the WCTU, the B&PW, church auxiliaries, the Nurses Association, the YWCA and so on—who would gather in Raleigh before each session of the Legislature, often in mid-December, to form an agenda of goals for the upcoming session. An office would be opened on the mezzanine of the Sir Walter Hotel (in 1929, the Masonic Temple) and staffed through the session. Their agenda would be widely publicized, particularly in the Sunday papers, with the progress of the bills tracked week by week. The Council organized representatives to appear at hearings and more than once urged letter-writing and telegram campaigns on behalf of the cause of the moment. The executive secretary administered all this during the legislative terms, of which Mrs. Highsmith served for four: 1929, 1931, 1933, and 1935. In 1937 she was elected vice-president, and in 1939, president.

Her old friend Mrs. Jerman, the president, obviously put her up to it. (Vara also, perhaps, as she was third vice president.) The big piece that ran in the paper on 6 January 1929 included her photograph, at nearly 50 years old, and a detailed biography, emphasizing her work with the PTA. The inner circle is familiar to us, with Mrs. Doak as treasurer for a decade or more and figures like Kate Burr Johnson, Mrs. Bost, and Dr. Winston to be found at the helm.

The legislative program for 1929 session included five points: the secret, or Australian ballot, which had been defeated in 1925 and 1927; limiting the workday from 11 to 9 hours a day; two weeks' notice before marriage; increase in capacity and maintenance of the state farm colony for women ("vicious and diseased women," they said); state takeover of the Industrial School for Negro Girls at Efland; and a child labor bill preventing children 14 to 16 from working more than eight hours a day. Few of these concerns were resolved in any one Legislature, but when they were, each would be replaced with the next thing on an always pressing agenda. After the Legislature of 1943 the Council paused to take pride in an unusually successful year, with passage of a nine-month school term; the Training School at Efland; funds for public libraries; care and treatment of mentally handicapped children of all races; and new controls on the sale of beer and wine. But their policies on compulsory school attendance and state supervision of city and county jails had failed to pass, and raising the drop-out age from 14 to 16 had been tabled. At that meeting, in a not especially unusual tactic, Mrs. Highsmith was commissioned to go with Mrs. Jerman to talk with Governor Broughton about the need for a state board of control for mental health care. The Legislative Council advanced its agenda however and wherever it could.

One other duty of the Legislative Council's executive secretary was to keep in touch with the group that called itself the Sir Walter Cabinet, that is, the wives of the legislators and elected officers of the state.

Barely a year after taking on the State Legislative Council, when Annie Kizer Bost resigned her position as executive secretary of the North Carolina Federation of Women's Clubs to become state Commissioner of Public Welfare, Mrs. Highsmith succeeded to the position. Mrs. Bost had been the first to hold it, beginning in 1927. This office, like that of the Legislative Council, was located at the Sir Walter Hotel, made available to the Federation without charge. Eventually it moved to the Carolina Hotel and, in 1950, to a fine mansion on Hillsboro Street. The goal was a centralized place, near the seat of government, to conduct Federation business, and the Sir Walter was certainly that. She was executive secretary of the State Federation from early 1930 until she resigned in 1935 to return to the Board of Health. It was a good move from a policy perspective: from here on out the executive secretary would write the press releases, as she was already doing, and would receive a small salary.

Her spirited defense of the Woman's Club movement that appeared in October 1929 was in response to an article in the September issue of *Harper's Weekly:* "Is the Women's Club Dying?" It was a reasonable question to ask in that era of rapidly evolving attitudes toward leisure time. The article cites radio, bridge parties, and politics as rivals for women's attention and predicts that without reprogramming "the cultural club will go the way of the horse and buggy, the cotillion, and the cross-word puzzle." One might also add the obvious draw of the automobile road trip. But Mrs. Highsmith and her cohort were not to be swayed from their missions, and they found any number of ways to respond. One interesting argument was that the investment in infrastructure—club houses—was so formidable as to keep the ladies' attentions. In fact the clubwomen were quick to adopt radio to their own purposes and continually to refocus their projects and proposals on the issues of the day.

In 1932 and 1933 she wrote and published a record number of Sunday columns, some of them quite long, and was almost constantly before the public. For one thing the Women's Clubs embarked on a broadcasting project that saw the Raleigh club presenting a weekly 15-minute spot on WPTF. And yet she managed to undertake ambitious trips frequently, for instance a 10-day car trip to Florida for the Christmas holiday at the end of 1931, taking along her husband and sisters Jean and Mary Belle. In June she and Vara went to the General Federation meeting in Seattle, traveling outward by special train via Lake Louise, Banff, and Vancouver and back through Oregon, California, and such must-sees at the Grand Canyon and Pike's Peak. In 1933 she took ten weeks to visit ten countries in Europe, later writing about the League of Nations and World Court in The Hague. Her party of six had been organized by a Duke French professor, Dr. Edward H. Young.

She held a three-year office, 1932–35, with the General Federation of Women's Clubs, the national organization, as one of five press officers in the Department of Press and Publication. Her beat, about which we know little, was the editorial content of the state magazines. In the next triennium, 1935–38, she became national chair of Press and Publicity for the General Federation, now reckoned—a little grandly—to include 2,000,000 women in the US and Canada. Her job was not to write but to stimulate writing, to which end she promoted a "Back to School" movement for the 10,000 or so club reporters in the country: "every writer of state publicity a trained writer" was her objective. A program of cash prizes in a series of national contests for best press release by a club woman was funded by the New York *Herald-Tribune*'s Bureau of Club Women. In North Carolina she sponsored a club institute called "Write it Right" and prevailed on the School of Journalism at UNC to offer summer and correspondence courses for local reporters.

Even when writing for clubwomen her subject matter was sometimes less than delicate. But for the fact that Dr. Highsmith was himself inundated with the issues facing high schoolers every day, you'd wonder how uncomfortable the dinner conversations were in so refined a household. In April 1938, for instance, the *Health Bulletin* began with the observation: "Elsewhere in this issue under the title of 'Best Health Security Is Home Sanitation,' Mrs. Highsmith has discussed some of the intimate details about home sanitation which only a woman can properly write about." Here she returns, by the way, to flies.

This doubtless puts the lie to a favorite family story of mine. Sometime in 1953, before my grandfather died, we were all seated at table in the big dining room, probably for Thanksgiving. Aunt Louise's husband Louis, the obstetrician, was new to us and, I thought, quite debonair. (I had a particular relationship with him, I felt, as he and I had swept rice off the front porch after Aunt Lula Belle's wedding; it's practically my first very clear memory.) Uncle Louis praised my dad for knowing and quoting Shakespeare at table, to which Aunt Louise remarked "Oh, Louis, if it doesn't have a uterus you don't know what it is." I'm quite sure it was the first time I had heard the "u" word, and I often wondered afterward if it was the first time such a word had been uttered at table. But given Grandmother's professional involvement with the details of venereal disease, to say nothing of birth control, pregnancy, infant mortality, endemic and epidemic disease, and personal cleanliness, I imagine Aunt Louise's remark was thought only mildly scandalous, if that.

In fact the interests of Dr. and Mrs. Highsmith overlapped frequently, especially on the matter of health education in the public schools. She prevailed upon him to teach a course, "Know Your Child," at the Raleigh Woman's Club in the autumn of 1923, when she headed the Education Department. Their closest co-work came, I think, during the Depression, where they helped deliver a Relief program for unemployed teachers. Dr. Highsmith was eager to engage "needy unemployed persons competent to teach adults to read and write English. ... This refers to teaching those who are usually termed illiterates." Successful candidates would be paid 40 cents an hour not to exceed $12 a week. Mrs. Highsmith covered the project in two different Sunday articles (February 12 and October 22, 1933).

Dr. Highsmith had a leading role in the 1938 Health Institutes initiative in the state, which brought together the State Board of Education, where he worked, and the State Board of Health, where she did. On behalf of 900,000 students and 24,000 teachers in the state they worked to form a united health service, supported in part by a Rockefeller Foundation seed grant. Thirty-four health institutes that year trained 7,880 teachers in the latest approaches to public health, a good beginning by any measure.

He also persuaded her, later, to undertake the women's arrangements for a statewide Rotary convention in Raleigh under his guidance. The spouses were called, and in some places still are, Rotary-Anns.

The hardships of the Great Depression were felt across all the sectors of the North Carolina economy. Club women, on the whole comfortably positioned in society, were shocked at its abrupt onset and stark realities. Women's clubs lost members and purchasing power. Crippling cuts in the budget were proposed for both the State Board of Health and the Department of Public Instruction, exacerbating layoff of teachers and medical personnel in the counties and erasing the school lunch program. Food ran short everywhere, so the membership was enjoined to take up canning every last morsel of summer abundance for leaner times, and to teach others how to do it. Club advice the following spring urged planting gardens, and the women compiled source lists for the seeds. By 1931 Mrs. Highsmith was addressing women's groups on unemployment relief, suggesting measures that could be taken by the individual home-maker to provide jobs around the house.

The employment crisis left male employees of the textile mills jobless, while women and children did the same work during a much longer work week at very much lower pay. Overproduction on the farm had led to price collapse. Mrs. Highsmith and her constituents supported Governor Ehringhaus and Frank P. Graham in their drive to adopt a new North Carolina constitution to address those problems in its overhaul of the tax code. In the Tobacco Revolt of 1933, at the peak of the annual state tobacco market, they similarly backed the governor as he declared a "voluntary marketing holiday" before prices could fall any further. In the wake of that episode came the state's first experiments in acreage control.

Officers at every level of the Women's Clubs—national, state, and local—tried to offer words of encouragement and solid ideas for coping. Mrs. Hobgood, State Federation president in the fall of 1931, asked constituents for solidarity with the various relief agencies and the PTAs and other civic organization, especially in finding food and clothing. "We will give as we have never given before of our money—if we have it—of our store of food and clothes and certainly of our oldtime energy of which we have a plenty." "Whistle," she said; "keep courage, and march forward." In her Sunday piece for January 18, 1931, Mrs. Highsmith quoted the better part of the inspirational New Year's greeting from Mrs. John F. Sippel, national president:

> I would that we Club Women might be as lighted candles at this time, making the rooms we enter brighter and happier and our abiding places veritable temples of light.

> Doubtless we shall not reach within a few days or within a few weeks the same degree of prosperity that we enjoyed a few years ago, but it will come and it will be a saner prosperity; it will be wealth that has a stable underpinning; it will be set upon a firm foundation and we shall be stronger men and women for having overcome.

At some point she gave notice of terminating her long (12-year) tenure as press and publicity officer of the North Carolina Federation, retiring from that work at the conclusion of the statewide meeting in Elizabeth City in May 1935. Between her appointment in May 1923 and her elevation to the national equivalent of the same office, she had submitted just short of 200 articles to the newspapers of the state, mostly in the area of 600–750 words but sometimes running to twice that. From every perspective it's a monumental *œuvre*, chronicle not only of clubwomen and their concerns, but also of governmental affairs both state and national, and of the radical assaults foisted by the era on the public welfare—and of the solutions that sometimes began to hold sway.

The Social Security Act of 1935, signed by President Roosevelt on August 14, sharply affected for the better the delivery of medical and social service programs in the states. Its particular provision for prenatal and infant care at the state and local levels fell directly into Kate Highsmith's area of expertise. It also provided the funding that brought her, probably itching for a new crusade, back to the Board of Health and *The Health Bulletin.* Here she promoted in the dailies and weeklies, one might say with the fire of her youth, new programs and advances in pre- and post-natal care. She contributed a major piece, now signed, to nearly every *Bulletin* from May 1936 through spring 1939. Here we find the major pieces of her maturity: "Marihuana," "Saving Babies from Syphilis," "Ripe Old Age" (with the portrait of her grandmother). A photograph on the cover of the October 1937 *Health Bulletin* depicts the mail room, suggesting the scope of the operation, where 43,000 copies of the publication were mailed every month.

She drew repeated attention to advances in the early diagnosis and treatment of cancer, to which she had lost a sister, talking of the wonders of radium and x-rays; and kept her readers informed on the latest understanding of the dread but treatable public health menaces: rabies, malaria, typhus, and of course tuberculosis.

Her term of office as national chair of press and publicity for the General Federation expired with the triennial meeting in Kansas City in May 1938, leaving her freer to accept assignments where her heart lay, at home in North Carolina. Her elevation to both the Raleigh Woman's Club and State Federation presidencies was widely deemed to be just a matter of time: she was sure to be a candidate for one or the other post as of the elections of 1941. It was doubtless with that in mind that she left the Board of Health at the end of 1938. The Depression had receded and many of the New Deal policies she had championed were gaining sway, even as momentum toward renewed world war gathered its inexorable strength.

The press that attended her Raleigh Woman's Club appearance in March 1938, toward the end of her terms with the General Federation, was unusually detailed, presenting her now-familiar biography:

> Mrs. Highsmith, who is one of the nine women in the United States to be chosen as chairman of a department in the General Federation, has been invited by the Raleigh club to attend in her official capacity and extend greetings from the General Federation. The club will make this an occasion

for honoring a member who has won such signal distinctions in the National organization as a recognition of her talent and ability as a writer.

Mrs. Highsmith, one of the most prominent and accomplished members of the Raleigh club, has held many positions of honor not only in her native state but in the entire nation. She has served as director of publicity for the State Board of Health and for the State War Savings and Liberty Loan committees, as State director of the saving societies of the Fifth Federal Reserve District, as special publicity writer for the American Social Hygiene Association, as chairman of publicity for the North Carolina Federation of Women's Clubs, and is now serving as assistant director of health education of the State Board of Health.

The same text ran twice in the Sunday papers, the second time with a new photograph. At 58, she is mostly gray-haired with a simple brush coiffure—greatly less formal than the tight, blue-washed permanent she would adopt in the 1940s. Her almost beatific gaze is reassuring but unquestionably resolute.

She ended her career as essayist with moving pieces for the *Health Bulletin* issues of February and April 1939, both concerning mothers and their babies.

Mrs. J. Henry Highsmith, c. 1943

President and Past President

In January 1939 Mrs. J. Henry Highsmith began a six-year tenure as elected president of the State Legislative Council, serving for the Legislatures of 1939, 1941, and 1943. She had been first vice president for the 1937 session and before that executive secretary for 1931, 1933, and 1935. Forward motion on women's agendas was mostly slow, with central planks of their platforms tabled or defeated again and again. A chief concern remained laws governing marriage licenses, because measures they had seen adopted in 1921 and 1929, requiring health clearances from both applicants, as well as a waiting period, had been scuttled in 1933—this on account of complaints from the hotel industry that neighboring states were getting the wedding-and-honeymoon trade. The Council remained focused, as it had been since the Depression began, on what it termed a "crying need" for better state labor laws, especially as to length and conditions of the work week. To the 1941 session it was asserted that young male employees often worked 60 to 70 hours a week; and ice workers, 12 hours a day, seven days a week. (In 1933 the lobby had been for a 55-hour week and 10-hour day for women.) Once there was a 48-hour week for men, merchants came to Raleigh in droves to demand exemption for their particular industry.

Mrs. Highsmith and her co-crusaders hammered away on matters of incarceration, probation, and parole; on highway safety and beautification; merit-based salary systems for public employees; state-funded alcohol education, now that the 21st Amendment, repealing prohibition, had passed. (North Carolina became dry in 1908 by a vote of 62% to 38%, and never ratified the 21st Amendment.) The Legislative Council and the women's organizations that were its backbone welcomed the inauguration of the progressive new governor, J. Melville Broughton, in January 1941. Both he and his wife Alice were from Raleigh, and longstanding friends of the Highsmiths.

Now free of weekly press releases and monthly essays on public health, she was abler to direct her activism toward the things that mattered most to her personally. In some respects the pinnacle of her work with the State Board of Health came with the "Better Babies Conference" in Raleigh in February 1939—not to be confused with the commercialized, register-your-baby-to-win Better Babies Days sponsored in those weeks by department stores, including Raleigh's Boylan-Pearce. The Raleigh conference bought together health professionals from seven states and 74 North Carolina counties under the aegis of the National Council for Mothers and Babies, there to address the unacceptably high maternal and infant death rate in the state, among the worst in the nation. Eminent national speakers took the stage alongside

Mrs. Highsmith and her colleagues from the Board of Health. Dr. Carl V. Reynolds's keynote summarized:

> When we can take tragedy out of the deaths that occur as the result of the daily hazards of life and place it where it belongs—in preventable deaths— our battle for life preservation will have kept step with scientific progress.

This, in fact, was the very premise of many of the best essays of her maturity, that death from motherhood was preventable.

She spoke widely on women in government and agreed to serve on executive boards of every sort: the NC Commission on Interracial Cooperation, for example. And she moved ever upward in Duke alumni affairs, thanks in part to her close friendships with the president's wife, Mrs. William Preston Few—a Trinity classmate—and with Alice Baldwin, Dean of Women at Duke (after whom Baldwin Auditorium is named). Dean Baldwin was a frequent weekend guest at 832 Wake Forest Road.

Vacations with her family and the relatives from Sampson County had a central place in the yearly routine. In the summer of 1939, after Louise had returned from Girl Scout Camp and Lula Belle from a house party in the mountains, they all went off—Vara, too—to Nags Head, staying at the Fearing Cottage. The Fearings, of Elizabeth City and Roanoke Island, were established patricians of the Albemarle since Colonial times. The personal connections were with Mrs. J. G. Fearing, Eliza, prime mover of the Elizabeth City Woman's Club, and apparently too with D. Bradford Fearing of Manteo, whose idea it was to stage a pageant about the Lost Colony. That summer, the Highsmiths attended the gala 100th performance of *The Lost Colony*. A few days later we find them at the New York World's Fair, for which Mrs. Highsmith had served on a women's matters national committee.

In March 1940 she motored with Vara and mutual friends to a Methodist Missionary Council meeting in New Orleans, stopping in Mobile and Natchez to admire the gardens. Summer 1940 was largely given over to Katherine's debut at the North Carolina Debutante Ball on Labor Day weekend, escorted by her cousin Geddie Herring. There's a stunning portrait of Kate and Katherine made in the living room at 832 Wake Forest Road that weekend.

She lobbied, and rallied, consistently against the rearmament of the country and the munitions trade—for instance, at a raucous "Keep America Out of War" debate at the Wake County Courthouse in July 1940—and promoted any number of initiatives for women studying paths to world peace. Her work with local PTAs was ongoing, and she was a frequent speaker to the Business and Professional Women's Club and Nurses Association.

At the 39th annual convention of the Federation, meeting in Winston-Salem, she lost the presidential election to Mrs. P. R. Rankin, *née* Catherine Frances McCauly, of Mount Gilead. Mrs. Rankin, an acquaintance of long standing, was a church organist admired for her Carolina heartland family values and envied for her home, called Friendship. Mrs. Highsmith was named, instead, third-vice president, thus the director of department activities statewide. She went right to work to produce unusual printed programs of the Federation's goals and aspirations for 1941–42. Just after the convention she accompanied Mrs. Rankin and Mrs. Latham to Atlantic City for the Golden Jubilee convention of the General Federation. There she successfully presented Mrs. Latham's candidacy for national treasurer. Her elegant essay of nomination had been published the previous February: "North Carolina honors one of her best-loved women, affectionately known throughout the state as Mamie Latham."

Shortly after getting back to Raleigh from Atlantic City, she learned that the newly elected president of the Raleigh Woman's Club, Mrs. Harold Glascock, *née* Jessie Lee Mayhugh, had given notice that she could not serve after all, owing to illness. Mrs. Glascock had been a member of the club since 1908 as well as an activist on behalf of the PTA and the Daughters of the American Revolution. (It was with Dr. and Mrs. Glascock that Kate Herring had traveled with from Raleigh to Dunn in 1915, "in an automobile.") The executive board of the Raleigh Woman's Club thus chose Mrs. Highsmith for the presidential term 1941–43. She was installed on June 11, succeeding Mrs. Doak. "My purpose," she said, "shall be to promote in a very real sense a phase of the national defense program—The Enrichment and Preservation of the American Way of Life."

Mrs. Doak, incidentally, went on to become executive secretary of the State Federation, with headquarters now at the Carolina Hotel. She was the fifth to hold that office, after Mrs. Bost, Mrs. Highsmith, Mrs. Bunn, and Miss Susan Iden of the *Raleigh Times*.

Kate Herring Highsmith's presidency of the Raleigh Woman's Club thus coincided with her country's return to war. Within a week of her inauguration, the clubhouse on Hillsboro Street was opened for social gatherings for men in uniform. Not long afterward, young ladies would assemble there on Friday evenings to be bussed to Fort Bragg for dance parties. There were community drives for aluminum, wool sweaters, and books for servicemen. There were calls for volunteer plane spotters and volunteers for the Women's Army Corps. The Highsmiths housed a soldier at Christmas that year; Edenton Street housed 25 "boys" during the holidays, and the Fidelis Sunday School Class fed them breakfast. She served the local council on Civil Defense and a statewide nutrition study group. She raised flags, gave devotionals, and chaperoned dances. The Woman's Club Get-Together Dinner that October used "Women in Defense" as a theme, with patriotic decor that included V for Victory banners and name tags made by Girl Scout Troop 6, hundreds of paper flags, and red-white-and-blue after-dinner mints.

Her statement to the districts, as the Federation's third vice president, read:

> Clubwomen throughout the nation including those in North Carolina for 20
> years or more have worked and prayed for the adoption of arbitration as a
> method settling disputes between nations. From study and observation they
> were convinced that this method offered a road to possible permanent peace.
> With sickening hearts they watched and feared that the world was on the road
> to another war and they had hoped that our nation might escape involvement
> and continue at peace. Now in spite of all efforts we find it at war. We shall
> take our places and render the full measure of service of which we are capable
> in the defense of our country and the attainment of a just peace.

Given her professional experience during the previous war, it was
natural that she emerge as a leader in the War Bonds and Saving Stamps
campaigns and pledge drives. Women were encouraged to have Pin Money
Books for their stamps; civic groups could "buy a bomber" with their name on
it, part of the "Air Armada for Our Navy." The State Federation joined with
the Nurses Association and Home Demonstration Clubs to "buy" the Hague
Convention hospital ship USAHS Larkspur, actually a refurbished German
vessel interned in World War I. (Later it was used to transport war brides and
their dependents to the United States.) One of Mrs. Highsmith's first duties
as Federation president was to travel to Wilmington for the launch of the
Liberty merchant ship, SS Sallie S. Cotten, named for the matriarch of the
State Federation—then immediately renamed Ole Bull, after the Norwegian
violin virtuoso, eventually to become part of the royal Norwegian fleet.

She was also a strong proponent of the NC Tobacco War Bond Program,
with a goal of raising $28,750,000 in bonds at the tobacco warehouses, as five
cents would be diverted from the receipts for every pound of tobacco sold.
Clubwomen staffed the booths.

As the 1942–43 club year began, Mrs. Jerman began to circulate a resolution
endorsing Mrs. Highsmith for the presidency of the State Federation. The
resolution was adopted unanimously in Raleigh in September, by District
8 in October, and by the Charlotte clubs later on. "Mrs. Highsmith insists
that she will make no campaign, though she permitted her club and district
to endorse her for the honored office," reported the Sunday papers that
November. A highly laudatory biographical piece by the noted Charlotte
journalist Mrs. J. A. Yarbrough appeared in the Sunday *Observer* in early
January 1943, as though promoting her candidacy.

As the somber holiday season of 1942 got under way, she received at a
Woman's Club tea on November 25, part of Women and War Week, for every
Wake County mother with a son in service. Two days later she presided
for the last time over a meeting of the Legislative Council, from which she
was to retire after three terms, six years. She was succeeded by Dr. Ellen

Winston. At an affectionate farewell dinner as her Woman's Club term came to an end, she was serenaded with "K-K-K-Katie," the World War I song, and "Let Me Call You Sweetheart." Her fairy godmother appeared for the biographical sketch of her life and works.

Between that event on April 21, 1943, and the State Federation meeting in High Point a week later, Dr. and Mrs. Highsmith announced the engagement—just before she was awarded her Bachelor of Arts degree at Duke—of their daughter Katherine to Kern Holoman. The wedding would take place in June whenever he could secure leave. There were no invitations, only announcements later, to the wedding, which ended up taking place on June 23 at Edenton Street Church with her sisters and three close friends as bridesmaids and Kern in his army uniform. The reception, of course, took place at the Woman's Club.

Kate Highsmith's election as president of the North Carolina Federation of Women's Clubs, on April 29, 1943, in High Point, was unopposed and enthusiastically celebrated. "She is widely known and greatly beloved, a woman of long experience and fine executive ability," wrote the *Charlotte News*. The nominating committee had been chaired by Mrs. McKee, now a state senator.

"Only Mrs. J. Henry Highsmith of Raleigh was considered to head the organization for the two critical years ahead," wrote Mrs. Doak in the Sunday papers. "This able, experienced clubwoman and fine citizen takes the presidency with the love, confidence and hearty support of the entire organization."

The splendid cover portrait of the *North Carolina Clubwoman* that fall bore the caption:

> Trained, experienced, efficient, wise;
> Possessor of life's permanent values:
> The serenity that comes with faith
> The courage that comes with hope
> The devotion that comes with love—
> She will help us to
> "Build for the future a life without fear,
> A faith without doubt, and a world without war!"

The accompanying lead story cites a piece in the *Raleigh Times* welcoming her to the job. It is one of the best descriptions we have of her personal aura at the time:

> Mrs. Highsmith is a charming person with whom to come in contact socially or in civic affairs. She dresses in excellent taste; her voice is low and pleasing; she has a ready smile, and she has none of the earmarks of the successful aggressive clubwoman, but no one would hesitate to call her a progressive woman. Her ability to hear a statement of the other woman's point of view is one of her appealing qualities. Probably no other woman in the State has

contributed more to its welfare, yet with this, she has never neglected her family. The Highsmiths live on Wake Forest Road in Raleigh, and their home is a place of real hospitality. ... With all her honors and her public work she remains a gentle, kindly woman.

Her first letter to her constituents, published in *The Clubwoman,* May–June 1943, summarized her thoughts and goals:

> No greater opportunity for world service has ever come to women, or probably ever will come, than the call for their participation in determining the kind of peace plans the world will adopt after the war. Clubwomen in particular are being asked to study the world situation and to inform themselves concerning the many peace proposals so that they may be able not only to mould constructive public opinion, but also to work through their Congressmen for the terms and the principles they believe will make for a just and lasting peace. Neither American men nor women knew enough about the peace plans proposed following World War I to save them from becoming partisan political issues, and we have as a result World War II. Statesmen are saying that only an informed public opinion and the voice and efforts of thinking Christian women will save the peace plans of today from being mangled at the hands of politicians.

The aspirations she envisaged for her administration began with the hope of recapturing "the fearless spirit, indomitable faith, and will-to-do that actuated clubwomen of pioneer days and made them dare to undertake big things for themselves, their families, and their generation." They concluded with her theme:

> "Build for the Future a Life Without Fear, a Faith Without Doubt, and a World Without War."

She tended her flock faithfully, despite the circumstances and hardships of travel, twice making the traditional October visits to all sixteen Club districts in the state. She kept to her agenda of planning for peace and meanwhile seeking solace and promise in faith. Her thinking seems focused on post-war life, what a life without war and a lasting peace might look like. She was determined that the school curriculum should include religious instruction. "One of the main projects of her administration," we read in late 1944, "was to have Bible taught in the schools." She implored her constituents to study subject matter and be prepared for what was coming in order to cast their votes properly. She pushed her constituents, as best policy and politics allowed, toward supporting the Equal Rights Amendment, to which there was strong opposition in some women's circles. It was no secret, however, that Mrs. Highsmith "works steadily for adoption of the equal rights amendment to the Federal Constitution."

Outside of public addresses, her main writing in this period is in the form of published letters circulated to her constituencies, particularly the presidents of the local clubs. While we do not have that correspondence, as far as I know, big chunks are preserved in the form of quotations in the Woman's Club column in the Sunday papers, now written by Mrs. Doak. Just after the Normandy invasion the presidential message began:

> My message to the clubwomen, now that actual process of liberation of enslaved peoples has begun, is, first, to quicken their interest in all phases of war service; and second, to be constant in prayer for the success of our cause. The petition of our great President on D-Day may well serve as the model to guide them in their supplication, in its portrayal of the cause for which we fight, in its spirit, and in its acceptance of the divine will.

Her reference is to Franklin Roosevelt's famous D-Day prayer, aired over the radio on June 6, 1944.

It's to be remembered that she'd witnessed the homeland in wartime once before, in 1914–18. This time, however, she had a son-in-law in harm's way: my father, who was in France that June.

By the November 1944 election she was urging women not only to vote but also—an ongoing theme of her writings—to study before they did. "Women should be interested in politics, it is the science of government. It has been said 65 per cent of the votes this year will be women's votes, so please, women, know your candidate and vote intelligently."

The annual convention of the State Federation was in Charlotte in late April 1944, in preparation for which she made several trips there, every meal and overnight an occasion of notice in the press. Eddie Rickenbacker, World War I flying ace who had purchased Eastern Air Lines and shepherded it into one of the largest and most successful commercial services in the world, was the featured speaker. In Charlotte, too, I believe, she first advanced her notion that the Federation would purchase a building in downtown Raleigh to serve as permanent state headquarters.

Travel conditions deteriorated from there. Her term as president of the NCFWC was meant to conclude at the next annual convention, May 1945, scheduled for Raleigh in her honor. But early in the year the U. S. Department of Transportation forbade gatherings that brought more than 50 people from out-of-town, in order to save on gasoline. Instead, an "expanded board meeting" was held in Raleigh on May 29–30 for a group of that size. The evening before, she entertained her outgoing executives at her home, presenting them each with a gift. Her daughters Katherine Holoman and Louise Highsmith served as her pages for the sessions. Mrs. Karl Bishopric of Spray was elected to succeed her, and by June 1, at the age of 65, she had entered the exalted ranks of past presidents—thus to be an honored guest wherever and whenever she appeared.

The basics of her last prolonged crusade, on behalf what was called the Youth Conservation movement, began to take shape in her mind during the October 1944 tour of the sixteen state districts, where she found that "delinquent, indigent and neglected children" were a chief concern of her constituents. The numbers were staggering: 60,000 children between 14 and 17 had recently dropped out of school; there had been a 56.8% rejection rate for NC draftees, the highest in the county, owing to physical unfitness and illiteracy. In her effort to learn more, she invited the remarkable Anna M. Kross, whose idea Youth Conservation may have been to start with, to deliver the keynote address to the 1945 "expanded board meeting."

Judge Anna M. Kross, another blockbuster activist, was a sitting magistrate in New York City and director of the General Federation's efforts in Youth Conservation, announced as the primary feature of the national club agenda for 1945 and beyond. She served on those boards through 1950, meanwhile advancing her progressive ideas on the welfare of incarcerated women and adolescents, and on the establishment of family courts. She was eventually New York City Commissioner of Corrections; the women's detention building on Rikers Island was named the Anna M. Kross Center in 1978, and before her death she was recognized by Lyndon Johnson with an Eleanor Roosevelt medal. Her idea was no less than "to save the country's most precious possession, its youth."

In North Carolina, Mrs. Karl Bishopric, as Woman's Club president, and Mrs. Highsmith, as immediate past president, went to work distributing a letter of appeal to the 300-and-some clubs statewide, asking each to appoint a Youth Conservation chairman who would complete a questionnaire designed to assess the true situation of youth across the state. The survey was also to reach churches, government providers, schools, and the YMCAs and YWCAs. When the questionnaires were collected and evaluated, she prevailed on Governor Gregg Cherry and Mrs. Bisophric, jointly, to call a Youth Conservation Conference in Raleigh on January 25, 1946, over which she presided. Cherry's published call termed youth "the State's most precious resource."

The result of the conference was a draft program of nine categories: health services, mental health, school attendance, nutrition, recreation, vocational and employment education, financial matters, and labor law. A Family Life Week would be anchored by Youth Conservation Sunday, perhaps to coincide with National Family Week or National Sunday School Week, the second week in April.

A sample of her other activities as past president might focus on the Equal Rights Amendment, which had been introduced in every Congress since 1923, or on jury service for women, which passed the Legislature in 1945, when the words "man" and "men" had been replaced with "person" and "persons." She began to appear with a dozen other civic notables on a Raleigh Radio Forum broadcast by station WRAL. This program considered matters deemed controversial, such as minimum wage, state-sponsored medical care, and the like. The experts would talk for 20 minutes and take phoned-in questions for 10.

For the 1945 Legislature she advanced an aggressive plan to restore the primacy of public education in post-war North Carolina, leading a coalition of the teachers' union (NCEA), PTA, and others in favor of cost-of-living adjustments, compulsory school attendance to age 16, mandated physical education and recreation, vocational and special education especially for returning veterans, and a ten-month contract for principals.

Kate Highsmith's past-presidency, then, was nearly as full as ever, the annual sequence of teas and receptions unrelenting, likewise the calls to serve on all manner of committees to the civic good—a new building for the YWCA, for instance. She had reported to her constituents on the Bretton Woods and Dumbarton Oaks Conference in 1944; now she followed and spoke on the organization and birth of the United Nations.

Along with Mrs. Bost and Mrs. Doak, she organized Mrs. Jerman's funeral on March 13, 1946, arranging for three distinguished speakers: Josephus Daniels (a childhood friend), Kate Burr Johnson, and Harriet Elliott, dean of UNC Woman's College in Greensboro. The music was by the St. Cecilia Chorus, Raleigh's oldest musical organization, in which Mrs. Jerman once sang.

Political leadership in North Carolina, and the Progressive and New Deal agendas with which Mrs. Highsmith had long been associated, evolved radically owing to a series of unexpected deaths in office (and Franklin Roosevelt's death in Georgia in 1945). Senator Josiah Bailey had been replaced in the United States Senate by William B. Umstead; defeated in the 1948 election by J. Melville Broughton, he was then elected governor, only to suffer a near-fatal heart attack two days after his inauguration. Meanwhile Senator Broughton died in office after two months. A new governor, W. Kerr Scott, appointed former UNC president Frank Porter Graham to fill Broughton's Senate seat.

Graham and his wife were well known to the Highsmiths, and Mrs. Highsmith took a leading position in supporting him for election to the Senate in the 1950 Democratic primary. The ugly election revolved around the racist views of the candidate Willis Smith. ("White People, Wake Up Before It's Too Late," said a central print piece. "Do You Want Negroes working beside you, your wife and daughter in your mills and factories? ... Frank Graham Favors Mingling of the Races.") Among Smith's supporters was the young Jesse Helms. Unusually, Mrs. Highsmith and her posse of clubwomen came out strongly for Graham at a Woman's Club convention in Raleigh. One ¾-page newspaper ad featured her portrait as a mature leader (now 70), also pictures and statements of Mrs. Bost and Mrs. Latham among some 14 worthies. Her endorsement was printed again and again that May: "I recognize in [Frank P. Graham] the qualities of Christian leadership and character that all women value and are willing to fight for. I see in Graham a hope for better understanding and more friendly relations among the nations."

Graham narrowly lost the primary and went on to work at the United Nations as a mediator; Smith served briefly in Washington, succumbing to a heart attack in 1953. Kerr Scott ended up in his Senate seat but died, too, of a heart attack in office.

At the end of 1950 the North Carolina Federation completed negotiations to purchase a large house and grounds at 1509 Hillsboro Street to serve as Federation Headquarters. Mamie Latham was prevailed on to relocate from Asheville and become the resident hostess there. Upstairs were some apartments and guestrooms for visiting clubwomen; downstairs, sitting rooms, receiving areas, and administrative offices.

Mrs. Highsmith's report to the Raleigh club on the Legislative session of 1951 was glum; their "stand on world government and on [preserving] Moore Square [from being turned into a parking lot] was upheld, ... but the platform supported with the Legislative Council of broad social reforms was almost entirely defeated." The child labor laws, she feared, were again under attack.

I was born in 1947, followed by the eight grandchildren listed in the dedication above, in total four Holomans (Katherine's children), four Wilkersons (Louise's children), and Henry Rich (Lula Belle's son). She was as devoted to us grandchildren as her daughters were to her, appearing at every one of our birthdays, taking us after church, often as not, to the S&W Cafeteria beside the Sir Walter Hotel—where Joe the headwaiter was always fussing over her—or to fancier places for Easter and Mother's Day. We sensed she was important and universally loved, but would not have been able to pinpoint exactly why.

In addition to our cousin Henry Rich, Dr. Highsmith had two grandchildren in Florida, children of John Henry and Eva. He proudly gave his granddaughter Lula Marion away at her wedding in Green Cove Springs in June 1950, where, earlier in the day, Lula Belle had overseen the cake cutting. Dr. Highsmith turned 75 in 1952, still retaining his title as director, Division of Instructional Service, North Carolina Department of Public Instruction. He was also at the time chairman of accreditation for the Southern Association of Colleges and High Schools, speaking to PTAs ("What Is Happening to Our Children?"), introducing the state's teachers to a new line of French and Spanish textbooks, and so on. We find him presenting Raleigh high school valedictorians with books at a Phi Beta Kappa Association meeting at the end of April 1953.

In early May, Mrs. Highsmith traveled to the NCFWC convention in Wilmington, and while she was away, Dr. Highsmith was found to have died in his reading chair. Grandmother was located by the long-distance operator at Lumina Pavilion at Wrightsville Beach and driven home, if I remember the story aright, by the Highway Patrol. "Since his young manhood," remarked the *Charlotte Observer* in announcing his death, "he had had no other business or profession than the schooling of the children of this state."

Dick and I, and possibly our cousin Louise, were aware of our bereavement but were thought too young to attend the funeral. We went out to the cemetery the next day to see the flowers. Our younger cousins, however, will not have remembered their grandfather.

Grandmother is said to have been have been shocked and overwhelmed. They had been a domestic couple for more than three decades but, just as significantly, co-crusaders on behalf of the welfare of North Carolinians for all their adult lives. Grandfather's reading chair was off limits for some time, and his study, untouched, became, more and more, a kind of memorial.

She had reemerged into public life by the time of the 1954 State Federation convention in Asheville, where she's pictured, with Mrs. Bost, Mrs. Latham, and Mrs. Land, on the front page of the *Asheville Citizen* Society page of April 29; and for the Golden Anniversary of the Raleigh Woman's Club that year, where Katherine appeared as her mother Kate in a costume pageant. She's pictured with the other living past presidents—a mighty bunch, ten in number, including Mrs. Josephus Daniels, Mrs. Bost, Mrs. Doak, and Mrs. Simms—at an anniversary event that January. A photograph of Katherine-as-Kate ran in the paper on October 1. She continued to serve as trustee of the State Federation.

She made a few forays beyond Raleigh, including to a Virginia Woman's Forum on "Woman's Place in a Changing World," and to the General Federation convention in Philadelphia in 1955.

In 1956, while Kern and Kaye Holoman were abroad on their Grand Tour, she suffered a mild stroke, necessitating alternative weekend arrangements for her grandchildren Kern and Dick. Lula Belle took the lead on her care, and she had a reasonable recovery.

During the holiday season of 1960, possibly Thanksgiving, she retired after lunch to take her nap in Dick's and my room at the end of the house. She took a fall and was carried off in an ambulance, soon to be diagnosed with a broken hip. From then through the summer, she was "confined" at Mayview Convalescent Home, then returned home at the first of September to a life of walkers and wheelchairs. The downstairs library was converted into her bedroom, and wheelchair ramps were built at 832 Wake Forest Road and at our home on Hostetler Street.

She resumed her calendar as she could, appearing as past president of her organizations, attending the Littleton College reunions with her remaining sisters, and going to church every Sunday. We find her still in public life in March 1964, when she rides in a parade of antique cars from Cameron Village to the Memorial Auditorium, a steam calliope leading the way; and when, the same week, she endorses her old friend Dan K. Moore for governor.

She declined rapidly after that and had to return to Mayview, where she died on October 2, 1966. Katherine, Louise, and Lula Belle tried to visit her every afternoon, and my brothers and I often went along. My high school graduation party in 1965 was at her bedside. That Christmas 1965, Aunt Lula Belle smuggled in a Mason jar of holiday eggnog and more or less poured it down her throat. After a few minutes, she sat up to say "That was good!" So far as I know, those were her last words.

KATE HERRING HIGHSMITH
AS WRITER

She herself thought that "the best part of the work she did was in the field of writing, doing promotion work for the State Board of Health as a pioneer in health education." Her most passionate writing for the Woman's Club—and PTA and State Legislative Council and Tuberculosis Association—nearly always centers on public health and welfare, or on promoting progressive social causes like the secret ballot and public libraries. She was recognized as a pioneer publicist and journalist, and as a woman, for her skill at advancing arguments and bringing non-professionals around to understanding the sometimes complex evolution of health care and social thought. She was by no means the only woman in the press corps—think of all the women who wrote for the Society pages—but her attendance at nearly-all-male Press Association meetings was noticed approvingly, and her subject-matter expertise admired. Her departure from the Board of Health in 1918 to join the war financing effort was the occasion for such a great burst of compliments in the press that I've included a selection below (chapter 1918). "Her best work has been in popularizing the department and in carrying health propaganda to the remotest parts of the State," they said. "She has been able to do this by mastery of the news rather than the editorial side."

Her duties included plenty of drudge work and too much cut-and-paste: chunks of other people's reports, convention agendas, countless lists of names. But her reputation for making science and politics comprehensible and the ladies' activities vital was well earned.

The formidable sample of her work included here is, however, necessarily incomplete. The essays attributed to her in the papers and *Health Bulletin* represent just a portion of items she actually wrote or co-authored. Her autobiographical sketch, for instance, mentions weekly public health mailings. And much of every monthly issue of the *Bulletin* under her leadership feels like she might have written it. There's no telling what appeared in the dozens of other publications, impossible to trace or lacking attributions, with which she was affiliated: *The Weekly Guide* of Dunn, *The Southern Methodist* magazine, *The Christian Home,* the national *Health Digest,* and of course the *North Carolina Clubwoman,* which she invented and edited for ten years.

The *Health Bulletin* had been published by the North Carolina State Board of Health since the 1860s. With rare exceptions the articles of that era lack attributions, and Herring is never included in the Official Staff listing. She almost certainly edited the majority of vols. 20–22, 1915–16 to 1917–18, thus was probably responsible for the sometimes jovial Editorial Brevities at the top of each 24-page number. There we encounter her crusades and her language: "What is food for flies is poison for man. Where they feed you should not feed."

"Eat vegetables," orders the *Bulletin*, presumably in her voice.

I like to think she is responsible for the cover of vol. 34, no. 7 (July, 1919), which was entirely devoted to a new state law on privies. (Her supervisor was state expert on the subject, and the *Bulletin* often ran excruciatingly detailed advice for the "improved" model, with photographs.) On the cover are juxtaposed "A Law of the State of North Carolina, Enacted A.D. 1919": "Every residence located within three hundred yards of another residence must have an improved privy of a type approved by the State Board of Health" with, to the left, "A Law of Moses, Judge of Israel; About 1491 B.C.": "Thou shalt have a place also without the camp, whither thou shalt go forth abroad: and thou shalt have a paddle upon thy weapon; and it shall be, when thou wilt ease thyself abroad, thou shalt dig therewith, and shall turn back and cover that which cometh from thee.—(Deut. 23: 12–13)." Office humor, you might say.

Her signed work on behalf of War Savings Stamps and related efforts begins to appear in the dailies in the spring of 1918, but she's also obviously the author of many dozens of press releases that mention her by name, often as organizer of the Thrift Exhibits that traveled through the Fifth Federal Reserve District in the county and state fair season of 1919. Nor do we have anything signed from her year with the Social Hygiene projects. She probably wrote most of the press originating in Maryland, pieces that deal with the "moral, physical and economic ravages" of vice and venereal disease.

But this is, too, the period of major signed works, both heartrending (the piece on Kiffin Rockwell, May 1918, that was featured in the Sunday *Atlanta Constitution* a few weeks later) and powerful ("How the Southern Negro is Supporting the Government," in November 1918; "The Negro and War Savings in North Carolina," the following January 1919).

Mrs. J. Henry Highsmith's heroic stint as chief publicity officer for the North Carolina Federation of Women's Clubs, which lasted from 1924 until she left in 1935 to return to the Health Department, overlaps with her long service to the State Legislative Council. (For that matter, the Council office was often the same physical location as Woman's Club headquarters. So whether the press releases originated from the Federation or, during the odd-year sessions of the Legislature, the Council, they figured in what people saw as her familiar Sunday columns, Society page 1. The subject matter is the staggering array of issues that drew the attention of powerful women and women's organizations of the time: the long struggle to rectify the work environment for women and children, mandatory medical evaluations for marriage, conditions of incarceration, adult illiteracy, sanitation and cleanliness, a statewide eight-month school year and mandatory schooling to age 16, highway beautification, national parks, hunger and unemployment during the Depression, driver licensing and driver education, King Cotton, marijuana, several Constitutional amendments, Christmas trees, libraries, art museums, the North Carolina Symphony, slang. Leading her personal concerns, always, were the plagues that cost North Carolina too many lives: tuberculosis, infant and maternal mortality, preventable loss of sight, polio, cerebral palsy, cancer. Poverty in general. She led some of these battles and followed in many others, but hers was, often as not, their primary voice.

Her return to the Health Department and major monthly essays in the *Health Bulletin,* 1936–1938, was meant to focus on mothers and babies, and did so, but she treats other threats as well: rabies, malaria, hunting accidents. She also draws sharp focus on any number of issues in public education, from school lunch to child health screening to teacher health and janitor health. This particular concern of her last round of published columns strongly foreshadows the subject of her last public crusade, the Youth Conservation movement.

She worked at a 1930s-vintage Underwood office typewriter, a wonderful see-through riot of mechanical device, the letters on black keys and the functions on green, a toggle to move from red to black ink on the bi-colored ribbons, and the large corporate monogram peering at the typist from behind the platin. I was hypnotized by it, and even though we weren't supposed to touch, I spent a lot of time trying it out—the original source of my fascination with typewriters and writing.

Her hundreds of speeches exist, so far as I know, only in quotations from the daily press and a few announced titles: from "Helping the Child to Find Himself" to "Sex Education in the Home" offered to PTAs; or "Intelligent Voting" to the Business and Professional Women. Little but the titles are known of her many program contributions to the Twentieth Century Book Club, but even these prompt insight into her curiosity: Huguenots and Quakers, modern China, India.

Over the radio she was most often heard during Federation Hour on WPTF, largely devoted to legislative matters. But there were also topics like "Our State Wild Flower Reserve" for the Raleigh Garden Club radio show (January 1937) and, now and then, local politics, as in her support for the council–manager form of government in the Raleigh election of 1935, or front-page partisan struggles, as in her staunch (and permanent) opposition to the repeal of prohibition, from 1937. She was author, too, of countless resolutions, any number of which carried to good end result: the nomination of Mrs. E. M. Land as a national vice president of the Women's Clubs, for instance, and a 1930 proposal for a North Carolina Art Museum. Very occasionally she wrote endorsements of candidates for political office.

Newspaper style, as she learned it, favored as little punctuation as possible and positively shunned the comma. Mrs. Highsmith tended to write very long sentences, squeezing in a lot of information before eventually arriving at the period stop. Add to that the accident-prone atmosphere of editing, typesetting, and laying out a big daily paper and you find yourself staring at some pretty forbidding paragraphs. But she does not mince words, and her point is always clear.

Although she lived her life in the bosom of what is considered white privilege, we rarely find her in overtly problematic territory. This I would attribute to her having grown to maturity on the farm and to her inalterable, Christian, belief in the fundamental equality of her fellow beings. The Confederacy has no place in her writings (the word "Confederate" nowhere appears), even as her pieces run alongside articles in the Society section on Confederate Flag Day and celebrations of Robert E. Lee's birthday. As to race she is careful always to include what she thought of as the Negro experience in her assessments of the public welfare. She lived in a place and time defined by racial segregation, of course, but counted as staunch allies such organizations as the North Carolina Federation of Negro Women's Clubs, founded 1909. Overcoming poverty in every community of the state was the common denominator of her life's work.

Where today's reader flinches is at her vocabulary for mental health, which makes common reference to the "feeble minded" and the "mentally deficient." This was acceptable clinical terminology of her day, of course, but grates mightily in the 21st century. So too are her fleeting references to "eugenics" and "improvement of the race," but in the 1920s and '30s, this had to do with her belief in progress of humankind as a whole and was, as she saw it, primarily a matter of eliminating disease and assuring the wellness of mothers and their babies.

Resist the temptation to skim over the Woman's Club pieces because of their tendency toward long lists of ladies' names and towns of origin, and transcripts of convention programs upcoming. If you do you will miss such *aperçus* as the cost of the four-day Havana add-on to the 1932 Miami Convention of 1932—$49.50 all expenses paid—and the special 18-day return rail fare from Raleigh to Miami, which was $44.85, plus $10.13 for a Pullman. Or, to cite another example, Mrs. Highsmith's shock to discover that of 3 million North Carolinians, 2 million lacked access to a public library (and libraries had been a focus of women's clubs since the outset).

The articles from the 1930s and early '40s are a stern reminder of the Depression as it was experienced in the agrarian South, and of the finances and daily lives of everyday people struggling to keep their families and communities intact until the dawn of a new era of world peace. Nestled in those long lists of names are a good hundred or more pleasing characters:

Dr. Ernst Derendinger, for instance, art historian of Catawba College and visiting lecturer at Harvard, always ready with remarks. Or Katherine Clark Pendleton Arrington, tenacious and ultimately successful advocate for a North Carolina Art Museum. Or the divine Mamie Latham (Mrs. R. H. Latham), Woman's Club grandee at the local, state, and national levels, whom Grandmother talked into moving to Raleigh to become hostess of the newly acquired mansion that would serve as Federation Headquarters. Dick and I remember her fondly as a sort of surrogate grandmother, with a staircase descent that could only be called regal. In all, the essays comprise a virtual encyclopedia of Progressive-era and New Deal characters and thinking. The women's movement, as Mrs. Highsmith lived it, was seldom disinteresting.

So find your own favorites. Among mine, an ever-changing list, are:
"How the State Fights Great White Plague" [the North Carolina Sanatorium in Hoke County] (1915)
"Paul and Kiffin Rockwell" (1918)
"The Negro and War Savings in North Carolina" (1919)
"No Sinister Motives Behind Club Women's Request for Survey of Women in Industry" (1926)
"Prejudice of Men Most Difficult Obstacle Movement Has Had to Overcome" (1926)
"Art Museum for State Big Need" (1926)
"Women Are United for Australian Ballot Law" (1929)
"Child Labor Day" (1931)
"Club Women to Observe Book Week" (1932)
"Why Mothers and Babies Die Needlessly in North Carolina" (1936)
"Marihuana" (1938)
"Saving Babies from Syphilis" (1938)

It's not difficult to see the ways the Highsmith legacy passed down to our generation. Aunt Lula Belle, who earned a Master of Science in Public Health, went on to have nearly the same title at the Health Department, Chief of Health Education, and to serve on the editorial board of the *Health Bulletin*. My mother Katherine Holoman lived clearly in awe of her mother's example and determined to emulate it, which she did on multiple fronts. She succeeded her mother at the State Legislative Council, North Carolina Conference for Social Service, and of course at the Woman's Club, where they were noted as the first (but not last) mother–daughter pair of state presidents.

At both the State Legislative Council and the Conference for Social Service, mentors passed executive responsibilities to their disciples in lineages strong with the distinguished women we meet in these pages: Kate Burr Johnson, Annie Bost, Ellen Winston. Virginia Greer had been executive secretary at the Conference since 1948, when Dr. Winston was president; Katherine succeeded her, more or less at Mrs. Greer's request.

Aunt Louise, who was also involved in Woman's Club work, developed the Highsmiths' commitment to singing (inherited, it must be said, primarily from Dr. Highsmith's love of singing and choirs, and that of his sister, our Aunt Margaret) into an enduring profession that served as a model for her own family and ours too.

At our house my mother was herself forever on crusades. One of her first photographs as a club woman shows her assisting at a chest x-ray clinic. She often visited Samarcand Manor and other homes and correctional institutions for young women. She disliked purchasing wild Christmas holly and mistletoe, thinking it unsound stewardship of natural beauty; those things needed to come from our own yard. See, then, Mrs. Highsmith's essay on the same subject of December, 1924. Several of Katherine's other concerns—mandatory automobile inspection, fluoride in the water, family planning—are direct outgrowths of her mother's agenda. Kate had attended the 1950 White House Conference for Children and Youth; Katherine, excited by the precedent, attended the 1970 White House Conference, as did Dr. Winston.

One of the sub-headlines to Mrs. Highsmith's Sunday article of February 3, 1924, mentions a "Plan to Wipe Out Illiteracy." Her daughter Katherine was convinced that universal adult literacy could be achieved in North Carolina under her watch, and before her untimely death was actively working toward that end.

I inherited Grandmother's typewriter.

PART I

KATE M. HERRING

1905–1906

——————◁◈▷——————

1880

18 September — born at Herring's Crossroads near Newton Grove in Sampson County, NC, the second (after Vara Louise) of the nine children of Rufus King Herring and his wife Paulina Anna Westbrook Herring

1898

16 May — death of her father, Rufus; family remains in Herring township

1901

8 June — returns (as Miss Katie Herring) home after visiting Miss Maggie Simmons of Raleigh

1902

17 March — attends and ushers at revue, "Old Times Made New," given by alumnae of Littleton Female College; Vara played Joan of Arc

28–29 May — graduates Littleton College (as "Katie Maude Herring") in a class of five; at the graduation exercises, she presents the valedictory essay, "More Light"; ushers that night at the college Annual Concert

1903

7 April — bridesmaid at Randall–Culbreth wedding in Falcon, NC; the groom, Charles Randall, was a family friend in Dunn

6 August — visits Miss Georgia Biggs in Rockingham, listed as "of Clinton"

1904

5 May — as assistant principal, participates in commencement at Newton Grove Preparatory School, where Prof. Plato Tracy Durham of Trinity College is speaker

Fall — enters Trinity College, the future Duke University, as a member of the Junior Class

1905

19 October — visit of Theodore Roosevelt to Trinity College, for which she writes ode, "A Welcome to the President," published in the November issues of *Trinity College Archive* under the name Katie M. Herring

December — publishes "The Heart Interprets For the Eye" in December issue of the *Trinity Archive*

1906

4 April — attends Trinity Class of '06 reception, where she delivers a toast

April — publishes a valedictory poem, "No Letting Down," in April issue of *Trinity College Archive*

6 June — receives the AB degree *cum laude*, Trinity College, in the name of Katherine Maude Herring

19 OCTOBER 1905

A WELCOME FROM TRINITY TO THE PRESIDENT

By Katie M. Herring

Hail to thee, our nation's Chief!
   Hail to thee, our people's Pride!
Hearts we bring that bear no grief,
   Hearts and hands are open wide.
We welcome thee, a nation's Seer;
   We welcome thee, a Prophet, great;
We wait with one loud, mighty cheer,
   To greet thee at our College Gate.
Old Glory yonder welcomes thee;
   A symbol true for what we stand.
For Freedom, waves she, gloriously,
   For God and this, our native land.
Our College bell peals forth with might,
   A plain and simple salutation;
Again we catch it in the night,
   A sweet and solemn adoration.

Note: Theodore Roosevelt visited the Trinity Campus on 19 October 1905.

The Trinity Archive, November 1905, p. 89

December 1905

The Heart Interprets for the Eye

By Katie M. Herring

1. Eugene to Clara
Nashville, Tenn.,
Vanderbilt University, Nov. 17, 1903.

Dear Clara:—Your letter was of the greatest interest and pleasure to me. After reading every word over carefully, I felt better fitted for several hours of hard study.

Thank you, Clara, for the invitation to attend your Thanksgiving reception; no other pleasure would be greater than to spend the day at home and go to your party that evening—not so much in attending the party as being with you once more. Yes, they expect me to spend the day at home, but having only one day off and much work pressing, I am going to be a good boy once and deny myself the pleasure of seeing you.

I send you the latest issue of "The Observer." I found it to be very interesting, and marked several passages which greatly impressed me, and I hope will affect you likewise.

Wishing you success, and much pleasure at your party, I am, as ever yours,
Eugene

2. Clara to Eugene
Glenriff, Tenn., Nov. 30, 1903.

Dear Eugene:—I am glad to see you growing more conservative as you grow older, but it seems rather strange to me that you so hastily decided "to be good." My invitation seems to have helped you to decide at once, but you are right, I suppose, since you could enjoy yourself better elsewhere.

The party was thoroughly delightful, and all seemed a merry crowd. Janie spent Thanksgiving with me, and what do you think? Percy went all the way from C— to see her, and she was with me. Poor girl! I was so sorry for her, but sympathy would not bring to her the one she wished to see.

I am going to spend several days before Christmas with my aunt in Centerville, and I'm quite busy, as I leave tomorrow. You will pardon this short letter.

Very sincerely,
Clara James

3. Eugene to Clara
Vanderbilt University,
Nashville, Tenn., Dec. 10, 1903.

Dear Clara:—I hope you enjoyed your visit to your Aunt's. I wish I were with you now to hear you tell all about it.

Clara, I sincerely repent for "being good," and not going to see you Thanksgiving. Your invitation had nothing at all to do with my spending the day here. It made me all the more anxious to go, but as I said before, my work would not permit me. You seem not to understand, but if I were with you I could explain it all, and I'm sure you would forgive me. It was my one regret the whole day, and you know there's nothing pleasant akin to regret.

Did you get the magazine? You did not mention it, perhaps you haven't had time to read it.

Do write soon; you have no idea how long the time seems when I have to wait.

> Your own true friend,
> EUGENE

4. Eugene to Clara

You will be surprised, Clara, to get this note from me, but I just could not wait to hear from you to tell you that my very good friend, Max Rowland, from North Carolina, whom you have heard me speak of so many times, is going home with me to spend Christmas. I'm sure you will like him, but I hope not too well. I enclose a small snap of him that you may see how he looks. This is one I got on the sly while he was "loafing" in front of Kissam Hall. By the way, don't you think it would be fine to have Janie to spend the holidays with you? You know four can always get along better than three. Then there's not an odd one always to be troubling.

> Yours,
> EUGENE WATTS
> December 16, 1903.

5. Clara to Eugene

DEAR EUGENE:—I would have written earlier but was detained on my visit several days longer than I expected and then it takes sometime, you know, to get to be yourself again.

Pardon me, Eugene, for not thanking you for "The Observer." I heartily appreciate your sending it and enjoyed it. The marked passages were interesting, perhaps all the more so by being marked. Not knowing in what manner they impressed you, I cannot say that they impressed me likewise. I especially enjoyed the Thanksgiving poem.

I am delighted to hear that "Max," as you call him, is coming home with you. I will do all I can to make it pleasant for him, for I know I'm going to like him. I think that is one of the cutest pictures I have ever seen. Does he look as well as his picture? Yes, I'll be sure to invite Janie to spend the time with me and you must not fail to bring him. I have just been discussing some plans for receptions, dinners, etc., all for Max's pleasure you see.

While glancing over a back number of the Columbia Daily Herald today, I came across an item that at once took my eye. I do not understand it, although I am not surprised. I wish you to explain. I send the clipping.

Very truly,

CLARA

Glenriff, Tenn., Dec. 19, 1903.

The Clipping

"Among those registered at the Bethel Hotel is Mr. Eugene Watts, of Nashville, who has come to attend the Thanksgiving german [dance party] to be given by the Elks' club in Elks' Hall."

6. Eugene to Clara

DEAR CLARA:—Examinations are on and I have only a few minutes to write and tell you that Max and I will be home the evening of the 23d. If the train is not too late, we'll come around that night, otherwise next morning, and will then know your plans. I would like to write you more, but English exam. is on for today.

Hoping to see you soon,

EUGENE

P. S.—I don't understand what you mean by the clipping, but will take it along and we'll discuss it in full while home.

E.

7. Eugene to Clara
(After the Holidays.)
VANDERBILT UNIVERSITY,
NASHVILLE, TENN., Jan. 6, 1904.

MY DEAREST CLARA:—We arrived safely on the Park yesterday. There's quite a rush as the boys are not all in yet. There's not more than half back; perhaps they had the same inclination, and I might say temptation, to stay over that we had. I now see wherein they were wise to heed; for, Clara, never did I want to see you as I do tonight. If you only knew how Max and I hated to leave, and how tame it is to come back to this humdrum life! I don't believe I can ever wait until June to see you. I feel tonight as if it were five years since I was with you, and what will five long months seem? Clara, I love you more tonight than I ever did. You looked so fair and beautiful—more than I ever saw you—the night we told you good-bye.

I can never thank you enough for the genuinely pleasant time you gave my friend and me. It is useless for me to attempt to tell you how much we enjoyed it, but I never spent a more pleasant Christmas, and Max says he never will unless he can spend it with you. I know he has told you all this; I will never forgive him for taking all my time from you when Janie was there. And, Clara, when you went to ride and stayed so long I almost said you were to blame; and when we would call at night and would see Max follow you over to the sofa in the corner—I wished I had never seen Max Rowland. Poor Janie; I know I made it miserable for her, and she never did like me. I don't see why Max didn't pay her more attention. She's a fine, clever girl.

Max sends you quite a number of messages which I hardly know how to express.

Please write soon, for I will be anxiously waiting to hear from you.

Devotedly yours,
EUGENE

8. Clara to Eugene

DEAR EUGENE:—I hope you and Mr. Rowland have gotten settled and down to work before now. It is awfully hard to apply yourself after a long rest; but speaking of leaving, those leaving never fare so badly as those left. They have nothing of interest to occupy their time till they can somewhat recover, while those leaving are meeting new scenes and faces constantly.

It was indeed nice of you to speak of my entertaining as you did. But could anyone have done other than her best when her guests were so charming? Really, I think Mr. Rowland is one of the most attractive men I ever met; as for you, Gene, you know my views there. But I congratulate you on your excellent choice of friends.

Janie left yesterday and I was almost as lonely as when you left—lonely enough to cry, but tears often make worse instead of mend * * *.

Remember me always kindly to Mr. Rowland.

Your old friend,
CLARA
Glenriff, Tenn., January 12, 1904.

9. Eugene to Clara

MY DEAR CLARA:—I am troubled. I can never rest until I understand and then I fear it will be the ruin of me. Oh! Clara, you that have made me so happy so many times and who have been all the world to me, why is it you wish to crush the very life out of me? Can one so fair, and at one time so good and true, be so heartless and cruel? It is useless for me to tell you for you know it all and it needs no explanation. Forgive Max? Let me never see him again, yet he knows not of my great grief. I have told you all this. It will break my heart to give you up, but if you say so, it will be so with all the strength of my manhood.

EUGENE
March 3.

10. Clara to Eugene

Will you please explain your rage, Eugene Watts, without further pouring volley upon me, or let me know wherein I am the cause? Very rude of you in the least.

CLARA JAMES

Glenriff, Tenn., March 4.

11. Eugene to Clara

NASHVILLE, TENN., March 6, 1904.

Your innocence, Clara, is indeed uncalled for. If you really knew nothing and are ignorant of my great trouble, it would be indeed rude of me. But can my eyes fool me—the most trustworthy of my senses? Can my heart deceive me? Would that my eyes had never seen and my heart had never felt! And, Clara, if I must tell you it was that while in Max's room I unintentionally saw in a letter to you just begun, one sentence that kills me and separates us forever. This is sufficient; with this I close.

EUGENE

12. Eugene to Clara

MY DEAREST CLARA:—Why can't we judge as we'd be judged? Clara, I can never forgive myself for doubting you and saying the harsh things I did. Just a few minutes ago, Max came in for a friendly chat, and while asking me of you incidentally remarked about "his Clara" down in North Carolina. Oh, how mean and wretched I felt! Nothing could ease my mind but to sit down and tell you all about it at once and beg your forgiveness. You see I thought there was no other Clara in the world but "my Clara," and thereby misjudged my good friend Max, and my friend that is all the world to me. Little girl, won't you forgive me? I never knew that love was so sweet until I thought I had lost yours. Write me forgiveness and love at once. I cannot wait.

Yours forever,

EUGENE

Vanderbilt, March 11, 1904.

13. Clara to Eugene

After several days of suspense, I received a note of apology from you, and one I assure was sorely needed. Forgive you? How hastily you judged when so much depended on the turning of the balance. And how could you have ever made so great an error through a simple name? But, I remember— yes, I forgive you—when I thought that the Eugene Watts, from Nashville, registered at the Bethel Hotel, was "my Eugene." I forgive you all and since we find ourselves in the same error let us never again let hearts full of suspicions and doubts interpret for the eyes.

As ever yours,

CLARA

Glenriff, Tenn., March 14, 1904.

Telegram
NASHVILLE, TENN., March 14, 1904.

No heart can ever again interpret for my eyes.

    E. W.

The Trinity Archive, December 1905, pp. 131–37

APRIL 1906

NO LETTING DOWN

By Katherine Herring

"Let there be no letting down,"
  Are the words we often hear,
"Keep directly to the point,"
  Spur us on throughout the year.
Voices, dear, of college days
  Help us to the goal,
Lest we falter by the way
  When we've left thy fold.

May there be no letting down
  When our work we take,
May we keep up to the point
  And ever wide awake.
For life is dark, the future gray,
  And good is found through ill;
May we then the echo hear
  Though the voice be still.

Let there be no letting down
  When duty calls us forth,
To serve, to wait and ever love—
  What more in life's of worth?
Voices, dear, may strength be thine
  To reawake the deadened soul,
In life to know the greater truths,
  In God to know the whole.

The Trinity Archive, April 1906, p. 297

1914–1917

———————⸎———————

1906–07, 1907–08
Teacher of English, Kinston High School

1908

30 June — serves as bridesmaid (as Katherine M. Herring) in Clinton for her first cousin Donnie Mae Royal

15 August — honored (as Miss Kate M. Herring, of Clinton), with Annie V. Crews of Oxford—a lifetime friend—and others, at a "delightful barge party" on the Perquimans River, under full moon; a lawn party followed at Herford, constituent of a longer house party organized by Miss Celia Winstead

1908–09 and Fall 1909 (three semesters)
Teacher of English and German, Louisburg College

12 October — honored at a reception by Mrs. Ivey Allen, *née* Mary Davis, president of Louisburg College, for the two new members of he faculty.

24 December — receives at a reception given by President and Mrs. Rhodes in Durham for Littleton College alumnae living in Durham or attending the Annual Conference of the Methodist Church there

1909

April — attends a Japanese Party in Louisburg of The Younger Set literary society, where papers on Japan, past, present, and future were read

29 November — returns "home" (as Miss Katherine Herring) to Dunn from Louisburg Female College; soon separates from Louisburg College

1910

18 January — visits Raleigh

22 July — receives (as Miss Katie Herring, of Dunn) at an at-home given by Mr. and Mrs. J. W. Whitehead at their elegant residence on King and Harnett Streets, Dunn

76

1911–14
Associate Editor, The Orphans' Friend
Oxford Orphan Asylum

1911

January — promoted to associate editorship of the *Orphans' Friend and Masonic Journal;* moves to Oxford

11 February — attends a bridal shower in Oxford co-hosted by Annie V. Crews

22 July — attends meeting of the Press Association in Asheville, representing the Dunn *Weekly Guide*

25 November — press release from Oxford congratulates her for the Thanksgiving number of *The Orphans' Friend*

1912

25 January — death of her mother, Paulina, at the family home in Dunn

1913

4–6 June — attends commencement exercises at Trinity College in Durham

16 June — serves as mistress of ceremonies at a bridal shower given by the Thursday Evening Book Club in the "hospitable home" of the Misses Herring in Dunn

8 July — Kate and Pauline Herring entertain "at their attractive home on Harnett Street," Dunn, honoring Annie V. Crews of Oxford and Ellen McPhail of Mt. Olive; Eugenia ("Miss Gene") and Lucy assist

13 October — death of her grandmother, Elizabeth McPhail Herring, at 102

1914

16 January — returns to Dunn after visiting friends in Goldsboro, including Mrs. Leslie C. Lane

12 February — attends Thursday Evening Book Club, Dunn, with Vara

Spring — establishes residence in Raleigh, boarding at 118 North Wilmington Street; joins Raleigh branch of Southern Association of College Women

10 June — assists, as does Pauline, at reception after Hicks–Goodwin wedding in Dunn

18–19 June — attends North Carolina Epworth League Conference at Fifth Street [now Fifth Avenue] Methodist Church, Wilmington, representing Dunn

June 1914 – December 1917
Director of Publications, North Carolina State
Board of Health Editor, *The Health Bulletin*

30 June — first salary payment from State Board of Health ($31.67; $50 / month after that)

9 October — attends, as former staff member now "of Raleigh," President

Ivey Allen's reception for new teachers at Louisburg College

Christmas — holidays in Dunn

1915

29 March — major piece on tuberculosis in the Raleigh *Farmer and Mechanic*

19 June — hosts Lucy, who has attended a house party in Durham

20 June — leaves Raleigh, with Lucy, for a short stay in Aberdeen, near Pinehurst

Fall — exhibits at fairs across the state, attracting wide notice

28 December — leaves Raleigh to spend a week in Dunn

1916

January — acts for her superior, Warren H. Booker, assistant secretary of the State Board of Health, while he is Ohio during the illness of his mother

January — addresses Raleigh branch of Southern Association of College Women on State Board of Health, part of a year-long series on state government agencies

February — addresses Raleigh branch of SACW on State Historical Commission

17 March — after visiting the Hall of History, addresses the SACW meeting on the institution

late March — Lucy visits from Dunn, to attend *Birth of a Nation*

14 May — attends and assists at final meeting of SACW

1 June — first meeting of Raleigh Woman's Club in the elegant new clubhouse at 314 Hillsboro Street

7 June — attends Trinity College commencement in Durham, then class of 1906 tenth reunion, offering a toast: "1906–1916: Contrast and Fulfillments"

20 August — Vara, Pauline, Eugenia, Lucy, and Mary Belle move from Dunn to Raleigh, joining their sister Kate in a house at 709 Hillsboro Street

August — joins Raleigh Woman's Club for 1916–17; Vara joins the following year

25 September — leaves for Spruce Pine and Waynesville, Mitchell County, for exhibitions of principles of health and disease prevention, among several fairs that autumn

10 October — leaves for Louisburg exhibition

31 October — exhibits at Rockingham exhibition

7–9 December — attends State Newspaper Institute at UNC in Chapel Hill, noted in the press

Christmas — holidays in Dunn

1917

14 July — leaves Raleigh for journalism class at Pulitzer School of Journalism, Columbia; Eugenia visits in August and accompanies her home, arriving c. 20 August

14 December — hosts SACW at her home on Hillsboro Street to discuss "Advance of Science by the War"

KATE HERRING HIGHSMITH
AND THE STATE BOARD OF HEALTH

Memoir, c. 1960

By Kate H. Highsmith

My connections with the State Board of Health began in 1914, but my interest in public health work dates back to several summers before, when I lived in the country on a farm. Our nearest neighbor lived a quarter of a mile back of us on another farm. I usually spent my summer vacations at my home in Sampson County, and for four summers, practically every other year, I witnessed a scene that racked me with pain and puzzled grief. Regularly every two years, my neighbors would add another grave in their family plot—a baby grave. Now there were four. And each time Jane would cry out in agony, "My baby, oh, my precious baby! My arms ache with emptiness for my baby." And each time there was nothing to do but lead her hopelessly away from the little freshly-made mound back to the empty cradle and grief stricken home.

In those distressing days when I watched Jane's last baby sicken and die with summer diarrhea as the other three had done, I said surely, surely this should not be, but who was I to try to do anything? There was the doctor who only gravely shook his head as he closed his medicine case and departed. And yet the agonizing cry of Jane—"my arms ache for my baby"—came to me over and over and would not long leave me.

A short time later when I was sitting at my desk in the office of the *Orphan's Friend and Masonic Journal,* which I had been called to edit at the Oxford Orphanage, there came to my hands a copy of the *Health Bulletin* published by the State Board of Health, the first copy I had seen. There before my eyes was the story of how flies carried the germs of diarrhea, how the germs grew and multiplied in milk, and how if flies were kept from babies, food, and milk, and the latter sterilized, that diarrhea could largely be prevented.

Did my neighbors have flies? Yes, plenty of them. Everybody had them. It was no disgrace then. And the milk? Yes, Jane's babies were all bottle-fed. But how was I to get this information to Jane and her husband? This article was written by a doctor, and much of its meaning was hidden behind medical terms. Diarrhea was called enteritis, and when there was mention about preventing this disease, the term "prophylactic" was generally used. Flies were referred to at times as *Domestica Musca*. There was too much said about filth, flies, and dirt as the source of this disease for me to mark it, send it to Jane and her husband, and run the risk of insulting them. Jane prided herself as a housekeeper and took special pride in her kitchen. But I have seen her bright, shiny milk pail hanging in the sun swarming with flies.

Medical science was just now making available its findings regarding the causes of certain well-known diseases—hook worm, tuberculosis, typhoid, and diarrhea among babies. At last there was hope. The deadly diseases could be prevented to a large degree if only the people knew what to do. Oh, if only I could write and tell them in everyday language what the doctors knew and what medical science was discovering daily about the cause, the spread, and the means of preventing these dread diseases, how grateful I would be!

Next spring found me on my way to the office of the State Board of Health to apply for a job that was new and untried: to write about health as news. I wanted every Jane and her husband and their neighbors throughout the state to know that babies did not have to keep on dying from summer diarrhea, that summer should not be dreaded as the season of typhoid fever, and that there was hope for those suffering with tuberculosis, then the great killer. How were they to know this except through the newspapers?

Only one man in the office would listen to my proposition. Finally he said "Try your hand at this," tossing a letter toward me on the table. It was from the mayor of Greensboro, saying that the town had passed an ordinance prohibiting the keeping of livery stables within the city limits. This was done as a means of keeping down the breeding of flies and in the interest of better health for the citizens of the town. Greensboro was the first town in the state to adopt such measures. An article of about three hundred words was written and typed. Soon the reporters from the two daily papers in Raleigh made their rounds of the State Departments for new items. With "How's this?" the article was handed to the news men. They read it scrutinizingly and said, "Good stuff. We'd like more of it." Next morning on the front page of the *News and Observer* was the headline, "Greensboro To Become a Flyless Town."

There was no money in the treasury, but I was told to come back within two weeks if I could live on $50.00 a month. Of course, I could. It was only a toe-hold I was asking for.

For three and a half years, till war came, an article on some phase of health work went out daily to the daily and semiweekly newspapers of the State, and a special article went to the weeklies. In addition, writing for the *Health Bulletin* each month and assisting with editing it became a regular duty. The Press News Service of the State Board of Health became known far and wide. Request after request came from other State Health Departments for permission to reprint the articles. Many visitors came to see how such a far-reaching health education program was carried on.

My connection with this Service was abruptly ended in 1917 when I was drafted to do the publicity work for the State War Savings Campaign. The newspaper men of the State unanimously elected the publicity "man" on the State Board of Health for the job, and it was not known by them at the time that that man was a woman. It was discovered when Mr. R. R. Clark, editor of the Statesville *Landmark,* wired the State Board of Health for my release.

Kate H. Highsmith
Raleigh, North Carolina

> *Note:* A typescript of this text, prepared on an electric, self-justifying typewriter, was found in Katherine Holoman's papers after her death in 1997; shortly thereafter, I keystroked it, as an early exercise in converting documents to digital format, to save on a floppy disc. The same story is told in almost the same order in Blanche Brian's 1960 feature story on Mrs. Highsmith. I am guessing that Grandmother dictated this story to her daughter Katherine to type up, being by that time unlikely to be at the typewriter herself.

15 JULY 1914

GREENSBORO THE FLYLESS

The Gate City Sets the Pace and Challenges the State Board of Health to Make a Fly Inspection

[attributed –ed.]

Raleigh, N. C., July 15 — That Greensboro is to be an absolutely flyless town by the end of this week is the determined aim of that town's progressive and wide awake citizens. Not one thing is left undone in that town this week to drive out and destroy those pesky filth and disease carriers—flies—and to better the health conditions of its people.

The State Board of Health is invited to inspect the work of the anti-fly crusade, and to make such suggestions as will render this town absolutely flyless, therefore safe and healthful, if any fly breeding material can be found by the Board inspectors. Their standard is a flyless town.

What Greensboro has done and is doing, other towns can do. As citizens make a town, not flies, it is in the hands of the citizens to have a flyless town. If you want a flyless town, Greensboro proves to you you can have one. It's up to you.

> *Note:* I suggest that this is the text Miss Herring wrote in Mr. Booker's office as described in her memoir. At about 180 words, it's within range of what she remembered writing. It's attributed to a Health Department release in

one of the papers that carried it. And the concluding sentence sounds very much like her. It was carried verbatim in many state papers that week and gathered into stories on the Greensboro experiment in a number of others.

Press release, North Carolina State Board of Health

Carried by the *Alamance Gleaner,* Graham NC, 16 July 1914, p. 2
and Asheville *Gazette-News,* Salisbury *Evening Post,* Wilmington *Dispatch,* Concord *Daily Tribune* and *Times,* all July 16; New Bern *Daily Journal,* Wilmington *Morning Star,* Monroe *Journal,* all July 17; Charlotte *News,* July 18; *Robesonian* of Lumberton, July 20; Gastonia *Gazette,* Elizabeth City *Advance,* July 21; *Randolph Bulletin* of Asheboro, July 22; and on through Kings Mountain *Herald,* August 13, and *Jackson County Journal* of Sylva, August 28.

29 MARCH 1915

HOW THE STATE FIGHTS GREAT WHITE PLAGUE

State Sanatorium One of Most Powerful Agencies in Wiping Out the Young Man's Scourge; Wonderfully Situated; Efficiently Managed; Beneficial in Results; But Woefully Inadequate to Meet Demands Made Upon It

By Kate M. Herring

"Why is it that I have never heard of this institution, this sanatorium for the treatment of tuberculosis till recently? If I had known only three years ago that there was a place in North Carolina where consumptives could go and get well, my son, oh, my son! he would have been living today. I did not know. He died through ignorance. I did not know then that tuberculosis could be cured. But today I am told that here in our own State men and women who have this terrible disease are getting well and strong again. Oh! the ignorance of it! If I had only known!"

On hearing these words from a sorrowing mother I realized the curse of ignorance, especially in its connection with tuberculosis. I thereupon resolved that every mother's son should know about it, that he should have a fighting chance with this disease, the young man's scourge, as far as it is possible to reach him with the information. He shall know that tuberculosis is preventable, that it is curable, that there is in North Carolina a sanatorium where patients are being restored to health and strength. Furthermore, the people shall know that they have at the sanatorium an institution that is worthy of their support and that it is dependent upon them for success in fighting the Great White Plague.

A Wonderful Institution.

On returning from a recent visit to this institution I was asked by one and then another, "What do you think of the sanatorium?" "It is wonderful," I said. "It is wonderful as to its climate and location. It is situated in the recently famed sandhills in Hoke County on an elevation that gives it a commanding view of the country around for ten, twenty and thirty miles, in every direction. There is nothing else like it in North Carolina and nothing that surpasses it on this side of the Rockies. The atmosphere is dry and rare and the breezes are cool in summer and mild in winter. The location is ideal for the purpose it is serving and for the larger purpose it hopes to serve.

"It is wonderful in the work it is doing. Here are men, business men—merchants, farmers, tradesmen; professional men—lawyers, doctors, preachers and teachers: and young men just starting out in life; here are women, young women in the bloom of life, teachers, stenographers, housewives, mothers, all being restored to lives of usefulness and homes of happiness. This restoring to health and saving life at its most valuable period, is it not wonderful?

"It is wonderful, again, how that the heart and soul of the man who is at the head of it became actuated through the vision that tuberculosis, an ignorance-cursed evil in our land, could be driven out. His vision became real. His confidence inspired confidence in others and today he stands at the head of a mighty band, that State's troops, marshalling his forces onward in the fight. He has never doubted and he is as courageous as he who sees victory ahead."

New Life There.

"Then the sanatorium is really a success?" I was asked. "A success? Could you see those ninety or more hopeful, determined patients getting well, gaining anywhere from one to six pounds a week, happy and grateful, looking out anew on life's road with hopes refreshed, you would say, 'Were this all, it has not failed.' And when you consider the 248 treated and returned home as tuberculosis missionaries, the work of last year, and the hundreds that are now on the waiting lists entreating entrance, to say nothing of the possibilities of the future, you'll agree that its success has already been attested to."

The Wants of the Sanatorium.

"What impressed you most about the place?" I was asked. "The lack of available room and equipment," I replied. Perhaps it was the long waiting list—their cries were piteous and anxious—that made me feel it so. Oh, that the needs of this institution met the demands! In one room, not a large room, is the superintendent's private office, the bookkeeper's office and filing cases, the stenographer's desk, the head nurse's office, the drug room, the sterilizing room, the nurses' chart room and a stairway. Yet, I never saw such efficiency for such straitened economy. Perhaps what impressed me most was the efficiency of the staff—the nurses, the officers—and their faithful devotion to their work and charge. Their enthusiasm was contagious. It might have been from this source that the patients received their cheer. Whether they were up or in bed they laughed and seemed grateful. All seemed happy and satisfied.

"Speaking of their needs, what do they need most?" one asked. "Well, among the big things, they need a new building for office rooms and bed rooms for more patients." Perhaps the saddest impression that came to me was the fact that this proposed new building consisted of a main body with two wings which the management conceived to be a modest request from the General Assembly and sufficient to meet only the most immediate needs of the institution—that only one wing of this building was provided for by the Legislature. To me it is regrettable that the other part of the building which is so badly needed will have to wait two years hence. Then there is a heating plant that is badly needed, but there are lots of smaller things that might be called needs of comfort. Doubtless there is no class to whom comforts become essential as those recuperating. They need books, papers and magazines to read, but not magazines and papers a year old or even a month old. They need subscriptions to the best monthly and weekly magazines and to the daily papers. At present only one as a donation paper goes to the Sanitorium and that is "The Orphan's Friend," sent by a good Mason. They need music. This is almost essential to the spirit and progress of their getting well. Nothing would be a more acceptable gift than a piano. Graphophone records are always welcome. Comfortable chairs—rocking chairs—tables, desks, pictures and all those comforts that are needed to make a house a home—they will be greatly welcomed. These needs could easily be furnished by clubs, societies and the various organizations that have a spirit of helpfulness, if too large for individual purses.

Biggest Thing in the State.

"You have great hopes for the Sanatorium, then?" "Some day," said I, "it will be the biggest thing in the State, doing the biggest work, and then some day," I added, "there'll be no need for it as a tuberculosis sanatorium—but as a resting place for worn out nurses, doctors, teachers and those who strove to drive tuberculosis out of the land."

> *Note:* The North Carolina Sanatorium for the Treatment of Tuberculosis was established near Aberdeen, Hoke County, NC, in 1908, the first state institution of its kind. From 32 beds in 1980 it grew to 650, with sections for children, African Americans, and prisoners. It served through 1973, then, as tuberculosis was essentially eradicated, became a prison hospital, closing in 2010.

The Farmer and Mechanic, Raleigh, p. 12

20 JULY 1915

AS I WAS A-SAYIN'

[generic column title]

"Don't talk hot weather. Don't quote the thermometer. Don't get heat on your brain and the brains of those about you. Especially don't talk hot weather on Sunday!"

That is a series of summer comfort commandments by Miss Kate M. Herring interpreted from psychology in the terms of common sense for the benefit of those who would make the best out of life as it is. Miss Herring, for those who do not know, is the writer of health bulletins of the State Board of Health, and the voice crying in the wilderness of an indifferent State for the wiping out of every disease that is preventable.

"The custom of continually talking hot weather," Miss Herring continues, "is a baneful habit; and whoever persists in doing it shows that he has little regard for his own comfort and the feelings of other people. Talking heat, keeps it constantly on the mind. Then the mind gets all fussed up causing more heat and more discomfort.

"But there is one advantage, it must be admitted, in talking about the weather. That is a continuous flow of conversation, with the minimum use of brain cells. The little nothings so brilliantly and bravely asserted about the weather call for no brain work either on the part of the speaker or the hearer, and such bromides as 'it's a scorcher,' 'ain't it fierce?' serve only to intensify the heat.

"The sensible thing to do is to adjust one's food, clothing and exercise to the season and then dismiss the matter from the mind. Much of the suffering in hot weather is mental rather than physical. It has been frequently noted that people suffer more when the thermometer is at ninety-five on its way up than when is at 95 on its way down."

Raleigh *News and Observer,* p. 4

7 AUGUST 1916

HEALTH WORK IN THE SCHOOLS QUICKLY BRINGS GOOD RESULTS

By Miss Kate M. Herring
Publicity Manager for State Board of Health

"An education without health—what's the use?" The value of a sound body is more appreciated today than it has been at any time in history, even than in the days of the Hellenes. This renaissance or rebirth of the recognition and appreciation of the worth of a normal, healthful body may be said to have been called into existence through that great force or dominant idea known in the world today as efficiency. As civilization advances with its sharp law of competition and the demand for efficiency increases, a still greater valuation will be placed on the physical man. That fitness that calls for and is dependent on a sound mind in a sound body will be the universal need and likewise the universal demand. To meet that need is the problem of today. It is a problem the solution of which lies mainly with the public schools.

Health work has gone into the public schools largely through the conviction that merely mind decoration is not enough, that mind culture acquired at the expense of health culture is not efficiency and does not meet the test. In other words, education without health is useless. Education comprehends the whole man and and the whole man is mainly what he is physically. His education calls for the development of the body along with the training of the mind. Schopenhauer says: "The greatest of follies is to sacrifice health for any other kind of happiness, whatever it may be, for gain, advancement, learning or fame." Someone else has plainly expressed the relation between health and education thus: "No use to spend time, money and hard work on the mind and no health—just to droop and die. A sound mind is a sound body—if you have it you must study for it just the same as you do for book knowledge. An education without health—what's the use?"

Health work as a general thing has been slow to work its way into the public schools, but once inaugurated it has been quick to accomplish results. This is due to the fact that it has had to break down barriers centuries old. It has had to beat down prejudices and outrule superstitions, some of which belong to the dark ages. It is a noticeable fact that wherever health work has made progress, it has been always on the heels of prejudice, superstition and ignorance. For instance, medical school inspection work made its way into the school only on uprooting and banishing many an old mossback [i.e., old-fashioned] notion pertaining to education and public health, one of which was that children at school are invariably dullards or mental defectives by the will of an inscrutable Providence and not in many instances on account of their diseased bodies or other physical defects, a great many of which could be easily remedied or prevented. It is not known that children are backward or delinquent not because they are mentally or morally deficient but because they are physically deficient. Another notion or two done away with in this connection is that frail bodies contain the brightest minds and that whatever we are God made us, even though we are crippled with rheumatism from bad teeth or are sick from typhoid fever from eating filth. What is still another notion to go is the belief that people naturally have to be sick and that God deals out sickness as he does sunshine and rain. We don't believe any longer that an epidemic of typhoid fever has a Divine origin, consequently we don't wait for God to remove the cause which man alone is responsible for. We are realizing that sickness and defects are man's work and that it's man's duty to prevent or remedy them.

Of the various forms of health work now in use in the public schools, perhaps medical school inspection [i.e., in-school screening] is the most extensive and at the same time the most valuable. Its value in bettering the health of school children, in safeguarding them from epidemic diseases, in enabling them to make the best of their educational opportunities, has been recognized by both educators and health workers. Medical school inspection was founded on the close relationship between the mind and the body and the consequent dependence of education on health conditions. Since its establishment, good results have followed in its course. Physical defects have been remedied, epidemics have been cheeked and school conditions as well as health conditions have been improved.

In North Carolina, this educational health work has been confined more or less to the counties and towns employing whole-time health officers, except in a few towns where special provision for this work has been made. Last year in the eleven counties employing whole-time health officers and the three counties—Northampton, Wilson, and Alamance—that arranged for this work to be done by the State Board of Health, more than 25,000 school children were examined and it may be said here that not one objected. Judging from the reports that are filed in the office of the State Board of Health, at least 25 per cent of the defects discovered have been treated. But this does not take into account the educational value, particularly from a health standpoint, that came to the school from these examinations and the lectures and exercises that attended them.

The school health club is perhaps the second most valuable form of health work that has been started in the public schools. This health educational feature was in use last year in the schools of five or more counties of this State. Probably Johnston County has developed the school health club idea further than any other county as a whole, but there are individual schools in town and in the country that have adopted the school health club idea with splendid results. The scope of work contained in a report of the Moss Hill Health Club in Lenoir County furnishes an idea of not only the work a club may do, but of its organization, also. The report was in part as follows:

"The floors and windows have been scrubbed once each month and cleaned in general. The floors have been swept every day. The yards have been cleaned of rubbish and stumps and logs removed. An old well has been filled up and a new pump placed on the grounds. Swings were put up, a flower garden prepared and flowers planted. Dirt has been hauled to fill up all holes on the ground to prevent standing water. A tennis court for healthful exercise has been fixed. Every pupil in school has been enrolled as a member of the club and every member is required to wash his hands before and after eating and to wash his teeth once a day. The officers of the clubs look after the health conditions of the school in general—its ventilation, temperature and cleanliness—and make monthly reports on going out of office. The officers arrange for debates, also for illustrated lectures and free health literature which may be obtained from the State Board of Health."

One of the latest and best additions to our health educational forces is the school nurse. Wherever the school nurse has been employed, her services have been indispensable to the school course. Like the public health nurse, the school nurse is first and last a social worker. She works in the school and in the home, with the mother and with the child. She knows the home conditions of the child and when there is trouble with the child, she knows how and where to correct it. She is nurse, teacher, sanitary inspector and social worker. Probably the most valued services of the school nurse [are] in connection with the medical examination of school children. She administers minor treatment and looks after having made the more important treatments. Her follow-up services in connection with medical school inspection makes the work more effective in its results. A number of schools in North Carolina employ school health nurses and find their services most valuable.

Another feature of health work carried on in the public school of the State is that done by the State Board of Health through exhibits, illustrated lectures, free health literature and health moving pictures. These are sent to the teachers, moving pictures excepted, at their request and are free unless a minimum charge is made for transportation.

Health moving pictures is a new educational feature in North Carolina which the board has adopted to make the teaching of health popular, attractive and impressive. So far their success has been wonderful. This feature of health work will be used in connection with the school work this fall.

> *Note:* The Fifteenth Annual Education Edition was a 48-page supplement to the Raleigh *News and Observer,* 7 August 1916. It contained several dozen articles alongside ads for the state's schools and colleges.

Raleigh *News and Observer* (Sunday), Educational Edition, p. 44

1918

23 January — attends meeting, in Governor's Mansion, of Child Welfare Department of the Wake County Council of National Defense; discusses public health shortcomings in Raleigh; is appointed to committee on midwives

25 January — attends meeting of Southern Association of College Women, Raleigh chapter, focusing in part on illiteracy of young men of draft age; is appointed to follow up with a report on educational conditions in NC

1 February 1918 – 1 January 1919
Publicity Director
North Carolina War Savings Campaign
Winston-Salem

1 February — begins eleven-month leave of absence from Board of Health to serve the War Savings Campaign in Winston-Salem; the appointment noted widely in the papers, her work with the Board of Health copiously praised

4 February — arrives in Winston-Salem, begins work

12 February — returns to Raleigh, with others from her office, to present a War Savings Institute

1 March — joins Winston-Salem Lafayette Association

16 March — reports, in a release, that over 500 War Savings Societies representing 25,000 members have been organized in the State, primarily in the schools

15 April — visits sisters on Hillsboro Street for a few days

9 May — participates in large conference/rally of Winston-Salem District of War Savings Stamps, with "patriotic and inspirational" speeches, where new drive and $50 million goal announced; probably attends subsequent rallies that week in Charlotte, Fayetteville, Wilmington, New Bern, and Elizabeth City

18 May — Lucy arrives in Winston-Salem to visit her sister at the Hotel Frances

23 May — probably attends NC Bankers Association meeting in Raleigh; contributes to the *News and Observer* special edition that day

4 June — attends first major Trinity College Alumnae luncheon reunion in Durham during commencement week; addresses the group on her work

5 June — participates in a working session in Winston-Salem with officials including representatives of the Nebraska State Committee, with a goal to emulating the successful Nebraska Plan; Mary Shotwell among the other employees attending

26–28 June — visited by Eugenia

31 August — attends a reception in Winston-Salem given by Col. and Mrs. F. H. Fries in honor of an office worker recently married

11 September — conducts War Savings Stamps campaign teachers' institute in Concord

22 September — departs Winston-Salem for business meeting in Washington, D. C., and to visit her sister Lucy there

28 September — attends Winston–Salem branch meeting of Southern Association of College Women

6–21 November — at the height of the influenza epidemic in the state, participates in "final" Victory Drive through a series of district conferences: Elizabeth City, November 6; Washington, November 7; Tarboro, November 8; Raleigh, November 9; Bryson City, November 12; Hendersonville, November 13; Marion, November 14; Hickory, November 15; Statesville, November 18; Hamlet, November 19; Wilmington, November 20; and Greensboro, November 21.

30 November — hosts and speaks at meeting of Southern Association of College Women

4 December — attends "Industrial Enterprise" emergency conference in Winston-Salem, to address $1,500,000 shortfall in victory campaign

24 December — leaves Winston-Salem to return to Board of Health in Raleigh

SELECTED COMMENTARY FROM THE PRESS ON MISS HERRING'S APPOINTMENT TO THE WAR SAVINGS CAMPAIGN

27 JANUARY 1918

DIRECT PUBLICITY FOR WAR SAVINGS

Miss Kate M. Herring, of State Board of Health, Takes Up New Work for Year

Miss Kate M. Herring, who since June, 1914, has been in charge of the newspaper publicity for the State Board of Health, will be publicity director for the War Savings Campaign in North Carolina beginning February 1. The State Board of Health has granted Miss Herring a leave of absence until January 1, 1919. She will leave Raleigh Thursday to take up her work in Winston-Salem, headquarters of the War Savings Campaign.

Miss Herring is a trained newspaper woman, having made her work during her service with the State Board of Health meet with the needs and the limitations of the daily and weekly newspapers of the State.

As an A.B. graduate of Trinity College, who since her graduation took a special course in journalism at Columbia University, Miss Herring has put into her work for the State Board of Health a very healthy grasp of the human equation which, combined with a clear conception of news, has made her material generally acceptable to the press of the State. Miss Herring has been more than a health propagandist: she has been an unbiased reporter of the health conditions in North Carolina, and a ready conveyor of progressive movements.

With brevity, conciseness and the news idea as the basis for her writing policy, Miss Herring carries into her new work precisely what is needed to put a State-wide publicity campaign of the sort across. Her successor for the year at the State Board of Health has not yet been selected.

Raleigh Sunday *News and Observer,* p. 5
Winston Salem *Twin-City Sentinel,* 28 January 1918, p. 3
Winston-Salem *Journal,* 29 January, p. 5

5 FEBRUARY 1918

MISS HERRING TO WRITE FOR PAPERS

Publicity Expert Assumes Duties in State War Savings Headquarters; Comes From Health Board

Miss Kate M. Herring arrived yesterday from Raleigh to assume charge of the newspaper publicity work of the State War Savings campaign. Her work will be done in State headquarters, this city, under the direction of Col. F. H. Fries, State Director. Miss Herring has already begun her work, which will consist of supplying the various newspapers of the State with practical reading matter concerning the campaign.

Miss Herring is a trained journalist, who for some time has had charge of the publicity work of the State Board of Health, at Raleigh. The following letter concerning Miss Herring's work with the department has been written, for The Journal, by Mr. Warren H. Booker, chief of the bureau:

"Recently several very complimentary editorials have been noted in the State papers in regard to the press service issued by the Board. I assure you these compliments are highly appreciated by this Board, and it is only fair that the editors of the State should know who is personally responsible for this material. I write to say that this department is deeply indebted to Miss Kate M. Herring for this work. In this same connection I am writing to say that after February 4th, Miss Herring will sever her relations with the Board for the remainder of the year in order to take up the publicity work in connection with Col. F. H. Fries of Winston-Salem, who is State Director of the War Savings Stamp campaign.

"In asking this Board for the loan of Miss Herring's services until January 1, 1919, Col. Fries made it very plain that he, together with his executive committee, had canvassed the field thoroughly and decided that Miss Herring was the person for the place.

"Miss Herring and this Board view the matter as a call to a patriotic service that could be answered only in the affirmative.

"In taking up her new work, the Board bespeaks for her the same full measure of splendid cooperation in this patriotic Service she is undertaking that you have shown her endeavors in the past.

"Miss Herring's successor has not been selected as yet, but announcement will be made as soon as a decision is reached.

> Yours very truly,
> WARREN H. BOOKER,
> Chief of Bureau.

Winston-Salem *Journal*, p. 3
Raleigh *Christian Advocate,* 7 February 1918, p. 15

4 FEBRUARY 1918

A FIRST CLASS "PUBLICITY MAN"

Miss Kate M. Herring, "publicity man" for the State Board of Health, has answered the call to service and for the rest of this year will be publicity expert for Col. F. H. Fries, of Winston-Salem, state director of the War Savings Stamp campaign. The State Board of Health readily gives Miss Herring full credit for the excellent press matter the board has been sending out; and we want to say, too, that of all the "propaganda" The Star is asked to assist, no press matter we receive is better prepared or more enticing from the standpoint of the news editor, and as a result all of it gets in the papers. They couldn't have found a better "publicity man" in the state than Miss Herring for the thrift campaign work.

She is a young woman of recognized capability and her splendid work is proving that Colonel Fries secured a well equipped assistant when he attached Miss Herring to his campaign staff. With reference to Director Fries' search for a publicity manager, The Charlotte Observer thus speaks his "discovery":

"After a canvass of State possibilities he selected Miss Kate M. Herring of Raleigh. It develops that it is Miss Herring who has been doing the press service for the State Board of Health, and her work has been so well done as to have attracted general comment. She leaves that service today for the purpose of taking up the War Savings Stamps assignment, and Dr. Warren Booker of the Board of Health makes it the occasion for divulging the name of the person responsible for the excellent health press service the board has been giving through its bulletins. It is understood that Colonel Fries has only 'borrowed' Miss Herring from the board, but it is safe to say that once 'discovered,' a young woman of her capabilities may be said to have placed her foot on the ladder of promotion, especially when the discovery is made by a man of Colonel Fries' appreciative characteristics."

A master hand has been evident in the Board of Health publicity, for that work has been done with such effectiveness as to make it inconceivably valuable to the whole State. Of course, North Carolina has one of the most capable and best equipped health departments in this country and it was proving its own claim to efficiency when it discovered that Raleigh lady for the work of reaching the people of the State through the Health Bulletin and the communications that are issued so promptly from Raleigh when vital health matters of the State are concerned.

For a long time we have been struck with the remarkable gifts and qualifications of quite a number of women who have been given an opportunity to serve the public in various capacities. Their name is legion in North Carolina. There will be a whole lot of "discoveries" in this State during these war times.

Wilmington *Morning Star,* p. 4

4 FEBRUARY 1918

EXCELLENT CHOICE

In selecting Miss Kate Herring as head of the state newspaper publicity work for the war savings campaign, the executive committee has made an excellent choice. We venture to say that the press of the state will be supplied with such articles from her pen as will aid the movement very decidedly.

For some time, the press articles of the North Carolina Board of Health have been attracting no little attention. They have been brief, snappy and to the point, and many people who otherwise would not have read them at all have been led by the interesting style in which they were written to absorb the health information contained in them.

This work has been under the direction of Miss Herring, and much of the success of the board of health propaganda has been due to her way of presenting it. There is every reason to believe she will be equally successful in the war savings publicity work.

Winston Salem *Twin-City Sentinal,* p. 4 (Editorial page)

21 FEBRUARY 1918

MISS HERRING'S FINE WORK

Miss Kate M. Herring, who has been newspaper publicity agent for the State Board of Health, is to direct the publicity work for the state war savings certificate and thrift stamp campaign. Colonel Fries, the state chairman, is fortunate in securing the service of Miss Herring. She has done a fine work for the State Board of Health. By knowing what to say and how to say it; and having the sense and capacity not to use columns of space to express a quarter column idea, she has secured much newspaper publicity for the State Board of Health, and has furnished matter of much educational value to the people. Miss Herring will write good copy for the thrift stamps and war savings certificates. —Statesville Landmark.

Greensboro Daily News, p. 4, attr. to Statesville *Landmark*

24 DECEMBER 1918

MISS HERRING TO RETURN TO DEPARTMENT OF HEALTH AT RALEIGH

State War Savings Headquarters Will Not Be Maintained During Coming Year, and Publicity Director to Return Home

Will Have Publicity Work In This State

Miss Kate M. Herring, who has been director of publicity for the North Carolina War Savings movement with headquarters in this city, will leave this morning for Raleigh. where she will again resume her duties with the State Board of Health. Miss Herring won fame in North Carolina by her publicity work in the State health department, and that department loaned her to the war savings headquarters for the year.

While the war savings movement will be conducted during the coming year, State headquarters will not be maintained, but the work will be redirected through the Federal reserve banks and through the postoffices.

While Miss Herring will have charge of the publicity work of the State health department, it in understood that she will be given a much wider field than heretofore in promoting greater educational efforts for the betterment of public health.

Miss Herring's work in this city has been notable, and the results obtained in the State in the promotion of thrift have been satisfactory. However the campaign in this State may terminate, it has been most successful in the creation of a new spirit of thrift on the part of the people. It is understood, too, that thrift will be taught in the public schools during the coming year.

Fine interest has been enlisted in the War Savings movement, and while no State organizations will be maintained during the coming year, savings stamps have become so popularized that the demand for them will continue for a long time.

While her numerous friends in this city regret to see Miss Herring leave, they wish for her every success in her work for the continued betterment of the State through the State Department of Health.

Winston-Salem Journal, p. 4

---

23 MAY 1918

BANKS SHOULD PUSH SALE OF WAR SAVINGS STAMPS

Publicity Director of State Committee Chides Financiers Because of Backwardness In This Respect—It Means The Securing of Increased Deposits

By Kate M. Herring
Publicity Director, State War Savings Committee

There are 283 banks in North Carolina playing a losing game, at least they are not prospering as they should, if Mr. Jerome Thralls of the American Bankers Association is correct in his conclusions when he says:

"We find in actual experience that the banks which are active in the War Savings and Thrift campaign are enjoying increasing deposits while those in institutions that are not active are actually sustaining losses in deposits."

This number of 283 banks, which represents the money institutions of the State that are not acting as agents for the sale of War Savings Stamps, is over half of all such institutions in the State. And [that] more than 50 per cent of the banks of the State are not interested in promoting Thrift by becoming sale agents for the Thrift and War Savings Stamps is a big reason why North Carolina has fallen short of raising her quota thus far.

Nebraska proves this to be true. That State has already subscribed over four million dollars over her quota and raised over 50 per cent of her sales, having sold to April 1st $11.06 per capita or about $15,000,000 of Stamps, and she has been able to do this, according to Mr. Ward M. Burgess, State Director, through the support of the banks. He attributes his success largely to the fact that every bank in Nebraska not only accepted the appointment as an authorized Treasury agent, but became actively engaged in pushing the sale of stamps. Every bank established at least ten sub-agencies and financed these in addition to keeping them constantly stimulated to sell the stamps.

Missouri is the next leading State in the Union in the amount of War Saving Stamps she has sold and Mr. Festus J. Wade, State Director and a leading banker in the Missouri valley, attributes his success to the co-operation of the banks of his State. He says in a letter to the bankers of Missouri:

"Where bankers show an apathy in patriotism in these hours of turbulence and strife, it has a bad effect upon the local community where the financier is a slacker. We have hopes that the unpatriotic banker who has failed to purchase a supply of war stamps from the Federal Reserve Banks would mend his ways and join our array of Thrifters. There are still a few days left for these bankers who have thus far failed to do their duty to come forward and do their bit."

That the War Savings Campaign is not detrimental to the business of banks, but on the other hand is a boon to it, is the testimony of many banking institutions in this country. The president of the Federal Reserve Bank of Dallas, Texas, says:

"The banks have only recently begun to recognize that instead of the war savings campaign taking money out of their banks and community, that it will ultimately result in more benefit to them than to any other class. I am particularly struck in this connection with the fact that a large percentage of a given amount of money invested in War Savings Stamps in a given community will be in that community in 1923, instead of having been in the meantime dissipated through expenditures for non-essentials."

The president of the Federal Reserve Bank in San Francisco says:

"Aside from the patriotic endeavor to help the government, which is, of course, paramount at this time, there will rebound to the public through the banks and enormous and profitable business later, which is worthy of careful consideration. The habit of thrift and saving will become ingrained in the nature of millions of our citizens, and this alone is of such financial importance that it is beyond computation. Children who start savings now, at from twelve to sixteen years of age, will be young men and women when this loan is returned. They will have an interest in and a familiarity with finance and banks such as never has existed before. The savings banks in particular will absorb a major part of these savings and their prosperity will reflect the general financial health of the nation."

Mr. Thralls says: "We have urged the banks to participate in this campaign, not only as a patriotic duty, but as a business proposition. Banks have spent hundreds of thousands of dollars in spasmodic Thrift campaigns. The present moment affords the first and only opportunity through which the power of every factor in the nation can be coordinated in an effort to teach the people thrift and industry. Every new saver that is created is a prospective bank customer. Millions of new savers and millions of new savings have already been created, through the movement. The savings of these people will go a long way towards financing the year, will protect the present business of the banks, and will place America in the position to make a credible flight for a fair share of the world's commerce after the war."

For those who are still doubtful as to the effect of the War Savings Campaign will have on the banks and other savings institutions, Great Britain's experience, as told by Basil F. Blackett, of the British Treasury, to the Savings Bank Section of the American Bankers' Association in Atlantic City last fall, will be of interest.

"It is a remarkable fact," he says, "that in spite of the special attractions of the War Savings certificates and of the large sums—nearly $500,000,000—invested in them, the War Savings Campaign has given an impetus to every one of the older institutions for encouraging savings. The Postoffice Savings Banks, the other savings banks, the building societies, and other cooperative societies, all show record increases in their deposits, and those responsible for them have in consequence nearly all been hardy and valuable workers for the War Savings movements."

Only six states in the Union last month made a poorer showing in the number of banks selling War Savings Stamps in North Carolina, and these, like North Carolina, showed a low per capita sale of stamps.

Raleigh *News and Observer,* Banker's Edition, p. 26

26 MAY 1918

MOTHER OF PAUL AND KIFFIN ROCKWELL

By Kate M. Herring

Whoever had known the heartbroken, rebellious mother of Paul and Kiffin Rockwell on their leaving for France four years ago would never believe that she is now awaiting her passport to go to France. Furthermore, she says, "if I had a dozen sons I should want them to fight for France."

It was in a hotel in a western North Carolina town that I met recently, after a separation of several years, Dr. Loula A. Rockwell, mother of Paul and Kiffin Rockwell, the latter whose name has become immortal through his heroic deeds and death as an aviator in France, the former a wounded soldier now living in Paris. She was there in the interest of her profession. I was there in the interest of Liberty Loan Bonds. Our first meal together was breakfast. The morning newspaper carried cross-page headlines of the aggressions made by the German army on the western front and the retreat from several important positions of the French and British soldiers.

The guests at breakfast talked excitedly of the apparent victories of the enemy. Dr. Rockwell's face was sad. The soft, low tones of her voice and the suppressed sighs betrayed the feeling in her heart. Long before any other guest at the hotel had done so, she had read the newspaper account of the German attack on Ypres and their attempt to recapture Arras. These positions and all held by the Allied armies were familiar points to her, as was every village and battlefield in the war zone. These places meant more to her than "Somewhere in France."

Few words had passed between us at breakfast before I realized the sacrifice that this mother had herself made for France. I saw that she had made a fight as brave as any of her two sons, and had won. She told me that when her boys left to enlist in the French army she was rebellious, that she could not understand their motive and considered it on their part a wild adventure of youth. Kiffin was only twenty-three, she said, and had always conferred with her upon all other matters of important interest to him.

"I guess I was selfish," she said, "but I did not understand. I could not see where my two boys meant anything to France, whereas they meant something to me. Their life was mine. When my husband died, six years after our marriage, leaving me with three babies—for babies and books, he said, were all that preachers had in this world—my life became theirs. It was my purpose to train them for careers of scholarship, and my hope and inspiration in this task was that they would be my comfort and stay in old age.

"Perhaps I was a silly mother," she continued, "but I made every possible effort to have my boys taken out of the army and returned to this country. During the months following their departure I was almost frantic with grief, for I felt that I should never see them again. I wrote letters to the War Department, both at Washington and at Paris. I had reason to believe that they would not be accepted in the French army, and it was only by chance they were allowed to enlist even in the Foreign Legion from Africa, at a penny a day for their services. They served only one year in this regiment when Kiffin received a wound in the hip and was sent to a hospital at Rennes. This was in a bayonet charge at the battle of Arras. Before this battle Paul had received a wound which incapacitated him for life as a soldier. He was sent to a hospital in Paris. It was while Kiffin was in the hospital at Rennes recovering from his wounds that he wrote me the letter that brought me to my senses, and I am glad that he lived to know that I knew that he was right and I was wrong. I shall never forget that day.

"I was on my way to see a patient one morning when his letter was handed to me. I sat alone in my little car and there read his letter for the first time without shedding a tear. I saw then, for the first time, what impelled them to go to France, and saw it in the light that they saw it."

The letter referred to by Dr. Rockwell is found with other letters, photographs and souvenirs of her son Kiffin in the Kiffin Rockwell cabinet in the Hall of History at Raleigh. The letter reads:

"Dear Mamma:—Paul tells me that when he got to Paris he found that we were widely advertised, and not wholly to our credit, by some rather wild letters you had written to everybody trying to get us out of the French army. Now we appreciate that you have done all of this for love, but you might have known that when we were once in the French army nothing but death or physical disability could get us out. Besides, we don't want to get out. Although you raised us to be "too proud to fight," we know a just cause when we see it, and if you could see the French women as I see them, you would be proud that you had two boys to give. So I have sent Paul back to Paris to the War Department to straighten things out, for I want to ask some favors of them when I get out from here. I told him to tell that you were not dependent upon us and that you would not let us support you when we were at home. Moreover, I have laughed many times at a letter of advice you wrote me as to how to act if I were taken prisoner. Now, I never intend to be taken prisoner, but if I should and were to follow your advice, I would be immediately tied up to a tree and shot. Now I know you love me, and I hope some day you will be proud of me, but you will have to let me run my affairs over here."

"It was this letter," said Doctor Rockwell, "that brought me to myself. I realized that my sons were no longer boys to be dictated to, but men, and I felt the seriousness of their purpose. I was proud of their forefathers' fighting spirit that I saw in them, and I honored them for this vision of justice and right that they had caught. Realizing that my sons were warriors, I steeled my heart for any fate. When the word came two years later that Kiffin was killed in an encounter with three enemy airplanes, I could thank God that he died facing the enemy of civilization as he had expressed a wish to die. And while I am proud of the record he made as a soldier and the standard he set for those who shall fight after him, I am proudest of the character that I have seen develop, through their letters, in both of my boys. I would not change it if I could, and if I had a dozen sons I should want them too to fight for France."

Mrs. Rockwell is a true mother. While the world has done honor that would become a general to Kiffin Rockwell's memory, she has felt the same love and honor for Paul that she has for Kiffin. She affectionately couples the name of Paul with that of Kiffin, and rarely speaks of one without referring to the other in the same conversation. In fact, it was with more than usual emphasis and a degree of pride that she said it was Paul who took the initiative in their going to France. That Paul's wounds have so impaired him physically as to unfit him for a soldier, and his own disappointment and discontent at being out of the fight, stirs the heart of his mother with pathos and motherly sympathy. Just before his marriage to Mademoiselle Jeanne Leygues, daughter of the Minister of Marine for France, who two years before nursed him in her mother's chateau, which had been converted into hospital for wounded soldiers, Paul wrote to a friend in America:

"A great battle is now going on and though my chances for happiness are greater now than ever before, I would stake it all for the strength to face [the] enemy with my old musket. I once had ambition to be a great writer but I have not been able to make a great soldier, and nothing else now seems worth while."

On the occasion of Kiffin's death, he wrote:

"Kiffin's death has hit me hard, yet I know that he fell as he wished, facing the enemy of civilization. For me I find it harder to live than it would be to die, now that he has gone and I cannot take up arms again. I have much to console me in that Kiffin did not fail his fellow man in the greatest crisis the world has ever known. He hated Germany's mad principles and he did his best to crush them."

Paul Rockwell is now War correspondent for the Chicago Daily News. In spite of his wounds and ill health keeping him out of the army, he spends more than half of his time at the front, back of the trenches, gathering war news for his American readers.

Dr. Rockwell, as a devoted mother would, finds peculiar solace in the beautiful tributes of love and honor paid to the memory of her son by the French people. The words of Captain Thenault, commander of the American Aviation Squadron, of which squadron Kiffin Rockwell was often called the soul, are most comforting to her. He said, in pronouncing the funeral oration of her son:

"He was a great soldier with a high sense of duty. This he performed simply and valiantly without boasting and without ambition. On the night of his death when we were gathered together, I said to his comrades: 'The best and bravest is no longer here,' and never was commendation more merited. Rockwell never considered that he had done enough."

Kiffin Rockwell's own letter, the last he wrote his mother, is particularly comforting to her. In this letter which was written just before his leaving to fly in the Verdun sector where a great battle was raging, for "where Kiffin Rockwell flew the enemy did not," said the French people, he said:

"If I die I want you to know that I have died as every man ought to die, fighting for what is right. I do not feel that I am fighting for France alone but for the cause of all humanity which is the greatest of all causes."

A picture of Kiffin Rockwell's grave at Luxueil, covered with Alsatian daisies and canopied over with floral tributes and expressions of the French people's love and appreciation, represents to this mother as no other relic or tangible thing does, the hero that her son was and the esteem in which he was held by every soldier and officer who knew him. The picture shows hanging at the head of the grave a scroll bearing the inscription,

"Kiffin Rockwell, American Aviator pilot slain by the enemy, the 23rd day of September 1916, at Rodern, Alsace."

On the scroll, the picture shows, are three badges of honor won by the aviator. These are the Medaille Militaire, the Croix de Guerre and his commission as lieutenant of the French army, which was awaiting him the day of his death.

Of the many letters received by Mrs. Rockwell after her son's death, several of which are now in the North Carolina Hall of History, two are particularly interesting. Ambassador Jusserand wrote her this brief but assuring letter:

"All France mourns with you. Your son will live forever in the hearts of the French people."

Lieutenant Z. Pichkoff's letter reads:

"Dear Madam: I have not the honor of knowing you, but I know both your boys, Paul and Kiffin. They are my friends. Kiffin was in my company in the Foreign Legion. I have just read in the paper of the glory of Kiffin's, of his heroic, worthy of every brave man's death. I do not wish to speak to you words of consolation, for the mother of so great a hero must be heroic herself. I only wish to express to you all my admiration for Kiffin, for I have known him well and have always seen him at the height of his task, and the duty which he voluntarily took upon himself. I have known him in the Champagne in the winter of 1914 and '15. I have known him in Paris. Just two weeks before I sailed for the States I was lunching with him at Mrs. Weeks. He died a brave heroic death facing the awful foe, and every soldier will envy him such an end. The name of Kiffin Rockwell and that of all brave American volunteers will go down in history, and proud may be every family that can say, my son fought for justice and civilization.

"Most affectionately yours."

Lieutenant Pichkoff is the adopted son of Maxim Gorky. He was just returning from this country to Russia when the war broke out, finding him in Paris. He enlisted in the Foreign Legion with Paul and Kiffin Rockwell. He was Corporal in the bayonet charge of the Battle of Arras in 1915, in which battle Kiffin was wounded in the hip, and he lost his right arm. For the latter's bravery on this occasion he was decorated and made Lieutenant. After his recovery he was sent to America by the French government to do propaganda work, and was in Washington at the time of Kiffin Rockwell's death.

The Mrs. Weeks referred to in Lieutenant Pichkoff's letters is Mrs. Alice S. Weeks of Boston and Paris. Her son who was killed in the Battle of Arras was Kiffin's best friend. After his death she became a devoted friend of Kiffin

Rockwell and took him into her home in Paris. Mrs. Weeks now holds open her home under the direction of the American Home Service to all American soldiers in France. Here any American soldier may find a welcome when off duty.

Mrs. Rockwell is a prominent physician of Asheville and Winston-Salem and enjoys a large and appreciative patronage in both of these North Carolina towns. This day she would have been serving the wounded soldiers in France but for an illness she suffered just prior to her sailing last September, and the arrival of her little grandson, Kiffin Rockwell Hayes. It was only a few days after the birth of her grandson that Mrs. Rockwell was informed of the birth of a granddaughter in Paris, Anne Loula Rockwell. Her heart is now divided between her grandson, Kiffin, the son of a North Carolina Methodist preacher, and her granddaughter, Anne Loula, daughter of a French Noblesse.

While Dr. Rockwell's plans of going to France have been temporarily deferred, she has by no means released the hope or abandoned the idea of visiting the country which now claims both of her sons. To see again her living son and visit the grave of her dead hero is an impulse in her heart hardly more strong than that to do what she can for the sick and wounded soldiers of the Allies fighting for the freedom and righteousness. As Kiffin Rockwell announced a short while before his death that he was paying his debt to Lafayette and Rochambeau, so Mrs. Rockwell has it in her heart to pay whatever remains of her debt that is yet unpaid.

> *Note:* Kiffin Yates Rockwell (1892–1916), a North Carolinian, was the first American pilot to shoot down a German plane in World War I and was himself killed in an aerial battle over Alsace not long afterward. His brother Paul Ayres Rockwell (1889–1985), a young journalist who had enlisted in the Foreign Legion with Kiffin, was wounded early on and became a Paris-based newspaper correspondent. The bibliography on Kiffin is large (for instance: *War Letters of Kiffin Yates Rockwell, Foreign Legionnaire and Aviator, France 1914–1916,* ed. Paul Ayres Rockwell [New York: Doubleday, 1925; rpt. Shane Kiffin Ayers, 2008]), and there are numerous memorials to him. One of these is a display in the North Carolina Hall of History (now Museum of History) which was familiar to Kate Herring—even more so after she became Mrs. Highsmith, since the Hall of History was located in the building where Dr. Highsmith worked for most of his career. The Rockwell archives, including dozens of photographs, are easily accessible.

> Their mother, Loula Ayres Rockwell (1866–1959), is the subject of this interview, which stemmed from an encounter of Herring and Rockwell in Asheville "after a separation of several years." I doubt Loula Rockwell actually made it to France in 1918. Paul's return to the United States in July 1919 was noted in multiple American newspapers, as he was by that

time a well-known journalist. He had married Jeanne Leguyes, his former nurse and, said the papers, "a member of one of France's wealthiest and most influential families." Indeed, her father Georges Leygues (1848–1933) was *de facto* prime minister of France (1920–21) in the Millerand presidency. Note, too, that the boys' superior officer in the French Foreign Legion, Zinovy Peshkov (1894–1966) was the son of the Russian-Soviet writer Maxim Gorky (true name Peshkov).

Kiffin is especially remembered for remarking, even before he was a member of the Lafayette Escadrille, "I pay my debt for Lafayette and Rochambeau." That is the title of Edgar Lee Masters's elegy to him.

Raleigh Sunday *News and Observer,* p. 7
Sunday *Atlanta Constitution Magazine,*16 June 1918, p. 1

9 NOVEMBER 1918

DISTRICT MEET W.S.S. WORKERS

**Representatives From Twelve Counties
To Hold Conference Here Today**

$11,500,000 NEEDED TO WIND UP DRIVE

Colonel Fries and Corps From Winston Are Here For Meeting

[attributed –ed.]

The Raleigh District Conference of War Savings workers, meeting to map out the plan of action for the Victory Drive, will be held in the Wake County Court House today at 11 o'clock with Col. F. H. Fries, State Director, presiding. All war workers, bond salesmen, relief solicitors, and representatives of the press in Wake, Alamance, Chatham, Durham, Granville, Vance, Warren, Franklin, Harnett, Johnston, Orange and Lee counties have been invited to the conference here today which is the fourth of twelve being held in various sections of North Carolina.

From War Savings headquarters in Winston-Salem, Col. Fries, Gilbert T. Stephenson, John L. Gilmer and Miss Kate M. Herring have arrived to attend the conference here. They reached Raleigh last night from Tarboro.

North Carolina lacks $11,500,000 of reaching the State quota of $48,500,000 and this amount must be raised between November 27 and December 6. This State, with Tennessee, now leads the South, and Col. Fries and his staff of workers are confident that North Carolina will go well beyond the goal during the remaining weeks of the campaign.

Since the War Savings campaign was taken over by the Treasury Department, a plan proposed by North Carolina headquarters has been adopted for national use and will be followed in every State in the Union until the close of the campaign in December. This provides for a house-to-house canvass in every community and a call upon all who have pledged to either double their pledges or to make an additional pledge for a proportionate part of the unraised quota. During the next few weeks, special stress will be laid upon redeeming the pledges made last June when nearly $38,000,000 of the State's quota was subscribed.

Raleigh *News and Observer,* p. 10

14 NOVEMBER 1918

WAR STAMP WORKERS PLAN FOR DRIVE IN ASHEVILLE DISTRICT

District Now Stands Second in Sales and Third in Pledges— Hendersonville Conference Prepares for Hard Work to Put Six Counties Over Top

[attributed –ed.]

A meeting of workers in the War Savings Stamp campaign was held at the courthouse in Hendersonville yesterday afternoon. Representatives from the counties of Buncombe, Henderson, Haywood, Madison, Transylvania and Polk met with Judge Colbert T. Stephenson, state director of the service of the war savings committee; Miss Kate M. Herring, director of publicity, and John L. Gilman. state chairman of the retail merchant's division.

Plans for putting the six counties comprising the Asheville district over the top were outlined and figures showing the present standing of the various counties were furnished as follows:

County	Allotment	Pledges	Sales	Rank in State Pledges	Sales
Buncombe	$1,095,440	$921,497	$716,700	30	3
Henderson	357,760	365,000	131,784	11	30
Madison	442,900	265,000	157,888	70	32
Transylvania	158,200	90,000	44,979	75	54
Polk	168,080	109,720	29,576	63	35
Haywood	462,440	396,514	254,099	27	6

No county in the Asheville district has yet sold anything like its allotment, and it was brought out in the discussion that some very hard work would have to be done throughout the entire district between now and the end of the year to maintain the state's reputation of 100 per cent on war work activities. The district as a whole stands second in sales and third in pledges; the merchants' section of the Asheville division stands first in the state, having sold 140 per cent of its quota.

The Victory Drive to secure the balance of North Carolina's war savings allotment begins November 27 and ends December 6. Every effort will be made to put North Carolina across but it is clearly understood that some

very hard work is ahead of the solicitors.
Asheville *Citizen,* p. 10

20 NOVEMBER 1918

HOW THE SOUTHERN NEGRO IS SUPPORTING THE GOVERNMENT

By Kate M. Herring
Director of Publicity
North Carolina War Savings Committee

What to do with the Negro in the War Savings Campaign was one of the most puzzling questions that confronted the National Committee. The proposition to apportion to each State its allotment of War Savings Certificates on the basis of twenty dollars per capita was earnestly objected to by representatives from the South. They claimed that this method of determining the quotas was inequitable to the South for the reason that a large part of its population consists of Negroes, and that they cannot buy an average of twenty dollars per capita of War Savings Certificates. They urged the Committee to put the apportionment upon some other basis than population. But the Committee was obdurate and held the South to the same basis of apportionment as other sections.

When the National War Savings Committee saw fit not to make the Negro an issue or an exception in the War Savings Campaign, but to consider him an American citizen with responsibilities the same as other citizens, all the States of the South, except South Carolina, proceeded with their campaigns, altogether ignoring race. South Carolina, however, made a reapportionment of her quota, assigning to the Negroes only two dollars per capita and to the white people enough over twenty dollars to make up the balance. North Carolina made no distinction between the races, expecting Negroes to invest twenty dollars per capita in War Savings Certificates the same as white people.

One of the first things to be attempted by the North Carolina War Savings Committee was to plan for the colored people. The State Director asked each of his county chairmen to name the most representative and influential Negro in his county to be called to a conference to make plans for promoting the War Savings Campaign among the Negroes. As a result of this conference the State was divided into ten districts, in each of which a leading Negro was appointed supervisor of the War Savings activities. In addition to this, separate War Savings headquarters for the colored people, with a capable colored man as executive secretary, were established. This office has been in close touch with and operated under the supervision of State headquarters for the white people.

In North Carolina very much the same educational work has been done for the Negroes as for the whites. The colored War Savings Committee considered that the greatest need of the colored people was to be informed both as to what

War Savings securities were and what they as patriotic citizens should do about them. One of the first efforts of the Committee to educate their people in thrift as well as patriotism was to issue the following leaflet:

To The Colored People of North Carolina—Greeting

Our interests are collective, but they are also racial and individual. They are indissolubly wrapped up in the issues of the war. If the United States and her allies win, it will be, in an important sense, our victory, and will herald the dawn of a new day. If the enemy win, it will be, in a vital sense, our loss, and will betoken the approach of another long night of gloom.

You must see this matter from the point of view that your individual, personal attitude and activity MUST and WILL help to win this war, or lose it. YOU CANNOT BE NEUTRAL! You cannot say as Pilate: "I wash my hands of this matter." To assume an attitude of indifference or even of passive sympathy is to give comfort and help to the enemy. "HE THAT IS NOT FOR US IS AGAINST US!"

How You Can Help

☐ 1. Conserve speech. Be careful to utter no word calculated to beget mischief.

☐ 2. Conserve food. Waste no flour, sugar, meat, or other staples.

☐ 3. Conserve fuel. Burn no more wood, coal, gas, or oil than comfort and safety require.

☐ 4. Conserve time and energy. Find some useful, gainful employment. Do some constructive work putting in full time.

☐ 5. Conserve money. Save every penny of your money and buy Thrift and War Savings Stamps. By so doing you will develop self-reliance, independent manhood and womanhood, and become a creditor to the Government. You will fire a deadly missile at the enemy.

Your Thrift and War Savings Stamps are the best investment in the world. They are mortgages on the United States of America. They are tangible evidence of your loyalty. They insure the success of our Army.

Our fathers left us a proud heritage of faithfulness, patriotism, and valor, but for the first time in our history we are called upon to help furnish the sinews of war. Shall we be less faithful, patriotic, and valorous? A thousand times, No!

Patriotic meetings of colored people have been held in their schools, churches, and community centers, at which War Savings speeches were made by both white and colored field workers. War Savings Societies have been organized in their day schools, Sunday schools, churches, lodges, and working places the same as among white people. In fact, the first War Savings Society organized in the State was among colored people. This was the Warren Place War Savings Society, at Pendleton, Northampton County, and was composed of the tenants of the Warren plantation. The President and moving spirit of this organization is W. J. Lassiter, a Negro tenant, who subscribed $200 to the War Savings Campaign and who has already bought that amount.

Few white citizens of the State have given more liberally of their time and money than a score or more of loyal colored citizens. Negro educators, ministers, and business men of ability have labored unceasingly and without remuneration to arouse their people to a full sense of their full duty toward the Government's requests and to their responsibilities as American citizens. Prominent among those who have labored most faithfully to carry the gospel of thrift and patriotism to the people of their race, even in the remote corners of the State, are: Dr. R. B. McCrary, a leading business man of his race and Chairman of the Colored War Savings Committee; S. G. Atkins, Principal of the Slater Normal School, Winston-Salem, and Executive Secretary of the Colored War Savings Committee; C. S. Brown, Principal of the Watters Normal School, Winton; T. S. Inborden, Principal of the Bricks School, Enfield; Bishop G. W. Clinton, A. M. E. Church, Charlotte; H. L. McCrory, W. H. Coler, Colonel James H. Young, John Merrick, E. G. Storey, S. H. Vick, and C. M. Epps—men of prominence and ability.

Colored people have considered and accepted the calls that have come to them in the War Savings Campaign as privileges of service and as a direct summons from the Government. The quick and whole-hearted response made by the Negroes of Greene County in the pledge drive of June 23–28 illustrates this fact.

Early one morning in June Ambrose Best was notified that he had been appointed chairman of an adjoining township to raise the War Savings quota of the colored people of the township in pledges. On receiving his summons he left his mule and plow in the field in the hands of his young son, and went afoot over into the township assigned to him. Before sunset he had visited every colored person's home and actually had secured an over-subscription of his allotment.

Jesse Williams was another colored township chairman of Greene County who on June 28 was not found deserting his post. He arranged for a schoolhouse meeting Friday night, and kept his audience until three o'clock in the morning signing War Savings pledges. As a result of his energy and enthusiasm he raised his War Savings quota in pledges three times over.

As a result of all these activities of the colored people in the War Savings Campaign, the records show that they have bought and have pledged to buy War Savings Stamps far more extensively in comparison with their ability than the white people.

From inquiries made of War Savings directors of other Southern States, it appears that their experience with the Negro has been not unlike North

Carolina's. Florida reports that the ten counties in that State making the best showing in the War Savings pledge drive in June had from forty to fifty per cent colored population, and that the ten counties making the poorest showing had from thirty to forty per cent colored population. Mississippi reported that the Negroes of that State have given a support to the campaign that in proportion to their means equaled or surpassed that of the white people. Unofficial reports from other Southern States show that the record of the Negro, in the loyal support he has given the War Savings Campaign, has been extremely gratifying. Apparently the misgiving in the beginning lest the Negro would handicap the directors of the Southern States in raising their quotas on a basis of population was unfounded. On the contrary, it would seem that the loyal support of the Negro has more than made up for his poverty.

In justice to the Negro as well as to enthusiastic War Savings workers, particularly pledge canvassers, it can be and should be said that the spirit to coerce the Negro into buying and subscribing for War Savings Stamps has not existed, not even in individual cases, in North Carolina. No threats, scares, or other means of intimidation have been used to make him pledge or buy either in keeping with or beyond his ability. On the other hand, wherever the Negro has been informed as to his duty as a patriotic American citizen, regardless of other calls, he has responded most liberally and cheerfully. It has been a noticeable fact that he responded most readily to the patriotic appeal. The plea that Uncle Sam needed him to uphold his hands while he delivered the blow that would crush the Hun was argument enough for him. The plea that War Savings Stamps are a good investment, that they bear four per cent compound interest and are non-taxable, meant not half so much to the average Negro as the fact that Uncle Sam and the boys at the front needed him and his money to drive back the Germans across the Rhine and to make the world safe for women and children.

But the real explanation of the Negro's co-operation and success in the War Savings Campaign in North Carolina lies in the fact that he has been recognized as an American citizen and given responsibilities the same as white men. Moreover, he has been made to realize the opportunities that have come to him through this call of the Government, and, like the colored soldier at the front, he has responded in a spirit of service and sacrifice that marks him a worthy patriot.

> *Note: The Outlook* was a Christian weekly published in New York. The 20 November 1918 issue included under the rubric "The Patriotism of the Negro Citizen" two essays, of which Kate Herring's was the second.

The Outlook, vol. 120, no. 11, pp. 452–53
widely reprinted, including:

> *Greensboro Daily News,* 26 November, p. 4
> Raleigh *News and Observer,* 2 December 1918, p. 8

4 DECEMBER 1918

GREAT CONFERENCE FOR WAR SAVINGS WORK TO BE HELD HERE TODAY

What Industrial Enterprises of State Can Do to Help Put State Over Will Be Considered at the Conference Today

Many Out-Of-Town Men To Be In Attendance

[attributed –ed.]

An important conference known as the industrial enterprise conference will be held this morning at 10 o'clock in the directors' room of the Wachovia Bank and Trust Company when quite a number of out-of-town and local business men will gather to consider in what ways the industrial enterprises of the State can help raise the State's War Savings quota.

The following local men will be in attendance: F. H. Fries, Miss Kate Herring, and Messrs. R. O. Self, G. T. Stephenson, J. K. Norfleet, H. E. Fries, H. O. Chatham, W. N. Reynolds, H. F. Shaffner, P. A. Gorrell, A. H. Bahnson, R. F. Huntley, J. L. Gilmer, Charles Creech, H. A. Pfohl, A. W. Cornwall, Wilson Gray, James G. Hanes, Van Melchor, Will Maslin, L. W. Lawrence, A. H. Galloway and Frank Griffith.

The following gentlemen from out of the city will be in attendance: Messrs. John G. Lewis, J. S. McNider, Paul Leonard, J. Clinton Smoot, B. D. Haines, L. S. Tomlinson, D. F. Giles, F. W. Dixon, Charles K. Reynal, J. G. Stikeleather, S. P. Burton, M. E. Block, Beverly Lake, W. J. Berryman, T. K. Pettus, E. J. Barnes, G. L. Clendennin, J. E. Brim, A. W. Dixon, J. H. Matthews, L. T. Vaughn, W. B. Strachan, William Perlstein, Eugene Holt, A. F. Sharpe, and Archibald Nichols.

The above gentlemen have signified their intention of attending the conference. Invitations were extended to quite a number of other out-of-town people to attend the conference and it is probable that a number of others will be here for the conference.

State headquarters is busily engaged this week in making plans for putting the State over. The officials have a determination to put the State over, and as only about $11,500,000 is necessary, the task can be accomplished if the people rally to the cause. When it is considered that this is the only war measure in which the State has not raised the required amount, the people should as a matter of State pride get solidly behind the movement with a view to giving a clean slate so far as its war activities are concerned.

Winston-Salem Journal, p. 3

1919

January 1919
Assistant Secretary, North Carolina State Board of Health

February–December 1919
Publicity Officer and Director of War Savings Societies
War Loan Organization
United States Treasury
Fifth Federal Reserve District, Richmond

January — returns to State Board of Health as Assistant Secretary, to general satisfaction of press

22 January — her move to Richmond announced

22 January — death of Lula V. Johnson, the first Mrs. J. Henry Highsmith, in Raleigh during the influenza epidemic

9 February — recovering from an illness of two weeks, is delayed in her arrival in Richmond

Mid-February — her article on "The Negro and War Savings" attracts wide national attention

21 March — attends Fifth Federal Reserve District meeting on Victory Liberty loans as director of savings stamp societies

10 April — visits Winston-Salem for a few days on business

9 May — visits Concord on business

14–22 June — spends week in Raleigh with the Misses Herring; Annie Crews also visiting

26 June — speaks in Morganton on thrift and savings societies to teachers attending summer school

1 July — reports in the press on her tour of Durham, Greensboro, and Winston-Salem, remarking that both colored and white normal schools (teacher academies) have pledged to her campaign

22 July — returns to Richmond after her "Western pilgrimage" to 10 summer institutes and 1,000 teachers, where the slogan was "A War Savings Society in Every School Room"

1 August — on behalf of her supervisor, Albert S. Johnson, scheduled to read major paper, "Financing the American Future," to North Carolina Press Association meeting in Wrightsville Beach; crowded off program, though the remarks are published

5 August — visits the Misses Herring in Raleigh

Fall — oversees War Loan Thrift Exhibit at fairs across the Fifth Federal Reserve District; Pauline in charge of events in Tarboro and Elizabeth City

2 November — returning from Columbia SC, arrives in Raleigh to spend several days with her sisters

Christmas — holidays with the Misses Herring on Hillsboro Street, a "family reunion" along with siblings Troy (and wife and son), Lucy, Mary Belle (of Belmont NC), Joe, and Rufus

28 December — her appointment to a two-year program with the Maryland Social Hygiene Society / American Social Hygiene Association is announced

1 JANUARY 1919

THE NEGRO AND WAR SAVINGS IN NORTH CAROLINA

By Kate M. Herring

That the South failed to raise its War Savings allotment for 1918 cannot be attributed to the Negro. When the National War Savings Committee met to formulate plans and decided to make the apportionments to the states on a basis of population, representatives from the South objected to the plan on the ground that the Negro could not buy $20 per capita of War Savings Certificates. The committee, however, held to its original plan, expecting the South to make of the Negro no issue or exception in this war measure.

North Carolina at no time felt that the Negro would be a handicap to her in War Savings work. From the beginning, Col. F. H. Fries, State Director, made plans whereby the Negroes could work independently as citizens and do their part as patriots. His plan of state organization included an organization for the white people and one for the colored, each with a separate state headquarters. Both headquarters were established at Winston-Salem, and the one for Negroes was operated under the supervision of, and in close touch with, the one for the white people. Dr. R. B. McCrary, a prominent business man of Lexington, was made chairman, and Prof. S. G. Atkins, Principal of the Slater Normal School, Winston-Salem, was made Executive Secretary. Other prominent colored men who have been active in War Savings work are C. S. Brown, Principal of the Watters Normal School, Winton; T. S. Inborden, Principal of the Bricks School, Enfield; Bishop G. W. Clinton, A. M. E. Church, Charlotte; H. L. McCrory, President of Biddle University, Charlotte; and W. H. Goler, Salisbury; Col. James H. Young, Raleigh; John Merrick, Durham; E. G. Storey, Wilmington; S. H. Vick, Wilson; and C. M. Epps, Greenville—all business men of ability and prominence.

The War Savings records for North Carolina show that the colored people pledged to buy War Savings Stamps far more in keeping with their ability than the white people. A comparative study of the counties that subscribed 100 per cent of their War Savings allotment and the counties that have the greatest percentage of Negro population shows that the Negro is not responsible for the state having failed to raise its entire War Savings allotment.

To December 1, North Carolina had subscribed for three-fourths of her entire War Savings allotment, which was $48,500,000. The population of North Carolina is 68 per cent white, 31.6 Negro, and the balance Indian. Nineteen counties in the state subscribed their entire War Savings quota. These, with the percentages of their War Savings subscriptions and the percentages of their Negro population, are:

County	% of W.S.S. Subscribed	% of Negro Population
Greene	128	47
Forsyth	120	30
Wilson	119	44
Gates	117	45
Martin	108	50
Jones	108	47
Pitt	107	50
Anson	105	52
Franklin	103	47
Edgecombe	102	61
Henderson	102	11
Chowan	102	55
Mecklenburg	101	38
Nash	100	42
Union	100	28
Lenoir	100	45
Iredell	100	22
Perquimans	100	50
Cabarrus	100	23

Taking an average for these nineteen counties, one finds that with 42 per cent of their population Negroes, they subscribed 106 per cent of their War Savings allotment, while 31.6 per cent is the average Negro population of the state, and 76 per cent is the average War Savings allotment raised by all the counties of the state. Moreover, six of the nineteen counties lie in the Black Belt, that is, that section of the state where the Negro population is greater than the white. From the foregoing it appears that the counties making the best showing in the War Savings Campaign had a greater percentage of Negro population than the average for the state.

But to approach the question from another angle, what showing have the Black counties made? Fourteen counties, of which over half the population is Negroes, comprise what is known as the Black Belt of the state. The percentages of their Negro population, also the percentages of their War Savings allotment raised are:

County	% of Negro Population	% of W. S. S. Subscribed
Warren	65	67
Halifax	64	77
Edgecombe	60	102
Hertford	59	88
Bertie	58	93
Northampton	58	89
Craven	56	59
Scotland	55	81
Chowan	54	102
Anson	52	105
Caswell	51	48
Vance	51	76
Perquimans	50	100
Pasquotank	50	63

With 56 per cent of their population Negroes, these fourteen counties subscribed over 80 per cent of their War Savings allotment, which is 4 per cent more than the average for the state. It appears that whether the race composition of the counties is considered, or the support that the counties with a large Negro population have given the War Savings Campaign, the result is the same. The Negro has not been a weight about the neck of North Carolina in its War Savings work.

For the reasons that the white and colored people have not been differentiated in the War Savings work of North Carolina, and that separate records of the subscriptions made by each were not kept, it is impossible to know how the subscriptions of one race compare with the subscriptions of the other, either in number or amount. But it is known that the Negroes who were able to subscribe large amounts have done so.

Scores of colored men, and not a few colored women, have become Limit Club members by purchasing $1,000 worth of War Savings Certificates. Anson County has a colored Limit Club of nine members. One of the first men in the state to purchase $1,000 of War Savings Certificates for himself and each member of his family, a total of $4,000, was Dr. C. H. Hines, of Edenton. On giving his check for this amount, he said, "I would as gladly give it as lend it if giving it would any sooner end the war."

On the other hand, it is known that the people with small means have subscribed in keeping with their ability. Some have made genuine sacrifices to meet their obligations called for in the War Savings Campaign.

An old man who had been saving for years that he might own a home and a plot of land in his own life time said, when he was called on to buy War Savings Stamps, that he had waited this long to own a home and that he would gladly wait five years longer, if lending his money to the Government would help win the war.

A colored washerwoman, whose labors are the sole support of her blind husband and three children, said that it was her blind husband's wish that he could buy a bond or $50 worth of stamps as his part in helping win the war. "Put him down for fifty dollars," she said, "I will continue to wash and save until I pay for it."

Colored school teachers have shown a most intelligent response to the purposes and plans of the thrift movement. Winnie Williams, a colored school teacher of Warren County, furnishes an example of their enthusiasm and co-operation in the War Savings activities of the State. Friday, June 28, in the absence of the township chairman, she called a meeting of the patrons of the district at her schoolhouse and took their subscriptions for $1,800 worth of War Savings Stamps.

Prof. H. F. Woodhouse, of Elizabeth City, Negro teacher-preacher, has been a most zealous thrift missionary to the colored people of Pasquotank county. He has organized nine War Savings Societies with a total membership of 2,988. He says that 2,973 of this number are buying War Savings Stamps by the "thrift card route," while the remaining fifteen are able to buy War Savings Stamps directly. Professor Woodhouse says that the doctrine of thrift has been the greatest blessing that could come to his people, and that it will be the saving grace of the next generation of Negroes.

Apparently North Carolina's experience with the Negro in the War Savings Campaign is not unlike that of other Southern States. From an inquiry made of the War Savings Directors of several states of the South as to the co-operation of the Negro in the War Savings Campaign, it was found that the support he has given has been extremely gratifying. Florida reported that the ten counties of that State making the best showing in the War Savings pledge drive in June had from 40 to 50 per cent colored population, and that the ten counties making the poorest showing had from 30 to 40 per cent colored population. Mississippi reported that the Negroes of that State gave a support to the campaign that equaled that of the white people.

What is the explanation of the support given by the Negroes of North Carolina to the War Savings Campaign? In the first place, the counties which have made probably the best showing in War Savings and which have the largest Negro population lie in the most fertile agricultural sections of the state. The blackest counties are the richest counties. In the second place, the first three Liberty Bond campaigns did not reach the farmers of the state to any great extent. The War Savings campaign was the first call of the government to reach all the people, and it found the agricultural sections a rich vein. In the third place, North Carolina recognized the Negro as an American citizen and gave him responsibilities the same as white men. He was made to know that he was expected not only to meet these responsibilities but to recognize them as opportunities offered him by the government for building up a strong and patriotic citizenship. Like the colored soldier at the front, he heard the call and responded.

South Atlantic Quarterly, vol. 18, no. 1, pp. 36–40

4 FEBRUARY 1919

MANY UNREDEEMED W. S. S. PLEDGES IN THE STATE YET TO REDEEM

[attributed – ed.]

Miss Kate M. Herring in Richmond, assisting the War Loan Organization of the 5th district, says:

War savings pledges unredeemed in 1918 War Savings Stamps to be redeemed in 1919 stamps. While this arrangement of the Government allows the individual more time in which to purchase his stamps and by so doing keep faith with the government, it does not allow the amount to be credited to the 1918 sales. All stamps bought in 1919 will be of the blue series and will be credited to the 1919 record. They will mature in 1924.

The amount of North Carolina's outstanding War Savings pledges is estimated to be between eight and ten million dollars. This means that there are over ten thousand people in the state who have pledged to buy War Savings Stamps but who have not yet redeemed their pledges. The government is not only expecting those people to keep their pledges but is allowing them an extension of time in which they may, if need be, raise the money and meet their patriotic obligations.

War Saving Stamps sell during the month of January this year for $4.12, and are redeemable in 1924 for $5.00. Thrift Stamps are the same as those of last year and sell for twenty-five cents each. Thrift Stamps left over from last year can be converted into 1919 stamps. Sixteen Thrift Stamps and twelve pennies can be exchanged for one War Saving Stamp.

North Wilkesboro *Hustler,* p. 2

3 JULY 1919

HEARTY WELCOME IS GIVEN THRIFT SPEAKER

[attributed *–ed.*]

Richmond, Va., July 2.—Miss Kate M. Herring, one of the directors of the War Loan organization of the Fifth Federal Reserve District, reports that both colored and white normal schools in North Carolina are pledging their support of the government's educational thrift campaign.

At Durham the superintendent of schools has arranged to give the course in thrift that the government is authorizing for all teachers taking the summer course. The National Training School for Teachers there, which is colored, has also instituted the thrift course, and War Savings Societies are to be organized at once.

The Normal College and the colored A. and M. of Greensboro will both offer the course in thrift at the summer schools and the teachers there have already signified their desire to organize War Savings Societies.

Professor S. G. Atkins, of the Slater Normal College at Winston-Salem, extended a warm reception to Miss Herring and a hundred per cent cooperation for the thrift movement was assured.

"I am more convinced than ever," said Miss Herring, "that the greater part of the educational work of this organization should be done and can be done through the institutes and teachers' meetings that will be held prior to the opening of school in the fall."

Raleigh *News and Observer,* p. 11

22 AUGUST 1919

STATE FAIRS TO HAVE THRIFT EXHIBITS

[attributed *–ed.*]

Richmond, Va., Aug. 22.—According to an announcement made today the War Loan Organization of the Fifth Federal Reserve District will put on thrift exhibits at the State fairs of Maryland, Virginia and the two Carolinas.

Arrangements are now being completed for these exhibits, and Miss Kate M. Herring, director of War Savings Societies of the district, has been appointed to take charge of the work. A number of attractive features have been arranged to show how thrift habits may be encouraged and illustrating the practical results of systematic saving.

In some States the fair associations have decided to offer War Savings Stamps or cash to winners of certain premiums.

Salisbury *Evening Post,* p. 6, with dateline 21 August
widely carried in Federal Reserve Fifth District newspapers, for instance Bristol [TN] *Herald Courier,* Winston-Salem *Twin-City Daily Sentinel,* Annapolis *Evening Capital and Maryland Gazette,* 23 August; *Washington Times,* 24 August; Kinston *Daily Free Press,* 26 August; Raleigh *News and Observer,* 27 August

26 AUGUST 1919

ANNOUNCES BROAD EDUCATION PLANS

War Loan Organization Is Pushing Sale of Government Securities

[attributed –ed.]

Richmond, Va., Aug. 25.—Announcement of extensive educational and sales plans is made by the War Loan Organization of the Fifth Federal Reserve District which has its headquarters in this city. This organization, which directed the Victory Loan campaign in this district and which is closely affiliated with the Federal Reserve Bank, directs the sale throughout the Fifth Federal Reserve District of all government securities marketed by the Treasury Department through the Federal Reserve Bank. The securities now being offered are Treasury Certificates of Indebtedness, a new series being issued on the first and fifteenth of each month, Treasury Savings Certificates, War Savings and Thrift Stamps.

In addition to marketing current offerings of the Treasury Department, this organization is conducting an extensive educational campaign among club women, business women, school children, industrial employees, fraternal orders, seeking to develop among them habits of systematic saving and wise investment, particularly in government securities, and pointing out the intrinsic worth of Liberty Bonds and War Savings Stamps in an effort to protect the public against the unscrupulous activities of the loan shark, the fake stock promoter and the swindlers who traffic on the ignorance of many people who for the first time in their lives are owners of government securities.

Albert S. Johnstone is director of the organization. Alan Johnstone, Jr., until recently director of the Industrial and Commercial Division, has been appointed director of the newly created Investment Division. Allen Cox, who was in charge of the Agencies Division, becomes associate director of the Investment Division.

Frank C. Wood, formerly field director for Virginia of the Industrial and Commercial Division, has been made district director of this division, and has named Glenn Thomas, who managed one of the War Trophy trains during the Victory Loan Campaign, field director for Virginia. For Maryland, Mr. Wood has appointed Lawrence F. Simmons of Cambridge, Maryland,

successor to Stephen Tighe, who goes to the Investment Division. To this
Investment Division have also been recently transferred Thomas W. Tannor,
of Virginia, W. T. Joyner, of North Carolina and P. S. Armor, formerly
representing the Agencies Division in Maryland.

By functioning along wider and wider lines now being developed the
War Loan Organization will be able, it is believed, to perform a greater and
more lasting public service. Not only will the savings movement be pushed
with vigor, it is announced, but a greater popular distribution of treasury
certificates of indebtedness and treasury savings certificates will be sought.

Certificates of indebtedness issued by the United States Treasury in
anticipation of Liberty and Victory Loan and tax payments, have heretofore
been bought in this district almost exclusively by the banks. Now, however,
because of their attractive investment features, high rate of interest and
tax exemptions, an increased effort will be made to obtain for them a
greater popular distribution, as for instance, among investors generally
and custodians of trust funds. Between August 1st and the end of the year,
the United States Treasury expects to issue about $3,500,000,000 of these
securities. They are issued semimonthly and run for five months,

Treasury savings certificates are issued in the $100 and $1,000
denominations and are exchanged for the proper complement of 1919 War
Savings Stamps. They bear 4 per cent interest compounded quarterly, and
are exempt both as to principal and interest from all State, county, city and
local taxes, except estate or inheritance taxes and from all normal federal
income taxes.

Raleigh *News and Observer,* p. 11

27 SEPTEMBER 1919

THRIFT EXHIBIT WILL BE SHOWN IN STATE

**Raleigh Selected As One of Places For Exhibition
During Fair Week**

[attributed –ed.]

Raleigh has been selected as one of the places at which, if present plans are
consummated, the Government Thrift Exhibit, which is one of the first of its
kind ever to be put out under the auspices of the United States Treasury,
will be shown. The plan is to display it during the whole period of the Fair
at Raleigh.

The exhibit will be in a tastefully arranged booth. It will contain
numerous posters and charts showing the value and necessity of saving.
The various features of the work of the Savings Division in this district will
be emphasized and literature will be distributed explaining the various
government investment securities. Of great interest will be the Liberty

Loan quotations, which will be given every day at the booth, the figures being direct from the New York Stock Exchange and showing the market fluctuations on Liberty Bonds and Victory Notes of all issues.

Miss Katherine Wicker, of Washington, will be in charge of the booth at all of the North Carolina Fairs. The exhibit has been prepared and arranged by Miss Kate M. Herring, of Raleigh, Miss Herring being the director of exhibits for the United States Treasury Department, in the Fifth Federal Reserve District. Her headquarters are at the office of the War Loan Organization, Richmond, Va.

According to the present plans the Government Thrift Exhibit will be shown at several of the principal fairs of North Carolina. It will also visit Maryland, Virginia, and South Carolina, being displayed at State, county and district fairs.

Raleigh Sunday *News and Observer,* p. 2

22 SEPTEMBER 1919

THRIFT EXHIBIT SHOWS ADVANTAGE OF SAVING

**Tells Story of Successful Dollar at a Glance;
Prepared by Miss Kate Herring**

[attributed –ed.]

Richmond, Va., Sept. 21.—A brand new thrift exhibit showing the power of systematic saving, the first of its kind that the United States Government has ever undertaken, has been prepared by Miss Kate M. Herring, Director of War Savings Societies of the War Loan Organization here, to be shown at state, district and county fairs in the Fifth Federal Reserve district.

Never before has the government attempted to visualize thrift, its efforts in the past having been confined to the printed and spoken message, but in the exhibits that Miss Herring has prepared the story of the successful dollar is told at a glance.

The exhibit is offered to fair managers without charge. It is built to occupy a space ten by fifteen feet which the fair officials are asked to donate together with the help necessary to place the exhibit in position. A representative of Miss Herring's department will be in charge of the exhibit.

Besides posters, charts and graphic illustrations the exhibit contains object displays and several novelty attractions electrically lighted. Thrift, saving, investment and the substantial character of government securities are treated in attractive ways through the most effective methods developed in display work.

A number of applications have been received from fair authorities asking for the government exhibits and it is planned to show them at the Virginia, North Carolina and South Carolina State Fairs during the next month.

Raleigh *News and Observer,* p. 11

26 OCTOBER 1919

THRIFT EXHIBIT WILL BE AT COLORED FAIR

**Government Instructs How To Save Through
Purchase of Liberty Bonds**

[attributed –ed.]

The Government Thrift Exhibit, which was one of the newest and most interesting exhibits at the State Fair last week, will remain in place for the Colored Fair this week, which opens Wednesday, October 29th. The daily New York market price of Liberty Bonds and Victory Notes will continue to be shown daily, also the rate of income on bonds purchased at the market price today. The safely and other attractive features of government securities will be clearly pointed out.

The exhibit, which was prepared by Miss Kate Herring, the first exhibit work ever authorized by the U. S. Treasury Department, is designed to teach thrift, saving and investing, advocating the different securities offered by the government as a medium of saving. The high cost of living—six ways to reduce it—is an additional subject that attracts attention.

Raleigh Sunday *News and Observer,* p. 2

1920

January–December 1920
Director of Publicity / Educational Secretary
Maryland Social Hygiene Society, Baltimore

1 January — assumes new post in Baltimore

late February — returns to Raleigh to attend to Pauline and Eugenia, "quite sick" with influenza but by 28 February improving

29 March — attends the installation of the Beta Chapter of Phi Beta Kappa at Trinity College and is initiated as a charter member, as is her future husband; stays several days in Raleigh

mid June — Eugenia, returning from Boston, New York, Niagara Falls, and Toronto, visits several days in Baltimore

early July — vacations over July 4 holiday with the Misses Herring

18 August — ratification of the 19th Amendment, granting women the right to vote

FEBRUARY 1920

MARYLAND SOCIETY COMPLETES ORGANIZATION

Outlines Plans for First Two Years' Activities; Executive Staff Appointed and Campaign Opened

[attributed –ed.]

Among recent additions to the organizations in the social hygiene field is the Maryland Social Hygiene Society, the Maryland representative of the American Social Hygiene Association, which has established offices in the Hoen Building, Baltimore, with an executive staff in charge consisting of Alan Johnstone, Jr., executive secretary, Stephen Tighe, assistant executive secretary, and Miss Kate Herring, educational secretary.

Dr. Hugh H. Young is president, his associate officers being Vice-Presidents Eugene Levering, Sr., Walter B. Brooks, Howard A. Kelly, and Jacob M. Moses; Secretary William P. Constable, and Treasurer Robert Garrett.

Alan Johnstone, Jr., was in charge of law enforcement in the southeastern states for the army during the war, and his record in promoting the various measures adopted by the government for controlling the venereal diseases caused him to be chosen for his present post by the Maryland Society. His assistants are experienced in the fields of publicity, law enforcement, education, and social legislation.

The purpose of the society, as set forth in its preliminary announcement, is to "act as the representative of the city of Baltimore and the state of Maryland in acquiring and diffusing knowledge on social health and in conducting a thorough and vigorous attack on vice and venereal disease in an effort to check the moral, physical. and economic ravages of these scourges."

"The business and professional men and women of Maryland are willing and anxious to give the experiment a thorough work-out," said Mr. Johnstone, in discussing the organization of the society, "and our present plans call for a budget of $40,000.

"Maryland is a particularly good field for laboratory work in many respects, as it is neither North nor South; it has an equal rural and urban population; it has a large Negro population; and it is centrally located."

The Social Hygiene Bulletin 7/2 (February 1920), p. 11

1921

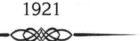

January–May 1921
Director of Publicity
American Social Hygiene Association
New York City

January — moves to New York, lodging at 404 W. 116th Street by the Columbia campus

mid February — the Misses Herring move from 709 Hillsboro Street to 604 North Blount Street

21 May — her engagement is announced at a tea in New York; notice carried widely in NC papers

30 May — returns to Raleigh from New York

25 June — marriage of her brother Rufus Herring to Gladys Jerome ("Aunt Gladys"), in Winfall, NC; Mary Belle, "of Raleigh, presided at the organ"

27 June — is entertained at a porch party by Miss Flora Creech at the home of Mrs. Palmer Jerman, noted clubwoman, on Lane Street

29 June — secures marriage license at Wake County Register of Deeds

30 June — marries J. Henry Highsmith at Edenton Street Methodist Church; departs for "extensive vacation" in the mountains of North Carolina

7 July — honeymooning at Mountain Meadows Inn

12 July — the newlyweds pass through Lenoir en route to Boone, where Dr. Highsmith addresses summer session of Appalachian Training School (now Appalachian State)

c. 20 July — returns from mountain honeymoon to 604 North Blount Street

end July — the newlyweds spend several days at Wake Forest College

1 August — Dr. and Mrs. Highsmith at home at 322 New Bern Avenue

16 August — probably attends picnic of 200 State officials in Pullen Park

organized by Jane McKimmon; after a "bounteous picnic lunch" in the pavilion, Dr. Highsmith leads the singing

Christmas season — chair of publicity for Tuberculosis Christmas Seals; she retains a lifelong association with Christmas Seals

25 November — the Highsmiths attend banquet of North Carolina Teachers' Assembly, jointly with Wake County Trinity College Alumni Association, at Edenton Street

Dr. and Mrs. J. Henry Highsmith

22 May 1921

The Engagement Announcement

New York (May 22): The engagement and approaching marriage of Miss Katherine M. Herring, formerly of Raleigh, to Mr. J. Henry Highsmith, also of Raleigh, was announced Saturday at a tea given by Miss Elizabeth Bain and Mrs. John McCurdy at the latter's apartment in "The Terrace," 405 West 118th St. The wedding will take place in Raleigh, June 30th.

Both parties are prominent in North Carolina. Miss Herring, who is director of publicity for the American Social Hygiene Association with headquarters in New York, held a similar position for several years with the North Carolina State Board of Health. During the war she served with the State War Savings Committee as publicity director with headquarters at Winston-Salem, and later was a member of the staff of the War Loan Organization for the Fifth Federal Reserve District at Richmond, Va. She is a graduate of Trinity College.

Mr. Highsmith is one of the leading educators of North Carolina. For a number of years he was professor of education and philosophy at Wake Forest College, which position he resigned to become a member of the State Board of Examiners and Institute Conductors. He is now State Inspector of high schools with headquarters in the State Department of Education at Raleigh. He is a graduate of Trinity College and of Teachers' College, Columbia University.

Miss Herring and Mr. Highsmith have a wide circle of friends both within and without the State. They will make their home in Raleigh.

Charlotte Sunday Observer, 22 May 1921, p. 8
Sampson Democrat, 26 May 1921, p. 2

June 1921

The Wedding Invitation

Miss Vara Herring requests the honor of your presence at the marriage of her sister, Miss Katherine Maude Herring, to Mr. John Henry Highsmith, on

Thursday, the 30th of June, at 6 o'clock in the afternoon at Edenton Street Methodist church, Raleigh, N. C.

[Enclosed card:] At home after the first of August, [3]22 New Bern avenue, Raleigh, N. C.

Winston-Salem *Twin-City Daily Sentinel,* 21 June 1921, p. 3

1 JULY 1921

HIGHSMITH—HERRING

The marriage of Miss Katherine M. Herring to Mr. J. Henry Highsmith, both of Raleigh, took place at the Edenton Street Methodist church yesterday afternoon at six o'clock. Rev. W. W. Peele, pastor of the bride, officiated, using the ring ceremony.

Before the bridal party entered, a musical program was given by Mrs. Kate Hayes Fleming and Miss Margaret Highsmith. The latter sang "Beloved It Is Morn" and "Dost Know?"

Acting as ushers were Mr. J. O. Herring of Clinton; Mr. W. J. Highsmith, of Durham; Mr. J. R. McPhail, of Fayetteville; Dr. H. W. Glascock, Dr. W. S. Rankin, and Mr. T. E. Brown of Raleigh.

Miss Lucy Herring of Washington, D. C., sister of the bride, was maid of honor. She wore a dress of orchid chiffon taffeta, and an orchid hat to match. Her flowers were pink Russell roses heliotrope.

The bride entered with her brother, Mr. T. I. Herring of Roseboro. Her dress was grey Canton Crepe, embroidered in crystal beads and cut roses. She wore a large grey hat, with shoes and gloves to match. She carried a shower bouquet of orchids and lilies of the valley.

The groom entered from the vestry, attended by his brother, Dr. L. L. Highsmith, of Kingsport, Tenn.

Palms, ferns and Queen Anne's lace were used as decoration for the church.

Immediately after the ceremony Mr. and Mrs. Highsmith left for an extended stay in the mountains of North Carolina.

They will be at home at 322 New Bern Avenue after August 1st.

The out of town guests here for the marriage were Mr. T. I. Herring, Mr. and Mrs. Rufus K. Herring, of Roseboro; Mr. J. O. Herring, of Clinton; Miss Lucy Herring, of Washington, D. C.; Mrs. J. E. Royal, of Clinton; Miss Annie Crews, of Oxford; Miss Mary Shotwell, of Richmond; Mr. J. R. McPhail, of Fayetteville; Mr. W. J. Highsmith, of Durham; and Dr. L. L. Highsmith, of Kingsport, Tenn.

Raleigh *News and Observer,* p. 7
Asheville *Sunday Citizen,* 3 July 1921, p. 14
Winston-Salem Journal, 3 July 1921, p. 15
Charlotte Observer, 3 July 1921, p. 6

J. Henry Highsmith, c. 1940

J. HENRY HIGHSMITH MEMOIR

c. 1935

Born in Sampson County, reared in Durham, attended elementary and secondary schools in Durham, graduating in 1896. Entered Trinity College on a scholarship awarded to Durham High School in 1896 and was graduated with the A.B. Degree in 1900. Received the Master of Arts Degree in 1902. From 1901 to 1904 served as Principal of the North Durham High School. Mrs. Warren (Jule B. Warren's mother) and I began the work of the session in a one-room building in the Pearl Mill Section and moved into the new North Durham School building in December 1901. Served as Principal for three years with six teachers in the School—Miss Hallie Holeman, Miss Annie Lee, Miss Bessie Battle, Miss Matthews and Miss Nellie Stephenson and Mrs. Warren. Duncan Tilley was janitor of the school and had a lot to do with how things went on. One of the incidents which I recall vividly was the smallpox scare which we had, for when we fumigated to kill the smallpox germs the fumes killed all of our potted plants. Mr. J. A. Matheson was Superintendent of Schools and took an active interest in all his schools, principals, teachers and students. I recall with interest that the other principals serving at that time were W. D. Carmichael at Morehead, Ernest Greene at Edgemont and W. J. Brogden at Fuller School.

Having taught for three years at a salary of $50.00 a month the first year, $60.00 the second and $75.00 the third, having served what I regarded as an apprenticeship in teaching, I went to Teachers College, Columbia University for two years—1904–1906. This was an unusual experience and a big change for a person who had taken his training in a college with about 300 students and in a town the size of Durham at that time.

After two years at Teachers College I accepted an invitation to teach at Meredith College, then called, I believe, Baptist University for Women, at that time located just one block from the Governor's Mansion, the building being called now Mansion Park Hotel. I was Professor of Philosophy and Bible, but I taught things that were neither Philosophy nor Bible to the extent of about eighteen (18) hours a week, regarded then and now as a heavy load for a college professor. At the end of the year at Meredith in the summer of 1907 I accepted a position at Wake Forest College as Professor of Education. Upon the death of Dr. Charles E. Taylor, a former President of the College, I was asked to teach the course in Moral Philosophy as well as the courses in Education. An effort was made to train young men for teaching positions in the high schools of the State and for several years some 20 to 25 persons were located as high school teachers, not only in private schools of which there were more at that time than now, but also in public schools.

In 1917 I resigned at Wake Forest to accept a position as member of the State Board of Examiners and Institute Conductors upon appointment by Governor T. W. Bickett. After three years of work on this Board the plan had been changed from two weeks institutes every two years to six weeks summer schools at the colleges in the State, and the certification requirements had been set up and the program was well underway. Professor N. W. Walker resigned as State High School Inspector and I was appointed to the position in 1920, serving in that capacity until 1931, when I became Director of the Division of Instructional Service, which has to do with both elementary and secondary schools so far as instruction is concerned.

In addition to my work as college professor or member of the State Department of Public Instruction I have taught in summer schools at the University of Louisiana, at NC State College, Raleigh, at the Woman's College, U.N.C., Greensboro and at Duke University.

One of my most interesting experiences was that of reorganizing the high schools in Oklahoma in 1928 and in Mississippi in 1929, working as a representative of the General Education Board in this reorganization program. This work in Oklahoma and Mississippi followed the program of high school reorganization in this State which began in 1925—and which had, I may say, a good deal to do with the high school program and development subsequently. I shall not undertake to evaluate my services except to say that I have seen tremendous growth in the high schools since 1920. We graduate from high school in any one year more students than were enrolled in all high schools whatsoever only a few years ago. Furthermore an effort is made in the high schools to meet the needs, not only of the few who enter college, but the thousands who for one reason and another will never attend any institution of higher learning. As a matter of record I may say that I have received honorary degrees [of] LL.D. from Catawba [Catawba College, 1925]; Doctor of Education from Wake Forest College [1934] and was elected to membership in Phi Beta Kappa and ODK [Omicron Delta Kappa, national leadership honorary] at Duke University.

> *Note:* His typescript, which is in the family archive, covers events through 1934, focusing particularly on his life story to about 1920.

PART II
MRS. J. HENRY HIGHSMITH

1922–1923

—— ⬥⬥⬥ ——

1922

24 January — hosts newly formed Raleigh Association of Trinity College Alumnae organization to discuss a Fanny Carr Bivens memorial fund; elected president

6 February — entertains at tea at her home on New Bern Avenue

14 June — birth of Katherine Herring Highsmith

26 July — attends, with Dr. Highsmith, a dinner at Bland Hotel for former students of Dr. Edwin Mims, dean of students at Vanderbilt, who had taught at both Trinity College and UNC

22 December — gives small tea honoring Mrs. Walter A. Stanbury, wife of new pastor at Edenton Street

1923

1923–35
Chairman, Press and Publicity
Founding Editor, *North Carolina Clubwoman*
North Carolina Federation of Women's Clubs

2–5 May — probably attends NCFWC convention in Winston-Salem, where Mrs. Jerman is elected president; the same morning, May 5, she is named statewide chairman of publicity

July — Highsmith family relocates to 832 Wake Forest Road, also called North Person Street; resides there for the rest of her life

29 July — first NCFWC article for the Sunday papers

August — following indictment of the superintendent of the State Sanatorium, is appointed director of a new press bureau to focus the public eye on the work of the North Carolina Tuberculosis Association, the North Carolina Sanatorium for the Treatment of Tuberculosis, and its extension work including Christmas Seals

13 September — in Asheville, addresses meeting called to reorganize Southern Tuberculosis Conference and Southern Sanatoria Association

23 September — announced as chairman, Educational Department, RWC, with bold agenda of lectures and courses, including Fall course "Know Your Child," led by Dr. Highsmith

30–31 October — attends third annual meeting of North Carolina Conference on Tuberculosis, Charlotte; addresses the Wednesday afternoon session

29 JULY 1923

WHAT CAROLINA CLUB WOMEN ARE DOING AND THINKING

By Mrs. J. Henry Highsmith

Club Women Asked to Help Counties Put Mother's Law to Work.

Club women in at least 50 counties in the state are being called on by Mrs. Kate Burr Johnson, Commissioner of Public Welfare, to urge their county commissioners at their meeting the first Monday in August to take action to secure their county's quota of the mother's aid fund and put the law to work in their counties. As it is, only 42 counties have taken advantage of the state's offer, leaving 58 counties yet to qualify.

The 50 or more counties which are being urged at this time by Mrs. Johnson to match the sum allotted by the state to each county for the work of aiding worthy mothers care for their children at home, are those which have superintendents of public welfare or other officials for administering the duties of the mother's aid law, but which have not yet signified their intention of undertaking the work.

"There's no excuse," says Mrs. Johnson, "for such counties not taking action at once and getting the benefit of the mother's aid fund. It would not be such an urgent matter," she said, "if there were not mothers in every county needing this help."

The counties which have taken advantage of the state's offer and which are now prepared to help a number of mothers to keep and care for their children at home instead of placing them in institutions are: Rutherford, Cleveland, Mecklenburg, Cabarrus, Union, Anson, Stanly, Iredell, Forsyth, Davidson, Moore, Scotland, Robeson, Columbus, Brunswick, Cumberland, New Hanover, Wake, Franklin, Vance, Orange, Granville, Edgecombe, Beaufort, Pitt, Lenoir, Nash, McDowell, Davie, Buncombe, Harnett, Halifax, Durham, Guilford.

Club women throughout the state worked faithfully for the passage of the mother's aid bill. They were successful. To put this act into effective operation in all the counties is the next step in getting the full benefits the law. To this end Mrs. Johnson is calling on the club women to go before their county commissioners at their meeting the first Monday in August and urge that they make an appropriation sufficient to obtain their county's quota provided for in the mother's aid fund.

State Federation Officers for 1923–1924.

The officers of the North Carolina Federation of Women's Clubs for 1923–1924 are: Honorary president, Mrs. R. R. Cotten, Bruce; president, Mrs. Palmer Jerman, Raleigh; first vice president, Mrs. Thomas Lenoir Gwyn, Waynesville; second vice president, Mrs. Thomas O'Berry, Goldsboro; recording secretary, Mrs. E. L. McKee, Sylva; corresponding secretary, Mrs. F. R. Perdue, Raleigh; treasurer, Mrs. Clyde Eby, New Bern; General Federation director, Miss Margaret L. Gibson, Wilmington; publicity director, Mrs. J. Henry Highsmith, Raleigh; auditor, Mrs. Fred F. Bahnson, Winston-Salem.

The chairman of the various departments of the Federation are: Art, Mrs. Rufus Gwyn, Lenoir; civics, Mrs. George Byrum, Edenton; conservation, Miss Julia Thorne, Asheboro; education, Mrs. H. W. Chase, Chapel Hill; health, Mrs. Rufus Allen, Waynesville; home economics, Mrs. Rosiland Redfern, Wadesboro; library extension, Miss Mary DeVane, Goldsboro; literature, Miss Marion Blair, Winston-Salem; music, Mrs. Chas. B. Wagoner, Concord; social service, Mrs. Chas. E. Quinlan, Waynesville.

Chairmen of the standing finance committees are: Finance, Mrs. A. H. Powell, Oxford; legislation, Mrs. C. A. Shore, Raleigh; membership; Mrs. John L. Gilmer, Winston-Salem; districts, Mrs. Thomas O'Berry, Goldsboro.

Presidents of the districts are: Mrs. F. Duke Hay, Black Mountain; Miss Louise Roth, Elkin; Mrs. J. R. McClamrock, Greensboro; Mrs. H. P. Adams, Waxhaw; Mrs. W. P. Horton, Pittsboro; Mrs. F. H. Brooks, Smithfield; Mrs. R. G. Lassiter, Oxford; Miss Ruth Burke, La Grange; Mrs. J. W. Farrior, Warsaw; Mrs. S. R. Fowle, Washington; Mrs. Quincy Gilkey, Marion; Mrs. E. H. Williamson, Fayetteville; Mrs. T. S. Hedgepeth, Elm City; Mrs. J. G. Fearing, Elizabeth City.

Last Year Broke Membership Record.

The year 1922–1923 was a record breaker in the increase of membership in the Federation. Mrs. B. H. Griffin, chairman of the membership committee, reported at the meeting of the Federation at Winston-Salem that 116 clubs with a membership of 9,991 had [been] admitted from June, 1922, to May, 1923.

The clubs admitted were classified as follows: Women's Clubs 30; community clubs 3; Parent-Teachers 7; Literary 10; Home Demonstration 23; clubs withdrawn 3; membership of clubs withdrawn 138; membership of clubs merged with Woman's Clubs 19; membership of Woman's Clubs admitted 1,480; membership of affiliated organizations admitted 8,511; membership of Woman's Clubs, and affiliated organizations admitted, 9,991; total membership of federated clubs 14,917; total membership of affiliated organizations 38,448; grand total of federated clubs and affiliated organizations 52,839.

Mrs. Palmer Jerman, State Federation president, and Mrs. R. R. Cotten, honorary president, will address the farm women of the state at their annual convention at North Carolina State College, Raleigh, Tuesday July 31. Mrs. Jerman's subject will be "The Union of North Carolina Women for North Carolina." Mrs. Cotten, who is herself a farm woman, will bring new ideas to the members of the convention.

Mrs. J. Henry Highsmith, chairman of publicity for the Federation, is asking all the district presidents and other Federation officers to send her all club news as soon as possible, and if possible, before it happens. From October to June, she will furnish the news of club activities to the Sunday papers of the state twice monthly. It is her ambition to give the club women of the state only live news and constructive, interesting reading matter, and to this end she is asking for the co-operation of all club women.

> *Note:* This appears to be the first of more than a hundred articles Mrs. Highsmith submitted as Chair of Press and Publicity for the NCFWC, 1923–1935.

Charlotte Sunday Observer, p. 10

4 NOVEMBER 1923

WORK FOR PEACE WOMEN'S SLOGAN

Uppermost Thought in Minds [of] Club Members as Armistice Day Nears

MRS. PALMER JERMAN SOUNDS THE KEYNOTE

President of National Federation of Clubs in Message to North Carolina Members Emphasizes Same Thought; Gleanings from Council Meeting

**By Mrs. J. Henry Highsmith
Chairman of Publicity**

There is a tide in affairs that brings now one and now another matter uppermost. With the approach of Armistice Day, November 11, which is also World Court Sunday, and with the call for the observance of World Court Week from November 5 to 10, undoubtedly the thought that is uppermost in our minds and the prayer that is in our hearts is peace—the doing away with war.

At this time, when 130,000 churches in America have been called on to use their influence in securing a world peace program looking toward a warless world, it seems fitting to call to the attention of the 53,000 federated and affiliated club women of North Carolina the keynote messages of the presidents of both the State and General Federation.

Mrs. Palmer Jerman in her presidential message says: "Among those of chief importance we earnestly desire the adoption of every means looking toward better national understanding and that permanent peace may be established."

Mrs. Thomas G. Winter, president of the General Federation of Women's Clubs, in her message to North Carolina club women, says:

"Every one of us hate war; then it behooves us to do more than express our hatred in vague terms, but to set to work to substitute international law and all the agencies by which law and justice can become operative for the lawlessness of war. We can do it. We can assist the government of our country to realize that we refuse to allow this issue to become the plaything of partisan politics or to become befogged by minor issues instead of the central ones. Which shall we have—war and lawlessness—or law and the court of law?"

The Council Meeting.

On recalling the royal welcome, the gracious hospitality and the delightful entertainment accorded the members of the council at their fall meeting at Hickory, Oct. 25 and 26, those fortunate enough to attend are still experiencing a great pleasure. To the Community Club of Hickory, of which Mrs. Carrie Gamble is president, to the Kiwanis Club, the Country Club and to all other organizations and individuals who contributed to the pleasure and success of the coming meeting, and not only the council members themselves, but the State Federation, feels deeply grateful.

Mrs. Palmer Jerman, president of the State Federation, spoke with force and optimism regarding the ability of the club women of the State to achieve great things during the next two years. She emphasized the importance of co-operation and Federation loyalty, from the lowest to the highest office.

Mrs. R. R. Cotten, honorary president of the Federation, made a special plea for finishing the endowment fund. Two thousand dollars of the $10,000 pledged several years ago, to be raised as an endowment fund, is yet to be raised. Mrs. Cotten urges that efforts be concentrated on this one thing, until the endowment is finished.

Mrs. A. W. Chase of Chapel Hill, chairman of the department of education, reported that 11 young women are in college this year as beneficiaries of the Sallie Southall Cotten Loan Fund. To date, 60 young women have been aided by this fund.

The attitude of the Federation toward moving pictures was reaffirmed by the council as being one of watchful waiting.

Mrs. Rufus Allen, of Waynesville, chairman of the department of health, announced that a new division had been added to her department, that of narcotics, with Mrs. Edwin Gregory, of Salisbury, chairman. According to Mrs. Allen, care of the teeth will be emphasized in the schools this year as a special feature of health work.

The outstanding feature of the work of the social service department, of which Mrs. Charles M. Quinland is chairman, is to be the promotion of a reformatory or farm colony for women prisoners, those that have passed the age limit for Samarcand. Mrs. Quinland and her corps of workers are emphatic as to the need of such an institution.

Mrs. Kate Burr Johnson, Commissioner of Public Welfare, gave an interesting report on the workings of the mothers' aid law. Fifty-seven counties have qualified for receiving aid from the mothers' aid fund. All the counties, she reported, had shown an interest in the law, as more than one hundred applications have been received, but not all the counties were yet ready to administer the law. The type of woman that is being helped, said Mrs. Johnson, is pleasing. And, one man applied for aid. He had one arm, one leg and three children. On learning that the law made no provision for men to receive aid, he immediately made application for a wife.

Mrs. S. E. Leavitt, of Chapel Hill, who is compiling a volume of prize poems and stories of the Federation for publication, announced that the book will be from the press and on sale in time to be used as Christmas presents. The volume will include the stories and poems for the period of 1915 to 1923. The foreword will be by Mrs. Sallie Southall Cotten. All clubs are expected to sell at least five copies of the book in order to finance its publishing.

Mrs. John S. Gilmer reported the addition of eight new clubs with a membership of 591.

All clubs are asked to raise a contribution during the year to meet the pledge of $1,500 made to the headquarters of the General Federation at Washington, D. C. Already $1,100 of the amount have been paid.

The committee on legislation, of which Mrs. C. A. Shore, of Raleigh, is chairman, will support four particular measures during the next two years. These are a movement on the part of the colored women's clubs of the state to erect an industrial school for colored girls similar to the one at Samarcand for white girls, a farm colony or reformatory for women prisoners, an eight-hour law for children employed in industry, and the State Public Welfare Department.

Miss Gertrude Weil, of Goldsboro, has been appointed North Carolina's representative on international relations. On explaining the work of her new office, she gave as its main object the promotion of friendly relations between the nations. The organization, through which Miss Weil works, "The Federal Council of the Churches of Christ in America," has three objectives, namely a Permanent Court of International Justice as a means of World Peace, the Outlawry of War, and the League of Nations.

Mrs. Charles R. Wagoner, of Concord, emphasized the importation of having trained music teachers in the public schools. The council heartily concurred with Mrs. Wagoner in this great need. It leaked out during the council session that one of Mrs. Wagoner's compositions, "The Mecklenburg March," was now being arranged by Creatore for Victrola records.

The plan for affiliation between the North Carolina Federation of Home Bureaus and the North Carolina Federation of Women's Clubs was given by Miss Maud Wallace, assistant state Home Demonstration agent. She said in part: "in each county where the Home Demonstration Clubs have been federated into a county council or Home Bureau, this council is entitled to send two delegates with the power to vote in its district meeting of the Federation of Women's Clubs. There are 14 such districts, and the Home Bureaus represented at each district are entitled to elect one delegate which will represent the district in the State Federation meeting. This gives the State Federation of Home Bureaus a representation of 14 delegates with the power to vote in the State Federation of Women's Clubs. The annual dues of the State Federation of Home Bureaus and Women's Clubs are $2.00 for each district."

Tarboro District Meeting.

The thirteenth district meeting will be held in Tarboro, Nov. 10, with the Tea and Topics Club hostess. Mrs. Palmer Jerman, Mrs. Thomas O'Berry and Mrs. R. R. Cotten will be present and will take an active part in the program.

According to Mrs. Thad Hedgepeth, district president, all Federation clubs and Home Demonstration clubs have been urged to have a full representation at the meeting. The non-federated clubs also have been given a cordial invitation to attend. As the "box lunch" plan recommended by the Federation for district meetings will be used, Mrs. Hedgepeth says, no club member need feel a hesitancy in coming. All club representatives are asked to bring and present their individual problems for discussion and probably for a solution. A splendid program has been prepared.

Meeting of County Federation.

The Gaston County Federation of Women's Clubs, the one and only county Federation in the State, and with a membership of 700 representing seven different federated clubs in the county, held its first meeting at Belmont Oct. 18, with Belmont's Woman's Club as hostess. A program looking to the uplift of the county and to the mutual helpfulness of all the clubs in the work they have undertaken was successfully carried out. A large delegation was present.

> *Note:* Creatore, mentioned in association with Mrs. Wagoner's "Mecklenburg March," was Giuseppe Creatore (1871–1952), the Italian bandmaster—the same Creatore in the patter before "Seventy-Six Trombones" in *The Music Man.*

Sunday Raleigh *News and Observer*, p. 8

19 DECEMBER 1923
WOMEN OF STATE WANT FIVE BILLS

National Program of Legislation For State Federation of Clubs

By Mrs. J. Henry Highsmith
Chairman of Publicity

Club women of North Carolina are interested in five bills that are now before Congress. They are: The Child Labor Law, The Uniform Marriage and Divorce Amendment, The Creation of a United States Department of Education with a secretary in the President's Cabinet (heretofore known as the Towner-Sterling bill, this department is deemed necessary by the organized women of the country as preliminary to a successful campaign toward the elimination of illiteracy in America); a bill for a Federal prison for women in Virginia, and the Modified Immigration Bill.

Drama Week, January 20–25.

Drama Week is to be observed in North Carolina January 20–25, writes Miss Marian H. Blair of Winston-Salem, chairman of the literature department of the Federation. Clubs are urged to present historical pageants or plays during this week in connection with their study of State history. The observance of Drama Week, says Miss Blair, is in co-operation with the Drama League of America and with the plan of the General Federation. She says further:

"The Drama League has prepared thirteen programs of all sorts, elaborate and simple, to meet the needs of any club and every community. The following is a list of some of the material which is available:

1. Great Dramatists of the Ages
2. Types of Drama — Tragedy, comedy, farce, etc.
3. Racial Aspects of Drama
4. High Lights in Modern Drama
5. Scenery and Plays of the Past and Today
6. Informal Programs for small clubs.

"These programs may be secured free of charge from the Drama League office, 59 E. Van Buren St., Chicago, or from your state chairman.

"Literature departments and clubs should see that a copy of 'Carolina Folk Plays,' edited by Dr. Koch of the University, is in every library in the state and in the private library of each individual member. If the Carolina Playmakers have not been to your town, make an effort to secure an engagement with them. The work which they are doing under the direction of Dr. Koch is of nation-wide interest, and deserves our enthusiastic support."

Book of Stories and Poems Ready.

"Stories and Poems from the Old North State," which is the title of the book of prize winning stories and poems entered in the literary contests held under the auspices of the North Carolina Federation of Women's Clubs from 1915 to 1923, has the following table of contents:

Foreword by Sallie Southall Cotten.

Introduction.

A Singin' Lad, by Zoe Kincaid Brockman.

The Message of the Tuscania, by Zoe Kincaid Brockman.

A Race for Honors, by Susie A. Bardin.

Land of Dreams, by Zoe Kincaid Brockman.

At the End of the Way, by Mary C. Robinson.

The Apotheosis, by Ellen Ellwanger Hanford.

The Wraith of Autumn, by Zoe Kincaid Brockman.

The Still Born, by Zoe Kincaid Brockman.

The Soul of the Pilgrim, by Susie Morris Whitehead.

The Call of the Country, by Mrs. Roscoe L. Wall.

The Ex-communication of Mother Hubbard, by Mary Pressly.

A Cry, by Carolina A. Trowbridge.

Tranquility, by Edna Baker Serimger.

The Seeker, by Zoe Kincaid Brockman.

The Merciful Governor, by Nell Battle Lewis.

My Day, by Mrs. Roscoe L. Wall.

The House of Life, by Mary Pressly.

The House of Loneliness, by Mrs. J. Bryan Grimes.

Such A Little Bit Q'Baby, by Daisy M. Hendley.

They's Liars Here, by Joy Kime Benton.

Bill an' Me, by Ella A. Lackey.

My Baby, by Sally Stewart Niemyer.

The Moonstone, by Mrs. Al Fairbrother.

The Prodigals, by Mary E. Wells.

The March Wind, by Edna Baker Scrimger.

Alternative, by Joy Kime Benton.

Cynthia's Voyage, by Mrs. Richard B. Willis.

Sally and Her Bonnet, by Mrs. C. A. Jordan.

The Silver Bell, by Mrs. Al Fairbrother.

Silent Trees and Singing Men, by Joy Kime Benton.

The Minstrel Sings, by Maura Burton Miller.

Non Omnis Moriar, by Emily P. Shapiro.

Echoes, by Mrs. Charles Ives.

Limitations, by Mrs. Charles Ives.

Research, by Mrs. Charles Ives.

Small Town Memories, by Mrs. Charles Ives.

Modus Operandi, by Mrs. Charles Ives.

At Night, by Mrs. Charles Ives.

The book which is now ready for delivery sells for $2.00. Address Mrs. S. E. Leavitt, Chapel Hill, N. C.

Clubs Asked to Observe Thrift Week.

Club women of the country are asked to celebrate Thrift Week, January 17–24. The Thrift committee is teaching that much of character is dependent on money affairs, and that improved economic standing in the individual brings about a better citizenship. Clubs are asked to endorse Thrift Week; to make January a thrift month; to ask merchants to mention Thrift Week in advertisements; to foster talks on Thrift and Savings; to urge children to start bank accounts. Full information may be had from Thrift Headquarters, 347 Madison Ave., New York City.

Mrs. Palmer Jerman, of Raleigh, and Mrs. Margaret L. Gibson, of Wilmington, will attend the board meeting of the General Federation of Women's Clubs to be held in Washington in January. They will remain over for the Illiteracy Conference that will be held the two days following the General Board Meeting.

Miss Adelaide Fries, of Winston-Salem, a prominent club woman, an author and the first woman to serve as president of the North Carolina Literary and Historical Association, captivated her audience as the presiding officer at the meetings of the State Literary Historical Association recently held in Raleigh. Her charm and poise as well as her face and tact, won her admiration and honor.

Note: Stories and Poems from the Old North State online at Google Books.

Raleigh *News and Observer,* p. 12

1924

9 January — Raleigh Association of Trinity College Alumnae, founded by her in 1922, announces student loan fund of $250 annually

19 May — named to Raleigh citizen's committee in campaign to fund Student–Alumnae building at North Carolina College for Women, Greensboro (now UNCG)

19 September — elected vice president, Raleigh Jr. High School PTA, for 1924–25

26 September — first school-year meeting of Senior High School PTA, organized the spring before; Dr. Highsmith is program committee chairman and Mrs. Highsmith, member of social committee

5 October — birth of Louise Westbrook Highsmith

20 October — attends Jr. High School PTA meeting

late November — vol. 1, no. 1 of the *Bulletin* of NCFWC, six pages, appears under her editorship; noted in papers nationwide; this becomes the *North Carolina Clubwoman*

December — Duke Endowment established as Trinity College becomes, under President William Preston Few, Duke University

13 JANUARY 1924

WOMEN URGED TO FIGHT FOR PEACE

North Carolina Federation Starts Off New Year With Good Resolutions

By Mrs. J. Henry Highsmith
Chairman of Publicity

Mrs. Alice Ames Winter, president of the General Federation of Women's Clubs, sends the following New Year message to the club women of the country:

"Of pressing and immediate interest to all club women is the question of the steps that this country can take to bring about the substitution of justice, legal methods and international understanding for the old brutalities of war. We cannot repeat too often that the considerations of our attitude in these matters should be far above partisan or personal points of view and it is the belief of the Department of International Relations that the General Federation—a body of women of all parties yet all determined to do what they can looking toward international peace—may form a determinate element in holding these subjects above party. As voters and as women combined in organizations we ought to let our government representatives know in no uncertain words that we demand that they shall see that the United States takes her proper part in the settlement of international difficulties through orderly judicial processes. Let every club pass a well considered resolution and send it to President and Senators."

Attended General Board Meeting.

Mrs. Palmer Jerman, president of the North Carolina Federation of Women's Clubs, attended the annual meeting of the General Federation Board which met January 8, 9 and 10, in Washington.

Following the meeting of the General Federation Board Mrs. Jerman attended the Illiteracy Conference, which was held by the Federation of Women's Clubs, the Department of Education, the American Legion and the National Education Association. Mrs. Jerman attended the conference by virtue of her office as president of the State Federation. She was also appointed by Governor Morrison to represent the State of North Carolina at the conference.

Miss Margaret Lovill Gibson, of Wilmington, who is General Federation director of North Carolina, attended the General Federation Board meeting as the official representative of the State Federation.

Club Women Called On To Set Standard.

Mrs. J. T. Alderman, chairman of safety under the civics department of the Federation, has seized the opportunity of her office to teach the club women of the State some of the sane and practical principles of safety. To this end she has prepared a twelve page illustrated booklet of the most helpful and sensible suggestions in the interest of preventing fires, accidents and injuries in the home. The book deals with all the fire hazards from curling tongs to lightning rods, and in addition gives helpful information concerning poison oak and poison ivy, including a remedy for the same.

A chapter on rubbish contains much timely advice. As the writer says, rubbish is not only a source of annoyance and anxiety at all times, but whether it is inside or outside the home it is a menace to the health and safety of the family.

Mrs. Alderman, who is with the North Carolina Insurance Department at Raleigh, appeals to the club women of the State to become leaders in adopting more intelligent methods in their homes in preventing fire and other disasters. She says:

"It is good business for a club woman to set a high standard of safety in her own home for her neighbor will follow her lead in this as she does in equipping her house with modern labor-saving devices and the latest styles in dress.

"If the president of the Woman's Club decrees that it is bad form to have a stove without metal protectors around and beneath it, local hardware men will soon face a shortage in sheet iron. If she releases the idea that it is old fashioned and a too dangerous risk to start fires with kerosene oil, the big oil tanks will soon diminish in size and usefulness."

The State Department of Insurance, recognizing the influence of the 53,000 club women in the State, published the booklet prepared by Mrs. Alderman, entitled "Safety in the Home," for free distribution among club women. Copies for distribution may be had by any club member writing to the State Department of Insurance, Raleigh.

Mrs. Alderman urges every club not having a department of safety to organize one at once and to make plans for observing "Safety Week" early in the spring. She will send material for programs and suggestions concerning the observance of Safety Week.

Working For a Club Home.

The Woman's Club of Dunn, although one of the newest in the Federation and as yet having only three organized departments, has ambitious plans for the future. In addition to broadening its activities and increasing its usefulness, the club is looking forward to owning a club home and will work to this end.

Mrs. N. A. Townsend is president of the club; Mrs. W. S. Snipes is secretary; Mrs. V. L. Stephens is chairman of the Civics Department; Mrs. Carl Fitchett of the Home Economics Department, and Mrs. W. E. Coltrane of the Music Department.

The outstanding features of the Civic Department during the fall months has been the sale of tuberculosis Christmas seals and aiding in organizing a library. Through the home economics department, the housewives of Dunn have had helpful lectures and demonstrations in cooking, sewing and other features of housekeeping. The music department has arranged for a year's study of the opera.

Since the organization of the Woman's Club of Dunn a few years ago, its force has been felt at every single angle where the club's activities touched the life of the community. The social, civic and educational life of the city has been greatly improved through the efforts of the club.

National Music Week.

National Music Week will be observed in April, 1924, according to Mrs. Chas. B. Wagoner, state chairman of music. "The Music Week Idea," she says "involves the participation of all elements in the community and we want industrial plants, department stores, bands, and supervisors, leaders in clubdom, welfare workers, leaders in civic offices, orchestra leaders, public school music artists and teachers, business men, and churchmen, all to contribute their share of the entertainment. Musical programs of all sorts from large spectacular programs to modest programs in the home are to be offered. Music Week is not simply a name, and cannot be put over merely by announcing that it will be held, without the development of the necessary local machinery. We recommend that each town take up the plan, develop its proper organization, and inaugurate a Music Week for the last week in April, or at whatever time seems best suited to local conditions. Perhaps ultimately it will be possible to put on a simultaneous state-wide Music Week."

Takes Straw Vote For President.

The Mount Airy Woman's Club was not idle during the full months as was shown in a report of the club's activities given by Miss Cora L. Earp. The social service department reported at the December meeting that a home for a young girl trained at Samarcand has been secured and that subscriptions to a number of magazines have been sent to the girls at Samarcand and to the boys at Jackson Training School as Christmas remembrances. At this meeting the fine arts department gave a Christmas entertainment including vocal and instrumental music and a play.

Another feature of the club's work was taking a straw vote to determine the feeling of the club women toward possible candidates for the nomination for president of the United States; ballots used were those sent out to clubs all over the nation from the publishers of one of the leading magazines. The ballots resulted as follows: McAdoo, 46; Coolidge, 14; Underwood, 4; Henry Ford, 3; Woodrow Wilson, 3; Hughes, 1; Hoover, 0.

Time of Prose Contest Extended.

The time of closing the General Federation Prose Contest according to Mrs. L. A. Miller, general chairman of literature, has been extended to February 1. Mr. Frederick A. Stokes, of the New York Publishing House, has added $100 to the General Federation prize of $25 contributed by Mrs. Winter for the best prose article, not exceeding 500 words on the subject, "What Do Two Million Women Want From the Publishers?" Mr. Stokes does this in the belief that the answers will prove helpful. The rules have not altered. Contestants must be members of a Federated club. Name and address of writer, and name of her club must appear on each page of the manuscript. Contributions should reach the State chairman by February 1st.

The prizes will be apportioned as follows: First, $50; second, $35; third, $25, and fourth, $15.

Mrs. Miller emphasizes the fact that frankness and sincerity of opinion, understanding of the situation in regard to American letters and the ability to concentrate the most constructive thought as possible within the limited space will count for more than literary style. This is an opportunity for the club women to define their place in the reading public of America. Only a few can win the prizes but every sincere lover of literature may and should contribute to this effort. The replies will be tabulated and the general opinion determined as nearly as possible.

All manuscripts should be typewritten, if possible, and sent to Miss Marian H. Blair, Winston-Salem, State Chairman of Literature.

Drama Week.

"Drama Week, January 20 to 25," writes Miss Marian Blair, chairman of literature, "is fast approaching. Several clubs have sent in requests for the programs issued by the Drama League of America. Your chairman still has a number of these programs on hand, and will be glad to supply them on request. If you have an interesting plan for the observance of Drama Week, send it in to the Department Chairman. If it is not practicable for your club to devote a meeting to the study of drama, then present a copy of 'Carolina Folk Plays' or some good collection of pieces to your school or public library. In this way every literary club can participate in the observance of Drama Week."

Raleigh Sunday *News and Observer,* p. 7

3 FEBRUARY 1924

CLUBS ARE URGED TO PLAN FOR BETTER SPEECH WEEK

Scope and Purpose Given in Leaflet Issued by Educational Division of General Federation; Plan to Wipe Out Illiteracy; Work For Towner-Sterling Bill; Club Notes To Appear Weekly Until State Convention

By Mrs. J. Henry Highsmith
Chairman of Publicity
North Carolina Federation of Women's Clubs

There is nothing more timely and more needed, it seems to us, than the movement to raise the standard and improve the quality of the English language as it is spoken by the large majority of people today. Why not make our language the universal medium of civilization for the people of the world? Is it because our language as it is spoken is lacking in culture and refinement that it is not accepted as the universal medium of expression? This charge against it is frequently made. To improve the quality of our spoken English, to create a respect for our language in keeping with that we have for our flag, is the purpose of the Better Speech Movement of America. This movement is a national undertaking sponsored by the National Council of Teachers of English, the National Federation of Women's Clubs, the American Academy of Arts and Letters and the Society for Pure English. It urges all patriotic citizens to rally under the banner: "One Country, One Flag, One Language."

"Better Speech Week" will be observed in North Carolina February 17 to 23: Clubs, schools, homes and every one who is a friend to "Better Speech" will be called on that week to co-operate in raising the standard and improving the quality of our speech. Mrs. C. C. Haworth, of Burlington, who is State chairman of the Better Speech Movement, is calling on every club in the State directly and on the schools, homes and other agencies indirectly to make plans for observing Better Speech Week. She will furnish suggestions and literature for programs.

The scope and purpose of "Better Speech Week" is further set forth in a leaflet issued by the educational division of the General Federation of Women's Clubs. It reads:

Better Speech for Better Americans: The English language is our most precious possession. To love it and preserve it is our patriotic duty. Respect for our flag should carry with it respect for our language—and loyalty to it. Let us use it, not abuse it.

Better Speech for Better Business: Business men know the value of correct and effective speech. Poor speech is a poor salesman, and slovenly speech is a poor advertisement. Let us look to our speech. It is an advance agent and may mend or mar our fortunes. Speech, like apparel, oft proclaims the man. Better speech means better jobs.

Better Speech for Better Homes: The home, the church and the schools are the three educational agencies of society. All education should begin in the home. Better speech should begin there. "As the twig is bent, so is the tree inclined." As parents we owe it to our children, both by precept and by practice, to arouse in them a consciousness of speech, and to incite in them a desire for improvement. The sooner begun the sooner done.

Better Speech for Better Friends: Good speech will open the way into the best of company. Many are the friends of a man or a woman who can talk well. Correct and pleasant speech is at once a social asset and a social grace. Become a friend of good speech and good speech will make many friends for you. Respect your language and others will respect you.

Better Speech for Better Schools: It has been said that if our schools would rise to their opportunity and raise English into a culture worthy of its qualities, there seems no reason why it should not become the universal medium of civilization for the world. But the schools cannot accomplish such a result singlehanded. Everybody must help. "Everybody who prays for a better America—whether in school or out, whether a professional man, a shop girl, or a mother of a family—should cooperate to raise the standard and improve the quality of our speech." The schools, through their students, are now attempting to arouse your interest and to enlist your support.

No Illiteracy in 1930.

The General Federation of Women's Clubs asks that there be "no illiteracy in the United States in 1930," and to accomplish this desired goal it suggests that "each one teach one." Mrs. Cora Wilson Stewart, of Frankfort, Ky., who is chairman of illiteracy of the General Federation, has an excellent one-hour program which she will send to any club desiring a program on this subject. Miss Elizabeth Kelly, of Raleigh, who is State chairman of illiteracy, also has valuable suggestions and help for putting on an illiteracy program.

Mrs. H. W. Chase, of Chapel Hill, State chairman of education, is asking all clubs having a department of education to put on at least one program on the subject of illiteracy during the year.

Work for Towner-Sterling Bill.

The 68th session of Congress is now convening. One of the bills which will come before Congress this year and which has the endorsement of the General Federation of Women's Clubs is the Towner-Sterling bill. This bill in brief proposes:

(1) To create a Department of Education with a secretary in the President's cabinet.

(2) To create a national council of one hundred representative educators and laymen which will meet annually at the call of the secretary.

(3) To give Federal aid to encourage the States in the solution of five educational problems fundamental alike to good citizenship in both State and Nation.

(a) The removal of illiteracy;

(b) The Americanization of the foreign born;

(c) The promotion of physical education;

(d) The training of leaders;

(e) The equalization of educational opportunities.

Mrs. H. W. Chase, of Chapel Hill, chairman of education, urges all club women not only to become familiar with the provisions of the bill, but to be ready to write to their representatives in Congress to vote for it.

Ask Help From Club Fund.

Through the Sally Southall Cotten Loan Fund, fifty-nine girls to date have been aided in getting an education. The sum of $2,730 has been loaned this year to eleven girls, the rates ranging from $50 to $400. Two girls whose graduation this spring depends upon further assistance from this loan fund [are] now calling for help. Mrs. E. M. Land of Goldsboro, chairman of the Sally Southall Cotten Loan Fund, is asking for generous contributions from all clubs which have not already responded to this meritorious work.

Club Notes to Appear Weekly.

The chairman of publicity [Mrs. Highsmith herself] announces that from now till after the meeting of the Federation in May, this department of club news and activities will be issued every Sunday instead of every other Sunday. This division seems advisable for the reason that the greater half of the club work of the year is to be done between now and the annual Federation meeting, and it is the desire of the chairman to serve the department and all club interests of the State as much as possible through these columns. She invites the chairmen of the various departments of club work to call on the publicity department whenever its services are needed.

Miss Gibson Concludes Report.

Miss Margaret L. Gibson, of Wilmington, State director of the General Federation, concludes her report of the general board meeting at Washington, January 7 and 8. The first part of Miss Gibson's report was published in last Sunday's issue of Federation news.

"The advantage of headquarters in Washington was strongly impressed upon us when we were able during one evening to listen to short addresses from twenty women heading different bureaus or special work in the Capital City.

"Headquarters is still in need of your help. Twenty thousand dollars remains unpaid upon the pledges of the country; and North Carolina has by no means paid all of hers. The clubs will be called upon in the near future to complete this promise, so that when Mrs. Winter's administration closes at the Los Angeles biennial in June, your director will be able to report North Carolina as over the top.

"It was our pleasure to see Maude Adams in everyday life. Miss Adams appeared before the board to speak for a national theatre. Mrs. Herbert Hoover, who heads the Girl Scouts of America, came before us to receive the Home Sweet Home house which was presented to the Girl Scouts by the General Federation of Women's Clubs.

"The board was received by Mrs. Coolidge in the White House, and the following day by President Coolidge in his office on the White House grounds. Col. and Mrs. Theodore Roosevelt also gave a reception for the members of the board. At the Congressional Club the board had the opportunity of hearing addresses from the heads of several of the leading publications for women.

"A press breakfast in the headquarters tea room brought before us the value and difficulties of a State magazine. Many States have most creditable publications, which carry the club message to every individual club member in the State.

"On the day preceding the board meeting, members who were in the city had the privilege of attending a meeting of the Women's Joint Congressional Committee, which is composed of representatives of seventeen national organizations of women. The purpose of the committee is to unite forces for the passage of bills and to inform the various organizations of the progress being made.

"During the evening of the same day the board was given a dinner in Alexandria by the Cameron Club at which the candidates for the presidency spoke—Mrs. W. S. Jennings, of Florida; Mrs. Wallace Perham, of Montana, and Mrs. John D. Sherman, of Colorado—and also the Hon. William J. Burns of the United States Department of Justice. Mr. Burns told of the dangers from the Reds in America, and cited many incidents of criminals captured and of other features of his remarkable detective work.

"Following the board meeting was the illiteracy conference to which all members of the national board were delegates."

On May 7, 1924, the world will celebrate the one hundredth anniversary of the first performance of Beethoven's immortal Ninth Symphony. [Sidney] Lanier, the Southern poet-musician, once said: "when we have played Beethoven's symphonies as they should be played, and shall have revealed to us all the might, all the faith, all the religion, the tenderness, the heavenly invitations, the subtle excursions down into the heart of man, the brotherhood, the freedom, the exaltation, the whisperings of sorrow unto sorrow, the messages of God which these immortal and yet unmeasured compositions embody, then will America give to music the place it deserves."

Cooperative Work Of Federation.

The North Carolina Federation of Women's Clubs co-operates with the following organizations and activities: The United States Government in its work of Americanization, the State Insurance Department through the Safety Leagues and fire prevention work, State Forestry Association, North Carolina Conference on Social Service, North Carolina Tuberculosis Association and the Extension Division of the State University.

Note: The Towner-Sterling Bill failed to pass. The United States Department of Education began to function in 1980.

Raleigh Sunday *News and Observer,* p. 11

2 March 1924

Ask Club Women To Push Gardens

Coolidge and Hoover Issue Appeal For Garden Week

By Mrs. J. Henry Highsmith
Chairman of Publicity
N. C. Federation of Women's Clubs

President Coolidge and Herbert Hoover are sponsoring two fundamental movements that are near to the hearts of all club women. These are National Garden Week and the Better Homes Movement.

Both of these movements were unanimously endorsed by the General Board of Directors at their recent meeting in Washington. Great impetus has recently been given to the Better Homes Movement by becoming organized with Mr. Herbert Hoover as chairman and with funds provided from the Laura Spellman Foundation. But club women are asked not to confuse this entirely altruistic movement under the leadership of Mr. Hoover with certain commercial interests which use the same name. President Coolidge is particularly interested in Garden Week and urges all club women to lend assistance in promoting this fundamental movement. Both Garden Week and the Better Homes Movement appeal to club women. Expression has already been given to their attitude toward better homes as follows:

"We want homes where the big things are made big and the little things are made unimportant, where children can be well-born and joyous and grow up to noble citizenship, where the family income is made to serve the highest family interest, where there are vigorous American bodies and minds. We want communities that are extensions of the home, where we shall be friends with each other, we people of all races and creeds where good schools, high standards of public health, recreation, beauty, shall tempt the finest type of people to come and live with us and bring up their children.

"There are big tasks lying before women—tasks that need such wisdom as we get from combined study, tasks that need the altruism we get from working together, tasks that need the energy we get from combination of effort."

Law Enforcement Timely Issue.

"Law enforcement is undoubtedly one of the greatest issues before club women," says Mrs. Alice Ames Winter, president of the General Federation of Women's Clubs. She says:

"Not only the prohibition amendment, violation of which is undermining the respect for law and order in every community, but it stretches out into all forms of crime and punishment. When we realize that in London last year there were only nine cases of murder in the first degree, and not one of them unsolved; and in New York alone in 1921 there were 260 murders and only three convictions in the first degree; when we know that thieves, swindlers and frauds rob of us of over two and a half billion dollars every year in addition to what bootleggers and grafters get out of us, we can not escape the fact that we are far down in the scale of civilization so far as law and the execution of law is concerned. And yet law is the first requisite of a self governing democracy, if it is to live."

Southern Pines Club at Home to Tourists.

Mrs. Robert N. Page of Southern Pines, state chairman of civics, and president of the Southern Pines Civic Club, writes that the club is doing construction work in all of its departments, which are seven in number. The club had as its guest recently Mrs. Palmer Jerman who spoke helpfully on timely topics of club work. This club, like many other progressive clubs in the State, is working for a new club building. At a recent entertainment given by the club, one hundred dollars were added to the building fund. On February 29, the club will be at home not only to all Southern Pines people but also the tourists.

Mrs. Edwin H. Williamson of Fayetteville, president of the Twelfth District, brought together on February 6, at a well appointed six course luncheon at her home, representatives from the six counties comprising her district. The purpose of the luncheon was to make plans for enlarging the work of the district and for encouraging those who are responsible for carrying on the work.

Mrs. Williamson's guests were: Mrs. J. A. Robeson, Elizabethtown; Mrs. N. A. Townsend, Dunn; Mrs. M. J. McQueen, Laurinburg; Mrs. G. W. Tompson, Fairmont; Mrs. Hester, Whiteville; Miss Sara Williams, of Fayetteville and Mrs. Paul Steward, secretary of the Twelfth district.

Under the supervision of Mrs. Williamson as president of the Twelfth district, a chairman has been appointed in each county to assist in federating new clubs and to strengthen those needing help.

Book of Prize Stories and Poems Off the Press.

Mrs. S. E. LeLavil, of Chapel Hill, announces that the book of prize stories and poems which she was authorized by the State Federation to compile for publication is finally off the press and is ready for distribution. She is urging all clubs to send in their orders for the books at once.

National Music Week In April.

"National Music Week will be observed the last week in April," writes Mrs. Charles B. Wagoner, of Concord, State chairman of music. "The Music Week idea involves the participation of all elements in the community," she says, "and we want industrial plants, department stores, bands and orchestral leaders, public school music supervisors, leaders in clubdom, welfare workers, leaders in civic offices, artists and teachers, business men and churchmen, all to contribute their share of the entertainment. Musical programs of all sorts from large spectacular programs to modest programs in the homes are to be offered. Music Week is not simply a name, and cannot be put over merely by announcing that it will be held, without development of the necessary machinery. We recommend that each town take up the plan, develop its proper organization, and inaugurate a Music Week for the last week in April, or at whatever time seems best suited to local conditions."

Defer Action on Education Bill.

Mrs. H. W. Chase of Chapel Hill, State chairman of education, is asking all educational chairmen to defer action on the Towner-Sterling bill until they have further notice from her. She says that opposition to the Towner-Sterling education bill has arisen and that to work for this bill intelligently, certain facts concerning the opposition must be had. Until that time, Mrs. Chase is asking club women to defer action.

Raleigh Sunday *News and Observer,* p. 27 (section 2, p. 1)

12 MARCH 1924

NEW CLUB HOUSE FOR GOLDSBORO

Women Trade In Real Estate and Accumulate Some Cash

By Mrs. J. Henry Highsmith
Chairman of Publicity
N. C. Federation of Women's Clubs

The occasion is at hand when women should talk more, when they should speak up and express themselves on certain important questions now before Congress that will soon be settled for once and for all and for right or wrong. This is the opinion of William F. Bigelow, editor of Good Housekeeping, who says that from now until Congress adjourns and from then until election day there should be an unceasing discussion of the things that should be settled now and must be settled right.

"One of these," says the editor, "is the question of education. This, one of the most important concerns of the American people, perhaps the largest single enterprise in the nation, is conducted by forty-eight different partners who have themselves only the loosest kind of control over their particular parts of it. In other words, education is largely a local matter, being good or bad in proportion to the interest and ability of the locality. The Education Bill provides for the dignifying of education by placing in the President's Cabinet a man whose duty shall be to look after the interests of education as Secretary Hoover looks after the interests of commerce, Secretary Davis of labor and

Secretary Wallace of agriculture. Education is now in the Department of the Interior, where it got $161,990 of the $328,000,000 appropriated last year. But money is not in the heart of the Education Bill. Whether the $100,000,000 which the bill as introduced calls for is appropriated or whether that sum is cut in half or quartered is not the main point, which is national recognition of the fact that education is a national problem, and should be dealt with nationally. Get education into the Cabinet. It will pay for itself. Talk it up."

New Club House for Goldsboro.

The latest activity of the Woman's Club of Goldsboro is buying and selling real estate. The club recently sold a portion of its lot on the corner of James and Mulberry Streets to the Standard Oil Company and purchased a new site for the building of their club house on North William Street. It is understood that both sales were cash transactions, involving in the aggregate the sum of approximately $32,500.

The new site obtained by the club is 90 x 200 feet and is a corner lot. The portion of the lot on Mulberry Street, which the club still owns, is 70 x 110 feet.

It is the purpose of the club to erect on the new property in the next few years a commodious fireproof club building. The lower floor is to contain a large auditorium, kitchen, banquet room, assembly rooms and guest rooms where the club affairs may be conducted and where visitors on occasions may be accommodated. The upper floor will contain several apartments for rent, the income from which will support the upkeep of the lower floor.

Four years ago the Goldsboro Woman's Club established a fully equipped cafeteria. While the cafeteria necessitated a large initial outlay, it is now practically free from debt, and will be operated in the future to add to the club's building fund.

In recognition of the splendid and unselfish service rendered the Women's Club of Goldsboro by three of the public spirited men of the city, the club recently admitted to honorary membership Capt. Nathan O'Berry, Mr. Joe A. Parker, and Mr. Joe Rosenthal.

League Meet In Durham.

At the invitation of the Woman's Club of Durham the North Carolina League of Women Voters held its Fourth Annual Convention in Durham March 4 and 5. Not only members of the League were invited to attend, but all women interested in the aim of the organization, which are: education in citizenship, more efficient government and progressive legislation.

Miss Belle Sherwin, first vice president of the National League, and Mrs. Elliot Cheatham of Atlanta, third regional director of the National League, were the honor guests and principal speakers on this occasion. Miss Mary O. Graham, Democratic National Committeewoman, and Mrs. Lindsay Patterson, Republican National Committeewoman from North Carolina, also Miss Elizabeth Kelly, president of the North Carolina Teachers' Association, were on the list of speakers.

Some of the accomplishments of the conference were the endorsements of the World Court and Hughes Harding plan, the Towner-Sterling Educational Bill, and the recommendation that the compulsory school law be based not only upon age, but also upon attainment, and that all children be required to finish the fourth grade at least.

It was also recommended that political and civil disabilities of women should be removed by special legislation, rather than by blanket legislation, either State or Federal.

The League expressed appreciation that the State's two Senators had endorsed the Towner-Sterling bill.

Mrs. Sherman Nominee For President.

The Colorado Federation of Women's Clubs announced that it will present the name of Mrs. John D. Sherman at the Biennial Convention at Los Angeles in June 1924 as President of the General Federation of Women's Clubs. Mrs. Sherman served as Recording Secretary of the General Federation from 1904 to 1908 and was 2nd Vice-President from 1910 but was forced to resign on account of illness. She is now Chairman of the Department of Applied Education of the General Federation.

Mrs. Sherman is nationally known through her work as Chairman of the Committee on Conservation of National Resources, particularly in preserving the national parks of the United States.

Illiteracy Largely Made In America.

Illiteracy is largely made in America as shown by the National Illiteracy Conference held in Washington in January. There are 5,000,000 adult illiterates in the United States and of these scarcely more than one fifth are foreign born. Most of our illiterates are made in America. Finland and Iceland have not one illiterate resident; Denmark, Sweden and Switzerland have only two per cent of known illiteracy; Germany has five per cent; Netherlands .08; Norway one; Scotland 1.6; England and Wales 1.8; France 4.3, but the United States at the head of the list in resources and in gold stands at the bottom with a black six per cent of known adult citizens who can neither read nor write.

Raleigh Sunday *News and Observer*, p. 9

27 April 1924

North Carolina Federation of Women's Clubs

By Mrs. J. Henry Highsmith
Chairman of Publicity

Announcement is made by Mrs. Josephus Daniels, chairman of the program committee, that final and complete arrangements have been made for the 32nd Annual Convention of the State Federation of Women's Clubs which meets in Raleigh May 6 to 9 inclusive. The program of the Convention printed below is so arranged that every department of club work will receive due consideration and all of the sessions will be well balanced, the heavier parts interspersed with those of lighter vein. The program follows:

Tuesday, May 6, 1924.

11:30 A. M.—Meeting of Executive Board at the home of Mrs. Josephus Daniels, President, Raleigh Woman's Club.

1:00 P. M.—Luncheon to the Executive Board—Mrs. Josephus Daniels, hostess.

1:00 P. M.—Luncheon for the past presidents—Mrs. Clarence Johnson, hostess.

3:30 P. M.—Meeting of Board of Trustees—Sir Walter Hotel.

4:30 P. M.—Meeting of Board of Directors—Ball Room, Sir Walter Hotel.

Evening Sessions, 8:00 o'clock—Ball Room, Sir Walter Hotel; Music—Directed by Mrs. J. W. Kellogg; Invocation; Welcome from Mayor E. E. Culbreth; Welcome from Club Women of Raleigh, Mrs. Josephus Daniels; Response—Mrs. E. L. McKee; President's Address, Mrs. Palmer Jerman; Announcements; Reception at Governor's Mansion—Governor and Mrs. Cameron Morrison.

Wednesday, May 7.

District Presidents, Mrs. Thomas O'Berry, presiding; Presidents of Literary Clubs and Chairmen of Literature Departments, Miss Marian Blair, presiding; Health, Civics, Social Service, Joint hostesses: Mrs. R. L. Allen, Mrs. R. N. Page, Mrs. Charles E. Quinlan.

Morning Session, Sir Walter.

9:00—Presentation of credentials.

10:00—Business Session, collect of Club Women of America; assembly singing; report of Committee on Rules and Regulations; appointing of Special Committees; reports of officers; reports of Trustees; report of Credential Committee; Election of Nominating Committee, report of Membership Committee; Introduction of Finance Committee.

1.00 o'clock—Luncheon—Presbyterian Sunday School Room, Christ Church Parish House.

2:30 o'clock—Afternoon session, report of Chairmen of Districts, report of one-half of district presidents—Mrs. Thos. O'Berry, 2nd vice president, presiding. Report of chairmen of departments: Civics—Mrs. R. N. Page; Education, Mrs. H. W. Chase; report of S. S. C. Loan Fund—Mrs. E. M. Lund; Health—Mrs. R. L. Allen.

4:30 to 6:00 o'clock, tea at Woman's Club, tea at Wakestone [home of Mr. and Mrs. Josephus Daniels], complimentary to delegates and to visiting and local club women.

Evening Session, 8:00 P. M., Fine Arts Evening.

Music, report of chairman of Music—Mrs. Chas. B. Wagoner, presentation of Florence M. Cooper cup, presentation of Duncan cup.

Music, report of chairman of Art, presentation of Robert Lamar Beall, presentation of prizes for best interior decorating, music, report of chairman of literature, presentation of Separk Poetry Cup, Joseph Pearson Caldwell Cup, music.

Thursday, May 8.

Breakfast Conference, 8:00 A. M., Yarborough House and Sir Walter Hotel, presidents of departmental clubs—Mrs. Josephus Daniels, presiding. Home Economics—Mrs. Rosalind Redfearn, presiding. Art, Music—joint hostesses: Mrs. R. L. Gwyn, Mrs. Charles B. Wagoner. Education, Conservation, Library Extension—joint hostesses: Mrs. H. W. Chase, Miss Julia Thorne, Miss Mary DeVane.

Morning Session.

9:15 o'clock: Collect, assembly singing, report of one half of district presidents, report of Home Economics—Mrs. R. A. Redfearn. Report of Library Extension Committee—Miss Mary DeVane. Report of Social Service Chairman—Mrs. Chas. Quinlan. Message from N. C. Social Service Conference by Miss Minnie Harmon. Report of Publicity Chairman—Mrs. J. Henry Highsmith. Report of Custodian—Mrs. Clarence Johnson. Report of General Federation Director—Miss Margaret Locell Gibson. Report of Southeastern Council—Mrs. Sidney P. Cooper. Report of Bureau of Information—Miss Nellie Roberson. Report of Committee on International Relations—Miss Gertrude Weil. Report of Anti Narcotic Committee—Mrs. K. C. Gregory. Report of Stories and Poems from the Old North State—Mrs. S. E. Leavett. Report of Co-Operative Efforts between Home Bureaus and State Federation—Mrs. R. E. Redfearn. A message from State Chairman, Home Demonstration Work—Mrs. Jane S. McKimmon. Report of Nominating Committee and Election.

1:00 P. M. Luncheon—Christ Church Parish House, Presbyterian Sunday School Room.

Afternoon Session.

2:30 P. M.—Report of Legislative Chairman—Mrs. C. A. Shore. Report of Committee on Resolutions, Amendments to Constitution—Miss Margaret L. Gibson. Federation Dinner 6:00 P. M., Sir Walter Hotel, Mrs. R. R. Cotten, presiding.

Evening Session 8:00 P. M.
State Theater.

Address: "Women in Government Work"—Helen H. Gardener, United States Civil Service Commissioner. Recital by St. Cecilia Club—Mr. W. H. Jones, Director.

Friday. May 9, 1924—9:00 A. M. Assembly Singing. Collect. Unfinished Business. Adjournment. Meeting of Board of Directors. Meeting of Executive Board.

Four Club Women Appointed to National Democratic Convention.

The appointment of four prominent club women of North Carolina, Mrs. Palmer Jerman of Raleigh, Miss Hattie Berry of Chapel Hill, Mrs. J. G. Fearing of Elizabeth City and Miss Mary Henderson of Salisbury, as delegates at large to the National Democratic convention which meets in New York City in June, has been received with interest and gratification not only by the club women of the State, but by club women throughout the country.

These women who have been called to serve their state and nation in some of the higher duties of citizenship received their training in the apprentice school of a local woman's club. Mrs. Jerman, who is now president of the State Federation of Women's Clubs, has long been an ardent worker in the club activities of her city. She has rendered the Raleigh Woman's Club valuable service in many capacities, particularly during its building campaign and since in shaping its policies and programs. She is often called by club members the "Watch Dog of the Constitution."

Miss Hattie Berry, who is now secretary of the N. C. Good Road Association, has been active in the club work of Chapel Hill, particularly in the departments of Civics and Health. Mrs. Fearing who is one of the State Representatives of Safety Education was one the founders of the live[ly] Woman's Club of Elizabeth City. She is also president of the Fourteenth District of Federated Woman's Clubs.

Miss Mary Henderson, who is now parliamentarian of the Woman's Club of Salisbury, has been active in social and political circles. She is also vice president of the State Democratic Executive Committee.

Mrs. Rufus [Allen] May Day Chairman.

Mrs. Rufus L. Allen of Waynesville, chairman of the Health Department of the State Federation, has been appointed State chairman of May Day for North Carolina. This appointment came through Mrs. T. W. Bickett of the Bureau of Infancy and Maternity of the State Board of Health. Mrs. Bickett explains the purpose of May Day as follows:

"On May Day we enlist the support of the press, the churches, the schools, the radio broadcasting stations, the motion picture industry and other agencies to take to the people of America serious thoughts on the health of their children. As an outward symbol we would encourage local observances of May Day which will emphasize the ideal of joyous outdoor health. This can be done by holding May Festivals and other appropriate May Day exercises."

Mrs. Allen is asking the Health Departments of the clubs of the State to put forth efforts to promote child health during the month of May which is the most effective and practical way of observing May Day. Some of the club health departments will study infant care and feeding as a means of warding off summer diseases. Other clubs will hold baby clinics where instruction will be given mothers concerning the care of their babies during the summer months. Mrs. Allen asks every club to do something for child health at this time.

Mrs. Jerman Addressed Wilson Club.

Mrs. Palmer Jerman addressed the Woman's Club of Wilson Friday afternoon on the subject of "The Relation of a Woman's Club to its Community." The Wilson club is one of the best in the State and is undertaking big things for its community.

Gave Silver Tea for Endowment Fund.

The Waynesville Civic League raised its quota to the Federation Endowment Fund by giving a Silver Tea. All clubs that are delinquent in making their contributions to the Endowment Fund might get a tip from the Waynesville club.

Asheville *Sunday Citizen,* p. 22

4 MAY 1924

NORTH CAROLINA FEDERATION OF WOMEN'S CLUBS

By Mrs. J. Henry Highsmith
Director of Publicity

All Raleigh is ready and waiting for the annual meeting of the State Federation of Women's Clubs which meets here this week, May 6 to 9 inclusive. Looking forward to being hostess to the largest body of women that assembles at any time in the State, the city is feeling a little flutter of mingled excitement and delight in anticipation of her pleasant duties and privileges. All her citizens, eagerly awaiting the arrival of the convention dates that will bring friends and delegates from "Cherokee to Currituck," have greetings and warm words of welcome for one and all. It is their desire that every member of the Federation will not only enjoy and be benefited by her stay in the Capital City, but that she should carry away with her memories of the most enjoyable Federation meeting ever attended.

The chief features of the opening session, Tuesday evening, in the Assembly Room of the Sir Walter Hotel, will be the presidential address by Mrs. Palmer Jerman, and the reception afterwards given by Governor and Mrs. Cameron Morrison at the Executive Mansion. No club woman who has ever heard Mrs. Jerman will want to miss her speech on this occasion. While in Florida last fall attending the meeting of the Southeastern Council of Federated Club Women, she was called on to speak a number of times and thereby won the name of the "silver-tongued orator from North Carolina."

The reception given by Governor and Mrs. Morrison promises to be one of unusual brilliancy and interest. Not only Raleigh people but North Carolinians all over the State consider the social occasions at the Governor's Mansion most delightful experiences.

While the morning session on Wednesday will be given over to business, it will be none the less interesting to club women. As a matter of fact, the annual meetings of the Federation of Women's Clubs are now looked upon primarily as the time for transacting club business, the importance of which is not clouded or surpassed by other interests. Many of the most important reports of Federation work will be made at this meeting.

At the luncheon at 1 o'clock, which will be complimentary to the delegates from the Raleigh Woman's Club, half of the guests will be served in the Sunday School rooms of the Presbyterian Church and the other half at Christ Church Parish House. Reassembling at 2:30 o'clock a business session will be held at which meeting Mrs. Thomas O'Berry will preside. Reports of the district chairmen and several department chairmen will be given at this meeting.

The social feature for Wednesday afternoon from 4:30 to 6 o'clock will be two complimentary teas and a ride over the city. One tea will be given at the Raleigh Woman's Club and the other at "Wakestone," the home of Mr. and Mrs. Josephus Daniels.

The evening session of Wednesday will be Fine Arts Evening. The program for this meeting will be furnished by the Music and Literature Departments. A feature of particular interest is the announcing the winners and awarding the cups and prizes to the successful competitors in the music and literary contests held by these departments. This [promises to be] one of the most interesting occasions of the convention.

Beginning at 9:15 o'clock Thursday morning, another session will be given to transacting business. At 1 o'clock the delegates to the convention will be the guests of the Rotary, Kiwanis, Civitan and Lions Clubs of the city, at a luncheon to be served in the Presbyterian Sunday School Rooms and in Christ Church Parish House as the day before.

The chief feature of the afternoon session Thursday will be the proposition to amend the constitution. Miss Margaret L. Gibson will lead the discussion.

The annual Federation Dinner to be given at 6 o'clock at the Sir Walter Hotel will be the social feature of Thursday. At this delightful get-together meeting Mrs. R. R. Cotten will preside. Laughter, music and good cheer will be in addition to the tempting menu.

The outstanding feature of the entire convention will be the address of Mrs. Helen H. Gardener of Washington, U. S. Civil Service Commissioner at the State Theatre, Thursday evening at 8 o'clock. Mrs. Gardener's address will be followed by a recital by the St. Cecilia Music Club.

Mrs. Gardener an Author.

Mrs. Helen H. Gardener, who will be the honor guest and principal speaker at the Federation meeting in Raleigh this week, is an author as well as a lecturer and distinguished statesman.

She has written seven books. One of her semi-scientific articles was translated into eight languages by the Medical Journals and used for years as basic research work. Her work on heredity was also accepted by the medical profession as scientifically valuable although written in the form of fiction. A new edition of one of her greatest books, "An Unofficial Patriot," has recently been published.

Mrs. Gardener spent about ten years in travel around the world lecturing at many of the universities in Japan, France, England and Italy. On her return she gave illustrated University Extension lectures on the comparative social conditions of women in twenty countries. She was decorated by the Japanese Government some years ago and by France for her public work. She is a member of Societe Academique d'Histoire Internationale, Paris, and also of the Lyceum Club of London, Paris, and Rome.

Commissioner Gardener has devoted her life to public and civic work. She is small in stature, has brown eyes and a crown of wavy silver hair. She is vivacious, sympathetic, and has a keen sense of humor, constituting distinct charm of personality. It is never difficult to see her and she feels that the Government and the Government employees have a right to the best that she has to give.

The following club women have been appointed by Mrs. Palmer Jerman as members of the Credentials Committee to serve during the convention: Mrs. James H. Brodie, Henderson, Chairman; Mrs. Clyde Eby, of New Bern; Mrs. W. G. Brogden, of Durham; Mrs. N. A. Townsend, of Dunn; Mrs. R. D. W. Connor, of Chapel Hill and Mrs. F. R. Perdue, of Raleigh.

Chairmen of local committees: Mrs. Josephus Daniels, General Chairman of Program; Mrs. W. T. Bost, Vice-Chairman; Automobiles, Mrs. J. Crawford Biggs; Arrangements, Mrs. Sam T. Smith; Breakfast Conferences, Miss Sally Dortch; Decorations, Mrs. Hubert Royster; Finance, Mrs. A. T. Horton; Federation Dinner, Mrs. T. E. Browne; Hospitality, Mrs. R. Y. McPherson; Hotels, Mrs. Clarence Johnson; Information, Mrs. W. H. Pittman; Luncheons, Mrs. J. J. Bernard: Music, Mrs. J. W. Kellogg; Pages, Mrs. James R. Cordon; Printing, Mrs. E. L. Layfield; Publicity, Mrs. J. H. Highsmith.

At the Friday morning session, all unfinished business will be attended to.

Breakfast Conferences.

An interesting and important feature of the Convention program not mentioned above is the Breakfast Conferences which will be held at 8 o'clock, Wednesday and Thursday mornings, at the Yarborough and Sir Walter Hotels. Breakfast conferences will be held for the different departments as follows:

Household Economics Department—Mrs. R. W. Green, local committee in charge.

Music and Art Department—Mrs. J. W. Kellogg and Mrs. P. F. Keil, local committee in charge.

Literary Clubs and Chairmen of Literature Departments—Mrs. E. L. Layfield, local committee.

District president—Mrs. Kenneth Gant, local committee.

Presidents of Departmental Clubs—Mrs. Josephus Daniels, local committee.

Social Service, Civics and Health Department—Miss Mary Shotwell, Mrs. Clarence Poe and Mrs. W. A. Withers, local committee.

Library Extension and Conservation Departments—Mrs. J. H. Highsmith, local committee.

Asheville *Sunday Citizen,* p. 11

24 AUGUST 1924

MRS. SHERMAN IS ACTIVE LEADER

New President of National Federation In Club Work Fifteen Years

STATE WILL ASSIST IN BEAUTIFYING HIGHWAYS

State Chairman of Music Suggests Music Week As Part of Program In Schools and Clubs; Also Urges Club Women To Work For Music Supervisor In Schools

By Mrs. J. Henry Highsmith
Chairman of Publicity

Not club women only but men and women not connected with club life are interested in knowing what manner of woman is Mrs. John D. Sherman of Colorado, the new president of the General Federation of Women's Clubs—the woman who succeeds the brilliant Mrs. Thomas G. Winter and assumes the leadership of America's 2,800,000 club women for the next two years. Club women for the most part know of Mrs. Sherman through her many works. For fifteen years she has been actively engaged in work for the General Federation. At the time of her selection to the presidency she was chairman of the largest department of work in the Federation, that of Applied Education, which is an organization of 23 separate federations in itself. As founder of Garden Week and a co-worker in the Better Homes Movement, her name has been largely before the public during the past two years. In Washington she is known chiefly as the National Parks Lady who has stood guard over America's playgrounds blessed by nature to protect them from the constant encroachment of commercial interests. During the war Mrs. Sherman was the one woman director on the board of the National War Garden Commission. As chairman of the conservation department she helped to establish the Rocky Mountain National Park, going before Congress to show the fitness and the need of its immediate establishment.

Mrs. Sherman is particularly interested just now in the American Home. Through her interest a new department of the Federation was recently created, this to be called the American Home Department. The purpose of this department is to attempt to find an answer to the question asked on every side, "What is the matter with the American Home?" As summarized by Mrs. Sherman herself, "the general purpose of this new department is to emphasize the home as the fundamental social institution for learning and practicing the business and the art of living."

Mrs. Sherman is said to be not only a great admirer of her predecessor, Mrs. Winter, but to be like her in many charming qualities, in that she is modest, democratic, brilliant of mind, big of heart, kindly in word and heart, a constructive leader in educational effort and a writer of ability. The new president has already announced that the work undertaken during Mrs. Winter's administration will be pushed to completion. "There will be no breaks in the activities now under way in the General Federation," declared Mrs. Sherman in her first official message to the club women of America.

Atlantic City Next Biennial Host.

Atlantic City is to be host to the next biennial convention of the General Federation of Women's Clubs. This will be in June, 1926. The invitation was given by the State Federations of New Jersey and Pennsylvania.

The meeting place of the 1925 biennial council will be decided at the meeting of the executive committee to be held in Washington, September 23–25.

Will Beautify Highways.

The State Highway Commission assures the club women of the State that it will co-operate in every way possible in assisting them in their work of beautifying the highways of North Carolina. Leslie R. Ames, chairman of the highway beautifying committee, in writing to Mrs. R. G. Lassiter, state chairman of Forestry, pledges not only the cooperation of his department but that of Mr. H. M. Curran, forester specialist of the Agricultural Department, and Mr. Holmes of Chapel Hill, State forester, N. C. Geological Survey. In addition he says that the patrolmen along the highways will be instructed to assist in the planting of shrubs and trees and to preserve any work which may be done along this line.

In this connection it may be said that Mr. Frank Page, State highway commissioner, deplores the fact that neither the Highway Commission nor any other agency has any legal status to enable it to prevent any depredation or abuse to the trees, shrubs or flowers along the highway. Evidently a law to protect the beauty is what is most needed at this time.

Worthwhile Community Event.

The Gaston County Federation of Women's Clubs has to its credit the production of what the newspapers termed the most magnificent and most spectacular drama ever presented in that section of the State. We refer to the historical pageant "Visions Old and New," given on July 4 at the Gaston County fair grounds to an audience of two or three thousand people. The object of the pageant in portraying the history and progress of Gaston County from the time of the first settlement to the present time was to awaken a widespread interest and love in the community's welfare and progress. Consequently it was a community event quite worth while. It was an excellent example of community co-operation. Over a thousand of Gaston's own people acted the parts that revealed the life of a great people—their ancestors. The various episodes were presented by the Woman's Club of some one of the towns of Gaston County, and in many instances the parts were taken by those who were direct descendants of those whom they portrayed.

In bringing together in a oneness of purpose—that of perpetuating the county's history—the event had, in addition to its historical viewpoint, a greater social and educational value.

To the club women of the county and to Mrs. Adelaide Smith Beard of Belmont, president of the county federation, both the county and the State owe a debt of appreciation.

Mrs. E. E. Randolph of Raleigh, State chairman of Music, in submitting her suggestions to the chairman of the various music clubs and departments of the Federation, does so at a time when they will be of most value to the chairman and certainly most acceptable—before the club work of the year is half over or has even begun. (It is a great mistake for State chairmen not to get in touch with the local chairman whom they are supposed to serve, till after the club year is well on its way and the year's program has already been made out.) To the already splendid programs which the majority of music departments of the Federation have given from year to year, Mrs. Randolph is asking the chairman to add an attractive, live music week program. She says, "Have a Music Week program not only for your department and for the club, but for your town and the neighboring communities. Take to the county schools your most interesting programs; help them put on the music memory contest, and encourage all the schools to add music books to their libraries."

Another suggestion offered by Mrs. Randolph is, "If you do not have a music supervisor, work for one in your own city and interest the Parent-Teachers' Association in helping you. Then after studying the musical needs of your county schools, see if you do not think that the Department of Education of North Carolina needs the office of a state supervisor."

"Have a 'Home Artists' Program," suggested Mrs. Randolph. "Charge a fee and pay them for their services. It will encourage them. Give with the aid of home talent and the phonograph evenings of opera. Take this program to the schools of your town and community and to the public institutions. Prepare your audience for the program by having the story of the opera and a sketch of the composer told in the schools and published in the newspapers."

In conclusion Mrs. Randolph says, "Now is the time to call attention to the cups offered for original compositions. The Duncan Loving Cup is awarded for the best vocal number, and the Florence M. Cooper Loving Cup for the best instrumental number. Since we cannot tell how great a composer a little encouragement may discover, ask your club members to advertise the Original Composition Contest. The State Library at Raleigh has on file a number of original compositions by North Carolinians and we want to add others to the list this year."

Entertain C. M. T. C. Boys.

While the regular activities of the Woman's Club of Fayetteville were postponed during the summer months, there was one committee whose work was a real service to humanity, appointed by the club and headed by Mrs. John H. Anderson. The work of this committee was to assist in entertaining the 1200 C. M. T. C. [Citizens' Military Training Camps] boys who were students at Fort Bragg during the month of July. The committee defied the hot weather and provided many programs of wholesome amusements and entertaining pastimes for the 1200 boys in training at the camp.

Their efforts were most thoroughly enjoyed and appreciated. Not only the boys themselves but the officers also gave testimony to the splendid recreation and pleasure afforded them through this entertainment committee.

> *Note:* Mary Belle King Sherman (1862–1935) was a noted activist, author, expert on parliamentary law, and conservationist. She was a major force behind the establishment of the National Park Service.

Raleigh Sunday *News and Observer,* p. 10 (Society, p. 2)
Asheville *Sunday Citizen,* p. 15

2 NOVEMBER 1924

PLANS MADE AT COUNCIL MEETING

Women's Clubs Prepare For Active Year Throughout The State

MRS. JERMAN PLEASED WITH YEAR'S PROGRAM

Federation Will Accept Offer of Women's College to Publish Bulletin
In Interest of North Carolina Federation of Women's Clubs;
First Copy Will Appear In Nov.

By Mrs. J. Henry Highsmith
Chairman of Publicity

Well made plans and practical, constructive programs outlining the year's work and submitted by the officials and chairmen of departments of the State Federation of Women's Clubs at the council meeting held recently in High Point have brought forth the prediction that this will be the best year in woman's club work that the State has yet known.

Mrs. Palmer Jerman, president of the Federation, is much pleased with the prospects of the year's work and feels that the women at the head of the various departments and of the standing committees have mapped out a wonderfully fine program. It was voted that many new phases of work in addition to the regular subjects will be undertaken by the several departments.

The Civics Department, of which Mrs. Robert N. Page, of Southern Pines, is chairman, will emphasize the importance of training for right citizenship, especially the training of children to obey. "Can any one be a useful, happy citizen who has not been trained to obey?" she asks. According to the program presented for the Education Department, of which Mrs. W. H. Chase, of Chapel Hill, is chairman, special study will be given to the motion picture question. The program of the Health Department, presented by Mrs. K. L. Allen, of Waynesville, chairman, pleads for the co-operation of all clubs in helping the State to enforce the marriage and narcotic laws. Mrs. R. A. Redfearn, of Wadesboro, chairman of the Home Economics Department, made an appeal for a State-wide effort to have trained leaders in home economics in high schools of every county in the State. Mrs. W. T. Shore, of Charlotte, chairman of Public Welfare, stated that the two main objectives toward which her department would work were increased appropriations for mothers' aid and a farm colony for women prisoners.

Announce Contests.

Mrs. E. E. Randolph, of Raleigh, Music chairman; Mrs. R. L. Gwyn of Lenoir, Art, and Miss Marian Blair, of Winston-Salem, Literature, announce the several contests to be conducted by their departments during the year. They asked for a cooperation that would create a wider interest and secure a large number of contestants.

As hostess to the sixty or more club women assembled in her borders, High Point was at her best. Her men's clubs joined hands with her woman's club to make their stay most delightful and they well succeeded. The Kiwanis, Rotary and Civitan clubs of the city entertained the visitors at lunch at the Country Club on Friday.

Those attending the council meeting will not soon forget the masterful address made by Miss Lavinia Engle, of Baltimore, on the subject "Legislative Programs and Methods." Her suggestions for carrying through a legislative program were instructive and helpful and most warmly received. Her advice that every legislative program be based on a real need for a law and not on the club's need for a program was characteristic of the sound doctrine she gave her enthusiastic audience for one hour. North Carolina club women always hear Miss Engle with keen pleasure and appreciation.

One important and most progressive step taken by the council at its recent meeting was its decision to accept the offer made by the North Carolina College for Women to publish a monthly bulletin in the interest of the North Carolina Federation of Women's Clubs. While all the detailed plans for this publication have not yet been made, the first copy in trial form is expected to appear about November 15. Mrs. J. Henry Highsmith, of Raleigh, State chairman of publicity, will become editor and Mrs. W. W. Martin of Greensboro will be associate editor. Mrs. Martin, who has recently come to North Carolina from Missouri, is a trained club woman, having had six years of experience as press chairman of the Missouri Federation.

The publication of the proposed leaflet will not do away with or alter the regular publicity service through the Sunday papers.

Mrs. Jerman's Itinerary.

Mrs. Palmer Jerman attended six of the fourteen district meetings during the past week and addressed each meeting on some important feature of club work. Her itinerary led her Monday, October 27, to Burlington; Tuesday to Hendersonville; Wednesday, Marion; Thursday, Lincolnton; Friday, Lumberton, and Saturday, Wadesboro. On Tuesday, November 4, Mrs. Jerman will attend the sixth district meeting at Selma and on the following Thursday she will go to Maysville. She will conclude her fall itinerary by attending the district meeting at Roanoke Rapids on Tuesday, November 11; at Windsor on Saturday, November 15, and at Faison on Saturday, November 22.

Free Music Libraries.

Mrs. E. E. Randolph, State Music chairman, calls the attention of all music departments and all music clubs affiliated with the Federation of Women's Clubs to the following announcement:

The Music Division of the G. F. W. C. announces that free loan libraries will be available after November 1. These music libraries will consist of a set of six programs on "Hearing America First," the subjects being:

Indian Music; Negro Music; Music in Colonial Days; Pioneer Music; Civil War Period; Present Day Composers.

In addition there will be single programs on "Edward MacDowell" and "American Women Composers."

These libraries will give outlines for papers, books for reference in preparing these papers, sheet music for illustrations, and player piano rolls and phonograph records for use when clubs have no available talent.

Any club belonging to the General Federation, in towns under five thousand in population, may secure these sets free of charge, by guaranteeing the express and the return of sets in perfect condition. Write to Mrs. Max B. Oberndorfer, National Chairman of Music, 520 Fine Arts Building, Chicago.

Music Memory Contest.

Mrs. Randolph announces further that her department will assist the rural schools of the State in putting on Music Memory Contests. Some of the counties, she says, under the direction of the rural supervisors, have already started this work. A State-wide contest for the rural schools will be held in Raleigh next spring. The music memory contest list for the rural schools of the State is:

Anvil Chorus, Verdi; Minuet in G, Beethoven; Anitra's Dance, Peer Gynt Suite, Grieg; In the Hall of the M't'n King, Grieg; Humoresque, Dvorak; Narcissus, Nevin; Melody in F, Rubinstein; The Swan (Le Cygne), Saint Saens; Spring Song, Mendelssohn; To a Water Lily, MacDowell; Largo, Handel; Andante Cantabile (string quartet), Tschaikowsky; Bridal Chorus (Lohengrin), Wagner; Pilgrim's Chorus (Tannhauser), Wagner; Marche Militaire, Schubert; Blue Danube Waltz, Strauss; Toreador Song (Carmen), Bizet; Pomp and Circumstance, Elgar; Hallelujah Chorus (Messiah), Handel; Swing Low, Sweet Chariot, negro spiritual; The Bee, Francois Schubert; Minute Waltz, Chopin; Funeral March of a Marionette, Gounod.

> *Note:* Lavinia Margaret Engle (1892–1979) was a Maryland politician and national leader of the suffrage campaign, later a longtime leader of the Social Security Administration.

Raleigh Sunday *News and Observer,* p. 24 (Sports, p. 6)

1925

6 April — addresses Junior High School PTA dinner for mothers and daughters: "Companionship of Mother and Daughter"; Margaret Highsmith, her sister-in-law, begins program with "America, the Beautiful"

4–6 May — attends 23rd annual NCFWC convention, Pinehurst, including outings to State Sanatorium and to Samarcand; asks that her publicity committee be renamed press committee

14 May — at RWC meeting reports on *Bulletin* and the press conference in Pinehurst

15 May — hosts Duke University Alumnae

26 September — co-hosts, with Margaret Highsmith, bridge luncheon at her home on North Person Street honoring Miss Julia Wetherington; a two-course luncheon was served, with "little Miss Lula Bell[e] Highsmith" (who was 13), assisting

28 September — named social chairman, Raleigh Junior High School PTA; immediately announces social hour and refreshments at the next month's meeting

7 October — named to advisory board, Raleigh PTA

29 October — attends District 8 conference of NCFWC, Chapel Hill.

7 November — visits Roseboro and Clinton with "little daughters Katherine and Louise"

23 November — speaks at Senior High School PTA

25 November — attends inauguration of Elmer Rhodes Hoke as president of the new Catawba College in Salisbury, where the principal address "The Function of the College," is delivered by J. Henry Highsmith, on whom the degree of Doctor of Laws (LL.D.) is then conferred

15 December — extends the greetings of the Woman's Club at dedication of the new Hugh Morson High School, at the corner of Person and Hargett Streets; all three of her daughters will graduate from Morson

4 JANUARY 1925

WOMEN URGE PLAN FOR FARM COLONY

Measure To Come Before Legislature Sponsored By Women's Clubs

MRS. JOHNSON GIVES ADVANTAGES OF COLONY

Commissioner Says State Prison System Makes No Provision For Adult Women Offenders; Most Serious Women Offenders Sent To State Prison

By Mrs. J. Henry Highsmith
Chairman of Publicity

A properly managed farm colony for women offenders to cost no more to maintain than what the State is now spending to keep its women prisoners in jails and county homes is one of the measures that will be brought before the approaching Legislature by the Legislative Council of North Carolina Women.

Mrs. Kate Burr Johnson, State Commissioner of Public Welfare, who knows the situation and its needs and who considers well and speaks advisedly on such matters, points out the conditions that a properly managed farm colony for women would remedy. She says: "Within the last twenty-five years it has become pretty generally recognized that women offenders should be separated from men and placed under the supervision of women. The demand for separate prisons will be easily understood by those who know anything of the position of women in prisons in which men are also confined and which are in charge of men.

"North Carolina's prison system does not make any special provision for its adult women offenders. Occasionally a woman guilty of one of those offenses which are held to be most serious is sent to the State Prison. Here the management has provided a matron, but the prison is a prison for men. The State thinks of it as such, and provides for running it in the conventional way of running a prison for men. But the great mass of women offenders, the majority of those most dangerous to society, as well as those who might be saved by the right kind of treatment, are not sent to the State Prison. There are only eleven white women there at the present time. Others are in the county jails, occasionally in poorly supervised workhouses, or county homes for the aged and infirm, or are turned loose on unsupervised suspended sentence, or conditional suspended sentences that are not merely futile but are positively vicious. Such, for instance, as ordered them to leave town in a given time. Thus Raleigh feeds her women offenders, mostly prostitutes, to Durham, Durham to Greensboro, Greensboro to Charlotte, and so on till the vicious circle starts all over again.

Mecklenburg Has Reformatory.

"One county, Mecklenburg, has a reformatory for women offenders, and Buncombe county maintains the Lindley Training School, which gives temporary care to delinquent girls. As a rule county institutions are not recommended unless they serve more than one county. The population is too limited and the overhead expense too great.

"Reports from two-thirds of the counties of the State for half the present year, on file in the office of the State Board of Charities and Public Welfare, show that many of the women imprisoned in the State are mere girls—just above the age admitted to Samarcand. In these reports are the names of 612 white and 185 Negro girls between the ages of 16 and 20 years, and 148 white and 214 young Negro women between 21 and 25 years old. Those numbers were reported from 69 counties in an average of a little more than five months. The figures indicate that nearly one-fourth of the prisoners were serving sentence. Assuming that the average for these months and these counties will hold for the whole year and the whole State, 700 women will serve in county jails in the State this year. To these must be added hundreds that come from the city courts.

"The girl, guilty most often of sex offenses or of theft, is thrown into jail where there is usually nothing to appeal to her better nature, but everything appeals to all that is base in her. Frequently she is diseased and no medical care is provided for her. She is held in idleness at the expense of the taxpayers, and to her own damnation. Only two jails in the State employ a women matron to care for women prisoners. The following incident is an illustration of the need of such matrons. Recently a girl was confined in one of the small jails of the State. One of the men picked the cheap padlock on the door separating her room from the men's quarters and spent one night in her room. The next night he took her into the men's quarters. He contracted syphilis. Another prisoner took the precaution to protect himself against contracting this disease. To accomplish this it was necessary to send to the next town, which he was able to do. The infected men continued in jail without any adequate facilities to prevent the infection of the other prisoners.

"These are the conditions that a properly managed farm colony for women would remedy. It would cost no more to maintain it than we are now spending on the keep of women prisoners in jails and county homes."

Mrs. W. T. Shore, of Charlotte, chairman of the Public Welfare Department of the N. C. Federation of Women's Clubs, is to be congratulated on her booklet, Public Welfare and the Community, recently issued by the Extension Division of the University of North Carolina. The book is published, according to Mrs. Shore, with the view of co-ordinating the efforts of the Public Welfare Department of the State Federation of Women's Clubs with those of the State Board of Charities and Public Welfare. Its project is to serve the 50,000 club women of the State as a handbook of information concerning the need of a bigger, better public welfare program in North

Carolina. The writer asks that every club member interested in public welfare work write to the University for this bulletin and help to make it serve the cause for which it was written.

Raleigh Sunday *News and Observer,* p. 25 (Editorial, p. 1)
Charlotte Sunday Observer, p. 30 (section C, p. 8)

8 MARCH 1925

CLUB WOMEN TO MEET IN PINEHURST

Dates of Federation Changed To May 4–6 To Avoid Conflicts

SANDHILL SECTION TO ENTERTAIN WOMEN

Arrangements For Entertainment Include Visits To
Samarcand and Sanatorium

By Mrs. J. Henry Highsmith
Chairman of Publicity

The dates of the annual convention of the North Carolina Federation of Women's Clubs at Pinehurst have been changed from May 5 to 8 to May 4 to 6 inclusive. This change was found necessary to avoid a conflict with the State Bankers Association, which holds its convention there May 7, 8, and 9.

The Carolina Hotel will be headquarters for the club women. Monday of convention week will be given to the three board meetings—the board of trustees, the executive board and the board of directors. The opening session will be Monday evening.

Mrs. Palmer Jerman, who recently visited Pinehurst to make arrangements for the convention, says that not only Pinehurst and the Carolina Hotel are counting on making the approaching convention the best the Federation has ever known, but that the whole Sand Hill country is asking for a share in the entertainment of the State's club women. A number of invitations to social features have had to be declined, she says, owing to the shortness of time the convention will be in session and the amount of important business there is to be transacted. However, Mrs. Jerman assures us, there will be recreation and social features a plenty to break the tedium of the conference work.

Arrangements will be made for those attending the convention to visit the two institutions that perhaps appeal most strongly to the club women of the State—Samarcand Manor and the State Sanatorium for the treatment of tuberculosis. In the establishment and work of these institutions the women will see the things for which they worked years ago realized. In the service that they are rendering to humanity and to the State, they will, no doubt, find encouragement to press on with their present program which apparently has found little favor in the eyes of the average legislator. Club women did not give up when their bill to erect and maintain a reformatory for girls was rejected by the Legislature the first time or the second time. A visit to Samarcand will convince the most skeptical club woman that it is worth while to keep up the fight for a farm colony for women prisoners too old for Samarcand and for a reformatory for delinquent colored girls.

A new feature of the convention will be a press luncheon. The main topic for discussion at this conference will be the Federation Bulletin. While the Bulletin will not be a year old its lusty growth and the possibilities for its further development and more effective service call for counsel and co-operation on the part of the convention delegates. Many questions pertaining to the Bulletin will be answered at the luncheon.

It might be said here that the Federation Bulletin has met a reception that not even the most hopeful of its promoters anticipated. Judging from the welcome that has been given it and the prompt and willing responses of the members who have been called on to contribute to its columns, it is evident that the Federation had reached the point where to continue its growth and increase its usefulness it needed an organ of its own. To those who have made the Bulletin possible the members of the Federation are deeply grateful.

Mrs. R. L. Gwen, state chairman of Art, is calling attention to the ten dollar prize offered by the director of General Headquarters in Washington for a design suitable for a book plate to be used permanently in the headquarters library. The design is to be suitable for use by the General Federation of Women's Clubs and therefore should symbolize some phase of its work. All communications should be directed to Miss Lida Hafford, 1734 N Street, Washington, D. C., before May 1.

Women Ask For Larger Part In Government.

Appointment of a woman assistant Secretary of Labor, a woman assistant Secretary of the Interior and a woman assistant Secretary of Agriculture is asked of President Coolidge by the board of directors of the General Federation of Women's Clubs, representing approximately 5,000,000 women voters.

The board asks further that qualified women be appointed as assistant to the U. S. Surgeon General and on a number of commissions, notably the Tariff, Railroad and Interstate Commerce commissions, and that the government's policy of naming women assistant Attorney Generals be continued. It is recommended that women also be named among commissioners having to do with rent, civil service and employee's compensation.

Fifty Dollars For Advance Story.

A prize of $50 is offered by the press and publicity department of the G. F. W. C. for the best advance story of a club event, written by a club woman and published in a newspaper. The contest closes May 3 and the winner is to be announced at the Mid-Biennial Council to be held at West Baden, Indiana, the week of June 1.

The story must deal with some club event which is about to occur in the State from which the contestant enters. It must contain not less than 300 words and not more than 700. Proof of publication in the form of a clipping, with the name of the newspaper, date, name and address of author, these verified by the club of which the writer is a member. All stories entered in this contest must be mailed to Miss Vella Winner, Oregon Journal, Portland, Oregon, not later than May 1.

Raleigh Sunday *News and Observer,* p. 23 (Sports, p. 3)
Asheville *Sunday Citizen,* p. 8

29 MARCH 1925

WOMEN TO PRESS SAME BILLS AGAIN

Defeated Legislative Program Will Be Offered Again at 1925 Session

ISSUE OFFICIAL CALL PINEHURST CONVENTION

Attractive Program Arranged For Meeting On May 4, 5 and 6;
Will Spend Day Following Convention at Chapel Hill;
National Radio Program Set For Same Week

By Mrs. J. Henry Highsmith
Chairman of Publicity

The call for the twenty-third annual convention of the North Carolina Federation of Women's Clubs to meet in Pinehurst, May 4, 5 and 6, has been issued by order of the President, Mrs. Palmer T. Jerman. The Woman's Civic Club of Southern Pines, with Mrs. Charles R. Whitaker as president, will be the hostess to the convention. The Carolina Hotel will be official headquarters.

According to the program committee, of which Mrs. Whitaker is chairman, a full and interesting three day program has already been prepared. The forenoon of Monday, the fourth, will be given to the regular meeting and luncheon of the executive board. The afternoon will be given to the meeting of the Board of Trustees and the Board of Directors. The opening session will be Monday evening in the ball room of the Carolina Hotel. The keynote of the convention will be "The American Home," a new department recently established by the General Federation.

Several breakfast and luncheon conferences appear on the program. The groups holding breakfast conferences Tuesday morning will be the district presidents with Mrs. Thomas O'Berry presiding, and the presidents and chairmen of literary clubs and departments with Miss Marian Blair presiding. The groups holding luncheon conferences on Tuesday will be that of Household Economics with Mrs. Rosalind Redfearn presiding and that of Art and Music with Mrs. R. L. Gwyn and Mrs. E. E. Randolph as joint hostesses. On Wednesday morning the presidents of the departmental clubs will hold a breakfast conference with Mrs. Charles R. Whitaker presiding; also the departments of Education and Civics with Mrs. H. W. Chase and Mrs. R. N. Page as joint hostesses. Luncheon conferences will be held Wednesday by the Health and Public Welfare departments with Mrs. R. L. Allen and Mrs. W. T. Shore as joint hostesses and by the Press and Publicity committee with Mrs. J. Henry Highsmith presiding.

One of the most enjoyable features planned for the delegates and visiting club women will be the Federation dinner at the Carolina Hotel Wednesday evening.

To Spend Day at Chapel Hill.

In order for the members of the Federation Council to accept the invitation from the University of North Carolina to spend the day following the adjournment of the annual meeting of the Federation at Pinehurst, the convention will adjourn Thursday morning, May 7. Members of the council accepting this invitation, which was extended at the council meeting in High Point last fall, will be expected to go from Pinehurst to Chapel Hill Thursday morning by automobile, arriving in time for lunch. In the afternoon the party will have the pleasure of attending the dramatic institute of the Carolina Dramatic Association which begins that day, or they may wander about the campus and town familiarizing themselves with the State University.

All Club Women Welcome.

All club women whether they are delegates or not will find a welcome not only to all sessions of the convention, but to Pinehurst as well, says Mrs. Jerman, who has recently returned from Pinehurst and Southern Pines where she conferred with those who will have charge of the entertainment of the club women. She says that all signs, one of which is the good roads leading to Pinehurst, point to a record-breaking attendance and a most interesting and enjoyable meeting. She urges clubs that have not already done so to elect their full quota of delegates at once, that they make their plans to attend.

Women's Bills Not Dead Yet.

Even though not one of the measures sponsored by the Legislative Council of North Carolina Women became a law at the hands of the State Legislature recently adjourned, the members of the council are not one bit dismayed and have already voted to adopt the same legislative program for 1927. They consider the measures which they so diligently worked for and lost too important to be dropped, and claim that they are as essential to the welfare of North Carolina next year and ten years from now as they are today. Since it will take more than one blow to send the "women's bills" to their death, they will likely spring to life just before the next primary. The council suggests that women and men who are interested in the measures interview candidates before the primary and get their opinion on these matters before their election.

At a recent meeting of the council letters of thanks and other expressions cf appreciation were sent to all "who helped to make the measures seen, not as 'women's bills.' but as efforts to improve conditions in North Carolina."

Radio Stations to Observe Music Week.

Every radio broadcasting station in America has been asked by the Music Division of the General Federation to co-operate in putting on a program of American music during National Music Week, May 3–9. The program, including the introductory remarks and short analysis of numbers to be read, will be furnished by the Music Division of the General Federation. Club women are asked to co-operate with the station in their community in putting on this program

Art Event of a Century.

The opportunity of a lifetime to study American art presents itself, says Mrs. Rose V. Berry, general chairman of art. She has reference to the One Hundredth Anniversary of the National Academy of Design, which will be celebrated this year. Of this event she says:

"It is impossible anywhere in the United States to see a collection of paintings and bronzes which cover in sequence—year by year, the achievement of the American painter and sculptor. Such an exhibition will establish for the American public for all time the excellence of the American painter and sculptor whom Europe has recognized and honored for more than a hundred years. It is suggested that every club prepare itself for this event by an intensive course of study. The subject is well worth it. No country has done so little for its artists as the United States; no country has recognized art less, or supported it less, than the United States; it is the only country of its extent which has no national collection and no way of honoring its creative groups. It is suggested that 'Art Education by Ownership' be a part of the effort made to understand the excellence of the American artists, that the State art chairman shall secure a painting or a bronze for the public schools, and that every home be enriched by a purchase of a bronze or a painting, which it has earned or saved for during the year.

Raleigh Sunday *News and Observer,* p. 3

18 APRIL 1925

NORTH CAROLINA FEDERATION OF WOMEN'S CLUBS

By Mrs. J. Henry Highsmith

The completion of the full and final program for the annual convention of the State Federation of Women's Clubs to be held at Pinehurst May 4 to 6 has been announced by Mrs. Palmer Jerman, President of the Federation. Many attractive features are mentioned in the program, and taken as a whole, it appears to be one of the best and full of interest throughout. Mrs. Chas. R. Whitaker, of Southern Pines, is Chairman of the Program Committee. Mrs. Robt. N. Page is Vice-Chairman and Miss Mary Schwarberg is Secretary.

Two Noted Speakers.

According to the program, the convention is to be favored with two noted speakers, Dr. Louise Stanley, of Washington, D. C., and Mrs. Ida Clyde Clark, of New York City. Dr. Stanley is head of the Bureau of Household Economics of the Department of Agriculture of the United States Government. She speaks Tuesday afternoon at a section given over to the Home Economics Department and before the Home Demonstration delegates. Her subject will be "Uncle Sam and the Home Maker." Mrs. Clark, well known as a lecturer and journalist, is associate editor of the Pictorial Review. She was one of the speakers at the Biennial Convention held last June in Los Angeles where she made a most fascinating address. She will speak Wednesday evening on the subject, "A New Woman Looks at an Old World." Being a native of Tennessee, she has the Southern viewpoint and sympathies which have been developed by wide contact with people and affairs. Other speakers will address the various conferences with helpful messages.

Social Features.

A wide as well as a warm welcome will be extended the convention guests if the plans of the Sandhill section go not awry. As a matter of fact more courtesies and social pleasures have been planned for the club women than there will be time to accept. One of these was an invitation from the Woman's Club of Carthage to the Federation delegates to drive over in the afternoon to a reception to be given in honor of Mrs. Palmer Jerman, their former townswoman. Another invitation that was declined with regrets was from Mr. and Mrs. Jacques Bushel who invited the Federation to a barbecue luncheon at the famous Jugtown potteries. The social features that will be participated in will be a reception given Monday evening by Mr. and Mrs. Leonard Tufts complimentary to North Carolina club women, a tea at Southern Pines Country Club Tuesday afternoon with the Woman's Civic Club of Southern Pines as hostess; this to be followed with a drive to the State Tuberculosis Sanatorium; a drive to Samarcand Manor Wednesday afternoon and the Federation Dinner Wednesday evening at which Mrs. R. R. Cotten, honorary President, will preside.

Opening Session.

The opening session Monday evening, May 4, will be featured with the President's address by Mrs. Palmer Jerman, and three addresses of welcome. Hon. R. N. Page will extend welcome from the Sand Hills; Mrs. R. W. Allen, of Wadesboro from the Fifth District, and Mrs. Charles R. Whitaker from the Hostess Club. Response will be made by Mrs. Thomas O'Berry of Goldsboro. The invocation will be offered by Rev. T. A. Cheatham.

Tuesday evening will be given over to a program prepared by the Fine Arts Department. Mrs. F. F. Bahnson, first vice-president will preside. At this session, the awarding of the cups and prizes offered for the best original productions in music, art and literature will take place. Several of the winning selections in music and literature will be given. Miss Margaret Bedell of Raleigh will sing a special group of songs. Dr. and Mrs. Pfohl and children of Winston-Salem will give several selections from a home orchestra.

Committees Appointed.

Mrs. R. D. W. Connor, of Chapel Hill, has been appointed Chairman of the Credentials Committee. Other members of this committee are Mrs. N. A. Townsend, Mrs. C. P. Rogers, Mrs. Phil Thomas, and Mrs. C. D. Grier.

Miss Mary DeVane of Goldsboro has been appointed chairman of the Committee on Resolutions. Persons wishing to present resolutions should send copy of them to Miss DeVane before May 4.

Mrs. Jerman's Travels.

Mrs. Jerman went to Wilson on Wednesday of last week to participate in the dedication of the recently completed club house. The club women of that city celebrated their achievement with appropriate exercises in an afternoon and evening meeting. From Wilson, Mrs. Jerman went to Cottendale to spend a day with Mrs. R. R. Cotten and on Friday she attended the annual meeting of the 10th District at Farmville. Last week she attended the annual meeting of the 14th District at Hertford and reports a record breaking attendance and a most helpful meeting.

Would Change Districts.

For some time it has been apparent that the fourteen districts of the state are not laid off to the best advantage to the people whom they would serve. Accordingly, the district presidents met in Raleigh recently and discussed the advisability of redistricting the territory. A number of changes were recommended which will be presented to the convention at Pinehurst for ratification. Mrs. Thomas O'Berry of Goldsboro, president of the districts, presided at the conference.

Asheville Citizen, p. 10

1926

3 February — appointed by RWC, with Mrs. R. N. Simms, Mrs. Palmer Jerman, and five others, to a committee in support of a $1.5 million bond issue for Raleigh public schools

10–17 March — serves as publicity chair for 16th annual Women's Missionary Council of the Methodist Episcopal Church South, at Edenton Street, with 600 delegates; Vara is program chairman

15 March — attends, with Vara, Pauline, and Lucy, Littleton College Alumnae event in Raleigh honoring Rev. and Mrs. J. M. Rhodes, the former president and his wife; Vara presides; Kate presents the honorees with flowers

28–29 April — assists at annual well-baby clinic offered at RWC

4–7 May — attends 24th annual NCFWC convention, Asheville; presides at press luncheon on Thursday, 6 May

21 May — addresses NCFWC District 8 presidents meeting in Raleigh: "How the Club President Can Assist the Press Chairman"

24 May – 5 June — attends Atlantic City meeting of GFWC, one of 14 delegates from NC

8 June — attends Duke Alumnae Association luncheon at commencement there; elected president

10 June — offered directorship of Survey of Women in Industry by the Child Welfare Commission

c. 21–28 June — travels to Washington, D. C., to finalize arrangements for Survey of Women in Industry

13–15 July — survey reaches crisis point with emergency meetings ending in the Governor's office; the idea is abandoned

7 August — entertains at luncheon to announce Pauline's engagement to Sergeant James R. Sloo; garden flowers presented the bride-elect's niece, "little Miss Katherine Herring Highsmith"

13 August — attends bridge party, with Eugenia, Lucy, and Mary Belle, for Pauline

18 August — wedding of Pauline to James Sloo, 604 North Blount Street

12–14 October — attends NCFWC council meeting in Wilson, which proposes a wear-cotton day, to establish headquarters at Sir Walter in Raleigh, and plans for Durham convention; reads report of Mrs. R. L. McMillan proposing State Art Museum.

29 October — death of sister Lucy C. Herring, of breast cancer, at 604 North Blount Street; funeral the next day there

6 November — attends reception of Educational Department of RWC honoring Lucy Gage, noted professor of early education at George Peabody College in Nashville (now part of Vanderbilt University)

12 December — her stepson John Henry Highsmith, Jr., sophomore at NC State in the School of Science and Business, is struck by a hit-and-run automobile on Hillsboro Street; he remains unconscious for some time

24 JANUARY 1926

URGES WOMEN TO GO FORWARD

Mrs. McKee, State President of Federation, Reviews Work of Year

By Mrs. J. Henry Highsmith
Chairman of Publicity
North Carolina Federation of Women's Clubs

In her New Year message to North Carolina club women, Mrs. Gertrude Dills McKee, president of the State Federation, calls for a measuring of the distance yet to be made to the goal that was set for each club and club member last fall. Half the club year has passed, she reminds us, but adds there is still time for fulfilling every purpose and realizing every ambition. Mrs. McKee pleads for a continuation of that fine spirit of co-operation that has characterized the North Carolina Federation of Women's Clubs throughout the 23 years of its existence.

Mrs. McKee was wonderfully impressed with the influence that one feels and sees emanating from the 300 federated clubs of the State on making the proverbial trip from Murphy to Manteo, as Mrs. McKee did last fall, visiting 15 of the 16 district meetings. Every conceivable sort of community work is being done from one end of the State to the other, she says. Her letter follows:

"Dear Club Women of North Carolina:

"At the beginning of the New Year, club women, with all the rest of the world, pause for retrospection and prospection.

"Half the club year has passed. It is a good time to measure the distance we have covered. Are we halfway to the goal we set for ourselves last fall? Every club, every club member, every officer, every chairman, every district president should ask this question seriously and answer it honestly. There is still time to fulfill every purpose, to realize every ambition. Herein lies the value and importance of this New Year deliberation. With our faces now turned toward the annual convention, let us press forward in each of our sixteen districts, in each of the eight departments through which our organization functions, in every endeavor in which an individual club is interested. Above all, let us hold fast to that fine spirit of co-operation that has characterized the North Carolina Federation of Women's Clubs throughout the 23 years of its existence.

"After making the proverbial trip from Murphy to Manteo last fall, visiting 15 of the 16 district meetings, I realize as never before that the influence of our organization permeates every nook and corner of the State. Truly, it warmed my heart to hear the reports at these district meetings. Every conceivable sort of community work is being done from one end of our State to the other; public and circulating libraries established and maintained; parks and playgrounds for children established and equipped; school grounds beautified; and books provided for public schools, in order that those schools might be placed on the accredited list of the State; trees planted, towns cleaned and beautified. A bed of flowers at a railroad station heralds to the visitor or passer-by the fact that a woman's club exists in that town. Even the most casual observation reveals a vast difference between the town or village with a federated club and one without. Never before did I grasp the full significance of Mrs. Jerman's ambition for a club in every cross-roads in North Carolina. It was not the mere addition to the Federation that she had in mind, it was the opening of opportunities to the cross-roads.

"But, wonderful as are these tangible results of club work in our State, there is an influence even more far-reaching emanating from our organization. Each of the 300 clubs of which it is composed is not only a unit for public service, it is also a source of inspiration for civic pride and community spirit to all who come within a radius of its influence. This fact is recognized by discerning people everywhere and has won for our organization the respect and esteem of all who are interested in the development throughout our State of a spirit of public service and of State and community loyalty.

"Going back to the district meetings, I want to say that they were of inestimable value to me. The delightful friendships, the evidences of rare ability in leadership, everywhere a wholesome desire for service, the splendid attendance, all these were a never failing source of pleasure and encouragement. My life has been made richer by these contacts, in fact, I am convinced that nothing in our plan of organization is so worth while to the president at least as the district meetings.

"With all good wishes, I am,
"Sincerely yours,
"GERTRUDE DILLS McKEE"

Deep Sympathy for Mrs. Cotten.

Club women throughout the State feel the deepest sympathy for Mr. and Mrs. R. R. Cotten, of Farmville, in the recent death of their son, Capt. Lyman R. Cotten, of the United States Navy. While Mr. and Mrs. Cotten did not reach the bedside of their son before his death, they were able to go to Washington and attend his funeral. He was buried in Arlington Cemetery. Mrs. Cotten, who prior to her son's death was spending some time with her daughter in Boston, is now at her home at Cottendale.

Attend General Board Meeting.

Mrs. E. L. McKee, president, and Mrs. S. P. Cooper, State director of the General Federation, attended the Board of Directors meeting of the General Federation recently held in Washington, D. C. They write that they were much impressed with the big, worthwhile things that the General Federation is undertaking and is interested in. The most important business transacted at the meeting was the adoption of the program for the biennial meeting to be held in Atlantic City in June.

While in Washington Mrs. McKee and Mrs. Cooper attended the funeral of Capt. Lyman Cotten and his burial in Arlington Cemetery. It is gratifying to the members of the federation that Mrs. McKee and Mrs. Cooper could act as their representatives on this occasion and be in person with Mrs. Cotten in this sad hour.

New Club Presidents.

Miss Annie Perkins, of Farmville, recording secretary, reports that the following clubs have elected new presidents:

Wilson's Mills Woman's Club, Mrs. Lula L. Uzzle.
Franklinton Woman's Club, Mrs. George Gilliam.
Henderson Woman's Club, Mrs. J. T. Alderman.
Macon Community Club, Miss Sallie Allen.
Norlina Woman's Club, Mrs. G. K. Marshall.
Madison, Dolly Madison Book Club, Mrs. Howard Penn.
Randleman Betterment Association, Mrs. N. N. Newlin.
Dover Woman's Club, Mrs. W. L. Bell.
Mount Gilead Research Club, Mrs. C. F. Scarborough.
Gastonia Woman's Club, Mrs. Frost Torrence.

Henderson Sans Souci Club, Mrs. W. W. Wester.

Clayton Halcyon Club, Mrs. Hugh A. Page.

Garland Woman's Club, Mrs. B. G. Cromartie.

Granite Falls Community Club, Mrs. Lula Hickman.

Hendersonville Woman's Club, Mrs. George Wing, Jr.

Meege Woman's Club has been changed to Chowan Woman's Club.

Raleigh Sunday *News and Observer*, p. 7
Sunday *Charlotte News*, p. 30 (section C, p. 4)

14 FEBRUARY 1926

STATE FEDERATION NOTES

What the Club Women of North Carolina Are Doing

By Mrs. J. Henry Highsmith
Chairman of Publicity

Mrs. McKee Urges Women to Study Politics.

Now is the time and the primary or the convention is the place for women to take the first step in discharging their responsibilities as citizens, declares Mrs. E. L. McKee, State President of the Federation of Women's Clubs. She not only advises women to take an active interest in politics and to vote in the elections, but she urges them to study their city and State governments that they may vote the more intelligently and thereby make the better citizens.

To take part in the selection of candidates, she says, is a woman's first duty as a citizen, for when she merely votes blindly with her party in the general election she has served well neither her party nor her State. Therefore Mrs. McKee is urging club women to get ready for the primaries and the conventions that will be held in June by having a hand in naming the candidates for the general election.

Mrs. McKee sees no reason for women shying at politics or politicians. In fact, she says, in these days the woman who is not informed and interested in politics is neither an intelligent nor a patriotic citizen. She cannot, if she would, get away from the duties of citizenship, and these duties involve an understanding of and participation in the politics of her State.

Mrs. McKee urges all club women to make use of her strongest weapon, the ballot, for after all, she says, no matter how much we may want to see conditions improved, there is only one way actually to achieve reform and progress and that is through the ballot.

Mrs. McKee speaks as follows:

"The original clubs of our country had as their sole objective, self-culture. There are scores of clubs today that have the same worthy purpose, but the time has long passed when club-life ends with self-culture. Every problem that has to do, either directly or indirectly, with the well-being of the home, the child, the community, the State, comes within the province of women's club work. North Carolina's sons have led her in a material progress that has attracted the attention of the entire Nation. But, North Carolina can not reach the full glory of her development by material progress alone. Men, by nature and training, are materialists, women are humanitarian, and, friends, beyond the shadow of doubt, women must be the leaders in that part of our State's development. Whose heart, but a woman's, beats so responsive to the call of the defective or the wayward child, the orphan, or the unfortunate man or woman? We, you and I, and others like us all over the State, are in very truth, their keepers. We need to indulge in no maudlin sentiment about it; we must simply use the full force of our organization in bettering the conditions of the State's unfortunates and its underprivileged, and in making North Carolina in every way a safer, healthier, more beautiful place in which to live. Herein lies the value to the State of organized womanhood.

"It seems providential that just as women were thoroughly aroused to these responsibilities, the ballot came to them [1920: the 19th Amendment]. I say this seems providential, because, after all, no matter how much sentiment we have about these things, no matter how much we may want to see conditions improved, there is only one way actually to achieve reform and progress, and that is through the ballot. We may, in our local clubs, and in our State meetings, pass all the resolutions we like, couching them in the most elegant terms, the most high-sounding phrases, but if they end with that they are worth nothing except what they may accomplish in directing and molding public thought and sentiment. To make those resolutions truly effective, we must be willing to put ourselves, individually and collectively, behind them, and see that they are embodied in the policies of the State. If any one doubts our ability to do this, a round of visits to the districts and individual club meetings would dispel any such misgiving. There are 53,000 of us, and very few candidates would like to have the combined sentiment, conviction and influence of 53,000 club women against them.

"The North Carolina Federation is a non-partisan organization, but that does not mean that we do not believe in the party system of government. We know that government by one party alone would result in despotism. There is not the slightest desire or disposition on the part of the Federation to cause any disruption in our existing parties, rather, do we seek to encourage and stimulate women to take an active interest in the affairs of their respective parties, and, furthermore, above all, to take that interest at the proper time. The woman who merely votes blindly with her party in the general election has served neither her party nor her State well. She has served her party well only when she has had a part in the selection of those candidates for whom she votes.

"In only short time, the primaries and conventions will be held, and right now is the time for us to take an active interest in the welfare of our parties. If we, as citizens, are to be of any service whatsoever to the State, we must take a hand this year in the selection of candidates. And we must not wait until the professional office-seekers have announced themselves. Often it is difficult to get a good man to come out for office after another candidate has announced himself. Let us select or help select our men, or women, perhaps, and see that they are announced first. To let the opportunity of having a part in the selection of candidates pass by, and then attempt to make selections from the tickets at the general election is, in my opinion, an injustice to both parties. Some one has said that the well-being of the Nation depends wholly upon enlightened conscientious citizenship, and that the first step in good citizenship is the recognition of the duty of registration and voting, and I would add, voting in the primary or convention as well as in the general election.

"Time was when women thought of politics as something a little unsavory. I wonder if all of us today have a really clear idea of what politics is? Webster tells us it is the science of government. Now, what could be objectionable in that? Some politicians may have reputations that are somewhat unsavory, but by no means are all politicians of that type. Some of the finest men in our State are politicians who make up the real body and strength of our political parties—church men, church women, Masons, Rotarians, Kiwanians, club men, club women. Anything wrong with those folks? I see no reason in the world for shying at politics or politicians; in fact, in these days, the woman who is not informed and interested in politics is neither an intelligent nor a patriotic citizen. She cannot, if she would, get away from the duties of citizenship and these duties involve an understanding of and a participation in the politics of her State—raising its standards, and, in short, bringing to this new role of being a citizen the same lofty ideals, sound judgment and common sense she has always possessed."

Sunday *Charlotte News,* p. 22 (section B, p. 6)

28 FEBRUARY 1926

NO SINISTER MOTIVES BEHIND CLUB WOMEN'S REQUEST FOR SURVEY OF WOMEN IN INDUSTRY

By Mrs. J. Henry Highsmith

Emphatically denying that there are sinister motives and out-of-state influences behind the efforts of the sixty thousand organized women of the State to have a survey made of the working conditions of women in North Carolina, Dr. Delia Dixon Carroll, State Chairman of Legislation of the Federation of Women's Clubs, and the Federation's spokesman in this particular issue, says that the accusation is a fabric and altogether without foundation. Furthermore, she says, it is the same old game which employers resort to whenever this or similar requests are made.

As a matter of fact, Dr. Carroll says, the agitation for a survey or for some means of obtaining information concerning women in industry was begun in the Federation of Women's Clubs about six years ago. The Department of Social Service, organized primarily to study and serve the industrial and social needs of women and children in industry, was thwarted at every turn made in their behalf for the reason that no information concerning them was to be had. Why, asks Dr. Carroll, do employers of women withhold this information? If conditions are good is there any objection to the public knowing it?

The Federation took action in 1923 when the State Convention in session at Winston-Salem passed a resolution in favor of asking the Women's Bureau of the Department of Labor at Washington to make an investigation, using government experts to secure and tabulate the information, and this to be done at the government's expense. This resolution was offered with the understanding that if a large group of people requested it, this service was to be had free from the Labor Department, and for the further reason that the Legislature and other agencies of the State had been appealed to for this survey, but always with the reply that there were neither funds nor trained workers to be had for this work.

Not willing that the issue should drop with the need of information and legislation growing more and more acute, the Federation at its convention held last year at Pinehurst adopted another resolution pledging its co-operation with the Y. W. C. A. in a survey of conditions governing women in industry, such survey to be made by the best agency available. Mrs. C. L. Hook of Charlotte, past president of the Federation, submitted this resolution.

The question as to who makes the survey and who pays the bills is not the issue with which the club women of the State are most concerned, according to Dr. Carroll. They want most of all reliable information secured by workers who know their jobs and who know how to tabulate and present their findings that they become permanent and accessible records. Nor is the survey requested by the women because they believe conditions surrounding women in industry in the State intolerable or even generally bad. But, she asks, how can accusations to that effect be denied in the absence of the fact as to the real conditions?

Survey Not Related To Students Survey.

Dr. Carroll would make one other point clear. The survey that the club women are working for has nothing whatever to do with the investigation asked for by the Institute of Social Research at the University of North Carolina. There is no relation, she says, and one should no longer confuse one with the other. The only reason for confusing them, she explains, is that they both broke into print about the same time. Explaining further, Dr. Carroll says that the survey that the University students sought to make was altogether an industrial one while the one the women have asked for covers not only the conditions of women working in cotton factories, but also of those working in stores, hotels, cafes, laundries, canning factories, on piece work in homes, and wherever the health and welfare of women and children are likely to be affected by the conditions under which they are required to work.

Appointment of Mrs. Bost Pleases Club Women.

The action of Governor McLean in appointing Mrs. W. T. Bost, of Raleigh, as a member of the board of trustees of the North Carolina College for Women at Greensboro not only meets the approval of the alumnae of that institution, but also of the club women of the entire State, particularly those who have worked closely with her and know for what she stands and with what enthusiasm and self-forgetfulness she gives in serving others.

Mrs. Bost is, first of all, a club woman, for she believes that women work most effectively through some form of organization. She was president from 1921 to 1923 of the Raleigh Woman's Club, an organization at that time of between six and seven hundred members. She is now legislative chairman of the State League of Women Voters, president of the Parent-Teacher Association of the Murphey School in Raleigh, director of the Raleigh Community Chest, director of the Olivia Raney Library and a member of the City Board of Adjustment.

And yet there's another organization in which Mrs. Bost is most active. She loves her church and all its interests, the Lutheran church, in which she teaches a large class of young business women.

Mrs. Bost makes the fourth woman appointed on the board of directors of her alma mater. The other three are Mrs. Joseph A. Brown, of Chadbourn; Miss Easdale Shaw, of Rockingham, and Mrs. Cameron Morrison, of Charlotte. Mrs. Bost fills the vacancy made by the death of Edward E. Britton. Her appointment will be confirmed by the next Legislature.

Three Men Belong To Woman's Club.

A distinction possessed by the Goldsboro Woman's Club and probably by no other woman's club in the State is that three men are enrolled as members, even though they are honorary members. These are Nathan O'Berry, Joe Rosenthal, and Joe Parker. Membership was extended them for the valuable assistance and paternal watchfulness these men have given particularly to the Woman's Club at a time it needed it most.

Recently on the occasion of Captain O'Berry's seventieth birthday, the club presented him with a handsome silver loving cup, which the members of the club felt that it was, in truth, a loving cup. The president, Miss Mary Faison DeVane, introduced Mrs. W. R. Hollowell, president of the club when it was founded in 1899, who presented the cup to Mr. O'Berry. The cup, a large silver urn of classic design, ten inches high, was made by Tiffany and Company, New York City.

New Club Organized.

The Robersonville Woman's Club met recently and organized with 43 charter members enrolled, a constitution submitted and adopted, officers elected and the club voting unanimously to federate with the State Federation of Women's Clubs—all this at its initial meeting. At the same time the club members pledged themselves to stand together for the moral, spiritual, education and civic development of their town and community. The district president, Mrs. J. M. Hobgood, of Farmville, was present and addressed the club.

Raleigh club women are highly pleased with the exhibit of paintings by Emil Fuchs, internationally known for his etchings and his paintings as well as his books on art, which is now being shown at the club building. Mr. Fuchs brought to Raleigh last fall an exhibit of his etchings. His paintings that are probably attracting moat attention are the portraits of Marquis [de] Soveral, Adrienne de Carriere, and of Miss Reba Owen.

Raleigh Sunday *News and Observer,* p. 13 (Society, p. 1)

7 MARCH 1926

DISCRIMINATION GAVE BASIS FOR WOMEN'S CLUBS

Inferiority Complex, Says Mrs. R. R. Cotten, Responsible For Organizations

FELT UNCOMFORTABLE IF NOT SUFFERING

Prejudice of Men Most Difficult Obstacle Movement Has Had To Overcome; Discriminations Against Women Still Exist But Are Being Slowly Eliminated

By Mrs. J. Henry Highsmith

At first derided, then tolerated as a passing fad, then acknowledged as good for women and the world—these were the stages through which the Woman's Club movement passed in evolving from a lower order as an organization of women to its present status of respectability and usefulness, says Mrs. R. R. Cotten, pioneer club woman not only in North Carolina but in the country, in her History of the North Carolina Federation of Women's Clubs just issued. Into this unique and entertaining record covering the activities of the State Federation of Women's Clubs from 1901, the year prior to its organization through the convention at Pinehurst in 1925, Mrs. Cotten has put her very best self, her mature judgment, her keen sense of fairness, her delightful wit and humor, and, most of all, her love and untiring labor for a cause that lies close to her heart. The story of the Woman's Club movement in this country is delightfully told in the first chapter entitled "The Awakening of Womanhood." The essential facts of this chapter are reproduced in this article.

Sex Discrimination A Factor.

An '"inferiority complex," brought about by sex discriminations, from which women were made to feel uncomfortable if they did not actually suffer, in the early days of the Woman's movement, is shown by Mrs. Cotten to have been a large factor in the breaking away by women and organizing clubs of their own sex and for their own sex's pleasure and edification. She tells the story of the organization of the Sorosis of New York City, which was the first public protest by women against sex discrimination and which was the first woman's club to become the focus of the limelight of publicity. This is the story:

"In 1868, Charles Dickens, the famous author, made a tour of the United States. On the eve of his departure for England the New York Press Club gave him a complimentary dinner. Some brave and brainy women, themselves doing press work and other literary work, asked permission to hear the toasts and after dinner speeches. Such a natural desire! Such a simple request! Not to sit at the banquet table but in the gallery or ante-room and listen to the wisdom of the Lords of Creation. The managers of the banquet were horrified at the effrontery of the women and denied their request. Having prepared the tables and seen that all was ready the proper thing for them to do was to go home. Rebellion was inevitable. "We will form a club of our own," said brilliant June Croly, herself a reporter and writer of note. "We will give a banquet to ourselves and not invite a single man." So they did, and that explains why women's organizations are called clubs."

Tree of Knowledge Greater Factor.

But the real beginning of the Woman's Club Movement dates further back than the organization of Sorosis (from Soror, a sister) of New York City, according to Mrs. Cotten. As a matter of fact it has been traced back to Eve, when she, not content to sit in idleness in the Garden of Eden, sought to know more of the Tree of Knowledge. Mrs. Cotten says: "It is an interesting fact that woman's activities beyond her own home began with an effort for more knowledge, more culture, and a demand for universal education. From the Garden of Eden to the present day the Tree of Knowledge has allured her, and her persistent application of her knowledge to the betterment of human life has contributed much to the onward march of civilization."

Woman in club work has made her greatest progress in seeking after knowledge. Her efforts to this end have been the least offensive to old ideals, partly in the judgment of Mrs. Cotten because it was recognized that educated womanhood was absolutely essential to develop "the female of the species" into proper mates for educated manhood, and for the fulfillment through them of God's law of evolution which forever calls for higher types.

Soul of Womanhood Stirred.

Underlying woman's pursuit of knowledge was a psychic call from the Infinite which, says Mrs. Cotten, stirred the soul of womanhood—a call for emergence from selfish individuality into a broader service to the world. These inner stirrings of undeveloped powers in the souls of women were not confined to any one country or people. While Susan B. Anthony in the United States was struggling with prejudice in her demands for justice to women, Olive Schreiner, in South Africa, was writing and clamoring for the emancipation of women from the trammels of the past. So this Divine discontent, like a spirituous ferment, stirred the souls of women throughout the world and urged action. They responded without analyzing and understanding its full meaning. Results have been made manifest in organized womanhood.

Speaking of the dawning of this new era in the world's history known as the Woman's Movement, Mrs. Cotten says, it was a revolution, bloodless but not purposeless. Without knowing why woman started on the adventure of self-development, facing with courage past race habits and traditions, masculine ridicule, once so hard to bear, and all the handicaps incidental to the attainment of an acknowledged equality with man. At this point the great need for strength and co-operation led to the forming of many organizations among women, all of them being for the benefit of humanity. Two of these pioneer organizations were the Woman's Christian Temperance Union and the Suffrage Association. Then came the Woman's Club movement which through years of faithful striving has reached the point where as a force it has to be reckoned with in the affairs of the Nation.

Man's Prejudice An Obstacle.

On the upward climb made by Women's Clubs, many obstacles had to be overcome, and one of the most difficult has been man's prejudice. Man has been hard to convince, says Mrs. Cotten, of the difference between men's clubs and women's clubs—one being for pleasure and self-indulgence, the other for culture and reform. Man dislikes the word reform, she says. It intimates a lack of perfection, which he is slow to acknowledge. Now the leaven has acted and new clubs formed for men's activities, all have altruistic objects and follow lines of public benefit and patriotic stimulus. While many sex discriminations continue to exist in the law and in the social life, says Mrs. Cotten, these ultimately will be removed as many have already been removed by man's voluntary action. Individual security has yielded to the call for race progress, and in that progress woman is a large factor.

Woman's Club Has Marvelous Growth.

Twenty-one years after the organization of Sorosis of New York City, this club decided to celebrate its birthday by inviting all Women's Clubs in the United States to a banquet, which should be made the occasion of uniting them all in a national body. The response was a surprise even to Sorosis itself. The invitation to the banquet in New York was sent to ninety-seven widely scattered clubs. Delegates from sixty-one of those clubs appeared for the meeting and letters of regret were received from six others.

The meeting was a revelation to every woman present. To become united in effort, to feel the strength which comes from union of purpose and activity, gave to each delegate courage and enthusiasm for their declared purpose of working for all women.

At that New York meeting the General Federation of Women's Clubs was formed, composed entirely of individual clubs.

Maine has the honor of having first had a vision of greater strength from local union, and in September 1892, formed the first State Federation of Women's Clubs, which immediately joined the General Federation. Utah was next to follow and then Iowa with 45 clubs in membership. Like an epidemic the State Federation idea spread from State to State. In six years, thirty State federations were formed and all joined the General Federation.

Music Contest Closes March 15th.

Mrs. E. E. Randolph, of Raleigh, State Chairman of Music, announces that all manuscripts for the Duncan and Florence M. Cooper Music cups must be in her hands by March 15th. These cups are offered for the best original compositions in vocal and instrumental music.

Both cups were won last year by Mrs. C. C. Wagoner, of Concord. The Cooper Cup was awarded to Mrs. Wagoner for setting to music Kipling's poem "When Earth's Last Picture Is Painted." The Duncan Cup was awarded her for the instrumental composition "At the Circus." Mrs. Wagoner gave both of these numbers at the meeting of the Fine Arts section at the Pinehurst convention last May.

Mrs. Randolph announces also that National Music Week will be observed the week of May 2 to 8. Mrs. J. G. Carrier of Hickory, Chairman of Music Week, will assist any club or community desiring to observe this week.

> *Note:* Sallie Southall Cotten's *History of the North Carolina Federation of Women's Clubs 1901–1925* is available online at docsouth.unc.edu. Mrs. Highsmith and the new *Bulletin* are mentioned on p. 201.

Raleigh Sunday *News and Observer*, p. 13 (Society, p. 1)

21 March 1926

Atlantic City Is Women's Mecca

**President State Federation Wants State
To Have Largest Delegation**

FOURTEEN DELEGATES WILL BE ELECTED

*Now Planned That Delegates from Georgia, North Carolina
and South Carolina Will Assemble For Trip In Charlotte;
Will Stop In Washington En Route*

By Mrs. J. Henry Highsmith

Rarely in a life time, says Mrs. E. L. McKee of Sylva, president of the State Federation of Women's Clubs, will come to the club women of North Carolina a happier combination as to the time, place and occasion for one of the greatest thrills of their lives—the Biennial meeting of the General Federation of Women's Clubs at Atlantic City, May 24th to June 5th.

"I am very desirous," says Mrs. McKee, "that North Carolina shall have one of the largest State representations present, for never before has a Biennial meeting had so much to offer in the way of business, pleasure and recreation." Furthermore, she says, club woman should take advantage of this occasion for the reason that the Biennial will not come East again in several years and certainly not nearer than Atlantic City."

State to Send Fourteen Delegates.

North Carolina is entitled to send 14 delegates which will be elected at the State Convention at Asheville in May, according to Mrs. McKee; and those who will go by virtue of their office will be Mrs. McKee, president; Mrs. S. P. Cooper, of Henderson, State Director of General Federation, and Mrs. Eugene Reilly, of Charlotte, honorary vice-president of the General Federation. The Marlborough-Blenheim Hotel will be headquarters for the State delegation. It is now being planned by the transportation chairman that the delegates from Georgia, South Carolina and North Carolina will get together at Charlotte or Greensboro and will stop over in Washington, D. C., en route to Atlantic City.

Many Attractions Planned.

Mrs. McKee is of the opinion that North Carolina women will not be able to resist the many attractions that are being held out by both the program committee and committee on recreation and entertainment. Among the interesting speakers who will appear on the program besides Mrs. John Dickinson Sherman, president, will be Herbert Hoover, Secretary of Commerce, who will be the chief speaker on the Public Welfare program, Gifford Pinchot, governor of Pennsylvania, who will talk on American

Citizenship, and Dr. John J. Tigert, United States Commissioner of Education, who will discuss the campaign against illiteracy and the furthering of adult education.

Among the interesting women speakers will be Mrs. Mabel Walker Willebrandt, assistant Attorney General of the United States, who will speak on Federal Prisons; Dame Rachel Crowdy, chief of the Social Section of the Secretariat of the League of Nations, which is devoted to the welfare of women and children all over the world, and Mabel Potter Daggett, the writer, who has just returned from a visit of several months to the Queen of Roumania.

Some of the recreations planned, besides the Boardwalk attractions, will be surf bathing and bathing the indoor sea water pools, yachting, fishing, golf, tennis and horseback riding, riding in hydroplanes, visits to the Wenonah Gardens and other great flower gardens of the East.

The entire Steel Pier has been reserved for the exclusive use of the club women during the Biennial. The big meetings will be held in the Auditorium on the Pier which will seat several thousand people and which has been equipped with amplifiers to carry voices from the platform to the delegates and from the delegates to the platform.

Hostesses Will Carry Japanese Parasols.

An innovation which the Pennsylvania and New Jersey club women will introduce at the Biennial will be gay Japanese parasols which hostesses will carry to designate themselves as such. They will gladly answer all reasonable questions asked by visitors. "Ask the lady with the parasol" will be the slogan of the streets, the Board Walk and Steel Pier of Atlantic City during the Biennial.

Monroe Club Women Organized.

With Mrs. Palmer Jerman, of Raleigh, ex-president of the State Federation of Women's Clubs, the principal speaker, the women of Monroe met last week and organized a Woman's Club of four departments, with a membership of over two hundred. Miss Mary Covington, of Monroe, a young attorney, was elected president.

Other Club News.

Smithfield Woman's Club, which has been struggling for some time to find a permanent president, succeeded in finding that person last week when Mrs. W. N. Holt was elected president. The other officers elected were Mrs. T. J. Lassiter, vice-president; Miss Ava Myatt, corresponding secretary; Mrs. Joe Davis, recording secretary, and Miss Bettie Lee Sanders, treasurer. The club proposes to go to work to raise funds for building their new club house at the corner of Market and First Streets. At this point it will overlook the Neuse River.

Williamston Woman's Club is working for a Home Demonstration agent for Martin County. It is also studying county government, including the Australian Ballot, with a view of taking a hand in choosing their representative to the State Legislature next year.

Asheboro Woman's Club was hostess recently to the club members of all the Federated Clubs of Randolph county—Archdale, Randleman, Liberty and Ramseur. Miss Louise Alexander, a Greensboro attorney, addressed the clubs on American Citizenship. She advised them to study politics, especially their State and county government and urged them to vote in the primaries and to know for whom they were voting.

Raleigh Sunday *News and Observer,* p. 13 (Society, p. 1)

18 APRIL 1926

CLUB WOMEN TO MEET IN ASHEVILLE

Mrs. E. L. McKee, State President, Issues Call For Federation Convention

GENERAL PRESIDENT WILL BE SPEAKER

Breakfast and Luncheon Conferences Have Been Planned While Interesting Program of Social Events Is Arranged For Entertainment of Visitors in Asheville

By Mrs. J. Henry Highsmith

The call for the twenty-fourth annual convention of the North Carolina Federation of Women's Clubs to meet in Asheville May 4–7, 1926, has been issued by Mrs. E. L. McKee, president. The Asheville Federation of Clubs will be hostess to the convention and Kenilworth Inn will be official headquarters. All club women, whether delegates or not, will find a cordial welcome. They are urged by Mrs. McKee to attend.

The outstanding features of the convention will be the presence and address of Mrs. John D. Sherman of Chicago and Estes Park, Colorado, president of the General Federation of Women's Clubs, who will speak Wednesday evening, May 5th. Another distinguished guest on this occasion will be Mrs. Rose V. S. Berry, of New York City, who is chairman of art of the General Federation. Mrs. Berry will be the chief speaker on Fine Arts evening, Thursday May 6th.

Many Social Features Planned.

The club women of Asheville assisted by the men of the city have planned many social features for the convention guests. One will be a drive to Hendersonville, where the Women's Club of Hendersonville will be hostess at a tea served in their attractive new club house. Another will be a drive and a tea at the Biltmore Forest Country Club; and another will be a reception given by the City Federation of Clubs of Asheville.

The Annual Federation Dinner, which is always one of the most delightful social occasions of the convention, will take place Wednesday at 6 p. m. at Kenilworth Inn. All delegates and visiting club women are eligible to attend this dinner.

Breakfast and Luncheon Conferences.

Arrangements have been made for both breakfast and luncheon conferences, says Mrs. McKee. On Wednesday morning, Mrs. Thomas O'Berry will preside at the breakfast conference on American Citizenship, and Mrs. R. B. Peattie will preside at the breakfast conference for presidents of literary clubs and chairmen of literature departments. Mrs. George C. Green will preside at luncheon conference Wednesday on education, and Mrs. J. A. Spiers and Mrs. E. E. Randolph at the luncheon conference on Art and Music. Thursday morning Mrs. W. T. Shore and Mrs. Chas. T. Hallowell will be joint hostesses at a breakfast conference on Public Welfare and Health; Mrs. Whit Gaskins will preside at a breakfast for the presidents of departmental clubs, and Mrs. E. H. Williamson will preside at a breakfast for district presidents. At a luncheon conference Thursday on the American Home, Mrs. Estelle Smith will preside and at the press luncheon the same day, Mrs. J. Henry Highsmith will preside.

The opening session of the convention will be held in the ball room of Kenilworth Inn, Tuesday evening. The president's address will be the principal feature of the evening's program. The executive board is called to meet at 11 o'clock Tuesday morning, after which the members will be served a luncheon at 1 o'clock by Mrs. O. C. Hamilton at her home in Ardmion Park, Asheville. A meeting of the board of trustees is called at 3:30 o'clock, Tuesday, and a meeting of the board of directors at 4:30 o'clock.

New By-Laws Affects Resolutions.

Mrs. McKee calls attention to the new by-laws adopted at the last convention in regard to resolutions. She advises that all resolutions to be passed on by the convention must be submitted to the chairman of the resolutions committee, who is Miss Adelaide Fries, of Winston-Salem, prior to the dates of the convention. She urges those who wish to present resolutions for adoption at the convention to send them at once to Miss Fries.

According to the convention program, several matters of a forward-looking nature are to come up for discussion and perhaps for adoption. One of these is State Headquarters. While this subject has been presented before, little serious consideration has been given it, but the time has come when some action must be taken lest the work of the Federation suffer.

Another matter to be discussed will be club institutes. This is something which is more or less new in clubdom, but which Mrs. McKee feels is worthy of the convention's consideration. Club institutes are for the training of club women for a better understanding and appreciation of their work.

Mrs. Sherman's Visit Rare Privilege for Club Women.

In the coming of the president of the General Federation of Women's Clubs, Mrs. Sherman, to North Carolina on this occasion, Mrs. McKee feels that the Federation is especially honored and that for the club women of the State who will take this opportunity to see and know Mrs. Sherman, their national leader, a rare treat is in store. She feels that the Federation is particularly favored in Mrs. Sherman's coming at this time as only a month ago she was bereft of her husband who died unexpectedly in a Chicago hospital, but with Mrs. Sherman by his bed.

Mrs. Sherman was elected president of the General Federation two years ago by the majority vote at the biennial meeting in Los Angeles, but the office to her is a sacred trust given into her keeping by a power higher and greater than the ballot box. Nor for the advancement of self, nor for the glory of the hour, nor for the approval of the masses does she give herself and all there is of her powers but to do the task that is set for her—to leave a constructive organization that can function to the fullest and continue long after the builder has gone. Her honesty of purpose, keen mind and one object in view— the greatest ultimate good for all concerned—gave her recognition among the leaders in Washington. These qualities have made it possible for her to secure co-operation in plans which she has visioned and had the courage to undertake, plans which have marked her the true leader because she is ahead of the masses in revaluation of present day conditions, and the possibilities of advancing those factors which make for onward march of civilization.

Those who know Mrs. Sherman personally say she has a most magnetic personality and is a leader who touches deeply the hearts of women. She has courage, faith and understanding as she probes deep into the great problems of life searching for their solutions. She makes straight toward truth and light, fearless of results to herself so long as she believes good will result for the cause she espoused. Those who know her best realize that she has a true woman's heart who loves deeply and loves to be loved.

Mrs. Berry Radio Art Lecturer.

Mrs. Berry, who is connected with the Grand Central Art Gallery in New York, is an art lecturer and writer of note. Last year, she addressed 35,000 people in the interest of American Art and issued about 40,000 leaflets. This year she is broadcasting from Station WEAF, New York, bi-weekly current art events.

By way of an introduction, Mrs. Berry says: "We are promoting the appreciation of American Art in three ways. We are urging small communities with fireproof school buildings to make of their school buildings an art museum, to make it an annual event that these communities shall buy at least one worthwhile painting or piece of bronze. Then we are asking the club families to pledge themselves to save enough or earn enough to buy each year a small bronze or a painting, to make it a home activity. Thirdly for the American sculptor, who is making a small bronze that never before in the history of art has been made, we are attempting to substitute this for the silver cup."

Convention Time for Re-Dedication.

In an appeal made to the club women of the State, Mrs. McKee says that the convention must be the time and the place for personal re-consecration and for re-dedication of time, energy and ability to the work. She says:

"This is your convention, planned and arranged entirely for you. Here you may bring your problems and receive help for the solution of them; here you may bring also the news of the success that may have been yours during the past club year, sharing it with others and inspiring them to greater effort; here you may come, aye you must come, for the renewal of that club spirit which must be kept aglow within you.

"In all I have said and done this year, I have tried to keep you mindful of your individual responsibility to the federation. No organization is better than its individual members; no organization can do more than accomplish the will of its members. I have a feeling that there is much to be done within our ranks. There is need of earnest, careful study of our various divisions of work, there is need of much personal re-consecration and re-dedication of time, energy and ability to the work.

"The coming year is fraught with wonderful possibilities and opportunities for service to our respective communities and to our state. Come, let us plan together, and receive from each other the stimulus and inspiration for the duties and responsibilities before us."

Raleigh Sunday *News and Observer,* p. 13 (Society, p. 1)

25 APRIL 1926

SURVEY PLEASING TO CLUB WOMEN

Gratified at Promise of McLean That Investigation Will Be Made

HAVE CONFIDENCE IN WELFARE COMMISSION

As To Who Will Make The Survey Has Never Been An Issue With Them; Thinks Trained Investigators Essential, Various Activities of Women's Clubs

By Mrs. J. Henry Highsmith

That the long sought survey of the working conditions of women in the State has been ordered by Gov. A. W. McLean is most gratifying to the women of the State, particularly to the organized club women who have been working for this survey for a number of years. Governor McLean states that he came to his decision to order the survey after a series of conferences with Mrs. E. L. McKee, president of the State Federation of Women's Clubs, who was a recent guest at the mansion and who convinced him that the women really did want the survey for which they have repeatedly asked.

That the Child Welfare Commission, assisted by the State Board of Health, is to make the survey is also highly satisfactory to the club women. Who should make the survey has never been an issue with them. All that they want is accurate data and reliable statistics—facts that can be depended on to represent the actual conditions of women in industry. The women's committee, Dr. Delia Dixon Carroll, of Raleigh; Mrs. Mary O. Cowper, of Durham; and Mrs. H. F. Seawell, of Carthage; representing respectively the State Federation of Women's Clubs, the State League of Women Voters and the Young Women's Christian Association, have been unanimous in their request when appearing before the Governor and the Child Welfare Commission that persons trained to make surveys be employed for the job. They feel confident that this important matter—an essential on which the whole value of the survey is based—will not be disregarded by those in authority.

Will Find Rich Fare Well, Poor Fare Badly.

As to what the investigation will find, it remains to be seen, but Governor McLean in forecasting says: "They'll find after all it's an economic question; the rich will fare well and the poor pretty badly. That's been so since history began." It's fearing just that condition—working women faring badly—that has challenged the womanhood of North Carolina to make repeated efforts to come to their relief. That the first step has been taken after six years of pleading and agitation is most encouraging.

It is noteworthy that the Governor did not say in his prediction as to the findings of the survey that what's been so since history will continue to be so till history ends. That too is encouraging. Club women instinctively feel that one class of people should not fare badly when their only economic relations are to a class, the rich, who fare well. Moreover they don't believe that economic questions are unanswerable, like the laws of the Medes and Persians, unalterable. They believe that just and equitable relations can be established, and by means of which workers can have wholesome and healthful conditions in which to live and work, and employers have happy, contented employees with a corresponding increase in efficiency and in the quality and quantity of output.

Negro Club Women Commended For Establishing Training For Girls.

North Carolina club women commend most heartily the work of the Negro club women of the State who have established and recently dedicated their

Training School for Delinquent Negro Girls at Efland. Mrs. Kate Burr Johnson, Commissioner of Public Welfare, said in receiving the key to the institution on the day of its dedication: "I have never received anything that I thought represented more determination, self sacrifice and real Christianity."

The institution which has been in operation about six months was established by the State Federation of Colored Women's Clubs, of which Mrs. Charlotte Hawkins Brown is president. The school today represents an investment of $17,500 by the Negro Club Women of the State. On the day of the dedication exercises, it is said that $2,000 were subscribed, the bulk of which was paid in cash. It is the plan of the Negro Club Women to offer the institution entirely free from debt to the State of North Carolina at the next session of the General Assembly.

It will be recalled that one of the bills sponsored by the Legislative Council of North Carolina Women at the meeting of the last Legislature called for the establishment of a state reformatory for delinquent Negro girls. The bill was defeated, but the 1927 Legislature is to have the opportunity to pass or reject the bill, the purpose of which will be to secure State support for this institution.

Raleigh Opens Day Nursery For Negro Children.

Another Negro welfare organization recently established is the Negro Day Nursery in Raleigh. The purpose of this institution is to provide care and safety for Negro children whose mothers work away from home and have no satisfactory place to leave their children. A trained nurse with an assistant will be in charge and the nursery will have a capacity for about 40 children. A small fee will be charged for each child. The institution will operate under a board of directors appointed by the mayor representing the various welfare organizations of the city. Mrs. Charles G. Doak is chairman. It is believed that the nursery will not only serve a real need, but will help to solve many problems touching both races.

Invitations To State Convention Issued.

Invitations to the State Convention of Women's Clubs, which meets April 4–7, at Kenilworth Inn, Asheville, have been issued by Mrs. E. L. McKee, president, and Mrs. Rufus Siler, corresponding secretary, to all officers, members of the Federation, club presidents and appointed delegates. An unusually large gathering of club women is expected. Prior to the invitations, credential cards were issued. These are necessary to being admitted to the convention, and any delegate not receiving hers is requested to write to Mrs. Rufus Siler, at Waynesville, and secure one.

According to Mrs. McKee everything is in readiness for the convention which the club women of Asheville, and the club men, are aiming to make the outstanding convention of the year. Nothing, she says, will be left undone for the pleasure and interest of the club women while they are the guests of the "Greatest Convention City of the South."

Raleigh Sunday *News and Observer,* p. 13 (Society, p. 1)

2 MAY 1926

REDEDICATION OF FEDERATION

Ceremony of Music and Pageantry Will Feature Asheville Meeting

PRESIDENT WILL SPEAK AT OPENING

Questions of Education Law Observance and Needed Legislation Will Come Up For Discussion During The Convention; Breakfast and Luncheon Conferences

By Mrs. J. Henry Highsmith

A novel feature to be introduced at the Convention of the State Federation of Women's Clubs to be held at Kenilworth Inn, Asheville, Tuesday, Wednesday and Thursday of this week is a "Rededication Ceremony" consisting of music and a procession and partaking of the nature of a pageant. The procession will be led by the Federation mascot, little Mary Louise Cooper of Henderson, who will carry the Federation flag, and following her will probably be Mrs. R. R. Cotten of Farmville, honorary president and mother of the Federation, carrying the State flag. Following in order will be the ex-presidents of the Federation, the board of trustees, the present president and officers, the department chairmen and heads of standing and special committees, district presidents, and presidents of local clubs.

In keeping with the purpose of the ceremony and Mrs. McKee's earnest appeal—the rededication of self, time, energy and ability to club work—the Club Women's Hymn composed by Mrs. R. R. Cotten will be sung during the line of march. The concluding verse reads:

> Let Carolina womanhood
> Arise in all its might;
> With purpose strong, to right the wrong,
> And make earth's pathways bright,
> God guide us in our work and play,
> God keep us brave and true,
> Our efforts bless, and bring success
> To all we strive to do.

At the conclusion of the hymn and the procession, the Collect of Club Women of America written, by Mary Stewart of Colorado, who has expressed the heart, spirit and purpose of organized club women as probably no one else, will be said in unison. It follows:

Keep us, O God, from pettiness; let us be large in thought, in word, in deed.
Let us be done with fault-finding and leave off self-seeking.
May we put away all pretense and meet each other face to face without self-pity and without prejudice.
May we never be hasty in judgment and always generous.
Teach us to put into action our better impulses straight-forward and unafraid.
Let us take time for all things; make us grow calm, serene and gentle.
Grant that we may realize it is the little things that create differences; that in the big things of life we are as one.
And may we strive to touch and to know the great common woman's heart of us all; and O Lord God, let us not forget to be kind.

It is expected that this ceremony will be adopted at the convention to become a permanent feature. Its observance was suggested by Mrs. Cotten at the council meeting in Durham last fall.

A definite place on the program has not yet been assigned to the "Rededication Ceremony," but it is likely it will be the first number on the program of the opening session, Tuesday evening. Lighted tapers, signifying the rekindling of the club spirit and the Federation colors, blue and white, are expected to add to the significance of the exercises.

Mrs. McKee's Address Chief Feature of Opening Session.

But the chief feature of the opening session will be the president's address by Mrs. E. L. McKee. Having already won the distinction of being a beautiful, gifted speaker, Mrs. McKee will on this occasion no doubt charm her audience as she discusses the big questions of today with which club women are having to do. While she has held the office as president but one year, in that capacity she has been called on to represent the women of the Federation on a number of important political, legislative and social questions.

During the convention many of the live questions of the day will come up for discussion—such as those pertaining to legislation, education, law observance, youth, homes, public welfare, citizenship, conservation and the advancement of the fine arts. Three other subjects bearing more directly on the affairs of the Federation are scheduled for discussion and action. These are a State Federation Headquarters with a secretary in charge, club institutes where training for a better understanding and appreciation as well as accomplishment of club work may be had by club women, and junior membership—the organization of junior clubs to work in harmony with and under the direction of the senior clubs.

Interest Centered on Breakfast and Luncheon Conferences.

More than usual interest is being centered on the Breakfast and Luncheon Conferences of this convention. Mrs. Thos. O'Berry, of Wilmington, who will preside at the Citizenship Breakfast Conference Wednesday morning, announces that Mrs. Palmer Jerman, of Raleigh, and Miss Gertrude Weil, of Goldsboro, will be speakers on timely subjects at this breakfast. Mrs. W. T. Shore, of Charlotte, who will preside at the Breakfast on Public Welfare Thursday morning, announces that Mr. L. G. Whitley, of Raleigh, joint inspector of prison camps and jails for the State Board of Health and the State Board of Charities and Public Welfare, will be the principal speaker. Mrs. J. Henry Highsmith, of Raleigh, who will preside at the Press Luncheon on Thursday, announces that Prof. W. H. Livers, of North Carolina College for Women, Greensboro, and Mrs. W. W. Martin, also of Greensboro, will be speakers at the Press Luncheon. The other breakfast conferences are Wednesday morning, the presidents of literary clubs and chairmen of literature departments with Mrs. R. B. Peattie, presiding; Thursday morning, presidents of departmental clubs with Mrs. Whit Gaskins, presiding; district presidents with Mrs. E. H. Williamson, presiding. The other luncheons are Wednesday education, Mrs. George O. Green, presiding; Art and Music with Mrs. J. A. Spires and Mrs. E. E. Randolph presiding. Thursday, The American Home, with Mrs. Estelle Smith presiding.

Mrs. Sherman's Speech Crowning Event.

The coming of Mrs. John D. Sherman, of Estes Park, Colorado, president of the General Federation of Women's Clubs and her speech on Wednesday evening will be the crowning events of the convention. Mrs. Sherman will tell North Carolina club women something of what clubwomen throughout the country have been able to do and what they are now attempting. She is a strong, pleasing, convincing speaker who is at home with questions large or small, having a national or local bearing, and who is keenly interested in everything having to do with the welfare of humanity.

Mrs. Sherman's interest at this time is centered on bettering the American home. It was at her proposal on becoming president of the General Federation that the American Home Department was established as one of the regular channels of the General Federation. Her two years in office have been largely devoted to organizing and setting to work the forces of this department.

Plans and Programs Complete.

Plans and programs are now complete and Asheville club women await the arrival of their four or five hundred guests literally from Currituck to Cherokee. Many side issues that have not yet been made known by hostess clubs will be introduced at the proper time for the pleasure and interest of the women attending the Federation. The social occasions planned will be in keeping with Asheville's hospitality and ability to do things well.

Raleigh Sunday *News and Observer,* p. 13 (Society, p. 1)

16 MAY 1926

UNIQUE PERSONALITIES AT STATE FEDERATION

Mrs. R. R. Cotten, Mother Of The Federation, Heads The List

By Mrs. J. Henry Highsmith

Among the lingering impressions that one gets from a meeting of the State Federation of Women's Clubs are those of a number of interesting personalities. Heading the list of Who was Who at the recent meeting of the State Federation at Asheville was Mrs. R. R. Cotten, of Farmville, the honorary president and mother of the Federation, without whose presence, sage counsel and genial wit no State meeting of club women is considered complete.

Mrs. Cotten who will be 80 years young and beautiful in June is North Carolina's outstanding pioneer club woman. She mothered the club movement in the State during the period of its infancy, and because of this service was admitted in 1900 to the National Society of Pioneers, no service later than 1900 being recognized as pioneer service.

Mrs. Cotten has served the Federation in nearly every office from president to historian. From the latter office she resigned at the present Asheville Convention after writing a 215 page history of the woman's club movement in the State from its beginning, when women felt the urge for self expression and demanded more knowledge, more culture and freedom from the trammels of the past through the period of organization and adjustment, to the present year—a period of more than 40 years.

Mrs. Cotten's love for the Federation has become a passion. She has missed but few of the annual meetings and even then has been present in spirit and helpful messages. She is ever watchful for the growth and increasing service of the Federation. To her as to no one else is due the firm financial basis on which the Federation rests. Her foresight and vision have led the club women on to progress and a finer development and into wider fields of service.

The rededication exercises which consisted of a procession, music and other forms of pageantry and which were held at the opening session of the Federation Tuesday evening, were arranged at the suggestion of Mrs. Cotten, made last fall at the council meeting in Durham. So pleasing was this rededication ceremony that it has been adopted as a permanent feature of the annual conventions of the Federation.

For charm, poise and marked ability as a presiding officer, Mrs. E. L. McKee, of Sylva, president of the State Federation, will be remembered by those whose pleasure it was to attend the twenty-fourth annual meeting. While this was Mrs. McKee's first opportunity to preside over a state convention of club women, she assumed gracious ease in her new role and carried through the three-day program with dispatch and good effect.

Mrs. McKee has emphasized during the first year of her administration the individual club woman's place and power in today's program, and has set a high standard for all club workers. At her instigation a number of forward looking measures were proposed at the convention to go into effect probably next year. Among these were the establishment of a State Headquarters for the Federation, the organization of club institutes, and work among junior clubs. Progress was noted in every line of work reported at the convention.

Mrs. McKee was appointed recently by Governor McLean as a member of the Educational Commission, which organization is to have charge of making an investigation of the State's educational system. Mrs. McKee has had the experience of having served four years as a member of the board of trustees of the State Normal School at Cullowhee, having been appointed to that position by Governor Morrison.

The commanding presence of Mrs. Palmer Jerman, of Raleigh, ex-president of the State Federation, never fails to leave its impress upon the visitor at an annual convention. Mrs. Jerman has all the qualities of a forceful executive, and wisely uses these in the accomplishment of her work. She is first of all a club woman. For a number of years she has taken an active interest in woman's club work in both her town and state and has rendered particularly valuable services in connection with the legislative measures in which club women have been interested. At present she is president of the Legislative Council of North Carolina Women and is an ex-president of the State League of Women Voters.

Mrs. Jerman's second interest is politics; however no office has yet tempted her sufficiently to run for it, much to the surprise of many of her friends of both sexes. Her advice on matters political and legislative is frequently sought.

Mrs. S. P. Cooper, of Henderson, State director for the General Federation and ex-president of the State Federation is always an impressive figure at the annual meetings. She is the mother of little Mary Louise Cooper, the Federation's mascot, who was born during her mother's administration as president. In addition to Mrs. Cooper's several years' service as a club woman, she has made a number of financial contributions to promote club interests of the State.

Mrs. Kate Burr Johnson, of Raleigh, state commissioner of Public Welfare, is another charming ex-president who steals away long enough each year from her daily labors to drop in on the convention, give greetings and leave a message of importance for club women to think over. Usually Mrs. Johnson presents a phase of her work in the prosecution of which she needs the co-operation of the club women, mother's aid work, clinics for crippled children, juvenile delinquency, and the like, all of which appeal to the mother heart of club women. In several of the resolutions adopted the convention pledged its support to a number of public welfare measures which are being sponsored by Mrs. Johnson's department.

Miss Adelaide Fries of Winston-Salem, another ex-president who was recently characterized as a tower of strength and the model of accuracy, is considered one of the pillars of the Federation's structure. She serves well and efficiently in whatever place she is called to fill. At the recent convention she served as chairman of the resolutions committee and was appointed historian of the Federation to succeed Mrs. Cotten. Miss Fries is the author of a number of books, which for the most part deal with the early history and settlement of the Moravians in North Carolina.

Mrs. Eugene Reilly, of Charlotte, honorary vice-president of the General Federation, also an ex-president of the State Federation, has been a loyal club woman and friend of the Federation since its early days. Her interest in club activities never wanes and her contributions in service have been invaluable. At the recent convention, she was the proponent of club institutes and was made chairman of a committee to investigate the needs and possibilities for establishing these in connection with summer schools.

Mrs. J. T. Alderman of Henderson, who was the second president of the Federation, attended the convention and will be remembered particularly for the brief and pleasing introduction she made in presenting Mrs. Rose V. S. Berry, of New York, who was the principal speaker on Fine Arts Evening. Mrs. Alderman served the Federation when much time given such a cause meant a real sacrifice.

The presence of two outstanding club women and ex-presidents of the Federation was sadly missing at the convention. These were Mrs. C. C. Hook, of Charlotte, and Miss Margaret Gibson, of Wilmington, who are both ill. The latter was the third president of the Federation and since its organization has been one of its most loyal supporters. Mrs. Hook, who has been a hard worker, is a gifted leader of club women.

Mrs. E. H. Williamson, of Fayetteville, second vice-president and chairman of districts, with her sixteen district presidents vying with each other for the best report, made a most favorable impression. Never before, it seemed, had club work made such rapid strides forward, but look at the personnel of Mrs. Williamson's co-workers—all gifted, experienced workers. Here they are:

Mrs. Charles E. Quinlan, Waynesville; Mrs. J. W. Huston, Asheville; Mrs. Carrie Gamble, Hickory; Mrs. F. H. Chamberlain, Lincolnton; Mrs. R. W. Allen, Wadesboro; Mrs. C. C. Hale, Mount Airy; Mrs. C. C. Haworth, Burlington; Mrs. W. J. Brogden, Durham; Mrs. N. A. Townsend, Dunn; Mrs. G. P. McKinnon, Maxton; Mrs. George W. Oldham, Kenansville; Mrs. J. J. Purdy, Oriental; Mrs. B. J. Downey, Nashville; Mrs. J. P. Brodie, Henderson; Mrs. J. M. Hobgood, Farmville; Mrs. E. F. Cordell, Sunbury.

Another group of efficient workers deserving special mention for work well done are: Mrs. Thomas O'Berry, of Wilmington, chairman of American Citizenship; Mrs. Estelle Smith, of Goldsboro, chairman of The American Home; Mrs. J. A. Spiers, of Wilson, chairman of Art; Mrs. Elizabeth C. Morriss, of Asheville, chairman of Adult Illiteracy; Mrs. C. T. Hollowell, of Edenton, chairman of health; Mrs. R. B. Peattie, of Tryon, chairman of literature; Mrs. E. E. Randolph, of Raleigh, chairman of music; Mrs. W. T. Shore, of Charlotte, chairman of Public Welfare; Mrs. Jane McKimmon, of Raleigh, chairman of Home Demonstration work; Dr. Delia Dixon Carroll, of Raleigh, chairman of Legislation; Mrs. Eugene Davis, of Wilson, chairman of finance; Mrs. S. E. Leavitt, of Chapel Hill, chairman of Revolving Book Fund; Mrs. O. C. Hamilton, of Asheville, chairman of program, and last but not least, Mrs. E. M. Land, of Statesville, chairman of Scholarships and the Sallie Southall Cotten Loan Fund.

No work of the Federation is more deservedly popular than that made possible by the Sallie Southall Cotten Loan Fund under the efficient management of Mrs. Land—educating young womanhood. To date 90 girls have been aided by this fund in getting a college education.

Mrs. R. D. V. Connor of Chapel Hill, who has served as treasurer for two years, was elected first vice-president of the organization; Miss Annie Perkins, of Farmville, was elected recording secretary; and Mrs. Eugene Davis, of Wilson, as treasurer. Mrs. Rufus Siler, of Waynesville, remains as corresponding secretary.

Raleigh Sunday *News and Observer,* p. 6

23 MAY 1926

NO CIGARETTES AND FEW BOBBED HEADS VISIBLE AT MEETING OF STATE FEDERATION

Exhibition of Community Night Schools Staged By Mrs. Elizabeth Morriss Is Eye Opener to Visitor From North

By Mrs. J. Henry Highsmith

That there was no cigarette smoking and only a few bobbed heads to be seen among the delegation of club women attending the recent convention of the State Federation at Kenilworth Inn, Asheville, evoked much favorable criticism from a rather distinguished visitor from the North who found pleasure in listening in on many of the convention sessions.

"What impresses me most, next to the lack of cigarette smoking and scarcity of bobbed heads," he said "is the fine type of womanhood that the convention seems to be composed of—a mature, level-headed, motherly type, who takes sane views on questions of today with attacking everything in the spirit of reform. I admire the business-like way," he said, "with which this body of women has attended to its affairs, going straight through with the program without discord or a jarring note. Such unity of purpose and harmony of action in so large a group of women," he said, "is most refreshing and encouraging."

A number of club activities which the women reported as doing or having done greatly interested the visitor. He characterized the work of the departments of Public Welfare and Citizenship as progressive and invaluable, and the work of the American Home Department and that of the Home Demonstration Clubs as the kind of work that is transforming the Southern home.

But the piece of work that was an eye-opener to the appreciative guest and to the majority of club women was the exhibition of the Community Night Schools of Asheville and Buncombe County staged by Mrs. Elizabeth Morriss, chairman of Adult Illiteracy. In addition to a large and attractive display of objects of woodcraft and the manual and industrial arts, all of which were made by the men and women attending the night schools, Mrs. Morriss had present living examples of her handiwork, several women whose lives and homes have been transformed by this new light that has been brought into their lives with its blessings of health, happiness and love. They told the story themselves and as impressive as were their testimonies, the climax was reached when they sang as seemingly it had never been sung before:

> I'm pressing on the upward way,
> New heights I'm gaining every day;
> "Lord plant my feet on higher ground."
>
> CHORUS
> Lord lift me up and let me stand,
> By faith on heaven's table land
> A higher plane than I have found
> "Lord plant my feet on higher ground."

At least one slogan was taken home by every woman attending the convention—a slogan that is somewhat contrary to the teachings of health and hygiene but that nevertheless was received as "balm of Gilead" by tired mothers and busy housewives. It is "Dust in repose is not dangerous." Mrs. Harry A. Burnham of Boston, Mass., who is chairman of Home Making of the General Federation and who represented Mrs. John D. Sherman, president of the General Federation, as honor guest and speaker of the convention, left this and other catch phrases with her audience as she appealed for more leisure wisely used in the home. She gave first place in the home to religion, with honesty and the open Bible in the forefront; second place to rhythm or possessing a sense of values, and third place to risibility or the need of humor. A laugh is a winner, she said.

Club women who have radios may have the pleasure of hearing again Mrs. Rose V. S. Berry of New York City lecture on art. On the first and third Monday evenings she broadcasts from Station WEAF on the subject of Art Reviews. On Thursday mornings at 10 o'clock she broadcasts from Station WRNY.

A healthy increase in the number of new clubs federated and in membership was reported by Mrs. W. H. Williamson, chairman of districts. While seven small clubs withdrew from the Federation, 37 were taken in with a membership of 770. This number brought the total regular membership up to 13,289 and the affiliated membership to 36,985, a grand total of over 50,000.

Mrs. J. M. Hobgood of Farmville, president of the 15th District, federated 10 new clubs and won the Cooper gavel, the prize offered for the largest number of clubs federated in one year. Mrs. C. C. Hale of Mt. Airy won second prize, and Mrs. E. F. Corbell of Sunbury, chairman of the 16th district, won the loving cup offered for largest attendance at district meeting.

Mrs. Jane S. McKimmon, reporting for the Home Demonstration Clubs affiliated with the Federation, stated that 1,200 clubs had been organized in 53 counties by means of which college instruction was being carried to the women and girls of those counties. Six counties have been organized for preaching the gospel of good homes to Negroes. She said that Negro ministers and school teachers were most helpful in and appreciative of this work. Revolutionizing kitchens has been a special feature of club work emphasized during the past year. Mrs. McKimmon asked the support of all club women in getting this work into the 100 counties.

A feature of the convention that deserves more than passing comment was the art exhibit, which represented for the most part the work of North Carolina club women. In the display were portraits, oil and water color paintings, pen and ink sketches, book plates, posters, pencil sketches and hand decorated china. There was an exhibit of pottery from the North State Pottery near Sanford, showing fine examples of this particular ware. Through the courtesy of Lawrence Mazzinovish of Tryon, a young American artist, many beautiful pictures of North Carolina mountains were exhibited. This collection was augmented by several paintings by living American artists from the Macbeth Galleries in New York.

To stimulate the study and appreciation of art in North Carolina, it was announced on Fine Arts Evening at the convention, that Mrs. Kate P. Arrington of Warrenton would duplicate every $500 raised by the high schools of the State by a like sum to be used in purchasing standard paintings for the schools.

Mrs. Rufus U. Gwyn of Lenoir won the $10 prize offered for the best portrait. The prize was offered for the first time last year by the Wilson Woman's Club.

Mrs. Graves Riis of Chapel Hill won the $10 prize offered for the best collection of sketches.

Mrs. J. L. Graham of Winston Salem won the Robert Lamar Beall cup for the best water color.

Mrs. Rosa Cox of Asheville won the prize for the best collection of decorated china.

Mrs. J. A. Spiers of Wilson, chairman of art, concluded her part on the program of Fine Arts Evening with E. Dunwoody's poem, the Vision.

> I thank my God that I may see the shadows of the clouds—upon the hills
> That I may have the undertone that in the forest thrills;
> That I may see a color and be glad
> That I may see a form and be at peace,
> Hear chords—and then be sad,
> And tho with pen or brush or stroke I may not bear a part,
> I thank God that I may bear the vision in my heart.

Mrs. C. A. Jordan of Raleigh won the Joseph P. Caldwell cup for what was characterized as a most fascinating piece of fiction—the best short story.

Mrs. Joy Kime Benton of Hendersonville won for the third time the Seapark Cup offered for the best poem. Mrs. Benton now becomes the owner of the cup.

Mrs. Charles B. Wagoner of Concord won for the second time the Duncan Music Cup offered for the best original musical composition.

A high peak was reached at the convention when $1,537.50 was pledged to the Sallie Southall Cotten Loan Fund, making the total sum of the loan in the neighborhood of $15,000. It was stated by Mrs. E. M. Land, chairman of the fund, that 19 girls now at college are receiving aid from this fund, making a total of 90 girls who have been assisted from this source in getting an education.

The prospects of the Federation owning a club house at Wildacres, made possible through the generous offer of Thomas Dixon of a lot on which to build a club house, furnishes a thrill to all the members of the Federation. It is hoped that the committee appointed to select the lot will lose no time in doing so and that plans will be made soon for erecting the building.

Incentive frequently comes to the Federation to cause it to do more and better work. This time it is in the form of a prize of $100 offered by the Asheville Chamber of Commerce to the club doing the best work along civic or humanitarian lines during the year. A joint committee from the Asheville Chamber of Commerce and the Federation will be the judges of the work.

While no drastic measures were adopted at the convention, many forward looking movements were considered and acted upon. The most outstanding of these were the establishment of club institutes in connection with summer schools, the establishment of a State Federation Headquarters, and club work among the juniors. The committee into whose hands the selection of a suitable location for Headquarters was placed was composed of Mrs. Palmer Jerman, of Raleigh; Mrs. J. A. Yarbrough, of Charlotte; Mrs. J. W. Huston, of Asheville; Mrs. Howard Rondthaler, of Winston-Salem, and Mrs. J. R. McClamrock, of Greensboro. This committee will report their findings at the council meeting in October. The work of organizing girls clubs was put into the hands of the first vice-president, who is Mrs. R. D. W. Connor of Chapel Hill.

Only three new officers were elected: Mrs. R. D. W. Connor as first vice-president; Miss Annie Perkins, of Farmville, as recording secretary and Mrs. Eugene Davis of Wilson as treasurer. Five new department heads were appointed: Mrs. A. C. Avery of Morganton, chairman of Public Welfare; Mrs. J. C. Kale, of Lincolnton, chairman of Music; Mrs. R. L. McMillan of Raleigh, chairman of Art; Mrs. W. T. Shore, of Charlotte, chairman of Legislation and Mrs. R. H. Latham, of Winston-Salem, chairman of Finance.

The following new district presidents were appointed:

Mrs. Charles Piatt, Charlotte, District Five.

Mrs. Charles S. Morris, Salisbury, District Six.

Mrs. F. R. Perdue, Raleigh, District Eight.

Mrs. Charles R. Whitaker, Southern Pines, District Nine.

Mrs. J. A. Brown, Chadbourn, District Ten.

Mrs. F. M. Brown, Roanoke Rapids, District Fourteen.

Raleigh Sunday *News and Observer,* p. 5

30 MAY 1926

WOMEN ATTEND CLUB BIENNIAL

Mrs. E. L. McKee Heads Delegation of Tar Heels Attending Meeting

FOURTEEN ELECTED TO REPRESENT STATE

Unusual Significance Attaches To Meeting Which Apparently Fulfills Prophecy of Matthew Arnold Made Over Half Century Ago

By Mrs. J. Henry Highsmith

North Carolina Club women headed by Mrs. E. L. McKee of Sylva, president of the State Federation of Women's Clubs, and Mrs. S. P. Cooper, of Henderson, State director of the General Federation, were among the first arrivals in Atlantic City to attend the biennial meeting of the General Federation, which convened Tuesday, May 25, and will continue through June 5th. Accompanying Mrs. McKee and Mrs. Cooper were Mrs. W. T. Shore of Charlotte, Mrs. Carrie Gamble of Hickory, Mrs. R. Duke Hay of Black Mountain, Mrs. R. L. Allen of Waynesville, and perhaps others. This number constituted the vanguard of the North Carolina delegation. Others who are interested in the program of the second week will go later.

The fourteen delegates elected at the State Convention in Asheville to represent the Federation at the biennial were: Mrs. Palmer Jerman and Mrs. J. Henry Highsmith, Raleigh; Mrs. Charles E. Platt, Mrs. W. T. Shore and Mrs. Hugh Murrill, Charlotte; Mrs. J. H. Brodie and Mrs. J. T. Alderman, Henderson; Mrs. R. R. Cotten, Farmville; Mrs. R. Duke Hay, Black Mountain; Mrs. E. M. Land, Statesville; Mrs. Charles R. Whitaker, Southern Pines; Mrs. Carrie Gamble, Hickory; Mrs. R. L. Allen, Waynesville; and Mrs. C. C. Hamilton, Asheville. The alternates were: Mrs. John L. Gilmer and Mrs. R. H. Latham, Winston-Salem; Mrs. C. C. Hales, Mt. Airy; Mrs. John Anderson, Fayetteville; Mrs. R. L. Gwynn, Lenoir; Miss Ethel Parker, Gatesville; Mrs. Mauney, Gastonia; Mrs. J. G. Fearing, Elizabeth City; Mrs. Thos. O'Berry, Goldsboro and Mrs. Riddle, Morganton, Mrs. McRae and Miss Ara Johnson.

Unusual significance is attached to this meeting of club women for the reason that, in the opinion of its leaders, it will fulfill the prophecy of Matthew Arnold who prophesied over half a century ago: "If the world ever sees the time when the women come together pure and simply for the good of all mankind, it will be a power such as the world has never seen."

Many club women throughout the country believe that the time spoken of by the prophet has come and that the General Federation of Women's Clubs, organized in 1890, is that new power. They say that there is no other organization in the world where Jew and Gentile, Catholic and Protestant, Republican and Democrat, American and foreigner, women of every class and creed are working hand in hand for the betterment of mankind like the women of the General Federation. It is made up of 50 State Federations, 15,000 individual clubs, 41 foreign clubs and 3,000,000 members.

Another claim made for the General Federation by its leaders is that it embodies the expression of the two essentials underlying world peace and progress, these being unfettered Christianity and true democracy. Religious intolerance is dying, they claim, and political prejudice is bound to crumble in the sunlight of such tolerance and intelligence as is found among the women of the General Federation.

Musical Events Unique.

A unique feature of the biennial music program will be the singing of operas written by four American women. Six of America's leading women composers will be there in person. They are Gena Branscombe, Fay Foster, Harriet Ware, Meta Schumaun, Floy Bartlett and Louise Ayres Garnett.

The four American women who have written outstanding operas that have been given productions by prominent companies are Mrs. Archibald Freer, of Chicago, "The Jester," produced by the Chicago Opera Company;

Mrs. Alfred Andrews, "Guido Ferranti," produced by the Chicago Opera Company; Clara Moore, San Francisco, "Narcissa," and Mrs. Celeste Hechsker, of New York, "The Rose of Destiny." Arias from these operas are to be sung by a tenor and soprano given to the Federation by Fortune Gallo of the San Carlos Opera Company.

Raleigh Has Lesson In Home Building.

Raleigh and the surrounding community have had recently a practical demonstration in home building. A model home combining beauty and economy has recently been constructed by the American Home Department of the Raleigh Woman's Club and by the Raleigh Times, the latter sponsoring the movement under the direction of the former. The model home was built and furnished to serve as an example of what the family of limited means can do in furnishing a home in good taste, beauty and harmony without assuming a burden of debt that will deprive the new home of much of its joy. The best of materials and workmanship went into the construction of the home as nothing else would be economical or satisfactory.

The home was built around the average American family of five members with the housekeeper's problem ever in mind. Special attention was given to those arrangements and conveniences most appreciated by her.

The Olivia Raney Library provided books, while almost every store, firm and organization in the city made a contribution.

The cost of building the model home, including the price of the lot, was $13,005.86. The cost of furnishing the home was $1,500. Architects and contractors' fees were $1,445.98. Landscaping and garden plans cost $150.

That the people of the community might derive the greatest benefit possible from the undertaking, the model home was open for inspection for a week. A committee from the American Home Department of the Woman's Club acted as host. Interesting entertainments were arranged for afternoon and evening visitors.

In providing this lesson of home building for the community, Raleigh is in line with a number of other progressive towns who have co-operated with the Better Home Movement of America.

Eighth District Sets the Pace.

Mrs. F. R. Perdue of Raleigh, president of the Eighth District, has taken time by the forelock and had not only made plans for the work of her district for next year, but has called the club presidents together and discussed with them the object to work for during another year. This conference was held recently in Raleigh with 12 of the 15 clubs of the district represented. Three main objectives were pointed as goals for the coming year. Mrs. Perdue announced these to be citizenship, the work of the Sallie Southall Cotton Loan Fund and a club home for every club in the district.

Other subjects stressed were: The Music Memory Contest by Mrs. E. E. Randolph; Publicity by Mrs. J. Henry Highsmith; Garden Clubs by Miss Susan Iden; District Work by Mrs. W. J. Brogden of Durham, the retiring district president; the Legislative program by Mrs. W. T. Bost. Mrs. Palmer Jerman spoke on Better Citizenship for Club Women.

The counties included in the Eighth District are Wake, Durham, Orange, Chatham and Person, all being represented except Person. Those attending the meeting were: Mrs. J. R. Harward, Apex Woman's Club; Miss Myrtle Phillips, Bonlee Woman's Club; Mrs. Clarence Chamblee, Zebulon Woman's Club; Mrs. Ethel Howard, Wendell Mothers' Circle; Mrs. Harry F. Comer, Chapel Hill Community Club; Mrs. W. J. Brogden, Durham Woman's Club; Mrs. H. L. Cohen, Raleigh Section of the Council of Jewish Women; Mrs. M. C. Todd, Mothers' Circle, Wendell; Mrs. S. W. Tucker, Durham Study Club; Mrs. Lonnie Smith, Apex Woman's Club; Mrs. James L. Griffin, Pittsboro Woman's Club; Mrs. R. Y. McPherson, Raleigh Woman's Club; Mrs. F. R. Perdue and Miss Susan Iden, president and secretary of the district.

At the end of the conference a luncheon was served during which a round table discussion on the problems of the club presidents was held.

Club Women Watching Sister's Bonnet.

Club women are watching with interest the political race of one of their number, Miss Mary Covington of Monroe, who is president of the newly organized Monroe Woman's Club and who has recently announced her candidacy for representative from Union County in the next General Assembly. Miss Covington is an A. B. graduate of Slater College, Rome, Ga., and had conferred on her in 1922 the degree L. L. B. by George Washington University of Washington, D. C. On examination she was admitted to the bar of the District of Columbia in October, 1922, and in February 1923 she was admitted to the North Carolina Bar Association. Since receiving her license for the practice of law, Miss Covington has spent some time in Boston where she was associated with the Judge Baker Foundation. Here she studied to equip herself for juvenile court work. She began the practice of law in Monroe in January, 1925, and recently won distinction in displaying marked ability in a murder trial.

On announcing her candidacy she said recently: "I shall not represent the men of Union County alone; I shall not represent the women of this county alone; but I shall represent the citizens of Union County. There is nothing that can be accomplished in the interest of the men which does not directly or indirectly affect the welfare of the women; nothing which can be accomplished in the interest of the women which does not directly or indirectly affect the interest of the men. There can be no lines of cleavage there. We are one citizenship. It is the little things of life that create differences; in the great things we are one."

Note: Mary S. Covington (1885–1961) does not appear to have won the election. She practiced law in Monroe until she moved to Durham to establish a law library at Duke. Among her students at Duke was Richard Nixon.

Raleigh Sunday *News and Observer*, p. 13 (Society, p. 1)
Asheville Sunday Citizen, p. 62 (Home, p. 18)

5 SEPTEMBER 1926

CLUB SEASON IS OPENING EARLY

Well Laid Plans and Programs For Year Among Federated Clubs

SIX NEW CLUBS ARE FEDERATED IN SUMMER

Total of 168 New Members Added Through New Clubs;
Chairman of District Work Expects To Add Fifty Clubs During Year;
District Meetings In October

By Mrs. J. Henry Highsmith

Indications are that the club year is opening unusually early and with better laid plans and more worthy objectives than has characterized any previous club year. Not a few clubs have already held their first meetings and gotten in good running order, while a large number remained active during the summer finding too much to do to go into summer quarters for three or four months.

Six New Clubs Federated.

Another proof of the growing interest in organized club work during the summer is that six new clubs, with a membership of 168, have been federated since May. This has been done through the efforts of Mrs. H. E. Williamson, of Fayetteville, who is State chairman of district work and who has set as her goal for the coming year to federate fifty new clubs.

The clubs recently federated are: The Fortnightly Club of Sylva with Mrs. Ben N. Queen as president; Saluda Book Club of Saluda, Mrs. John T. Coats, Jr., president; Mackpellah Woman's Club of Stanly, R. F. D., Mrs. J. F. Reinhardt, president; Roxboro Woman's Club of Roxboro, Mrs. A. M. Burns, president; The Book Club of Pinetops, Miss Sadie Belle Browne, president; The Ahoskie Woman's Club of Ahoskie, Mrs. Hugh S. Harrell, president.

District Meetings Scheduled.

Mrs. Williamson in announcing her schedule of district meetings calls attention to the fact that all the district meetings will be held during the month of October with the exception of the 16th District meeting which will be held September 28th at Ahoskie. Mrs. E. F. Corbell of Sunbury is president of this district. The schedule arranged for the meetings is as follows:

District No. 1 at Franklin, October 26th, Mrs. Charles Quinlan of Waynesville, president.

District No. 2, Asheville, October 25th, Mrs. Joseph Silverstein of Brevard, president.

District No. 3, Statesville, October 22nd, Mrs. Carrie Gamble of Hickory, president.

District No. 4, Forest City, October 23rd, Mrs. Frank Chamberlain, Lincolnton, president.

District No. 5, Charlotte, October 21st, Mrs. Charles E. Platt, of Charlotte, president.

District No. 6, Danbury, October 6th, Mrs. Claude Morris, Salisbury, president.

District No. 7, High Point, October 20th, Mrs. W. C. Hammers, of Asheboro, president.

District No. 8, Roxboro, October 8th, Mrs. F. R. Perdue, of Raleigh, president.

District No. 9, Sanford, October 19th, Mrs. Charles R. Whitaker, Southern Pines, president.

District No. 10, Clarkton, October 18th, Mrs. J. A. Brown, of Chadbourn, president.

District No. 11, Wilmington, October 16th, Mrs. George Oldham, Kenansville, president.

District No. 12, Morehead City, October 15th, Mrs. J. J. Purdy, of Oriental, president.

District No. 13, Pikesville, October 9th, Mrs. B. J. Downey, of Nashville, president.

District No. 14, Henderson, October 7th, Mrs. F. M. Brown, Roanoke Rapids, president.

District No. 15, Belhaven, October 14th, Mrs. J. M. Hobgood, Farmville, president.

District No. 16, Ahoskie, September 28th, Mrs. E. F. Corbell Sunbury, president.

State department chairmen are showing themselves keenly alert to their responsibilities as leaders for the local chairmen by preparing and issuing early, when the information is most needed, their programs of study planned for the year. Those who have submitted their programs for publication are Mrs. R. L. McMillan, of Raleigh, State chairman of art; Mrs. Charles R. Whitaker, of Southern Pines, State chairman of tuberculosis work and president of the ninth district; Mrs. Estelle Smith, of College Station, Raleigh, State chairman of the American Home department, and Mrs. J. Edward Kale, of Lincolnton, State chairman of music.

Living American Artists To Be Studied.

In addition to the elaborate art program which Mrs. R. L. McMillan has prepared for the clubs and which has already been described by this department, she has prepared a suggestive outline for clubs wishing to study living American Painters and sculptors. Her ten programs are: Ten Notable Americas Painters; American Women Painters; American Landscapists; Painters of Figure and Landscape; Painters of Notable Individuality; Painters of the Sea; Taos Society Painters of Southwest; Figure and Portrait Painters Living; American Sculptors and Women Sculptors of America. Two other courses of study that have been prepared by her are on Development of American Painting and Some American Artistic Activities of Interest.

Ninth District Council Meeting at Southern Pines.

Mrs. Whitaker announces that the council meeting of the ninth district will convene with the Southern Pines Civic Club, September 8th at 11 o'clock at the Woman's Club House. All officers of the clubs of the ninth district are invited to attend and bring a box lunch. As chairman of tuberculosis work, Mrs. Whitaker has asked the club presidents to plan for the study of tuberculosis at the first meeting in November and in ease there is not a local county tuberculosis association or some other local organization to sell Tuberculosis Christmas seals, to appoint a committee and make plans for the club to do this important piece of educational health work. She states that many clubs have handled the sale of Christmas seals with much success and great profit.

Personnel of American Home Department Named.

In the program of study prepared and issued by Mrs. Estelle Smith, chairman of the American Home department, it is announced that Miss Rebecca Cushing of Raleigh, will be chairman of the division of home economics teaching; that Mrs. Jane S. McKimmon, of Raleigh, will be chairman of the division of home extension service and that Mrs. Fred M. Brown of Roanoke Rapids will be chairman of the division of home making. Miss Florence Lytle of N. C. C. W., Greensboro, will serve as textile and clothing specialist; Miss Helen Estabrook of West Raleigh, as house furnishing specialist; Mrs. Anna L. Grimes, of Ayden, as nutrition specialist; Mrs. Cornelia C. Morris, of Henderson, as home budget specialist; Mrs. Eva S. Giddens, Goldsboro, as insurance specialist and Miss Mary E. Thomas, West Raleigh, as mothercraft specialist. Mrs. Smith, herself, will be chairman of the committee on education in the home. Miss Florence Slater, of Winston-Salem, will be available at times during the year for lectures on some subject of mothercraft.

Mrs. Kale, state music chairman, writes interestingly about her plans to increase the development of musical appreciation in North Carolina. She reports great interest in the music programs issued by the State music department.

Raleigh Sunday *News and Observer,* p. 7
Sunday *Charlotte News,* p. 24 (section B, p. 8)

3 OCTOBER 1926

MURPHY TO SPEAK AT COUNCIL MEET

**Club Women Will Meet at Wilson With Headquarters
As Lively Issue**

LEGISLATIVE PROGRAM WILL BE CONSIDERED

*Mrs. R. R. Cotten, Honorary President, Mounts Platform
For 8-Months School Term; Committee To Consider Headquarters
For Federation To Report*

By Mrs. J. Henry Highsmith

Walter Murphy, of Salisbury, will be the principal speaker at the fall council meeting of the North Carolina Federation of Women's Clubs, which will hold a two days' session at Wilson, Tuesday and Wednesday, October 12 and 13. As Mr. Murphy has been asked to speak on the legislative problems in which the women of the state are now interested. It is likely that the Australian ballot will be the major topic of his address.

Mr. Murphy will speak Tuesday evening at the public session of the council and will be introduced by Mrs. E. L. McKee, of Sylva, president of the State Federation. Other speakers will be on hand to discuss other phases of club women interests.

What the women want from the next Legislature and expect to get will come in for much discussion and probably some definite action at the council meeting. However, the programs planned for the regular work of the club year will not be overlooked. Due consideration will be given to the plans and outlines presented by the department heads and chairmen of committees for carrying on their work another year, and several new lines of work will probably be added.

State Federation Headquarters.

A lively discussion is expected to follow the report of the committee appointed at the State convention in Asheville to look into the possibilities of maintaining a State Federation Headquarters and its proper location. The committee appointed is composed of Mrs. Palmer Jerman, of Raleigh, chairman; Mrs. J. R. McClamrock, of Greensboro; Mrs. Howard Rondthaler, of Winston-Salem; Mrs. J. A. Yarbrough, of Charlotte, and Mrs. Thomas O'Berry, of Wilmington. The fact that the State convention empowered the council to act on the report of the committee at this meeting and the further fact that Raleigh, Greensboro, Charlotte and Winston-Salem each claim a peculiar fitness for having State Headquarters located in her boundaries, presents a situation that is causing much speculation as to what the final action of the council will be.

Club Institutes.

The report of the committee on establishing club institutes is also looked forward to with interest. Mrs. Eugene Reilly of Charlotte is chairman of this committee and she has given much study with the view of bringing to the club women of the State the information they need and that the plans adopted may harmonize with those adopted by other states. Several Southern states, South Carolina and Florida among them, have for several years conducted club institutes and have found them most beneficial aid to club women.

Junior Membership.

Another new feature of club work to be reported on at the council meeting is Junior membership. which is headed by Mrs. R. D. W. Connor of Chapel Hill. She finds the juniors eager to organize and get to work and already has federated a number of junior clubs.

Law observance and several other new subjects will be introduced for consideration during the meeting.

Wilson Waits To Welcome Council Guests.

Mrs. W. T. Clark, president of the Women's Club of Wilson, which is to be hostess to the council members, writes that not only the members but that the citizens of the city stand ready to welcome the council members as their guests. The commodious new club house, the pride of all Wilson people, will be headquarters for the council meeting. The first social feature planned is a luncheon to be served at the club house Tuesday at 1 o'clock. A meeting of the executive board will be held in the forenoon Tuesday and a general session in the afternoon.

Mrs. Cotten Pleads For Equal Opportunity For Rural Children.

That Mrs. R. R. Cotten, of Farmville, honorary president of the State Federation, has mounted the rostrum in behalf of an eight months school term is just what the club women of the State would expect of her if the opportunity presented itself, knowing as they do that she never loses an opportunity to speak for justice in equal opportunities for the country woman, the country home and the country child. Speaking before the Rotary Club in Greenville recently, she said:

"I may be attacking some of Don Quixote's windmills, but I had rather attempt the impossible and fail than never to attempt anything. The weak points in all things are the points which should be made strong and the weak point in our county system is the rural school, and we should study that weak point and try to strengthen it. The rural homes in our county are not all they should be—which I attribute to the tenant system—but over which I can have no control. The value of the home maker is underestimated. Education is the only lever by which we can elevate these homes, and we can only accomplish it through the better education of the younger generation, who will take to the home the knowledge gained at school. Are our foundations strong enough to bear a greater future? I say no because nothing is strong enough that is built on injustice. What then is wrong? It is the inequality of opportunity which retards the rural school—the rural home—the rural citizen.

The Raleigh Woman's Club enters upon its 23rd year of service this week. At the first meeting of the new club year Thursday will be launched one of the most extensive programs the club has ever undertaken.

A big feature of the year's work will be the enlargement of the present club house or the building of a new one. During the ten years since the present building was erected the club has grown so rapidly that larger quarters are necessary to accommodate its membership of 750.

Other special features of this year's program will be the Westminster Choir concert, the tea for the State Art Society, the concert by the St. Cecilia Club and Male Chorus, the fall and spring shrub exchanges, book week observance, receptions for city teachers, "better speech week" observance, educational moving pictures, a baby clinic, a get-together supper and a mid-winter reception.

In addition to this, a number of exhibits including the work of local artists, an exhibition of North Carolina textiles, another of clay pottery made in this State, and the annual fall and spring flower exhibits, will be held during the club year, while a number of prominent lecturers will be brought to Raleigh to speak on a variety of topics during the year.

The officers of the club are Mrs. R. Y. McPherson, president; Mrs. W. T. Bost, first vice-president; Mrs. L. A. Mahler, second vice-president; Mrs. Harold Glascock, recording secretary; Mrs. F. R. Perdue, corresponding secretary; Mrs. H. E. Satterfield, treasurer, and Mrs. H. C. Evans, auditor.

Ahoskie Woman's Club was hostess last week to about four hundred club women representing the twenty-three clubs in the Sixteenth District. Mrs. E. F. Corbell of Sunbury, district president, presided and in making her report said that the activities of the clubs of her district ranged from planting of flowers to the building of club houses, from sending funds to mine sufferers to equipping school buildings, from raising poultry to putting on a campaign for eradication of tuberculosis, from working for an election for a high school to raising money for school buildings, from weighing babies and planning their nourishment to making application to the orthopedic hospital for a child, from studying modern literature to sponsoring lyceum courses, from putting on music memory contests to observing National Music Week.

Neither Mrs. McKee nor Mrs. E. H. Williamson, chairman of district work, was able to be present, but Mrs. R. R. Cotten, of Farmville, honorary vice president, and other prominent club women made up much for their absence.

Fayetteville Woman's Club Works For Library.

The Woman's Club of Fayetteville of which Mrs. R. B. John is president will work this year for the establishment of a city public library. At the recent opening meeting of the club Mrs. John stressed the need of a public library and asked that its establishment be the paramount aim of the club for this year. The message was favorably received.

Raleigh Sunday *News and Observer,* p. 3

17 OCTOBER 1926

HEADQUARTERS MOVEMENT GETS WARM ENDORSEMENT

Women Regard This As Most Progressive Step Taken By Club

By Mrs. J. Henry Highsmith

The establishment of State Headquarters at Raleigh, with a paid secretary in charge by the State Federation of Women's Clubs, which action was taken at the council meeting of the Federation held recently at Wilson, is considered the most progressive step taken by the club women of the State in recent years. At present a room at the Sir Walter Hotel will be used for this purpose, and plans are afoot to have headquarters set up and operating by the meeting of the State Legislature in January.

The need of a local habitation for this State organization representing 53,000 women—a home and a meeting place—where it could mass its forces and centralize its efforts, has long been felt, but not until recently has the Federation deemed it best to undertake the financial obligations connected with such an undertaking. That the organization is now in a position to support a State Headquarters, which will not only place it in line with other progressive states in women's club work, but will put it in a position to increase its efficiency, to strengthen its work and to extend its influence, is most gratifying to club women throughout the State.

Walter Murphy Says Chances of Legislative Measures Excellent.

Optimism was widespread when Hon. Walter Murphy of Salisbury in addressing the council meeting at Wilson declared that the legislative measures which the club women are sponsoring and which they will present to the 1927 Legislature have excellent chances of passing. He said that he had analyzed them carefully and could find no objection to any part of them. On the other hand, he declared that he favored them and would work for their passage, not because they were sponsored by the women, but because they were eternally right and are asked in the interest of better citizenship, in the interest of better men and women. On reviewing three interesting periods in North Carolina history and dwelling upon the 40 years of gloom that followed the Civil War, Mr. Murphy showed that since that time the commonwealth had been in a state of rapid progress till two years ago. We've struck a snag, he said, somewhere and are not able to get off of it. He told the women that they have it in their power to change conditions, to help the State again to move forward, if they have a mind to. Your ballots, he said, will get you whatever you wish, provided you use enough of them.

Mrs. E. L. McKee, State president, in addressing the council declared that the success of the Federation thus far has not been by chance but by thinking and planning ahead, by showing the spirit of cooperation and harmony in all things and by working with a unified scheme—a combination which she declared was as essential to the future growth of the organization as it has been in the past. She stressed the case of the club women's attitude that was rapidly taking place, growing from the small community idea to State and nation-wide interests.

Mrs. Palmer Jerman, in discussing the legislative program, the survey and other interests of the club women, asked them first to study the measures that would be presented to the coming Legislature, to study the survey questionnaire and when the time comes to stand together and prove their strength.

Mrs. Kate Burr Johnson's Work Endorsed.

The work of Mrs. Kate Burr Johnson, State Commissioner of Charities and Public Welfare, was heartily endorsed by the representatives of the 60,000 women at the council meeting, and her action in withdrawing from the Survey "when it became evident to her that the Survey was not to be directed and carried out as the women's organization had requested and as she had been led to believe it would be done" was unanimously approved. A resolution reaffirming the desire of the Federation of Women's Clubs for a survey of women in industry was also passed.

The resolutions committee was composed of Mrs. W. T. Clark of Wilson, chairman; Mrs. A. C. Avery, of Morganton and Mrs. R. D. W. Connor of Chapel Hill.

State Art Museum Endorsed.

The project to establish a State Museum of Art where art treasures may be collected, preserved and exhibited, which project is sponsored by the State Art Department of the Federation and the State Art Society, were unanimously endorsed. It is understood that a room in one of the fire-proof State buildings will be set aside where the art collections of the State can be housed till a permanent art museum can be built. It is further understood that for lack of such a building the State is losing each year priceless specimens which it can never regain.

To Observe Cotton Day.

To observe one day of the annual convention to be held in Durham next May as Cotton Day was also passed in a resolution, which called on the program committee to plan for the observance of this day. The plan suggested is that all the women attending the convention on that day will wear dresses made of cotton goods manufactured in North Carolina. Prizes will be given to the best made cotton dress and for the best made cotton dress made by the wearer. The observance of Cotton Day was asked to help somewhat in relieving the cotton situation by increasing the use of cotton materials.

Federation Sends Eighteen Girls to College.

That 18 young women are in college today who probably would not have been but for loans secured from the Sallie Southall Cotten Loan Fund of the Federation is one of the most satisfying pieces of work that the club women are doing. The loans to these 18 girls amount to $3,950. Last year 14 girls went to college on loans that amounted to $3,420. That the Federation has never lost a penny of the money loaned to young women and that these young women have made good in their studies is not only most gratifying, but is an inspiration to continually increase the fund that more worthy girls may be aided in getting an education.

Prospects Bright for Best Club Year.

According to plans and programs outlined for the year's work now in its beginning, the prospects are bright for this being the best year the Federation has known. Each department head showed that she had a vision and had planned her work accordingly. Mrs. R. D. W. Connor presented her plan of organizing the Junior Clubs, a new work now being inaugurated in this state. Mrs. Thos. O'Berry, chairman of citizenship, reported on a study of thirty county governments and suggested many constructive changes to be made. Mrs. Estelle Smith outlined her programs which provided many worthwhile undertakings. Mrs. J. Edward Kale of Lincolnton, chairman of music, Mrs. C. T. Hollowell of Edenton, chairman of health and Mrs. A. C. Avery of Morganton, chairman of public welfare, gave comprehensive outlines of the work of their departments. Mrs. S. E. Leavitt of Chapel Hill, in reporting for Mrs. R. B. Peattie of Tryon, was offering a prize for the best one act play, the writer to choose his subject and period of North Carolina history.

The gracious hospitality of the Wilson Club women and all the citizens of Wilson on this occasion was unsurpassed. The courtesy of the Rotary, Kiwanis, and Lions Club of Wilson in entertaining the members of the Council at a luncheon at the Country Club was deeply appreciated.

The members of the Council in attendance were: Mrs. E. L. McKee of Sylva, president; Mrs. Robert R. Cotten, of Farmville, honorary president; Mrs. R. D. W. Connor, Chapel Hill, first vice president; Mrs. E. H. Williamson, of Fayetteville, second vice president; Miss Annie Perkins, Farmville, recording secretary; Mrs. Rufus Sifler, of Waynesville, corresponding secretary; Mrs. Eugene Davis, of Wilson, treasurer; Mrs. Sydney P. Cooper, of

Henderson, General Federation director; Mrs. Thos. O'Berry, of Wilmington; Miss Gertrude Weil, of Goldsboro; Mrs. Estelle T. Smith, of Goldsboro; Mrs. Jane S. McKimmon, Raleigh; Mrs. J. A Spier, of Wilson; Miss Mary DeVane, of Goldsboro; Mrs. Charles T. Hollowell, of Edenton; Mrs. J. G. Fearing of Elizabeth City; Mrs. Sturgis Leavitt, of Chapel Hill; Mrs. A. C. Avery, Morganton; Mrs. W. J. Brogden, Durham; Mrs. J. Henry Highsmith, Raleigh; Mrs. Clarence Johnson, Raleigh; Mrs. Palmer Jerman, Raleigh.

The district presidents were: Mrs. Charles E. Quinlan, Waynesville; Mrs. F. H. Chamberlain, Lincolnton; Mrs. Claude S. Morris, Salisbury; Mrs. F. R. Perdue, Raleigh; Mrs. Charles Whitaker, Southern Pines; Mrs. J. A. Brown, Chadbourn; Mrs. George W. Oldham, Kenansville; Mrs. J. J. Purdy, Oriental; Mrs. B. J. Downey, Nashville; Mrs. F. M. Brown, Roanoke Rapids; Mrs. J. M. Hobgood, Farmville.

Raleigh Sunday *News and Observer*, p. 22 (Society, p. 10)

31 OCTOBER 1926

WOMEN WILL DETERMINE OWN POLITICAL EFFECT

If They Are Negligible Factors It Is Matter of Own Choosing

By Mrs. J. Henry Highsmith

Women are a negligible factor in politics in North Carolina and will remain so, says Miss Mary Henderson, vice-chairman of the State Democratic Executive Committee, unless they deliberately elect to cease disfranchising themselves in their own party by neglecting to attend and take part in the official party gatherings. She says too many women expect to be the honoree at the precinct meeting and feel unable to attend without an engraved invitation.

In addressing the club women of the State through this column on What the Parties Expect of the Women and What Women Expect of the Parties, Miss Henderson speaks plainly and with conviction. Her counsel is nonpartisan. It is good advice for all the women of all the parties and is intended to make them think seriously on the eve of the approaching election. She says:

Women to Determine Their Place In Politics.

Any political party expects any woman who enters it to accept as a matter of course all the responsibilities and duties incident to membership, just as it has always expected this of men. The men of the parties accepted the inevitable as gracefully as possible, and promptly welcomed the women into the public party gatherings after the passage of the nineteenth amendment. They are waiting to see whether women take party membership lightly or seriously. Opportunity for all forms of party service is open to women; the rewards are theirs, if they choose to win them. In short, the future of women in politics is only limited by their own will. And yet, however important they may be numerically, no one can deny that women are still a negligible factor in practical politics in North Carolina. They will continue a negligible factor unless they become familiar with their party plan of organization and deliberately elect to cease disfranchising themselves in their own party by neglecting to attend and take part in the official party gatherings.

Voting on election day is only a small part of the party system. Women will never attain anything like equal party representation until they go to the meetings where representatives are elected, and nominate and vote for the women whom they wish to represent them on the party committees and in the party conventions. Yet very few women attend these meetings. They are losing their diffidence as voters, but some of them have acquired an odd notion that these business meetings are akin to social gatherings. Some social editor once added an absurd but descriptive word to our slang dictionary: honoree, a person in whose honor a party is given. Too many women expect to be the honoree at the precinct meeting and feel unable to attend without an engraved invitation. The usual inconspicuous little newspaper notice is all sufficient and I hope all of us will realize this in 1928, for the best of all practical political experience is the training acquired by actual participation in party work.

For some years the women have taken an active part in the work of the campaigns and have done yeomen's service in getting the voters to the polls. They expect a share in formulating the policies of the party as the logical reward for party work. Their influence is to be seen in the first paragraph on primaries and elections in the State platform. The women asked for an unequivocal endorsement of the Australian ballot system. They got something less than this, but still a paragraph that distinctly leaves the way open for the passage of such a law by the next Legislature. If the women desire representation on the State platform committee, they must attend their Congressional district meetings, nominate a woman and try to elect her. It will be a fair field and no favor and it would be an interesting experiment for some district. The National Executive Committee has recommended that hereafter a woman from each State should be named as a member of the National Resolutions Committee. These recommendations are usually accepted. Therefore, I assume a woman from North Carolina will have a voice in the framing of the next national platform. This woman will be elected by the North Carolina delegates sent to the next national convention.

Women Would Improve Party Platforms.

No woman expects to change the present style of writing party platforms at any early date, but certainly I know no woman of either party who does not groan in anguish of spirit over the great folios required for the multiplicity of issues touched upon. The important issues are almost submerged. Eventually, I am sure, women hope to see party claptrap eliminated from our national platforms. Perhaps some day we may help in cutting through to essentials, leaving only a leaflet with every issue so simply presented that the average voter will be willing to read it.

Says Legislative Program Should Be Given Fair Chance.

The Women's Legislative Council acts as our State clearing house for legislation sponsored by the women's organizations. The women's program goes before the Legislature again this year. I am sure I am voicing the feeling of the women of both parties when I say that they expect our legislators to forget that these bills are presented by women. They do not come before them as women but as citizens, with a well-considered program designed for the welfare of the State at large. They expect these bills to be reported out of committee and discussed on the floor. They wish to hear the arguments advanced against them if an attempt is made to prove any of them socially or economically unsound.

Mrs. Kate Burr Johnson Fine Type of Woman Official.

Women hold very few offices, either town, county or State. They hope they will never see a group of women demanding office as a reward for party service, indifferent to their own special fitness for the work. They are quite content to make haste slowly in the matter of office-holding. Women have, I think, a very clear conviction that the enforcement of law should be non-partisan. They believe that administration requires technical skill and knowledge and that partisanship is destructive of its best development. They have endorsed but one woman for an important administrative position. The women used all of their influence to bring about the selection of Mrs. Kate Burr Johnson for the position of Commissioner of Public Welfare. They endorsed her because of her very evident qualifications. She was elected to the position and after a test of more than four years they are proud that they should have showed such unerring judgment. She completely exemplifies the administrative type they most admire and has more than once proved her fearlessness and her sober determination to do her duty as she sees it without regard to personal detriment. The women of my party are watching with interest for an increase of appropriation to the State Board of Charities and Public Welfare. This department is an excellent example of economy and efficiency in administration. The results attained with the meager sum allotted are astonishing.

In a few days, election day will be upon us and I am wondering how many of us will vote voluntarily and how many of us will fail to remember there is any election at all.

We talk constantly of "pull" in American politics. One ribald political writer gave a dexterous twist to the word not long ago. "It is an unhappy, literal truth," he declared, "that the basic 'pull' is the tugging and hauling by the party leaders to drag the recalcitrant procrastinating voter to the polls." And yet, after party campaigns and "Get Out the Vote Campaigns" by non-partisan organizations in our last election just a little more than half the qualified voters cast a ballot. No wonder one of the favorite topics of magazines is the breakdown of our theory of government, the equal participation of all the citizens of a State in the periodical selection of its officials. Women acquired a vote just when the habit of letting the other fellow's vote decide the election became popular and respectable. I realize quite well that voting is often neither exciting nor interesting but it is a civic duty and about the only governmental function left on a purely voluntary basis.

Woman's Intelligent Vote May Save the Day.

So far as I can tell from all I hear and read, there is a growing hope that women may save the day and stimulate renewed interest in voting, for women have brought one fresh phase into politics—they show a growing determination to vote intelligently. New voters until recently were boys of 21, who, when they voted at all, voted usually with a cheerful and uncritical partisan fervor. Most women achieved their vote after reaching maturity. They are quite willing to acknowledge they know little about government but they are not willing to admit that they are too old to learn. They join parties but most of them seem determined to have a reason for the faith that is in them. Through courses in citizenship they are getting down to business. The education of the woman citizen is going on apace. If the League of Women Voters could be transformed into a League of Voters its educational program would be more far-reaching: too few men come to meetings avowedly feminine.

Club Women Urged to Emphasize World Peace On Armistice Day.

Miss Gertrude Weil, of Goldsboro, chairman of International Relations of the State Federation of Women's Clubs, has made an appeal to the club women of the State to use Armistice Day celebration as an occasion to emphasize world peace as the great objective. She tells them to remember, and make others remember, that this armistice whose anniversary we shall soon observe, ended a war whose avowed object was to end war. While we glorify heroism and courage, she says, let us educate our people to devote these noble qualities to maintaining peace among the nations.

Miss Weil believes that peace is to come through education for peace. She calls on the club women of the State to work for an understanding of international relations and a knowledge of the several ways that have been devised and settling international disputes other than war. She advises them to study causes of war, the League of Nations, the Permanent Court of International Justice, Arbitration, Security and Disarmament, National Defense Act, Monroe Doctrine and Problems of the Pacific.

Raleigh Sunday *News and Observer,* p. 10

7 NOVEMBER 1926

CLUB WOMEN ENCOURAGE LITERARY PRODUCTION

Many Valuable Prizes Are Offered By State Federation

By Mrs. J. Henry Highsmith

Owing to an increasing literary aspiration that is evidenced among the club women of the State and to encourage further interest and more worthwhile literary efforts, a new ruling has been made by the executive board of the State Federation of Women's Clubs which allows writers submitting their articles in the yearly contests held by the literature department of the Federation to retain magazine rights to their stories and poems. Heretofore the Federation has retained both the book and the magazine rights to all winning contributions, which prohibited the authors from offering their compositions for sale, and deferred publication for an indefinite period of time. The above ruling was made in the belief that if writers should hold magazine rights more of them would be induced to enter the contests and to submit their best works.

Book rights, however, are retained by the Federation. All prize winning contributions will appear in book form as soon as there is a sufficient accumulation. The book will be a second volume of Stories and Poems of the Old North State.

Sixty-one Poems and Thirteen Stories Submitted Last Year.

Unusual interest was shown in the contest last year. Sixty-one poems by 21 writers and 13 short stories by 10 writers were submitted. Only two prizes were offered; the O. Henry Cup, the prize offered for the best short story with a humorous vein, had the year before become the permanent property of its last winner. The Seapark Poetry Cup, offered for the best original poem, was won by Mrs. Joy Kime Benton of Hendersonville on the poem "In a Deserted Garden." The Joseph P. Caldwell [Cup] was won by Mrs. C. A. Jordan of Raleigh on the story entitled "Red Shoes and Green Stockings." The judges, in making the above awards, asked that honorable mention be made of two other poems, "In a Kitchen," by Mrs. A. J. Howell, and "Gipsy Love," by Mrs. C. A. Jordan. An essay for which no prize was offered but which received honorable mention was by Miss Clair Eulalia Reid of Forest City on "Three Southern Poets: Hayne, Timrod and Lanier."

In addition to the Seapark Poetry Cup and the Joseph Caldwell Cup for the best short story, another cup is offered this year. The Lanier Club of Tryon is offering a cup for the best one act play. As with the stories and poems, absolute liberty of theme, period and character is granted. Writers may retain their acting rights to plays but the book rights will belong to the Federation. As interest in dramatic literature appears to be stronger than in any other form at this time, several original and worthwhile plays are anticipated.

Other Prizes Offered.

A number of other prizes are open to North Carolina club women who have literary aspirations. One is in honor of Katherine Lee Bates, author of America the Beautiful, a prize of $25 offered by the Literature Division of the General Federation of Women's Clubs for the best poem of not less than 12 or more than 40 lines. Manuscripts, typewritten, containing name, address and club of author, should be sent to the chairman, Mrs. John B. Roberts, 1916 Pine St., Philadelphia, between February 1 and 15. Judges will be announced later. Another is a prize of $50 offered for the most practical plan adopted by a federated club for year-round promotion of children's reading. For the second best plan a prize of $25 will be given. These prizes are offered by the General Federation in co-operation with the National Association of Book Publishers. Further information may be secured from Mrs. John B. Roberts, 1916 Pine St., Philadelphia.

Valuable Bronzes Offered Through National Art Division.

Bronzes valued at approximately $20,000 will be given through the Art Division of the General Federation as prizes in a publicity campaign on behalf of a National Art Gallery. Lena Vaughn Hyatt-Huntington will give her superb Diana, which stands over seven feet in height. The value is around the $5,000 mark, and the bronze will be a glorious addition to the campus of some university or college. Harriet Payne Bingham gives a birdbath, the shallow basin being supported by a triple caryatid female figure. This piece will stand about five feet, and is a $3,000 bronze. Grace Talbot, a young sculptor who has just recently come into her own, will give one of her beautiful bronze figures. This young woman is especially interesting, for her work is full of promise, and she is only 24 years old. A fourth gift which is full of charm is the "Duck Baby" of Edith Barretto Parsons, which stands over four feet. A fifth gift comes from Harriet Frishmuth, whose fountain figures are among the most vivacious things which come in bronze. They are so delicately slender, so full of motion, and so possessed of the essence of life that her compositions stand alone among modern bronzes.

These women sculptors have contributed their gifts to the Federation's art work for the purpose of arousing interest in the National Art Gallery publicity campaign. The work will be done through the Art Division of the General Federation. It is the intention to offer these bronzes to the students of the universities, colleges and the high schools. They will be awarded for the best essay on American Art and the Need of the National Art Gallery. The Art Division of each state will be expected to enlist all its high schools, its colleges and its universities in the contest. The bronzes will not be given to the individual winning the contest, but to the Alma Mater of the successful winner. Ask Mrs. Rose V. S. Berry, Grand Central Art Gallery, New York, for details.

Twelve Books by North Carolina Writers Sent
to National Headquarters.

In complying with the request that North Carolina club women present to the library of National Headquarters of the General Federation of Women's Clubs, which is in Washington, 12 books, fiction excluded, by North Carolina writers. The 12 books presented are:

"Life of Woodrow Wilson," by Josephus Daniels, presented by Mrs. Palmer Jerman.

"The White Doe" and "Tales Aunt Dinah Told to Little Elsie," by Mrs. R. R. Cotten, presented by her club at Greenville.

"Moravians in Georgia" and "Records of the Moravians in North Carolina," by Miss Adelaide Fries, presented by Miss Fries.

"Carolina Folk Plays," presented by the Woman's Club of Chapel Hill.

Poems of John Charles McNeill, presented by Mrs. W. O. Spencer in the name of the literature department of the Winston-Salem Woman's Club.

"Records of the Moravians in North Carolina," second volume by Miss Adelaide L. Fries, presented by Miss Marian H. Blair.

"The History of North Carolina Federation of Women's Clubs," by Mrs. R. R. Cotten, presented by Mrs. E. L. McKee.

"The Easter People" and "Where the Star Still Shines," by Miss Winifred Kirkland, presented by Miss Adelaide Fries.

Raleigh Sunday *News and Observer,* p. 7

14 NOVEMBER 1926

TAR HEEL PRESIDENT IS ACCORDED SIGNAL HONOR

Mrs. McKee Head of Southeastern Council; State Work Progressing

By Mrs. J. Henry Highsmith

When Mrs. E. L. McKee, of Sylva, president of the North Carolina Federation of Women's Clubs, was made president of the Southeastern Council of Federated Club Women, which met recently in Charleston, S. C., it was, as the club women of the State know, the recognition of her unusually fine qualifications as club worker and presiding officer that won for her this high honor. The chairmanship of the council is second only to the presidency of the General Federation. The council comprises the State Federations of Alabama, Georgia, Florida, Kentucky, North Carolina, South Carolina, Tennessee, Virginia, and Cuba. Mrs. L. H. Jennings, of South Carolina, is the retiring president. Newport News, Va., was chosen as the next meeting place for the council.

Attending the council meeting at Charleston with Mrs. McKee were Mrs. Eugene Davis, of Wilson, treasurer of the State Federation, and Mrs. Robert N. Page, of Southern Pines, delegate-at-large. Mrs. McKee acted as

secretary of all the sessions. Mrs. Davis served on both the courtesy and
nominating committees. It was she who presented Mrs. McKee's name for
chairman of the council and had the thrill, as she expressed it, of seeing her
the unanimous choice of the convention. If North Carolina club women could
have seen Mrs. McKee and heard her address at the closing session when she
was presented in her new role, writes Mrs. Davis, they would have thrilled
with pride as the two North Carolina representatives did on that occasion.

North Carolina Club Work Outstanding.

North Carolina was at the forefront in almost all the progressive phases of
club work, according to Mrs. Eugene Davis. Writing of the meeting she says:
"You can imagine my delight to find that North Carolina leads in most of the
more important phases of club work discussed, particularly in the program
for eradicating illiteracy, in the loan fund for educating worthy girls, in plans
for establishing State Headquarters and above all in her financial condition.

"Mrs. McKee led the discussion on Junior Membership, a department of
work that is being inaugurated this year among the clubs of this State, and
thus far with success under the direction of Mrs. R. D. W. Connor, of Chapel
Hill. Other Southern States, however, particularly Florida, have stressed
junior club work for several years and are now reaping the benefits of their
labors in having trained young women to take up the work where older ones
lay it down.

"In reporting the activities and progress made by the clubs of the State,
Mrs. McKee reviewed the most outstanding accomplishments of the year and
at the same time stated some of the problems with which the club women
are having to deal. To her amazement, she said, she found the club women of
other States up against the same problem. But, she added: 'It was interesting
to find a striking similarity in the legislative programs of the eight States
included in the council, which fact, to my mind, is a splendid reason for the
organization of the Southeastern Council, and a strong argument for the
soundness of the measures included in the program'."

In writing of her impressions of the council meeting, which she described
as one of the most delightful and helpful meetings she ever attended, she
says: "I must give the club women of the State a thought or two gleaned from
the many fine addresses that we heard. I was much impressed by the address
of Dr. Cox, president of Emory University, in which he gave club women
some facts to think about, stating to ignore them made them none the less
true. One was the fact that the lowest 25 per cent of society is producing 50
per cent of the children, while the highest 25 per cent is producing only 2 per
cent of the children. He said also that while science is making the average
life longer, we are growing less sturdy as a race, which fact is proven by
statistics gathered during the late war. However, he expressed great faith in

the youth of today emphasized the part club women were taking and must take in solving the problems of the times.

"Dr. W. S. Rankin, a director of the Duke Foundation, was another speaker of whom I was justly proud as a North Carolinian. He stressed the necessity of having hospitals in our small towns and rural sections, giving the lack of such hospitals as a reason for the cities being crowded with doctors and the scarcity of them in small towns and the country, since doctors will not practice any more without hospital facilities.

"The social part of the meeting included a luncheon at the Country Club, tea by the D. A. R., one by the U. D. C., and another by the Colonial Dames. All delightful, and held in their respective chapter rooms, each of these a place of historic interest—U. D. C. the old market place, Colonial Dames the powder magazine. D. A. R. owns and used the handsome tea and coffee service from the 'South Carolina,' given them with the ship's bell by the U. S. Government.

"The most thrilling experience was the visit to Fort Moultrie. Colonel West invited Mr. Jennings and me to receive the review with him. We stood with him in front of his staff and were told that this was a most unusual honor, in fact, that it was one usually given to the President or Secretary of War or representatives of foreign countries. I know one thing—I was thrilled. Mrs. West, assisted by the officers and their wives, served tea at her home.

"Miss Poppenheim entertained about 20 of us at supper and it was a delightful evening—beautiful Charleston home, with the bell at the gate! It is filled with rare and beautiful antiques. I would gladly go back to Charleston just to have supper again with Miss Poppenheim."

Members of Federated and Affiliated Clubs Invited to Enter Contest.

Mrs. Elia W. Peattie, of Tryon, chairman of the Literature Department of the State Federation, cordially invites all members of all federated and affiliated clubs in the State to enter the literary contest. The Seapark Cup will be given for the best poem, the Joseph Pearson Caldwell Cup for the short story, and the Lanier for the best one-act play. Mrs. Pickens Bacon, of Tryon, has been appointed chairman of the contest. All manuscripts must be sent to her before April 1. Mrs. Carroll Rogers, of Tryon, is book chairman, and Mrs. S. E. Leavitt, of Chapel Hill, is chairman of Stories and Poems of the Old North State. Mrs. Peattie states that she will be glad to answer inquiries and correspond with any one on any subject relating to the literary work of the Federation.

$100 Offered by Asheville Chamber of Commerce for Best Civic Work.

Attention is called to the cash prize of $100 offered by the Asheville Chamber of Commerce to the Woman's Club performing the greatest service in the civic advancement of home, community or State. A joint committee from the

Chamber of Commerce and the State Federation will soon have prepared the rules and policies governing the contest. All federated clubs in the State are eligible to compete for the prize. The suggestion is made that clubs which are interested and which desire to know more about the plans and details of the contest write to the secretary of the Asheville Chamber of Commerce for this information.

Two Boone Women to Head Third District Work.

Mrs. J. M. Moretz, of Boone, president of the Worth While Club, was elected president of the third district of the North Carolina Federation of Women's Clubs at the district meeting held recently in Statesville, and Mrs. F. M. Huggins, also of Boone, was elected secretary. In addition to this the ladies from the metropolis of the mountains landed the next district meeting.

Mrs. Moretz succeeds Mrs. Carrie Gamble, of Hickory, whose term of office expires next May. Mrs. Huggins succeeds Mrs. Carl Wolfe, also of Hickory. The next meeting of the district will be held in Boone in the fall of 1927, either in late September or early October.

Raleigh Sunday *News and Observer,* p. 4
Asheville *Sunday Citizen,* p. 17 (section B, p. 5)
Charlotte Sunday Observer, p. 49 (section 5, p. 9)

21 NOVEMBER 1926

ART MUSEUM FOR STATE BIG NEED

North Carolina Losing Many Fine Paintings By Natives

MR. BLAIR SPONSORS MOVEMENT FOR ART

Mr. Haynes, of Winston-Salem, Furnishes Examples By Placing Sculptural Work In High School; What Other Cities Have Done

By Mrs. J. Henry Highsmith

The establishment of a State Art Museum in which paintings and other objects of art could be displayed from year to year would be the greatest incentive, says John J. Blair, president of the North Carolina State Art Society, to the cultivation and appreciation of art in the state. There are, he says, in North Carolina, a number of painters whose work has been approved and displayed in the galleries of New York and Philadelphia. If an exhibition of their art could be held every year here in the state capitol, it would certainly prove the greatest encouragement and incentive to further advancement.

Furthermore, he says, there are in different towns in the state fine examples of old masters and notable paintings which have been handed down or inherited from generation to generation. The owners of these would be only too glad to either loan or donate them in order that they might be seen and enjoyed by a large number of people. There are also many men and women of wealth who would be glad to donate valuable paintings provided they are properly displayed in a well lighted and fire-proof museum.

Mr. Blair's statement is in support of a movement sponsored by the State Art Society and the art department of the State Federation of Women's Clubs to secure a State Art Museum where the art treasures of the state can be collected, preserved end exhibited to the edification of the people of the state for all time to come. The movement was recently endorsed in a resolution adopted by the council of the State Federation of Women's Clubs in session at Wilson and prior to this by the board of directors of the Raleigh Woman's Club.

Mrs. R. L. McMillan, of Raleigh, chairman of the art department of the State Federation and also chairman of the Fine Arts Department of the Raleigh Woman's Club is most enthusiastic over the undertaking. She says that the state is losing each year valuable art gifts for the reason it has no place of security in which to keep these. A number of artists and art collectors who have visited Raleigh, as well as many of the fine old families of the state, she says, have expressed a willingness to turn over to the state some of their art treasures if only their preservation and safety could be assured.

Need Museum for Industrial Art.

Mrs. McMillan believes also that the state has reached a stage in its industrial growth where in order to develop further and keep pace with other industrial centers, it must foster the study and appreciation of art. In the matter of industrial designing, she says, the state has a long way to go to be in line with other states which have made provision for the study of art and for the development of native art. She deplores the fact that manufacturers of the state have to depend for the most part on out of state talent for their patterns and designs, when there is fine native talent waiting to be developed to produce just this kind of art. She quotes Robert W. DeForest, president of the American Federation of Arts.

"The museum in the future must stand side by side with the library and laboratory as part of the teaching equipment of the state. No people that aspires toward greatness can afford to neglect the pursuits of the intellect. Science, literature, music and art must be fostered and encouraged if a people is to achieve its greatest destiny. Art helps a people to finer vision and freer interests, and convenient access to great art is more necessary today than it was when belittling contact with the mediocre and vulgar was more restricted and difficult."

Twin City Man Sets Fine Example.

According to Mr. Blair, the time has come when citizens of North Carolina who have accumulated considerable wealth from different lines of industry will be glad to turn their attention to the encouragement and development of art. He cites Mr. Haynes of Winston-Salem as an example. He says:

"A notable example of this has been the gift of beautiful marble reproductions of three notable pieces of sculpture, namely, 'The Wrestlers,' the 'Discus Throwers,' and 'The Boy with the Thorn,' presented to the Memorial High School at Winston-Salem by Jim Haynes of that city. It gave him the greatest pleasure to award the commission for the execution of these pieces to one of the best known studios in Florence. This is an example of what others would do in case there was provided a suitable building in which they could be displayed, so that the people of the state could enjoy them.

"To the State Art Society has been presented the sculptor's model of the memorial monument recently presented by Mr. Boney to the city of Wilmington. This model was presented to us by Mr. Packer, the sculptor, but still remains in his studio in New York, on account of the city of Raleigh having no suitable place to put it. This monument took second prize at the international exhibition of sculpture and architecture in New York city in 1925.

"Beautiful examples of memorial museums are to be found in the cities of Charleston, Savannah, Memphis, and other cities throughout the United States. North Carolina is one of the 18 states which has no art museum.

"Such a building as the State Art Museum would add greatly to the beautiful group of state buildings which already, with our own artistic capitol, adorn the Capital City of our commonwealth."

Miss Leila Mechlin to Speak.

The annual meeting of the State Art Society will be held in Raleigh in connection with the annual meeting of the State Literary and Historical Association, December 2 and 3. On the evening of December 2, Miss Leila Mechlin, secretary of the American Federation of Arts, Washington, D. C., will address the society on American painting. On the afternoon of December 3, at 4 o'clock, she will speak on civic art. Slides will be used with both addresses. Miss Mechlin writes that the American Federation of Arts which she represents is much interested in what the state is attempting to do in the way of art and is willing to assist in a very material way.

While the State Art Society will not be quite two years old at the approaching annual meeting, it has already made its influence felt in the state. In the less than two short years of its existence art appreciation and art interest on the part of the public seem to have manifested themselves as they have never done before. Many forward steps have been made, one of which is the project of securing a State Art Museum. A further impetus is expected to be given to this movement at the annual meeting next month.

There are more than 125 art museums in the United States. These are located in about 60 cities. Eleven are maintained by public funds, 32 depend upon membership with or without municipal aid, 38 privately endowed, 20 affiliated with colleges and universities, five part of public library, two connected with art schools.

Note: The movement to establish a state art museum was first undertaken in 1924 by the North Carolina State Art Society. It began to acquire paintings in 1928 and to display them in 1929. A state-funded grant of $1 million in 1947, the first of its kind in the nation, established the core collection of European masterpieces. The North Carolina Museum of Art opened in 1956.

The monument referenced is the 1924 Confederate Memorial, formerly (until June 2020) in downtown Wilmington. Francis Herman Packer (1973–1957), a student of Saint-Gaudens, was the sculptor; the donor was (Corporal) Gabriel James Boney (1845–1915), who left a provision of $25,000 to that end in his will.

Raleigh Sunday *News and Observer,* p. 4
Asheville Sunday Citizen, p. 40 (section D, p. 4)
Charlotte Sunday Observer, p. 48 (section 5, p. 8)

5 DECEMBER 1926

WAGING WAR ON BILLBOARD EVIL

N. C. Club Women Join Hundred State and National Organizations In Crusade

CONSERVATION OF NATURAL BEAUTY

Seek To Enhance Attractiveness of Highways By Planting Trees and Shrubs and To Save Wildflowers and Winter Greens From Extinction

By Mrs. J. Henry Highsmith

Along with North Carolina's system of good roads came the bill board advertisers, apparently in droves. As soon as a new road was finished and often before it was opened to the public, the road sides in some sections became literally lined with commercial advertising. Panel after panel and poster after poster would greet the eye of the traveler as he sped from town to town, and the faster he traveled to get away from the flagrant would-be sellers that he might see the landscapes—the woods and fields in their natural beauty—the more advertisements would come into view.

Club women of the state have insisted for many years that one of North Carolina's greatest assets is her beautiful, natural scenery—her mountains and beautiful scenery, her hills and green valleys, her broad fields and wooded plains, and her lakes, rivers, and water front. These they considered were not commercial resources only. They have spiritual values, and who can say much of their refining influences have gone into the character-making forces of her people?

For many years the State Federation of Women's Clubs has urged conservation of the State's natural beauty. It has worked to save from destruction and ultimate extinction many of its wild flowers and winter greens—particularly used promiscuously for Christmas decorations. It has sought to enhance the beauty of highways and public places by planting trees, flowers, and shrubbery, and now it joins forces with the General Federation of Women's Clubs and more than a hundred state and national associations in an educational campaign to save the beauty of America, primarily by protecting the landscapes. All outdoor advertising shall be restricted to commercial districts where it will not injure rural or civic beauty.

The method proposed for accomplishing this is to awaken public opinion in all parts of the country, so that advertisers may realize the resentment aroused by the rural bill board. The campaign slogan is, The Landscape is No Place for Advertising.

Campaign Getting Results.

That the campaign is well under way and is succeeding is evidenced by the fact that 30 leading national advertisers have agreed to restrict their signs as rapidly as possible to commercial districts. Those are: Fisk Tire Co., Kelly-Springfield Tire Co., B. F. Goodrich Rubber Co., Hood Rubber Co., Champion Spark Plug Co., Reo Motor Co., Dodge Brothers, Nash Motor Co., Kirkman & Son, Pillsbury Flour Mills Co., Washburn Crosby Co., Mountain City Mill Co., Russell Miller Milling Co., Duluth Superior Milling Co., Ward Baking Co., Fleischmann Co., National Biscuit Co., California Fruit Growers Exchange, Cliquot Club Co., Anaco Proto Products Co., Armstrong Cork Co., Cluett Peabody & Co., International Harvester Co., Indian Refining Co., Gulf Refining Co., Sun Oil Co., Standard Oil Co. (N. Y.), Standard Oil Co. (Cal.), Standard Oil Co. (N. J.), and the Texas Company.

Public opinion too is making rapid headway in behalf of natural beauty. This opinion is reflected in the increasing number of city ordinances and state laws that have been passed recently to regulate the use of billboards, also in the strong resolutions passed by such influential bodies as the National Conference of City Planning and the National Real Estate Association.

But the club women of the state and country have it understood that they are not fighting outdoor advertising. They are simply asking that the billboards play in their own yard. The work in North Carolina is under the direction of Mrs. James Alderman Powers of Kinston who is state chairman of the Beautiful Poster Committee. The Woman's Club of Durham and the Community Club of Chapel Hill have done telling work in a war they waged on billboards and commercial signs on the highway from Durham to Chapel Hill.

"Enable the tourist and the home folks to see beautiful South Carolina" by removing objectionable roadside sign boards is the well organized plan of the club women of that state. Intense publicity campaigns and earnest addresses upon the subject are the methods by which they work.

To Observe Public Welfare Day.

Mrs. A. C. Avery of Morganton, state chairman of public welfare, is asking the clubs to observe the first club meeting day in January as Public Welfare

Day. She and her committee will arrange an entertaining, instructive program for clubs desiring this. Speakers on Welfare Work and Objectives will also be provided by Mrs. Avery for clubs who will notify her in advance.

The purpose of Mrs. Avery in asking the clubs to have a public welfare program early in January is, as she says, to have the mind of every woman in North Carolina centered on the welfare program of the state and to get them thinking, talking and praying in its behalf. At that time, she says, the State Legislature will be in session when the needs of the State Department of Public Welfare will be presented. Every club woman should know what these needs are and why they are presented to the Legislature.

Mrs. Avery has appointed the following sub-chairmen:

Miss Mary Covington of Monroe, chairman of Industrial and Social conditions; Mrs. W. E. White of Graham, chairman of Institutional Relations; Mrs. T. W. Lingle of Davidson, Work Among Colored Women; Mrs. A. M. Frye of Bryson City, Indian Welfare; Mrs. W. B. Puett, Belmont, Child Welfare; Dr. Mary Martin Sloop, Crossnore, Mental Hygiene: Mrs. Joe Kjellander, Morganton, Organization of Welfare Department in Clubs.

Mrs. Avery is asking also that the work of the welfare departments of the individual clubs be centered this year on the care of the undernourished child. She calls attention to the work of one club last year, which gave a roll and a pint of milk each noon to forty children under weight, with the result that in two months all but four of those children had gained in weight from four to ten pounds. She adds that as the proceeds from the sale of Tuberculosis Christmas Seals can and often is spent for work of this kind that it is an incentive to buy all and sell all one can this Christmas.

Fayetteville Club Women Working For Public Library.

The Woman's Club of Fayetteville has as its main objective for this club year the establishment of a public library. It has taken the right steps in interesting the representatives of all organization, firms and the citizens as a whole in this undertaking. Mrs. T. M. Hunter is chairman of the Library Campaign.

At a recent meeting of the club a gain of 172 new members was reported, making a total of 210.

Spring Hope Club to Have New Club Home.

A new club house appears on the horizon for Spring Hope, and heartens the club members to the point of undertaking almost the impossible. Through the generosity of Mr. E. F. Vester, one of that town's public-spirited citizens, the club has purchased a house adjoining a playground which he had previously donated to the club, and it is their plan to remodel this house when it is paid for to accommodate the club's needs.

Moyock Woman's Club is sponsoring this month a concert by a gifted singer, Mrs. Lamson, of Washington, D. C. They have set as their goal the sale of $100 worth of Tuberculosis Christmas Seals, having sold $93 worth last Christmas. This club has long passed the toddling stage not only in years but in service. It is business-like in its activities, having provided each member with an attractive year book containing well arranged programs for the year. The club is making its influence felt for good in its community.

Raleigh Sunday *News and Observer*, p. 37 (Editorial, p. 1)
Charlotte Sunday Observer, p. 63 (section 6, p. 7)

12 DECEMBER 1926

IS VIRGINIA DARE ART OR ATROCITY?

Brings Up Old Question of "What Is Art and Who Are We To Follow?"

LACK OF AGREEMENT APPEARS DESTRUCTIVE

Appreciation Built Up By One Group of Interpreters of The Artistic Destroyed By Another Group; Anyhow Much Discussed Statue Has Own History

By Mrs. J. Henry Highsmith

Whatever else the statue of Virginia Dare by Miss Louise Lander, which came to the State through the efforts of Mrs. R. R. Cotten, of Farmville, and which now resides in the Hall of History, having been formally presented by Mrs. Cotten at the recent meeting of the North Carolina Literary and Historical Association, may or may not be in the way of art, it brings up two old and important questions, what is art? and whom shall we believe?

As it now stands the people of North Carolina do not know whether they have in the statue of Virginia Dare an atrocious impostor in white marble or something fine and beautiful. As a work of art it looks to the average person much like the marble figures that have been pointed out to them in art galleries as masterpieces. But according to a few critics it belongs in no such company.

This state of bewilderment arises from the fact that those who have set themselves up as critics and whom the community has been accustomed to look to as guides in art appreciation are at variance in their estimates of the art value of the Virginia Dare statue. One calls it in all sincerity fine and beautiful. Another calls it hideous. Still another says it's a "botch from an artist's point of view." And as many or more speak well and appreciatingly of its merits and the sculptor's conception as they who give it unfavorable criticism. So what is the general public to believe?

This lack of agreement on the part of art critics is undoubtedly destructive to art appreciation and art interest on the part of the people. They at once feel that they are without a true interpreter and realize that there are no standards which they can accept. They give up trying to arrive at a place where they themselves for their own pleasure can safely and satisfactorily interpret the more common forms of fine art. One critic scorns the taste and judgment of another critic. One attempts to tear down what another spent a life-time to build up, and so one wonders whether they are all blinded by ignorance, jealousy, or conceit.

A well known Raleigh woman said a few days ago that she had long ago given up trying to know a good painting, a good picture, piece of sculpture or any work of art when she saw it. She said that too often she had all the decisions she had reached under the study and guidance of one set of interpreters torn down and shaken to pieces at the hands of another set.

It is just this feeling, no doubt, that exists among the masses today and consequently there can be no great progress made in the interest of art. And not until well recognized standards can be established, and what is more important, the restoration of confidence on the part of the people in their leaders of art, will North Carolina make any appreciable progress in her art career.

Credit Goes To Mrs. Cotten.

But regardless of the merits or demerits of the Virginia Dare statue, great credit goes to Mrs. R. R. Cotten for securing for North Carolina this work of art. She who is ever watchful of North Carolina's progress, and the welfare of her people and who has been a close student and writer of her legions and history, says that Miss Lander's gift is a memorial to, and is not intended even as an imaginary likeness of, as some people seem to think, the first child of English parents born in the United States. She tells what romantic encounters this marble statue had in its journey from Italy to Raleigh, North Carolina. According to Mrs. Cotten:

"It was carved in Italy from Carrara marble by Miss Louisa Lander, one of a very gifted family embracing poets, sculptors, painters, jurists and writers, all highly educated and accomplished.

"Miss Lander was born in Salem, Mass., September 1, 1826, later became a resident of Washington, D. C. In choosing to become a sculptor she defied the traditions of her generation and consequently encountered many handicaps, which now appear ridiculous and unnecessary. Sculptors were few in America at that time and women entering that field of creation were known as sculptresses, for in that day everything had its sex distinction.

"She strove long, but failed to master the secrets of modeling for no reason except that she was a woman and the male sculptors kept religiously the secrets of their craft from an invader into their field of art.

"Her father, a wealthy man, agreed to take her to Italy to continue her study of art. En route to Italy they lingered some time in London, and at the British museum she became interested in the records relating to the early English settlements in the United States. The pathos of Raleigh's Lost Colony fascinated her, and she resolved to carve a statue of Virginia Dare, the maid of mystery. She executed her intentions, never dreaming that ultimately her statue would find its final resting place in North Carolina, the birthplace of Virginia Dare.

"After several years of study and effort she succeeded in making many busts, statuettes and statues, thus demonstrating to the world that art has no sex. In that time she carved this statue of Virginia Dare. It was modeled in Rome in 1859 and completed in 1860, after 14 months of arduous labor, and perhaps many dreams of fame. It was shipped from Italy to Boston, Mass., on a vessel called the Souter Johnny, which encountered a terrible storm and was wrecked off the coast of Spain. The statue was subsequently recovered, but so many delays attended its reshipment that it was surrendered to the underwriters, and finally Miss Lander had to buy from them her own property, she, in the meantime, having safely reached her home in Massachusetts.

"After an exposure of two years in the salt water, the salty baptism had stained the original purity of the marble, but Miss Lander restored it to its pristine beauty and it was placed on public exhibition in Boston. It was greatly admired and finally sold to a man in New York for $5,000—name unknown.

"The studio building in which it was exhibited in some way caught fire and after its baptism by salt water, our statue was in danger of a baptism by fire. Fortunately by closing some folding doors our statue was saved from the flames and from the deluge of water used to extinguish to, it being untouched even by smoke.

"In the meantime the man who had bought the statue died, his executors refused to confirm the sale, and Virginia Dare remained the property of its creator—Miss Lander. Then the Chicago World's Fair came on. North Carolina decided to participate and an effort was made to erect at Chicago a North Carolina Building. Mrs. R. R. Cotten was made chairman of the woman's committee of the North Carolina Commission and her work in promoting the proposed building and to have the Virginia Dare desk used in the Woman's Building at Chicago caused the scheme to get much publicity.

"Virginia Dare was literally resurrected, and many papers hitherto unfamiliar with her history began to give it space. Miss Lander read in a Washington paper of the proposed North Carolina State Building and wrote to Mrs. Cotten offering to sell us the statue as a most appropriate ornament for that building. Being very frank and honest, Mrs. Cotten, without any evasion, wrote her that the plan for North Carolina Building had been abandoned for lack of funds, and the purchase of any statue, however desirable and appropriate, was impossible. In her letter Mrs. Cotten also suggested that Miss Lander present the statue to North Carolina, where the history of Virginia Dare would never cease to be interesting. Then Mrs. Cotten, being a Lady Manager on the National as well as the State World's Fair Board, was called to Washington to serve on a World's Fair Committee.

Having previously an invitation to call on Miss Lander when possible, she improved the opportunity and called to see her. She found her a charming woman and saw the beautiful statue called Virginia Dare. She renewed her plea for it to come to North Carolina as a gift. Miss Lander took it under consideration. Col. A. B. Andrews and Governor Elias Carr also called on her in Washington and saw the statue.

"The idea of giving the statue pleased Miss Lander, and several dates were named for her to come to the State and present it, but her feeble health and other handicaps prevented, and our plans never materialized. Miss Lander was a spinster and lived alone in her beautiful home, and seemed to regard the statue as a daughter and companion. She finally decided it would add to her happiness to keep it during her life and in her will to bequeath it to the State. Mrs. Cotten suggested that the Historical Association would be a proper recipient and would assume the rare and protection of the statue, which Miss Lander accepted.

"Through the intervening years Mrs. Cotten saw her many times. Once at Miss Lander's request, Mrs. Cotten read her poem, the White Doe, standing beside the statue in Miss Lander's drawing room. She seemed much pleased with the poem, Mrs. Cotten presented her with the book used, and that evening she finally decided to put in her will that the statue should come to North Carolina. Mrs. Cotten promised if she lived longer than Miss Lander that she would present the statue for her, and see it installed in a safe place. After more than 30 years of interest in and work for it, that promise now becomes a realization.

"To summarize the facts and coincidences which connect this statue with the State of North Carolina may be of interest. They are as follows:

"It was carved by an Anglo-American woman. It embodies her ideals of an Anglo-American woman. The idea of carving such a statue was conceived in London where Sir Walter Raleigh's letters-patent for discoveries and colonization in the New World were granted by Queen Elizabeth, and where the authentic records and illustrations made by Governor White of the Lost Colony are treasured in the British Museum.

"It is a memorial to the first child of English parents born in the United States, and the first born Anglo-American infant to receive baptism in the United States.

"It was carved in Italy the birth place of Columbus, who discovered America.

"After leaving Italy, it was shipwrecked just as were the hopes of Columbus so long as he remained in Italy. The shipwreck occurred off the coast of Spain.

"After being rescued from the ocean it was finally reshipped to America from Palos, Spain, the very port from which Columbus sailed on his voyage of discovery and reached America in safety.

"It was presented to the North Carolina Historical Association by the original sculptor—Miss Lander, and the citizens of this State can feel that in coming to North Carolina Virginia Dare has come home, and it seems most fitting that this statue should have a place in the Hall of History where so much of historical interest has been collected by one of the State's most loyal sons."

> *Note:* The statue of Virginia Dare (1856) by Louisa Lander (1826–1923) rests today quietly in the Elizabethan Gardens on Roanoke Island, near the outdoor theater where Paul Green's symphonic drama *The Lost Colony* is staged. Aside from her affection for Mrs. Cotten, Mrs. Highsmith was intrigued by the artifact owing to her long association with the Hall of History, which was in the building where Dr. Highsmith worked.

Raleigh Sunday *News and Observer,* p. 35 (Editorial, p. 1)
Charlotte Sunday Observer, p. 58 (section 5, p. 10)

19 DECEMBER 1926

URGING USE LIVE CHRISTMAS TREE

Club Women Over State Renew Protests Against Destruction of Greens

RALEIGH MAY SET EXAMPLE TO STATE

*Mayor Culbreth Suggests Use This Year of Live Trees Outside House
For Christmas Trees Draped With Vari-colored Lights and Snowy Tinsel*

By Mrs. J. Henry Highsmith

After many years of agitation by North Carolina Federation of Women's Clubs, and more recently garden clubs and other organizations, for a more sane and moderate use of winter greens used for decorating purposes at Christmas time, it appears that something is about to be accomplished. In Raleigh, for instance, the Mayor, E. E. Culbreth, is working to have his people adopt a new method of observing Christmas in the use of the Christmas tree. He is urging them to use live trees or evergreens out of doors, and in their own yards if possible, instead of betaking themselves to the woods where on property likely not their own they destroy a half dozen or more young trees perhaps in an effort to get one that is just what they want. Else they seek the wagons from the country which have brought in thousands of trees and branches to be sold for decorating purposes, leaving the wooded spaces that were once a joy to the eye now bare and bereft of a single holly untouched and standing upright, but with the ground littered with the shorn trunks and broken branches.

Mayor Culbreth sees in the use of live green trees or evergreens out of doors, made to glow with vari-colored electric lights and snowy tinsel, far more beautiful Christmas trees than people have yet known, not because they are in their natural setting with the stars overhead, or glistering with rain-drops or freshly fallen snow, but because their symbolism becomes richer and more real. Their light and cheer and the true Christmas spirit which they typify are not confined within four walls but are shared with every one in the community.

The plan of substituting real trees for artificial ones and live ones for those that are dead or dying did not originate with Mayor Culbreth. But while visiting in a Northern city during the Christmas season a year or two ago, he saw how beautiful a city could be made as well as how successfully and pleasing the Christmas spirit could be broadcast over an entire community by observing this plan. Imagine, he says, Blount Street, or any other street of the city having one or more trees in each yard aglow with lights on Christmas eve and Christmas night. And this he says can be done easily and without much expense by attaching an electric cord to a socket on the porch or to one inside the house through the window; and to this cord attach another cord that is fitted up with small electric bulbs and sold for decorating purposes. The expense necessarily will depend on the length of the cord and the number of lights used. For homes not having electric lights, Mr. Culbreth finds after investigating that electric batteries can be purchased for from $2.50 up. These will furnish an electric current sufficient to light a tree for two or more nights and are especially suitable for Christmas entertainments in the country.

While the idea of decorating a tree or evergreen bush in the yard with lights at Christmas is not altogether new in Raleigh, several homes having furnished a great deal to the spirit of Christmas last season, it is not yet done to the extent that it can be called a custom nor to the extent that the movement can have any appreciable effect on saving the evergreens, particularly the holly, from woeful destruction. But never before has there been so strong a sentiment for preserving Christmas greens and seldom if ever has there been a more practicable and effective method suggested as the use of live trees for Christmas trees. Consequently Mayor Culbreth's effort to bring about a more moderate use of evergreens at Christmas is most timely and commendable. In what other way could Raleigh, Charlotte, Winston-Salem, or Asheville promote the good and beautiful more effectively than by becoming a model town, a leader in this respect? From a commercial viewpoint and as a community enterprise, the plan could be made to pay many times over in the amount of National and State advertising it would receive, and what is more valuable it would create an aesthetic atmosphere that would be an invaluable asset to any town or community.

Another beautiful idea in connection with establishing this custom would be the increased use and growth of evergreens about the house. No home would think of not growing one or more evergreens suitable for a Christmas tree than they now think of not decorating in some way for the occasion. This feature alone as an outgrowth of the movement, it seems, would justify the experiment.

Raleigh Sunday *News and Observer*, p. 33 (Editorial, p. 1)
Asheville Sunday Citizen, p. 25 (section C, p. 5)

1927

26 January — attends formal opening of NCFWC State Headquarters at Sir Walter Hotel; Mrs. Bost, whom she will succeed in 1930, is first executive secretary

2 February — addresses Raleigh Garden Club on the planting of annuals and perennials

3 February — nominated Corresponding Secretary, RWC

11 February — attends presentation of portrait to Sallie Southall Cotten Dormitory at NC College for Women, Greensboro

10 March — attends, with other civic leaders, presentation of Dr. W. A. Parker of the National Recreation Association

16 March — eulogizes, to Duke Alumnae, Joseph G. Brown, president of Duke Board of Directors, who had died 30 January during Sunday service at Edenton Street

22 April — addresses a committee meeting at Edenton Street to promote a new Methodist church on the corner of Person and Franklin Streets, a very short distance from her home

2–5 May — attends 25th annual convention of NCFWC, Durham; presides at press breakfast on Tuesday, 3 May

18 May — elected president of Hugh Morson High School PTA for next school year

1927–28, 1928–29
President, Hugh Morson High School PTA

8 September — following death of RWC president, advances from corresponding secretary to first vice president

14 September — hosts executives of Hugh Morson PTA for a planning meeting at her home; Dr. Highsmith is chair of library committee

20 September — elected president of the Twentieth Century Book Club

20 September — presides over first Morson PTA meeting of the year, in the new school auditorium

12–13 October — hosts visiting delegates to the 45th annual state convention of the WCTU

5 October — attends Get-Together Luncheon at RWC as first vice president; then hosts third birthday party for "Little Miss Louise Westbrook Highsmith" and 25 little guests

6 October — attends memorial for Mrs. R. F. Perdue, deceased president, RWC

13 October — attends Eighth District NCFWC meeting in Zebulon

2 November — offers luncheon toast at a district meeting of the PTA hosted by Hugh Morson High School

8–10 November — represents Hugh Morson PTA at the state convention in Charlotte; is elected corresponding secretary

17 November — attends luncheon at Sir Walter Hotel for Mrs. Walter Miller, NCFWC chair of public welfare and publicity director of American Child Health Association, concerning Sheppard-Towner Act of 1921, an early social security measure funding infant and maternal care

early December — accompanies Dr. Highsmith to meeting of Southern Association of Colleges and Secondary Schools in Jacksonville FL and reports back on the beautiful new Woman's Club there

c. 20 December — Pauline undergoes emergency appendectomy at Mary Elizabeth Hospital on Wake Forest Road

2 JANUARY 1927

STATE FEDERATION TO OPEN OFFICES

Headquarters Will Be Conducted By Mrs. W. T. Bost, Executive Secretary

FEDERATION READY EXPANSION PROGRAM

President of Organization, Mrs. E. L. McKee, Addresses New Year Message To People of State, Particularly To Those In Public Life

By Mrs. J. Henry Highsmith

For an open mind and a humanitarian spirit in the heart is the wish Mrs. E. L. McKee, of Sylva, president of the State Federation of Women's Clubs, is making this New Year for the citizens of North Carolina, particularly, she says, for the men and women who will be active in public affairs, for upon the attitude of their minds and hearts will depend largely the success and progress of the State for the next biennium.

In this and in other parts of her New Year message, which follows, it is clear that Mrs. McKee has in mind as the main object of her wish the success of the legislative program which the State Federation, along with several other State organizations of women, will present at the approaching session of the State Legislature. Because of the humanitarian principles on which the measures are based, and because they are asked in the name of right and justice and for the protection of the weak and inarticulate, Mrs. McKee speaks in behalf of these things at this opportune time, when she says, hearts are "swept clean of all materialism, prejudice and distrust by the blessed spirit of the Christ-child—the spirit of good will toward men." So her New Year message is addressed primarily to those who will have it in their power during the next two months, to grant or refuse those things that will make the State "a good place to live and bring up children in as well as good place to make money in."

Her message follows:

"It has always seemed to me a fortunate thing that we can enter the New Year with our hearts swept clean of all materialism and prejudice and distrust by the blessed spirit of the Christ-child—the spirit of good-will toward men. I trust that in North Carolina men and women are thus prepared for the duties of the year 1927, particularly those men and women who will be active in public affairs, for they face the fact that the success and progress of North Carolina for the next biennium depends largely upon their attitude of mind and heart.

"Therefore, my New Year's wish is for an open mind and a humanitarian spirit in the heart of every citizen of North Carolina, both private and public, so that the one may ask for intelligently and the other grant wisely and unselfishly those things which will make our State stand out among other States as a good place to live and bring up children in as well as a place to make money in. May there be no antagonism among the various groups of citizens, but may we move forward in harmony and good-will toward the end which all are seeking—a better, healthier, safer, more beautiful State—a State in which, in reality, "the weak are protected by the strong in order that they may become strong, and in which strong thereby become great."

—Gertrude Dills McKee.

In the opening of State Federation Headquarters in the Sir Walter Hotel, Raleigh, on Monday, January 3, with Mrs. W. T. Bost as executive secretary, the club women of the State realize one of their fondest dreams. While the actual opening of the headquarters office will take place and the machinery set to work that date, and Mrs. Bost will enter upon her duties as executive secretary, the formal opening will take place at a later date, at which time club women from all over the State will assemble to do honor to the occasion. An interesting program is being arranged for that day.

With the establishment of headquarters as the first step, the Federation is now ready to enter upon a program of expansion and more efficient work. Mrs. McKee has outlined this program in an article which she prepared for the January issue of the State Federation bulletin. She says that maintaining State Headquarters where the working forces of the organization can be brought together and strengthened is nothing but good business. She points out the fact that a great deal of the work of the Federation can be done not only more efficiently at a central distributing point but that a great saving can be effected.

While the first State Federation Headquarters was established in 1917, fifteen States now have well established quarters operating successfully, and fifteen States maintain bureaus of information. The States having headquarters, all of which are financed wholly or in part from State Federation funds, are Alabama, California, Colorado, Florida, Georgia, Illinois, Iowa, Massachusetts, Michigan, Minnesota, Nebraska, New Jersey, North Carolina, Ohio, and Texas. From the foregoing list will be observed that North Carolina is the fifth Southern State to fall in line with this progressive idea.

Mrs. Bost announces that her hours will be from 11 to 3 o'clock every day in the week, and she extends a cordial invitation to club woman to visit her. She will gladly render any service that comes within the bounds and equipment of her office.

[Asheville and Charlotte papers continue:]

Attend Board Meeting.

Mrs. Sydney P. Cooper of Henderson, State director, and Mrs. E. L. McKee of Sylva, president, will attend the meeting of the Board of Directors of the General Federation of Women's Clubs, to be held January 12, 13 and 14 at headquarters, 1734 N. Street N. W., Washington, D. C. The board consists of the officers, state directors, trustees and department chairmen. State presidents and division chairmen attend board meetings as conference members.

The meeting, which will be attended by about 65 women, will be presided over by Mrs. John D. Sherman, president of the General Federation. The Federation foundation for the adequate financing of Federation projects heads the list of special subjects which will be presented for consideration. The enlargement of the Federation News will be another important subject and there will also be discussion of the several types of propaganda now being employed and directed toward women's organizations. Present and projected work of the several departments will have full consideration. The Board meeting proper will be preceded by two days of committee meetings and conferences.

President Coolidge will receive the Board and on January 12 Mrs. Herbert Hoover will entertain the members of the Board at a tea at her

home. A reception will be held at Headquarters the evening of the 11th.
Mrs. Virginia White Speel, president of the State presidents, will entertain
with a conference luncheon at her home. A visit to the Bureau of Standards,
called the "house of wonders," is also scheduled. The Mayflower has been
designated as the official hotel.

Raleigh Sunday *News and Observer*, p. 17 (Society, p. 1), incomplete
Charlotte Sunday Observer, p. 41 (section 3, p. 9)
Asheville *Sunday Citizen*, p. 27 (section C, p. 5)

9 JANUARY 1927

FEDERATED WOMEN'S CLUBS TO OPEN STATE HEADQUARTERS IN RALEIGH ON JANUARY 26

**Invitation Has Been Extended to All Club Women of North
Carolina to Be Present—Most Progressive Step Federation
Has Ever Taken—General Federation Not Responsible for
Legislative Program in This State—Women Want Housekeeping
Made a Profession**

By Mrs. J. Henry Highsmith

Announcement is made by the Executive Board of the North Carolina
Federation of Women's Clubs that State Headquarters will be opened
formally at the Sir Walter Hotel, Raleigh, Wednesday afternoon, January
26th. The opening will be in the nature of a reception from 3 to 6 o'clock
to which all North Carolina club women are invited. Invitations have
been issued personally to all the officers of the Federation, to all heads of
departments and chairmen of standing committees, to all club presidents
and through them to every club woman in the state. Hundreds of club
women from every section of the state are expected to be present for the
occasion. The invitation reads:

> The executive board of the North Carolina Federation of Women's
> Clubs invite all North Carolina club women to be present at the
> opening of State Headquarters, Sir Walter Hotel, Wednesday
> afternoon, January the twenty-sixth, nineteen hundred and twenty-
> seven from three until six o'clock, Raleigh, North Carolina.

Mrs. E. L. McKee, state president, who was in Raleigh the greater part
of last week attending conferences of the educational commission, said
that she considered the establishment of State Headquarters the most
progressive step the Federation has ever taken and that she believes it to
be a step taken toward a period of growth and unprecedented expansion in
Federation activities. She made it clear in both private and public statements
that headquarters was not set up solely for political purposes but that it is
permanent—and was established to meet the long felt needs of a statewide

organization to have its working forces co-ordinated and centralized for more efficient work.

Another point which Mrs. McKee would have made clear is that Federation Headquarters it not to be confused with the headquarters of the Legislative Council of North Carolina Women at 109½ Fayetteville Street, Raleigh. However she says the State Federation of Women's Clubs is one of the seven state organizations of women forming this group, and that the legislative measures which the federation endorses are sponsored by these seven statewide organizations, comprising nearly 75,000 North Carolina women who know conditions in North Carolina at first hand and who in the interest of humanity are asking that legislation be enacted to remedy these conditions.

State Federation Not Dictated To By General Federation.

Mrs. McKee states emphatically that the General Federation of Women's Clubs has had nothing to with dictating or formulating the legislative program which the State Federation is interested in and hopes to have passed at the present session of the state legislation. She says that the General Federation has no more to do with the plans and policies of the State Federation than Congress has to do with the State Legislatures; that the national body like Congress deal with national and international affairs leaving state and local problems to the jurisdiction of the state.

[Asheville paper continues:]

Asks That Home-Making Be Made Profession, Put On Census List.

A movement is on foot to secure from the United States Government in Washington recognition of the home maker or housekeeper as either a profession or industry. As it is today, home making is not listed as an occupation in the census department, consequently it receives no consideration or help from the government as would be the case were it on the Census list.

Secretary Herbert Hoover, in whose department is the Census Department of the United States, is being besieged with floods of requests from club women all over the country to have the American Home Maker listed in the next census as having a definite occupation and as contributing definitely to the nation's social and economic progress. It is said that the United States Census Bureau knows how many looms and spindles, how many typewriters and adding machines, how many tractors and reaping machines, are used in the various trades, industries and professions. But it ignores the greatest and most universal of our national industries, that of home-making.

It is this situation that brought about the nation-wide survey of home equipment that was put on and conducted by the General Federation of Women's Clubs. In this survey, the house-keeping equipment in 7,911,630 families was looked into with results that were startling but not discouraging.

The survey, as one of its results, has riveted attention upon defective housekeeping facilities in American homes and what these mean in the waste of human energy and material resources. Analyzed, the defects concern (1) sanitary equipment, (2) labor saving facilities, (3) cooking fuel, (4) heating methods and (5) light and illumination. The General Federation is at work on a program whereby the Art of home making will be placed where it rightly belongs. One phase of this program is to ask the United States government to place the profession of home making on the Census list.

Mrs. John D. Sherman, president of the General Federation of Women's Clubs, speaking on this subject says:

"Giving the Home-maker a status and recognizing home-making as an industry will place the needed emphasis upon the home as the basic unit of society and government.

"The Home will continue to be inadequately equipped until it has similar recognition in the machinery of the government that serves and protects the American people.

"There are nearly three million women in the various women's clubs of the country, the majority of them home-makers, who when given such recognition as is being asked from the government, would be stimulated to better equipped homes, higher standards of living and a more profound determination to lead in their profession."

Asheville *Sunday Citizen,* p. 20 (section C, p. 4)
Charlotte Sunday Observer, p. 22 (section 3, p. 8), incomplete

16 JANUARY 1927

BILLS UNDER CONSIDERATION TO BE GIVEN INTENSIVE STUDY
DURING BALANCE OF JANUARY

**No Doubt to Be Left in Mind of Legislature as to Where the
Women Stand on Matters Affecting Their Interests—One Measure
Sponsored by Council Has Already Been Presented and Is
Receiving Favorable Comment—Social Conditions Particularly to
Be Given Close Scrutiny**

By Mrs. J. Henry Highsmith

Taking their cue from editorial statements published recently in one of the State's afternoon dailies, "if North Carolina women are in a real campaign for legislation, it is certain that what they want will be provided," and "one would like to be more certain that it represents the positive interest and vote of the North Carolina women," the club women of the State will at once set themselves to the task of removing these doubts if they really exist.

Accordingly, the first thing which they will undertake is to wage a legislative campaign with such intensity and earnestness that the genuineness of it will never again be questioned; and the second will be to disabuse the minds of those legislators, if there are any, who claim that they are not sure that their women constituents back home are in favor of the bills.

Mill Begins to Grind.

As the legislative mill is already grinding and one of the bills which the Legislative Council of North Carolina Women is sponsoring has been presented and has received more or less favorable consideration, it is clear that quick action on the part of club women to carry out the above program is most imperative. Those on the inside and in close touch with the lawmakers advise club women throughout the state to lose no time in communicating with their representatives in the Legislature, leaving no doubt in their minds as to how they stand on the five measures and as to the way they, as their representatives, are expected to vote on each measure.

For the purpose of strengthening the ranks, women's clubs have been asked to give one meeting in the month of January to the study of the five bills contained in the legislative program and to other questions affecting the social welfare conditions of the state. Mrs. A. C. Avery of Morganton, chairman of public welfare, is making this request and offers to assist any club desiring a speaker or a program for this meeting. She says that no club woman is even slightly indifferent to the legislative program who knows anything at all about the measures.

Bills That Women Want.

The five bills which club women throughout the state are supporting are here given with an unanswerable reason as to why each should be written into the laws of the state:

1. Why a state-wide Australian ballot law? Because we need a system of voting which requires order at the polls, allows a private and un-coerced vote, provides for speed, ease and accuracy in voting and in counting the votes cast.

2. Why a law limiting the working day of children under 16 to 8 hours a day in industrial and mercantile pursuits? Because a child of 14 or 15 who works the 11 hours a day or 60 a week that our law allows is injured physically by the strain and is prevented from further education, even in night school.

3. Why the establishment of a farm colony for women offenders other than those received at Samarcand? Because the State needs to be protected from vicious and diseased women by their being cured and taught to support themselves in a lawful manner, or if this is impossible by their permanent removal from society, in a self-supporting farm prison.

4. Why two weeks' notice before marriage? Because history proves that

such a law prevents hasty, unwise marriages and so causes respect for sanctity of the home. Good marriage laws are more important than divorce laws.

5. Why the reformatory for colored girls? Because the State makes no provision for the care of delinquent Negro girls, though it does for the boys. Girls are left free to be a menace to society instead of being taught to be self-supporting and law-abiding. The reformatory is successfully running now.

The council has also endorsed the program of the State board of public welfare and the program of the State Department of Education.

Other state organizations of women beside the State Federation of Women's Clubs supporting the above measures are: Federation of Business and Professional Women's Clubs; League of Women Voters; State Nurses Association; Woman's Auxiliary, Protestant Episcopal Church, Diocese of North Carolina; Women's Missionary Society of the N. C. Conference, Methodist Episcopal Church, South; Woman's Christian Temperance Union.

Mrs. Chamberlain Speaks.

Mrs. J. R. Chamberlain of Raleigh addressed the literature department of the Fayetteville Woman's Club, Wednesday of last week on "The Latter Day Novel." She is giving a series of lectures on "The Development of the Novel" at the Raleigh Woman's Club before a huge and an appreciative group of Raleigh club members. Mrs. Chamberlain is not only a lecturer and author of more than state-wide reputation, but also a trained and enthusiastic club worker. She has served the Raleigh Woman's Club as president and as chairman of the education department. It was during her term as chairman of the committee on legislation of the State Federation that the measure providing for the establishment of Samarcand was enacted into law. The History of Wake County and the Life of Cordelia Phillips Spencer, the two books of which Miss Chamberlain is the author, have created wide interest.

Charlotte Sunday Observer, p. 37 (section 3, p. 9)
Asheville *Sunday Citizen,* p. 21 (section C, p. 5)

23 JANUARY 1927

IDA CLYDE CLARKE LAUDS CLUB WOMEN'S PROGRAM

Commends Governor's Interest in Art; Praises Mrs. Johnson's Work

By Mrs. J. Henry Highsmith

A high compliment was paid the club women of North Carolina by Ida Clyde Clark of New York City, noted lecturer and author, who on her recent visit to the State looked in on a number of women's clubs and saw and heard for herself what they are actually doing. "I think I can say," she said, "that the

North Carolina Federation of Women's Clubs has a finer, more constructive program than any other State Federation that I've come in contact with. You women are at work on big worthwhile things," she said, "and are not spending your time on trivials and non-essentials." "Let me say this," Mrs. Clark continued, "that as long as you undertake big tasks, as long as you are not afraid to tackle big problems and to fight them through you will not only develop big women with vision and leadership but you will be able to hold them. In a number of states where I am more or less familiar with club affairs I know of a dozen or more big women who have been lost to the Woman's Club movement simply because the club program was not big enough to hold them. I became interested in your Federation and the work it is doing two years ago," she added, "when I spoke to you at Pinehurst and I'm glad to see that you are still working harmoniously together for the things that count most, particularly for those measures affecting the welfare of women and children."

Without being questioned Mrs. Clark stated that her mission in Raleigh primarily was to get acquainted with Mrs. Kate Burr Johnson and know something firsthand of the work she is doing. She said that when in other states she sought to learn something of progressive social welfare measures and accomplishments she was referred to the Commissioner of Public Welfare of North Carolina and her corps of welfare workers. Their work, she said, is attracting attention all over the country.

Mrs. Clark expressed surprise at what she called the "wonderful work in humanics" that Mrs. Johnson is doing. She regretted the fact that she had only a few hours to give to the work when, to do it justice, would require several days.

Commends Governor McLean On Interest in Art.

Mrs. Clark thinks North Carolina is to be congratulated on having a Governor that has a mind and taste for more things than those that are strictly political and she added that this is most unusual to find among governors. She said that in the delightful conversation she had with him, she found him interested in a number of projects that would mean a richer and more beautiful state and a happier people. "I found him much interested in Art," she said. "He tells me that a State Art Museum that will be fireproof and adequate for all time will soon be erected. He agreed with me that apparently the State needed to turn its attention to the promotion and cultivation of Art, or suffer by comparison."

Large Crowds Expected at Opening of State Headquarters, Wednesday, the 22nd.

State-wide interest is being shown in the formal opening of Federation Headquarters in Raleigh at the Sir Walter Hotel, Wednesday, January 26th, from 3 to 6 o'clock. Indications are that a large number of club women from every section of the State will be present for the occasion. Mrs. W. T. Bost, executive secretary, says that judging from the plans of the local committee with Federation representatives, the affair will be one of the most delightful social gatherings that the club women have recently attended. Mrs. E. L. McKee, State president of the Federation, who will come to Raleigh a day or two in advance of the opening, states that there will be no ceremony connected with the opening of State Headquarters but that she is anxious for the club women of the State to come together in an informal social gathering to do honor to the occasion which she believes marks an epoch in women's club work in North Carolina. Invitations have been issued directly to the officers, department heads, and chairmen of standing committees of the Federation, to all club presidents and through the club presidents, to every club woman in the State.

Three Junior Clubs, one each at Henderson, Norlina, and Forest City, have been organized and are at work on some worthwhile, community program, writes Mrs. R. D. V. Connor, of Chapel Hill, who is State chairman of Junior Club work. The Henderson club, of which Elizabeth Mills is president and Mrs. J. L. Wister is chairman, has 40 members. The Norlina club, of which L. D. Howard, Jr., is president, has 14 members and the Forest City club with Sara Ruth Daggett, president, and Miss Katherine Goggans, chairman, has 38 members. The Forest City club is composed of the pupils of local music teachers and their present interest is the music memory contest. A prize is offered to the one playing the best hymns from memory.

Mrs. Connor was appointed at the convention held last May in Asheville to head up the Junior Club work in North Carolina—a new feature of club activities. After six months work in setting up her organization and getting it into action she writes that she is most enthusiastic over the possibilities for good that the Junior work promises. She explains the object of the Junior Clubs to be mainly the training of young girls and women to become ready-to-hand instruments to be used by the senior clubs. The organization is especially designed, she says, to give to the large class of girls who finish high school but who do not go to college the opportunity for continued study and training. Furthermore, she says, it meets the need of the young college girl who on her return after four years' absence from her home frequently finds herself without organized association with other young women. In the junior section she will find congenial club members and much of the spirit she found at college.

Two Music Cups Again Offered.

Mrs. J. Edward Kale of Lincolnton, State Music Chairman, announces that only two months remain for competition in the "Original Music Composition Contest," which closes April 1, 1927. All manuscripts must be in her hands by that date, she says. Two Loving Cups, the Duncan and the Florence M. Cooper Music cups, will be awarded this year, one for the best original vocal composition and the other for the best original instrumental composition. Last year and the year before Mrs. Charles B. Wagoner of Concord won the Duncan cup. Her composition, "Take Thou the Rose With All Its Beauty Red," won the cup last year, while the year before her winning composition was "When Earth's Last Picture is Painted," a beautiful setting of Kipling's well known poem.

Mrs. Kale states that the object of the music composition contest is to encourage creative work and musical appreciation in North Carolina. She says much good talent now lies dormant in every community and only needs to be discovered and developed. She hopes by means of the contest that some of this native talent will be developed. She expects a large number of competitors. Last year 20 manuscripts were submitted.

Rural Schools to Hold Music Memory Contests.

To carry the Music Memory Contest to the rural schools of every county in the State is the plan of Mrs. E. E. Randolph of Raleigh, chairman of the Music Memory Contest of the State Federation, and Miss Hattie S. Parrott, assistant State supervisor of rural schools, who have prepared a special bulletin for the purpose which has been published by the state Superintendent of Public Instruction. The object of the contest, says the foreword of the Bulletin, is to develop music appreciation among a larger per cent of the rural school children of the State.

According to Mrs. Randolph, the Music Memory Contest in the rural schools during the two years it has been attempted has been most successful. Last year 26 counties promulgated the work and approximately 75,000 children were given the opportunity to know more music. Mrs. Randolph is expecting one hundred counties to take up the work this year.

Raleigh Sunday *News and Observer,* p. 7
Charlotte Sunday Observer, p. 26 (section 2, p. 12)

30 January 1927

Women Gratified At School Report

Faith In Three Club Women On Educational Commission Fully Justified

MRS. M'KEE FIGURES IN IMPORTANT WORK

Declares She Believes That Work of the Commission Was Well Worth While; and Has Confidence in Ultimate Victory For the Eight Months' Proposal

By Mrs. J. Henry Highsmith

When Governor McLean appointed three prominent club women, Mrs. E. L. McKee of Sylva, Mrs. J. A. Brown of Chadbourn and Mrs. J. G. Fearing of Elizabeth City, as members of the Educational Commission, the club women of the State were highly pleased and felt that they would be of valuable service to the commission. Now that the work of the commission is finished and the majority and minority reports on the eight months' term have been submitted to the Governor and made known to the public, club women are more than gratified that their faith in their three representatives was fully justified.

The stand taken by the three women members of the commission and two of the men members (this constituting the minority report submitted to the Governor) that the State should have an eight months' school term and have it by constitutional amendment, is most heartily approved by the women of the Federation.

Mrs. McKee, who was in Raleigh attending the official opening of the State Federation Headquarters at the Sir Walter Hotel Wednesday afternoon of last week, stated that she believed the work of the commission had been worth while. Although she regretted a minority report had also to be made on the eight months' term, for which she was partly responsible, Mrs. McKee stated that in no other way could she be true to her conscience, to the information she had received from a study of the educational needs of North Carolina, and especially to the 150,000 white rural school children that were looking to the commission for educational opportunities substantially equal to those of city children. Continuing, Mrs. McKee said:

"After an eight months' study of the educational system of the State, including the six months' school term, the eight months' school term, consolidation, teacher training supervision, and many other pertinent things, I am convinced that we are attempting to build an imposing superstructure upon an utterly inadequate foundation. The longer that this condition is allowed to exist," declared Mrs. McKee, "the more difficult and costly will be the adjustment. If it were possible," Mrs. McKee went on to say, "to remedy this situation in less time than three years—the time it will take to put into effect a constitutional amendment—I would heartily favor it, for each year sees thousands of country boys and girls turned out as graduates when as a matter of fact their training equals only standard eighth grade achievement." "This is no guess work," said Mrs. McKee. "Tests made of all high school seniors last spring revealed the fact that according to national standards, the majority were in reality eighth grade pupils, a condition due to lack of educational opportunity."

"The plan suggested to improve and make the most of the six months' school term till a more convenient season to adopt an eight months term, is out of the question," said Mrs. McKee. "In the first place no well-trained teacher will teach in a six months' school when she can teach in an eight or nine months' school. In the second place, she pointed out, no child can do in six months in a rural school the work that is mapped out for a child to do in eight or nine months in a town school. Therefore, when rural school children who finish the elementary grades are transported to a town high school, as statistics show, they, on account of their unpreparedness, often retard the class they enter from a third to a half of its normal progress. The six months' elementary school, then, is a serious drawback to both the city and the rural high school; and consolidation and transportation as effective as they have been, are not able to overcome this deficiency."

Mrs. McKee's acquaintance with the six months' school has come from personal observation and first-hand knowledge. "Since visiting several six months' schools recently," she said with some feeling, "and seeing there 15- and 16-year-old boys and girls doing fifth grade and sixth grade work, not because they are dullards or repeaters, but because they are victims of a State educational system that denies them a decent chance, I am more than ever convinced that the elementary schools should have first consideration and take precedence over all other educational matters, they should have first claim and not the last on the State's resources."

"As it has been heretofore," declared Mrs. McKee, "the rural school children of the State have had no advocate at court and theirs has been the remnant—a mere pittance." She added that it remains for the manhood and womanhood of the State who can see and feel the need of this neglected and inarticulate group of our citizenship to speak out and sponsor their cause.

As to financing an eight months' school term, Mrs. McKee said that she believed a state which has already provided $85,000,000 in bonds for building good roads and now proposes to provide an additional $30,000,000 can certainly find $5,000,000 to equalize the burden of educating her rural school children. She expressed herself as not favoring the State's assuming the whole burden of elementary education, but rather that the burden should be divided between the counties and the State, with the State bearing a much larger part than at present through a greatly increased equalization fund.

While Mrs. McKee recognizes that North Carolina has made progress in an educational way, she feels that it has reached the limit of its educational progress until the State's public school system had been placed on a firm foundation. This can be done only after the State has a minimum eight months' term for all children—rural as well as city. The only practicable, if not the only possible way, of securing an eight months' terms, Mrs. McKee declared, [is] through the expression of the will of the people. She believes that the present General Assembly should have impressed on it the importance of submitting this at this session, so that the people may have the chance to vote two years hence, so that the children may have the opportunity of an eight months' term three years hence.

"I believe," she concluded, "I know the people of my State have the will to educate."

The official opening of State Federation headquarters, held at the Sir Walter Hotel, Raleigh, Wednesday afternoon of last week, met all the delightful expectations of the official members, with one exception, that of the weather, which prevented as large numbers attending the reception as would have been the case if the weather had been favorable.

Hundreds of club women from all over the State were present and in an atmosphere of good feeling and much rejoicing over the realization of one of the club women's fondest dreams, the assembly as it circled the entire mezzanine floor on which headquarters opens, presented a beautiful occasion.

The Raleigh Woman's Club, of which Mrs. R. Y. McPherson is president, was hostess to the visiting club women. Officers and members of the Raleigh club assisted the officers and chairmen of the Federation in receiving. Music was furnished by the Ray Orchestra of Raleigh.

Among those who were present and received were Mr. and Mrs. E. L. McKee, Mrs. Robert R. Cotten, Mrs. R. D. W. Connor, Mrs. E. H. Williamson, Miss Annie Perkinson, Mrs. S. P. Cooper, Mrs. Palmer Jerman, Governor and Mrs. A. W. McLean, Mr. and Mrs. Josephus Daniels, Mr. and Mrs. B. H. Griffin, Miss Carrie McLean, Miss Mary Henderson, Mrs. Kate Burr Johnson, Mrs. J. T. Alderman, Mrs. F. M. Brown, Mrs. J. M. Hobgood, Mrs. Thomas O'Berry, Mrs. Estelle Smith, Miss Gertrude Weil, Mrs. W. J. Brogden, Mrs. W. T. Shore, Miss Nellie Roberson, Mrs. W. T. Bost, Mrs. R. Y. McPherson, Mrs. L. A. Mahler, Mrs. T. W. Bickett, Mrs. Jane McKimmon, Mrs. H. G. Connor, Dr. Delia Dixon Carroll, Mrs. Harold Glascock, Mrs. R. N. Simms, Mrs. E. E. Randolph, Mrs. Louis Cohen, Mrs. Mary O. Cowper, Mrs. Frank B. Sherwood, Mrs. Brock Barkley, Mrs. H. L. Evans, Mrs. J. S. Mitchener, Mrs. M. Rosenthal, Miss Isabel Bowen, Mrs. Murray Allen, Mrs. T. E. Browne and Mrs. Kemp Neal.

Raleigh Sunday *News and Observer,* p. 11 (Society, p. 1)

6 FEBRUARY 1927

CLUB WOMEN INTERESTED IN RESTORATION OF KING COTTON TO PLACE OF SOVEREIGNTY

Committee Named to Make Plans for Wider Consumption of Cotton Products—Federated Clubs Consider Holding "Cotton Day" at State Convention in Durham—Scars on the Highways Receiving Attention of the Women State Headquarters

By Mrs. J. Henry Highsmith

With the feeling that the 53,000 club women of North Carolina through concerted action might at least give a share as their part in the effort that is being made to restore King Cotton to his throne, a committee has been appointed by Mrs. E. L. McKee, president of the State Federation of Women's Clubs, to study the situation and to adopt a program to be carried out by all the club women of the State. The committee composed of Mrs. E. H. Williamson of Fayetteville, chairman, Mrs. C. W. Bradshaw of Greensboro, Mrs. James H. Brodie of Henderson, Miss Ruth Burke of La Grange, Mrs. John L. Gilmer of Winston-Salem, Mrs. S. W. Tucker of Durham and a club member to be named, of Charlotte, met recently in Raleigh the day of the official opening of State Federation Headquarters and formulated plans by which the committee feels the club women of the state can make a worth while contribution to the cotton interests.

According to Mrs. Williamson, chairman of the committee, this is not merely a sentimental move but an undertaking which requires practical common sense and one hundred per cent co-operation to achieve results. In a letter addressed to club presidents, Mrs. Williamson expresses her faith in the earnest efforts of club women to help put King Cotton, who has been deposed and that by a silk worm, back on his throne. She believes that the solution of the cotton problem lies not only in the marketing of raw cotton but also in the consumption at home of cotton products and it is in the latter field that she believes the women by using their wits and combining their efforts will be able to do the greatest good.

Featuring lisle hose in co-operation with merchants, manufacturers, and the schools is one way by which the committee hopes to popularize and thereby increase the consumption of a home cotton product. As fashion already seems to have decreed that lisle hose are to be worn with sport, morning and the plainer costumes during the spring and summer, the first week in March has been set apart for displaying and creating interest in this home made product.

Political Sense.

Among many other ways suggested by the committee for increasing interest in cotton materials is the observance of Cotton Day at the State Convention to be held in Durham in May. On the second day of the Convention, according to the committee, every woman present will be expected to have on a cotton dress. Twelve prizes ranging from $25 and $15 as first and second prizes will be awarded to winning competitors in the cotton dress contest. Three classes of dresses—sport, house and afternoon dresses—will be considered in the contest. Details, rules and regulations governing the contest will be announced at an early date.

[*Charlotte Sunday Observer* continues:]

Scars Along Highways.

Mrs. J. S. Silverstein, of Brevard, president of the second district, writes interestingly about the scars left by progress along the highways and countrysides and asks the pertinent question whether or not progress in the future will be warranted in making as many scars as it has in the past. Where are those lovely groups of trees, those beautiful sections of woodland and picturesque hills along the roads that everyone can so easily recall? she asks.

Sacrificed to progress, she says, and in their places we now have the scars incident to our wonderful hard surfaced highways which are such a joy to all, but lacking in beauty, except in the graceful sweep of their curves. But these same highways, points out Mrs. Silverstein, need not remain devoid of beauty. She says that while trees and shrubs have been needlessly and ruthlessly destroyed because of the indifference of property owners and road workmen, that they should not remain so. But, she says, this work of restoring beauty and making attractive our wonderful system of state highways forming a network of excellent roads throughout the entire length of the state cannot be done by the property owners adjacent to them or by civic, patriotic or social organizations, but to be properly done it must be done by the state. She believes, however, that it is fitting that the club women of the state do whatever they can toward beautifying the highways, whether it is creating sentiment favoring a state improvement fund as well as a plan, or getting out and doing the work themselves. In this connection Mrs. Silverstein points out the fact that we are apt to think of the highway as being only a few feet wider than the paving or about 24 feet wide in all, whereas the actual width of the thousands of miles of narrow strips of land owned by the state and known as state highways is 60 feet. The highways were planned, she says, for the future as well as for the present and if the paving were to be widened to 40 feet there would still remain a strip of land 10 feet wide on either side where selected trees and shrubs could be planted without ever injuring the pavement.

Literary Contest.

Mrs. Elia W. Peattie, of Tryon, state chairman of literature, writes that unusual interest is being shown in the literary contests of this year and she believes that the discovery of much new talent will be the result of this year's competition. It is recalled that three cups are offered this year: the Separk cup for the best poem; the Joseph Pearson Caldwell cup for the best short story; and the Lanier Club cup for the best one-act play having a North Carolina background. Stories are limited to 6,000 words; plays to one act; and poems should be of reasonable length. Manuscripts must be in the hands of Mrs. Pickens Bacon of Tryon not later than April 1. The Federation will retain the book rights to all manuscripts in order that those winning the prizes may be printed in "Stories and Poems of the Old North State" when sufficient material shall have been collected; but writers will own the magazine rights to all manuscripts and so will be able to sell their product. It will therefore involve no sacrifice for writers to send their very best to the

Federation contests. In regard to plays authors may retain the producing rights but the Federation will retain the book rights.

Opening of Headquarters.

Among the many enthusiastic and interesting club women who attended the opening of state headquarters a week or so ago was Mrs. J. M. Moretz of Boone, who came all the way from her mountain home, regardless of the weather, to be present at what she said was one of the happiest occasions of her life. Mrs. Moretz is president of the Worth While Club of her town and has been elected president of the third district to succeed Mrs. Carrie Gamble, whose term of office expires in May. Mrs. Moretz reported many worth while activities that her club is engaged in, one of which is their work with the young people of the community. She stated that at this time she is most concerned with formulating a constructive program to bring before the district clubs when she takes up her work in May.

Pittsboro Woman's Club deserves honorable mention for sending the largest representation of its members to the opening of state headquarters of any club outside of Raleigh. According to the visitors' book in which all visiting club women attending the reception were asked to register, 14 of its 48 members were present for the occasion. For a rainy, cold day in January this was considered an excellent representation. Other towns making a good showing in the number of representatives present were Farmville with five present; Greensboro, seven; Durham, eight; Fayetteville, six; Zebulon, seven; Clayton, eight; Burgaw, eight. Three came down from Statesville. Club women from 38 towns and cities were in attendance. Wilson, Goldsboro, Chapel Hill, Henderson, Charlotte and numbers of other towns were represented by three and four club women.

Charlotte Sunday Observer, p. 53 (section 3, p. 12)
Raleigh Sunday *News and Observer,* p. 29 (Editorial, p. 1), incomplete

13 FEBRUARY 1927

WITH CAROLINA CLUB WOMEN

By Mrs. J. Henry Highsmith

Having advocated the creation of the Great Smoky Mountains National Park since it first became known that such a park was a possibility, the club women of the State are now more than anxious as to the fate of the bill that is before the North Carolina Legislature, which bill authorizes a bond issue of $2,000,000 for the purchase of land to be included in the proposed park. At a recent state convention the club women passed a resolution favoring the creation of a National Park out of that portion of the Great Smoky Mountains lying between North Carolina and Tennessee and urging their senators and representatives at Washington to work in the interest of the park.

Mrs. E. L. McKee, of Sylva, president of the State Federation of Women's Clubs, has been an enthusiastic, active worker for the park, not only in her section of the State but all over North Carolina and in Tennessee. While attending a meeting of the Southeastern Council of Federated Club Women at Chattanooga about a year and a half ago, she presented a resolution and made a speech urging the states represented at the council meeting to work with North Carolina and Tennessee to secure the proposed National Park. The resolution was unanimously adopted.

Club women's first interest in the proposed national park has not been based on the viewpoint that it will be so fine a business investment that the State cannot afford to overlook it, as desirable as that may be, but on the fact that the State is afforded a rare opportunity for conserving just the things it has been losing on a wholesale scale and apparently is without power to check the loss. The club women have seen in the creation of a National Park in Western North Carolina not only virgin forests and some of the most unique and beautiful mountain scenery in the world preserved from spoliation and utter destruction by the ruthless hands of commercialism, but they have seen in it a place where people may go to rest, to play, to re-create themselves—a factor not to be lost sight of or undervalued in the complexities incident to a rapidly developing commonwealth.

Furthermore, the club women saw and appreciated the aesthetic asset that the creation and development of this park would mean to the State. They feel that the beauty alone that would be acquired would fully justify the State spending $2,000,000.

Portrait Of Mrs. Cotten.

The portrait of Mrs. R. R. Cotten, of Farmville, pioneer for the larger education of women, was presented Friday afternoon of last week to the Sallie Southall Cotten Building, a dormitory for girls in the North Carolina College for Women at Greensboro, built a number of years ago and named in honor of her.

In the midst of loved ones and a host of admiring friends, the latter made up of the members of the college faculty, the students, particularly those who occupied rooms in the Sallie Southall Cotten Building and styled themselves the "Boll Weevils," and a large number of intimate friends of the town and from different parts of the State, Mrs. Cotten was honored with a most impressive program and many beautiful tributes. The portrait was presented by her husband, R. R. Cotten, out of the love she feels for the institution and the great work it is doing for the womanhood of the State. It was received by Dr. J. I. Foust on behalf of the institution and will hang in the living room of the Sallie Southall Cotten Building. The portrait, which is a beautiful life size sitting, was painted by Mrs. Clous of Boston, a well known New England artist and a personal friend of Mrs. Cotten. The members of Mrs. Cotten's family who attended the presentation exercises were Mr. and Mrs. Douglas Wesson of Springfield, Mass., Mr. and Mrs. Russell Wiggins of Boston, Mrs. Lon Newton, her granddaughter, of Miami, Oklahoma, and Mrs. Lyman Cotten and son, John, of Salisbury. Among her Federation friends who were present were Mrs. E. L. McKee of Sylva, Mrs. Palmer Jerman, Mrs. Kate Burr Johnson, Dr. Delia Dixon-Carroll and Mrs. J. Henry Highsmith of Raleigh.

Club Women Encouraged.

A certain degree of optimism is felt by the members of the Legislative Council of North Carolina Women over the favorable treatment that the four or five bills which they are sponsoring have had at the hands of the Legislators thus far. This does not mean, however, that they are anticipating success for all of their bills, or even the greater number of them, but they are encouraged over the fact that a more intelligent and sympathetic interest has been shown them which far surpasses anything they received from the Legislature two years ago.

At the time this is written the Australian ballot bill, often referred to as the Fells-Broughton bill, has been reported out of the subcommittee to which it was sent on motion of the joint session of the Elections Committee, and it is expected that it will be out of the committee and voted on early next week. While few objections have been expressed openly against the bill, it is known that there are many who oppose it and who are working hard to defeat it. Miss Mary Henderson of Salisbury, who attended a recent joint session of the Elections Committee of the Senate and the House, spoke effectively in the interest of this bill.

The bill requiring a notice of fifteen days before a marriage license can be issued is now before a subcommittee for amendments and it is expected to be reported out of the committee and also voted on next week. The committee to which the bill was referred for amendments has as members William Dunn, Jr., of Craven, A. D. McLean of Beaufort, and T. J. Moss of Rutherford. At a recent public hearing of Judiciary Committee No. 1, Mrs. W. T. Bost made a most forceful speech in favor of the bill, sometimes called the "Stop and Think Law."

The bill to establish a farm colony for women offenders older than those received at Samarcand, and the bill asking the State to take over the Industrial School for Negro Girls at Efland, have been reported favorably by the Public Welfare Committee and are now awaiting the action of the Appropriations Committee. This will be the status of these bills till after the

Committee on Appropriations is heard from. Mrs. Kate Burr Johnson, Mrs. W. B. Waddill, Mrs. Palmer Jerman and Mrs. Charles G. Doak made strong speeches in the interest of those bills at recent hearings.

Another bill which the Council is most interested in is the "attainment as well as age" clause in the compulsory education law. This bill, which was introduced by Representative Tomas L. Creekmore of Wake at the request of the State Parent-Teacher Association, would require all children under 16 years of age who have not completed the fourth grade to attend school. Mrs. Wiley Swift of Greensboro, state president, spoke in its behalf. This bill has had a favorable report from the committee to which it was referred.

Mrs. McKee At Work.

A program of Federation extension is now being planned by Mrs. McKee, president of the Federation, assisted by Mrs. W. T. Bost, executive secretary of State Federation Headquarters, to be presented at the annual convention in May. Mrs. Bost has been requested to secure through the district presidents a list of the counties in each district having federated clubs and the number of members in each club, also a list of the counties having no clubs, at the same time ascertaining as far as possible why there are no clubs in these counties and the possibilities of organizing clubs.

In regard to this program Mrs. McKee says: "I should like to have this data gathered because I believe we are reaching a point in our growth where further expansion of the Federation should be conducted in a more systematic way and according to definite plans, otherwise we are in danger of becoming over-organized in some sections, while others suffer for lack of organization. I am convinced that wise and intelligent federation extension must be based henceforth on some such information as suggested above."

Mrs. Korner Rounds Out.

Mrs. J. Gilmer Korner of Kernersville, who for twenty-five years has served what is now the Kernersville Woman's Club as president, has resigned and Mrs. F. W. McFarland has been elected in her stead. The Kernersville club was organized in 1901 as an Embroidery Club but two years later it was changed to a woman's club. Of the charter members only two are living, Mrs. Korner and Miss Notre M. Johnson of Oak Ridge. The club has about twenty members and supports three departments—education, health and literature. Last year at the meeting of the Sixth District Mrs. Korner was made Club Mother of that district in appreciation of her long term of untiring service and her faithfulness and devotion to club work, not only in her town but in her district. The club women of her town feel that she has made a valuable contribution to the social and educational life of that community.

Asheville *Sunday Citizen*, p. 21 (section C, p. 8)

20 FEBRUARY 1927

CLUB WOMEN WILL CRUSADE ON SLANG

Federation Will Join National Drive Against Bad Language

FUNNY PAPERS WILL ALSO BE UNDER FIRE

Low Brow Complex and Lip Laziness Declared To Be Underlying
Causes of General Use of Poor English Throughout America Today

By Mrs. J. Henry Highsmith

This week, Feb. 20–26, the club women of the State will muster forces and with the club women of other States go out with their little hatchets, not to cut down cherry trees but to make war on badly spoken English. The first attack will be made on the Indian grunt "nmhum" and "unumph" which are usurping the place of a good American "yes" and "no" and at the same time the slovenly "ya," "yeh" and "nope" will be dealt a blow

The second attack will be made on slang, the variety used so excessively and ill advisedly by high school boys and girls to the disgust of their teachers and to the desperation of their parents. Slang is charged with cheating the user out of a good vocabulary. He uses slang not because it more adequately expresses his emotions and viewpoint but because it is more convenient. He does not have to think. Therefore slang used excessively impoverishes the vocabulary, cripples thought, stunts ideas and marks the user as a "polly" [a parrot] continually repeating what he has picked up from others.

A third attack will be made on the coarse and often vulgar English of the "Funny Papers." This source of bad English is considered a serious one on account of its undermining influence, particularly upon the young. It works its greatest mischief upon the tiny tots who, when spread out on their "tummies" on the floor with their heels in the air, and in this receptive mood, drink in every word that falls from the lips of the would-be funny actors.

Another source of unrefined English as well as cheap sentiment is said to be that of the popular songs which sweep the country now and then like an epidemic of measles or whooping cough; first, through the cities and towns and thence out into the country districts. And the worst of it is, the young and the old are found to be susceptible at each visitation. One attack does not render immunity.

After searching for some of the underlying causes of so general a use of poor English which seems to be on the increase, two reasons have been assigned. The first is that we are afflicted with a "low brow" complex, and the second is that "lip laziness" is a most prevalent disease in America, affecting the speech of millions of people with nothing being done about it.

To the latter is charged the habit of careless pronunciation and chopping off more than one syllable words, which produces the effect of "Slovenly Speech Spoken by Slovenly Minds."

To the "low brow" complex is charged such offenses as belittling the use of pure and correct English, particularly the more expressive and well chosen words, when slang and the over-worked, commonplace varieties could have been used. As one writer expresses it, "It is that peculiarity of Americans to think it superior to be inferior." Another one says it is that consuming fear of being called "high brow."

While the club women of the country feel that the language will probably never be brought back to the dignity of the King James Bible and the works of Shakespeare, they are demanding at least a respectable handling of the mother tongue and they are counting on schools, colleges, churches, clubs, radios, and newspapers to take the lead in the campaign.

Mrs. Charles M. Platt, of Asheville, is chairman of Better Speech work in the North Carolina Federation of Women's Clubs. Every club in the Federation is expected to observe Better Speech Week in February or March, but the date is left to the convenience of the club. Mrs. Platt says that North Carolinians of all people in the country are expected to use good English on account of the fact that their parentage with the exception of three-tenths of one per cent is Anglo Saxon. For this reason she urges North Carolina club women to take the lead in the interest of Better Spoken English and to observe Better Speech Week in their communities this spring.

[Asheville, Charlotte papers continue:]

Paintings For Schools.

Mrs. Katherine Pendleton Arrington, of Warrenton and New York city, president of the North Carolina State Art Society, announces that to date 10 paintings valued at more than $10,000 have been purchased and placed in North Carolina public schools. The paintings were purchased according to the plan Mrs. Arrington suggested to the schools over a year ago, which was that to every $500 raised by the children of a school she would add $500, making $1,000 with which to buy a painting. Five of the 10 paintings go to high schools—one each to Durham, Wilson, Raleigh, Greensboro and Warrenton. One goes to a public school in Charlotte. One is to be presented as a prize for the best essay by a school boy or girl on art purchases for schools.

These pictures include representative works by Waugh, Sargent, Kendal, Jonas Lie, Jean McLane, Dougherty, Vincent, Couse and McIlhenny. Mrs. Arrington writes that the work of the State Art Society for this year will be directed toward raising funds for establishing a State Art Museum at Raleigh and to foster art appreciation by giving periodic exhibitions and lectures and by placing good pictures in the schools. Mrs. Arrington feels that the State is making substantial progress in the way of art and believes that its program of progress has only begun.

Picture Memory Contest.

A movement that promises to stimulate interest in good pictures and increase art appreciation is the picture memory contest, which Mrs. R. L. McMillan, of Raleigh, state chairman of art, and Miss Minnie Martin, of Raleigh, state chairman of picture memory contest, have planned for school children from the fifth grade through the senior high school. A distinct group of masterpieces in painting will be selected for study in the contest, the study grouped according to the interest and age of the children.

The state contest will be held in Raleigh the latter part of April or first of May. Cities and towns will hold preliminary contests to determine the representatives to be sent to Raleigh. The plan of conducting the picture memory contest will be similar to the music memory contest and as great results expected from the new undertaking as the older one has known.

Art Lecture.

George S. Dutch, art director, George Peabody College, has been chosen as one of the speakers on the general program of the state teachers' meeting which will be held in Raleigh, March 24, 25 and 26. Mr. Dutch will speak on "The Place of Art in the Curriculum." He will also address the section on art. Miss Minnie Martin who is chairman of the art section of the North Caroline Educational Association, feels that the cause of art education will receive an impetus to go forward on hearing Mr. Dutch on this occasion.

Raleigh Sunday *News and Observer,* p. 33 (Editorial, p. 1)
Asheville *Sunday Citizen,* p. 27 (section C, p. 5)
Charlotte Sunday Observer, p. 24 (section 2, p. 12)

27 FEBRUARY 1927

WITH CAROLINA CLUB WOMEN

By Mrs. J. Henry Highsmith

To save the home from the junk heap to which it seems to be destined, along with the family couch, the spinning wheel and grandmother's trailing skirts, is one of the chief concerns of club women today all over the country, North Carolina club women included, who are engaged in serious efforts and study to find out the true status of the American home. Such questions as What's wrong with the home? Why doesn't it function? And, where's the good old home of yesterday? are not to go unanswered.

Statements to the effect that crime for the most part is traceable to the home, that failures are homemade and that the wrongs of church or state usually have their origin in the home, are to be carefully analyzed and questioned as to whether or not they are truthful assertions.

The pessimist's doctrine that the home is a failure, that it is no longer maintaining its high standards of living, that it is an artificial institution not able to meet the challenge of this age of science and democracy, and that as such, just as well as discarded along with other things that have lost their usefulness, is to be considered for whatever it is is worth.

Club women feel that an attack upon the home is an attack upon their citadel. It is an invasion upon their rightful domain. And while they feel called upon to defend it from abuse and desecration, at the same time they are not unmindful of the fact that the home as an institution has not kept pace with other institutions in progress and development and is today reaping censure for its backwardness. They realize that the home is now in the confusion and uncertainty of a transition period, and that in order to have it pass safely through and make a new and wise adjustment, it must he kept intact and guided in the right direction. This they feel is their place and time of action, a call to come to the rescue of the American home and help a new generation to build a structure of physical and spiritual beauty that will meet the profoundest needs of humanity.

To this end, the club women of the country will spend four days next week, March 8, 9, 10 and 11, in Des Moines, Ia., studying all the problems of the home. The meeting is known as the First American Homes National Congress and has been called by Mrs. Mary Sherman, president of the General Federation of Women's Clubs, who never tires of working for a more efficient and happy home. She says of this congress: "I think that it is well worth our while in these crowded, unsettled times, when substitutes for the genuine things of life are being sought on every hand, to spend four days of concentration upon keeping the American home intact as we propose to do at our First American Homes National Congress to be held in Des Moines March 8 to 11.

"For such an institution as the home there can be no substitute. Our citizenship is based upon it. Let us protect it and improve it. Let us, both men and women, regard homemaking as a profession and as a God-given duty, conducting it with the same attention and precision that we give to our business institutions, adding to these efforts the spiritual qualities that tend to keep life in the right channels."

A definite accomplishment in the interest of home-making which the club women hope to bring about this year is securing recognition in the census of the United States for the housekeeper or homemaker—to have homemaking rated as a profession or trade and to receive the same consideration from the government as other professions or trades.

Is All Well With Working Child?

When the Legislature killed in short order recently the bill to limit the working day of women and children, also the attainment as well as age bill that would require all children under 16 years who have not completed the Fourth grade to attend school, the impression went out that all was well with the working children in the Old North State. There was little or no discussion of the subjects and there was left a general feeling of well-being except in the hearts and minds of those who know.

A study made of the child labor laws in ten Southern states by the Legislative Council of North Carolina Women shows that North Carolina ranks lowest in care of her children. Children under 16 years of age may be worked 11 hours a day or 60 hours a week in North Carolina but not in any other Southern state, except Georgia. South Carolina has a 10-hour day or a 55-hour week; Florida has a 9-hour day or 54-hour week; and the six other states have an 8-hour day or either a 44 or 48-hour week. All have earlier hours for quitting work. Seven of the ten states forbid the working of children under 14 years, but in this state boys between 13 and 14 by ruling of the child welfare commission may work 8 hours a day except in certain prohibited industries. Furthermore, no limit is put on the number of hours children under 16 years may work in stores and other places not considered factories or manufacturing establishments.

In view of the lack of interest that is now being taken in the child labor situation, the editor of the Woman's Home Companion most pertinently asks: "Has the slavery of boys and girls been abolished? Are there no more greedy parents and employees? Do youngsters who ought to be in school or at play no longer work in factories, in mines, in sweatshops or on the streets at night? That is nonsense of course. Conditions are just as bad and perhaps worse than they were three years ago when the campaign for a constitutional amendment was at its height.

"Deceived by lies, confused by false statistics, scared by tommyrot about states' rights, the voters rejected the amendment. At that time many large promises were made that if the constitution were left untouched the several states could be depended upon to pass their own laws restricting child labor. What of those promises?

"Meanwhile children are laboring all day long and every day; they are being injured, weakened in health, dying; they are being cheated out of their schooling and their right to play."

Asheville Sunday Citizen, p. 27 (section C, p. 7)

13 MARCH 1927

LOAN FUND IS AID TO HUNDRED GIRLS

Sallie Southall Cotten Loan Fund Now Totals Over $15,000

KEEPS 25 GIRLS IN COLLEGE THIS YEAR

*While Fund Is Supported Largely By Volunteer Donations Made
By Clubs, Many Individuals Make Personal Donations Annually;
203 Clubs Participate*

By Mrs. J. Henry Highsmith

Having aided 104 girls to get a college education and not having lost a penny, is the record of the State Federation of Women's Clubs through its educational loan fund, known as the Sallie Southall Cotten Loan Fund. The value of this fund today is $15,000. The amount of the fund that is available this year is $4,000 and is being used to keep about twenty-five girls in college.

During the fourteen years existence of this educational undertaking of the club women, 220 notes covering loans to over a hundred girls have been carried by the Federation with no losses and with the most satisfactory results in scores of grateful, talented young women having been equipped with a college education. To Mrs. E. M. Land, of Statesville, the present efficient chairman of the fund, and to Miss Carrie Hoffman, of Statesville, and to Mrs. Charles E. Platt, of Charlotte, the other member of the committee, is attributed much credit not only for the careful use and wise administration of the fund but also for the phenomenal growth it has had during the past three or four years.

While the Fund is supported largely from volunteer donations made by the clubs, many individuals make personal pledges annually. Two individuals have made loans of $100 each for a period of four years without interest. When the four year period has passed, one of the loans was reloaned for another four years. At the annual meeting of the Federation in 1923 at Winston-Salem Mrs. S. P. Cooper, of Henderson, presented in the name of her little daughter Mary Louise Jackson Cooper a $1,000 North Carolina bond to the Fund to be used for a period of fifteen years without interest. Donations from the clubs have shown a steady increase from $250 in 1913, the year the loan fund was launched, to $2,100, the amount donated by the clubs in 1926. The number of clubs contributing has increased from 67 in 1925 to 203 in 1926.

But the gift that probably more than any other made the loan fund possible and the personality that has been the inspiration of the movement and not a small factor in determining its success have been those of Mrs. R. R. Cotten, in whose honor the education loan fund was named. At a meeting of the Federation held in New Bern in May, 1913, the Sallie Southall Cotten Loan Fund was established and was named for Mrs. Cotten not because she was then the retiring president and not merely because it would be a fitting tribute to the mother of the Federation, as Mrs. Cotten is affectionately called, but because the education of young women was her hobby. Every club woman who knew Mrs. Cotten knew with what zeal she championed the cause of educational opportunities for young girls. She labored in season and out that women might have educational opportunities equal to those of men. She worked faithfully with the legislators in the interest of all measures having to do with the uplift and education of the young womanhood of the State. And today while Mrs. Cotten has already passed her eightieth milestone, there is not a more ardent advocate of an eight months school term for all the children of the State than she, and no one would more willingly ascend the platform to urge its adoption.

Recognition of Mrs. Cotten's interest in and work for the education of young women was made several years ago when the trustees of what is now the North Carolina College for Women at Greensboro named for her one of the large dormitories for girls—the Sallie Southall Cotten Building. President J. I. Foust, writing recently, said "I am writing to endorse most heartily the Sallie Southall Cotten Loan Fund. In the first place the North Carolina Federation of Women's Clubs could not select anyone whom they could more fittingly honor than Mrs. Cotten. Mrs. Cotten's service to North Carolina has been unique and helpful in every way."

The first gift to the Sallie Southall Cotten Loan Fund, $500, was made by Mrs. Cotten's children in appreciation of the honor accorded her at the time the movement was launched. Another contribution made by Mrs. Cotten herself was the writing of a booklet of Negro folk-lore stories, "What Aunt Dorcas Told Little Elsie," the proceeds from the sale of which booklet were to be applied to the educational fund. By this means a substantial sum has been added to the fund.

This Year Greatest in History of Loan Fund.

Mrs. Land predicts that this year will be the greatest year in the history of the loan fund. She says that while the pledges of this year were $1,500, the treasurer has already received $1,700 and that April is usually the month in which the bulk of the donations is made. Furthermore, Mrs. Land says that demands for loans have been greater than ever before and that the club women are responding with an interest and enthusiasm that she has never seen before. In regard to turning away girls who ask for help, Mrs. Land says it is a serious thing. It may mean denying them the opportunity which they are seeking through education of finding themselves. But she explains that consideration is given to the girls already in school before extending aid to new applicants. Money is loaned without interest during the girl's term in college and for two years after leaving college. She is given two years in which to meet the payments after she becomes self-supporting.

Mrs. C. C. Hook, of Charlotte, Mrs. S. I. Dill, Jr., of New Bern, and Mrs. J. S. Williams have each served as chairman of the fund.

Raleigh Sunday *News and Observer,* p. 9 (Society, p. 1)
Asheville *Sunday Citizen,* p. 29 (section C, p. 7)
Charlotte Sunday Observer, p. 30 (section 3, p. 4)

20 March 1927

Club Women Meet In Durham In May

New Feature of Federation Will Be Club Institute On May 5

By Mrs. J. Henry Highsmith

The twenty-fifth annual convention of the North Carolina Federation of Women's Clubs will be held in Durham, May 2–5, at the Washington Duke Hotel with the Woman's Club of Durham as hostess. Mrs. E. L. McKee of Sylva, president of the Federation, and Mrs. W. J. Brogden of Durham, president of the Durham Woman's Club, are both engaged in making plans for the convention, which they declare will surpass any previous state meeting in attendance and in points of interest. Four full days instead of three as formerly will be given to conducting the affairs of the Federation.

While the program is not yet complete it is understood that a number of prominent club women known throughout the country not only for the high positions they hold, but also for the outstanding accomplishment they have been able to achieve, will attend the convention and will take important parts on the program. In addition, many new features of unusual interest to club women are being introduced into the four-day program by this year's convention.

Club Institute Will Be Held.

One new and interesting feature of the convention will be the launching and holding of a club institute on Thursday, May 5, the last day of the convention, for the purpose of studying and adopting more efficient methods for carrying on the work of local clubs as well as of the Federation. The main object of the institute will be to instruct club women as to the best methods of running the machinery of their clubs or departments so as to get the maximum of efficiency with the minimum of effort. The committee in charge of arrangements for the institute are Mrs. Eugene Reilly, of Charlotte, chairman; Mrs. J. T. Alderman, of Henderson, and Mrs. John L. Gilmer, of Winston-Salem.

A practical and forward looking program containing subjects of vital interest to every enterprising club woman has been prepared by the committee. The names of those appearing on the program for talks and discussions are Mrs. E. L. McKee, Mrs. R. R. Cotten, Mrs. J. T. Alderman, Mrs. John L. Gilmer, Mrs. C. C. Hook, Miss Adelaide Fries, Mrs. Palmer

Jerman, Mrs. Kate Burr Johnson, Mrs. Jane McKimmon, Mrs. S. P. Cooper, Mrs. J. A. Yarbrough, and Mrs. J. Henry Highsmith.

The institute will be opened Thursday morning by Mrs. McKee, who will make a short address setting forth the plans and needs for a club institute. Mrs. Cotten will outline the main objectives to be accomplished through a one-day institute. Mrs. Alderman will discuss club organization, including the three kinds of clubs, namely, cultural, civic, and the department club, and will also discuss the qualifications and responsibilities of officers, committees and chairmen. Mrs. Gilmer will lead the discussion of the different methods of electing officers. Mrs. Hook will treat general finance and Miss Fries, the budget.

Mrs. Jerman will talk on the value of having a Legislative Council, also the purpose of passing resolutions. Mrs. Johnson will discuss the relation of the Woman's Club to civic and welfare groups; Mrs. McKimmon, the relation of city to rural clubs; Mrs. Cooper, the relation of the General Federation to the State Federation and to local clubs. Club ethics and platform courtesies will be discussed by Mrs. Yarbrough and the place of publicity by Mrs. Highsmith.

While the club institute idea is new in North Carolina, club women feel that it will be firmly established with this endeavor and will become a fixed institution in connection with club and educational affairs in the State.

South Carolina was a pioneer State in holding club institutes, having conducted these regularly for fourteen years in connection with the State Normal College at Rock Hill. Many other States have followed in her steps.

But the club institute plan was developed and made general under the direction of Mrs. Thomas G. Winter, then president of the General Federation, at Chautauqua, New York, July, 1923. Since then a large number of states have established the club institute as a regular feature of club work.

[Continues in Asheville and Charlotte papers:]

Congratulate Miss Fries.

The women throughout the state are rejoicing with Miss Adelaide Fries over the recent publication of her third book on the History of the Moravians of North Carolina and particularly over the high praise that has been given her work by the press and by prominent historians of the state. Her third volume covers that interesting period of North Carolina between 1776–1779 and is of particular interest as it preserves a contemporaneous account of life in western North Carolina in those eventful days. Col. S. A. Ashe, of Raleigh, than whom there is no a more able and just critic, particularly of historical merit, in North Carolina, says of Miss Fries' work: "By the publication of her third volume on the Moravians of North Carolina, Miss Adelaide Fries has added greatly to the obligation the state recognizes because of her difficult achievement in translating the records of the Moravians in North Carolina.

As far as I know, she stands at the head of all the women in this country in such excellent literary work. In this state there certainly is no other who approaches her." "Again," he says, after reviewing her book, "let me give unbounded praise to Miss Fries for her great achievement. Those who wish to promote literary effort and culture here at home cannot do better than by manifesting in every way their appreciation of Miss Fries' work and their admiration of her great performance."

Miss Fries' continued success in writing the history of North Carolina along with that of the Moravians of the state is most pleasing to her club friends. At the convention of the Federation in Asheville last year she was made Historian of the Federation. Since the founding of the Federation in Winston-Salem in 1902, Miss Fries has been closely associated with all of its activities and interests. She served as president from 1913–1915 and has headed a number of important departments and committees.

Asheville Prize.

As the club year begins to draw nearer to its close and accounts are taken of achievements, more inquiries are being made by the clubs in the interest of the $100 prize which the Asheville Chamber of Commerce is offering to the club which performs this year the greatest service in civic advancement of home, community or state. A number of clubs which have been active in community work and which feel through their accomplishments that they are eligible to compete for the prize are awaiting anxiously to know the details and regulations governing the prize. In fairness to the clubs competing and in the interest of a high type of club service to the community which the offer of the prize is supposed to stimulate. It is time that full information concerning the prize be given out. Perhaps this information may be had from the secretary of the Asheville Chamber of Commerce. A joint committee from the Chamber of Commerce and the Federation were to adopt rules and regulations governing the contest.

For years art workers and enthusiasts have endeavored to stimulate an interest in art that would eventually lead to a general awakening and appreciation of art in North Carolina. Thus far results have been slow to manifest themselves. But here and there are signs which show that their efforts have not been in vain and that a greater interest and appreciation of art in North Carolina than ever before. Furthermore it is now known that the right beginning has been made with the school children. The recent interest taken by the high schools of the state in the art contest staged by the Grand Central Art Galleries of New York, and the success of the Wilson High School, particularly the honor won by Harry Finch of Wilson in securing the prize picture, "Filet Blue," by Harry Vincent, an oil painting of ships in dock, valued at $1,250, is indicative of the new interest in art that is rapidly becoming statewide.

Grand Central Prize.

That the Wilson High School through the paper of Harry Finch and under the auspices of the Woman's Club of Wilson, won the Grand Central prize over the high schools of other states in the union is considered by the club women of the State as a great victory for the whole state. The offer was made by Walter L. Clark, president of the Grand Central Art Galleries, of New York, to any state in which as many as five paintings or bronzes with a value of $1,000 or more each are purchased for schools through that association in a single year, the prize given to be a picture or bronze of equal value. North Carolina came within the conditions of the contest as Mrs. Peter Arrington, of Warrenton, president of the North Carolina Art Society, had aided seven high schools in the state in the acquiring of seven pictures each having a value of from $1,000 to $2,000, she paying half of the cost of each and the schools the other half. The seven schools that purchased pictures with Mrs. Arrington's aid are those at Raleigh, Wilson, Warrenton, Charlotte, Greensboro, Wilmington, and Durham. Essays were sent from all these schools on the subject of the best way to raise funds for the purchase of pictures under the Arrington offer. Decision was made by a committee of New York judges. The class of 1927 of the Wilson High School raised the money for the half payment of "Under the Moon," one of the seven pictures distributed by Mrs. Arrington. The work was done under the auspices of the art department of the Woman's Club of Wilson, Mrs. Margaret W. Spiers, chairman of that department.

> *Note:* Adelaide Fries (1871–1949), an archivist, was a distinguished scholar and historian of the Moravian Church in and around Winston-Salem.

Asheville *Sunday Citizen,* p. 29 (section C, p. 7)
Charlotte *Sunday Observer,* p. 30 (section 3, p. 4)
Raleigh Sunday *News and Observer,* p. 24 (Sports section, p. 4), incomplete

27 MARCH 1927

TWENTY-FIFTH CONVENTION NORTH CAROLINA FEDERATION OF CLUBS
MEETS IN DURHAM

**Mrs. John D. Sherman President of the General Federation
Will Be Guest of Honor—Cotton Reception Will Be Feature of
the Meeting—Four Days Replete With Interest Will Be Offered—
Breakfast and Luncheon Conferences Will Be Arranged**

By Mrs. J. Henry Highsmith

Featuring the twenty-fifth annual convention of the North Carolina Federation of Women's Clubs, to be held in Durham May 2–5, will be the address and presence of Mrs. John D. Sherman of Chicago and Estes Park, Colorado, president of the General Federation of Women's Clubs, celebration of the twenty-fifth anniversary of the founding of the State Federation, a "cotton" reception and a club institute.

Call For Convention.

According to the call for the convention recently issued by Mrs. E. L. McKee, president of the Federation, the convention will open Monday evening and close Thursday at noon. The Washington Duke Hotel will be headquarters for the convention.

Local clubs are asked to send their full quota of representatives, but a general invitation and a cordial welcome is extended to all interested club women to attend the business sessions and social functions.

Breakfast and luncheon conferences which have proved so beneficial at previous state conventions have been arranged for this convention. Monday, the first day, will be given over to the meetings of the executive board, the board of trustees and the board of directors. The opening session Monday evening will be featured by the address of Mrs. McKee, president. Mrs. Sherman's address will be Tuesday evening and the celebration of the Federation's twenty-fifth birthday will be held Wednesday evening. Thursday morning's session will be given over to the club institute. On Wednesday afternoon a "Cotton" reception will be held and at 6:30 Wednesday evening will be the annual Federation dinner.

Mrs. McKee calls attention to the fact that all resolutions to be presented to the convention must be in the hands of the resolutions committee two weeks prior to the opening of the convention. Miss Adelaide Fries of Winston-Salem is chairman of the committee. The other members are Mrs. W. T. Bost of Raleigh, Mrs. C. C. Hook of Charlotte, Mrs. W. B. Waddill of Henderson, and Mrs. Jane McKimmon of Raleigh.

Rural Women's Clubs.

An active club that is serving well its community is the Chowan Woman's Club of Meege, twelve miles from Edenton on the public highway. With twenty-five live women as members, this club not only keeps abreast with the larger clubs of cities in the kind and quality of their work but they leave them behind when it comes to raising money for community enterprises. Recently the club spent $950 to furnish the Chowan High School auditorium with an attractive and serviceable stage equipment. This consisted of an indoor scene, an outdoor scene, a set of lights of different colors and a drop curtain for local advertisements. Prior to this the club purchased a heavy velour curtain for the stage which adequately completes their auditorium stage equipment. Another donation made recently by the club was $91 to the basket ball team of the high school.

The club meets regularly twice a month. Programs of public welfare citizenship and literary studies are carried out. One meeting each month is with the Home Demonstration agent. Mrs. J. L. Savage is president of the club. Other active members are Mrs. K. K. Hollowell, Mrs. E. N. Elliott, Mrs. B. W. Evans and Miss M. W. Winborne, secretary pro tem.

Every home in the Rhodes-Rhyne village in Lincoln County can now boast of a peach, apple and fig tree as well as a grape vine as a result of a community wide fruit-tree planting which took place there last week when officials and operatives of the mill with the assistance of the county agent set out over a hundred trees. The school children also took part in the tree planting exercises.

As a part of her work as president of the fourth district of Federated Women's Clubs, Mrs. F. H. Chamberlain conceived the idea of planting fruit trees in all the mill villages in this district, believing that in each case the trees would be a valuable asset not only in the amount of fruit to be obtained but in building up a more contented class of laborer. D. F. Rhodes, president of the Rhodes-Rhyne mill concurred in the idea and immediately purchased 100 trees for his village.

Mrs. Cotten's Picture.

Members of the Woman's Club and Literary Club of Farmville have asked the privilege of giving to State Federation Headquarters a picture of Mrs. R. R. Cotten who is known as the mother of the Federation and a who is now its honorary president. Mrs. Cotten is a member of both the Farmville clubs. Mrs. W. T. Bost, executive secretary of headquarters, in acknowledging the offer made by Mrs. J. G. Spencer, secretary, says that she knows of nothing that would make the club women of the state feel more at home on their visits to Federation Headquarters than a picture of Mrs. Cotten always here to greet them.

Elizabeth City Elects.

The Woman's Club of Elizabeth City at a recent meeting elected officers and committees for the next year. Mrs. J. G. Fearing will serve again as president; Mrs. J. H. White, Mrs. W. D. Glover, and Mrs. W. L. Cohoon were elected vice presidents; Mrs. E. F. Aydlett, recording secretary; Mrs. J. C. Rodney, corresponding secretary; and Mrs. E. T. Burgess, treasurer.

At this meeting the treasurer's report showed that $1,000 has been paid during the past year on the indebtedness of the club house, leaving a balance of $2,781.25 and interest of $190.60 yet to be paid. But the club [expects] to meet all payments as they come due and have their club home free of indebtedness in a few more years.

Charlotte Sunday Observer, p. 23 (section 2, p. 9)

3 April 1927

Fleecy Staple Regaining Its Popularity With Women

Wear Cotton Movement Spreading Over Nation Says Mrs. Williamson

WORK OF FEDERATION OF WOMEN'S CLUBS IS ATTRACTING
ATTENTION EVERYWHERE—NEW YORK AND PHILADELPHIA
HAVE SHOWN A SYMPATHETIC INTEREST SINCE THE
BEGINNING—LARGE DEPARTMENT STORES DISPLAYING
DRESSES—COTTON DAY AT FEDERATION CONVENTION

By Mrs. J. Henry Highsmith

Whether or not the club women of the state have had little or much to do
with the fact that cotton is coming back and that cotton fabrics are declared
to be one of fashion's latest decrees, it is certain that a nationwide movement
is getting under way to bring cotton to its own, and North Carolina club
women are proud that they have been given a place in the forefront of the
profession, says Mrs. E. L. Williamson of Fayetteville, chairman of the
committee appointed by the State Federation of Women's Clubs to promote
the interest of cotton goods.

Interest Exhibited.

According to Mrs. Williamson to Mrs. Williamson, who has just returned
from New York and Philadelphia, where she went in the interest of the "Wear
Cotton" movement, the work of the committee of the Federation of Women's
Clubs is attracting much attention in other sections than the south. New
York, she says, has shown a cooperative and sympathetic interest from the
beginning. Letters of inquiry and interest have come from different parts of
the country where there are cotton interests, and their spirit has been one
also of appreciation and cooperation.

"I was most encouraged," says Mrs. Williamson, "on returning to New
York this time to find everywhere a favorable sentiment being manifested
towards cotton goods. The large department stores were displaying cotton
dresses of the most expensive models and elaborate designs, and the persons
with whom I talked, those who are in a position to know, say that they have
reasons to believe that in the near future cotton will regain the popularity it
held a number of years ago.

Support Given.

"As to the success of the movement here in the state, I have been most
gratified with the enthusiastic responses which our suggestions have met
and with the wholehearted support that has been given our programs not
only by the clubs but also by the schools, merchants, newspapers, and the
various civic and social organizations. Nearly every town in the state has
had or is planning to have some kind of a 'wear cotton' demonstration, and
as a result of these the sale of cotton goods is said to be increasing."

The merchants of one town, says Mrs. Williamson, after observing cotton week in their stores, mainly by attractive widow displays of cotton goods, special advertising on the part of the merchants and the wearing of print cotton dresses by the clerks, reported that their sale of cotton goods showed an increase of approximately 50 per cent, and that the outlook is for the best business in cotton piece goods that they have had in recent years.

But the victory is not won, declares Mrs. Williamson, who is urging women's clubs and civic organizations to carry on until King Cotton is again enthroned. While a most favorable beginning has been made, says Mrs. Williamson, success in the end will depend upon the women who wear and buy the larger part of all cotton products. Their cooperation must be had and to secure this is the particular work of the women's clubs.

Cotton Reception.

Cotton Day at the annual convention of the State Federation that is to be held in Durham, May 2–5, will be featured by a reception held Wednesday afternoon, May 4. from 4 to 6 o'clock, at which time a cotton dress contest will be held. All club women attending the convention and reception, whether delegates or not, will be expected to wear cotton dresses and take part in the contest. Dresses competing for prizes are to be made by the wearer.

According to the committee, three classes of dresses will be given consideration in the contest: sport, afternoon and house dresses. The first prize offered is $25; the second, $15; and the third and fourth are manufactured articles such as spreads, towels, sheets pillow cases, dress goods and hose.

Another feature of the contest will be an exhibition of the prize-winning dresses from the high schools of the state. Prizes will be awarded the winning schools at the same time they are awarded winners in the Federation contest. The other members of the committee who are assisting Mrs. Williamson are: Mrs. C. W. Bradshaw, Greensboro; Mrs. James Brodie, Henderson; Miss Ruth Burke, La Grange; Mrs. S. W. Tucker, of Durham, and Mrs. J. L. Staten, of Charlotte.

Music Memory Contest.

The music memory contest of the rural schools of the state will be held at the Woman's Club in Raleigh Friday, April 29, at 11 o'clock. Mrs. E. E. Randolph, of Raleigh, chairman of the rural contest committee, says that this is the third music memory contest in which rural school children have taken a part and that it promises to be the largest yet held.

Miss Ethel Kelly, rural supervisor of Caldwell County, says that 478 pupils of that county are entering the county music memory contest and that 400 more pupils are listening in and receiving training. Miss Carrie D. Wilson, rural supervisor of Nash county, says that 40 pupils will enter the contest to be held early next month and that representatives will be sent to the state contest to be held in Raleigh. The music memory contest for town and city schools will be held in Lincolnton, Saturday, April 9, at 10 o'clock in the high school auditorium. Mrs. J. Edward Kale, of Lincolnton, chairman of the town school contest, reports that unusual interest is being shown in the approaching contest. Two prizes arc offered: one a silver loving cup given by Mrs. Kale, will go to the high school winning in the contest; the other, a portable Columbia phonograph given by the Columbia Phonograph Company will be given to the elementary school winning. Two contestants from each of the 16 districts are eligible,

Present Pictures.

An outstanding event in the art circle of the Wilson Woman's Club and the Wilson High School will be the visit of Walter L. Clark, of New York city, president of the Grand Central Art Galleries, and Mrs. Kate Pendleton Arrington, of Warrenton and New York, who will come to Wilson for the presentation of the two pictures recently acquired from the Grand Central Galleries. The presentation of the pictures is scheduled to take place Saturday evening, April 2 at the Woman's Club, at which time the art department of the club will hold a reception in honor of the senior class of the high school, which class is given much of the credit for securing the pictures.

Mrs. J. A. Spiers, chairman of the art department of the Wilson Woman's Club, recognized in the proposition Mrs. Arrington made to the State Federation when in convention session last spring at Asheville "the finest opportunity we have ever had to develop art appreciation in our schools." At the opening of the high school in the fall she set about to interest the school in Mrs. Arrington's offer to give $500 or more to any school or community of North Carolina raising a like amount for the purpose of purchasing a picture painted by a contemporary American artist.

The proposition was accepted by the senior class and in less than six months they had not only secured one painting but two. The second was won through an essay contest in which a member of the class won signal honor net only for his school and town but for his state.

In her work with the Wilson school, Mrs. Spiers has demonstrated that Mrs. Arrington's proposition is both practical and feasible. As chairman of art education by ownership of the Federation art department, Mrs. Spiers is urging the art derailments of clubs to accept Mrs. Arrington's offer, which is still open. She will advise any chairman or person interested in the undertaking.

Mrs. Gaskins In Charge.

Mrs. C. Whit Gaskins, of Asheville, state chairman of civics, has been put in charge of the civics contest in which the Asheville Chamber of Commerce is offering a $100 prize for the best piece of club work that will give information concerning the rules and regulations governing the contest. The prize will be awarded the winner at the meeting of the State Federation in May.

Charlotte Sunday Observer, p. 33 (section 3, p. 5)

10 APRIL 1927

WITH CAROLINA CLUB WOMEN

By Mrs. J. Henry Highsmith

Club women's greatest gain from the 1927 Legislature was not the passage of three of their five measures, as significant as that was, says Mrs. Palmer Jerman of Raleigh, president of the Legislative Council of North Carolina Women, but it was in the lessons they learned, not only in regard to general political methods and psychology but also in regard to their own methods and policies. While women in politics have come a long way in a few short years, she says, there's much for them to learn in order to make much headway or attain any degree of success.

"And at this point," says Mrs. Jerman, "I want to congratulate the club women who worked during the past Legislature well informed and certain as to how their women constituents stood in regard to the measures contained in the women's legislative program."

"Defeat of the Australian Ballot Bill was the club women's greatest disappointment," according to Mrs. Jerman, in whose opinion the passage of the bill has only been deferred till the session of the next Legislature. She says that the bill has passed from the academic into the political stage, that its abstract theories have all been established and that it now has to pass the stage of political bickering to become a law. She believes it will have easy passage two years hence.

The three bills of the women's legislative program that were enacted into law were the two measures asking for appropriations, one for the support of the Efland Industrial School for wayward colored girls; the other, for the establishment of a farm colony for women offenders older than those received at Samarcand. The former received an appropriation of $1000 over the two-year period, and the latter, $60,000. The third measure was establishing the principle of the 8-hour day for children at work between 14 and 16 years of age.

In the passage of these bills, Mrs. Jerman said, it was a great source of gratification to her and the other members of the council to have had the interest and support of the women of the state who did fine education work before the Legislature began; of the leading newspapers particularly their editorial columns; and of Governor A. W. McLean who gave sanction and support of the two bills calling for an appropriation.

Lessons to Learn.

In regard to lessons which women may learn with profit from their recent experience with the Legislature, one is, according to Mrs. Jerman, that they must learn to compromise in details that the main objectives for which they work may be realized, but never so far as to sacrifice the principle. Another is that they must come to know political methods, not that they shall makes general use of these, she advises, but that they may be able to protect their bills and save them from trickery and deceit.

But knowledge alone of political methods, explains Mrs. Jerman, is not women's greatest strength and must not be depended upon. They must look to the merit of their bills and rely on this. They must have a good program and work for it with patience and persistence. And the final test of this program, says Mrs. Jerman, must be not how many bills will be popular and will likely pass, but does the program represent women's best thought in government as far as they are able to ascertain it? And is its purpose the unselfish devotion of its interests to the good of the state, as a whole?

Women are just beginning to try their powers in the interest of government, says Mrs. Jerman, and the work of Miss Carrie McClean in the recent Legislature is another confirmation of their fitness and ability to render valuable services to their state and country. While Miss McClean did not represent women and women's interest alone, it was as it should be, said Mrs. Jerman, and I'm glad the sentiment for more women as members of the Legislature is rapidly increasing.

As to the woman's legislative program for the next two years, Mrs. Jerman says that as she is able to foresee it that the Australian Ballot bill will again head the list and that the measures which failed to pass, will be retained. But the new program, she says, will conform to this principle: keep what is good of the old program, work to defeat bad legislation, and promote good new legislation.

Ready for Convention.

The Woman's Club of Oxford apparently is ready for the State Convention which meets in Durham May 2–5 inclusive. According to the report of the activities of the club during the past year under the leadership of Mrs. R. L. Brown, by Miss Edna White, corresponding secretary, all financial obligations have been met, including a payment of $600 on a debt and monthly payments on building and loan shares. The club has sold twenty copies of Mrs. Cotten's History of the State Federation and bought and paid for an Encyclopaedia Britannica for the city library.

The Music department of the club, which was organized last year, has prepared and presented monthly programs using local talent. A study of the operas has also been made. But the club considers its community work its best work. During tobacco season the club house was kept open as a rest room for women from the country. A permit has recently been given by the Boy Scouts of the town to place a temporary building on the club lot.

May 1–6 National Music Week.

Mrs. J. Edward Kale of Lincolnton, State Music Chairman, is calling for a statewide observance of National Music Week which begins the first Sunday in May and continues throughout the week. She says, "America must sing this year as never before and let the melody of the 'Old North State' be heard above all the others. Plan a variety of musical programs for home, church and school and end the week with a community musical 'get-together.' Give one program using our own state composers and musicians."

Club Women and Forest Week.

Club Women in North Carolina and throughout the country are urged to give some recognition to American Forest Week, April 24–31, which week has been proclaimed by President Coolidge for nation-wide observance. Forest conservation is one of the activities in which both the State and General Federation of Women's Clubs have long been interested. The chief objective of the General Federation's program for Forest Week is "To fix in the minds of our citizens the usefulness and beauty of our forests and the value of keeping our country tree-green."

In recent years thousands of trees and shrubs have been planted annually in North Carolina by club women and this year will likely be no exception. Two motives seem to have inspired the tree-planting movement now so popular. One is to beautify the fine system of state highways, otherwise attractive enough and the other is to memorialize the heroic deeds and sacrifices of the World War veterans. This may be in the form of a tree, a grove, avenue or roads of remembrance. Both ideas and sentiments are fine and are in keeping with the principles in observing National Forest Week.

Asheville *Sunday Citizen,* p. 28 (section C, p. 6)

17 APRIL 1927

WOMEN OBSERVE 25TH ANNIVERSARY

Miss Louisa Poppenheim Will Be Guest and Speaker at Club Meeting

FORMER PRESIDENTS WILL BE ON PROGRAM

Each One of the Presidents Who Have Served Federation During Twenty-five Years of Life Is Still Active In Club Work In State

By Mrs. J. Henry Highsmith

Observance of the twenty-fifth anniversary of the organization of the State Federation of Women's Clubs will be a big feature of the approaching State convention to be held in Durham, May 2 to 5, inclusive. Miss Louisa

Poppenheim, of Charleston, South Carolina, who was instrumental in forming the North Carolina Association and who issued the call and presided at the initial meeting, will be the honor guest and chief speaker. The eleven ex-presidents and Mrs. E. L. McKee, the present president, will have parts on the program. Each will characterize her administration by dressing in the style that prevailed at the time of her presidency and by depicting or representing in some attractive way the outstanding events or accomplishments of her term of office. Anniversary exercises will be held Wednesday evening at 6:30 o'clock in connection with the annual Federation dinner at the Washington Duke Hotel. Mrs. R. R. Cotten will preside.

Those having served the Federation as president for a term of two years each, with the exception of the first president who served three years, and who will feature the anniversary program are: Mrs. Lindsay Patterson, of Winston-Salem; Mrs. J. T. Alderman, of Henderson; Miss Margaret Lovell Gibson, Wilmington; Mrs. Eugene Reilly, Charlotte; Mrs. Robert R. Cotten, Farmville; Miss Adelaide L. Fries, Winston-Salem; Mrs. Thomas W. Lingle, Davidson; Mrs. Clarence Johnson, Raleigh; Mrs. Charles C. Hook, Charlotte; Mrs. Sydney P. Cooper, Henderson; Mrs. Palmer Jerman, Raleigh; and Mrs. E. L. McKee, Sylva. Music toasts and reminiscences will have a place on the program.

The fact that during the twenty-five years of the Federation's existence death has not visited the line of its presiding officers, and that each remains an interested and active club worker, is both noteworthy and gratifying. Nothing is so inspiring at the meetings of the annual conventions as the unselfish devotion and enthusiasm manifested by those who have held the reins and led the way in former years. Their loyalty and ever renewed interest in club affairs is not only a beautiful example for younger hands who take hold but it is an inviting and impelling force. By means of it young, eager minds are attracted to the field and the gaps are kept filled with willing workers.

The program arranged for the anniversary celebration affords the opportunity of looking back over the twenty-five years and noting the changes and developments that have taken place during this interesting period— the period when the Woman's Club movement evolved from a "passing fad," derisively termed, into its present state of usefulness and respectability, composed of 15,000 women holding direct membership and 40,000 women holding affiliated membership. Dropping of the "inferiority complex," which state of mind was more or less common in the earlier days, will likely be one of the most noticeable changes to have been made. There's little now about a woman's club meeting, particularly a state convention, which suggests inferiority of any kind, conscious or subconscious. The committee in charge of the program are: Mrs. J. Henry Highsmith, of Raleigh, chairman; Mrs. Harry Comer, Chapel Hill; Mrs. J. L. Morehead and Mrs. C. W. Toms, Jr., of Durham.

Federation Organized at Winston Salem.

On May 26, 1902, in Winston-Salem, the North Carolina Federation of Women's Clubs came into being. Miss Louisa Poppenheim, then president of the South Carolina Federation and corresponding secretary of the General Federation, in the office of the latter, had sent a call to the North Carolina clubs asking that they send delegates duly authorized to join the Federation. The meeting was held at the home of Mrs. H. R. Starbuck. Miss Poppenheim was made temporary chairman, and Mrs. A. J. Howell, of Wilmington, temporary secretary.

At this meeting the State organization was formed, its constitution adopted and the machinery of the organization set into motion. The next day, May 27, the organization met in the chapel of the Moravian Church in Salem for taking final action in effecting the organization and for adopting plans for work. The departments of work were assigned on the lines of education, library extension, village improvement, and State charities. The clubs enrolled at the first meeting were: Sorosis Round Table and Embroidery Club of Winston-Salem; North Carolina Sorosis of Wilmington; Goldsboro Woman's Club; Circulating Book Club of Salisbury; and the Alpha Club of Statesville. The officers elected were: Mrs. Lindsay Paterson, of Winston-Salem, president; Mrs. R. R. Cotten, first vice-president; Mrs. W. R. Hollowell, second vice-president; Miss Margaret L, Gibson, recording secretary; Miss Clayton Candler, corresponding secretary; Mrs. Charles Price, treasurer.

Cotton Reception Unique and Entertaining.

The "Cotton Reception" which is to be held Wednesday afternoon during the State convention and which is to be sponsored by Mrs. E. H. Williamson, of Fayetteville, chairman of the Cotton Day program committee, promises to be a unique and highly entertaining feature of the convention. According to Mrs. Williamson, increasing interest is shown every day and wholehearted co-operation is being given by club women, school teachers, merchants, and the public generally. She announces that in addition to the Cotton Dress contest that will be staged and the exhibition of prize winning dresses from the high schools, there will be a style revue of selected models from the best houses in the country. Four classes of dresses will be considered in the contest—sport, house, afternoon and evening dresses. A number of prizes will be awarded.

The work of Mrs. Williamson and her committee in the "Back-to-Cotton" movement is attracting more than statewide attention. The editors of Commerce and Finance, published in New York, commend Mrs. Williamson for her well planned program and the successful results she seems to be achieving. Mrs. Williamson has a well written article appearing in the April issue of Commerce and Finance which issue is devoted to cotton and its products.

Mrs. R. Duke Hay of Black Mountain, State chairman of transportation, announces that the identification certificate plan will be used in going to the council meeting to be held in Grand Rapids, Mich., May 30 to June 4. She hopes a number of North Carolina club women will avail themselves of this great inspirational meeting and she will gladly explain the identification certificate plan to any and all who go and who will write her beforehand. It is the same plan, she says, that was used last year in going to Atlantic City to attend the biennial meeting.

Credential cards were mailed with the call to the convention the last of March to all officers, past presidents, chairmen of departments and standing committees, district presidents, club presidents and delegates. If any woman fails to receive her credentials she is asked to notify Mrs. W. T. Bost, executive secretary at State Headquarters in Raleigh.

Raleigh Sunday *News and Observer,* p. 33 (Editorial, p. 1)
Asheville *Sunday Citizen,* p. 26 (section C, p. 6)
Charlotte Sunday Observer, p. 32 (section 3, p. 4), incomplete

24 APRIL 1927

NATIONAL CLUB FIGURE COMING

Club Women Looking Forward To Presence of General President in May

WILL BE SPEAKER AT DURHAM MEETING

Mrs. John D. Sherman, of Chicago, is Expected To Speak On "The American Home," a Subject That Is Close To Her Heart, In Her Address

By Mrs. J. Henry Highsmith

More than usual interest is felt the approaching convention of State Federation of Women's Clubs this year which meets in Durham Monday of next week, May 2, and continues through Thursday, on account of the unusually interesting numbers contained in the program. Chief of these, perhaps, is the coming of Mrs. John D. Sherman, of Chicago, president of the General Federation of Women's Clubs, who will be honor guest and chief convention speaker. Her address will be delivered Tuesday evening in the convention hall of the Washington Duke Hotel.

Mrs. Sherman's address will likely revolve about a theme that is known to lie close to her heart, the American home, raising its standard spiritually, intellectually, socially and materially. Mrs. Sherman never misses an opportunity to proclaim the gospel of better homes, better families and better citizens. It is stated that the one aim of her administration is to bring about a reform and changes of standards for housekeeping as a profession. She and the 140,000 clubs in the General Federation are working for the recognition in the new United States census of the 92 per cent of women who do their own work and who are now listed as having no occupation. She would have housekeeping rated and classified along with other trades and professions.

Mrs. Sherman will come to North Carolina from New York City, where she will have attended a committee meeting on the Cause and Cure of War. On her way she will stop over in Washington for a visit at Federation Headquarters. After addressing the North Carolina club women on Tuesday evening, May 3, she will go to Nashville, Tenn., where she will address the Tennessee club women on May 5, and thence to Paducah, Ky., where she speaks to the Kentucky Federation May 6. Her itinerary for this spring includes nine state Federations of Women's Clubs.

Unusual interest is attached to Mrs. Sherman's visit this year owing to the fact that her visit was keenly anticipated a year ago when she was prevented from coming on account of the sudden death of her husband. She expresses delightful anticipation in the visit she expects to make to the State and particularly to the club women who, she says, are doing worthwhile things.

Many Social Features Planned.

Through the courtesy of the Durham Woman's Club, hostess to the convention, many social features have been planned for the recreation and entertainment of the visiting club women. Dullness is not to be the result of four days at work interspersed with no play. On Monday evening after the opening session the Woman's Club of Durham will hold a reception in honor of their visitors in the parlors of the Washington Duke Hotel. On Tuesday afternoon the women will be driven over to Chapel Hill where the Community Club will entertain at a tea at the new Woman's Building on the University campus, after which they will be escorted by the women students through the University grounds and to its many points of interest. A particularly pleasing feature of this entertainment will be the opportunity given the mothers who have sons attending the University to have tea with them. The sons will also be guests at the tea.

A unique and interesting social feature will be the Cotton reception at 4 o'clock Wednesday after noon in the hotel parlors. The committee in charge is planning to make of this event a beautiful and significant occasion.

The annual Federation dinner, which is looked upon as probably the crowning social event, will be held Wednesday evening at 6:30. A special feature of the dinner will be the anniversary exercises which immediately follow.

Club Institute to Be Held.

An entirely new feature of the convention will be a Club Institute to be held Thursday, May 5, the last day of the Federation meeting. The committee having in hand the arrangement of plans for the Institute are Mrs. Eugene Reilly, of Charlotte, chairman; Mrs. J. T. Alderman of, Henderson, and Mrs.

John L. Gilmer, of Winston-Salem. The purpose of conducting the Institute is to provide an opportunity for studying together the best methods and plans for obtaining greater efficiency in club work, in other words to adopt a business basis for conducting club affairs. The main objective of the Institute may be said to be to instruct club women as to the best methods of running the machinery of their clubs so as to get the maximum of efficiency from the minimum of effort.

All club women are invited to attend the Institute and to take part in the discussions. All instruction is free. While the Institute at this time will be in the nature of an experiment it is the purpose of the convention to make it a permanent institution, and to plan for its larger growth and usefulness. Consequently this initial meeting is looked upon as having more than ordinary significance.

An interesting and instructive program has been prepared by the committee.

The Institute will be opened Thursday morning by Mrs. E. L. McKee, who will make a short address setting forth the plans and needs for a Club Institute. Mrs. Cotten will outline the main objectives to be accomplished at this time. Mrs. J. T. Alderman will discuss club organization including the three kinds of clubs, namely cultural, civic and the departmental clubs; and will also discuss the qualifications and responsibilities of officers, committees and chairmen; Mrs. J. L. Gilmer will lead the discussions on the different methods of electing officers. Mrs. C. C. Hook will treat general finance, and Miss Adelaide Fries the budget. Mrs. Palmer Jerman will talk on the value of having a Legislative Council, also the purposes of passing resolutions. Mrs. Kate Burr Johnson will discuss the relation of the Woman's Club to civic and welfare groups; Mrs. Jane S. McKimmon, the relation of city to rural clubs; Mrs. Sydney Cooper, the relation of the General Federation to the State Federation and to local clubs. Club ethics and platform courtesies will be discussed by Mrs. J. A. Yarbrough, and the place of publicity by Mrs. J. Henry Highsmith.

Regulations Governing $100 Prize Offered by Asheville Chamber of Commerce.

Mrs. C. Whit Gaskins, of Asheville, State chairman of Civics, in a letter to club presidents, calls attention to the $100 prize offered at the last convention by the Asheville Chamber of Commerce to the federated club putting on the best piece of civic work in its community. The regulations furnished by the Chamber of Commerce are as follows:

First: The award is to be made to the North Carolina club which has accomplished the most important civic improvement during the club year. Local conditions and needs are to be considered in determining the importance of the achievement.

Second: Only clubs affiliated with the State Federation are eligible.

Third: The judges will be named by the president of the State Federation and must be entirely disinterested.

Fourth: Reports in writing signed by club president and two members of her executive board must be submitted to Mrs. C. Whit Gaskins, 18 Vance Crescent, Asheville, N. C., State chairman of Civics, before April 20.

Fifth: The prize will be announced and delivered at your next annual convention.

Sixth: The winner will supply the Asheville Chamber of Commerce with a complete written and photographic record.

Seventh: The Federation will give the Chamber of Commerce a detailed report of the contest results.

May Day Child Health Day.

May Day will be observed by women's clubs throughout the State and country as Child Health Day. As most club women are mothers, the observance of the day has a strong and universal appeal. Every Home a Health Center is the theme of the National Child Health Day program. Herbert Hoover, Secretary of Commerce, and president of the Child Health Association, says the object of observing the day is to obtain a square deal for every child in the United States. The child's home, habits and living conditions will be given special consideration. Regular health examinations, including dental examinations, will be emphasized and urged.

Raleigh Sunday *News and Observer,* p. 29 (Editorial, p. 1)
Asheville *Sunday Citizen,* p. 34 (section C, p. 12)
Charlotte Sunday Observer, p. 36 (section 3, p. 6), incomplete

1 MAY 1927

DURHAM IS READY FOR CLUB WOMEN

**Opening Session Will Take Place At Eight O'Clock
On Monday Night**

CONFERENCES WILL FEATURE CONVENTION

First Business Session Will Be Held Tuesday Morning; President of General Federation, Mrs. John D. Sherman Will Deliver Address Tuesday Evening

By Mrs. J. Henry Highsmith

With every plan made and every committee at attention to serve, announcement is made that Durham is ready and awaiting the arrival of the six hundred club women who will gather there Monday for the Twenty-fifth Annual Convention of the State Federation of Women's Clubs. Not only will the Woman's Club of Durham be hostess to the convention, but the different men's organizations will play the host, and all of Durham will unite in extending a welcome and providing for the welfare and comfort of the visiting club women. Furthermore, Chapel Hill clubwomen will extend a hand of cordial hospitality and ask that the club women be their guests Tuesday afternoon from 4 to 6 o'clock.

According to the program just issued the opening session of the convention will take place Monday evening at 8 o'clock in the ball room of the Washington Duke Hotel, which will be convention headquarters. The invocation will be said by Dr. W. P. Few, president of Duke University. Welcome from the City of Durham will be extended by Mayor John M. Manning. Welcome from the hostess club will be given by Mrs. W. J. Brogden, president, and welcome from the men's organizations of the city will be extended by Dr. R. L. Flowers, president of the Durham Chamber of Commerce.

Response to the addresses of welcome will be made by Mrs. Eugene Davis, of Wilson, treasurer of the Federation. The place of prominence on the evening's program is given to the address of the president, Mrs. E. L. McKee of Sylva.

A most delightful feature will be the musical program arranged for this meeting. The numbers are by the Constable Orchestra, Mrs. P. N. Constable, leader, and Mrs. J. A. Weatherford, accompanist; quartet, by Dr. George Reade, P. N. Constable, R. T. Howerton, and J. C. Hundley, and a solo, "Unless," by Miss Louise Cooke, accompanied by Miss Mary Todd, both of the Southern Conservatory of Music. Following the meeting will be a reception given by the Women's Club of Durham in the hotel parlors to all the visiting club women.

On Monday at 11 o'clock the Executive Board will meet in the Fountain Room of the hotel. At 3:30 o'clock in the same room the Board of Trustees will meet, and at 4:30, the Board of Directors. At 1 o'clock Mrs. W. J. Brogden will be hostess at a luncheon to the Executive Board, and at 6:30 o'clock Mrs. S. P. Cooper will be hostess to the past presidents at dinner.

Breakfast and Luncheon Conferences.

An interesting and instructive part at the convention program will be the breakfast and luncheon conferences. Departments holding breakfast conferences Tuesday morning at 8 o'clock are Art and Music, with Mrs. R. L. McMillan and Mrs. J. Edward Kale, presiding; Illiteracy, with Mrs. Elizabeth Morris, presiding, and the Press with Mrs. J. Henry Highsmith, presiding.

Mrs. McMillan will have as speakers for her breakfast conference Miss Minnie Martin of Raleigh, Mrs. J. A. Spires of Wilson, Miss Isabel Busbee and Miss Ida Poteat of Raleigh. The latter will conduct a round table discussion. Miss Nell Battle Lewis of Raleigh will be the principal speaker at the press conference.

Luncheon conferences to be held Tuesday will be one on American Citizenship with Mrs. Thomas O'Berry of Goldsboro, presiding, and one for the presidents of departmental clubs with Mrs. A. M. Jordan of Chapel Hill, presiding. At the conference on Citizenship, Dr. E. C. Branson of Chapel Hill will speak on County Government in North Carolina. As chairman of the civics department, Mrs. C. Whit Gaskins has secured Mrs. W. C. Brownson of Asheville to speak on Garden Clubs.

Breakfast conferences scheduled for 8 o'clock Wednesday morning are on Education with Mrs. George Green presiding, one for the presidents of literary clubs and chairmen of literature departments with Mrs. R. B. Peattie, presiding; and one for district presidents with Mrs. E. E. Williamson presiding.

Luncheon conferences to be held at 1 o'clock Wednesday will be one on Public Welfare and Health with Mrs. A. C. Avery and Mrs. Charles T. Hollowell presiding, and one on the American Home with Mrs. Estelle Smith presiding.

The first business session of the convention will be held Tuesday morning at 10 o'clock, at which time reports from officers, special committees and department heads will be heard. After the afternoon business session which begins at 2:30 o'clock the club women will be driven over to Chapel Hill where the Community will be hostess at a tea at the Woman's Building on the University campus.

The evening session on Tuesday will be given over to the addresses of Mrs. John D. Sherman, president of the General Federation of Women's Clubs and to a program of music by Durham musicians. Those taking part will be Miss Mary L. Knight, Mrs. S. W. Venable, Mrs. W. W. Rankin, Miss Alice Hundley, Mrs. D. W. Newsom and a group of Durham high school girls who will sing a number of songs, "The Cantones," directed by W. P. Twaddell.

At the business session on Wednesday which convenes at 9:15 o'clock Mrs. E. H. Williamson, second vice-president, will preside, at which time will be given the reports of the chairmen of districts and one-half the reports of the district presidents. At this meeting will also be given the report of the Sallie Southall Cotten Loan Fund by Mrs. E. M. Land, to be followed by the taking of pledges for this fund. Another interesting feature will be the election of officers, including a president for the next two years.

Following the afternoon business session a Cotton Reception will be held at 4 o'clock with the local Woman's Club as hostess. A cotton dress contest will feature the reception. Mrs. E. H. Williamson of Fayetteville will be manager of the contest.

At 7 o'clock the annual Federation dinner will take place in connection with which will be the celebration of the Federation's twenty-fifth anniversary. Mrs. R. R. Cotten will preside.

Chief Justice Stacy Speaks.

At the evening session beginning at 8:30 Wednesday, Mrs. R. D. W. Connor, first vice-president will preside. The chief feature of the program will be the address of Hon. W. P. Stacy, Chief Justice of the Supreme Court of North Carolina, on the subject "Constitutional Government." Preceding the address will be a violin solo by Mrs. Waldo Boone and a group of North Carolina Folk Songs by Miss Nola Jane Gentry, assisted by Miss Mary Kestler, both of Duke University. The Girls' Glee Club of Duke University will also sing a group of songs.

An interesting number on the evening's program will be the awarding of prizes offered in the art, music and literary contests, the cotton contest and in the civic contest, the prize of which is $100 offered by the Asheville Chamber of Commerce for the best piece of civic and community work done by a club during the past club year. Introduction of new officers will also take place at this meeting. Thursday, the last day of the convention, will be given to a new undertaking of the Federation, that of conducting a club institute and making plans for establishing a permanent club institute.

Art Exhibits Secure for Convention.

Mrs. R. L. McMillan, state chairman of art, announces that she has secured two unusually fine and interesting art collections to be on exhibition at the State convention. One is an exhibit of block prints by Miss Mabel Pugh of Morrisville and New York. The group consists of 23 designs, two of which have been accepted by the National Academy of Design. These two were the old school house at Morrisville and an old church at Hillsboro. Two other of her block prints are in the International Print Makers Exhibition in California at this time. Miss Morris at present is making illustrations for books for Doubleday Page and Company, New York.

The second exhibition will be of original illustrations assembled by the American Federation of Arts. William James Aylward, who depicts with appealing charm the spirit of romance and adventure invariably associated with ships and the sea, will have on exhibition four studies of the West Wind, two in oil and two in crayon-water colors. Mrs. Huger Elliott will have five water colors. Maxfield Parrish, who is called "a sort of Peter Pan among artists" and who has charmed the world with his marvelous colors as well as with his delightful clowns, will have on display fourteen Knave of Hearts illustrations for which he is most renowned. Seven pictures by Frank E. Schoolover, noted painter of American Indians and Canadian trappers, will be among the number on display. Jessie Wilcox Smith whose sympathetic and beautiful interpretations of childhood have endeared her to millions of readers of American magazines and books the world over will have four of her works on exhibition and N. C. Wyeth, who has become an authority of renown upon the subject of pirates, old ships and all the colorful costumes of the 16th and 17th Centuries, will be represented by six of his best paintings, Thornton Oakley will have four illustrations from "Westward Ho."

Two important committees of the convention will be the Credentials Committee composed of Mrs. Eugene Davis, chairman, Mrs. Pritchard Carlton, Mrs. John Anderson, Mrs. James Brodie, Mrs. R. W. Crews, and Mrs. R. H. Patterson; and the Resolutions committee composed of Miss Adelaide Fries, Mrs. W. T. Bost, Mrs. Charles C. Hook, Mrs. W. B. Waddill, and Mrs. Jane McKimmon. Chairman of local committees on arrangements are Mrs. W. J. Brogden, Mrs. C. H. Livengood, Mrs. C. F. Williams, and Mrs. J. H. Epperson.

Raleigh Sunday *News and Observer,* p. 35 (Editorial, p. 1)
Asheville *Sunday Citizen,* p. 34 (section C, p. 12)
Charlotte Sunday Observer, p. 48 (section 3, p 16)

15 MAY 1927

PRESIDENT OF CLUB WOMEN TO PUSH PRESENT PROGRAM
EMPHASIZING CITIZENSHIP

Plan Will Be to Train Club Women in an Understanding of Government and Its Problems—Mrs. O'Berry is Heartily in Favor of Proposed Survey of Women in Industry—Eight Months School Term is Another Question on Which She is Fully Committed

By Mrs. J. Henry Highsmith

While not yet having formulated plans and policies by which the State Federation of Women's Clubs will be directed for the next two years, Mrs. Thomas O'Berry of Goldsboro, the new president, who was a visitor the past week at Federation Headquarters, stated that it is her aim to push those measures already endorsed by the Federation and to which the club women of the state have pledged their support meanwhile working out a larger and more progressive program that will challenge the strength of the entire organization. Citizenship, particularly as it applies to county government, will likely be the keynote most strongly emphasized in Mrs. O'Berry's administration. A long study of this subject has fixed indelibly upon her mind the importance of having a better informed and more intelligent citizenry in regard to this basic unit of government.

Better Citizenship.

However, Mrs. O'Berry's keen interest in better citizenship does not preclude interest in other questions uppermost in the minds of club women. When asked as to how she stands in regard to a survey of the working conditions of women in industry, she replied, "O, I'm heart and soul for it and I believe we are going to get it—not a white-washed affair but a thorough investigation that will give us accurate and reliable data." In this connection she said she felt that the sentiment for an impartial survey was growing and that whereas many industrial heads have heretofore opposed a survey the time is rapidly coming when they will welcome the opportunity to let the public know the working conditions of their employees. As a matter of fact, she said, they cannot afford not to cooperate in this movement as opposition would only bring suspicion upon their own heads.

The eight months school term is another question to which Mrs. O'Berry is fully committed. She believes that the means will soon be found for providing for rural school children the same advantages as those enjoyed by city school children. Mother's Aid work and the program of the State Welfare Department under Mrs. Kate Burr Johnson will also have Mrs. O'Berry's hearty support. For several years she has been identified with and an ardent worker for some of the most progressive measures adopted by the state in its program of social and humanitarian work. Preventive tuberculosis work, visiting nurse service and mother's aid have from their beginning been aided by her.

Civic improvement which includes beautifying the highways and making towns, villages and homes safer, healthier and better places in which to live, appeals particularly to Mrs. O'Berry. She feels that any worthwhile civic program depends upon the efficiency and far sightedness of the local governing, body hence the necessity for an efficient well organized county government.

Mrs. O'Berry assumes leadership of the 15,000 club women in the state after a period of training not only in Women's Club work but in charity and civic organizations. For sixteen years she served on the board of what was the Charity Organization of Goldsboro, and is now the Bureau of Social Service. For two years she was president of this, the oldest civic organization in Goldsboro. At present she is first vice president of the Goldsboro Woman's Club, in which organization she has been an active worker for many years having served at the head of some of its most important committees and departments.

Her service to the Federation already numbers seven years. For three she was president of the Tenth District, now the Thirteenth. For the next two years she served as second vice president of the Federation and was state chairman of district work and for the past two years she has been chairman of the American Citizenship Department, during which time she has led many clubs into a study and an investigation of the machinery of this county government.

In recognition of Mrs. O'Berry's interest in better citizenship and better local governing bodies, Governor A. W. McLean appointed her a member of the Commission to Study County Government in North Carolina, and to report to the next convention of county commissioners which body made the request for this study. According to Mrs. O'Berry, the Commission, with Dr. E. C. Brooks as chairman, based its study on the records of a survey of county governments in the state having been previously made by the Social Research Department of the University of North Carolina under the leadership of Dr. E. C. Branson.

In emphasizing American Citizenship in the club program for the next two years Mrs. O'Berry says that her main objective will be to help club women overcome the ignorance, indifference and lack of civic consciousness that prevails in most counties in regard to their county governments, and as a consequence to bring about a more efficient system. She says that there is now a movement on foot to standardize the methods of conducting county governments so as to define duties and place responsibilities, to prevent overlapping of jurisdiction, to secure greater efficiency and eventually to reduce taxation. She believes that club women can render their counties a real service at this point by informing themselves as to the duties and detailed functions of their county offices and then to work untiringly to secure the most capable men or women to fill these offices. She appeals to club women to study their county government in all its branches, for on it rests their state government.

Mrs. O'Berry, who before marriage was Miss Annie Land, was born and reared to young womanhood in Littleton, North Carolina. There she attended Littleton College. Later she graduated from Peace Institute, Raleigh. She moved with her brother, E. M. Land, to Kinston and since her marriage has made Goldsboro her home.

Charlotte Sunday Observer, p. 51 (section 4, p. 5)

29 MAY 1927

MRS. M'KEE TURNS ATTENTION TO EDUCATIONAL ADVANTAGES FOR CHILDREN OF THE STATE

Retiring President of Federation of Women's Clubs Will Work for Equal Opportunities for Rural and City Pupils—Sees Growth and Development as Outcome of Her Administration—Confident That State is Desirous of Helping

By Mrs. J. Henry Highsmith

No sooner did Mrs. E. L. McKee, of Sylva, pass to other hands her job of conducting the affairs of the club women of the state than she took up the interests of the children of the state. She says: "More than anything else I am interested in the welfare of the state's children. I long to see every country child have educational advantages in grammar and high school equal to those of the city child. I believe it to be his inherent right." Continuing, she says "circumstances are such that many children must contribute to the maintenance of the family, and knowing this to be the case I long to see the condition of those children made as favorable as possible to see them given as fair a chance in life as possible."

Helping Defectives.

Mrs. McKee says further: "I long to see every defective child in North Carolina given the proper attention and to see legitimate means provided for decreasing the alarming number of these defectives.

"My heart goes out to the juvenile delinquent, who is usually the product of unfavorable surroundings."

But Mrs. McKee does not believe in adopting militant methods in order to get things done. She says: "I do not advocate nor approve militant methods of securing those things we so much desire. I am confident that our public officials and the state at large have great respect for the purposes and the motives of organized women and are willing to co-operate with them in finding the best methods to secure those things which all agree are for the upbuilding of our state and for the protection and help of our unfortunates."

When asked as to what she considered the outstanding accomplishment of her administration, Mrs. McKee said: "I do not hesitate to say that it was the strengthening of the bonds between the individual clubs and the State Federation." By way of explaining she said: "In the beginning an analysis of the club situation revealed these facts: Our ideals and purposes were very noble and unselfish; our plan of organization could scarcely be improved; we had large numbers—yet notwithstanding these things, notwithstanding the fact that the local clubs were so vital a force in their respective communities our state organization was not the force in the state we had a right to expect. The strength of the Federation did not represent, by any means, the combined strength of the individual clubs; in other words there was a tremendous loss of strength somewhere between the individual clubs and the state organization.

Remedy Situation.

To remedy this situation was the task to which Mrs. McKee devoted the strength of herself and her organization for two years. Her first act was to issue a call to the club women to become "50,000 vibrant strands of steel woven together into a cable of such strength that it could stand whatever tension was placed upon it."

Her second was to increase the efficiency of the Federation by making it more usable. To this end her efforts have been directed toward the establishing of a State Federation Headquarters and of a club institute. The object of the latter was to familiarize club women with the work and works of the Federation. "And so," she concludes, "I should say the outstanding achievement of the administration has been not simply the establishment of these two agencies, but rather that which comes as a result of their establishment, to wit, the strengthening of the bond between the clubs and the Federation, for thereby and only thereby may we ever hope for the Federation to represent the combined strength of its individual clubs."

A source of strength and usefulness which Mrs. McKee has been able to develop has been linking up the Federation with and having it to take a larger part in the affairs of the state. The result has been a better understanding and appreciation on the part of state officials of the Federation's purposes and plans on one hand and an increasing interest in state affairs lending to a sympathetic and statewide view point on the part of the club women on the other hand. The state government with its departments and the workings of its machinery has been brought home and made real and interesting to the club women in even the remote sections. It is a noticeable fact that interest in local, county and state government is growing as a result of which more efficient government is expected.

Wonderful Growth.

Mrs. McKee expresses herself as having seen signs at the recent state convention of a most wonderful growth and development within the ranks. She mentions the serious business-like, punctual way in which the body as a whole attended all the sessions; the large percentage of women from small towns and communities; the large number of voting women in attendance; the character of the reports, their conciseness and brevity, and the grasp of essentials which they showed. "As to the club institute," she said, "it succeeded my most sanguine expectation. I had said before if 50 women were present I should feel that it was worth while; if a hundred were there I should be more than gratified. There were 200 and their interest, their apparent desire to learn from the speakers and from each other, the questions asked, the splendid idea advanced, all contributed to making the club institute the outstanding event of the convention and assured it a prominent place in the future life of the Federation."

Charlotte Sunday Observer, p. 30 (section 3, p. 4)
Asheville *Sunday Citizen,* p. 24 (section C, p. 5)

12 JUNE 1927

MAKE DRIVE TO ABOLISH ADULT ILLITERACY IN SEVEN COUNTIES

Buncombe Leads Literacy Campaign Which Is Taken Up By State Federation Club Women

By Mrs. J. Henry Highsmith

With Buncombe County leading not only the state but the national campaign against adult illiteracy, the race is set and the movement is rapidly getting under way in a majority of the forty-eight states. The goal of the campaign, which is being conducted jointly by the National Bureau of Education and the General Federation of Women's Clubs, is to remove the blight of illiteracy so far as possible before the taking of the 1930 census—to change the standing of the United States among the larger nations of the world from the tenth to a place nearer the top in its percentage of illiteracy [*recte:* literacy].

According to the program planned by Mrs. John D. Sherman, president of the General Federation of Women's Clubs, and Dr. John J. Tigert, U. S. Commissioner of Education, each state is to make a beginning by making a survey of all of the native adult illiterates in a type county and therefore by working out a program with the State and county school officials to the end that these illiterates be taught to read and write. The club women of the state have been called on to take the lead in this educational work and their response has been most enthusiastic and heartening to the cause.

When Mrs. Elizabeth C. Morriss of Asheville, director of Buncombe County Community Schools and chairman of Adult Illiteracy in the State Federation of Women's Clubs, was asked to comply with the general program, Buncombe County was not only the first county to arrive with all of its adult illiterates listed but it brought with it a well worked out plan that had been tried out and found practical and feasible for greatly reducing illiteracy if not entirely eliminating it.

According to Mrs. Morriss during the six years that the community schools have been operated—called community schools rather than night schools because they are community projects designed to make better citizens— approximately 4,000 native white adults have been enrolled. Their average age is 30 years and most of them have a number of young children. They were taught two hours an evening, two evenings a week for five months during the summer and fall. They were given a chance to master the simple tools of learning—reading, writing and arithmetic. The result is that about 1,000 have completed the equivalent of the third grade at school, 1,000 the second grade and 2,000 that of the first grade. The estimate is that there are about 4,000 other persons in the county beyond school age who have not yet reached the third grade in their education and that 1,500 of these are wholly illiterate according to the Army Standard which is that a person to be literate must be able to "read a newspaper and the Bible and write his own letters."

But learning to read, write and figure is not all that one gets in one of the Buncombe County community schools. Here the pupils are taught also the elementary rules of health, sanitation, home management, proper food, care of children and community welfare. Every community school conducts at least one project, the aim being to leave the community better than it was before the school was held. The first paper that one group of pupils ever signed was a petition to the county authorities for a special tax to permit the extension of the school term.

So favorably received has been the Buncombe County plan that Mrs. Morriss was called to Grand Rapids, Mich., recently to address the council meeting of the General Federation and to hold conferences with the various state committees interested in this particular work. At this meeting definite plans for a larger and more systematic campaign were worked out.

Counties of Sixth District Will Stage Demonstration.

Instead of making a demonstration of one county as called for in the general program, North Carolina, having already made that experiment, will, with Mrs. Morriss again at the head of it, stage a demonstration of seven counties, those comprising the Sixth District of the State Federation of Women's Clubs. These counties are Davie, Davidson, Forsyth, Rowan, Surry, Stokes, and Yadkin. This district was chosen on account of the very fine work done by Mrs. Claude S. Morris of Salisbury. Mrs. Elizabeth Morriss herself says: "Such outstanding work has been done in the Sixth District under the president, Mrs. Claude S. Morris, that the seven counties of the district have been chosen as the demonstration counties in the literacy campaign. A paid, trained, whole time worker will be put in charge, and with the co-operation of the clubs of the Federation, there is here a most promising outlook."

Feeling that the 53,000 organized club women should be put to work on this problem of teaching the 200,000 illiterates in the State to read and write, Mrs. Morriss as chairman of the illiteracy committee with Mrs. Morris, president of the Sixth District, as vice chairman and Mrs. Howard G. Etheridge, of Asheville, secretary, has worked out a State plan embracing eight objectives with a chairman in charge of each objective. Mrs. J. G. Fearing of Elizabeth City will secure the co-operation of the educational officials of the State, county and town, also of the teachers and the school commissioners. Mrs. J. H. Anderson of Fayetteville will secure the cooperation of all representative literate organizations, as women's clubs, men's clubs, patriotic, civic and church organizations. Mrs. R. W. Crews of Thomasville will be in charge of making the census of native adult illiterates. Mrs. C. W. Bradshaw of Greensboro will have charge of the work of securing trained teachers and Mrs. D. E. Giles, of Marion, of financing teachers' salaries. Miss Ruth Burke of La Grange and Mrs. Billy Davis of Sylva will aid in securing adequate textbooks and other necessary equipment, and transportation. Chairmen for posters and publicity have not yet been named.

The large objective in the literacy campaign planned for the State, according to Mrs. Morriss, is to secure for the education of native adult illiterates a definite place in State and county educational systems.

To encourage the work the committee is offering a number of prizes among the women of the Federation. The first is a $20 prize to the District not including the Sixth District, which makes the most adequate census of the adult illiterates in all of it counties before April 15, 1929. A $10 prize is offered to the District which first secures $5 from each of its counties for the Citizens' Reference Books for adult illiterates in Community Schools, in the seven demonstration counties; and $5 is offered for the best set of three posters showing how removal of illiteracy will make of North Carolina's 200,000 illiterates wiser parents, more intelligent citizens and happier men and women. This contest is open to all members of clubs affiliated with the State Federation of Women's Clubs.

In addition to the above prizes, a $30 prize is offered by the World Federation of Education Associations for the best illiteracy poster submitted at its meeting in Toronto, Canada, August 7–12. The contest is open to students of elementary and high schools, State normal schools and teachers colleges. The poster should be designed to depict some phase of illiteracy and its handicap to a nation, a community or an individual.

Community Schools Different.

Many unusual elements enter into the general plan of conducting the community schools. Much of their remarkable success has been attributed to Mrs. Morriss' insistence on having specially trained teachers and in order to have these it has been through her efforts that the Asheville Summer School is now offering the only training course for teachers of adult illiterates available in the State. This school has given the course "Methods for Teaching Adult Illiterates" for the past four years.

Another distinctive point is that a specially prepared text book has been found necessary. Consequently Mrs. Morriss set about to write a text book that would meet her needs, and now two volumes of the Citizen's Reference Book, a text and reference book for adult beginners, have just been published by the North Carolina University Press at Chapel Hill. Dr. Howard Odum, director of the School of Public Welfare of the University, says that this book "conforms to the newer and larger programs of adult education being developed in this country and abroad." The book has the approval of such specialists as Dr. E. L. Thorndike and E. P. Keppel.

As to the place of meeting there are no such restrictions. Any available place will do—a school building, a church, vacant rooms over a store or a railroad car. But the instruction must be individualized, permitting each pupil to work to capacity a task, a plan or a project. He must be taught why the problems and projects and why do them in such and such a manner. For every group there must be a definite objective planned and a minimum requirement outlined. There must always be recognition for achievement. Consequently certificates are given for completion of the third grade course.

Adult Education Paying Investment.

In addition to the many lonely benighted lives made happy and contented by having this new light come to them, the work is declared to be paying dividends to the county in higher property values, in better health, and less law evasion. Furthermore, attendance at day school has shown an increase because of the attendance at night schools of the children's parents. The observation is a parent taught means a child in school. And yet a far more significant result has followed Buncombe County's efforts.

So firmly is County Superintendent Reynolds convinced of the ever-lasting good that comes from adult education that he says: "Education is for everybody whether he be eight or 80 years old. With this idea as the big objective in the educational policies of the county, the board of education has incorporated the adult schools in the regular county system and provides for adults the same privileges end opportunities that are provided for children in the day schools."

> *Note:* Elizabeth C. Morriss (1877–1960) was a pioneer in Adult Education, director of the Community Schools for Adult Beginners of Asheville, in Buncombe County. Mrs. Claude S. Morris, Emma-Lewis, was founder of the Rowan [County] Public Library, Salisbury.

Raleigh Sunday *News and Observer*, p. 18 (Society, p. 8)
Charlotte Sunday Observer, p. 30 (section 3, p. 4)
Asheville *Sunday Citizen*, p. 27 (section C, p. 7)

1928–1929

15 January — attends, with Eugenia, funeral in Clinton for their aunt, Arabella Westbrook Royal, who had died on the 13th

17 January — attends work group at Governor's Mansion on establishing an Adult Eduction Commission

24 January — presides at Hugh Morson High School PTA; Dr. Highsmith offers invocation and reports on new library furniture and a staff librarian

30 January — Eugenia takes and passes State Bar Examination, licensed 3 February; noted with photograph in the *News and Observer*

3 February — hosts Raleigh branch of AAUW, studying the pre-school child

21 February — receives, with Dr. Highsmith, at formal reopening of RWC clubhouse after remodel

6 March — speaks at Boylan Heights School, part of Better Speech Week

c. 20 March — judges National and International Oratorical Contest for secondary schools

2–5 April — assists in membership drive for Raleigh Civic Music Association, sponsoring touring concerts at 1,250-seat Hugh Morson auditorium

29 April — has an automobile accident on Falls of the Neuse Road, causing some $600 damage to each vehicle, to be resolved in court (1 February 1930)

1–3 May — appears not to have attended 26th annual convention of NCFWC, in High Point

27 May — of 49 children examined by the City Health Department for entry to Murphey School, Katherine (age 6, pictured) is one of 7 to be "physically perfect"

18 August — the Highsmiths, including John Henry, Katherine, and Louise, return from motor trip through western NC: Asheville, Lake Junaluska, Blowing Rock, Lenoir, with trip cut short by the violent hurricane season

14 September — entertains executive board of Hugh Morson High School PTA to make plans for year on the theme "The Wise Use of Leisure Time"; Dr. Highsmith continues on library committee; Lula Belle is 16

21 September — presides over first meeting that year of Hugh Morson PTA, introducing new teachers

late September — addresses Woman's Club of Pittsboro

28 September — attends Get-Together Luncheon of RWC, as first vice president

November — serves on women's committee of Community Chest annual drive

11 November — joins a coalition of NC notables to address the lack of public libraries in North Carolina; with 46 counties having no library facility, NC ranks last in the nation

13 November — attends state Parent-Teacher Congress of 500; Dr. Highsmith is corresponding secretary; she is chair of nominating committee

7 December — death of her brother, Joe (Joseph Oscar, or J. O.) in Durham; funeral 8 December at 604 North Blount Street

17 December — speaks and leads round table discussion on Social Hygiene at Hugh Morson PTA

1929

1929–30, 1931–32, 1933–34, 1934–35
Executive Secretary, Legislative Council of
North Carolina Women

1929–35
President, Wake County League of Women Voters

9 January — assumes duties as elected executive secretary of State Legislative Council, succeeding Mrs. Bost; picture and biography in *News and Observer*

21 January — cosigns, with Mrs. Jerman, president, telegram from Council to legislative leaders demanding their position on the Australian ballot bill, failed in 1927 Legislature

12 March — attends final meeting of 1929 Sir Walter Cabinet, an informal evening with jokes, stunts, and music

3 April — presents short session on parliamentary law to PTA Council

4 April — elected Fine Arts chairman, RWC, for 1929–30

25 April — addresses WCTU on "The 1929 Legislation"

30 April – 3 May — attends 27th annual convention of NCFWC, in Charlotte

30 April — attends reception for Dorcas Club of Durham (wives of Duke faculty) given by Vara on North Blount Street, assisted by Eugenia, Mary Belle, and Annie Crews

4 May — death of Sally Southall Cotten (Mrs. R. R. Cotten), "mother of the State Federation"

9 May — presides at RWC meeting, partially in tribute to Salle Southall Cotten

15 May — leads parliamentary drill at Hugh Morson PTA Council Institute

28 May — hosts last meeting of season for Twentieth Century Book Club, "one of the most delightful for the season"; guests include Mrs. Peyton Brown (Aunt Margaret), Vara, Eugenia, Mary Belle, and Annie Crews

6 June — at RWC, installed as Fine Arts chairman (and chairman of sub group on Music), concludes service as first vice president.

August — vacations for two weeks at White Lake with Lula Belle, Katherine, Louise, and Mary Belle; returns c. 14 August

26 August — assists at tea at RWC for convention of State American Legion Auxiliary

29 September — birth of grandson John Lewis Highsmith, in Raleigh

2 December — elected president, League of Women Voters

3 December — addresses Hayes-Barton (later Myrtle Underwood) School PTA on "Character Training in the Home" substituting for scheduled speaker

20 JANUARY 1929

WOMEN ARE UNITED FOR AUSTRALIAN BALLOT LAW

No Group of Organized Women Meets Without Sanctioning Secret Voting Law

By Mrs. J. Henry Highsmith
Executive Secretary
Legislative Council of North Carolina Women

Whatever else may divide the womanhood of North Carolina, it is one and together for the Australian Ballot system of voting. Women may have differed in their preferences for party candidates in the recent election, and they may be divided on such questions as prohibition and divorce, but on one thing they are a unit—on the need of a law guaranteeing to every citizen the right to cast his or her vote free of interference, embarrassment or spying.

Since the day of their enfranchisement in 1920, when it became their privilege for the first time to go to the polls and vote, the women of North Carolina have openly declared themselves for a free and fair means of casting their ballot. They would have some method that would secure order at the polling places, that would prevent the jostling and crowded conditions that usually prevail there. They would have privacy that they might cast their ballots in secret without fear or favor of any one; and they would have an accurate count and whatever methods can be devised for the prevention of fraud and for an easy, honest and speedy method of voting.

So united are the women of the state for some reform in the voting system that scarcely no group of women brought together in the interest of social or public welfare adjourns without sanctioning the Australian Ballot System. For four years it has headed the program of the Legislative Council of North Carolina Women, and while it has met defeat at the hands of the last two Legislatures, it is again presented to them with renewed faith and optimism.

Senator J. M. Broughton of Wake County, who has made a thorough study of the Australian Ballot system and who worked so ably in its behalf during the General Assembly of 1927, has prepared and introduced a bill in the Senate which in many particulars is believed to be better than any of its predecessors. It will receive consideration at the hands of the election committee early in the week. The bill has not yet been introduced in the House.

That some form of the Australian Ballot method of voting is operating well in forty-seven states of the Union, some of which are uniformly Republican and some Democratic, argues against the claim of its opponents that it would jeopardise the chances of the party in power. As a matter of fact it works with perfect satisfaction to either party.

Students of government and teachers of political economy have for a number of years advocated this method of voting, and even among the so-called practical politicians, sentiment in its favor has been on the increase, till today it is conceded by the best minds to be the surest and safest way of conducting an election whose methods will be above reproach.

Among the bill's strongest supporters is Governor O. Max Gardner, who has worked for this measure a number of years. He ranks it among the first recommendations for which he has asked legislative enactment at the hands of this Legislature.

While the arguments and reasons for adopting the Australian system are to many well known, it may not be amiss to show here how the Australian system compares with the present North Carolina system, as is set forth in a leaflet issued by the Council of North Carolina Women:

"1. The former makes voting easy and quick. The latter, with its from two to ten separate ballots, is confusing, slow and difficult.

"2. The former tends to prevent intimidation, coercion and bribery by providing for complete privacy in voting. The latter tends to encourage these evils, intolerable in a democracy.

"3. The Australian system tends to prevent fraud by its numbered ballots which are given out only at the polling place by an election official. The present system of giving out ballots wholesale is wasteful and conducive to careless voting, intimidation and fraud. It is easy to put several ballots into the box.

"4. The Australian system is dignified, and engenders respect for our form of government. The present system is undignified, inefficient, extravagant, careless, annoying, and causes disrespect for the primary duty of a citizen. And it must be remembered that a form which makes fraud easy for one party or person makes it easy also for another, and so is no advantage to anyone in the long run."

Raleigh Sunday *News and Observer,* p. 18 (Society, p. 8)

27 JANUARY 1929

NO FEARS FOR DEMOCRATIC PARTY'S SAFETY BY ADOPTION OF AUSTRALIAN BALLOT PLAN

By Mrs. J. Henry Highsmith
Executive Secretary
Legislative Council of North Carolina Women

No fears are felt for the safety of the Democratic Party in North Carolina by O. M. Mull, chairman of the state Democratic executive committee, in the adoption of a state-wide secret ballot law. On the other hand, it is his opinion that the party has much to gain by having the will of the voters expressed freely and unhampered. He denounces the use of antiquated election machinery that in no way, he says, keeps pace with the progressive spirit of the state and the present age.

Confidence Of People.

While the record of the Democratic Party in the past has been such as to win the confidence of the people and safeguard its position, there are two possibilities, thinks Mr. Mull, where political defeat might at any time become imminent. These are through failure by prejudice or passion, he says, to consider the vital issues of the hour, and the continued use of an antiquated election machinery that will not register might at any time become imminent. This latter contingency, he says, can now be eliminated by providing a secret ballot simple in operation and safe-guarded against fraud and undue influences.

The Legislative Council of North Carolina Women not only endorses Mr. Mull's viewpoint that a new and fair and easy method of voting is needed in North Carolina but it too entertains no fears with the party's safety entrusted to the Australian ballot system which they have been advocating for eight years.

Chairman Mull's Views

Mr. Mull's views stated in full are:

"I am positively of the opinion that the only road to sustained political success is the highway of helpful service. Measured by this standard I am sure that the record of the Democratic Party in North Carolina for the past 28 years and more is such as to merit the confidence of the people and win the support of a large majority of our voters. While the Democratic Party thus continues to serve the essential needs of our state government in its moral, social and financial growth and development, we need have no fear of political defeat unless same results from one of two causes: that is by prejudice or passion we fail to consider the vital issues of the hour or by the use of antiquated election machinery the will of the people is not registered at the polls. This latter contingency can now be eliminated. We have created a new and progressive state, yet we are using an old and antiquated method of conducting our elections. This should be changed and North Carolina should be given election laws in keeping with the spirit of the state and the present age. We should provide a secret ballot simple in operation and safeguarded against fraud and undue influences so that the will of the voters could be freely expressed. The record of the Democratic Party is such that it has nothing to fear but rather much to gain by an expression of the free and unhampered will of the voters.

What The Women Want

"The women of the state have for years advocated the secret ballot. By their loyalty and efficient service to the Democratic Party they deserve consideration.

"The leader of our party, Governor Gardner, has for years advocated the secret ballot. The voters of the state have accorded him this position of leadership and I believe the time is now at hand for the enactment of a secret ballot law."

> *Note:* Governor Max Gardner's effort was successful; see "Secret Ballot," in *NCpedia*.

Charlotte *Sunday Observer,* p. 27 (section 2, p. 15)

3 FEBRUARY 1929

LOYALTY OF WOMEN VOTERS TO DEMOCRACY JEOPARDIZED BY PRESENT VOTING SYSTEM

By Mrs. J. Henry Highsmith

Politicians who would hold to the present system of voting in order to save the state for Democracy four years hence stand a good chance to lose it, according to Mrs. Thomas O'Berry, of Goldsboro, who was in Raleigh yesterday returning from a trip to Charlotte and the western part of the state, where she had been in the interest of the State Federation of Women's

Clubs. Mrs. O'Berry is president of this organization, and in connection with her duties as chief executive, she has been brought in touch with a great many women of the state and is able to speak for them politically as well as in other club relationships.

Mrs. O'Berry feels that the success of the party may be endangered in the next election if the politicians maintain that the means of saving democracy is through the open ballot. This admits, she says, that manipulation of the ballot may be employed, which is an affront to honest thinking men and women. This position if allowed to defeat the Australian ballot will lose to the party thousands of votes of conscientious and straightforward thinking men and women. Women, she says, will not stand by a party, the practices of which are such as will destroy their confidence in the party's principles. They have come too recently into the exercise of citizenship and are by nature and training averse to the methods of expediency frequently used by political parties to gain an end.

Men of strong party allegiance have declared themselves opposed to any method which interferes with a fair and free expression of the will of the people. Neither can the young men who have been trained to think and act independently, and who have not the strong party affiliations of their fathers, be counted on to uphold the party if it fails to provide a device for intelligent and honest voting. And it is the young men and women to whom the party must look for its future.

"I honestly doubt that the women can be counted on to continue to work for the party as they have in the past," says Mrs. O'Berry, "if this party continuously denies to them their rights for clean election laws." The Democratic Party, she says, has held up to the women ideals of justice, honesty and progress, but it has yet to answer to them why North Carolina is the only state in the union without a secret ballot law. She declares that the faith as well as the loyalty of women is undergoing a severe test at this time and it remains for the party to uphold its honor.

Charlotte Sunday Observer, p. 26 (section 2, p. 10)

10 FEBRUARY 1929

WOMEN OF NORTH CAROLINA WOULD THROW RESTRICTIONS ABOUT
MARRIAGE SACRAMENT

**Requirement of Notice of Intent to Marry Might in Many Instances
Frustrate Hasty and Ill-Considered Unions—Would Give Parents
and Guardians Time to Interfere When Contract Is Obviously
Unsuitable—The Necessity for Physical Examination**

**By Mrs. J. Henry Highsmith
Executive Secretary
Legislative Council of North Carolina Women**

The next bill sponsored by the Legislative Council of North Carolina Women to be introduced at this session of the general assembly is known as the notice of intention to marry. This bill simply means that before the issuance of a marriage license there shall be a five days' notice in advance. This delay is asked primarily as a protection to hasty and impulsive young people who frequently rush headlong into marriage without due deliberation and advisement, and that there be time for the proper physical examinations which are required by our present marriage laws.

Time To Do Something.

This bill is presented by the Women's Legislative Council in answer to the question that is so frequently tossed to them: "Why don't you women do something to prevent the increasing number of divorces and marriage wrecks?" That there is need that something be done and that be done quickly every one agrees. That one marriage in every six or seven flounders on the rocks and ends in the divorce courts is argument enough that some reform in our marriage laws is necessary. An interval of five days between the time of applying for the license and marriage has been found of real value, according to the experiences of the states having this or similar laws.

Not only women's organizations favor this measure. The clergy of the state are committed to it, as are health workers, social workers, judges and solicitors, particularly the two named last as it falls to them to deal with the wreckage resulting from hasty and ill-advised marriages. Records of the courts of domestic relations show that 60 per cent of all divorces sought are of couples who either ran away or entered the marriage contract without serious consideration. Dr. Chas. O'H. Laughinghouse, state health officer, says concerning this bill:

"I see every argument in favor of the law and no reasonable argument against it. One of the most common objections raised is that it interferes with personal liberty. There is no contract in the world that interferes with personal liberty as greatly as does marriage and it seems to me that a few days meditation before entering into such a contract would be well-advised."

Many Hasty Marriages.

"There are too many hasty marriages," he said. "I know of two cases in the last week when young folks went to a dance, got 'lit to a million,' decided on the impulse of the moment to be married, and woke up the next day—sober, married, and startled.

"Any law which would lend seriousness to the marriage contract would be helpful."

Mrs. Kate Burr Johnson, commissioner of the State Board of Charities and Public Welfare, cites this incident which happened in Greensboro recently and which shows the need for such a law:

"A mentally defective boy, who was suffering from a vicious form of venereal disease, married a feeble-minded girl. The father brought a complaint against the doctor who issued the certificate of health to the boy, and who was also said to have given the young man medical treatment several times during the past two years. At the time of the marriage, the boy was absent without leave from a hospital where he was being treated for mental trouble.

"Publication of the intention to marry would doubtless have prevented this union. The father of the boy and others who had knowledge of the participants consider it deplorable."

A summary answering why a notice of intention to marry is so essential in the regulation of the marriage laws of the state has been prepared by Mrs. W. T. Bost of Raleigh. It is briefly this:

"1. Enough time should be provided between the application for a marriage license and its issuance for proper physical examinations which are required by law, and which, if rigidly carried out, would prevent in many cases the union of diseased or mentally sick people physically unfit to marry and perpetuate the race.

"2. It would place obstacles in the way of illegal and irregular marriages through public notice of the marriage application. Bigamy might be prevented as well as the marriage of minors. A careful study into conditions in North Carolina will show that too often a girl of 15, 14, 13, and even 12 and 11 enters into marriage with or without her parents' consent. Often the age is misrepresented and it is in such cases that the law requiring an interval between publication of intention to marry and the marriage will be of most value.

"3. It would be a protection to hasty and impulsive young people, hundreds of whom rush headlong into marriage without thought or serious consideration, with the result that desertion and divorces from such marriages are multiplying rapidly. It would give these young people a chance to deliberate and take it under advisement with either parents or guardians and in some cases it would enable the parents or guardians to protect these minors from unsuitable marriages."

Charlotte Sunday Observer, p. 49 (section 4, p. 7)

20 OCTOBER 1929

INTEREST IN CLUB WORK NOT WANING AMONG WOMEN

Falling Off of Attendance at Club Meetings Does Not Mean That Club Women Will Sit By and See Great Movement Fade Off Stage

By Mrs. J. Henry Highsmith

Is the Woman's Club dying? Does it have the hold on women seeking improvement for themselves and their children that it had 20 years ago?

Does it have the same place in the community as a social, civic and cultural center that it once had? These sinister suggestions now in circulation may be the voice of a friend or an enemy, or perhaps both, but while they are making the rounds the true status of the Woman's Club movement in North Carolina might as well be looked into.

Beliefs and assumptions as answers to these questions might satisfy the club devotee, but the doubtful critic must have his proof—facts and figures.

The signs that are interpreted to mean the early death of the woman's club—its passing from the high place which it once held in life and affairs of organized women—appear to be observations not generally obtaining but true perhaps to individual clubs. That unfavorable conditions do exist in some clubs, as in some churches and other organizations, is not doubted, but it does not hold that the whole system of the woman's club or the church is doomed because one club or one church does not function as it was originally intended.

The first and most unmistakable symptom of the club's early demise, as pointed out by the critics, is the falling off here and there in attendance at club meetings. Another fateful observation is that the woman's club program is superficial—that it does not deal with subjects related to the life of its members and that it is no longer the medium through which women may work to meet the needs of their community.

Another arraignment made of the woman's club of today is that it is static, while the forces of life are active and progressive. The modern woman, they say, no longer finds what she needs and wants in the woman's club. It is claimed that the club of today is run just as it was organized and run 20 years ago, with little or no adaptability in its programs, and with no defined job objectives.

But probably the greatest enemy eating at the root of the life of the Woman's Club, according to one of the critics, is talk—not malicious talk by its enemies or competitors, but pointless, futile talk by the leaders and those claiming to have the best interests of the club at heart.

It is pointed out further that there is the radio, bridge parties and politics to compete with in holding the club woman's interest, the inference being that the club is the loser. Having made these observations and interpretations, one critic summarizes the situation thus: "The truth is unless club leaders wake up to the true situation and inject some invigorating serum into their programs and activities, the cultural club will go the way of the horse and buggy, the cotillion, and the cross-word puzzle."

Club Leaders Not Discouraged.

No two women know better the status quo of the Woman's Club movement in North Carolina than Mrs. Thomas O'Berry, of Goldsboro, who was president of the State Federation of Woman's Clubs for the past two years and is now the General Federation State director, and Mrs. W. T. Bost, of Raleigh, who is executive secretary of the State Federation Headquarters in Raleigh. Through the offices that these women hold, they have been able to keep their fingers on the pulse of the real situation in this State, and their judgments should be given due consideration.

As regards the rumor that women everywhere are losing interest in the Woman's Club, Mrs. O'Berry says:

"There is in North Carolina today every indication of increasing usefulness and strength in the Woman's Club, a proof of which is found in the increased attendance at State and district meetings.

"The recent convention at Charlotte was the largest in the history of the Federation, both in registered delegates and in the number of visitors. The district meetings of 1927 showed an increase of 338 over the preceding year. More than 3,000 women attended these district meetings last Fall. It must be taken into consideration that about half of these women drive from 70 to 90 miles to the one-day meeting. This to me very obviously signifies increased interest.

"The greatest inspiration I have ever experienced," says Mrs. O'Berry, "was to see and to talk to the interested, eager and intelligent women attending these meetings. I was so much impressed with the large number of young women not only attending the meetings, but assuming places of responsibility, that I have often spoken of it in subsequent talks. Twenty new Junior clubs came into the State Federation last year, and not a single Junior club has withdrawn, an evidence of the awakening interest of the younger women."

Mrs. Bost not only discredits the rumor that women are losing interest, but wonders at the fact that the Women's Club is the force it is in the country in spite of the encroachments made upon it by numerous other organizations, all of which claim women's interest and time. She says:

"Granted that there is a shrinkage in numbers in this club or that, that attendance at departmental meetings is somewhat smaller, can it be said that the Woman's Club 'is not what it used to be,' or is not the force it once was? The marvel to me is that in spite of all the encroachments that have been made upon it; in spite of the numerous claims upon club women for services here, there and everywhere; in spite of the complexities of our modern life that plunge us into a veritable vortex of fast living—the marvel to me is that the Woman's Club has held its own and is the living, vibrant force that it is in the country today.

"I frequently hear," she says, "club women complaining of the small attendance at their meetings, but I also hear members of the Parent-Teacher Associations, church societies, Leagues of Women Voters and other organized groups, make the same complaint, but are we to be led by such symptoms to believe that all these institutions are going to the wall?"

A possible explanation of why a club might not expect to continue increasing its membership or even to hold all its members is here given by Mrs. Bost:

"Twenty-five years ago the Woman's Club was practically the only medium through which women might seek self-improvement or render public service, but today there are dozens of other mediums organized along special lines all appealing to her interests. However, we believe that in the majority of communities, the Woman's Club will be the main organization through which women will be given an opportunity to stimulate their cultural and social life, and serve their communities. Its many-sided program makes an appeal to the average woman who prefers membership in one organization rather than in four or five.

Furthermore, Mrs. Bost believes the Woman's Club is a permanent public institution, "as fixed and as definite a civic enterprise and as forceful a one as any element entering into community development," she says:

"The building of club houses all over North Carolina, costing from a few hundred dollars for a remodelled building to $100,000 or more for new ones, is additional proof that the Woman's Club is a permanent institution. North Carolina club women have over $600,000 invested in clubhouse property. And why? Primarily that they may have the proper tools and equipment for facilitating the work. We hear it said that the Woman's Club has a roof over its head and is here to stay, for has not the rooftree always been regarded as the symbol of permanency? Club women will not so lightly abandon the thing that meant sacrifice and service in the building thereof.

Mrs. Palmer Jerman Has No Fear.

Mrs. Palmer Jerman, of Raleigh, who is recognized for her wisdom and club experience not only in her native State, but throughout country, has for many years kept a watchful eye on the club situation. She says, "I love the Woman's Club for what it has done and for what it is still able to do through its diversified program. One of the club's finest features, she says, "is its flexible program, readily adaptable to local and specific needs."

Another fine feature of the Woman's Club, thinks Mrs. Jerman, is its autonomy in local matters. Neither the State or the General Federation dictates the policies to or places limitations upon any club's activity in local work. For this reason clubs have been able to engage in big local projects and carry forward momentous undertakings that were unthinkable 15 or 20 years ago.

> *Note:* Mrs. Highsmith references Anna Steese Sausser Richardson, "Is the Women's Club Dying?," *Harper's Magazine* 159/9 (30 September 1929), pp. 605–09.

Raleigh Sunday *News and Observer,* p. 11 (Society, p. 1)

1 DECEMBER 1929

EXPLAINS WHY SURVEY OF WOMEN IN STATE INDUSTRY WAS DROPPED

**Mrs. J. Henry Highsmith, Appointed to Make Survey,
Gives Story of Its Collapse**

By Mrs. J. Henry Highsmith

The question of a survey of women and children in industry in North Carolina is like Banquo's ghost—it will not down. No sooner does one group of persons get together and resolve that a survey of the working conditions of men and women is the one thing needed in this State, than another group gets together and makes the same resolve. But so far it's to no effect. And so far the scenes of the year 1926, when the women of the State labored for a survey, are being re-enacted.

But things are different now from what they were in '26. Not a few developments, particularly in the textile industry, have taken place. Whether it was just woman's intuition or the use of her gift to divine, she foresaw the trouble, said so and went about to prevent it. Then there were only slight symptoms, as unmistakable as they were, to tell that all was not well with North Carolina's pet child, the cotton mill industry; but today there's no mistake about this being a sick industry, seriously ill and needing expert attention. No one will deny that there's something radically wrong with the system somehow and somewhere. That the mills are not functioning properly, not producing to full capacity and with their accustomed ease, having rigors within and without, suffering now and then violent convulsions and being, therefore badly in need of treatment is the generally accepted diagnosis.

Public opinion demands that this child be given a thorough physical examination, that expert clinicians study the case, assemble the facts, and with these facts in hand determine the proper treatment. No fake remedies or temporary palliatives will do. Only an examination that will reveal the trouble and open the way for a permanent recovery will suffice.

With the foregoing said about the present demand for a survey of the industrial conditions of the State, I return to the summer of '26, to the controversy that arose when representative groups of women of the State endeavored to have made a survey of women in industry, which to this day, they believe, would have prevented many of the labor troubles that are about to cost the State its good name. I feel as [British journalist] Philip Gibbs felt when writing later the facts about the World War, "Now it can be told," the title he gave his great book [1920]. Furthermore, I feel that the women, in their efforts to serve the State, particularly, the childhood and womanhood of the State, have been fully vindicated. The tragic events which have happened partly as a result of having no accurate information regarding the hours, wages, and living conditions of that large mass of working men and women show clearly enough that the women were justified in speaking out as they did for this inarticulate group.

That the survey was not accomplished was not due directly to any one person or one thing. In the first place the manufacturers were against it, all except a few isolated ones who would have welcomed any kind of investigation. The Governor himself said he saw no reason for a survey; everything was well enough as it was. The attitude of the manufacturers became fully known a few months prior to this time when the Institute for Research in Social Science at the University of North Carolina asked for permission and co-operation in making a study of the cotton mill industry of this State. Their offer was declined.

On the other hand, the women who for years had labored in season and out for a survey brought such pressure to bear as the Governor could not evade. He saw they were in earnest. They were conscientious. Something had to be done. And yet there were the manufacturers, of whom he was one, to be reckoned with. He did not dare displease them. Consequently he found himself in an uncomfortable position on top of the fence. And it was this position that he endeavored to keep throughout the proceedings—acceding to the women just far enough to stay off revolt in their side, meanwhile assuring those on the other hand that their interests would not suffer.

To affect a combination of a peace offering and a compromise was the only hope in this situation. And never was it intended by the Governor and his advisers that there should be a bonafide survey, just such as the women wanted, and which had been promised them.

That this was the true equation was repeatedly borne out in the subsequent transactions having to do with making the survey.

To keep history straight, Governor McLean consented to having a survey made provided the Child Welfare Commission make it. That commission was composed of Mrs. Kate Burr Johnson, State Commissioner of Public Welfare, Mr. A. T. Allen, State Superintendent of Public Instruction and Dr. G. M. Cooper, who was acting executive secretary of the State Board of Health. Mr. E. F. Carter was executive secretary of the commission. The women were insistent at one point and that was that the survey be made by a thoroughly competent and impartial agency. They said they would not accept a survey made by Mr. Carter, as he would be surveying his own field and the results would be the same as if he were auditing his own books. A compromise was effected when it was agreed to by all to put a woman in charge of making the survey. I was that woman. When I was called to Mrs. Johnson's office I found in conference with her Mr. Allen, Dr. Cooper and Mr. Carter. On being asked if I would accept the position as director of the Survey of Women in Industry, naturally I asked them to explain just what the work would be. Not one but all had a part in the explanation. I was told that I would have full supervision of making the survey, assembling the facts and writing the report which was to be ready by the meeting of the Legislature in January. I was told that I would have the assistance of Mr. Carter and the facilities of his office in so doing. Furthermore, it was suggested to me at that same meeting that I go to Washington and confer with the heads of the Women's Bureau as Mr. Carter had already done, in order to get ideas and the instructions, blanks, schedules and questionnaires necessary for making a worthwhile survey. Besides having it in written form, receiving so much salary per month, that I was to be the director of the survey, the newspapers next morning published the fact in headlines and at the same time carried the statement that Mr. Carter and his office would assist me in making the survey. I accepted the position with this understanding and went to work.

I was given a desk temporarily in Mr. Carter's office. Every courtesy was shown me. Preparations were being made to fit up several rooms on the second floor where I was to have an office and where all the work of the survey was to be done. Things went well at first. I went to Washington for the suggested conference with Miss Mary Anderson and other heads of the Woman's Bureau and was accompanied by Miss Pattie Gee Hill, Mr. Carter's secretary, at his suggestion.

Soon copies of questionnaires, schedules and blanks were studied, worked over and adapted to meet the needs, and a sufficient number turned over to have printed. At this point what seemed unreasonable delays became noticeable.

The question of employing the field workers, particularly those who were to have charge of making the investigation, was recognized at the beginning to be a very important one. As the value of the survey depended solely on the accuracy, intelligence, and thoroughness with which the investigators made their studies, filled out their blanks and answered their questionnaires— and some of these forms were far from simple—it naturally became my duty to select men and women whose training, experience, personality and sense of fairness best fitted them for these positions. But I soon found that I did not have the power to employ the field workers, but only to recommend them for employment. After much delay I learned that my recommendations were remaining recommendations while Mr. Carter himself was preparing a list. It then became known that his list was composed of men and women, for the most part, who had a mill background, or who had had connections directly or indirectly with the mills. After days of delay, and in order to get going, the members of the Child Welfare Commission advised a compromise made up of names taken from both lists. Before this difference could be settled, it became known that it was the plan of the executive secretary to have all the schedules or forms containing the information gathered by the field workers first opened, and checked over downstairs in his office before sending them upstairs to the survey offices. This matter was likewise referred to the commission for settlement. But neither Mr. Allen nor Dr. Cooper saw any irregularity in this and so failed to stand with Mrs. Johnson who held that the returns or information sent in by the investigators was survey property and should be sent directly to the survey offices and there opened checked, and tabulated. This preak precipitated the question who was responsible for making the survey? Who was the director? The decision of this question apparently carried too much responsibility, more than either one of the male members of the Commission was willing to bear, and so it too was referred to the Governor. More delay.

Finally word came from the Governor through Mr. Allen that Mr. Carter was supposed to have general supervision of making the survey and that I was only an assistant.

This complete reversal of policy and agreement on the part of the Governor and the two male members of the commission, Mr. Allen and Dr. Cooper, brought the whole matter to an impasse. The issue was clear. If Mr. Carter was going to have charge of making the survey, then it would not be the survey the women had asked for, and had been promised, for was it not well known that Mr. Carter's sympathies had always been on the side of the mill interests?

Mrs. Johnson feeling this she could not keep faith with the women whom she represented if she in any way sanctioned such a survey, asked the Governor to relieve her from having further responsibility or connection with it. The survey was immediately called off.

One word more as to the nature and scope of the attempted survey. At the time the survey was requested there were approximately 170,000 women in industry in North Carolina. But there were no reliable data by which one could judge as to the conditions under which these 170,000 women worked and lived. There were no authoritative facts by which one could deny or stave off unjust and malicious criticism either in or outside of the State. Neither were there statistics on which to base constructive and helpful legislation as well as inaugurate wise social programs. Other states have this information on file. All other Southern States except probably one have had industrial surveys and the findings have become a matter of record. That North Carolina should continue her policy of refusing to give this information to the public, especially in the light of her recent labor troubles, cannot be understood. But the women's interest in this matter is not abated. They will continue to work for a comprehensive impartial survey until it is accomplished.

It was the plan of the survey to reach ten per cent or 17,000 working women in carefully selected industries representing cotton factories, tobacco factories, stores, laundries, hotels and restaurants. The information sought concerned working hours, wages, night work, sanitary conditions, heat, ventilation, fatigue, home work, home working mothers, tuberculosis and general living conditions.

In addition plans had been made with the State Board of Health to conduct a survey of three typical agricultural counties of North Carolina, the purpose of which was to obtain information pertaining to women who work on the farm. This information was considered important in order to valuate correctly much of the information gathered with respect to the living conditions of the mill village people.

Furthermore it was one of our plans to make a restricted survey of domestic servants. As no other State has done this the information received would not only have been interesting and helpful but would have been much in demand.

Raleigh Sunday *News and Observer*, p. 24 (Sports, p. 6)

1930

14 January — presents program at Twentieth Century Book Club meeting with her neighbor, Mrs. R. N. Simms

25 January — as new president, presides over Wake County League of Women Voters

2 February — jury trial in Wake County Superior Court finds her co-responsible for car accident in 1928; no damages assessed

10–12 February — attends state convention of NC League of Women Voters in Goldsboro; responds to official welcome at opening session

22 February — the Highsmiths depart by car with three guests, including Mrs. Peyton Brown (Aunt Margaret), to attend National Educational Association meeting in Atlantic City

9 March 1930 — her appointment as Executive Secretary at NCFWC State Headquarters in Raleigh is announced, with biographical summary and photograph; succeeds Mrs. W. T. (Annie Kizer) Bost, the first executive secretary, and is succeeded by Mrs. J. Wilbur Bunn

1930–1935
Executive Secretary, State Headquarters
North Carolina Federation of Women's Clubs

3 April — honored, with Mrs. Bost, at RWC tea

10 April — at Thompson School PTA, makes an appeal for YWCA

11 May — Louise scores 100% at pre-school examination for Murphey School, one of 3, and is pictured in the paper, as was Katherine two years before

13–16 May — attends 28th annual NCFWC convention in Pinehurst

27 May — reported as member of Raleigh committee supporting for Josiah William Bailey for U. S. Senate

30 May — issues statement that she was placed on [Josiah] Bailey [for U. S. Senate] Committee without her knowledge and consent; supports U. S. Senator [Furnifold] Simmons

2 June — attends League of Women Voters session on first use of Australian ballot for the upcoming primary on 7 June; Lula Belle appears in the demonstration skit

17 June — judges essay contest of North Carolina Cotton Growers' Co-operative Association, on "How Can the Benefit of the Agricultural Marketing Act be brought to the Farmer?"

21 June — becomes further embroiled in the senatorial election at the Wake County precinct level; joins a coalition running for Democratic State Convention and is briefly mentioned for statewide party ticket; Mrs. Jerman now a member of Democratic National Committee

11 August — returns from 10-day White Lake vacation with Lula Belle, Katharine, and Louise, also Eugenia and Mary Belle; Dr. Highsmith joins them for the weekend

12 October — hosts Mrs. E. M. Land and Mrs. J. M. Hobgood, NCFWC officers, during their 16-district visits

14 October — hosts reception for Mrs. Josiah Evans Cowles of Los Angeles, honorary past president of GFWC, and her husband Dr. Cowles, at State Headquarters

20 October — presides over Wake County League of Women Voters discussion of constitutional amendments proposed for November election

3 November — conducts class on parliamentary law, open to women of Raleigh

26 November — presides over Wake County League of Women Voters meeting; Mrs. Jerman of the Legislative Council explains program for the 1931 Legislature; Mrs. Bost reports on White House Conference on Child Care the previous week

4 December — at RWC meeting of her art department, featuring *tableaux vivants* presented by Wiley School children, she reports on departmental projects

4 December — at annual meeting of NC Art Society, presents co-authored resolution on State Art Museum, which passes

14 December — Legislative Council announces reopening of headquarters, re-election of Mrs. Highsmith as executive secretary, and four-point legislative program; Mrs. Jerman is president, Mrs. Land vice president, and Mrs. Doak, treasurer

6 APRIL 1930

FEDERATION TO HOLD ITS CONVENTION AT PINEHURST

By Mrs. J. Henry Highsmith
Press Chairman

The official call for the twenty-eighth annual convention of the State Federation of Women's Clubs recently issued by Mrs. E. M. Land, of Statesville, State president, announces that Pinehurst is the place and May 14–17 is the date of the 1930 convention. Official headquarters will be at the Carolina Hotel.

Owing to the central location of Pinehurst and good roads making it easily accessible, an unusually large number of club women is expected to attend. All club women, whether delegates or not, will be cordially welcomed to all business sessions and to all social functions.

On the opening evening of the convention, Wednesday, May 14, Mrs. Ambrose Diehl, of Pittsburgh, Pa., chairman of the committee on Motion Pictures in the General Federation of Women's Clubs, will be principal speaker. The president's address will also be given on this evening. At the close the evening's program a reception will be tendered the convention by the management of the Carolina Hotel.

The second evening will be given to Fine Arts. The departments of Art, Literature and Music will provide an artistic program which will include an hour of music furnished by North Carolina artists.

The crowning event of the convention will be the Federation dinner, Friday evening, May 16. At this time Mrs. Grace Morrison Poole, first vice-president of the General Federation of Women's Clubs, will be honor guest and speaker. An additional feature for that evening's entertainment will be groups of readings and songs by Mrs. Lawson Turner of Lynchburg, Va.

In addition to the reception held at the Carolina Hotel the first evening, there will be a tea at the Country Club on Thursday afternoon and an archery contest on Friday afternoon.

Miss Adelaide Fries, of Winston-Salem, has been appointed chairman of the Resolutions Committee. Clubs having resolutions to present at the convention are asked to submit these to the chairman of the Resolutions Committee two weeks before the convention.

Presiding at the district presidents' dinner Wednesday evening will be the second vice-president, Mrs. J. M. Hobgood, of Farmville. Presiding at the president's breakfast conference Thursday will be Mrs. W. A. French, of Wilmington. Mrs. O. M. Meekins, of Elizabeth City, will preside at the breakfast conference on music, and Mrs. J. E. Hardin, of Greensboro, will preside at the breakfast conference on civics the same morning.

At the luncheon conference of junior membership, Thursday, Mrs. R. D. W. Connor, of Chapel Hill, will preside. At the luncheon conference of literary clubs and literature departments on Thursday, Mrs. Annie Miller Pless will preside. Miss Ethel Parker, of Gatesville, will preside at the American citizenship luncheon the same day.

On Friday morning Mrs. L. R. Johnston, of High Point, will preside at the breakfast conference on art and Mrs. T. E. Johnston, of Salisbury, will preside at the breakfast conference on education. The luncheon conference Friday on the American home will be presided over by Mrs. T. E. Browne, of Raleigh, and the public welfare luncheon conference that day will be presided over by Miss Ruth Burke, of La Grange.

Featuring the first day's program will be a meeting of the executive board at 1 o'clock and a luncheon at 1 o'clock. Meetings of the board of trustees and directors will be held in the afternoon. Opening session of the convention will be at 8:30 o'clock Wednesday evening in the hotel assembly hall.

Time Extended for Literary Contest.

On account of the interest that is being taken in the literary contests, Mrs. Annie Miller Pless, of Marion, chairman of Literature, announces that the time for receiving manuscripts as entries for the contest has been extended to May 1, instead of April 1, as first announced.

Raleigh Sunday *News and Observer,* p. 13 (Society, p. 1)

20 APRIL 1930

CONVENTION AT PINEHURST

Three Nationally Known Club Women to Speak on Interesting Program

By Mrs. J. Henry Highsmith

Among the outstanding features of the twenty-eighth annual convention of the State Federation of Women's Clubs to be held at Pinehurst, May 14–17, will be the addresses of three nationally known club women, Mrs. Grace Morrison Poole, Mrs. Ambrose Diehl, and Mrs. Saidie Orr Dunbar, one an officer and the other two chairmen of important committees of the General Federation of Women's Clubs. These able and distinguished visitors, by their presence as well as by their speeches, will add interest and inspiration to the three day sessions of the convention.

Speaker At Banquet.

First of these is Mrs. Grace Morrison Poole of Brockton, Mass., first vice president of the General Federation, who will be the banquet speaker Friday evening and who will be introduced by Mrs. Thomas O'Berry of Goldsboro, who is also a member of the executive board of the General Federation. Her subject will be "What Is It All About?" Mrs. Poole is a noted lecturer. In addition to having been, and now is, a busy club woman, she has served seven years on the school board of her home town. One of her present activities is conducting classes in current history in Massachusetts and New Hampshire. She says her favorite recreation is homemaking and her hobbies are a Sunday school class of high school boys and two little nieces which are seldom out of her mind. But the thing she loves best to do, she says, is to "travel far and near in this world of ours, which is a part of my very life and affords me the greatest joy of living."

Mrs. Ambrose Diehl of Pittsburgh, Pa., chairman of the Motion Picture committee of the General Federation, will be the principal speaker on the opening evening, Wednesday, May 14. She will relay to the convention a message from Mrs. Thomas G. Winters, who has recently accepted a position with the Studio Relations committee of the Moving Pictures Producers Association, whose work with the committee is to interpret to the studios the feeling and wishes of the organized women of America.

Welfare Luncheon.

Mrs. Saidie Orr Dunbar of Portland, Oregon, who is chairman of Public Welfare of the General Federation, will be the honor guest and speaker at the Public Welfare luncheon conference on Friday. Miss Ruth Burks of La Grange will be present at the luncheon conference.

Another attractive woman speaker and entertainer will be Mrs. Lucile Barrow Turner of Lynchburg, Virginia, who will be given a prominent place on the program at the Federation dinner, Friday evening. Mrs. Turner is a noted reader and impersonator. Among her selections that evening will be a number of Negro spirituals which she herself will sing.

And not least of the attractive speakers who appear on the convention program is the state president, Mrs. Edward M. Land of Statesville. She will make her address at the opening session, at which time she will review the accomplishments of the club women during the past year, and outline the plans and policies for them to follow for another year. Mrs. Charles R. Whitaker of Southern Pines will make the address of welcome, and Mrs. J. M. Hobgood of Farmville, second vice president, will make the response.

An additional very interesting as well as instructive feature of the convention program will be the parliamentary law classes held each morning from 9 to 10 o'clock with Miss Bettie Windley of New Bern as instructor. These classes which proved to so popular last year at the Charlotte convention are offered again at club women's request.

A number of delightful social functions have been arranged for the pleasure and recreation of the club women. Among them are the reception on Wednesday evening in the Carolina Hotel parlors, a tea at the Pinehurst Country Club Thursday afternoon and an archery contest and tea Friday afternoon.

Picture Memory Contest.

Mrs. R. L. McMillan of Raleigh, chairman of the Picture Memory contest, announces that the statewide Picture Memory contest will be held in Raleigh at the Hugh Morson High School on May 3. The children will be guests of the art department of the Woman's Club at luncheon on that day. During the luncheon hour an interesting program will be presented by the children of Miss Margaret Leavering's grade at Wiley School. With the assistance of Miss Mary Tilley of Meredith College, a number of tableaux of living pictures will be given. Among the pictures selected will be Mother and Child by Frans Hals, Boy with Rabbit by Raeburn, Girl with the Cat by Hoecker, Miss Bowles by Reynolds, The Torn Hat by Sully, Madonna of the Chair by Raphael, The Song of the Lark by Breton, The Pastry Eaters by Murillo, Age of Innocence by Reynolds, The Artist's Mother by Whistler, The Blue Boy by Gainsborough, and the Boy with the Sword by Manet.

After the luncheon the children who enter the contest will be entertained by Mrs. J. W. Bunn, president of the Raleigh Woman's Club, at a garden party. Dr. and Mrs. F. C. Brooks will entertain them at the beautiful new home of the president of State College, and Mrs. O. Max Gardner will receive them at the Executive Mansion.

Mrs. Chamberlain To Lecture.

Club women of the state will be interested in the announcement that Miss Hope Summerell Chamberlain will be available next year to Women's Clubs to lecture or make informal talks on North Carolina History, North Carolina Women, Early Americana, Art, American Novelists, Recent American Poetry, and Book Reviews. Mrs. Chamberlain's fame as an author and lecturer is already well established in North Carolina. She has recently returned from an extended stay in Europe where she traveled and studied, preparatory to lecture work at home.

Charlotte Sunday Observer, p. 30 (section 3, p. 6)

4 MAY 1930

SPECIAL MEMORIAL SERVICES FOR MRS. SALLIE S. COTTEN
BY WOMEN'S CLUBS OF STATE

Mrs. Cotten Was Instrumental in Organization of State Federation and Was Its First President—Sallie Cotten Loan Fund Has Helped Hundred Girls to Secure Higher Education—Wrote a History of Federation and Other Works

By Mrs. J. Henry Highsmith

In a special memorial service to be held at Pinehurst Friday morning, May 16, the club women of the state assembled here in their twenty-eighth annual convention will pay tribute to Mrs. R. R. Cotten, mother of the Federation, who passed from earth just a year ago today at the age of 82.

This service set for 11 o'clock Friday morning of convention week will be the first state wide memorial held by the club women for Mrs. Cotten, as her death occurred the day after the convention closed at Charlotte last year. Action was taken at the council meeting at Chapel Hill in October to hold a special memorial service to Mrs. Cotten during the 1930 convention.

Tribute To Mrs. Cotten.

Among those who will pay tributes to Mrs. Cotten will be Mrs. Sydney P. Cooper of Henderson who will deal with Mrs. Cotten's early life as a pioneer and citizen. Mrs. W. T. Bost will tell of Mrs. Cotten as a club woman, reviewing her services in behalf of the causes and interests of club women throughout the state and particularly her love for and work in the State Federation. Mrs. Palmer Jerman will pay her tribute as counsellor and friend. The club woman's hymn, written for the Federation by Mrs. Cotten, will be sung at the opening of the services. Friends and relatives of Mrs. Cotton from far and near will attend the exercises. Her children and grand-children will attend.

Following the memorial services will be the presentation of the Sallie Southall Cotten loan fund, which is not only one of the Federation's most outstanding achievements, but which is in itself a living memorial to Mrs. Cotten. During the 16 years of it existence the fund has grown from a small loan in 1913 to over $20,000 in 1930. To the present time $31,436.33 has been loaned, and $14,409.33 has been repaid. The remaining unpaid amount is still in use. More than 100 girls have been aided by this fund to secure a college or higher education, and in all the transactions of making and repaying the loans not a dollar has been lost. Every cent has been repaid. Today 28 girls have the use of this money and 50 more are on the waiting list.

Education Of Girls.

Mrs. Cotten, to whom the education of girls was a great passion, said in reference to this loan: "It gives me a thrill of joy every time I remember that after I have passed on the Sallie Southall Cotten loan fund will continue to help North Carolina girls and keep me in the memory of the women who have made it a success."

Mrs. Cotten is lovingly known as the mother of the State Federation she was instrumental in forming. It was largely through her efforts that the state organization at Salem Academy, now Salem College, [was established] at Winston-Salem in May, 1902. The next year, 1903, and again through her efforts the newly formed state association joined the General Federation of Women's Clubs. Mrs. Cotten represented the General Federation in North Carolina a number of years before the state organization was formed and admitted. She attended her first biennial meeting held in Milwaukee in 1900, and for her service and connection with that convention she was admitted to the Society of Pioneers, an organization recognizing no service later than 1900.

Outstanding Services.

One of the most outstanding services of Mrs. Cotten to the Federation in addition to serving it as president and honorary president, the latter up to the time of her death, was the writing of the history of the Federation. The period covered was from 1901 to 1925, almost half a century [sic] of club work in North Carolina. In addition to her history she has written the White Doe, a legend of Virginia Dare, and Tales Aunt Dorcas Told Little Elsie, a collection of Negro folk lore stories.

Charlotte Sunday Observer, p. 37 (section 3, p. 5)

11 MAY 1930

PROGRESSIVE FEATURES FOR NORTH CAROLINA FEDERATION
OF CLUB WOMEN THIS WEEK

Complete Program Includes Number of Entertaining Speakers— Attendance Expected to Be Largest in Recent Years—Special Memorial Services for Mrs. Sallie Southall Cotten—Breakfast and Luncheon Conferences—Archery Contest

By Mrs. J. Henry Highsmith

Indications are that the annual convention of the State Federation of Women's Clubs, that will be held Wednesday Thursday and Friday of this week at Pinehurst, will be not only one of the most largely attended but also one of the most interesting and forward-looking conventions the Federation has yet held.

The three day program carries many new and entertaining features of which one will be the speeches of the three prominent and nationally known club women, Mrs. Grace Morrison Poole, Massachusetts, first vice president of the General Federation; Mrs. Ambrose Diehl, of Pennsylvania, chairman of motion pictures of the General Federation, Mrs. Saidie Orr Dunbar of Oregon, chairman of public welfare.

Entertaining Speakers.

Another attractive and entertaining speaker will be Mrs. Lucile Barrow Turner of Lynchburg, Va., noted speaker and impersonator, who with Mrs. Poole, will feature the banquet program on Friday evening. Mrs. Diehl will speak on Wednesday evening at the opening session and Mrs. Dunbar at the public welfare luncheon at noon Friday.

The special memorial services to Mrs. R. R. Cotten, whose death occurred a little over a year ago, which services have been set for 11 o'clock Friday morning, will be of particular interest to every club woman. In addition to the tributes that will be paid Mrs. Cotten by Mrs. Sydney Cooper, Mrs. W. T. Bost and Mrs. Palmer Jerman, there will be two songs, "The Club Woman's Hymn," which she herself wrote, and Geoffrey O'Hara's "There Is No Death." Mrs. E. M. Land, president of the Federation, will preside at the services, following which Mrs. W. J. Brogden, of Durham, will present the Sallie Southall Cotten loan fund, a living memorial to Mrs. Cotten and one of the club women's greatest accomplishments. Contributions to the fund will be taken at this time.

Among the interesting breakfast and luncheon conference speakers will be Col. J. W. Harrelson of Raleigh and Paul Van Lindley of Greensboro, who will speak Thursday morning at the civics breakfast, over which Mrs. J. E. Hardin of Greensboro, presides. Mrs. B. A. Hocutt of Clayton, is also on the program. Colonel Harrelson's subject is "Economy and Social Value of Landscape Beauty."

Music Conference.

At the music breakfast conference Thursday morning, Professor Harold S. Dyer, director of music at the University of North Carolina, will speak. His subject will be "Discrimination in Radio Music." Other speakers will be Miss Annie Cherry, Miss Hattie Parrot, Mrs. Cora Cox Lucas and Mrs. A. S. Kennickell, Jr., Mrs. E. E. Randolph of Raleigh will preside at this breakfast in the place of Mrs. I. M. Meekins of Elizabeth City, state chairman of music, who continues ill.

At the breakfast conference held for the presidents of departmental clubs, over which Mrs. A. W. French of Wilmington will preside, Mrs. M. F. Grote of Zebulon, Mrs. Frank Shaw of Enfield, Mrs. N.H. Hopson of Varina, and Mrs. E. L. McKee of Sylva will speak.

Mrs. R. D. W. Connor of Chapel Hill will preside over the luncheon conference held on Thursday for the Junior club members. Her speakers will be Misses Pauline Smith, Jessie Stanley, Martha Galloway, Catherine Blalock, Annie Battle Miller and Mrs. Billy Davis.

Mrs. Annie Miller Pless of Marion will preside over the conferences for literary clubs and literature departments with Mrs. Hope Summerell Chamberlain, of Raleigh, as speaker.

At the same hour, Miss Ethel Parker of Gatesville will preside over the conference on American citizenship. The speakers at this conference are Dr. Fred Morrison, of Raleigh, and Miss Harriet Elliott, of Greensboro.

Study Of The Arts.

Following the afternoon session of Thursday will be a tea given by the courtesy of the Civic Club of Southern Pines in their attractive new club house.

Thursday evening will be given over to the Fine Arts—music, art, and literature. Mrs. Charles E. Platt of Charlotte, first vice president, will preside. The principal speaker of the evening will be Dr. Ernest R. Derendinger, on the subject of art's glorious mission, which lecture will be illustrated with lantern slides. Dr. Derendinger is professor of art at Catawba College, Salisbury, and is visiting lecturer on art at Harvard University summer school. He did graduate work in Europe, receiving his Ph. D. from Berlin for work done in excavating and recreating Munichaurach near Erlangen, Bavaria, built in the year 1128 by Hirsauer Bauschule.

Another artist on the evening's program is Miss Nanna Johnson, of Winston-Salem, who with Mrs. Cora Cox Lucas at the piano will give a song and piano recital. Miss Johnson is a lyric soprano. She graduated in voice from Salem College and has done extensive study in New York. She is a graduate of Westminster Choir School, of Dayton, Ohio, and she toured Europe last year with the famous Dayton Westminster Choir. She has had wide experience in church oratorio and concert work. At present she is soloist at Reynolds Presbyterian Church of Winston-Salem, and is soprano soloist at Salem College commencement this year.

Awarding Of Prizes.

The awarding of cups and prizes for the best creative work in art, music and literature will be made at this session.

At the breakfast conference on art Friday morning, over which Mrs. L. R. Johnston of High Point will preside, [missing]. Speaking at this conference will be Mrs. R. L. Gwynn of Lenoir and Mrs. R. L. McMillan of Raleigh.

At the breakfast conference on education, at which Mrs. T. E. Johnston of Salisbury will preside, Miss Frieda Heller and Prof. E. J. Coltrane will speak.

An interesting feature of Friday afternoon's session will be a play, "Life Experiences," by pupils of the night schools of High Point, directed by Miss Eva Edgerton, instructor. This demonstration of a night school at work using the pupils themselves—nine of them who have learned to read and write this year—is sponsored by the Woman's Club of High Point, under whose auspices this work has been done. Showing its approval of the night school work, the city council of High Point recently made an appropriation of $5,000 for carrying on the work another year.

Mr. Hugh McRae of Wilmington will be the principal speaker at the American Home luncheon Friday. Mrs. T. E. Brown of Raleigh will preside. Another feature of the luncheon program will be a skit directed by Mrs. C. G. Doak of Raleigh.

At the public welfare luncheon presided over by Miss Ruth Burke of La Grange, Mrs. Saidie Orr Dunbar of Portland, Ore., will speak.

Archery Contest.

An archery contest and tea held at the Pinehurst Country Club, will be the social feature of Friday afternoon.

The climax of the convention will be the Federation dinner on Friday evening, with Mrs. Land presiding. Music for the dinner will be furnished by Flora Macdonald College.

Mrs. Thomas O'Berry of Goldsboro will introduce the dinner speaker and convention guests. [The speaker will be] Mrs. Grace Morrison Poole of Massachusetts, first vice president of the General Federation. Mrs. Poole's subject will be "What Is It All About?"

Following Mrs. Poole will be some songs, readings, and impersonations by Lucile Barrow Turner of Virginia.

Mrs. Charles L. Scott of Sanford, president of the ninth district is taking the place of local hostess. She has chosen an able corps of assistants from her district who will look after the needs and pleasures of the visiting club women.

Mrs. T. B. Upchurch of Raeford, the incoming president of the district, will make the address of welcome from the district, and will also serve the convention as chairman of the committee of information. Mrs. Charles R. Whitaker of Southern Pines will extend a welcome on behalf of the Civic Club of Southern Pines and will also serve as chairman of the convention hall. Mrs. U. L. Spence of Carthage will supervise the arrangements for breakfast and luncheon conferences; Mrs. Talbot Johnson of Aberdeen will have charge of decorations; Mrs. P. P. McCain of Sanitarium, of transportation and of badges and souvenirs; Mrs. R. L. Cloud of Hamlet, of exhibit rooms; Mrs. J. R. Ingram of Sanford, of hospitality; Mrs. Charles L. Scott, of entertainment.

The committee on credentials is composed of Mrs. Eugene Davis, chairman, Mrs. Ruth Pyron, Mrs. John D. Robinson, Mrs. H. D. McCall, Mrs. Howard Etheridge, Mrs. R. L. Poston, Mrs. John L. Gilmer and Miss Elizabeth Schwarberg.

Charlotte Sunday Observer, p. 43 (section 4, p. 7)

12 May 1930

Plans Complete For Club Convention

Many Prominent State and National Club Women on Program for Three-Day Session at Pinehurst May 14 to 17

By Mrs. J. Henry Highsmith

With the final touches made and all details whipped into line, convention plans of the State Federation of Women's Clubs, which meets this week at Pinehurst, are now ready. Mrs. E. M. Land, of Statesville, president of the Federation, announces that her program is replete with good things and that the committees on entertainment from the ninth district have everything in readiness for the arrival of the guests.

Mrs. Charles L. Scott of Sanford, president of the ninth district, is taking the place of local hostess. She has chosen an able corps of assistants from her district who will look after the needs of pleasure of the visiting club women. Mrs. T. B. Upchurch of Raeford, the incoming president of the district, will make the address of welcome from the district and will also serve the convention as chairman of the committee of information.

In addition to the reception held in the parlors of the Carolina Hotel Wednesday evening, and the one at the Pinehurst Country Club on Thursday afternoon, the Civics Club of Southern Pines will entertain the convention delegates and visitors at tea at their attractive new club house, on Friday afternoon.

The opening session will be Wednesday evening when Mrs. Edward M. Land, president, will make her address outlining the plans and policies of the Federation for another year, as well as reviewing the achievements of the club women during the past year. Mrs. J. M. Hobgood of Farmville, second vice president, will respond to the address of welcome. The principal speech of the evening will be made by Mrs. Ambrose Diehl, of Pittsburgh, Pa., chairman of the Motion Picture Committee of the General Federation. Mrs. Diehl will bring a message from Mrs. Thomas G. Winters, who has recently accepted a position with the studio relations committee of the Moving Pictures Producers' Association. Immediately following the closing of the first session will be a reception given by the Carolina Hotel to all visiting club women.

Three breakfast conferences will be held Thursday morning at 8:00 o'clock. The conference for presidents of Departmental Clubs will be presided over by Mrs. W. A. French of Wilmington. Her speakers will be Mrs. W. F. Grote of Zebulon, Mrs. Frank Shaw of Enfield and Mrs. E. L. McKee of Sylva. The music breakfast conference will be presided over by Mrs. E. E. Randolph of Raleigh. Her principal speaker will be Prof. Harold S. Dyer, director of music at the University of North Carolina. His subject will be Discrimination in Radio Music. Miss Annie Cherry of Roanoke Rapids, Miss Hattie Parrott of Raleigh, Mrs. A. S. Kennickell, Jr., and Mrs. Cora Cox Lucas of Greensboro are other speakers at this breakfast.

At the Civics breakfast conference at which Mrs. J. E. Hardin of Greensboro will preside, Colonel J. W. Harrelson of Raleigh, chairman of Conservation and Development, will speak on the Economic and Social Value of Landscape Beauty. Mr. Paul Van Lindley of Greensboro will also speak at this conference.

Each morning during the convention at 9 o'clock, there will be held a club institute, with Mrs. Eugene Reilley of Charlotte presiding. One of the most interesting as well as instructive features of the convention will be the parliamentary law class and practice conducted by Miss Bettie D. Windley of New Bern.

The first business session will be held at 10 o'clock Thursday morning. Luncheon conferences on Thursday will include one for the Junior Clubs presided over by Mrs. R. D. W. Connor of Chapel Hill; one for Literary Clubs and Literature Departments, presided over by Mrs. Annie Miller Pless of Marion; and one on American Citizenship presided over by Miss Ethel Parker of Gatesville.

The social feature of Thursday will be a tea at the Pinehurst Country Club given as a courtesy of the Carolina Hotel.

The evening session Thursday, known as Fine Arts Evening, will be presided over by Mrs. Charles E. Platt of Charlotte, first vice president. At this session seven silver cups and one silver vase will be awarded for the best creative work done in literature, music and art during the year. One of the principal speakers on this evening will be Dr. Ernest K. Derendinger, on the subject Art's Glorious Mission, which lecture will be illustrated with lantern slides. Dr. Derendinger is professor of Art at Catawba College, Salisbury, and is visiting lecturer on Art at Harvard University summer school. He did graduate work in Europe, receiving his Ph. D. from Berlin for work done in excavating and recreating Munichaurach, near Erlangen, Bavaria, built in the year 1128 by Hirsauer Bauschule.

Two breakfast conferences will begin the day on Friday. The art conference will be presided over by Mrs. L. R. Johnston of High Point, and the education conference by Mrs. T. E. Johnston, of Salisbury.

Featuring the morning session of Friday will be a special Memorial Service to Mrs. R. R. Cotten, who is called the Mother of the Federation. Mrs. Cotten's death occurred a year ago May 4, when Mrs. Cotten was eighty-two. Those who have been appointed to pay tribute to Mrs. Cotten are Mrs. Sydney P. Cooper of Henderson who will deal with her early life as pioneer and citizen; Mrs. W. T. Bost of Raleigh who will pay tribute to her as a club woman and Mrs. Palmer Jerman of Raleigh who will eulogize her as counsellor and friend. The Club Woman's Hymn, written by Mrs. Cotten and Geoffrey O'Hara's "There Is No Death" will be sung as part of the memorial services. Following the services will be the presentation of the Sallie Southall Cotten Loan Fund which is not only one of the most outstanding achievements of the Federation, but which is a living memorial to Mrs. Cotten. Mrs. W. J. Brogden, of Durham, chairman of the loan fund, will make her report and receive contributions to the fund.

The crowning event of the convention will be the banquet held Friday evening. An especial attraction of the evening's program will be the entertainment of Mrs. Lucile Barrow Turner of Lynchburg, Va., who is a noted reader and impersonator. Among her selections will be a number of Negro spirituals which she herself will sing. Another and chief attraction of the banquet program as well as of the entire convention will be the address of Mrs. Grace Morrison Poole of Bracton, Mass., first vice president of the General Federation. The subject of her address will be "What Is It All About?"

Statesville *Landmark,* p. 6

26 MAY 1930

GENERAL INTEREST CENTERS IN FEDERATION CONVENTION TO BE HELD AT DENVER, COL.

North Carolina Will Send Seven Representatives—Mrs. Land Will Report on Home Accidents Survey in This State—Keynote of Meeting Will Be "Woman's Service as Citizens"—Five Thousand Expected From Every State in Union—Real Achievements

By Mrs. J. Henry Highsmith

Club women in North Carolina as well as in every other state in the union will have their interest for the next few weeks centered about the biennial convention of the General Federation of Women's Clubs to be held at Denver, Colorado, June 5–14.

Carolina's Quota.

North Carolina will have its full quota of delegates present. These will be Mrs. Edward M. Land, of Statesville, president of the State Federation; Mrs. Thomas O'Berry, Goldsboro, state director and trustee of the General Federation, and Mrs. Palmer Jerman, of Raleigh, regional director of the foundation fund of the General Federation, all three of whom will go by virtue of their offices, and the following who were elected delegates at the state convention held recently at Pinehurst: Mrs. Eugene Davis, of Statesville; Mrs. Adolph Oettinger, of Goldsboro; Miss Jennie Coltrane, of Concord, and Mrs. Charles R. Whitaker, of Southern Pines.

The North Carolina delegation will leave June 1 on the South Eastern special, going by Atlanta, Birmingham and Kansas City, and returning by Yellowstone Park, Chicago and Cincinnati. Mrs. Land will visit friends in Raton, New Mexico, before returning. The Standish Hotel in Denver will be headquarters for the North Carolina women attending the convention.

The keynote of the convention will be "Women's Service as Citizens." Around this subject has been built a program enlisting a score or more women and men of national reputation as speakers. Mrs. John F. Sippel, of Baltimore, president of the General Federation, will preside. Approximately 5,000 club women representing every state in the union and many foreign countries are expected to attend.

Final Report.

Mrs. Land has been honored in being called on by Mrs. Sippel to give the final report of the Home Accident Survey recently conducted in North Carolina by the Federal Bureau of Standards and the National Safety Council in cooperation with both the State and General Federation of Women's Clubs. This report will be made on Saturday morning, June 7. And on the evening of the same day at what is known as state presidents' night, Mrs. Land will give an account of what she considers the most outstanding piece of club work accomplished in this state this year. This will be, she says, the Educational Pilgrimage to Washington of the 86 men and women who this year have learned to read and write. Other accomplishments will be included in the report, one of which will be the survey and study of North Carolina highways,

Denver is a city of 350,000 inhabitants. It is situated 13 miles from the foothills of the Rocky Mountains at an elevation of one mile above sea level. It is the first city in America to outline a definite city plan to which all civic development must conform. In putting this plan into operation hundreds of buildings were razed and thousands of dollars expended. Denver's civic center is a central park of approximately twenty acres enclosing the Greek Theater, public library, state capital and other public buildings.

Municipal Auditorium.

The Municipal Auditorium, where the convention will be held, seats 12,000 people, but by a feat of engineering, it can be transformed into a smaller theater with hippodrome stage and an audience chamber of 3,500. The Greek Theater, center for outdoor gatherings, plays and concerts, with a seating capacity for more than 5,000 will also be used for some of the meetings of the Convention.

Charlotte Observer, p. 7

7 SEPTEMBER 1930

ART SCHOOL OPENS DOORS FOR SECOND YEAR'S WORK

Youngest Educational Institution In Raleigh Determined To Grow

By Mrs. J. Henry Highsmith

Little has yet been heard of the Raleigh School of Fine and Applied Arts—the city's youngest educational institution, barely out of its infancy but promising vigorous growth and development in the future. And while young in years—not yet two—it has set out strongly determined and ably equipped to achieve its glorious mission—"to create a school that will foster art in general and become an asset to the State and entire South." On September 8 it opens its doors and enters upon its second year's work.

Mr. James A. McLean, director and founder, sees in the informal opening on Monday morning in his new, attractive, and commodious quarters the rapid development of an idea that has long been his inspiration and fond hope. It was his dream when a youth at art school to establish some day in the south, in his native state preferably, a School of Fine Arts. This dream is about to be realized. Last year he opened this school in small quarters on Fayetteville Street, and at once found there a demand for the work that he was prepared to give. Twenty enthusiastic pupils studied with him during the first year.

Not daunted by hard times nor having lost faith in his ideal, he has moved to a new site affording better facilities, an ideal surroundings, and an atmosphere congenial to the artists' minds. The new school occupies what is known as the old Hoke residence on Firwood Avenue near Peace Institute. The building is an early period brick mansion in the cupola and gable style, setting back in a large yard of oak trees. The building retains its old-fashioned luxury in spacious rooms, marble mantels, inlaid hardwood floors and walnut staircases. On the first floor of this building all classes will be conducted, while the second floor will serve as the residence of the director. Students will reside in town as the school is without dormitory accommodations. Night classes will be conducted for those who are unable to attend day classes. The building will be open to the visiting public on Sunday before the opening on Monday, September 18, and on successive Sundays.

The teaching staff of the new school will number five. Mr. McLean, himself, will instruct in portrait, figure, landscape, perspective, and composition work.

Miss Louise Giles Berry, who comes to Raleigh from Oklahoma City, will give instruction in lithograph, wood-block, etching, water color, still life, and color theory. Miss Berry studied at the Pennsylvania Academy of Fine Arts, Philadelphia, and was winner of a European Traveling Scholarship.

Miss Elizabeth Dortch of Raleigh will have charge of the children's class in painting and drawing. Miss Dortch has studied at Peace Institute, and at the Grand Central Art School of New York City,

Mr. Thomas Bowden of Raleigh who has studied at the Academy of Fine Arts in Philadelphia, also at the Roerich Art School in New York, will have charge of the sculpture department.

Mr. Norris Hadaway of Raleigh, who is Designer of Theatre Posters for the Publix-Saenger Theatres, Inc., in Raleigh, will give instruction in theatre poster designing—an opportunity no other art school in the South offers.

Mr. McLean is a native of Lincolnton. He received his training at the Pennsylvania Academy of Fine Arts in Philadelphia and was invited to exhibit his work in the exclusive art clubs of that city. His works have won prizes and honorable mention at a number of exhibitions. In 1927 and the year following, he exhibited pieces of his work at Jackson, Miss., under the auspices of the Mississippi Art Association. While studying in Philadelphia he won the William Emlen Cresson Memorial prize which was awarded for traveling and studying in European art centers.

An attractive feature of the school is the summer class work done each summer at some interesting place affording rare studies and unusual vocational opportunities. During the past summer the study classes were held at Atlantic, a small fishing village on the North Carolina coast, whose unique and quaint fisherfolk, houses, customs, etc., offered a great variety of subject matter for the students.

That the citizens of Raleigh and of North Carolina who are interested in the promotion of art may have an opportunity to aid in the advancement of this school, Mr. McLean is offering a number of memberships—life memberships, $100.00; year memberships, $10.00; perpetual memberships, $1,000.00. The board of directors and governing body is to be made up from persons holding these memberships.

Mr. J. J. Blair, director of school house planning in the State Department of Education, and one of the State's greatest apostles of Art, has faith in "Jimmy McLean's Art School," as he calls it. He says:

"It should be a matter of interest and value to the people of Raleigh and North Carolina to know that there has been established here in Raleigh a School of Fine Arts conducted by Mr. James McLean, who completed the course given by the Philadelphia Academy of Fine Arts in 1929 after having spent five consecutive years in study and practice.

"He is prepared to introduce the same methods of instruction which are given there, and at the same time furnish models and equipment of a similar type to those used in the best art schools of the country.

"During the summer, he successfully conducted his school at the town of Atlantic, having rented the teacher's home during the vacation period—in which excellent accommodations were given to the students who enrolled in the school.

"The instructors in the Philadelphia Academy have given Mr. McLean the very highest recommendations, so that the school in the past and will in the future continue to deserve the confidence and patronage of those who are interested in promoting and patronizing a school of Fine Arts in the South,

"An artist who saw the announcement catalogue which was recently gotten out by Mr. McLean said the work which his students did here last year compared favorably with that of any school with which he was familiar in the recognized art centers of the country."

That there in a need for such a school in North Carolina, Mr. Blair is fully convinced. He sees in the new Art School possibilities whereby thousands of North Carolina boys and girls may have a chance to study and practice art, that otherwise would never have had an opportunity. He says:

"Recently on a visit to the neighboring town of Dunn we happened to meet a girl who was leaving for Norfolk to take a boat to New York, to continue her studies along the line of Art and Drawing.

"The same week we met in Archdale, N. C., another girl who was preparing to leave for Philadelphia to study art during the coming winter. These are examples of students who have a talent for drawing and painting, having to go to northern cities in order to get an adequate instruction and training. Necessarily, the expense in each case is a big item to be considered. For instance the Announcement Catalogue of the Philadelphia Academy of Fine Arts says that one student can count on expending at least $75.00 a month, outside her regular tuition.

"It is a fact that there are no summer art schools south of Philadelphia along the Atlantic Seaboard. The schools on Long Island, Cape Cod, the Massachusetts and Maine coast have for years been patronized by people from the south."

Raleigh Sunday *News and Observer,* p. 4

5 OCTOBER 1930

AUTUMN COUNCIL MEETS THIS WEEK IN GREENVILLE

Interest of Club Women Throughout State Centered In Federation Gathering; Outstanding Program Will Be Address of Col. Joseph D. Sears of Illinois

By Mrs. J. Henry Highsmith

The interest of club women throughout the State will be centered this week on the autumn council meeting of the Federation to be held at Greenville Thursday and Friday, October 9 and 10. In importance and interest the council meeting is second only to the annual convention held in the spring. At the fall meeting the plans, programs and policies of the Federation's activities are decided upon.

The council is a working body with its membership made up of the executive board chairmen of departments, chairmen of standing committees, and district presidents. Past presidents of the Federation, chairmen of special committees and division chairmen attend as conference members.

Outstanding in interest on the council program will be the address of Col. Joseph D. Sears, of Bloomfield, N. J., vice-chairman of the National Prison emergency committee, on Tuesday evening. Colonel Sears will discuss some phase of prison reform. He became interested in prison reorganization work in his native state, New Jersey, and has worked with numerous organizations and committees in the interest of better prison conditions.

Colonel Sears is a graduate of Lawrenceville School and Columbia University. He served in the World War and now holds the commission of colonel in the Chemical Warfare Division of the Reserve Corp. He is also a past commander of the American Legion of New Jersey.

In addition to numerous articles, Colonel Sears is also primarily responsible for the New Jersey prison survey of 1916–1917 and the New York prison survey of 1919–1920.

Colonel Sears is at present directing the nationwide effort of the National Prison emergency committee to lay out a more scientific and humane method of dealing with the men and women committed to our penal institutions. Mr. Ogden H. Hammond, formerly U.S. Ambassador to Spain, is the national chairman of the committee, which includes such eminent names as William H. Woodin, treasurer; George Gordon Battle, president of the national committee on prisons and prison labor; Ellis P. Earle, George W. Wickersham, and Dwight Morrow, U. S. Ambassador to Mexico.

Mrs. W. T. Bost, State Commissioner of Public Welfare, who will introduce Colonel Sears, says that his coming to North Carolina is well-timed and that his message will be of great value to the prison committee appointed by Governor Gardner recently to study conditions in the State.

Mrs. E. M. Land, State president, has returned from her trip to Pittsburgh, Pa., where she attended last week the annual convention of the National Safety Congress. At this meeting Mrs. Land represented Mrs. John F. Sippel, General Federation president, and was accorded a prominent place on the program of October 3, to discuss the home safety program of the General Federation. She was the guest speaker over radio station KDKA Thursday, October 2, at 1:30 p. m.

Raleigh Sunday *News and Observer,* p. 9 (Society, p. 1)

19 OCTOBER 1930

PRESIDENT REPRESENTS FEDERATION AT COUNCIL

Mrs. Land Attends Southeastern Council Meeting and Places Wreath on Jackson's Tomb; State Headquarters Entertains Honorary President of General Federation of Women's Clubs

By Mrs. J. Henry Highsmith

North Carolina club women were represented at the annual meeting cf the Southeastern Council of the General Federation of Women's Clubs, which met Thursday, Friday and Saturday of last week at Nashville, Tennessee, by Mrs. E. M. Land, of Statesville, president of the State Federation. At the opening session held Thursday evening in the auditorium of Hotel Noel, Mrs. Land made the response to the address of welcome. Mrs. John F. Sippel, of Baltimore, president of the General Federation, followed as the chief speaker at this opening session.

An unusually interesting feature of the council meeting was the pilgrimage on Friday afternoon to the Hermitage, the home of Andrew Jackson. Each State president placed a wreath on the tomb of General Jackson and paid tribute to his memory. Mrs. Flora Myers Gillentine, of Nashville, president of the Southeastern Council, placed a wreath for the council, and Mrs. Sippel placed one for the General Federation. Mrs. Land placed one for North Carolina, the State of his birth.

The States comprising the Southeastern Council are Virginia, West Virginia, North Carolina, South Carolina, Georgia, Mississippi, Alabama, Florida and Tennessee.

On Friday morning Mrs. Land was accorded a place on the program to tell of the outstanding achievements of the clubs of the State during the past year. She told first of the work done in adult education and the educational pilgrimage to Washington. Then she spoke briefly of the two State-wide surveys conducted by the Federal government—Roadside Beautification and Home Accident surveys. Much interest was manifested in the achievements of North Carolina Club Women of last year.

Headquarters Entertains.

State Headquarters of the Federation at Raleigh had the unique pleasure last week of entertaining Mrs. Josiah Wane Cowles, of Los Angeles, Cal., honorary past president of the General Federation of Women's Clubs, and her husband, Dr. Cowles. Mrs. J. Henry Highsmith, executive secretary, was hostess.

A number of Raleigh friends and club women called to meet Dr. and Mrs. Cowles, who were spending a short time in Raleigh as guests of Mrs. R. O. Self. Dr. and Mrs. Cowles came east last spring and have spent the summer visiting the principal cities in the eastern states. Before returning to their home in California they will visit relatives in Durham, Statesville, Lenoir, and Asheville, Statesville being their former home.

Mrs. Cowles was president of the General Federation of Women Clubs from 1918–1922, entering office the year of the World War and serving a term of four years. She is known as the "World War President." The years since that time have not dimmed her enthusiasm in club work, nor has she lost any of her interest in the affairs of the General Federation. Mrs. Cowles expressed the belief that each new president brings to the Federation brighter vision and a service that enriches and strengthens it.

Those calling to meet Dr. and Mrs. Cowles were: Mrs. T. Palmer Jerman, Mrs. W. T. Bost, Mrs. Thomas O'Berry of Goldsboro, Mrs. T. W. Bickett, Dr. E. Delia Dixon Carroll, Mrs. Josephus Daniels, Mrs. B. H. Griffin, Mrs. J. Wilbur Bunn, Mrs. Jane McKimmon and Mr. and Mrs. R. O. Self.

District Meetings.

The itinerary of the District Meetings changes from the eastern to the extreme western part of the state. Mrs. Land, State president, and Mrs. J. M. Hobgood, chairman of districts, will be in Andrews Monday, October 20, where the meeting of the First District will be held. Mrs. Billy Davis of Sylva is president of this district and will preside over the meeting.

Asheville will be the place of meeting for the second district on Tuesday, October 21. Mrs. J. O. Wood of Black Mountain is president of this district and will have the meeting in charge.

On Wednesday, October 22, the third district will hold its meeting at Morganton, with Mrs. T. B. Finley of North Wilkesboro, district president in charge. Thursday, October 28, the fifth district meeting will be held at Concord with Mrs. J. D. McCall of Charlotte, district president, presiding. Friday, October 24 the sixth district meeting will be held at Mount Airy with Mrs. George Marshall of Mount Airy, district president, presiding.

The fourth district meeting will be held on Saturday, October 25, at Bessemer City, with Mrs. W. T. Alexander of Shelby, district president, presiding.

Raleigh Sunday *News and Observer,* p. 9 (Society, p. 1)

19 OCTOBER 1930

PARENT-TEACHER MEMBERSHIP GOAL SET BY MRS. BINFORD
AT FIVE THOUSAND FOR THE YEAR

By Mrs. J. Henry Highsmith

There's to be no let-up in the activities of the State Parent-Teacher Associations this year, if the goals and special projects which Mrs. Raymond Binford, of Guilford College, state president, has outlined as a program for the year is successfully carried out.

Increase In Members.

In the first place she expects an increase of members over that of last year. The state membership at the end of school a year ago stood at 20,027. At the end of the school year this spring it was 23,503, showing a gain of over 3,000 members. Consequently the membership goal set for this year is 5,000.

The second goal set by Mrs. Binford is for more standard and superior associations. Mrs. E. E. White of Greensboro, second vice president, calls attention to changes in the requirements for standard and superior ratings for the year 1930–1931, and asks that all standard and superior associations be listed with her before the annual convention at High Point, November 10–12.

Third goal set by Mrs. Binford is that there be more study groups of parents. She says that parent education is a serious need, for the best development of the child but also for the best development of the school and community. The time has come, thinks Mrs. Binford, when parents must be made to realize that their responsibility to their children does not end when they put them in school. That the parent assumes little or no responsibility for the welfare and success of his child after entering him in school, leaving it all up to the teacher, is an old notion that must be got rid of, she says, and it is the work of the Parent-Teacher group to do this. Parents should study along with teachers and pupils. Parents should know their jobs as parents as well as teachers know theirs as teachers, and both should work together for the good of the child.

Training Leaders.

Another objective named by Mrs. Binford is the training of leaders. The lack of trained leaders, she says, is the greatest handicap met in Parent-Teacher work. To overcome this drawback, the state association has been working in a number of ways for a number of years. Numerous training schools and summer institutes have been held for the specific work of training workers. The more recent of these were the Parenthood Institute held at Black Mountain last July with Dr. Frank Howard Richardson as head. In June a publicity and parliamentary practice conference was held in Greensboro at the North Carolina College for Women, and the third annual summer institute for parent-teacher workers was held at the University of North Carolina the last week in August. Seventy-six workers attended this institute, 19 of whom received certificates of achievement.

While these are the major projects named by Mrs. Binford, she urges that the work of providing milk and soup for undernourished children be carried on; that the parent's bookshelf maintained by the state congress be made use of; that school, local, and traveling libraries be worked for; that playgrounds be provided; that the summer round-up be made each year and that more associations celebrate Founder's Day. Year before last 74 associations celebrated the day and sent in a contribution of $199. This year 124 associations celebrated and their offering amounted to $249.

As our state is only the second from the top in its class in Child Welfare subscriptions, says Mrs. Binford, let us make a special effort to reach the top this year. More subscriptions to the Child Welfare Magazine means more parents studying and becoming acquainted with their problems as parents.

Charlotte Sunday Observer, p. 33 (section 4, p. [3])

28 OCTOBER 1930

HOME DISCOVERED NOT SAFEST PLACE FOR LITTLE CHILDREN

**Accident Prevention Campaign Planned for North Carolina
in Effort to Make People Safety-Minded—Federation Club
Women Have Accepted Challenge**

By Mrs. J. Henry Highsmith

That spot which has been regarded as the safest place in the world for
children, the home, has been found to be not such a safe place after all. At
least the North Carolina home is not.

According to statistics furnished by homemakers themselves, more
accidents occur in North Carolina homes than in North Carolina industries,
and it is said that about half of all the accidents occurring in the United
States annually are within the home, and to children under five year of
age. Ten in every 100 accidental deaths are of babies under five years of
age. And the startling fact connected with this is that the majority of these
accidental deaths could have been avoided by the exercise of reasonable care
and forethought.

Nationwide Survey.

This revelation and others as important have been learned through the
survey of home accidents made in this state last spring by the federal Bureau
of Standards and the State Federation of Women's Clubs.

As a result of the North Carolina survey, Mrs. E. M. Land of Statesville,
president of the State Federation, announced that a vigorous nationwide
program of accident prevention and first aid will be inaugurated this year
by the General Federation, the United States Bureau of Standards and the
National Safety Council, the purpose of which will be to make men, women
and children "Safety Minded." In making this announcement, Mrs. Land
says:

"The survey in North Carolina yielded results of such value that their
inescapable facts will form the background of a campaign to bring home-
makers to a realization of the dangers that are lurking in our homes.

"If it is true that 90 per cent of the home accidents are avoidable, we who
are responsible for the well-being of those within the protection of our homes
have before us a task that is a challenge. With these splendid co-operating
agencies seeking a remedy for present conditions we women must translate
into terms of daily living the timely suggestions of those who are striving to
make safe the American home."

Alarming Percentage.

"It has been estimated that about 100,000 serious and 24,000 fatal accidents occur annually in or about our homes. If some great catastrophe or epidemic were taking such an annual toll, all citizens would be up in arms, demanding that something be done. Perhaps enormous sums of money would be expended in an effort to avert such a calamity. In a home safety program the remedy is so simple that any woman without special training may be an active worker and participate in a cause which seeks to eliminate the frightful waste in human suffering which occurs each year. Many accidents are preventable, many are avoidable; many are the result of personal carelessness. To arouse women to the gravity of the situation is the task before us, and is worth every ounce of effort that can be put into it.

"Many of the serious and fatal accidents occurring to small children, as reported by club women, were through contact with unguarded fires, heated stoves, sharp-edged tools and toys, or from placing a child in a high chair too near stoves."

Tragic Occurrence.

One tragic report was that of a busy mother who left her small child in a high chair near the kitchen stove as she was preparing breakfast for her family one morning. The child stood in the chair to reach out for the handle of the kettle on the stove. The chair was over-turned, throwing the child against the stock [stove] and as he clutched wildly for something to break his fall, his hand caught the handle of the kettle, which he brought down on himself, receiving a death-dealing scald. When it is too late we can see how easily these tragic occurrences might have been avoided."

Charlotte Observer, p. 21

9 NOVEMBER 1930

STRONG LEGISLATIVE PROGRAM ADOPTED BY WOMEN'S COUNCIL

By Mrs. J. Henry Highsmith

Club women throughout the state will be interested and pleased to know that the program adopted by the Legislative Council of North Carolina Women at a recent meeting of the council in Raleigh includes practically all of the measures adopted at the annual meeting of the Federation of Women's Clubs at Pinehurst May 1.

The program adopted by representatives from the seven statewide women's organizations include the measures that will be presented to the 1931 Legislature and other measures which the council endorsed and to which it will give its support.

Well Represented.

The organizations represented at the council meeting, which was called by Mrs. Palmer Jerman, of Raleigh, president, were the State Federation of Women's Clubs, the State Federation of Business and Professional Women's Clubs, the League of Women Voters, the State Nurses Association, the Woman's Auxiliary of the Protestant Episcopal Church, the Woman's Missionary Society of the N.C. Conference, (Methodist); the Woman's Christian Temperance Union and the cooperating agency of the Y. W. C. A.

The representatives were: Miss Lena Glidewell, Mrs. T. W. Bickett, Miss Elsie Riddick, Mrs. Edward M. Land, Miss Harriet W. Elliott, Mrs. Palmer Jerman, Mrs. Thomas O'Berry, Mrs. M. O. Cowper, Mrs. W. H. Swift, Miss Virginia Marshbanks, Mrs. J. S. Holmes, Miss Sallie Dortch, Mrs. A. M. Gates, Miss Vara Herring, Mrs. F. S. Love, Mrs. Charles G. Doak, Mrs. T. Wiley Duke, Miss Clara Cox, Miss Alice Laidlaw.

Measures Program.

The measures making up the program are:

1. That the clause be removed that exempts children who have completed the fourth grade from the provision of the law establishing an 8-hour day and a 48-hour week for children under 16; that children between 14 and 16 be required to complete the sixth grade before leaving school for work; that the employment of children under 16 to oil and clean machinery in motion, to work around electric wires, to work with poisonous acids and dyes and to run elevators be prohibited, and that power be granted to the appropriate state commission to extend this list.

2. That night work for minors under 18 be prohibited and that an 55-hour week for women and all industries be established.

3. That the state take over the Industrial School for Negro Girls at Efland.

4. That more effective state election systems be studied, including a permanent registration law.

5. That the Highway Commission be given power to enforce the existing law regarding billboards and that the highway commission be authorized to spend 1 per cent of its appropriation on highway beautification, which amount will be met by the federal highway system.

Public Welfare Plans.

The council voted to endorse the State Public Welfare program, also the state educational program. It will co-operate with the proper agencies in establishing a women's and children's bureau in the Department of Labor and Printing, with adequate enforcing powers, and endorses the appointment of a legislative committee to study property laws and laws relating to spouses and equalization of rights.

Concerning the program, Mrs. Jerman expressed herself as being well-pleased. While it contains nothing of a startling nature, she said, it is carrying on the work that the women have been interested in for a number of years. In regard to the measures dealing with child labor and working hours for women, she says that it is most gratifying that the women's program has become widely accepted, not only by almost all civic and social organizations but more recently by various textile groups. She declared that the outlook for the passage of these bills is brighter than ever before.

Concerning the state election law which has engrossed the interest and attention of women for so long, she said they were fairly well pleased with the working of the present law but that there are phases of it that need correction. However, she said, the council does not intend to introduce any bill to that end during the coming Legislature. The council is interested in securing a more effective election law and with it a permanent registration system. More time for study and investigation was thought necessary.

Industrial School.

Hope was expressed by Mrs. Jerman that the Legislature would see fit to take over the industrial school at Efland for colored girls, as this is the last group of the state's population unprovided for; and that an appropriation be made for opening and maintaining the building just completed at the farm colony for women, near Kinston.

The one new item included in the program which has been favored by many women's organizations, and which is expected to be well-received, is the two measures regarding the highway beautification. In view of the fact that Mr. and Mrs. W. L. Lawton, of New York, in cooperation with the American Nature Association, the National Council for the Protection of Roadside Beauty and the State Federation of Women's Clubs, conducted a survey and study of the roadsides of North Carolina last year and included these measures in their recommendation, it was considered most timely and worthwhile that these be included in the program.

Charlotte Sunday Observer, p. 32 (section 3, p. 8)

9 NOVEMBER 1930

STATE PARENTS AND TEACHERS MEET THIS WEEK AT HIGH POINT

Over 23,500 Members Will Be Represented—Mrs. Raymond Binford is President—Number of Speakers of National Prominence in Program—Election of Officers Tuesday

By Mrs. J. Henry Highsmith

Beginning tomorrow, representatives of the 23,500 members of the State Congress of Parents and Teachers will assemble at High Point, where the twelfth annual convention will be held Monday, Tuesday and Wednesday.

The theme of the convention will be "The Call of Today" and headquarters will be at the Sheraton Hotel. A meeting of the board of managers has been called for 10 o'clock on Monday and registration begins at the same hour. At 2 o'clock a conference of local presidents will be held with Mrs. J. W. Burke, of Gibsonville, presiding. At the same hour a delegates conference will be held with Mrs. C. L. Weil, of Goldsboro, presiding.

Formal Opening.

The formal opening of the convention will be at 8 o'clock in the Wesley Memorial Church Monday evening. Mrs. Raymond Binford, of Guilford, state president, will preside. Featuring the opening session will be the president's message and the addresses of Miss Frances Hays of Washington, extension secretary of the National Congress of Parents and Teachers, and of Dr. Frank Howard Richardson, of Black Mountain. Miss Hays will speak on the subject "The Road Ahead," and Dr. Richardson will speak on "Growing Up, and Father." Harold D. Meyer, of the University of North Carolina, will respond to the address of welcome.

The first business meeting of the convention will be held Tuesday morning at 9 o'clock. Mrs. Binford will preside. Reports from the nominating committee, the treasurer and the auditor and committee on revising the by-laws will be presented at this hour. The nominating committee, of which Mrs. Frank Castlebury, of Raleigh, is chairman, will submit nominations for the first, third, and fifth vice presidents, recording secretary, treasurer, and historian.

At 10 o'clock Miss Hays will speak on "How to Use Publications." At 11 o'clock the convention will break up into groups for studying special subjects. Miss Ellen Lombard, of Washington, who is a specialist in home education, will address one group on organizing study groups; Mrs. E. P. White, of Asheville, will lead the group on membership; Mrs. Arthur Watt, of Sedgefield, will lead the group on publicity; and Mrs. E. E. White of Greensboro will lead the group on standard and superior associations.

Election Of Officers.

Election of officers and an address on parental education by Miss Lombard will feature the afternoon session.

The highlight of the convention will be the banquet Tuesday evening at the hotel, with Dr. Richardson as toastmaster. The speakers for this occasion are presidents of three state colleges in North Carolina: Dr. J. I. Foust, of Greensboro; Dr. E. C. Brooks, of Raleigh, and Dr. Frank Graham, of Chapel Hill. At this time the new officers will be presented and cups offered as prizes will be awarded. Mrs. Edgar Whitener, of High Point, is chairman of arrangements for the banquet, with whom reservations may be made.

The regular session on Wednesday will be featured by the addresses of N. J. Coltrane, of Salisbury, president of the North Carolina Educational Association, and addresses by Miss Lombard, on Home Education, and on Program Making, by Miss Hays. The round table groups following the addresses will be led by Mrs. C. O. Burton, of Greensboro, Miss Hays, and Mr. L. W. Connor.

Reports of local associations and city councils will feature the Wednesday afternoon session, which will be followed by a post-convention board meeting.

One of most interesting and worth while features planned for the convention will be the exhibit arranged and in charge of Mrs. Arthur Watt. Twelve national associations will send exhibits, and several state departments.

Furnishing Exhibits.

National agencies sending exhibits are: National Educational Association, National Recreation Association, American Library Association, American Child Health Association, Progressive Education Association, National Child Labor Committee, National Committee of Mental Hygiene, American Social Hygiene Association, National Kindergarten Association, American Medical Association, and the National Congress of Parents and Teachers.

The exhibit from the National Congress will be in charge of Miss Frances Hays, national extension secretary. Miss Hays will be present during the whole of the convention and will be an honor guest and speaker.

Many state agencies will also contribute to the success of the exhibit. Among these will be the exhibit of the State Library Commission, with a librarian in charge. She will have a traveling book truck on hand and will explain how the free library service is carried to all in the state who do not have access to library facilities.

Charlotte Sunday Observer, p. 36 (section 4, p. 4)

16 NOVEMBER 1930

P.-T.A. WOMEN URGED TO HEAR HOOVER AND WILBUR ON RADIO

Child Health and Protection to Be Conference Subject, Mrs. Binford Reminds

By Mrs. J. Henry Highsmith

Mrs. Raymond Binford of Guilford College, president of the State Congress of Parents and Teachers, is urging local groups and individual members of the Parent-Teacher Association to listen in on two important speeches to be broadcast over the radio this week.

The first is President Hoover's address to the White House Conference on Child Health and Protection, November 19 at 9 o'clock p. m. This address will be broadcast over a nation-wide hookup and will be heard by many

Parent-Teacher Associations throughout the country. The second is an address by Dr. Ray Lyman Wilbur, Secretary of the Interior and chairman of the White House conference, which will be given at 12:45 noon on Saturday, November 22. This address, which will sum up the conference, will also be broadcast over a nation-wide network of radio stations.

Mrs. Binford is not only asking North Carolina Parent-Teacher workers to tune in and hear these addresses, but also to so organize their communities that large numbers may hear them. She advises that members request their radio stations in advance to plan to broadcast these speeches.

These addresses have been especially timed and arranged that Parent-Teacher groups may have the opportunity of hearing President Hoover and Mr. Wilbur tell what the conference is accomplishing and hopes to accomplish for child welfare. In this connection Dr. H. E. Barnard, director of the White House conference, stated recently that knew of no other groups so well able to interpret the finding of the conference and to put into actual use the recommendations made as the 20,000 local Parent-Teacher Associations scattered over the country.

Mrs. Binford will address the State Convention of Negro Parents and Teachers which meets in Raleigh, November 14–15. Mrs. H. R. Butler, president of the National Congress of Colored Parents and Teachers, will attend and address the conference.

Charlotte Sunday Observer, p. 26 (section 3, p. 4)

23 NOVEMBER 1930

CLUB ACTIVITIES IN FULL SWING

By Mrs. J. Henry Highsmith

Probably no other period of the year makes as great demand on the club woman's time as the fall and particularly that period between Thanksgiving and Christmas. At the present time, however, it might be said that club activities are on in full swing, engaging the interests of all club women from the state president to the individual member.

Mrs. E. M. Land of Statesville, state president, attended the White House Conference on Child Health and Protection in Washington, D. C., last week. Prior to her leaving for Washington, she addressed the Industrial Safety Conference in session at High Point. Mrs. Thomas O'Berry of Goldsboro, State director and a member of the executive committee of the General Federation of Women's Clubs, joined Mrs. Land in Washington and also attended the conference.

Mrs. R. L. McMillan of Raleigh, chairman of the State Picture Memory contest, is urging the formation of picture memory groups in the schools.

She says the movement, which began about four year ago with twelve schools, has increased to more than a hundred. This spring one hundred and seventy-five children participated in the state-wide contest. Plans for another state-wide contest to be held in Raleigh in May have been made. Mrs. McMillan believes that the appreciation of pictures is one of the genuine and remunerative forms of wealth which one may possess and enjoy. It is "tax exempt," she says. Neither high taxes nor Bolshevism can destroy it. It is her opinion that much of the unrest and the violations of the law of today, and many of the manifestations of fanatical and extreme tendencies, develop from the reaction against the humdrumness or lack of inspirational work of our every day existence. She believes a cultivation of more of the things that will feed the soul would be a remedy for some of the unsettled condition.

Mrs. John D. Robinson of Wallace, chairman of Conservation, is announcing the offer of a prize for the largest number of living Christmas trees decorated and reported to her by a single club. She is also calling on the clubs to co-operate with the American Tree Association of Washington in its tree planting program by way of observing the bicentennial of George Washington. She is not only asking clubs to plant trees but individuals also. They are to be planted now and registered with the American Tree Association that they may be dedicated at the nation-wide dedication service on February 22, 1932.

Mrs. Chas. R. Whitaker of Southern Pines, chairman of the Division of Health of the Federation, is calling the attention of club women to the need of a greater sale of Christmas seals than has been made the past two or three years. She says that North Carolina club women have always taken an active part in the sale of seals, but that the needs for continuing and strengthening the tuberculosis program are greater this year than usual and doubly increased efforts will be necessary to meet the situation. She is urging all clubs to effect a seal sale organization ready to begin the active sale of seals immediately after Thanksgiving.

In a letter issued recently by Mrs. Land in behalf of the observation of Book Week, she asks that books which have been discarded from public libraries for the reason that they are badly worn or thumbed, be sent to county jails for use of the prisoners. A second request is that books and magazines be sent to the Industrial Farm Colony for Women at Kinston. She says that while the average of the girls there is nineteen, that the mental age is much lower. Therefore wholesome books for girls such as the Pollyanna series would be suitable.

Charlotte Sunday Observer, p. 28 (section 3, p. 4)

30 NOVEMBER 1930

LITTLE DEPRESSION FOUND AMONG STATE CLUB WOMEN

Leaders Travel Two Thousand Miles Over State Visiting Sixteen Districts—Department Programs Well Received—Two New Clubs Recently Admitted to Federation

By Mrs. J. Henry Highsmith

Mrs. J. M. Hobgood of Farmville, second vice president of the State Federation of Women's Clubs and chairman of districts, who with Mrs. E. M. Land of Statesville, president, and Miss Frieda Heller, of the State Library Commission, Raleigh, traveled 2,000 miles visiting the 16 districts of the Federation, is of the opinion that woman's club work in the state is just coming into its own and that club women have larger and truer conceptions of club service than ever before.

Harmony And Work.

The territory covered by Mrs. Hobgood, Mrs. Land and Miss Heller extended as far east as Gatesville and as far west as Andrews. More than a month was given to attending the district meetings.

Harmony and hard work were found among the different groups of club women, according to Mrs. Hobgood. She says: "It may be because I am one of them but, it appeals to me that club women are beginning to learn what the club movement is all about—its purpose and program. They are certainly better informed and have a much better grasp of the General Federation and its relation to our state than even last year. Everywhere there was harmony and the best of feeling toward everyone or else I was too dumb to notice it, and yet I am rather sensitive to atmospheres.

"One of the finest things about the women of the Federation," says Mrs. Hobgood, "is that they are so busy with their own projects that they have no time nor inclination to indulge in jealousies and criticisms of other organizations. I am not a sleuth by any means," she says, "but I see very little of self-seeking among the members of our family. It makes the work a joy."

Holding Up Well.

That club activities had not suffered a great decline like many other interests was both a surprise and relief to Mrs. Hobgood. She says: "As the time came for the district meetings, I found myself growing more and more despondent about the clubs and their work. The bottom had dropped so completely out of everything, I felt that the Federation had been hit too. The first meeting held which was at Gatesville was well attended, and fine interest shown, so our spirits picked up a bit. From then on as each meeting was held we grew more sanguine and happy. We found the women up and at it with the same old energy and enthusiasm." She said further: "Last year we had total attendance of 2,152 with a beautiful day for every meeting. This year, although we suffered a net loss of nine clubs, our total attendance was 2,116 and three districts held their meetings in torrential downpours. The reports were splendid and well given."

The department programs were all well received, some more than the others, said Mrs. Hobgood, particularly the literary program. It went straight to the heart of every woman. More than usual interest was shown in questions dealing with citizenship. But everybody was interested in libraries, especially after Miss Heller so charmingly and effectively presented the subject. From all indications work for libraries and work with adult illiterates will be the major activities next year.

New Clubs Admitted.

Two new clubs have recently been admitted to the Federation by Mrs. Hobgood. These are the Richlands Woman's Club with Mrs. L. C. Herring, president and Mrs. G. B. Whitted, treasurer. The membership is 20. The other club is the Veritas Club of Charlotte.

"The district presidents selected this fall are a fine lot—most of them young and enthusiastic," says Mrs. Hobgood. "I am looking to them for fine service and much progress."

Charlotte Sunday Observer, p. 33 (section 4, p. 3)

4 DECEMBER 1930

[NORTH CAROLINA ART SOCIETY] ADOPTS RESOLUTIONS

The following resolutions framed by A. R. Newsome, Mrs. J. Henry Highsmith and Dr. Clarence Poe, were adopted:

1. That we note with great pleasure the steady growth of art appreciation in North Carolina, the increasing interest in art in the public schools, the increasing attendance at the annual State art exhibit, the growing number of competent artists in North Carolina cities and towns, the improving standards of architecture both in public buildings and private homes, the almost astounding increase in well planned plantings of home grounds, the beautification of our highways, the establishment of a creditable School of Fine Arts at our State capital, and the progress of art departments in our colleges, the accumulating gifts for our future State Art Museum, and the general public interest in fostering the building of this State Art Museum as soon as financial conditions again become normal.

2. That the Board of Directors of the society take steps, at the first opportunity that may seem practicable to them, to secure a site in the city of Raleigh suitable for the location of a State Art Museum.

3. That our directors be instructed to formulate plans looking to having the next General Assembly of 1933 provide a fund to be used in the erection

of a State Art Museum and that if the Legislature does not provide the full sum necessary for the erection of such a building, it be requested to provide one-half on condition that its appropriation be available when the other half of such sum shall have been provided by private gifts.

4. That the General Assembly be requested to provide a fund for the purchase of inexpensive reproductions of famous works of art for the public schools of the State, on condition that certain minimum amounts be duplicated locally and that selections be made in accordance with recommendations and plans of the State Department of Public Instruction.

5. That the State be asked to set aside 1 per cent of its highway building fund for purposes of beautifying the highways of the State (this fund being duplicated from Federal funds) to the end that North Carolina roadways may become as famous for beauty as for excellence of construction and thus attract visitors from all over America in addition to enriching the lives and raising new standards of beauty for our own people. The elimination of the billboard evil is accepted as a necessary part of this program.

6. That we commend the Raleigh School of Fine and Applied Arts as deserving the support and co-operation of our society and all others interested in its purposes. We also commend the formation of the Southeastern Arts Association.

7. That the society is heartily thankful to all those citizens who, realizing the value of its projects to the State, have given it encouragement and assistance, and more especially to its president, Mrs. Katherine Pendleton Arrington, for her vision, her able and generous leadership and her untiring labors, and for her gifts to North Carolina schools and to the future State Museum, including the new marine by Paul Dougherty; to the directors and executive committee for their unselfish services, and to the patrons and patronesses and members who have assisted in our beautiful fourth annual art exhibit and other activities of the organization. Our thanks are also especially extended to the Grand Central Art Galleries, to the management of the Sir Walter Hotel, to the Junior League, and to the press of the city and State for their generous cooperation in connection with the State Art Exhibit; and to the Colonial Dames for their interest and contribution to a State Art Museum.

> *Note:* A. R. Newsome (1894–1951) was secretary of the North Carolina Historical Commission, later the Department of Archives and History, and editor of the *North Carolina Historical Review*. Clarence Poe (1881–1964) was editor of *The Progressive Farmer* (a forerunner of *Southern Living*). Katherine Clark Pendleton Arrington (1876–1955) was the moving force behind the NC State Art Society and the North Carolina Museum of Art.

Raleigh *News and Observer*, 5 December 1930, p. 13

1931

13 January — outlines Legislative Council agenda to Raleigh B&PWC

18 January — among 100 signers of petition by NC Conference for Social Service asking that a new tax code be adopted by the 1931 Legislature

27 January — addresses, as executive secretary of the Legislative Council, Sir Walter Cabinet

28 January — attends hearing for Sixth Grade Attainment Bill

5 February — nominated chairman of RWC Art Department, immediately calls meetings for 14 February

27 February — House Judiciary Committee follows advice of Mrs. Jerman, Mrs. Highsmith, and Mrs. Bost not to repeal the 5-day marriage banns law

2 March — attends dinner to organize a Phi Beta Kappa association in Raleigh

9 March — cosigns petition to Legislature to reinsert "not over" to the 55-hour work week labor law, to prevent "yellow dog" contracts

11 March — death of brother Rufus K. Herring in San Francisco, where he had gone for treatment two months earlier; his wife Gladys is there and accompanies the body to Raleigh, joined by Pauline in Memphis

25 March — arrival of funeral party by train; they depart by automobile for the (Masonic) funeral in Roseboro

14–16 April — attends 29th annual NCFWC convention, Greensboro; moves resolution, to enthusiastic applause, to reconsider tabled bill calling for sixth grade attainment

28 April — addresses Twentieth Century Book Club, studying "Early Days in America," on "Huguenots and Quakers, Their Origin and Customs"

1 June — closes Federation Headquarters for June, July, and August

24 July — speaks on WPTF Welfare Forum on State Board of Charities and Public Welfare: "What Restrictions Should the Community Place on Marriage?"

22 August — attends fifth reunion of Littleton College Memorial Association, Panacea Springs, near Littleton; Vara presides; Frances Renfrow Doak reads

24 August — Highsmiths spend the night in Statesville, guests of Mr. and Mrs. E. M. Land, en route to Asheville

6 September — listed, with Katherine Pendleton Arrington, Clarence Poe, etc., as a patron of Southern School of Creative Arts, formerly the Raleigh School of Fine Arts, a project of James A. McLean

8–9 October — attends NCFWC council meeting in Wilmington

22 October — receives at a PTA tea honoring Murphey School faculty

5 November — speaks for 15 minutes on WPTF endorsing Mrs. E. M. Land's candidacy for GFWC second vice president

18 November — offers short discussion on parliamentary practice to Murphey PTA

4 December — speaks on WPTF concerning unemployment relief among club women

8 December — hosts "splendid" meeting of Twentieth Century Book Club with guests from England and Texas, husbands of the members, Mr. and Mrs. Peyton Brown (Aunt Margaret and Uncle Peyton), and Vara and Eugenia

December — is included in a book on NC women of great service, by Harriette Hammer Walker of Asheboro (Seaman Printery, Durham): *Busy North Carolina Women*

11 JANUARY 1931

NORTH CAROLINA CLUB WOMEN BECOME LEGISLATION-MINDED; UNITED SUPPORT TO PROGRAM

Pleased With Mrs. McKee's Election to Senate—Sure That Poll of Full Strength Will Bring Results—Club Officials to Attend National Board Meeting in Washington—Will Be Received by President and Mrs. Hoover—Visit Historic Spots in Capital

By Mrs. J. Henry Highsmith

For the next two months, club women of the state will have their attention centered on the Legislature in the interests of the progress of the bills which their organization is sponsoring.

From all appearances club women this year are legislation-minded. They have faith in their program and know what they want. They are not willing as heretofore to leave the fate of their measures in the hands of a small group at the capitol but are prepared to throw the full strength of their influence behind the bills for their successful passage.

Mrs. L. B. Fleming of Oxford, state chairman of the child welfare division of the Federation, is calling on all club women to give particular study to the child welfare program of the Legislative Council of North Carolina Women. She says that the program is sound and deserves the support of every club woman, as it would relieve many of the problems connected with working children, should it be enacted into law. Mrs. Palmer Jerman, president of the Legislative Council, is asking for the united strength of the organized women of the state and says, "if we ever understand the power that lies in our hands when we work together in earnest, every member doing her part, then we shall be able to bring to pass easily the things whereunto we have set our hands." She says further, "I know the measures have your sympathy, but it will take more than sympathy to get our bills enacted into laws."

That Mrs. E. L. McKee of Sylva, former president of the State Federation of Women's Clubs, is the first woman to be elected to the North Carolina State Senate, is not only pleasing to her co-workers in the Federation and friends all over the state, but is indicative of the high place that woman is beginning to fill in legislative affairs in the state. She was given the honor seat, number 1, in the Senate Wednesday, when she took the oath of office among a host of admiring friends.

Mrs. E. M. Land of Statesville, president of the State Federation, Mrs. Jerman of Raleigh, trustee of the General Federation, and Mrs. Thomas O'Berry of Goldsboro, state director and member of the executive committee of the General Federation, will leave today for Washington, D. C., to attend the annual mid-winter meeting of the board of directors of the General Federation of Women's Clubs, which will be held at National Headquarters, January 13. Mrs. John F. Sippel, president, will preside. Club representatives from every state in the union will attend.

The business sessions of the board will begin the morning of the fourteenth and will continue through Friday, with three sessions a day. Among the problems to be discussed by experts will be that of unemployment, inter-American relationships, and the White House conference on child health and protection. The women will be received by President and Mrs. Hoover, and there will be a pilgrimage to the United States Naval Academy at Annapolis and to the Penal Farm at Occoquan, the first industrial farm for misdemeanants. Members of congress and their wives and other members of the official social life of the nation's capital will be received at a large reception to be given the evening of the thirteenth at the Federation Headquarters, one of the historically interesting mansions of Washington.

Charlotte Sunday Observer, p. 23 (section 3, p. 3)

18 JANUARY 1931

CLUB WOMEN ACCEPT DUTY OF KEEPING UP NATION'S MORALE DURING DEPRESSION PERIOD

Mrs. John F. Sippel, General Federation President, Calls on All Club Women to Carry On Cheerfully—Predicts Return of Saner and Lasting Prosperity

By Mrs. J. Henry Highsmith

Keeping up that intangible but most valuable asset called morale is the part that club women can play most effectively in helping to meet the ills of depression and restore our country to normal conditions, according to Mrs. John F. Sippel, president, of the General Federation of Women's Clubs.

In her New Year message to the club women of America she says:

"It is our task not only to fill in some of the chinks but actually to help build up the breaches in the walls that support our economic and social structure. Let us cement our building strongly," she says, "by sane buying, not wild orgies of spending now and paying next year; and not in the fearsome, doubtful mood, but calmly, wisely using our own good judgment and discernment, spending as we need to spend, buying as we need to buy, and cheerily."

It is Mrs. Sippel's opinion that a saner prosperity than what she has ever known is bound to come to America in the near future. "We cannot name the day or the hour on which it will come back," she says, "but undoubtedly it will. It is impossible that it will not, for America has all of the elements of prosperity—coal, iron, oil and other minerals beyond measure. We have half the gold in the world and half the machinery. Most of the automobiles and all of the sky scrapers. We have broad acres of fertile land, more than enough for our present population; we have the greatest home market in the world; wonderful transportation facilities; we have a climate that is varied and healthful. Moreover, we have a racial heritage that is rich in energy, initiative, enterprise, invention, and determination to succeed. We have men and women of ideals and courage and ability to translate their ideals into realities."

"Have faith in the future and in our ability to overcome," advises Mrs. Sippel. "Let it not be said that because we have been so prosperous in the past, we do not know how to accept adversity and carry on; that we are weak and flabby and are ready to sit down in the shadows of depression and be sorry for ourselves." On the other hand she says: "I would that we Club

Women might be as lighted candles at this time, making the rooms we enter brighter and happier and our abiding places veritable temples of light."

"Doubtless we shall not reach within a few days or within a few weeks," says Mrs. Sippel, "the same degree of prosperity that we enjoyed a few years ago, but it will come and it will be a saner prosperity; it will be wealth that has a stable underpinning; it will be set upon a firm foundation and we shall be stronger men and women for having overcome."

Charlotte Sunday Observer, p. 19 (section 2, p. 5)

25 JANUARY 1931

NATIONAL OBSERVANCE OF CHILD LABOR DAY TODAY

By Mrs. J. Henry Highsmith

Today is being observed in the United States as Child Labor Day. For twenty-four years the last Sunday in January has been observed in the interests of the working child in churches, in synagogues and in schools and public places. That it is still necessary, in this of all years, to set apart a certain day or days, to call the attention of the churches and the public in general to the seriousness of the conditions under which the children of this country are at work is to many a sad commentary on American civilization. Yet after twenty-four years of effort to do something to make easier and better the lot of the laboring child, IT IS NECESSARY. "The nation will look back with amazement and with perhaps little tolerant pity at a generation which is permitting serious unemployment and child labor to exist side by side," says the National Education Association.

In North Carolina today thousands of able bodied men and women are roaming the streets in search of a job or are standing idle against public buildings in disappointment and despair while children of fourteen and fifteen years are permitted to work eleven hours a day and sixty hours a week, and many of them do this without even the ability to read and write.

In North Carolina today the hum of the spindle is silent, not because men and women are unwilling to work, but because of the folly of a system which has permitted overlong hours for both women and children day and night. Furthermore, mills, factories, and work shops are closed and continue to remain closed because of piles and piles of unpurchased stock, thus creating a vicious cycle of over-production followed by unemployment.

And yet the situation is not without a remedy. The Legislative Council of North Carolina Women is presenting to the General Assembly measures which if enacted into laws will go a long way, it is believed, toward bringing about a solution to the problems. The measures are offered, however, not as cure-alls in every case, but as steps in the right direction.

The first of these measures requires the completion of the sixth grade at school by children between fourteen and sixteen years before they may leave and go to work. This measure if enacted into law will not only aid in the enforcement of our present compulsory school attendance law but will raise the standard of fitness of industrial workers.

The second measure would establish an 8-hour day and a 48-hour week for children under 16 years. This law would afford protection for the health of boys and girls during their adolescent period, and it would mean more efficient work and added years of productive labor.

A third measure would prohibit the employment of children under sixteen years to go to work in dangerous occupations.

A fourth measure would prohibit the employment of children between sixteen and eighteen years in mills, factories, and work shops throughout the night.

These standards have already been attained in one or more respects in from 38 to 47 states. They are timely and economically sound.

As unemployment of men and women, and over-production are two et North Carolina's most serious problems, the council advises: Give the work to the adults. Release the young child for school; or at least shorten his working day.

Mr. E. J. Coltrane, president of the North Carolina Education Association, speaking of the program of the Women's Legislative Council, says: "I should like to commend the child welfare legislative program of the Legislative Council of North Carolina Women. As an educational measure alone, it appeals quite strongly to me. Your goals for working children, when enacted into law, will do more than any other proposed measure to expedite the education of all children in the elementary grades. I know of no measure that will do more to solve the problem of the working child and at the same time aid in the solution of the educational problem."

Raleigh Sunday *News and Observer*, p. 15 (section 2, p. 1)

1 FEBRUARY 1931

CLUB WOMEN URGED TO HELP IN COMMUNITY RELIEF WORK

Called to Support of Red Cross Drive in Nation—Will Carry Out Program Suggested by Governor's Council For Relief of Unemployed

By Mrs. J. Henry Highsmith

Feeling that the club women of the state are ready and eager to serve their communities in what is considered the period of greatest financial depression the country has ever known, Mrs. E. M. Land of Statesville, president of the State Federation of Women's Clubs, is submitting to club members definite suggestions for giving relief and rendering valuable aid.

Mrs. Land's suggestions have the endorsement of R. W. Henniger, executive secretary of the council on unemployment and relief appointed by Governor Gardner. They not only supplement the council's program, said Mr. Henniger, but add materially to effectiveness in that they are practical and most timely.

Help Local Agencies.

Mrs. Land's first suggestion to the club women of the state is that they assist their local welfare agencies in relieving needy and destitute cases, particularly the homeless in their communities. She says:

"If the work of charity and welfare is not organized in your county, let your club serve as the agency to direct relief work. Try to give employment to some unemployed person at least one day in each week; register your unemployed, if possible; see what the industries will do to help in employing those who are idle; have that needed roofing, painting, or carpenter work done now. In the meantime, temporary relief must be given to those who neither have food nor clothes nor fuel nor work."

The second request made by Mrs. Land is that the club women assist the American Red Cross in its drive for $10,000,000. This organization, which was created by the American people to serve in times of great distress and emergency, is already giving relief to eighteen drought stricken counties in North Carolina, one county having been taken over wholly by the Red Cross. Mrs. J. F. Sippel, president of the General Federation of Women's Clubs, has been named by President Hoover as a member of this committee to assist in raising $10,000,000 for the Red Cross. In a radio talk recently given by Mrs. Sippel, club women were urged to take the lead in accepting this call to service and in meeting the responsibilities which it entails.

By way of making a further suggestion Mrs. Land says:

"You may have in operation a better plan than the one I am going to suggest, but I am passing on to you a suggestion which has been adopted in my own community, and which has met with such gratifying results. The Woman's Club of Statesville has placed in the grocery stores brightly painted barrels with a placard, 'For Charity.' Housekeepers have been asked as they make purchases for their own families to drop into these cabbage, a bunch of carrots, a can of tomatoes, some dried fruit or vegetables, maybe a pound or two of sugar, will serve to give variety to the restricted diet on which many children as well as adults are at present living. The city cooperates with the club, collects these barrels each week and turns over the supplies to the local charity organization for distribution."

Charlotte Sunday Observer, p. 37 (section 4, p. 9)

8 FEBRUARY 1931

CLUB WOMEN WILL ADVOCATE REGULATION OF BILLBOARDS

**Mrs. Palmer Jerman, President of Legislative Council, and
Mrs. E. M. Land, President of State Federation, Well Pleased
With Progress Made**

By Mrs. J. Henry Highsmith

In summing up the progress of the measures being sponsored by the
Legislative Council of North Carolina Women at this session of the General
Assembly, Mrs. Palmer Jerman, president of the council, expresses herself
as being well pleased with the progress that has been made thus far and
hopeful of final enactment for all of the bills that the council will present.

Will Receive Support.

She says that it has been most gratifying to find that the women's measures are
meeting with unusual sympathy and understanding which promises they will
receive strong support when they are up for action on the floor. Much time, she
says, has been taken up in getting the bills drawn properly and fully understood,
but having reached their final shape, she says, "I believe they will represent the
best thought of the women who sponsored their first movements."

The status of the bills to date as explained by Mrs. Jerman is that the
measure requiring children under 16 years of age to complete the sixth grade
before leaving school to go to work received a unanimous vote in its favor
from those present at its hearing before the educational committee of the
Senate. Consequently it will soon find its way to the Senate floor. This bill is
known as Senate Bill 69 and was introduced by Senator Baggett of Harnett.

The measure establishing an eight-hour day and a 48-hour week for
children under 16, and prohibiting the employment of children under 16
in hazardous occupations was introduced in the house this past week by
Representative Connor, of Wilson, and Crudup, of Vance. The bill is known
as House Bill 287 and will be given a hearing before the public welfare
committee early this week.

Stopping Night Work.

A bill calling for the elimination of night work for girls under 18 years in
mills, factories, canneries and manufacturing establishments between the
hours of 9 p. m. and 6 [a. m., and] between the hours of 3 p. m. and 6 [a. m.
has been introduced in] the house by Representative Newman of New
Hanover. This bill was also referred to public welfare committee.

A companion bill to the one introduced by Mr. Newman has been
introduced in the Senate by Senator Dortch, of Wayne. This bill would

eliminate night work for boys and girls under age 18 in the same places and between the same hours.

A bill having the endorsement of the North Carolina social service conference that would establish a 55-hour week week in all factories and manufacturing establishments, and that would prohibit night work for women and children in factories and manufacturing establishments between 16 and 18 years and between 9 p. m. and 6 a. m., has been introduced by Senator Gravely, of Nash.

Mrs. Jerman explained further that since the revenue bill having the endorsement of the present administration carries a provision for taxing and regulating advertising signs on the highways, which provision if enacted into law would go a long way toward attaining the ends for which the women are working through their highway beautification measures, the council will gives its support to the revenue bill. At a hearing of this measure before a joint meeting of the finance committees of both houses, Mrs. E. M. Land, of Statesville, president of the State Federation of Women's Clubs; Dr. Clarence Poe, Mr. Struthers Burt, and Mr. Graber, of the State Forestry Association, spoke in behalf of the bill.

Charlotte Sunday Observer, p. 23 (section 3, p. 3)

8 MARCH 1931

ANNUAL STATE CONVENTION OF FEDERATED CLUB WOMEN
TO BE HELD IN GREENSBORO

Mrs. John F. Sippel, General Federation President, Guest of Honor and Banquet Speaker—Other Women of National Prominence on Program—Interesting Social Features Planned—Night School Commencement Program April 15

By Mrs. J. Henry Highsmith

The twenty-ninth annual convention of Women's Clubs has been called to meet by the president, Mrs. E. M. Land, of Statesville, in Greensboro, April 14 to 17, inclusive. The King Cotton Hotel will be official headquarters, and the Woman's Club, Friday Afternoon Club and Reviewer's Club, all of Greensboro, will be hostesses to the convention.

Outstanding Speakers.

Among the outstanding speakers who will address the convention are Mrs. John F. Sippel of Baltimore, president of the General Federation, who will be honor guest and speaker at the annual banquet on Thursday evening; Miss Anita Browne of New York, poetry chairman of the General Federation, who will be honor guest and speaker on Wednesday evening at the fine arts meeting, and Mrs. Clara Cox Epperson, chairman of drama in the General Federation, who will be one of the luncheon conference speakers. Mrs. E. L. McKee, of Sylva, the first woman senator of North Carolina, will address the convention Tuesday evening at the opening session. Mrs. Land will make the presidential address at this meeting, also.

Among the social features planned for the visiting club women will be a reception the first evening following the opening session in the hotel parlors by courtesy of the Woman's Club of Greensboro. On Wednesday evening all club women attending the convention will be guests at dinner at the North Carolina College for Women, by invitation of Dr. J. I. Foust, the president. On Tuesday afternoon the three hostesses clubs will entertain at a tea, while the crowning social event of every Federation convention is the banquet to be held this year in the hotel dining room Thursday evening.

Night School Grads.

An outstanding event of the convention will be the state night school commencement on Wednesday afternoon, April 15, when pupils from the night schools of the state under supervision of local women's clubs, who have completed a prescribed course of study, will receive certificates that have been signed by the governor, state superintendent of public instruction and officials of the State Federation. Members of the state literacy commission, which will be holding its meeting in Greensboro at this time, will be present at this meeting. It is expected that a large number of pupils from several counties will attend this commencement.

Novel cotton badges, that have been designed by the Gastonia Woman's Club, will be worn by the pages, who will be selected from the members of the Junior clubs.

A most attractive feature of the convention will be an exhibition of paintings by the Southern Art League, also an exhibition of canvases by North Carolina artists. In addition there will be an exhibition display of North Carolina-made pottery, china and industrial arts.

Novel Entertainment.

The district presidents will stage a novel entertainment the first hour of fine arts evening, Wednesday. During the second hour the departments of literature, music and art will together present a fine arts program, with Miss Anita Browne as chief speaker.

This being a presidential year and that the meeting place is centrally located and easily accessible to all parts of the state, an unusually large attendance is expected.

Charlotte Sunday Observer, p. 40 (section 4, p. 8)

29 MARCH 1931

CLUB WOMEN PERFECT PLANS FOR FEDERATION CONVENTION
TO BE HELD AT GREENSBORO

By Mrs. J. Henry Highsmith

With all but a few final touches, the program of the twenty-ninth annual convention of the State Federation of Women's Clubs, to be held in Greensboro, April 14 to 17, is now complete. In making this announcement, Mrs. E. M. Land, of Statesville, president, says that all indications point to this as being one of the largest and most successful conventions the Federation has yet held.

Present Officers.

The officers of the Federation are, president, Mrs. E. M. Land of Statesville; first vice president, Mrs. John T. Hollister of New Bern; second vice president, Mrs. J. M. Hobgood of Farmville; recording secretary, Mrs. J. H. B. Moore of Greenville; corresponding secretary, Mrs. D. Lanier Donnell of Oak Ridge; treasurer, Mrs. R. H. Latham of Winston-Salem, and General Federation director, Mrs. Thomas O'Berry of Goldsboro.

The committee on credentials appointed by Mrs. Land are Mrs. R. H. Latham of Winston-Salem, chairman; Mrs. J. H. Separk of Gastonia; Mrs. J. C. Stewart of Wilmington; Mrs. H. W. Maler of Thomasville; Mrs. F. F. Bahnson of Winston-Salem, and Mrs. H. O. Woltz of Mount Airy.

Members of Junior clubs will serve as pages. Those that have already been appointed are Mrs. G. B. Justice, chief page; Miss Pauline Smith of Clayton, Miss Martha Galloway and Miss Virginia Graham of Raleigh and Mrs. Frank Spencer of Winston-Salem. Personal pages to the president will be Misses Caroline Long and Marianna Nicholson of Statesville.

Opening Session.

Beginning with a meeting and a luncheon to the executive board at the home of Mrs. D. Lanier Donnell of Oak Ridge, the convention gets under way Tuesday morning, April 14. In the afternoon at 2:30 an institute for club presidents will be held in the assembly room of the King Cotton Hotel, convention headquarters. A meeting of the board of trustees will be held at 3 o'clock in a private conference room of the hotel. At 4 o'clock a meeting of the board of directors will be held in the assembly hall. The past presidents' dinner with Mrs. Thomas O'Berry presiding will be held in one of the private dining rooms, at 6:30 o'clock. At the same hour the district presidents' dinner, with Mrs. J. M. Hobgood presiding, will be held in a private dining room. A dinner conference for club presidents with Miss Mary Taylor Moore presiding will be held also at 6:30 in the dining room.

The opening season of the convention will be held at 8 o'clock in the assembly room with Mrs. Edward M. Land, the president, presiding. The addresses of welcome will be made by Mrs. Cora Cox Lucas, president of the Greensboro Woman's Club; Miss Mary Taylor Moore, president of the Friday Afternoon Club; and Mrs. C. E. Hodgin, president of the Reviewers Club. Response on the behalf of the Federation will be made by Mrs. John T. Hollister of New Bern, first vice president. Featuring the evening session will be the addresses of Mrs. Land, the president, and Mrs. E. L. McKee, North Carolina's first woman senator. Immediately following this session will be a reception tendered by the three hostess clubs in the hotel parlors in honor of the visiting club women.

Breakfast Conference.

Beginning the day Wednesday, April 15, will be a breakfast conference for literary clubs and departments of literature. Mrs. Annie Miller Bless of Marion will preside. Speaker at this meeting will be Mrs. Clara Cox Epperson, chairman of drama, General Federation of Women's Clubs. A breakfast conference on civics will be held also at this hour with Mrs. J. E. Hardin of Greensboro, presiding. At 9 o'clock will be held a club institute program, with Mrs. Eugene Reilley of Charlotte, chairman. A parliamentary law class, conducted by Miss Bettie D. Windley of New Bern, will be a feature of the institute program and will be held in the assembly hall prior to the opening of the morning session at 10 a. m.

Of chief interest on the program of the morning session will be the report of the officers and special committees and the election of the nominating committee. This being a presidential year, much interest will be manifested in who the next president, second vice president, corresponding secretary and General Federation director will be.

Featuring Thursday's program will be two breakfast conferences, club institute program, report of resolutions committee, report of Sallie Southall Cotton loan fund, report of nominating committee, three luncheon conferences, one of which is for Junior clubs, with Mrs. D. F. Giles, presiding.

Night School Night.

Outstanding in interest will be the state night school commencement to be held at the Aycock Auditorium at North Carolina College for Women with Mrs. Elizabeth C. Morriss of Asheville, presiding. Following an address by Mr. Hodges, president of the state literacy commission, will be a demonstration by night school students and swarding of certificates of attainment.

The high peak of convention interest will be the annual Federation banquet in the ball room of the hotel, Thursday evening at 7 o'clock. Mrs. John F. Sippel, president of the General Federation, will be the honor guest and speaker on this occasion.

Charlotte Sunday Observer, p. 34 (section 3, p. 8)

31 MAY 1931

FEDERATION HEADQUARTERS CLOSE FOR SUMMER SEASON

By Mrs. J. Henry Highsmith

With June comes summer and with summer, vacation and the desire for play. Rare days in June to club women are those day when they can shake off the shackles of chairmanships, committee meetings and other club responsibilities and feel free to enjoy their homes, their gardens and their families undisturbed by the telephone. To close the club house door on June first not to open it until September or October first might seem the ideal way, but not since the club's motto is "Service" and the community cry is need of service.

In view of conditions as they have been and are likely to be worse this winter, Mrs. E. M. Land of Statesville advised in her last message as president of the State Federation that clubs not close their doors and go into summer quarters but that they remember the hungry mouths that had to be fed last winter and vision, of possible, worse conditions, perhaps for this winter, and prepare as far as possible to meet these needs. But for the food stuff, she said, canned by club women last summer, many a person might have gone hungry who was otherwise fed. "During the coming summer," she said, "let us conserve food when nature is so lavish with her supplies. Nothing from our gardens should be allowed to go to waste. Would it not be an excellent plan," she asks, "for club women to gather at the club house or in some member's home and can and preserve the bounty of their gardens and orchards for the needs of the winter?"

Furthermore, Mrs. Land suggests as a community project for relieving unemployment that idle hands be put to work on the idle tracts of land that are to be found in every town and village. "Surely," she says, "knowing our problem beforehand we can the better plan the ways and means of taking care of it."

What has heretofore been the club's greatest drawback, the inability to formulate and carry through interesting and constructive programs, mainly for lack of material, is this year being provided against by Mrs. T. E. Browne, of Raleigh, who as first vice-president is chairman of departmental work. Mrs. Browne and her nine department chairmen are preparing a series of program suggestions which they plan to soon put in the hands of the local chairman to be used in making up the programs and year books for next year. Much of the work has already been done by the department heads, says Mrs. Browne, and some of the programs that have already been placed with the printers will soon be ready to be distributed.

That the new plan of program making may be fully understood and put into effect at the time to be of greatest value, Mrs. Browne is inviting the chairmen of the nine departments of the Federation to a luncheon meeting at her home Thursday, June 4. The chairmen are Mrs. James Wiseman, of Elkin, American Citizenship; Mrs. J. M. Britt, of Lumberton, American Home; Mrs. J. J. Andoe, of Goldsboro, Art; Mrs. John D. Robinson, of Wallace, Civics; Miss Isabel Busbee, of Raleigh, Gardens; Mrs. B. P. Long, of Statesville, Literature; Mrs. C. J. Sawyer, of Windsor, Music; Miss Ruth Burke, of La Grange, Public Welfare; Mrs. Howard Etheridge, of Asheville, Education; and Mrs. D. F. Giles, of Marion, Junior Membership,

Headquarters Closed.

State Federation Headquarters at the Sir Walter Hotel, Raleigh, with Mrs. J. Henry Highsmith in charge, will close officially June first for June, July and August.

Raleigh Sunday *News and Observer,* p. 11 (Society, p. 1)

6 SEPTEMBER 1931

FEDERATION PRESIDENT PREDICTS GOOD SEASON

By Mrs. J. Henry Highsmith

With the advent of autumn and the opening of headquarters of the State Federation of Women's Clubs at the Sir Walter Hotel in Raleigh on September 1, the club activities of the state got under way and another club year was set in motion. Keen interest is awaiting the adoption and carrying out of the programs and projects planned during the summer for the new club year.

While the president, Mrs. J. M. Hobgood of Farmville, has spent much of the summer in Georgia, she has been able to keep her fingers on the pulse of the club situation at home and on returning reports that the prospects for another successful club year are most favorable. She feels that unusual interest has been manifested in club activities during the summer. Many clubs, she says, have neither closed their doors nor lost interest in the work of the club during the hot weather. They have canned and preserved not only in their own kitchens and in their club kitchens but they have gone out and helped others to can and thus prepare against hard times this winter. Many community problems have already been solved, she says, by the energy and foresight of its club women who not only canned fruit and vegetables while they were plentiful but who taught and otherwise made it possible for the poor to get and can their own food.

Members of one club in their own kitchen—the Statesville Woman's Club with Mrs. E. M. Land as director—have carried through a community canning project that is noteworthy. Members not only took to the club their surplus fruits and vegetables to can for emergency needs of the winter, but they purchased large supplies of these when they were most plentiful and brought in the housewives and mothers who needed them most and assisted them in canning their own food. As a result of the summer's work several thousand cans of fruits and vegetables adorn the shelves and tables of the club building to be used this winter in feeding the hungry, but what is more valuable the women of a community have been brought together in common service, sympathy and interests.

Other clubs have been outstanding in their summer services. The Woman's Club of Durham under the presidency of Mrs. W. J. Brogden has for a number of years conducted a fresh air camp for weak and undernourished children, enabling them to regain strength and prevent disease.

Raleigh Sunday *News and Observer,* p. 9 (Society, p. 1)

13 SEPTEMBER 1931

STATE FEDERATION PLANS SIXTEEN GROUP MEETINGS

First District Meeting Will Be Held in Elizabeth City October 12; State President, Mrs. J. M. Hobgood, Has Extensive Program of Conferences and Speaking Engagements

By Mrs. J. Henry Highsmith

The schedule of the sixteen district meetings of the State Federation of Women's Clubs, tentatively arranged, takes the president of the Federation, Mrs. J. M. Hobgood of Farmville, and the chairman of districts, Mrs. George E. Marshall of Mount Airy, from Elizabeth City in the east, where the first meeting will be held, October 12, to Bryson City in the west. The itinerary covers practically the club work of the entire State and the sixteen district meetings held annually and presided over by the district presidents bring the club women of every section into direct contact with the program as well as the officials of the State organization. The following schedule has been prepared by Mrs. Marshall:

16th District at Center High School, near Elizabeth City, Monday, October 12, with the Pasquotank Home Demonstration Club as hostess.

15th District at Washington, Tuesday, October 13.

12th District at New Bern, Wednesday, October 14.

9th District at Hamlet, Thursday, October 15.

10th District at Fairmont, Friday, October 16.

11th District at Rose Hill, Saturday, October 17.

13th District at Spring Hope, [Monday], October 19.

14th District at Oxford, Tuesday, October 20.

8th District at Pittsboro, Wednesday, October 21.

7th District at Burlington, Thursday, October 22.

6th District at Winston-Salem, Friday, October 23.

1st District at Bryson City, Monday, October 26.

2nd District at Brevard, Tuesday, October 27.

4th District at Belmont, Thursday, 5 October 29.

5th District at Charlotte, Friday, October 30.

A round of conferences and speaking engagements has been the program of Mrs. Hobgood for the past several days. On Tuesday and Wednesday, of last week she was a visitor at headquarters where she held conferences with a number of Federation chairmen and with representatives of the different State departments whose work is allied with that of the Federation. On Thursday she attended the Coastal Plains Field Day exercises and picnic where in an address she outlined the activities and objectives of the women's clubs of the State.

The announcement of a new phase of club work was made by Mrs. Hobgood recently. This was the Division of Radio Service in the Literature Department, to be under the direction of Miss Jenn Coltrane, of Concord. The purpose of this division is to extend the services of the Federation beyond the confines of its membership by broadcasting its programs of music, literature, art as well as by reaching the public with messages from its other departments. Miss Coltrane says that arrangements have been made with the W. B. T. Studio of Charlotte for broadcasting two club programs a week, with the possibility of the program being placed later on the Dixie Hookup.

Mrs. J. H. B. Moore, of Greenville, recording secretary of the Federation, announces that the Year Books of the Federation will be off of the press this week and will be mailed immediately to all officers and members of the Federation. She regrets the delay.

The fall council meeting of the Federation will be held in Wilmington October 8 and 9. The official call will be issued at an early date.

Raleigh Sunday *News and Observer,* p. 9 (Society, p. 1)

27 SEPTEMBER 1931

CLUB COUNCIL WILL HEAR DR. HENRY LEWIS SMITH

By Mrs. J. Henry Highsmith

Dr. Henry Louis Smith of Greensboro, president emeritus of Washington and Lee University, will address the council meeting of the State Federation of Women's Clubs at Wilmington, Thursday, evening, October 8. Mrs. Palmer Jerman of Raleigh will introduce Dr. Smith, who will speak on The Six Points of Leadership. Preceding Dr. Smith on the program will be the address of Mrs. J. M. Hobgood, president of the Federation, whose subject will be "The Tools of Preparation." The North Carolina Sorosis of Wilmington, of which Mrs. J. C. Stewart is president, will be hostess to the visiting club women and the Cape Fear Hotel will be headquarters.

The council program gets under way Thursday morning at 11 o'clock with an executive board meeting called to meet at the home of Mrs. J. C. Williams, president of the Eleventh District. Following the meeting a luncheon will be served the members of the board at the home of Mrs. Williams. At 1 o'clock at the Sorosis club house a luncheon will be served the other members and visitors attending the council meeting.

In the afternoon there will be meetings of the board of trustees, the finance committee and conferences of district presidents and department chairmen. Mrs. George E. Marshall of Mount Airy will preside over the district presidents conference and Mrs. T. E. Browne of Raleigh will preside over the department chairmen's conference. An automobile ride over the city will follow the conference meetings.

Featuring an open session to be held Thursday evening in the ballroom of the Cape Fear Hotel will be the addresses of Mrs. Hobgood, the president, and of Dr. Smith, the honor guest and speaker. Several musical selections by Wilmington musicians will be a pleasing feature of the meeting to which the public will be invited. Following this session there will be a reception in the hotel ballroom complimentary to the visiting club women by courtesy of the N. C. Sorosis.

Friday morning will be given over to the main business session of the council. At noon a luncheon will be served in the Cape Fear Hotel dining room. A business session will finish up the work of the two-day meeting.

Mrs. Hobgood visited headquarters last week on her way to Clayton, where she made the address at the Get-Together Dinner of the Clayton Woman's Club. She addressed the Woman's Club of Roanoke Rapids–Rosemary last week at its get-together meeting.

Raleigh Sunday *News and Observer*, p. 9 (Society, p. 1)

18 OCTOBER 1931

FEDERATION HEAD URGES WHISTLING FOR COURAGE

By Mrs. J. Henry Highsmith

Club women in Eastern and Central North Carolina are being urged to whistle, keep up courage and go forward during this prolonged period of depression by Mrs. J. M. Hobgood of Farmville, president of the State Federation of Women's Clubs, who is attending the sixteen district meetings previously arranged. Accompanying Mrs. Hobgood are Mrs. George E. Marshall of Mount Airy, chairman of districts, and Miss Frieda Heller of Raleigh, representing the State Library Commission.

Five district meetings are scheduled for this week which Mrs. Hobgood and Mrs. Marshall will attend as honor guests and chief speakers. These are: Meeting of the Thirteenth District at Spring Hope, October 19; meeting of the Fourteenth District at Oxford, October 20; meeting of Eighth District at Pittsboro, October 21; meeting of Seventh District at Burlington, October 22; and meeting of the Sixth District at Winston-Salem, October 23.

Passing from the eastern part of the state where the first of the sixteen meetings was held at Elizabeth City, the State officials will pass to the extreme western part, holding their first meeting of next week at Bryson City, Monday, October 26. The Second District meeting will be held at Brevard, October 27; the Third District at Maiden, October 28; the Fourth District at Belmont, October 29; and the Fifth District at Charlotte, October 30.

The message that Mrs. Hobgood is taking to the club women is a timely helpful and courageous "Forward, March!" In addition to carrying on the regular activities of the local club, she advises that club women throughout the state stand in readiness to join hands with the Governor's Council on Unemployment and Relief in carrying out the program adopted by the council. Two particular pieces of work, she said, had been assigned to the women's clubs along with Parent Teacher Associations, civic clubs and other volunteer organizations. These were securing, renovating, making and distributing clothing and securing, storing and distributing food. Mrs. Hobgood says:

"We will give as we have never given before of our money—if we have it—of our store of food and clothes and certainly of our old-time energy of which we have a plenty."

The Federation, too, has become air-minded. Not that it would take flight in some giant plane, but would remain anchored and have its ideals, purposes and programs soar to the uttermost parts. Through the courtesy of radio station WBT, of Charlotte, a program of Federation interests will be put on the air each Thursday, from 2 to 2:15 o'clock. The program will feature news, events, persons and programs of general interest. Music, art and literary addresses will be featured on the programs from time to time. On Thursday, October 22, Mrs. E. M. Land of Statesville will be the speaker. On the following Thursday, Mrs. Hobgood will take the time. Other speakers and programs will be announced from time to time.

Miss Jenn Coltrane of Concord is chairman of the radio division, which work comes under the Literature Department of the Federation, of which Mrs. B. F. Long of Statesville is chairman. Miss Coltrane announces that a radio program extending far into the winter months has been planned. She will be assisted in her programs by the chairmen of departments of the Federation and prominent club women of the State.

Raleigh Sunday *News and Observer,* p. 9 (Society, p. 1)

25 OCTOBER 1931

FEDERATION WILL PRESENT SERIES OF NINE PROGRAMS

Work As Outlined For the Various Departments of the N. C. F. W. C. Will Challenge Interests and Energies of All Clubwomen; Every Phase of Club Work Treated; Many Prominent Women Visit Headquarters

By Mrs. J. Henry Highsmith

There's to be no unemployment among club women of the State for at least two years, if the working plans of the State Federation are carried out as outlined in the programs of the nine departmental chairmen which have been prepared and presented to the clubs as their working-plans for this and perhaps next year. In fact, the whole Federation is to be put to work in one capacity or another. There's to be no idle class, and certainly no resting on laurels of past achievements.

Under the direction of Mrs. T. E. Browne, of Raleigh, third vice president of the Federation, the nine chairmen of departmental work and their division chairmen have prepared a series of nine programs which will challenge the interests and the energies of any club woman regardless of her tastes, gifts or accomplishments. It was the object of the program committee to put the club women to work using methods of the programs by which their work might be systematized and standardized. Progress was their objective and service their goal. The preparations and adoption of these programs have been the most forward step taken by the Federation in many years. Mrs. John F. Sippel, president of the General Federation, says that no State in the Union excels North Carolina in both her programs and her Year Book.

The department and division chairmen working with Mrs. Browne and the subjects they represent are: Mrs. J. J. Andoe, of Greensboro, chairman of art; Mrs. James Wiseman, of Elkin, chairman of citizenship; Mrs. J. N. Britt, of Lumberton, chairman of parent education; Mrs. John D. Robinson, of Wallace, chairman of civics; Mrs. E. S. Paddison, of Nashville, chairman of conservation; Mrs. Howard G. Etheridge, of Asheville, chairman of education; Miss Eva Edgerton, of High Point, chairman of adult illiteracy; Miss Frieda Heller, of Raleigh, chairman of library extension; Miss Isabel B. Busbee, of Raleigh, chairman of gardens; Mrs. B. F. Long of Statesville, chairman of literature; Mrs. Eugene Reilley, of Charlotte, chairman of Bible literature; Mrs. C. J. Sawyer, of Windsor, chairman of music; Mrs. E. E. Randolph, of Raleigh, chairman of music achievement contest for school children; Miss Ruth Burke, of La Grange, chairman of public welfare; and Miss Lilly Mitchell, director of the Division of Child Welfare of the State Board of Charities and Public Welfare.

Mrs. C. J. Sawyer, of Windsor, chairman of music, is asking the clubs in celebrating the birth of George Washington to use the music of his time. A collection of songs and pieces, she says, can be obtained from the United States Bicentennial Commission, Washington, D. C.

Among the recent visitors at headquarters were: Mrs. J. G. Fearing, of Elizabeth City; Mrs. E. M. Land, of Statesville; Mrs. B. F. Long, of Statesville; Mrs. Charles R. Whitaker, of Southern Pines; Mrs. J. W. Hunt, Mrs. E. B. Hatch and Mrs. Wade Barber, of Pittsboro; Mrs. C. J. Sawyer and Mrs. Sutton, of Windsor; Mrs. Eugene Davis, of Statesville; Miss Gertrude Weil and Mrs. Oettinger, of Goldsboro.

Raleigh Sunday *News and Observer,* p. 9 (Society, p. 1)

1932

5 January — returns home from a 10-day trip to Florida with Dr. Highsmith, Eugenia and Mary Belle; they travel down the west coast to Miami via Tamiami Trail, pausing to visit in Jacksonville, Daytona Beach, Winter Haven, and Arcadia; then home via the east coast back to Daytona Beach, Silver Springs, and Gainesville

4 February — at RWC meeting promotes visit to Raleigh of Flying Squadron, a group promoting prohibition

11 February — presides at RWC meeting to hear executive secretary of the Allied Forces for Prohibition

21 February — promotes exhibition of art pottery made by NC State student of Department of Ceramic Engineering, 3–5 March, the first of its kind

3–5 May 1932 — attends 30th annual NCFWC convention, Winston-Salem

24 May — addresses Wendell Woman's Club on "What a Woman's Club Means to a Town," retitled "The Place of the Woman's Club in the Community"

9–18 June — attends GFWC National Convention in Seattle, traveling with Vara by rail by way of Lake Louise, Banff, and Vancouver, and returning through Oregon, California, Grand Canyon, Pike's Peak; subsequently four NC women are named to national administration of Grace Morrison Poole

1932–1935
Division Chairman, editorials, state federation magazines
Department of Press and Publication
General Federation of Women's Clubs

October — oversees with two others, as part of NCFWC new radio service, series of weekly broadcasts on WPTF, Tuesdays from 1:15 to 1:30

4 October — attends Fall council meeting of NCFWC, Mt. Airy

11 October — addresses Dunn Woman's Club on parliamentary law

13 October — addresses Salisbury Woman's Club on "Club Women as Pioneers on the New Frontier"

25 October — Addresses B&PWC on "Women at the Crossroads," part of Get-Out-the-Vote campaign

1 November — pours at a tea given by Raleigh Junior Woman's Club at the Southern School of Creative Arts

4 November — assists Miss Anne Simms and her mother at a informal bridal tea at the Simms house on Wake Forest Road

9 November — addresses Wiley PTA on "A Challenge to Parents and Teachers," concerning the economic crisis

13 November — participates, representing League of Women Voters, in round-table "What Are We Doing For Peace?" concluding first Institute on International Affairs sponsored by United Church; reads Eugenia's paper, from B&PWC, in her absence

c. 15 December — her mandate as Executive Secretary, Legislative Council, is extended for the 1933 Legislature

10 December — assists, as does Eugenia, at Vara's tea honoring two former classmates of Littleton College

10 JANUARY 1932

JANUARY MEETINGS CLAIM ATTENTION OF CLUBWOMEN

North Carolina Will Be Represented at Meeting of Directors of General Federation in Washington January 13–16 and at Conference on Cause and Cure of War Few Days Later

By Mrs. J. Henry Highsmith

Two important January meetings will claim the attention of the club women of the State for the next two weeks. These are the mid-winter meetings of the board of directors of the General Federation of Women's Clubs held in Washington, January 13–16, and the National Conference on the Cause and Cure of War held in Washington, January 18–21. North Carolina will be represented at the board meeting of the General Federation by Mrs. J. M. Hobgood, of Farmville, president of the State Federation; Mrs. E. M. Land, of Statesville, State director of the General Federation, and a member of the executive committee; and by Mrs. Palmer Jerman, of Raleigh, member of the board of trustees of the General Federation. Prior to attending the Washington Board meeting, Mrs. Jerman will visit her son in New York. Mrs. Hobgood and Mrs. Lane will go by motor, leaving Raleigh Sunday after having attended an executive board meeting of the State Federation on Saturday at State Headquarters in Raleigh. They will be accompanied by Mrs. Robert K. Rambo, of Atlanta, Ga., General Federation director for Georgia, who will join them Sunday in Raleigh.

The sessions of the board meeting will be held at National Headquarters with Mrs. John F. Sippel, president, presiding. Attending will be club women from every State in the Union. The first meeting will be held Wednesday, January 13. On Monday before will be a meeting of the executive committee and on Tuesday the board of trustees and State presidents will meet. The outstanding social event will be a reception at headquarters when the visiting club women will meet their Senators and Congressmen and others in official life at Washington. The Cameron Club of Alexandria, Virginia, will entertain the visitors at dinner Thursday evening when interesting incidents in the life of Washington will be presented.

The conference on the Cause and Cure of War a week later will be attended by Mrs. Charles Hillett, of Charlotte, Mrs. Reverdy J. Miller, of Charlotte, and Mrs. Reuben Robertson, of Asheville.

The radio division of the Federation under the chairmanship of Miss Jenn Coltrane of Concord, announces the following program over radio station WBT, Charlotte: Thursday, January 13, at 2 o'clock, Mrs. B. F. Long on the subject: "Literary Contests Sponsored by the Federation"; Thursday, January 21, at 2 o'clock, Mrs. John D. Robinson of Wallace on the subject, "Highway Beautification"; January 28, Mrs. James Wiseman on American Citizenship; February 4, Mrs. J. J. Andoe on Art; February 11, Mrs. R. B. Etheridge on Education; February 18, Mrs. T. E. Browne, on Public Welfare, and on February 25, Mrs. Land on Safety.

In the campaign to further the business of being a club woman by securing subscriptions and giving a wider circulation to The Club Woman, G. F. W. C., one of the new projects entered into by the Federation this new year, Mrs. J. Henry Highsmith of Raleigh has been made chairman and the following club women have been appointed chairmen: District 1, Miss Margaret Gibson, Asheville; district 2, Mrs. J. S. Silversteen, Brevard; district 3, Miss Carrie Hoffman, Statesville; district 4, Mrs. F. H. Chamberlain, Lincolnton; district 5, Mrs. Chas. E. Platt, Charlotte; district 6, Mrs. John C. Bower, Lexington; district 7, Mrs. D. Lanier Donnell, Oak Ridge; district 8, Mrs. N. H. Hopson, Varina; district 9, Mrs. Charles L. Scott, Sanford; district 10, Mrs. J. B. Elliott, Chadbourn; district 11, Mrs. C. F. Taylor, Southport; district 12, Miss Margaret Bryan, New Bern; district 13, Mrs. B. A. Hocutt, Clayton; district 14, Mrs. F. M. Brown, Roanoke Rapids, district 15, Mrs. C. J. Sawyer, Windsor; district 16, Miss Ethel Parker, Gatesville.

Raleigh Sunday *News & Observer,* p. 13 (Society, .p 1)

13 MARCH 1932

CLUB WOMEN COOPERATE WITH ANTI-HOARDING PLAN

Mrs. John F. Sippel, President of the General Federation of Women's Clubs, After Attending President Hoover's Conference on Hoarding, Heartily Endorses Plan For Wise Spending

By Mrs. J. Henry Highsmith

North Carolina club women will cooperate with the President's program to overcome the hoarding of money. Mrs. John F. Sippel, president of the General Federation of Women's Clubs, who attended the President's conference on hoarding, approved heartily of the program adopted and says that it is altogether in line with the Federation's Wise Spending Study program. She is calling on the club women of the country to join their forces with those of local agencies to wage a campaign against the present practice of keeping money out of the channels of trade. She says hoarding is foolish saving, and she does not believe that those who are hoarding their money know the far reaching effects of such action. In trying to play safe for themselves, she says, they forget that in business as elsewhere "no man liveth to himself," and that idle dollars mean idle business, idle men, low prices and further depression.

Mrs. Sippel feels that since American women are considered the "big buyers of the nation" because they are engaged in business transactions to the amount of forty billions of dollars annually, and because they control from 75 per cent to 85 per cent of the retail buying, that it is up to them to know and cause others to know that money hidden away at home cannot at the same time be out circulating making more money and more jobs. Mrs. Sippel points out that a dollar hoarded not only ceases to perform its function as currency, but it destroys from $5 to $10 potential credit, and credit, she says is the very heart of our economic life. In conclusion she says:

"Let us give the same effort and enthusiastic support to the fight against this imp of depression, this foolish manner of saving, that we gave to the drives during the World War, in order that we may create a spirit of confidence instead of fear."

R. W. Henninger, executive secretary of the Governor's Council on Unemployment Relief, advises that war-salvaged material and surplus war articles now on hand will be sold at a nominal price to clubs and other welfare organizations (not individuals), providing the articles will be used in needy cases and will be given away and not resold. Clubs interested in providing for the needy of their committees either this year or next and desiring further information regarding the sale, will write to Mr. R. W. Henninger, Raleigh, N. C. The list of articles for sale includes blankets, coats, breeches, overcoats, hats, caps, shirts, shoes, socks, leggings, belts, gloves, underclothes, pillows and mattresses. The price of each ranges from one to five cents.

The State Picture Memory Contest sponsored jointly by the art department of the Federation and the State Department of Education, will be held in Raleigh, Saturday, April 16 at the Hugh Morson High School at 10:30 o'clock. The contest is planned for two groups of children; one of sixth and seventh grade pupils and the other of high school students. Each city may send four representatives; each town two and each county eight. Schools are asked to notify the State Department of Education by April 5, as to the number of children taking part in the contest.

Governor Gardner has endorsed the clean-up, paint-up week that Mrs. John D. Robinson of Wallace, chairman of civics of the Federation, is calling on the clubs to observe the week of April 3–9. He believes that such a movement if entered into by all the clubs of the State will accomplish much in the way of health, beauty and happiness for their people.

Raleigh Sunday *News & Observer,* p. 15 (Society, p. 1)

20 MARCH 1932

CLUB WOMEN COOPERATE WITH CHICAGO WORLD FAIR

Club Women of Entire Nation Cooperating in Project to Demonstrate at Century of Progress Exposition Accomplishments of Women Along Cultural, Philanthropic and Welfare Lines During Past Century

By Mrs. J. Henry Highsmith

North Carolina club women are cooperating with the club women of other states in a project to demonstrate at the Century of Progress Exposition to be held in Chicago in June, 1933, the accomplishments of women along cultural, philanthropic and welfare lines during the past one hundred years. Club women through the General Federation will unite with twenty other strong, national women's organizations under the head of the National Council of Women for the purpose of setting forth the part that women have played in the rise of civilization during the past century. In addition to putting on this comprehensive exhibit, it will also sponsor an International Congress of Women during the exposition. Attending this conference will be women of distinction and leaders of thought from practically all civilized countries.

Already the National Council has leased 2,400 square feet of floor space in the social science building at Chicago for the use of its member organizations. Here it will unfold the dramatic story of how women's organizations have developed from the small cultural club to the large influential groups of today. That there may be a more tangible record of achievements than a mere visual one, a nation-wide research into the history and progress of women's organizations has been started by Dr. Kathryn McHale, executive director of the American Association of University Women. The findings will be used as a basis of a book on the history of the woman's movement.

Forty-three schools have taken advantage of Mrs. Katherine P. Arrington's offer to assist schools in securing copies of famous pictures. Each of these schools has raised twenty dollars and has been given the same amount by Mrs. Arrington to buy fifty reproductions in color of famous pictures for class study and one large in color suitably framed for the school room. Mrs. Arrington's offer was made at the meeting of the State Art Society in Raleigh last December, and holds till the next annual meeting of the Society. Club women are urged to cooperate with the schools in obtaining through this offer famous paintings for their children to study in the schools.

Three North Carolina clubs have recently federated directly with the General Federation of Women's Clubs. These are the Eclectic Book Club and the Woman's Club of Statesville, and the Woman's Club of Evergreen. This makes an even fifty clubs holding membership in the General Federation through direct federation, while all the other clubs hold membership only through the state organization.

A new club to have been recently organized and federated with the State Federation is the Woman's Club of Unionville, Union County. The president is Mrs. Charles N. Griffin and the treasurer is Miss Verla Haigler. The club was organized by Mrs. Johnson McCall of Charlotte, president of the Fifth District.

Among recent visitors to State Federation Headquarters at Raleigh are Mrs. W. J. Brogden, of Durham; Mrs. John D. Robinson, of Wallace; Mrs. J. N. Britt, of Lumberton; Mrs. Guy Penny, of Garner; Mrs. J. M. Hobgood, of Farmville; Mrs. J. B. Joyner, of Farmville; Mrs. E. M. Land, of Statesville; Mrs. E. L. McKee, of Sylva; Mrs. Sydney Cooper, of Henderson; Mrs. Dennis G. Brummitt, of Oxford and Raleigh, and Mrs. Dan Poling of New York City.

Raleigh Sunday *News & Observer*, p. 15 (Society, p. 1)

27 MARCH 1932

STATE WOMEN'S CLUBS TO HOLD ANNUAL CONFERENCE

With State Convention of the North Carolina Federation of Women's Clubs Only Five Weeks Hence, Club Members Show Marked Activity in Preparing Reports of Work for Twelve Month Period

By Mrs. J. Henry Highsmith

With Spring comes the greatest activity of the woman's club year. This spring is no exception. With the State convention only five weeks away—May 3–6, club women have sensed its approach and are making ready for this the one great event of the year. While the convention does not mark the close of the club year nor mean the ceasing of club activities for the summer months, it does call for reports of all club work for a 12-month period. In the two months remaining—May and June—the local clubs will carry on their program of work till summer if not throughout the year.

Keen interest is being manifested at this time in the various contests sponsored by the Federation. Among these are the poetry contests under the chairmanship of Mrs. B. F. Long, of Statesville, who also has charge of the contests in writing short stories and one-act plays. Mrs. C. J. Sawyer, of Windsor, in charge of the music contests, says that the two music cups will likely be awarded this year. Mrs. J. J. Andoe, of Greensboro, reports much interest in the four art contests. These are for best water color, best landscape, or marine in oil, collection of sculpture and essay on Art in Precious Metals. Three money prizes are being offered by Mrs. John D. Robinson, Wallace, chairman of Civics, for the greatest improvement made by Clubs in Clean Up Campaign. The garden department under the chairmanship of Miss Isabel B. Busbee, of Raleigh, is offering a silver goblet for the largest per cent of homes beautified by planting, The education department under the chairmanship of Mrs. H. G. Etheridge, of Asheville, is offering two substantial money prizes to the district teaching one or more adult students in each county to read and write, and a prize is offered by the chairman of conservation, Mrs. E. S. Paddison, of Nashville, for the largest number of trees planted by a club. Mrs. J. N. Britt, of Lumberton, chairman of American Home, reports much interest in the contest: How Spend the Sabbath?

A Statewide music achievement contest will be held in Raleigh, April 2, at the Woman's Club. Each separate school in every city and county school system is entitled to enter one pupil from the elementary grades and one from the high school. Dr. A. T. Allen will present State certificates of award in music appreciation to each pupil properly registered in the contest. To the winner in the State contest, Mr. Jule Warren offers a cash prize of $50, the money to be used in purchasing a radio or other musical equipment for the school. In connection with the music achievement contest will be a hymn contest conducted by Mrs. Wheeler Martin, of Williamston. Mrs. C. J. Sawyer will be present on this occasion.

Mrs. J. M. Hobgood, of Farmville, president of the Federation, attended the organization meeting of the State Symphony Society in Chapel Hill last week. En route she visited State Headquarters at Raleigh and Mrs. W. J. Brogden, of Durham.

R. W. Henninger of Raleigh, executive secretary of the Governor's Council on Unemployment and Relief, in a letter to Mrs. Hobgood, advises that the club women of the State make the planting of gardens and the canning of surplus vegetables a major project of 1932. He further advises putting on a community seed drive, and says he will give further information for obtaining good seed to plant.

The Club of Twelve of Lexington recently donated twelve pecan trees to the Industrial School and Farm Colony at Kinston.

Raleigh Sunday *News & Observer,* p. 15 (Society, p. 1)

10 APRIL 1932

RUTH BRYAN OWEN TO TALK AT FEDERATION CONVENTION

**Congresswoman Owen of Florida Will Be Chief Speaker and
Guest of Honor at the Thirtieth Annual Convention of the State
Federation of Woman's Clubs in Winston-Salem, May 3–5**

By Mrs. J. Henry Highsmith

Congresswoman Ruth Bryan Owen will be the chief speaker and honor guest
at the thirtieth annual convention of the State Federation of Women's Clubs
which meets this year in Winston-Salem, May 3rd, 4th and 5th. Mrs. Owen
will address the club women and citizens of Winston-Salem on Wednesday
evening, May 4th, at the Reynolds Auditorium. She will be introduced by
Mrs. Palmer Jerman of Raleigh. On Wednesday afternoon, Mrs. S. Clay
Williams will receive at a garden party at her home in honor of Mrs. Owen
and visiting clubwomen.

According to the 1932 Convention Call recently issued by Mrs. J. M.
Hobgood, president of the Federation, arrangements have been made for
entertaining the largest convention the Federation has held in years. In
addition to comfortable quarters at reasonable rates at the Robert E. Lee
Hotel, convention headquarters, a full three-day program of engaging
interests and recreational pleasures has been arranged. Mrs. T. W. Watson
of Winston-Salem is chairman of the local program committee. The five
federated clubs of Winston-Salem, the Woman's Club, the Sorosis, Bon Air,
Utopian and the Sans Souci—will be hostesses to the convention.

Among a number of attractive features planned is an evening of music
to be given by Winston-Salem musicians on Thursday evening following the
Federation banquet. The speakers scheduled for the breakfast and luncheon
conferences will also be drawing features. The art exhibit promises to be
especially interesting this year. Miss Bettie D. Windley will again conduct
classes in parliamentary law which will be free to the delegates and visitors.

Novel badges featuring a likeness of George Washington will be worn by
the delegates while the pages will wear costumes of George Washington's
day.

An outstanding social event will be the tea at Historic Salem College
on Thursday afternoon. As the Federation was founded at this institution
30 years ago, and club women have been invited to visit the place every ten
years on holding their convention in the Twin City, there's a growing feeling
of love and veneration for this institution for the eventful part it played in
the Federation's early history. Another delightful social occasion will be the
reception given by the hostess clubs on the opening evening in the hotel
parlors immediately following the evening's exercises.

The Winston-Salem Junior Club will entertain on Thursday afternoon at the Woman's Club in honor of all visiting Junior Club members. The Junior Club luncheon will be held at the Robert E. Lee Hotel Thursday at noon with Mrs. D. F. Giles presiding.

The convention gets under way Tuesday morning with a meeting of the executive board at the Woman's Club, followed by a luncheon for the board at the club. In the afternoon a club institute will be held at the Robert E. Lee Hotel followed by a meeting of the board of trustees and this by a meeting of the board of directors. Three dinners are scheduled: One for the past presidents of the Federation, one for the district presidents and one for chairmen of departments and presidents of local clubs.

The opening session will be Tuesday evening at 8 o'clock in the ball room of the hotel. The president's address and special music will feature the session. The local public is cordially invited to attend this session, as well as the exercises the following night in the Reynolds Auditorium.

Raleigh Sunday *News & Observer,* p. 15 (Society, p. 1)

1 MAY 1932

FEDERATION CONVENTION OPENS TUESDAY EVENING

Full Program of Business and Pleasure Awaits Gathering of Club Women in Winston-Salem; Prominent Men and Women on Program as Speakers; Social Entertainments Planned

By Mrs. J. Henry Highsmith

With a three-day program replete with business and pleasure, the annual convention of the State Federation of Women's Clubs gets under way at Winston-Salem this week, beginning Tuesday and continuing through Thursday. The Twin-City will be the Mecca for hundreds of club women literally all the way from Manteo to Murphy. Those who will not attend in person will be there in spirit. Their accomplishments in club work—treasures of faith, hope, love and sacrificial effort—will be presented by their official representatives. Perhaps never before in the Federation's history have club women labored more faithfully more unselfishly and more sacrificially than during the past year. Calls to service were accepted as opportunities.

The opening session will be held Tuesday evening at 8 o'clock in the assembly hall of the Robert E. Lee Hotel. Mrs. J. M. Hobgood, president of the Federation, will preside. The invocation will be made by Rev. R. E. Gribbin. The address of welcome will be given by Mrs. Howard Ronthaler. Mrs. T. E. Browne, of Raleigh, will make the response. The president's address and special music by Miss Jessie Lupo, accompanied by Mrs. C. J. Sawyer, and by the Centenary Choir, directed by Harry E. Parker, will be the outstanding features of the evening's program. Greetings will be extended by Mrs.

Eugene Davis from the State Federation of Music Clubs and from Mrs. D. A. McCormick from the State Federation of Home Demonstration Clubs. Little Miss Mary Louise Jackson Cooper, of Henderson, the Federation mascot, will be presented.

Immediately following the evening session will be a reception in the hotel parlors in honor of the visiting club women as a courtesy of the five hostess clubs: The Sorosis of Winston-Salem, Bon Air Woman's Club, Utopian Club, Sans Souci Club and the Winston-Salem Woman's Club.

Beginning the day Wednesday will be two breakfast conferences: American Home with Prof. Ralph McDonald, of Salem College, and Mrs. Julius McInnes, of Raleigh, as speakers, and Education with Miss Lou Gray of Columbia, S. C., as speaker. At 9 o'clock on Wednesday and Thursday mornings a session of the Club Institute under the direction of Mrs. Eugene Reilley will be held at which time a class in parliamentary law will be conducted by Miss Bettie D. Windley of New Bern.

The first business session of the convention will be held Wednesday morning at 10 o'clock in the hotel assembly hall with Mrs. Hobgood presiding. Reports of officers, boards, committees and four district presidents—Mrs. J. D. McCall, Mrs. E. B. Hatch, Mrs. J. A. Robeson and Mrs. J. W. McIntosh— will be heard at this session. Mrs. C. J. Sawyer will report for the Music Department and Mrs. J. N. Britt will report for the American Home. Mrs. J. Henry Highsmith, executive-secretary of Federation Headquarters, will also make her report. New clubs will be introduced at this session and there will be special music by Wilson Angel, Mrs. Lorene Straley, Mrs. Julia Morris and Mr. Howard Conrad, accompanied by Miss Mabel Beatty.

Speakers at the three luncheon conferences on Wednesday will be Miss Helen H. Hodge of Charlotte, on Gardens; Dean C. G. Vardell, Jr., of Salem College, on Music, and Mrs. E. M. Land of Statesville, on Citizenship.

Reporting at the afternoon conference will be Mrs. Howard G. Etheridge on Education, at which time Certificates of Attainment will be awarded to night school pupils having completed the required course during this club year. Mrs. James Wiseman will report on Citizenship, Miss Gertrude Weil on International Relations, Miss Isabell Busbee on Gardens, Miss Harriett Elliott on Legislation and Miss Margaret L. Gibson on Constitutional Revision. Four district presidents reporting at this session will be Mrs. D. H. Tillett, Mrs. C. W. Graybeal, Mrs. Dudley Bagley and Mrs. R. A. Ashworth.

A delightful break in the day's program will be a visit at 4 o'clock to Wilscher, the gardens of Mrs. S. Clay Williams, where tea will be served honoring Mrs. Ruth Bryan Owen and the convention delegates and visitors. Of state-wide interest will be the speech of Ruth Bryan Owen, Congresswoman from Florida, at 8 o'clock in the Reynolds Auditorium. Mrs. Palmer Jerman will introduce the speaker and special music will be furnished by the Thursday Morning Music Club of Winston-Salem with Nils Bosom as director.

Two breakfast conferences will begin Thursday's program: Art with Miss Louise Hall of Duke University as speaker and Public Welfare with R. W. Henninger of Raleigh and Mrs. H. A. Cameron of Raeford as speakers. Featuring the business session of Thursday morning will be reports by Mrs. T. E. Browne on Public Welfare, Miss Adelaide Fries on Resolutions, Mrs. E. L. McKee and Mrs. Palmer Jerman on the General Foundation Fund, Mrs. Tully Blair on Transportation, Mrs. W. J. Brogden on the Sallie Southall Cotten Loan Fund, Mrs. D. F. Giles on Junior Membership, Mrs. J. J. Andoe on Art and Mrs. Jane S. McKimmon on Home Demonstration work. Of special interest at this session will be the report of the nominating committee, the election of new officers and the election of delegates to the Biennial Convention at Seattle. The four district presidents reporting at this time will be Mrs. D. M. Clark, Mrs. Janet Norma Winborn, Mrs. T. B. Upchurch and Mrs. Dennis G. Brummitt.

The luncheon conferences for Thursday are: Literature with Dr. Frank C. Brown of Duke University and Miss Elba Henninger of Greensboro College as speakers; Civics with E. B. Jeffress, State Highway Commissioner, as speaker and Junior Membership with Mrs. D. F. Giles presiding.

Featuring Thursday afternoon session will be reports by Mrs. Eugene Reilley on Club Institutes, Mrs. B. F. Long on Literature, Mrs. John D. Robinson on Civics, Mrs. E. M. Land on Safety, Mrs. J. Henry Highsmith on the Press and district presidents: Mrs. O. J. Mooneyham, Mrs. T. W. Watson, Mrs. J. S. Williams and Mrs. T. M. West. A separate session for Juniors will be held at 2:30 on Thursday.

The afternoon social features will be the tea at Salem College by courtesy of the college and a visit to the Wachovia Museum.

The climax of the convention will be reached Thursday evening with the holding of the Federation banquet in the ballroom of the hotel. The banquet speaker will be Mrs. Lindsay Patterson, the first president of the Federation. A program of music by the music faculty of Salem College will be an added delightful feature. The musicians taking part in the program will be Miss Hazel Horton Read, violinist, Miss Viola Tucker, piano, Miss Eleanor Shaffer, harp, Mr. Ernest L. Schofield, voice, and the Glee Club of Salem College, with Mr. Schofield as director. Miss Ruth Cumbie and Miss Harriet Ware will give several musical numbers Thursday morning.

Prize winning cups offered by the departments of Art, Music, Gardens and Literature will be awarded following the banquet program Thursday evening.

Mrs. George C. Hemingway, of Winston-Salem, is chief marshal. Her assistants will be Mrs. Henry Marshall, Mrs. Howard Grubbs, Miss Lois

Strickland, Miss Mary Crutchfield and Mrs. Hansell Hester. Personal pages to Mrs. Hobgood will be Mrs. Royster Lyle, Miss Elizabeth Field, Mrs. Harold Sugg Askew, Miss Evelyn Horton and Miss Edna Foust Harris, all of Farmville.

Governor O. Max Gardner has appointed Mrs. Hobgood as a delegate to the National Conference on State Parks to be held at Virginia Beach May 4 to 7, 1932.

With three North Carolina clubs subscribing 100 per cent to the Clubwoman GFWC, these being Clayton Woman's Club, Clayton Junior Club and the Chadbourn Woman's Club with a total of 83 subscriptions, prospects begin to brighten for the Old North State to have a chance to stand somewhere near the top among her group of states. Reports and receipts from other clubs and individuals indicate that the club women of the State are interested in the success of the campaign and in the standing of their state. It is hoped that before the campaign closes May 10th, that every club will subscribe to one or more copies of the magazine and that all officers and other individuals who receive free copies will renew their subscriptions by sending Mrs. J. Henry Highsmith, State Chairman, at Sir Walter Hotel, Raleigh, their checks for one dollar for one year's subscription or one-fifty for two years' subscription. Which will be the next 100 per cent Club? Which will join the Marie Land Booster Club?

To encourage art production, especially portrait painting, among North Carolinians, Mrs. S. Clay Williams is offering a silver vase through the art department of the Federation to the person painting and exhibiting at the Federation convention the best portrait. The exhibit will be in charge of Mrs. J. J. Andoe, of Greensboro.

Raleigh Sunday *News & Observer,* p. 15 (Society, p. 1)

15 May 1932

Club Women to Attend Biennial Convention

Large Delegation from North Carolina Expected to Attend Convention in Seattle June 9–18; Mrs. E. M. Land Will Be Presented as Candidate for Second Vice-President of General Federation

By Mrs. J. Henry Highsmith

North Carolina club women will now focus their interest and attention on the General Federation convention in Seattle, Wash., June 9–18, more especially because they are this year presenting a candidate for a national office—Mrs. Edward M. Land for vice-president of the General Federation of Women's Clubs. As was manifested at the recent State Federation convention when delegates to the Biennial Convention were elected, keen interest prevails and an unusually large number of club women from North Carolina will be expected to attend. Seven delegates, it was pointed out, may represent North Carolina at the General Convention. The seven delegates elected were: Mrs. E. L. McKee of Sylva, Mrs. J. Henry Highsmith of Raleigh, Miss Ethel Parker of Gatesville, Mrs. E. S. Groves of Gastonia, Mrs. George Hadley of Greenville, Mrs. H. A. Helder of Canton and Mrs. J. W. McIntosh of Lenoir.

The alternates were: Miss Jessie Moye of Greenville, Mrs. Eugene Reilley of Charlotte, Mrs. J. M. Moretz of Boone, Mrs. J. A. Moretz of Hickory, Mrs. Carrie Loftin of Asheboro, Mrs. A. A. Williford of Raeford and Mrs. Randolph Harper of Lenoir. Both Mrs. J. M. Hobgood, President of the Federation, and Mrs. Land, State director, will go as delegates by virtue of their offices. Mrs. B. F. Long of Statesville, mother of Mrs. Land, will attend as a delegate from the Eclectic Club of Statesville. Other clubs directly federated with the General Federation have the privilege and are urged to elect one delegate to the Seattle convention.

While the "Landslide Special" has been adopted as the official route of the club women of the Southeastern States going out to Seattle, it is not exclusive to others, either men or women, who desire to avail themselves of this opportunity to travel through the picturesque Canadian Rockies and visit the famous "Evergreen Playgrounds" of the world. The North Carolina party leaving June 2 will join the delegations from South Carolina, Georgia, and Florida at Asheville.

North Carolina Club Women who will attend the Biennial have been invited by the California Club Women to stop in California either en route to or from the convention. Mrs. Annie Little Barry, president the California Federation, who issued the invitation, says: "Any courtesy we may be able to extend your women in whatever place they may visit in our State we shall consider a privilege. We shall be glad to arrange for special gatherings where delegates may visit localities as a group. Will you kindly furnish me with information that will put me in touch with your delegates?"

The courtesy has been extended to the president of the North Carolina Federation, Mrs. J. M. Hobgood, inviting her to pour tea at the "Candidates Tea" in Seattle, Monday, June 13. On this occasion Mrs. Land will be honored together with the other nominees for office.

An unusual interest has been manifested this year in the contests conducted by the Federation, the interest having been state-wide, a list of the winners is here given: The Separk Poetry [cup] offered for the best poem was awarded to Mrs. Rush T. Wray of Charlotte. Her poem is entitled "The Storm." The Albert L. Berry cup offered for the best poetical composition went to Mrs. Zoe Kincaid Brockman of Gastonia. Her composition was "Lilacs." Honorable mention was given to Mrs. Pryor Nicholson of Varina for her poem "Color," and to Mrs. A. M. Bushnell of Saluda for her poetical composition, "Call of Spring." The Joseph P. Caldwell cup offered for best short story was awarded to Mrs. C. L. Philbrick of Raleigh, her story being named "Macaroni and Cheese." Honorable mention went to Mrs. C. A. Jordan, also of Raleigh. The Lanier cup offered for the best play was award Mrs. Pryor G. Nicholson of Varina.

The Duncan Music cup given for the best composition in instrumental music was awarded Mrs. Pearl R. Blades of Rutherfordton, for her composition called "Faitaise" ["Fantaisie"?]. The Florence M. Cooper Cup was won by Miss Gertrude Johnson of Asheville for her song "Breath of Roses."

The silver drinking cup donated by Mrs. James G. Stanton of Williamston for the club planting the most home grounds and gardens was won by the Varina Woman's Club.

The Margaret Nowell Graham silver vase offered for the best water color was won by Miss Hilda Ogburn of Greensboro. The James Westley White Cup offered for the best landscape or marine was won by William Pfohl of Winston-Salem, for his landscape "Salem Academy in 1845." The silver cup offered by Mrs. S. Clay Williams for the best portrait was won by Clement Strudwick, Jr., of Hillsboro. The prize for the best essay on art went to Miss Ethel D. Wood of New Bern, her subject being "Art in Precious Metals and as a Source of History." Honorable mention was given to Mrs. Margaret Nowell Graham of Winston-Salem and to Gene Erwin of Durham for water color designs.

Raleigh Sunday *News & Observer,* p. 15 (Society, p. 1)

29 MAY 1932

NORTH CAROLINA MEMBERS TO ATTEND GENERAL MEET

Large Delegation of North Carolina Women will Attend Biennial Convention of the General Federation of Women's Clubs to be Held in Seattle, Washington June 9–18; Leave June 1

By Mrs. J. Henry Highsmith

Exciting interest is felt by North Carolina Club Women in the Biennial Convention of the General Federation at Seattle, Washington, June 9 to 18, as June first approaches when the North Carolina delegation will take its departure. The party will join groups from other Southeastern states at Asheville and on the Landslide Special, named in honor of Mrs. Edward M. Land, of Statesville, who is a candidate for second vice president of the General Federation, will tour the Canadian Rockies, spending a day and night at the noted resorts, Banff Springs and Lake Louise. The trip will include visits to Vancouver and Victoria, also a day's sail on the Puget Sound.

Composing the party from North Carolina will be Mrs. J. M. Long, of Statesville, Mrs. J. Henry Highsmith and her sister, Miss Vara Herring, of Raleigh, Miss Ethel Parker, of Gatesville, Mrs. George F. Hadley and her sister, Miss Jessie Moye, of Greenville, Mrs. Eugene Reilley, of Charlotte, Mrs. E. L. McKee of Sylva, Mrs. E. S. Groves, of Gastonia, Mrs. A. M. Bushnell, of Saluda, Mrs. H. A. Helder, of Canton, Mrs. Randolph Harper, of Lenoir, and possibly Mrs. Carrie Loflin, of Asheboro, Mrs. J. M. Mortez, of Boone, Mrs. J. A. Mortez of Hickory and Mrs. J. W. McIntosh of Lenoir.

"Carry your cargo and make your port" will be the keynote of the convention, and the president, Mrs. John F. Sippel, of Baltimore, Maryland, will preside. Every state in the Union and many foreign countries will be represented in the several thousand delegates who are expected to attend, as the Federation comprises 14,600 clubs including 74 organizations in 24 foreign countries.

Unemployment, world peace, prohibition, child welfare, citizenship, education, conservation, motion pictures and many other pressing contemporary problems will constitute the cargo of the General Federation. Just how nearly the port has been made will be revealed by the reports of the chairmen of the more than 125 departments, divisions and committees. Speeches calculated to instruct and inspire the delegates to further effort will be delivered by internationally known women and men. Rev. Edmund A. Walsh, vice president of Georgetown University, Washington, D. C., and regent of the School of Foreign Service, will speak on Soviet Russia. "Law and the Citizen" will be the subject of an address by Judge Walter B. Beals, of the Supreme Court of the State of Washington. Mr. George A. Hastings, extension director of the White House Conference on Child Health and Protection, will speak on "The Challenge of the Child in a Changing Civilization." Dr. Aurelia Henry Reinhardt, president of Mills College, Oakland, California, will speak on "The American Community and the International Mind." "It's Up to The Women" will be discussed by Miss Catherine Oglesby, assistant editor of the Ladies Home Journal. Mrs. John D. Sherman, presidential commissioner of the George Washington Bicentennial celebration, will speak on "Our Participation in the George Washington Bicentennial." Dr. Estella Ford Warner, of the United States Public Health Service, will speak on "Some Assumptions and Facts in Community Health." Mrs. Ben Hooper, chairman of International Relations, who represented the [line dropped...] of officers. There is but one candidate for president, Mrs. Grace Morrison Poole, of Brockton, Massachusetts, a world traveler and professional speaker on current events and contemporary problems. Candidates for first vice-presidents are: Mrs. Eugene B. Lawson, Tulsa, Oklahoma, and Mrs. Henry C. Taylor, Bloomfield, Iowa. Candidates for second vice-president are: Mrs. Edward M. Land, Statesville, North Carolina; Mrs. Clarence Fraim, Wilmington, Delaware; Dr. Josephine L. Peirce, Lima, Ohio; and Mrs. W. E. Minier, Oakland, Nebraska. For other offices the only candidates are: Recording secretary, Mrs. Saidie Orr Dunbar, Portland, Oregon; treasurer,

Mrs. Edward Hammett, Sheboygan, Wisconsin. The term of office is for two years, with re-election the usual thing. A revision which will be voted on at this convention provides for one three-year term for all officers.

Wednesday, June 15, will be "Play Day." An all day boat trip on Lake Washington will be made with luncheon aboard, and tea aboard the government carrier Lexington at the Government Navy Yard at Bremerton. In the evening there will be a complementary showing of a motion picture. Playday arrangements and other local plans are in charge of Mrs. Charles G. Miller, president of the Washington Federation.

Raleigh Sunday *News & Observer,* p. 15 (Society, p. 1)

11 SEPTEMBER 1932

WOMEN GLAD OF RETURN OF FALL AND CLUB ACTIVITIES

Federation of Women's Clubs Report Many Propitious Signs to Great Club Year; Clubs Adopt Forward-Looking Programs For Year's Work And Eagerly Anticipate Fall Activities

By Mrs. J. Henry Highsmith

With September begins a new club year. North Carolina club women welcome the return of fall and club activities wherein they have opportunity for enriching their own lives and for bettering the lives of those about them. So eager have been many of the wide-awake clubs to be off and on the run that there's been "chafing of the bit" while waiting for orders. Now that the official starting time has arrived and every thing is in order, the word is given to go!

Communication from numerous clubs this summer show that hot weather has been no deterrent in carrying on the work of the clubs. The many attractive year-books sent to headquarters are proof of the earnest thought and labor that have been in planning the year's work. With these and many other propitious signs, it is easy to foresee a great club year just ahead.

Program suggestions have been prepared by six of the nine State department chairmen, and these will be issued this week to the club presidents together with the Federation Year Book that is just off the press. The program suggestions ready for distribution are on Art with Mrs. J. J. Andoe of Greensboro, chairman; American Home, Mrs. J. N. Britt of Lumberton, chairman; Civics, Mrs. John D. Robinson of Wallace, chairman; Gardens, Miss Isabel B. Busbee of Raleigh, chairman; Music, Miss Jesse R. Moye, of Greenville, chairman, and Public Welfare with Mrs. B. A. Hocutt of Clayton, chairman. Programs on Education including adult illiteracy, Literature and Citizenship are promised in the near future. These will be sent out by the respective chairmen: Mrs. Howard G. Etheridge, of Asheville; Mrs. B. P. Long, of Statesville and Mrs. E. L. McKee, of Sylva.

Mrs. George E. Marshall of Mt. Airy, chairman of districts, reported in early summer that already three new clubs had been brought into the Federation. These are the Worthwhile Club of Mount Gilead, the Dare Woman's Club of Manteo and the Woman's Club of Marshall. Probably by this time there are several more to be added to this list.

At the recent meeting of the State convention of Home Demonstration Clubs held at State College, Raleigh, the Federation of Women's Clubs was represented by Mrs. J. M. Hobgood of Farmville, president; Mrs. E. L. McKee of Sylva, ex-president and now chairman of citizenship; Mrs. Palmer Jerman, ex-president; Mrs. T. E. Browne, third vice-president; Miss Isabel B. Busbee, chairman of Gardens and Mrs. J. Henry Highsmith, executive-secretary of Federation Headquarters at Raleigh. Mrs. Hobgood extended greetings on behalf of the Federation to her affiliated sister organization and pledged to her anew the club women's cooperation in carrying forward their great program of community betterment. Mrs. McKee made the principal address using as her subject "Good Citizenship." She urged the study of state and county government as a means of becoming intelligent voters and good citizens. Mrs. D. A. McCormick of Robeson County, president of the State Federation of Home Demonstration Clubs, presided. Mrs. Dewey Bennett of Forsyth County succeeded Mrs. McCormick as president. The above mentioned club women were guests at a special luncheon directed by Mrs. Bennett and Mrs. T. L. Woodburn of Martin County.

It is good news to the club women of the state that the Federation Bulletin will be published and issued this year as formerly. All club women desiring to keep well informed as to club news and club interests will do well to subscribe to the Bulletin now, their subscriptions to begin with the October issue and to end with the May–June issue. The subscription price for the year is only fifty cents which should be sent direct to C. E. Teague, N. C. C. W., Greensboro, N. C. Only the officers of the Federation and presidents of local clubs receive the Bulletin free, but every club should see that its officers and department chairmen receive it regularly.

Raleigh Sunday *News & Observer,* p. 15 (Society, p. 1)
Asheville Sunday *Citizen-Times,* p. 15 (section C, p. 1)

18 SEPTEMBER 1932

CLUB WOMEN WILL HOLD FALL COUNCIL MEETING

Mount Airy Will Be Scene of Meet on October Fourth and Fifth; Schedule of Sixteen District Meetings Adopted; Clubs In Remote Parts of State To Be Visited by State Officers

By Mrs. J. Henry Highsmith

The fall council meeting of the State Federation of Women's Clubs will be held this year in Mount Airy, October 4th and 5th, with the local Woman's

Club as hostess. Dr. Walter L. Lingle, president of Davidson College, will address the council Tuesday morning, October 4th. At this meeting of the official family of the Federation plans and programs for carrying on the club year's work will be carefully considered and the working machinery of the clubs set in full motion.

Composing the membership of the council are the officers of the Federation, chairmen of the nine departments, heads of standing committees and the district presidents. Club members, however, are welcome to attend the open sessions of the meeting. Mrs. J. M. Hobgood, president, urges a full attendance of the members as important club matters are to be presented for consideration.

Following the council meeting in Mount Airy will begin the series of sixteen district meetings, the first to be held at Elkin, Thursday, October 6. Both Mrs. Hobgood and Mrs. George E. Marshall of Mount Airy, chairman of districts, will make the round of district meetings carrying from their offices the inspiration and information needed by the club women for carrying on their club work this winter. The following tentative schedule of the district meetings arranged by Mrs. Marshall has been adopted:

District No. 6. Elkin, Friday, October 6.

District No. 3. Banner Elk, Friday, October 7.

District No. 1. Cullowhee, Monday, October 10.

District No. 2. Asheville, Tuesday, October 11.

District No. 4. Henrietta, Wednesday, October 12.

District No. 7. High Point, Thursday, October 13.

District No. 5. Troy, Friday, October 14.

District No. 9. Southern Pines, Saturday, October 15.

District No. 14. Roanoke Rapids, Monday, October 17.

District No. 18. Murfreesboro, Tuesday, October 18.

District No. 15. Greenville, Wednesday, October 19.

District No. 12. Vandemere, Thursday, October 20.

District No. 10. Council, Friday, October 21.

District No. 11. Garland, Saturday, October 22.

District No. 13. Benson, Monday, October 24.

District No. 8. Garner, Tuesday, October 25.

The district presidents who will preside and otherwise have charge of their respective district meetings are: Mrs. D. H. Tillett of Andrews; Mrs. C. W. Graybeal of Old Fort; Mrs. J. W. McIntosh of Lenoir; Mrs. O. J. Mooneyham of Henrietta; Mrs. P. R. Rankin of Mt. Gilead; Mrs. A. D. Folger of Dobson; Mrs. R. E. Labberton; Mrs. Guy Penny of Garner; Mrs. T. G. Monroe of Hamlet; Mrs. J. A. Robeson of Council; Mrs. J. C. Williams of Wilmington; Mrs. J. M. West of New Bern; Mrs. R. A. Ashworth of Selma; Mrs. Wade Dickens of Scotland Neck; Mrs. W. S. Carawan of Columbia; and Miss Ethel Parker of Gatesville.

Among the many delightful visitors who have visited headquarters in Raleigh since its opening this fall are: Mrs. C. D. Bain, president of the Woman's Club of Dunn; Mrs. John S. Nowell, president of the Community Club of Macon; Mrs. Harry K. Kenyon, Mrs. J. M. Coleman and Mrs. E. H. Russell also of Macon; Mrs. Thomas O'Berry of Goldsboro; Mrs. Edward M. Land of Statesville and Mrs. J. M. Hobgood of Farmville. Mrs. Hobgood was honor guest and speaker at the Get-Together Dinner of the Clayton Club Wednesday evening.

That the Federation Year Book has been delayed another week is a source of regret to all. The printer assures us that it will be off of the press and ready to be sent out by September 19. Those receiving the Year Book free will be the presidents of all women's clubs, state officers, department and division chairmen and committee chairmen.

Raleigh Sunday *News and Observer,* p. 13 (Society, p. 1)

25 SEPTEMBER 1932

FOUR STATE CLUB WOMEN RECEIVE APPOINTMENTS

Mrs. Edward M. Land of Statesville, Mrs. Thomas O'Berry of Goldsboro, Mrs. J. Henry Highsmith and Mrs. Palmer Jerman, Both of Raleigh, Receive Offices in Federation

By Mrs. J. Henry Highsmith

Four North Carolina Club Women have recently received appointments in the General Federation of Women's Clubs under the new administration of Mrs. Grace Morrison Poole, president. These are Mrs. Edward M. Land of Statesville as chairman of juniors, Mrs. Thomas O'Berry of Goldsboro, district advisor in the department of public welfare, Mrs. J. Henry Highsmith as editorial writer for State federation magazines in the department of press and publication, and Mrs. Palmer Jerman who was retained as a member of the board of trustees. This recognition has come to the state, it is believed, in recognition of the unusual record made by North Carolina club women at the Seattle convention. They won no less than four first prizes and received a number of "honorable mentions" as well as prizes lower in the scale.

The Junior Woman's Club of Mount Olive had the distinction of winning two first prizes. For conducting the best paint-up, clean-up campaign and for writing the best essay on that subject. The latter was done by Mrs. Robert Peele Holmes II, the president. Miss Olive Miner, a junior club member of Greensboro, won first prize offered by the department of citizenship for her essay, "What My Country Has Done For Me." The junior club of Winston-Salem, of which Mrs. George Hemingway, Jr., is president, won first prize for submitting the best program of work.

According to the call for the fall council meeting of the Federation which will be held in Mt. Airy, Tuesday and Wednesday, October 4 and 5, the first session will be a meeting of the executive board at the Blue Ridge Hotel, Tuesday at 11 o'clock. Following will be a luncheon at the hotel for the board members, with Mrs. John Folger, Mrs. A. D. Folger and Mrs. George Marshall as hostesses. At 2:30 o'clock there will be a conference of district presidents with Mrs. George E. Marshall presiding. At the same hour there will be a conference of department chairmen with Mrs. T. E. Browne of Raleigh, presiding.

At an open meeting to be held Tuesday evening at the Rockford Street School Auditorium, addresses will be made by Mrs. J. M. Hobgood, president of the Federation, and Dr. Walter L. Lingle, president of Davidson College. Mrs. E. L. McKee of Sylva will introduce Dr. Lingle. A reception tendered as a courtesy of the Mt. Airy Woman's Club will follow the meeting. The main business session of the council will be held Wednesday morning, at which time Miss Maude Burgess of Washington, D. C., will address the club women. A complimentary luncheon courtesy of the local woman's club will follow and will conclude the program except for a short business session.

Mrs. T. E. Browne, chairman of departmental work, requests club presidents who received the program suggestions along with their Year Books to place these in the hands of their department chairmen without delay.

Miss Martha Gilbert of Statesville and more recently of Memphis has accepted the chairmanship of Library Extension of the Federation to succeed Miss Frieda Heller who has accepted a position with the University of Ohio at Columbus. Miss Gilbert will attend the council meeting at Mr. Airy and perhaps a number of district meetings to meet and know the club women of the State and serve them in their work of improving library facilities in their communities. Her address is in care of the State Library Commission, Raleigh, N. C. Miss Heller's work in Ohio will be in connection with libraries in high schools. Club women of the State congratulate Ohio on securing Miss Heller for this particular work.

Three North Carolina Woman's Club libraries have had recognition from the chairman of library extension of the General Federation in that an account of their activities will appear in an early issue of the Clubwoman GFWC. These are the Elizabeth City library, the Smithfield library and the Lenoir library—all of which have been sponsored by the local Woman's Clubs.

Raleigh Sunday *News and Observer,* p. 15 (Society, p. 1)

2 OCTOBER 1932

CLUB WOMEN TO ASSIST IN INSTITUTE OF GOVERNMENT

Mrs. J. M. Hobgood, President of State Federation of Women's Clubs, Pledges Whole-Hearted Support of Club Women in Carrying Forward Institute Program; Radio Service to Feature News

By Mrs. J. Henry Highsmith

North Carolina Club Women accept their call to aid in carrying forward the program of the Institute of Government as their long craved opportunity to have a hand in shaping the affairs of the government of the State. Mrs. J. M. Hobgood, president of the State Federation, in presenting the program of the Institute of Government to the club women for their study and consideration, says that the men realizing the highly unsatisfactory condition in which they have gotten the House of State are calling on the women to help them clean house.

As a member of the advisory board of the Institute of Government, Mrs. Hobgood has assured Prof. Albert Coates, of Chapel Hill, director, that the club women of the State can be depended upon for their whole-hearted interest and support in this undertaking. In writing to the clubs about this motto and urging that serious consideration be given it, she says:

"I feel that it is unnecessary for me to remind you that our governmental system has long needed a thorough house-cleaning. The old methods will no longer do. We must renovate, refurnish and modernize our House of State. Neither do I need to remind you that without women no house-cleaning was ever capably and efficiently managed. Many unsightly articles are always tucked away under curtains, piles of dust left in dark corners, and things in general left in a highly unsatisfactory state. The men realize this fact and are calling on us to help them. We have yearned to have a hand in governmental affairs, have shrunk from taking part because of many indications of untidiness in the way they are run and now this is our opportunity.

A State-wide radio service featuring Federation news, club interests and activities, inspirational addresses, and programs of music and other cultural subjects has been arranged with the five radio stations of the state. Miss Jenn Coltrane, of Concord, radio chairman of the Federation, announces that beginning Thursday, October 6, the Charlotte Station, WBT, will begin a weekly broadcast for the Federation, the hour to be from 1:45 to 2 o'clock. The first program is to be a message from Mrs. J. M. Hobgood, State president. On the following Thursday at the same hour, Dr. E. Derendinger will talk on some phase of art work. Mr. Hugh McRae, of Wilmington, will be the speaker at Federation hour on October 20.

Other radio stations cooperating with the Federation are WPTF, of Raleigh; WNNC, of Asheville, and the stations at Asheville, Greensboro, and Wilmington. At the last named station, Mrs. J. C. Williams will have charge of the programs which will be monthly. Mrs. J. J. Andoe will have charge of the Greensboro broadcasts, and Mrs. Howard G. Etheridge, of Asheville, both of which will be monthly programs.

In charge of the broadcasts from the Raleigh station, WPTF, which will be weekly, will be Mrs. J. Henry Highsmith, Miss Isabel B. Busbee and Mrs. C. G. Doak. The first program which will be a message from Mrs. Hobgood will go on the air Tuesday, October 11, from 1:15 to 1:30 o'clock. At the same hour on Tuesday, October 18, Miss Isabel Busbee will talk on the subject: "The Fall Is The Time To Start Gardening."

Speaking of radio programs, the American Women's Club of Paris, Inc., informs North Carolina club women that they are holding a gala dinner to be followed by a fashion show and a talk in English on fashions by the celebrated couturiers, Jean Charles and Jacques Worth, on Sunday, November 6. The talk, which will begin at 10 p. m. Paris time, will be broadcasted throughout America by courtesy of the National Broadcasting Company. Club women are advised to assemble in groups for listening in on this unusual program. Just what the hour will be in America they did not advise.

Raleigh Sunday *News and Observer,* p. 13 (Society, p. 1)

9 OCTOBER 1932

INCREASE IS SHOWN IN WOMEN'S CLUB WORK IN STATE, COUNCIL MEET HEARS

Remarkable Pick-Up is Shown Among Various Organizations; Mrs. Hobgood and Mrs. Marshall on Tour

By Mrs. J. Henry Highsmith

A remarkable "pick-up" in club interests and activities was noted in the two-day sessions of the fall council meeting of the State Federation of Women's Clubs Tuesday and Wednesday at Mr. Airy. Better times in women's club work were in full view and not seen around the corner. Proposed programs of work submitted by department chairmen and district presidents gave promise to this being one of the Federation's best years.

With the Woman's Club of Mt. Airy as hostess, of which Mrs. J. H. Folger is president, assisted by Mrs. George E. Marshall, second vice president of the Federation, and by Mrs. A. D. Folger, district president, the Mt. Airy meeting was as socially delightful as it was beneficial to club interests.

Club women's highest endeavors were challenged in the addresses of Mrs. J. M. Hobgood, president of the Federation, and of Dr. Walter L. Lingle, president of Davidson College, wherein they were urged to learn wisely the lessons of the world's latest catastrophe—the present depression. In concluding his address, Dr. Lingle said: "There is need for a moral and spiritual revival, in which the lives of men and women will be remade. We will have to go back and build into the character of our children and all our people the simple homely virtues of honesty, truthfulness and unselfishness."

Plans for the year's work adopted by the council included many progressive movements. Endorsement was given to the program of the Institute of Government, of which Prof. Albert Coats of Chapel Hill is president, with the recommendation that club women actively participate in carrying forward the provisions of the program. Consideration was given to the question of changing the Federation's biennial plan of electing officers and department chairmen to that of the triennial plan, thereby making it conform to the system adopted by the General Federation at its recent meeting in Seattle.

This question will be presented to the Federation for a decision at its convention at Raleigh in May. Announcement was made that during the month of October club women will be given the opportunity to add their names to a roster of 1,000,000 signatures which is being assembled by the National Council of Women. This subject will be presented by Mrs. Hobgood at the 16 district meetings of the Federation to be held during the month of October. The signatures, she explained, will be sent to foreign governments to urge the attendance of distinguished women at an international congress in Chicago, July 16–22, 1933. Mrs. Hobgood urged that club women who may not attend district meetings sign at Postal Telegraph offices and thereby help North Carolina to obtain her full quota of signatures. Any woman, whether a club woman or not, may sign.

To promote a wider interest in the work of music achievement and art appreciation among the children of the state, the council voted to offer a prize of $15 to the school whose pupils make the best showing in each of these special fields of work.

The day after the council meeting, Mrs. J. M. Hobgood and Mrs. George E. Marshall, the latter chairman of districts, set out on their round of district meetings. The first was held Thursday at Elkin with Mrs. A. D. Folger of Dobson, president of the sixth district presiding. Friday, they attended the meeting of the third district at Banner Elk, with Mrs. J. W. McIntosh of Lenoir, presiding. Their itinerary for this week will be Cullowhee on Monday, October 10; Asheville on Tuesday; Henrietta on Wednesday; High Point on Thursday; Troy on Friday and Southern Pines on Saturday. Their itinerary for next week will take them to the eastern part of the state: Roanoke Rapids on Monday, October 17; Murfreesboro on Tuesday; Greenville on Wednesday; Vandemere on Thursday and Garland on Saturday.

Charlotte Sunday Observer, p. 14 (section 2, p. 4)

23 OCTOBER 1932

CLUB WOMEN TO OBSERVE BOOK WEEK NOV. 13–19

Statistics Show That More North Carolinians Are Reading Books But Two Out of Three People Are Without Library Service; Women To Take Active Part in Making More Reading Materials Available

By Mrs. J. Henry Highsmith

Since the motivating force of many a woman's club has been the need of a community library, club women this year will not fail to celebrate National Book Week on November 13–19. And since there is a more definite need this year for books and good reading material as a means of offsetting the work of idle brains as well as idle hands, club women are urged to take the lead in making available reading matter for all the citizens of their community.

According to statistics compiled by the librarians of the State, more North Carolinians are reading today—making use of their public libraries—than ever before. North Carolina libraries then may be included in that group which "impartial observers say, with the exception of those agencies giving actual relief, the libraries of the United States are perhaps our most important institutions during times of business depression."

And yet according to the North Carolina Library Bulletin more than two million of our three million inhabitants have no library service. To be exact, 62 per cent of our people have not yet been reached with books and wholesome reading material. Forty-seven of our one hundred counties have no libraries of any kind. Whereas recognized library standards require the circulation of five books per capita, North Carolina circulates one book per capita, and whereas the standard requires a minimum income of $1.00 per capita per year, North Carolina's income is six cents per capita per year.

From the foregoing facts and figures, the field of library service in the State is white unto harvest. Club women will do well to get a new vision of the task that lies ahead, and rededicate themselves to its achievement—forty-seven counties without any library service, two out of every three people without books to read.

Miss Margaret K. Gilbert, field worker for the State Library Commission and chairman of library extension for the State Federation, says: "Book Week in its brief existence has already directed millions of people on the way to knowledge, wisdom and happiness. It has shown them how, for a few cents, or for the trouble of walking around the corner to the library, a man may find effective medicine for most of the ills of the human mind and spirit. He may find impregnable armour against boredom. In one tattered volume he may chance upon companions infinitely more witty, more charming, helpful and friendly than he would discover anywhere on earth even were he lucky enough to possess an Arabian Nights wishing mat for an airplane."

Announcement is made that the Federation is offering two prizes of fifteen dollars each to the school in the State whose pupils make the best showing in the work of the Music Achievement Contest and in the Picture Memory Contest. Club women are asked to bring this to the attention of their schools and request that their children be permitted to have one or both of these courses this year.

Among the recent visitors at headquarters in Raleigh have been: Mrs. Wade Dickens, of Scotland Neck; Mrs. W. S. Carawan, of Columbia; Mrs. Guy Penny and Mrs. Frank Penny, of Garner; Mrs. John S. Nowell and Mrs. Kenyon, of Macon; Mrs. Claude Morris, of Salisbury; Mrs. Paul S. Cragan, of Ruffin; Mrs. A. G. Johnson, of Lillington; Mrs. J. A. McRae, of Charlotte;

Miss Jenn Coltrane, Mrs. Charles Wagoner and Mrs. Grace Brown Sanders, of Concord; Miss Mary O. Graham, of Charlotte; Mrs. C. H. Chamblee and Mrs. A. A. Pippin, of Zebulon; Mrs. John D. Robinson, of Wallace; Mrs. W. F. Finley, of North Wilkesboro; Mrs. J. G. Fearing, of Elizabeth City; Mrs. E. L. McKee, of Sylva; Mrs. E. S. Paddison, of Nashville and Mrs. J. C. B. Ehring-haus, of Elizabeth City.

Charlotte Sunday Observer, p. 9 (section 2, p. 4)

30 OCTOBER 1932

FEDERATION TO PRESENT PRIZES FOR CLUB WORK

Federation Headquarters Issue List of Prizes Offered For Various Phases of Club Work, Including Art, Civics, Gardens, Music and Literature; North Carolina Receives General Federation Art Prize

By Mrs. J. Henry Highsmith

Whether it is because North Carolina Club Women won more National prizes than the Club Women of any other State at the Biennial Convention in Seattle, or whether they are just naturally interested and eager to get to work, or both, they are nevertheless prize-conscious and are showing an unusually keen interest in the various phases of work of the Federation. In reply to a number of requests that the list of prizes offered by the Federation for 1932–1933 be published in the Sunday newspapers the list is here given:

Art: The Margaret Norvell Graham silver vase for the best water color by a North Carolina artist. The Bernau silver cup for the best essay on "Art in Precious Metals and Its Effect on History." The James Westley White cup, for the best landscape or marine in oil by a North Carolina artist. The Mrs. S. Clay Williams cup, for the best portrait by a North Carolina artist.

Civics: The Nathan O'Berry cup, for the club doing the best piece of civic work during the year.

Gardens: The Fannie Chase Staton goblet, for the club having the largest per cent of the homes of its members beautified by planting during the year.

Music: The Duncan cup, for the most meritorious original musical composition. The Florence M. Cooper cup, for the second best original composition.

Literature: The Separk cup, for the best original poem. The Albert L. Berry cup, for meritorious composition in poetry. The Joseph Pierson Caldwell cup, for the best short story. The Lanier Club cup, for the best one-act play.

In addition to the state prizes will be offered a number of General Federation prizes later this Fall. On account of a comparatively new change of officers and department chairmen in the General Federation, programs of work and the list of prizes offered have not yet been announced.

Much interest and appreciation is felt in connection with the prize that has come to North Carolina in recognition of her art work through the clubs. Five reasons have been given by Mrs. Florence Topping Green, art chairman of the General Federation, which entitled the North Carolina Federation to this prize. These are:

Fine organization, programs, lectures and local art chairmen. Help and recognition given to North Carolina artists by exhibiting their works, paintings, prints, pottery, sculpture. Assisting 50 schools in the State in the purchase of copies of famous paintings. Two hundred children participating in State Picture Memory Contest with prizes offered. Fostering the work of creative genius in children through division of "Creative Interest of Children."

The prize is a distinctive pottery vase made and decorated by Viktor Schreckengost, a well known potter and painter. The work is done in dry point and the glaze is Egyptian blue. In presenting it to Mrs. J. J. Andoe of Greensboro, chairman of art for the Federation, Mrs. Green said: "Treasure this for it is indeed a lovely thing. If you had given paintings, prints or etchings instead of silver cups for prizes in your State, you would have received a higher prize."

Fourteen new clubs have been received into the Federation since May. These are: The Worthwhile Club of Mt. Gilead, the Worthwhile Club of Wadesboro, the Woman's Club of Marshall, the Dare County Woman's Club of Manteo, the Woman's Club of Ruffin, the Woman's Club of Draper, the Yadkinville Woman's Club, the Clarkton Woman's Club, the Buie's Creek Woman's Club, the Murphy Woman's Club, the Plymouth Woman's Club, the Vanceboro Woman's Club, the Mt. Olive Woman's Club and the John Charles McNeill, Jr., Club of Benson.

Raleigh Sunday *News and Observer,* p. 15 (Society, p. 1)

6 NOVEMBER 1932

CLUB WOMEN WILL MEET IN MIAMI AND HAVANA

By Mrs. J. Henry Highsmith

Of particular interest to Southern club women will be the meeting of the Southeastern Council of the General Federation of Women's Clubs in Miami, Florida, November 15–17, with a post meeting in Havana, Cuba, on the 19th. Mrs. E. C. Judd of Dalton, Georgia, president of the council will preside over the meetings. She will be assisted by Mrs. Meade A. Love of Quincy, Florida, president of the Florida Federation and by Mrs. S. S. McCahill, president of the Dade County Federation which is hostess to the council.

Special guests attending will be Mrs. Grace Morrison Poole, president of the General Federation of Women's Clubs, Mrs. Eugene B. Lawson, first vice-president, Mrs. John F. Sippel, immediate past president of the General Federation, and distinguished club leaders from the 11 states holding membership in the Southeastern Council. These are Delaware, Maryland, Virginia, West Virginia, North Carolina, South Carolina, Tennessee, Georgia, Kentucky, Alabama, and Florida.

Attending from North Carolina will be Mrs. J. M. Hobgood of [Farmville; +line dropped, Mrs.] George E. Marshall of Mount Airy, second vice-president; Mrs. Edward H. Land of Statesville, state director, Miss Mary F. DeVane of Goldsboro and Mrs. J. L. Shackelford of Farmville.

The opening meeting will take place Tuesday evening in Bayfront Park with Mrs. Poole as the principal speaker. Her subject will be "Our Broadcasting Horizons." Other sessions will be held at the Miami Woman's Club and at the First Presbyterian Church. The McAllister Hotel will be headquarters. Due to an 18-day round trip ticket which the railroads are now selling at an unusually low rate, and due further to the change in the by-laws of the General Federation which created triennial sessions, this regional council meeting is expected to attract large crowds of club women. The trip to Havana, a most attractive feature, is an all expense four-day tour which includes entertainment, sightseeing, transportation, hotel, Cuban tax and a trip into the interior of the island, Tickets for the trip are bought in Miami for $49.50. The 18-day trip return ticket from Raleigh to Miami is $44.85; with pullman one way $10.13.

Mrs. E. S. Paddison of Nashville, chairman of the Postal Signature campaign, reports lively interest being taken by the club women in this project, a number of clubs having already sent in their completed lists. She is asking club chairmen when sending in their lists to say whether or not they are competing for the five dollar prize that is being offered to the club sending in the largest number of signatures for the town or community. The winning number is to be based on the number of women in the town or community. She is asking that club women give in their report the number of women within the corporate limits of their towns. Attention is called again to the fact that any woman whether a club member or not may sign the petition.

Federation hour over WPTF will feature a message Tuesday from 2:15 to 2:30 from Dr. E. Derendinger of Catawba College on the Progress of Art in North Carolina. At the same hour on Tuesday, November 15. Catherine Oglesby, associate editor of the Ladies Home Journal, will send a special message to the club women of the state, and on Tuesday November 22, Miss Charl Williams of Washington, D. C., will send a message.

Over Station WBT, Charlotte, Thursday, November 10, E. Jones of Charlotte, president of the Pyramid Pilot Life Insurance Company, will talk on the subject: "How Women Can Educate Their Children Through Life Insurance." Mrs. P. R. Rankin of Mount Gilead, president of the Fifth

District, will have the broadcast for November 17. Miss Jenn Coltrane of Concord, chairman of radio of the Federation and in charge of the program over WNT announces that there will be no program on Thanksgiving Day.

Raleigh Sunday *News and Observer,* p. 13 (Society, p. 1)

13 NOVEMBER 1932

SEES TRIUMPHANT SPIRIT IN WOMEN'S CLUB WORK

By Mrs. J. Henry Highsmith

On finishing her fourth tour of the sixteen districts of the State Federation of Women's Clubs made this Fall in company with Mrs. George E. Marshall, Mrs. J. M. Hobgood, president, is of the opinion that club work in the State has struck a new and triumphant note and is moving forward in a most heartening and satisfactory way. For four years Mrs. Hobgood has toured the districts from mountains to coast, having attended 63 district meetings, traveled approximately ten thousand miles and visited every county in the state. And yet, after having heard around a thousand individual club reports, she says she is not tired and her interest in club work is all the more keen and appreciative.

Summing up her impressions of the status of club work in the State, especially as it has been affected by the Depression, Mrs. Hobgood says:

"During the past three years we have viewed the 'recent unpleasantness' from three points of vantage. In the Fall of 1930 we sorrowfully listened to many a report given in a half-hearted manner which carried the information that 'in view of hard times our club has lost many members and we have not been able to do many things we had planned.' Then, in 1931, we heard a new note. There was a set of the chin and a gleam in the eye as that same club reported, 'In spite of the Depression, we are carrying on and are doing our work, though on a much smaller scale.' And this year, with the lift of the head and the smile of one who has conquered, we heard, 'because of Depression, we have learned valuable lessons. There is a better spirit among our club members than ever before, we have several additions and are experiencing the best work of our existence.' Women's clubs have been 'weighed in the balances' and have not been found wanting."

Miss Isabel B. Busbee, chairman of gardens, calls the attention of club women to a phase of the federal relief work under direction of Dr. Fred Morrison of Raleigh, which is of special interest to them. It is the plan of Dr. Morrison to give work to the unemployed of a community by planting the highways and beautifying the school grounds. J. J. Blair of Raleigh, is to have charge of this work and he invites the cooperation of the club women of the State in carrying out this project. Miss Busbee believes that club women can be of great assistance to Mr. Blair, not only in the way of suggesting appropriate plantings, but in supervising the plantings to see that they are done properly, so as to insure them to live. Miss Busbee advises club women to communicate with Mr. Blair and Dr. Morrison in regard to this service for their local communities. She says that E. B. Jeffress, State highway chairman, also is ready to assist the club in any highway planting it wishes to make.

The Fannie Chase Staten Goblet, according to Miss Busbee, again will be offered to the club having the largest per cent of the homes of its members beautified by planting. It is recalled that the Varina Woman's Club, under the presidency of Mrs. N. H. Hopson, won this prize last year. A new silver goblet is awarded each year.

Miss Catherine Ogelsby, associate editor of the Ladies Home Journal, will give a message to the club women of North Carolina over the radio Tuesday at Federation Hour, from 2:15 to 2:30 o'clock. Her subject will be "It's Up to the Women." On Tuesday, November 22, at the same hour Miss Charl Williams, field secretary of the National Education Association, will send a message on some timely phase of educational work. Club women are asked to tune in on WBT each Thursday from 2 to 2:15 o'clock and on WRAM the first Friday at 8 o'clock in the evening. Excellent programs are given over these stations, which should be of interest to club women.

Raleigh Sunday *News and Observer*, p. 13 (Society, p. 1)

20 NOVEMBER 1932

CLUB WOMEN TAKE LEAD IN HEALTH SEAL CAMPAIGN

Mrs. Charles R. Whitaker of Lenoir, President of State Tuberculosis Association, Says Need of Seal Sale Greater This Year Than Ever Before; Urges All Club Women to Take Active Part in Work

By Mrs. J. Henry Highsmith

Another Tuberculosis Christmas Seal Sale is more of a necessity this year than probably any of the previous 26, says Mrs. Charles R. Whitaker of Lenoir, president of the State Tuberculosis Association and chairman of the Division of Health of the State Federation of Women's Clubs. While this tiny seal with its double-barred cross of hope, courage and life has done a big job during the past 26 years, its work is not yet done, she says. The tuberculosis situation in the State today is in a precarious condition due to unemployment, lack of nourishing food and sufficient clothing and that peace of mind that is a foe to disease and suffering.

Since the double-barred tuberculosis seal has been waging its fight against tuberculosis; Mrs. Whitaker points out that the death rate from this disease has been reduced two and one half times—a saving of approximately

150,000 lives a year. But tuberculosis remains the chief cause of deaths between 15 and 45 years. As great is our death rate from automobile accidents, she says, the deaths from tuberculosis are three times that from automobile fatalities. And while no cure by a vaccine or drug has yet been discovered, thousands are restored to health and usefulness each year. A regimen of rest, food and fresh air has been found to be the best method of treatment.

Mrs. Whitaker is calling on Women's Clubs to take the lead again in this timely health work. Last year, she says, 95 women's clubs sponsored the tuberculosis seal sale in their communities, and she feels that even a greater number will take the lead in this movement this year. Quoting from the Federation Year Book from 1931–1932, where only a few clubs reported their seal sale work, she finds that the clubs gave 21,202 free school lunches; 87 clubs looked after undernourished children, four clubs sponsored tuberculosis clinics, three clubs sponsored tonsil operations and many clubs reported numerous activities in the interest of preventing tuberculosis which had been made possible through the sale of tuberculosis Christmas seals. One club reported operating an open air camp for 32 children who had a tendency to tuberculosis at a cost of $1,200, this amount having been raised front the sale of tuberculosis Christmas seals.

Miss Gertrude Weil of Goldsboro, Federation Chairman of International Relations, is asking the club women of North Carolina to either see their senators—Josiah William Bailey of Raleigh and Robert R. Reynolds of Asheville, before they go to Washington, or to write to them at the Senate Officie Building in Washington, when Congress convenes December 5th, urging them not only to support the adherence of the United States to the World Court when the matter is introduced in the Senate, but also to use their influence in getting the debates on the subject started early in the session. Miss Weil is asking the club women to advise her what response they receive in reply to their request. "Why act upon the World Court this Winter?" is the subject of an illuminating article appearing in the December Federation Bulletin by Miss Esther Lape of the American Foundation, which was submitted by Miss Weil.

The speaker at Federation hour over WPTF Raleigh, Tuesday, 2:15 to 2:30, will be Mrs. C. G. Doak, who will give a message sent to the women of North Carolina by Miss Charl Williams of Washington, D. C., field worker for the National Education Association. On Tuesday, Nov. 29th at the same hour, Mrs. Charles R. Whitaker of Lenoir, president of the State Tuberculosis Association, will speak on "The Twenty-Sixth Sale of Tuberculosis Christmas Seals."

Arrangement has been made with WBIG, Greensboro Station, to give a series of art programs each Monday from 5 to 5:15 o'clock. The first will be

Monday, Nov. 21, and the speaker will be Dr. E. Derendinger of Catawba College. On Monday, Nov. 28 Dr. Derendinger will give a talk on Elliott Saingerfield, North Carolina artist, who recently passed away.

On Wednesday, Nov. 30, Walter Pach, famous lecturer, author, art critic and writer, will deliver a talk over Station WJZ New York through the National Broadcasting Company, on "Why You Should Have Paintings in Your Home." North Carolina Club Women are invited to tune in and hear this famous artist.

Raleigh Sunday *News and Observer,* p. 13 (Society, p. 1)

27 NOVEMBER 1932

MRS. HOBGOOD GETS POST IN SOUTHEASTERN COUNCIL

By Mrs. J. Henry Highsmith

The honor of being elected first vice-president of the Southeastern Council of the General Federation of Women's Clubs came to Mrs. J. M. Hobgood of Farmville, president of the North Carolina Federation, at the recent council meeting held in Miami and Havana, Cuba. Mrs. Julian G. Hearne of Wheeling, W.Va., was elected president. The council meets annually and is composed of the club officials of eleven of the Southern States. The three North Carolina representatives attending the meeting in Miami and the post meeting in Havana were Mrs. Hobgood, Mrs. Edward M. Land, of Statesville, and Miss Mary F. DeVane of Goldsboro.

At an elaborate tea given the fifty or more guests from the "Estados Unidos" by the club women of Havana at the El Encanto, Mrs. Land was one of several distinguished speakers. Many courtesies and delightful features of entertainment were shown the visitors by the Cuban club women.

Club women of the State are finding the study of Biblical Literature of increasing interest. The course of study prepared for their use this year by Mrs. Eugene Reilley, of Charlotte, chairman, is one of the Federation's most popular study courses. The subject is Women of the Bible. She says the program outlines are based altogether on the literary and historical significance of the subjects and not their theological aspects. She believes that club women should study the Bible because knowledge of it as a literary classic is essential to the full comprehension of our English literature. Our best poetry and prose is permeated with the language and influence of the Bible.

In preparing her outlines of study, Mrs. Reilley has divided the women of the Old Testament into three groups—namely: Pioneers and Founders; Daughters of Patriotism, and Queens and Captives; those of the New Testament come under two heads—the Beginnings of Faith and The Early Church. With the study of each group of women is one or more selections of music, art or drama of corresponding theme or interpretation.

A meeting of the Legislative Council of North Carolina Women has been called by Mrs. Palmer Jerman, president, for Thursday, December 1, at 11 o'clock at the Woman's Club in Raleigh. Lunch will be served at the club to the council members. Representing the State Federation of Women's Clubs on the council will be Miss Harriett Elliott, of Greensboro, Mrs. W. T. Shore of Charlotte, Mrs. B. A. Hocutt of Clayton and Mrs. E. L. McKee of Sylva. The object of the meeting is to elect officers for another biennial period and to adopt a legislative program to present to the 1933 Legislature.

Mrs. Charles R. Whitaker of Lenoir, formerly of Southern Pines, president of the State Tuberculosis Association, will be the speaker at Federation hour over WPTF, Tuesday, from 2:15 to 2:30 o'clock.

Mrs. W. J. Brogden of Durham, chairman of the Sallie Southall Cotten Loan Fund, is reminding the clubs that the second payment to the thirty or more girls who are borrowing from this fund to continue in college this year is to be met January 1st. Clubs that made pledges to this fund are requested to send a part if not all the amount to Mrs. J. D. McCall, treasurer, Law Building, Charlotte. Mrs. Brogden says that the club women have never disappointed the loan fund girls and that she is confident they will not this year.

Raleigh Sunday *News and Observer,* p. 13 (Society, p. 1)

4 December 1932

Woman Senator Endorses Institute of Government

Mrs. E. L. McKee, State Senator of 1931 Legislature and Chairman of Citizenship of State Federation of Women's Clubs, Urges Women to Take Part in Exercises Launching Governmental Program

By Mrs. J. Henry Highsmith

Mrs. E. L. McKee of Sylva, State Senator of the 1931 Legislature and chairman of the Citizenship of the State Federation of Women's Clubs, is urging the club women of the State to participate in the launching of the program of the Institute of Government in their respective counties tomorrow. She advises them that probably never before have they had an opportunity to serve their State and government in as constructive a way as they have at this time. She believes that the Institute of Government is one of the most timely, far-reaching and practical movements in public affairs ever undertaken in this or any other state in the Union. It is all the more significant, she says, since it grew out of the experiences and convictions of the State's own public officials and is approved by them from the Governor down.

A unique and important feature of the exercises to be employed in the 100 counties in launching the governmental program, is the installation of public officials in a public ceremony—the first ever held in North Carolina. In a large number of counties this will be at 8 o'clock in the evening, at which time a state-wide radio broadcast from Raleigh, setting forth the plans and purposes of the Institute, will be heard. In other counties it has been planned to have the installation of county officials in the forenoon at the county courthouse. "Regardless of the place and hour," says Mrs. McKee, "club women should be there to participate in this significant meeting."

In the county units of the Institute of Government which are now being formed, club women are being invited to serve on the local Board of Advisors.

Mrs. J. G. Andoe of Greensboro, chairman of Art of the Federation, attended the meeting of the State Art Society in Raleigh Wednesday and Thursday and the tea given by Mrs. Katherine Pendleton Arrington, president of the society, Wednesday afternoon at the Sir Walter Hotel. Mrs. Andoe reports that there are at present about 100 art departments in the Federation doing good work in the study of art. The studies of American painters and sculptors, including North Carolina artists, are creating the most interest.

Mrs. Andoe is arranging for a state-wide exhibit of North Carolina artists to be held in Raleigh in May in connection with the annual convention of the State Federation of Women's Clubs. In addition to the four prizes that are offered for the best portrait work, painting in oil, water colors, and for essay on Metals in Art, Mrs. Andoe says a number of new prizes will be offered possibly for block prints and etchings.

Mrs. John D. Robinson of Wallace, chairman of Civics, is calling attention to the fact that federal relief funds have been allocated to the counties can be used in paying for labor on local civic projects, provided the work is given to the unemployed. She suggests that chairmen of civics departments of the clubs undertake such projects as improving school grounds, playgrounds, public squares and parks, opening up and cleaning streets, erecting community houses, repairing public building, planting town approaches, parkways, and in general improve the looks of their communities.

Mrs. R. L. McMillan will be the speaker at Federation Hour on Tuesday, December 6, at 2:15 o'clock. Her subject will be "State Picture Memory Work." She reports a greater interest in this phase of educational art work than any previous year.

Club women are invited to attend the art exhibition at the Sir Walter Hotel in Raleigh which is sponsored by the State Art Society. It is the first exhibit that Raleigh has had from the American Federation of Art. The exhibit includes several pieces from California artists. The exhibit will remain in place until December 9.

Raleigh Sunday *News and Observer,* p. 15 (Society, p. 1)

18 DECEMBER 1932

COUNCIL WILL PRESENT MEASURES TO ASSEMBLY

Legislative Council of North Carolina Women Adopt Measures to Present to 1933 General Assembly; Would Amend Property Laws, Election Law and Alcohol and Narcotic Act

By Mrs. J. Henry Highsmith

A sane, practical and conservative program of legislation to be presented to the 1933 Legislature has been adopted by the Legislative Council of North Carolina Women, a member of which is the State Federation of Women's Clubs. Mrs. Palmer Jerman of Raleigh is president of the council, Miss Elsie Riddick of Raleigh is first vice-president, Mrs. Edward M. Land of Statesville, is second vice-president, Miss Iona Glidewell of Reidsville is third vice-president, Miss Alice Laidlaw of Raleigh is secretary and Mrs. C. G. Doak of Raleigh is treasurer.

Other state-wide women's organizations holding membership in the council are the Federation of Business and Professional Women's Clubs, League of Women Voters, State Nurses Association, Women's Auxiliary, Protestant Episcopal Church, N. C. Diocese; Woman's Christian Temperance Union, Women's Missionary Society of N. C. Conference, Methodist Episcopal Church, South. Co-operating with the council are the Young Women's Christian Associations and the N. C. Garden Clubs.

At a recent meeting of the executive board of the council, Mrs. J. Henry Highsmith was again chosen executive secretary, and the offer of the office of Federation Headquarters was accepted as temporary headquarters for the Legislative Council. Mrs. Highsmith will pilot through the Legislature the council's legislative program.

Among the measures sponsored by the council are four aimed at the further protection of children who work. The objective is to safeguard for North Carolina's children the rights set forth in the Children's Charter adopted by the White House Conference: For Every Child Protection Against Labor that Stunts Growth, either Physical or Mental, that Limits Education, that Deprives Children of the Right of Comradeship, of Play, and of Joy.

The program adopted is as follows:

1. To require children under sixteen years (1) to complete the sixth grade at school before leaving to go to work; (2) to continue in school until they are sixteen unless they are regularly and legally employed.

2. To remove the poverty exemption clause in the law establishing an 8-hour work day and a 48-hour work week for children under sixteen years.

3. To prohibit all night work for women and for all minors under eighteen years.

4. Establishment of Women's and Children's Bureau in the Department of Labor with a competent woman in charge and with adequate enforcing and investigatory powers.

5. Establishment of not more than a 55-hour work week and a 10-hour work day for women in all industries and in mercantile establishments.

6. Amendment to the Alcohol and Narcotic Act asking for not less than $1,000 for scientific temperance instruction in the schools of [the] State.

7. Amendment to property laws affecting husband and wife, so as to equalize the interests of each in the other's property, the share of neither to be less than one third.

8. Amendment to election laws, to restore the numbering of ballots and to curtail the use of absentee ballots.

9. The State to take over the Industrial School for Negro Girls at Efland.

Mrs. E. E. Randolph of Raleigh, chairman of the division of Public School Music of the Federation, will have charge of the program over station WPTF at Federation Hour, Tuesday, December 20th from 2:15 to 2:30 o'clock. Her program will feature Christmas carols. She will be assisted by other Raleigh musicians.

Raleigh Sunday News and Observer, p. 13 (Society, p. 1)
Charlotte Sunday Observer, p. 20 (section 2, p. 8)

1933

11 January — co-hosts tea for 500 with Mrs. James A. Hartness, 310 North Blount Street, honoring first lady Mrs. J. C. B. Ehringhaus and legislator Lily Morehead Mebane

mid-January — hosts Mrs. James G. Fearing of Elizabeth City, who had come to receive at the Hartness–Highsmith tea

17 January — speaks at a dinner sponsored by the Raleigh WCTU, at Edenton Street, celebrating thirteenth anniversary of national prohibition (18th Amendment) and opposing repeal (19th Amendment); other speakers include Lily Morehead Mebane, Mrs. Doak, and Dr. Highsmith

18 January — appears before state House Judiciary Committee to argue against repealing stringent marriage laws; is joined by Mrs. Jerman, Dr. Delia Dixon-Carroll, state health officer Dr. James Parrott, and others; their pleas fall on deaf ears and the Wilson-Taylor bills pass

15 February — at meeting of House Committee on Propositions and Grievances, leads assault on bill which would prohibit public employment of women married to other state employees; is joined by Dr. Dixon-Carroll, future governor J. Melville Broughton, and Mrs. Thomas O'Berry, vice chairman of state Democratic Party

21 February — attends luncheon for Mrs. Ehringhaus and others at Carolina Pines Club

22 February — hosts, as president of Wake County League of Women Voters, one-day convention of state League; speaks on bills before the Legislature

24 February — addresses Wake County League of Women Voters on "Public Welfare"

2 March — attends planning session for Raleigh convention of NCFWC

11 April — introduces, at Twentieth Century Book Club, G. K. Middleton of NC State to speak on China

27 April — accompanies Dr. Highsmith to banquet at Meredith College

3–6 May — attends 31st annual NCFWC convention, Raleigh; heads receiving line at reception, Sir Walter Hotel, alongside Mrs. Ehringhaus; delivers reports of executive secretary and of Press Committee

10 May — takes first place, "Arrangement of Flowers in Two Colors" at spring show of Raleigh Garden Club

13 May — attends ceremony in Governor Ehringhaus's office for Mary Moss Wellborn, envoy of the Kellogg Peace Pact; presides at a luncheon where Miss Wellborn speaks on disarmament

22–25 May — attends council meeting of GFWC in Richmond, as division chairman of editorials of State federation magazines

June – 29 August — visits ten European countries in ten weeks, including League of Nations in Geneva, World Court in The Hague, and England; by 10 September "she has resumed her duties at Federation Headquarters on the mezzanine floor of the Sir Walter Hotel and is again ready to serve the club women of the State"

3 September — participates in coalition to retain Prohibition (18th Amendment) at election of November 7, commonly called United Dry Forces (vs. United Council of Repeal); addresses a rally at First Baptist Church in order to introduce Mrs. J. M. Hobgood, NCFWC president, to speak against repeal

13 September — attends Get-Together Dinner of Clayton Woman's Club, where Mrs. Latham is guest of honor

30 September — addresses Raleigh chapter of Duke Alumnae Association on her recent trip

2–3 October — NCFWC council meets in Raleigh, not New Bern, after clubhouse there is wrecked by devastating hurricane on 16 September

12 October — addresses Sanford Woman's Club on "How Can A Woman's Club Best Serve Its Community?"

14 October — attends Eighth District Meeting in Durham, the meeting to conclude in time for the Duke-Tennessee football game

22 October — attends Dry Rally at Memorial Auditorium, Raleigh, featuring future governor Clyde R. Hoey (whose father-in-law is past governor O. Max Gardner)

24 October — signs open letter written by Mrs. Doak ("long-time worker for woman's suffrage and temperance") opposing repeal

7 November — repeal of prohibition roundly defeated in North Carolina, but 21st Amendment is ratified nationally in December, thus leaving the question to the states

28 November — re-elected president of Wake County League of Women Voters

7 December — honored, with other officers, at tea, RWC

Christmas — she and the Misses Herring host their sister Pauline and her husband, Sergeant and Mrs. J. R. Sloo of Memphis

8 JANUARY 1933

NATIONAL MEETINGS CLAIM ATTENTION OF CLUB WOMEN

Number of North Carolina Club Officials Will Attend General Federation Board Meeting and Conference On Cause and Cure of War to Be Held This Month at National Headquarters in Washington

By Mrs. J. Henry Highsmith

Two important national meetings are attracting the attention of club women this week. One is the annual mid-winter meeting of the board of directors of the General Federation of Women's Clubs to be held at National Headquarters in Washington January 10 to 14. The other is the conference on the Cause and Cure of War to be held in Washington, January 17 to 20. North Carolina Club women who will attend one or both of these meetings are Mrs. J. M. Hobgood of Farmville, president of the State Federation, Mrs. Edward M. Land of Statesville, state director, Mrs. Palmer Jerman of Raleigh, member of the board of trustees and Miss Gertrude Weil of Goldsboro, chairman of the committee on International Relations.

"These United States," the keynote of Mrs. Grace Morrison Poole's administration, will be sounded in many themes at the annual midwinter meeting of the board of directors of the General Federation, a galaxy of authorities on several of the many phases of the subject having been assembled for the different sessions. As this is the first meeting of the new board, considerable time will be given to a discussion of the new program of work and consideration of such projects as the National Economy League, Better Housing in America and the contribution the General Federation can make to aid in welfare work this winter.

Rear Admiral Richard Byrd, U. S. N., President of the National Economy League, will address the board on Wednesday evening on the plans and purposes of this organization, which has among its objectives the elimination of waste in governmental expenditures and the election of men and women worthy to serve "These United States." Other speakers will include representatives from the Department of State, the Department of Treasury, and the Department of Commerce. Miss Florence Hale, former president of the National Education Association and now vice chairman of the Department of Education in the General Federation, and Dr. Lillian Gilreth will also speak.

The first meeting of the board will be held Wednesday with the president, Mrs. Grace Morrison Poole, presiding.

Among the prominent speakers to address the conference on the Cause and Cure of War which will be presided over by Mrs. Carrie Chapman Catt, chairman, will be Dr. Mary E. Wooley, member of the American delegation at Geneva, who will speak on the Status of Disarmament. Other subjects that will be discussed will be: The World Today, The Depression, The Situation in Asia, Does It Help or Hinder the Coming of Permanent Peace? Moral Disarmament, Should the United States Join the League of Nations? War Provoking Influences of the Manufacture of Armament, The Lytton Report and The Control of the Sale of Arms.

The radio program for January over the Charlotte Station WBT, which is each Thursday from 2 to 2:15 p. m., under the direction of Miss Jenn Coltrane is: January 12, program of North Carolina poetry by Mrs. Rush Wray, of Charlotte, Jan. 19, program of music by Mrs. Lucie Duncan of Polkton, Jan. 26, Mrs. Edward M. Land as chairman of Juniors in the General Federation, will tell of her program for Junior organizations. Last week Mrs. J. J. Andoe, of Greensboro, Chairman of Art, spoke over WBT on American Paintings. Mrs. B. A. Hocutt of Clayton, Chairman of Public Welfare, spoke over WPTF, Raleigh, Tuesday on the subject of Club Women and Public Welfare. The radio division has been put under the department of Press and Publicity in the General Federation. Miss Coltrane says it is a delight that we are having radio programs over every radio broadcasting station in North Carolina this year. We have two weekly programs, one monthly and a number giving series of programs.

Raleigh Sunday *News and Observer,* p. 13 (Society, p. 1)

15 JANUARY 1933

JUNIOR CLUBS TO GIVE AID TO STATE PROJECT

By Mrs. J. Henry Highsmith

That the Junior Clubs of the State have adopted as a State project the Children's Home at Greensboro as an institution worthy of their support and interest is announced by Mrs. J. M. Hobgood of Farmville, president of the State Federation of Women's Clubs. A majority of the 35 Junior club presidents have expressed their approval of the project which meets also the approval of the State chairman of Juniors, Mrs. D. F. Giles of Marion and the General Federation chairman, Mrs. Edward M. Land of Statesville.

As Mrs. Hobgood sees it, the concentration of efforts on the part of the Juniors on this one project will not only bring these young club women into closer working relationships, but will also accomplish something big and worthwhile for the children of the State. In presenting this question for the consideration of the Juniors Mrs. Hobgood says:

"Some of the facts which commended the idea to me are these: The Children's Home in Greensboro is an institution which is centrally located and is not sponsored by any denomination or organization, being entirely dependent upon voluntary contributions and gifts. It has been in operation and under wise administration for a sufficiently long time for us to feel confidence in those in charge, to feel that it is a continuing organization and that it is filling a unique and obvious need in our State.

"My suggestion is that the Junior Clubs of the State contribute in various ways to this home. It is not necessary for any club to undertake this as its chief work, or that it shall curtail its present or local program in order to support the State project. Neither is it necessary for gifts of money only to be made. Dr. Phoenix, superintendent, writes that gifts of clothing for little folks of 3 years of age and under are most acceptable as are also household supplies. Layettes might be made, clothes for some certain little Tad might be sent or some really ambitious club might adopt a baby—just to clothe," she says.

Mrs. C. F. Strosnider of Goldsboro, chairman of Homemaking Division under American Home Department, announces that a homemakers institute has been planned as a project for the Women's Clubs of the State during the first or second week in April. The institute will be sponsored by either a local club or a group ofclubs or by the clubs of one or more counties. The institute program will be centered on the new philosophy of homemaking emphasizing (1) Balancing the home budget; (2) adapting the home to changing conditions; (3) family relationships.

A prize of $10.00 is being offered by the chairman of the American Home Department of the General Federation for the most constructive forward looking institute program. North Carolina clubs are urged to enter the contest and send copies of their institute program to Mrs. J. N. Britt of Lumberton, chairman of the American Home Department of the State Federation.

North Carolina is one of several States receiving honorable mention for the work it is doing in the Signature Campaign. Mrs. E. S. Patterson of Nashville, chairman, is sending out a rallying call to the club women to fill in their names and return them to her. The Campaign closes April 1. She announces that she has on hand petitions which she will send to any club writing for same. Thus far only 32 clubs have made reports to the number of signatures yet received.

Raleigh Sunday *News and Observer*, p. 13 (Society, p. 1)

22 JANUARY 1933

CLUB WOMEN SPONSOR BETTER ENGLISH WEEK

Mrs. M. M. Stewart of Raleigh, Chairman of Better English Week in the State Federation of Women's Clubs, Names Week of February 27 to March 6 For Campaign on Poor English

By Mrs. J. Henry Highsmith

For checking up on one's spoken English and encouraging the use of good speech among school children as well as among members of both men's and women's clubs, Mrs. M. M. Stewart of Raleigh, chairman of Better English Week in the State Federation of Women's Clubs, announces that the week of February 27 to March 6 has been set apart for observing Better English Week in North Carolina. Through the cooperation of the club women, the newspapers, libraries, schools and colleges, Mrs. Stewart hopes to reach all the citizens of a community with the desire and effort to improve their native tongue.

Better English Week is a national movement sponsored by a number of educational groups, among these the National Association of English Teachers. Its purpose is to improve the English in general of the American people and create in them an appreciation of the English language when correctly spoken. Better English Week calls attention to the importance in good speech of a pleasing voice, an enlarged and varied vocabulary and the cultivation of lucid forceful and uncorrupted diction. It warns against the use of "overworked" expressions, careless enunciation, grammatical errors and incorrect pronunciation.

Mrs. Stewart will outline the program which she has prepared for the women's clubs of the State in a talk over radio station WPTF at Raleigh, Tuesday, January 24 from 2:15 to 2:30 o'clock. Her suggestions will appear in the February issue of the Federation Bulletin.

Appearing also in the February Issue of the Bulletin is an interesting paper by Miss Margaret Gilbert of Raleigh, chairman of Library Extension of the Federation, showing the effects of the Depression on the reading habits of the people. Among a number of interesting observations she has made she mentions this:

"As a by-product of the present difficult times, there has come a great increase in the amount of serious reading. Libraries are furnishing not only recreational reading, the cheapest avenue of escape from personal depression, but practical reading to the extent that a library is no longer deemed a luxury but a public utility."

"For this serious reading," she says, "the books most in demand have been those relating to better ways of earning a living, to improving the professional or vocational skill, to increasing the family income, to understanding and meeting the economic crisis. The people," she says, "are trying to re-orient themselves to understand better the business of living. Their reading shows that they are interested in such subjects as trade crafts, home industries, gardening, pigeon raising, rabbit raising, making of hot beds, automotive engineering, electric work, religion, art and all information seeking a satisfactory philosophy of life.

"As the curve of business goes down," says Miss Gilbert "the curve of reading goes up. There is more at stake in municipal budgets than dollars and cents. We have to stave off social bankruptcy with one hand while we fight off financial bankruptcy with the other."

Raleigh Sunday *News and Observer*, p. 15 (Society, p. 1)

29 JANUARY 1933

OPPOSE MERGER OF HEALTH AND WELFARE DEPARTMENTS

Club Women Against Merger of Welfare and Health Departments

By Mrs. J. Henry Highsmith

The proposal of the Reorganization Committee of the General Assembly now in session to coordinate the activities of the State Department of Public Welfare with those of the State Department of Health came as a great surprise to the club women of the state. Year after year they have worked in close cooperation with the Department of Public Welfare in helping to take care of the state's unfortunates, and now at a time when demand for public welfare service is greater than ever before to have the recommendation made that such services be drastically curtailed, even though it be done in the interest of economy and the "extreme necessity of the State," is beyond their power to understand.

An intimate knowledge of the fields of work of both departments and of the set-up of each organization for performing its duties as required by law, shows that there is little or no duplication of services and that in no way can the divisions of each be coordinated into a working whole. The services rendered by the state Department of Health of a highly technical and scientific nature dealing with such subjects as epidemiology, bacteriology, sanitary engineering, stream pollution, sewage disposal and matters of similar type require specially trained men and equipment. The work of the Department of Public Welfare requires a group of men and women not less skilfully trained but in different subjects such as sociology, mental and social hygiene, family relationships, child care, mother's aid, home restoration, juvenile delinquency and the supervision and inspection of humane institutions.

Dr. James M. Parrott, secretary of State Board of Health and State Health Officer, expresses himself as being unqualifiedly of the opinion that this merger would be very unwise and urges that it not be attempted or done. Mrs. W. T. Bost, State Commissioner of Public Welfare, feels that such a step would nullify the extensive efforts over a number of years of those interested in building up a constructive social program for the State, and that such a plan would in no way work to the best interests of the State.

Through the efficient set-up of the machinery of the Department of Public Welfare in the counties of the State, it has been possible to put to work the funds of the Reconstruction Finance Corporation with the least possible delay and with an effectiveness that has brought commendation from those higher up who are in charge of dispensing the funds. Thousands have been given employment and relief in a way that has made the state a pattern to other commonwealths.

North Carolina club women have always felt an especial interest and pride in the state's public welfare work. It was largely through their efforts years ago that the work was extended and enlarged, thus enabling the state to take its place among the more progressive states of the union in the field of public welfare work. The two women who have so efficiently headed up this commission, Mrs. Kate Burr Johnson and Mrs. Bost, have been widely appreciated for their far-sighted vision and constructive programs employed in the public welfare field.

Another matter claiming the attention of club women of the state at this time is the Citizens Conference on Education that has been called to meet in the Raleigh Memorial Auditorium, next Tuesday, January 31st at 2:30 o'clock. Twelve statewide organizations, including the State Federation of Women's Clubs, sponsored the general invitation. Mrs. Hobgood, president of the Federation, issued the call to the 10,000 club members, stating that public education in North Carolina today is in graver danger than it has been at any time since the Civil War. Mrs. Hobgood will be one of the speakers on the conference program.

While it is a laymen's meeting and not one instigated by the school men, Clyde A. Erwin of Rutherfordton, president of the Teachers Association, has been invited to take the place of A. T. Allen as one of the speakers. Dr. Frank Graham, president of the University of North Carolina, is another speaker. Kemp Battle of Rocky Mount and Sanford Martin of Winston-Salem are others who have been asked to present the factual situation of education as they see it in the state today.

Raleigh Sunday *News and Observer,* p. 13 (Society, p. 1)

5 FEBRUARY 1933

MUSIC ACHIEVEMENT DAY TO BE OBSERVED APRIL 1

Music Memory Contest Will Feature Program To Be Held at Duke University Under Sponsorship of State Federation of Women's Clubs and State Department of Education; 100 To Take Part

By Mrs. J. Henry Highsmith

Music Achievement Day, sponsored by the State Federation of Women's Clubs and the State Department of Education, will be held this year at Duke

University on Saturday, April 1st. A feature of the day's program will be the annual music memory contest in which more than a hundred boys and girls from all over the State will take a part. Duke University, in extending an invitation to hold this year's Music Achievement Day program on its campus, assures the participants of the music memory contest that they will be given an opportunity to hear concerts by Lawrence Clark Apgar, organist and carillonneur, on the organ and carillon in the University Chapel.

Miss Hattie Parrott of Raleigh, in charge of this feature of school work, announces the following program: Registration at 10 o'clock; contest at 11 o'clock; organ and carillon concerts at 12 o'clock; and presentation of awards at 1 o'clock. The contest will be limited to the pupils of the sixth and seventh grades in the public schools. Each school is entitled to enter one pupil from each the sixth and seventh grades in the state contest. Each state contestant must be registered with Miss Parrott on or before March 27.

A cash prize of $50.00 offered by the N. C. Education Association will be awarded to the school represented by the winner. A second cash prize of $50.00 offered by the State Federation of Women's Cubs will be awarded to the school represented by the pupil making next to the highest score. Certificates of award in music appreciation will be awarded each contestant by Dr. A. T. Allen.

For four or five successive years the state music memory contests have been held in Raleigh and hundreds of boys and girls have gathered there to demonstrate the part that music plays in the lives of public school children. Last year the $50.00 prize was won by Miss Margaret McKaughan of Wake Forest and the second prize of $25.00, which was a scholarship in piano, was won by Miss Louise Lassiter of Woodlawn in Northampton County.

Club women are keenly interested in the proposed coordination of the State Library Commission with the State Library, if it in any way means the curtailment of any of the services of the commission. Women's Clubs and libraries are almost synonymous terms in the minds of many club women. All through the years, either the establishment or the support of a library has been considered a club's first duty to its community. To women's clubs goes the credit of establishing about 60 per cent of all the libraries in the State.

In this connection it is recalled that it was largely through the efforts of the Federation that the library commission was established. This was in 1909 when the Federation convention met in Raleigh in the Hall of the House of Representatives. After hearing Mr. Louis Wilson, a member of the newly created commission, tell of the plans and purposes of the Commission, the Federation voted to turn over all its travelling libraries to the commission. This gift included 92 travelling libraries in cases and several hundred not in cases.

Mrs. J. J. Andoe of Greensboro, chairman of Art, who has been giving a series of art talks over Radio Station WBIG, will conclude her series next Wednesday at 5 o'clock with a paper on "Art in Terms of Dollars and Cents." The subjects of Mrs. Andoe's talks which may be had by writing to her are "Eight Bells," by Winslow Homer; "Whistling Boy," by Frank Duveneck; "Toilers of the Sea," by Albert P. Ryder; and "Caritas" by Abbott H. Thayer.

Among the visitors who called at headquarters at the Sir Walter Hotel while attending the Citizens Educational Conference in Raleigh last Tuesday were Mrs. Kenneth Todd of Gastonia; Mrs. A. G. Johnston of Lillington; Mrs. John D. Robinson of Wallace; Mrs. Claude Morris, Mrs. T. E. Johnson, Mrs. M. H. Omwake and Mrs. E. W. Burt of Salisbury; Mrs. J. W. Hobgood of Farmville; Miss Annie Perkins and Mrs. Tabitha Devisconti also of Farmville; Mrs. Edward M. Land of Statesville, Mrs. E. L. McKee of Sylva, Mrs. J. J. Andoe of Greensboro and Mrs. C. O. Burton of Greensboro.

Raleigh Sunday *News and Observer,* p. 13 (Society, p. 1)

12 FEBRUARY 1933

UNEMPLOYED TEACHERS TO TEACH ADULT ILLITERATES

Plans For Establishment of Schools For Adult Illiterates Already Approved; Teachers Would Be Paid From Federal Fund and Would Conduct School For a Period of At Least Ten Weeks

By Mrs. J. Henry Highsmith

Club women of the State who have labored single-handed for years in the work of teaching adult illiterates welcome the announcement that schools for this group of citizens may now be established and taught by the unemployed teachers of the State, the teachers to be paid from the Federal relief funds of the county. Outlines of the plan, which has been approved by Dr. Fred V. Morrison, director of relief for North Carolina, have been sent to all county and city superintendents of schools by Dr. J. Henry Highsmith, director of the Division of Instructional Service of the State Department of Education and in charge of adult illiteracy, with the request that early action be taken and the program be put into effect.

The plan adopted, which will give help to worthy and needy teachers, contemplates providing educational advantages for adult illiterates or near illiterates in 100 counties for a period of at least ten weeks. Teachers will be selected by the county superintendent of public instruction and the superintendent of public welfare. They will be paid $7.50 per week or $10.00 per week provided the instruction is given at more than one center. Teachers will devote the same number of hours per week to teaching as is required of regular teachers, provided that hours spent in conducting evening classes may be counted as regular work.

A minimum of ten students will be required to constitute a school. These students may be taught individually or in groups, the most convenient arrangement possible being made to meet the needs of the students enrolled. Text books and teaching material will be furnished as far as possible by the State Department of Education. Reports and records on attendance and achievement upon completion of the course will be made to the Department of Education.

Mrs. Eva Edgerton Penland of Asheville, literacy chairman of the State Federation of Women's Clubs, has expressed her pleasure of having at least 100 new workers on "our job." She says that this aid has come at a time when it is most needed and will help to carry forward the State literacy program in a way that will get results. Mrs. Penland offered wholehearted cooperation of her group of faithful club workers in carrying out the State program.

Mrs. John D. Robinson of Wallace, chairman of civics, is again calling the attention of club women to the fact that Federal relief funds can be used to finance a town's general house-cleaning and spring planting, provided the work is given to the unemployed. Not a cent, she says, can go for material or for salaries. "This is too good a chance to miss doing all the civic work that has been put off for months and maybe years," she says.

Some of the things that Mrs. Robinson suggests doing with Federal relief funds allotted to the county are: clean-up and plant school grounds and cemeteries; beautify highways and town entrances; clean streets, build sidewalks, open up new streets, clean and tidy up vacant lots; clean and beautify town parks and make new ones; have equipment made for playgrounds; see that schools and public building have proper sewerage; undertake drainage projects where needed; and undertake any other project in order to make your town clean, attractive, healthful and a safe place in which to live.

Mrs. Robinson calls attention to the O'Berry cup which is offered each year to either the senior or junior club doing the best piece of civic work in the community this club year.

"Have you entered your town in the More Beautiful America Contest?" asks Mrs. Robinson. "It isn't too late," she says, "and I hope many North Carolina towns will be entered. This contest offers a wonderful opportunity to check on your town—its highways, parks, river fronts, railroad stations and many other things. The contest is open to individuals or groups, women's clubs, garden clubs, civic organizations or chambers of commerce. A prize of $1,000 will be given as first honor. Write to Better Homes and Gardens, Des Moines, Ia., for further information concerning More Beautiful America Contest.

Raleigh Sunday *News and Observer*, p. 13 (Society, p. 1)

19 FEBRUARY 1933

LEGISLATIVE MEASURES INTEREST CLUB WOMEN

By Mrs. J. Henry Highsmith

While the life of the marriage bill is still in jeopardy, the date for determining its fate at the hands of the Senate being set for the Tuesday morning session of the Legislature, there are other measures of interest to club women that are now before the Legislature. One of these is the sixth grade attainment bill, which is sponsored by the Legislative Council of North Carolina Women. The bill, which has been introduced in the House by Thomas Turner, Jr., of High Point, puts North Carolina in the class with forty-two other states which have some kind of educational attainment for its children who would leave school to go to work. Thirty-four states require the completion of the sixth grade or more, and fourteen the eighth grade.

Another bill of interest to women, particularly to married women, is one introduced by Victor R. Johnson of Chatham that would prohibit the employment of married women in any of the departments of State, county, or city government whose husbands receive as much as $125 per month. This bill that was vigorously protested against by representatives of organized women in the State received an unfavorable report from the committee on propositions and grievances.

A bill affecting the working hours of women and girls employed as clerks and salesladies in stores and of waitresses and cooks in restaurants, cafes and cafeterias has passed both houses and now establishes a 55-hour work week and a 10-hour work day as a maximum for the above groups. At present the State allows women employed in mills and factories to work 11 hours a day, which is the longest work day permitted by law, not only of any State in the union but of any country in the world.

A bill of general interest is the Murphy-Bowie bill to legalize the sale in North Carolina of light wines and beer in the event Congress legalizes the sales of such beverages. In this connection it is of interest to quote Mrs. Grace Morrison Poole, president of the General Federation of Women's Clubs. She says:

"Right here may I enter a plea for clear, straight thinking on the question of prohibition? Never to my knowledge has an officer of the General Federation of Women's Clubs claimed that its entire membership was in sympathy with the Eighteenth Amendment and the Volstead Act, but our vote record down through the years justifies us in saying that the large majority of our membership favors it.

"No one, for one moment, questions the right of individual club women to think and act as they please upon this social question, but we do expect officers of clubs and federations to give the stand of the General Federation when the subject is up for discussion."

Two other bills which affect the interests of women are to be introduced this week. One is a bill amending the property laws of the State as they affect the interest of the husband and wife in each other's property.

The other is asking that $1,000 of the appropriation allotted to the State Department of Education be designated for the purpose of teaching the effects of alcohol and narcotics on the human system. Another bill that has received much study and consideration in its preparations is an amendment to the present outdoor advertising law, that would tax and regulate hundreds of firms now advertising on the state highways without paying any state license.

Club women whose first interest is libraries are concerned greatly over the proposed budget as set up for the Library Commission by the Advisory Budget Commission. Since 1930, the total budget for this department will have been cut 47 per cent, with a cut of 51 per cent in salaries if the proposed budget goes into effect. This would mean a cut in average salary per employee of 44 per cent, which is by far the greatest cut in any State department. The budget for the Library Commission never has been large. In 1930–31 the budget was $19,413; in 1933 the proposed budget is $10,360.

Raleigh Sunday *News and Observer,* p. 13 (Society, p. 1)

26 FEBRUARY 1933

MARCH WILL PROVE BUSY MONTH FOR CLUB WOMEN

Better English Week and Homemakers' Institute Scheduled for Next Month; Women to Meet Tuesday For Purpose of Opposing Repeal of State Prohibition Law and of the Eighteenth Amendment

By Mrs. J. Henry Highsmith

With only two months remaining in which to finish up a number of club activities before the annual meeting of the State Federation of Women's Clubs in May, March promises to be a busy month beginning this week with the observance of Better English Week. The purpose of this special emphasis once a year on the use of good spoken English is, according to Mrs. N. W. Stewart of Raleigh, chairman, to create in children and grown-ups a greater appreciation of the English language when spoken correctly and in a pleasing voice; to create a desire for choice English and an enlarged and varied vocabulary; to create a sensitiveness to over-worked and slang expressions, careless enunciation, incorrect pronunciation and errors in grammar.

From the widespread interest that has been manifested in the observance of this week by schools, book clubs, women's clubs and a large number of individuals, it is expected that the King's English will have fewer abuses in the immediate future than it has had in the immediate past. Mrs. Stewart is calling on teachers, leaders and club workers throughout the State to make wide use of the program suggestions offered by her in the February issue of the February Bulletin. While the first week in March is usually observed as Better Speech Week, any week in the school and club year may be chosen with as good results.

Another project scheduled for March is the Homemakers Institute, which is being sponsored by the Homemaking Division of the American Home department. Mrs. C. F. Strosnider, of Goldsboro, is chairman. Her plan is to have one or more clubs, or a group of clubs as of a county, to cooperate in this community plan of studying the newest and best methods of making homes and raising the standard of living. She urges that this project be put on in March if possible. A prize of $10 is offered by the chairman of the American Home department of the General Federation for the best program outlined for a Homemakers Institute by any club or group of clubs in any of the States. Mrs. Strosnider is asking that a copy of every institute program be sent to Mrs. J. N. Britt, of Lumberton, not later than April 15. Mrs. Britt will select from the number the best to be sent to compete in the nation-wide contest. A large group of clubs is expected to enter the contest.

Club women of the State are hereby invited and urged to attend a meeting in Raleigh on Tuesday, February 28, for the purpose of securing united effort for action against the repeal of the State prohibition law and of the 18th Amendment. The meeting is being planned by the Women's National Committee for Law Enforcement and is one of a series of forty-eight that are being held in the capital cities of all of the states. Mrs. Henry W. Peabody, of Washington, D. C., is chairman of the committee and she in person will be the speaker on this occasion. In urging upon club women and other key women of the State and community the importance of their interest and cooperation in these matters at this time, she says that the crisis which our government is now facing is the greatest since 1861. As only one meeting of this kind will be held in the State, Mrs. Peabody urges a wide and representative attendance of thinking women. The place of meeting is the First Baptist Church in Raleigh, at 11 o'clock a. m. next Tuesday.

Mrs. D. F. Giles, of Marion, chairman of Junior Membership, who has recovered from a recent extended illness, has taken up her work again with the Juniors with renewed interest and enthusiasm. Her program of work for them this spring includes many fine undertakings worthy of the efforts and courage of this group of energetic workers.

Raleigh Sunday *News and Observer,* p. 15 (Society, p. 1)

5 MARCH 1933

CLUB WOMEN PLAN FOR STATE CONVENTION HERE

Annual Convention Will Be Held in Raleigh May 3, 4 and 5 With the Local Woman's Club as Hostess and the Sir Walter Hotel as Convention Headquarters; Interesting Program Planned

By Mrs. J. Henry Highsmith

Plans for entertaining probably the largest annual convention of the State Federation of Women's Clubs yet held have been made by Mrs. J. M. Hobgood, president, with the Raleigh Woman's Club as hostess and the Sir Walter Hotel as convention headquarters. The days of the convention this year are May 3, 4, and 5, Wednesday, Thursday, and Friday, which is one day later than the usual date.

Meeting with Mrs. Hobgood at Federation Headquarters last Tuesday for considering convention plans were Mrs. T. E. Browne, second vice president of the Federation, Mrs. J. Henry Highsmith, executive secretary and Mrs. J. V. Higham, first vice president of the Raleigh Woman's Club who represented Mrs. C. A. Shore, president.

According to Mrs. Hobgood, there is every indication that a record crowd will attend the convention in May. While only a tentative program was adopted, and many of the main features yet to be decided upon, enough was accomplished, she said, to insure every one entertainment, profit and pleasure during the three day convention. The speakers are nationally known and are among the country's best. The social features promise to be most delightful and entertaining. Many novel features are being planned by department chairmen who will have charge of the breakfast and luncheon conferences. The Juniors will have charge of the banquet program on Friday evening, which is assurance that it will be of a high order of amusement.

Mrs. J. J. Andoe of Greensboro, chairman of Art, announces that there will be an excellent display of North Carolina art in connection with the convention. She is inviting all North Carolina artists to enter some of their works in the exhibit not later than April 28. These should be sent direct to the Sir Walter Hotel, Raleigh.

Mrs. Andoe is calling attention to the four prizes that are offered this year for art achievements. These are: The Margaret Norvell Graham silver vase offered for the best water color by a North Carolina artist; the Bernau Silver cup offered for the best essay on "Art In Precious Metals and as a Source of History"; the James Westley White cup offered for the best landscape or marine in oil; and the Mrs. S. Clay Williams cup offered for the best portrait.

Beginning March 29, Mrs. Andoe will begin another series of art talks over radio station WBIG, Greensboro, at 5:45 o'clock. She has just concluded a series, the last being given last Wednesday on the subject, "Art for the Child."

Mrs. John D. Robinson of Wallace, chairman of Civics, requests all clubs that compete for the O'Berry cup, which is offered for the best piece of civic work during the club year, to send her a full report of same by April 15. Mrs. Robinson says that the clubs of her county—Duplin—are planning to put on a countywide Homemakers Institute. Any time in the month of March is specified for this project, but all institute programs are to be sent to Mrs. J. N. Britt of Lumberton by April 15. The best state programs will be entered in the national contest for the $10 prize offered by the American Home Department of the General Federation.

Mrs. Howard G. Etheridge of Asheville, chairman of Education, writes that renewed interest has been taken in teaching adult illiterates since the announcement that unemployed teachers will be paid from the Federal relief funds of the county who will organize and teach as many as ten students for a period of at least ten weeks. Teachers doing this work will be selected by the county superintendent of schools and the county superintendent of Public Welfare and will be paid $7.50 per week or $10 per week provided the instruction is given at more than one center. Those interested in this phase of work should write to Dr. J. Henry Highsmith, State Department of Education, Raleigh.

Raleigh Sunday *News and Observer,* p. 15 (Society, p. 1)
Charlotte Sunday Observer, p. 15 (section 2, p. 3)

12 MARCH 1933

FEDERATION COUNCIL WILL MEET IN RICHMOND IN MAY

Council of General Federation Will Convene in the Virginia Capital May 22–26; Event Is Anticipated by North Carolina Club Women Who Will Attend in Large Numbers

By Mrs. J. Henry Highsmith

An event that will be of special interest to North Carolina club women this spring is the council meeting of the General Federation of Women's Clubs to be held in Richmond, May 22 to 26. This occasion is attracting unusual attention for the reason that similar meetings for the past several years have been held in the West or Southwest, and this is the first opportunity North Carolina and Virginia club women have had in recent years in having a meeting of the General Federation to come so near their doors. It is expected that club women of the State will avail themselves of this opportunity to attend the meetings and acquaint themselves with the personalities as well as with the programs and policies of the national organization of which they are a member.

Mrs. L. J. Giles, president of the Virginia Federation, and Mrs. J. L. Blair Buck, Director and chairman of the Council Committee, as official hostesses announce in their general invitation that Richmond stands ready to welcome what promises to be one of the largest council meetings in the history of the Federation.

Mrs. Grace Morrison Poole, president, who will preside, has chosen "Thrift" as the keynote of the meeting. Mr. Lewis E. Lawes, famous penologist and warden of Sing Sing prison, will be one of the distinguished speakers. It is expected that his talk will follow the lines dealt with in his recent book "20,000 Years in Sing Sing." Mr. William Hard, nationally and internationally known newspaper man, magazine writer and political commentator, whose weekly broadcast is "Back of the News in Washington," will be another speaker. On May 25, Mrs. Anna C. Tillinghast, the only woman Immigrant Officer in the United States, will speak on Immigration and the Menace of Communism.

There will be only three work days of the convention. The day before the opening will be given over to smaller group meeting and the dinner tendered by the local Board to the members of the General Board. Friday will be "Play Day" when excursions will be made to historic Jamestown and Williamsburg. A visit to Alderson prison in West Virginia has been planned for Saturday.

Announcement of the final plans for the annual Music Achievement Day and Music Memory Contest that are sponsored jointly by the Federation and the state Department of Education has been made by Mies Hattie Parrott of the State Department. This year both the program and the contest will be held in Durham at Duke University, on Saturday, April 1st. The two or three hundred children from practically every county in the State will assemble in the Duke Chapel at 10 o'clock. Registration will begin at 10:30 and the contest at 11, in the Page auditorium. At 12 o'clock Lawrence Clarke Aggar will give both organ and carillon concerto. The awards will be presented at 1 o'clock in the chapel, after which lunch will be served in the College Union dining room.

Miss Grace Van Dyke Moore, director of Public School Music at North Carolina College for Women at Greensboro, will conduct the contest. A. T. Allen will present the certificates of attainment and Jule B. Warren will deliver the first prize of $50 for the North Carolina Education Association. Mrs. J. M. Hobgood will present the second prize of $15 for the State Federation of Women's Clubs. Mrs. E. E. Randolph, chairman of Public School Music for the Federation, will be in charge of the assembly and will assist Miss Parrott in the general management of the day's program.

The newest club to be organized and federated is the Woman's Club of Star with 14 members. Mrs. W. S. Griffin is president. Mrs. P. R. Rankin, president of the Fifth District, sent in the name of the new club.

Mrs. J. J. Andoe of Greensboro, chairman of art, was in Raleigh last week to confer with the local committee in regard to the Art Exhibit to be held in connection with the Federation convention in May. While here she addressed the Missionary Society of the Tabernacle Baptist Church on the Pueblo Indians.

Raleigh Sunday *News and Observer,* p. 13 (Society, p. 1)
Charlotte Sunday Observer, p. 15 (section 2, p. 3)

19 MARCH 1933

CLUB WOMEN TO SUPPORT EDUCATIONAL PROGRAM

By Mrs. J. Henry Highsmith

Mrs. J. M. Hobgood, president of the State Federation of Women's Clubs, feeling that club women's first interest is the safety of the schools of the state and that the life of their schools is at this time seriously threatened, is calling on the club women to back Governor Ehringhaus in his program for a balanced budget and an eight months school term supported by the state. Mrs. Hobgood urges immediate action on the part of the members of her organization in thinking through the school situation as it is now before the Legislature and in giving wholehearted support to the Governor's program that will save both the schools and the credit of the state.

Mrs. Hobgood calls attention to two schools of thought or plans of action concerning the schools now before the Legislature. One would reduce the state appropriation for schools from $23,300,000, the amount spent for schools last year, to $10,200,000, the total amount to be spent for schools next year. This plan, it has been pointed out, would reduce the school term to something like four months or make it inoperative altogether.

The other group advocates an eight months school term supported by the state from revenue other than that raised from taxes on land, which plan is contemplated in the Aycock bill and is endorsed in the resolution introduced in the Senate by Senators McLean and Bailey. In regard to this plan, Dr. A. T. Allen says:

"It is the only plan that is now seriously advocated that will keep the rural high schools operating in many sections of the state, and preserve the integrity of the rural school system. It will greatly improve the total efficiency of the whole system. It is an economy measure which makes it fit into the times. It provides, through reorganization, a possible saving of $750,000 before starting on the reduction of teachers' salaries. It opens the schoolhouse door to all children of the state on terms of equality. It makes the school system as strong as the state itself."

Realizing the crisis that now confronts the schools of the state, Governor Ehringhaus, in his message to the General Assembly, urged adoption of the 8 month plan to be supported from state revenue, which he estimates will bring a tax relief of 35 cents on the one-hundred dollar valuation of property. He visualized in this plan a "real chance to establish in our schools that equality of opportunity between the city and country boy and girl of which we have long dreamed and oft despaired."

Throughout the Governor's address, it was evident that he was relying on the folks back home to furnish the force to effect this plan. "The people will rally to our support and our cause will triumph," he said. Consequently, Mrs. Hobgood urges club women to lose no time in declaring themselves in favor of saving the schools regardless of the cost.

Club women particularly mourn the death of Dr. E. C. Branson of the University of North Carolina. He was one of the first professional men in the state to recognize the services rendered local communities and the state as a whole by this group of organized women. He not only helped the state to find itself but he aided individuals, organizations and institutions to know their capabilities and how to meet their responsibilities, Likewise he led them to see their defects and deficiencies. While he helped to destroy a number of "firsts" for North Carolina he helped to place her on a foundation on which she could make lasting progress.

While the 1933 Legislature will long be remembered for the many things it would abolish, repeal, or change the status quo, there are yet hopes that it will effect many good pieces of legislation before its adjournment. One of the shortest and yet most constructive bills to be introduced is one by Representative Watson of Nash which would provide that tenants shall have the right to have and cultivate on the land leased or rented a garden and potato patch and the right to maintain, keep and care for a cow, pigs and chickens on the rented premises.

Raleigh Sunday *News and Observer,* p. 13 (Society, p. 1)

26 MARCH 1933

CLUB WOMEN OPPOSED TO DECREASED HEALTH WORK

By Mrs. J. Henry Highsmith

Not long ago the club women of America received this significant statement: "The Nation's Womanhood Must Defend the Nation's Health." North Carolina club women at the time passed up the words of warning, feeling as they did that the State Department of Health was more or less adequately taking care of the health of the people. Today the message takes on new meaning. It strikes home. Club women do not feel so secure as to the safety of their children's health and that of their neighbors. They deplore the decreased activities of the Board of Health that have been ordered in the name of economy, and are fearful of what the future may hold in the way of epidemics and as a result of having to forego many valuable safeguards.

The facts are: The State Board of Health has been cut in its appropriation about two-thirds of what it received in 1930, if the figures of the Bowie-

Cherry bill stand. This means, according to Dr. James M. Parrott, State Health Officer, that the powers of the State Board of Health have been reduced beyond the point of providing adequate protection for the people's health. "If we have to carry on on the allotment that has been proposed for us," said Dr. Parrott, "our best will be only a pretense. The result, regardless of our efforts, would be a false security.

According to Dr. Parrott, public health work would be curtailed in 66 of the 100 counties, practically all of the rural schools, and in certain activities which affect the State as a whole. Between 30 and 40 per cent of the sanitary engineering service of the board would be lost, which would increase the hazard of epidemics, particularly that of typhoid fever. Dr. Parrott referred to the increase of typhoid among rural school children which is accounted for by lack of vaccination, but mainly by lack of sanitation and sewage control at the schoolhouses. There are 2,700 schoolhouses in the State, he said, that have no water supply, and 3,500 schoolhouses with no toilets worth the name.

Another service to be lost to the State which the people would suffer from would be that of the State Laboratory of Hygiene. Whereas doses of toxin-antitoxin sufficient to immunize against dread diphtheria have been made at a cost of 50 cents to the State, the same amount if bought in the open market will cost $5.00. Vaccine for the treatment of rabies has been had for $5.00, or free to persons not able to pay, whereas if bought in the open market will cost $20.00. All new health projects planned for the future will have to be foregone, one of these being the campaign for controlling the spread of venereal diseases, now said to be much on the increase.

But where club women are most concerned is over the fact that the children are to be the greatest sufferers from this policy of cutting to the heart and to the death of State institutions and departments of government to atone for the blunders of this generation. They agree with Dr. Parrott that it is cowardly to project the evils of this Depression into the next generation.

A glance over the list of health services to be dispensed with for the next two years for lack of sufficient appropriation at the hands of the 1933 Legislature shows that children will no longer have free protection from typhoid and diphtheria, dental service to school children will be tremendously crippled, all maternity and infancy work will be done away, and the services of six whole-time public health nurses will be abandoned altogether. This means that the poorer counties which have no health officers will be without public health service of any kind.

As a result of this enforced retrenchment—this letting down the bars, Dr. Parrott does not hesitate to predict [a surge of] diseases which at any time may reach epidemic proportions—diseases that are both preventable and controllable under proper safeguards.

Raleigh Sunday *News and Observer*, p. 13 (Society, p. 1)

2 APRIL 1933

WOMEN'S CLUBS TO SPONSOR PICTURE MEMORY TEST IN RALEIGH

School Children of State Will Have Chance to Win Prizes in Annual Event

By Mrs. J. Henry Highsmith

A state-wide picture memory contest, which is a course in art appreciation for school children, will be held in Raleigh at the Hugh Morson High School, Saturday, May 13. The contest is sponsored by the State Federation of Women's Clubs in co-operation with the state Department of Education. Miss Juanita McDougald of the state department is in charge of the work and announces that the program begins at 10 o'clock when registration for the contest begins. More than 100 school children are expected to attend, says Miss McDougald.

In charge of the contest which will be held from 11 to 12 o'clock will be Miss Mildred English and Miss Georgia Kirkpatrick, both of Raleigh. Lunch will be served from 12:30 to 1 o'clock at the Woman's Club with Mrs. R. L. McMillan and Mrs. J. S. Cox as hostesses. A feature of the luncheon hour will be art tableaux and music by the children of the Raleigh schools.

Dr. A. T. Allen will present the prizes after which a sight-seeing tour of Raleigh and vicinity, including the state buildings and the gardens of Mrs. Josephus Daniels and others, will be made.

Enrolled in the contest will be representatives from rural and city high schools, one to a school, and from the rural and city elementary schools. Schools may select their representatives in any way they choose. Pupils from schools whose term has ended may participate on the same basis as those still in session.

According to a tentative announcement of the prizes offered, to winners of first places in the four groups: elementary rural, elementary chartered, high school, rural, and high school chartered, a trip to Washington will be given. To winners of second places in these groups, framed copies of famous prints will be given. To winners of third places will be given a set of copper etchings of Duke University by Dr. Henry Dwire of Duke University. To winners of fourth places will go pieces of North Carolina pottery by Mrs. Jacques Bushes of Jugtown. To winners of fifth places will go photographs of North Carolina life by Mrs. Bayard Wooten.

Mrs. J. M. Hobgood, president of the Federation, while busily engaged in making convention plans and setting up a three-day program, finds time to visit several clubs, make speeches and wind up the affairs of her administration in fine order. She has recently visited and addressed the clubs of Ahoskie, Oxford and Goldsboro, where she addressed the Home-Makers Institute. Yesterday she attended the state music achievement day exercises and music memory contest at Duke University. She delivered the $15 prize offered by the Federation to the school whose pupil wins the second highest place.

Club friends of Mrs. T. E. Browne, third vice president of the Federation. deeply sympathize with her and Mr. Browne in the death of their son which occurred last week. Joseph Majette, known to the neighbors and his friends as "Jett," was one of the Browne twins and a favorite in the community. His bright face and kindly smile will be greatly missed by a wide circle of friends.

Those who heard the broadcast Wednesday afternoon sponsored by the International Flower Show at Miami Beach will agree with the writer, I am sure, that it was one of the loveliest things in all of its phases, including its purpose, ever to have been heard on the air. Think of fostering international harmony, friendship and co-operation among American countries through an interchange of flowers native to the individual countries! The flowers transported by the Pan-American Air Ways were for the most part priceless orchids—altogether fitting the import of the occasion. Why not say it with flowers—good-will, friendliness and a willingness to understand each other as nations—when nothing makes for friendliness and harmony among back yard neighbors like the exchange of plants or flower cuttings?

Charlotte Sunday Observer, p. 15 (section 2, p. 3)

9 APRIL 1933

WOMEN'S CLUB TO HOLD ANNUAL MEETING MAY 3–6

Full Three-Day Program of Business and Entertainment Planned; Raleigh Woman's Club In Charge of Social and Recreational Features; Prominent Out-of-Town Women To Be Present

By Mrs. J. Henry Highsmith

The thirty-first annual convention of the North Carolina Federation of Women's Clubs has been officially called to meet in Raleigh, May 3, 4, and 5, by the President, Mrs. J. M. Hobgood of Farmville. In the call recently issued, club presidents were advised as to the number of delegates their clubs were entitled to send, but they were assured that all club women, whether delegates or not, would be cordially welcome to all business sessions of the convention and to all social functions.

According to a tentative program that has been drafted, the opening session will be Wednesday evening at 8 o'clock in the Virginia Dare Ball Room of the Sir Walter Hotel, headquarters for the convention. In the forenoon of Wednesday at 10:30 o'clock there will be a meeting of executive board at the Woman's Club to be followed by a luncheon complimentary to the members of the board. At 2:30 o'clock, a Club Institute will be held in the Ball Room of the Sir Walter for the benefit of club presidents, district presidents and other club officials. At the same hour there will be a meeting of the Board of Trustees. At 3:30 o'clock the Board of Directors will meet in the Ball Room.

Three dinners have been planned for the first evening, for the past presidents, the district presidents and a dinner conference for chairmen of departments and presidents of local clubs. Following the opening session will be a reception tendered by the courtesy of the hotel and the hostess club to all visiting club women.

Starting the day Thursday will be two breakfast conferences: one on citizenship presided over by Mrs. E. L. McKee, and the other on civics presided over by Mrs. John D. Robinson. At the noon hour there will be two luncheon conferences, one on Literature, presided over by Mrs. B. M. Long, and the other on Education, presided over by Mrs. Howard G. Etheridge. On Friday morning there will be breakfast conferences on Gardens with Miss Isabel B. Busbee presiding, and on Music with Miss Jesse Moye presiding. Four luncheon conferences are scheduled for this day: Art, presided over by Mrs. J. J. Andoe; Public Welfare, by Mrs. E. A. Hocutt; American Home, by Mrs. J. N. Britt; and Junior membership, which luncheon will be held at the Woman's Club with Mrs. D. F. Giles presiding.

Parliamentary law classes will be held each morning at 9 o'clock preceding the business sessions. This service has been provided as a courtesy to the delegates and visitors. An art exhibit which is always an interesting feature of the convention has been planned by Mrs. Andoe, chairman of art, who has plans for an extensive exhibit of the works of North Carolina artists, including paintings, sculpture, pottery, china and industrial arts.

Among the out-of-town visitors and speakers will be Mrs. Edna G. Fuller of Orlando, Florida. A former member of the Florida legislature, Mrs. Fuller is recognized as one of the South's most brilliant women and an eloquent and convincing speaker. Other prominent speakers will appear on the programs of the breakfast and luncheon conferences. Raleigh musicians will contribute many fine numbers to the daily programs.

A number of delightful social events have been planned. One of these is the tea and garden party to be given as a courtesy of State College on the college campus. Another will be a drive over the city and out to Carolina Pines, Raleigh's newest country club development. The Raleigh Junior Club will entertain all visiting junior club members at a tea at the Woman's Club Friday afternoon.

The crowning event of the convention will be the Federation banquet on Friday evening. The Juniors of the State will have charge of the program which will consist of a variety of entertaining features. The Raleigh juniors will give a play and provide several musical numbers. A noted singer of North Carolina and New York has been invited to be the honored guest and special attraction for this occasion.

More than usual interest is felt in the approaching convention on account of its being election year. The new officers to be elected at this time are the president, second and third vice presidents, corresponding secretary and General Federation director.

Raleigh Sunday *News and Observer,* p. 15 (Society, p. 1)

16 APRIL 1933

MUSIC WEEK AND CHILD HEALTH DAY TO BE HELD

By Mrs. J. Henry Highsmith

Two national observances in which North Carolina club women will have a part are scheduled for May. These are National Child Health Day on May first, and National Music Week, May 7–14. Program suggestions for the latter have been prepared by Miss Hattie Parrott of Raleigh, chairman, and are to be had by writing to her.

The theme for music week this year, says Miss Parrott, is: "Give More Time and Thought to Music." The purpose is the awakening of the whole community to the importance of music as a factor in its life. This can be largely accompanied, suggests Miss Parrott, by the concentration of many musical events in a multitude of places into a single week. The variety as well as the multiplicity of the programs, all aimed at raising the standard of musical appreciation and achievement, will reach and demonstrate to the people that there is music which appeals to and helps the individual.

By way of organizing and making plans for observing music week, Miss Parrott makes these suggestions: "The initiative may be taken by one or more individuals or by a club interested in the musical and general cultural development of the community. Larger groups such as musical clubs, women's clubs, church choirs, schools, music teachers, professional musicians, music dealers and others should be called together. A chairman and secretary should be appointed, also several special committees. Emphasis should be made that the main function of the general committee is that of securing the cooperation of the entire community in the participation either as performers or listeners. On the number of people reached, the depth of impression made, and the chances of establishing permanent activities depends the success of the undertaking."

Plans for observing May first as National Child Health Day are being made by Mrs. D. J. Thurston of Clayton, chairman of the division of Child Welfare in the Federation, and Mrs. B. A. Hocutt of Clayton, chairman of the department of Public Welfare. They are calling on women's clubs and parent-teacher associations to cooperate with the schools in putting on suitable child health programs on this day. Through their superintendents, school teachers of the State have been asked to make the accomplishment of some definite local health need the object of the meeting. Mrs. Thurston suggests that such timely subjects as prevention of pellagrafi, tuberculosis and typhoid fever be given serious consideration, as these diseases are much on the increase at this time. She urges that malnutrition with its resultant effect of nervousness, retardation and lowered resistance to diseases be carefully studied, likewise the serious handicaps that children suffer from defective teeth and eyes. Material on the health of the child may be had from the State Board of Health at Raleigh, advises Mrs. Thurston.

A report of the Music Promotion Fund of the Federation at work in the schools shows that ten schools with an enrollment of 2,512 pupils benefitted from the phonograph and records furnished them this year through this fund. The number of pupils taking a regular music appreciation course using the phonograph and records was 1,876. The schools supplied with these musical helps were Bushnell, Highlands, Minneapolis, Davidson River, Prospect Hill, Wise, Winfall, Needham's Grove, Benhaven and Nathan's Creek. Mrs. Arthur S. Kennickle of Winston-Salem, is chairman of this fund. Miss Hattie Parrott of the State Department of Education supervises the work of it in the schools. In making her report to Mrs. Kennickle, Miss Parrott says: "In this work there is evidence of a permanent interest in good music in the schools and the appreciation of the best type of music is more apparent."

New clubs continue to come into the Federation. The latest is the Hubbard Fulton Page Book Club of Coats with 14 members. Mrs. W. E. Nichols is president of this enterprising new club and Mrs. C. J. Turlington is secretary-treasurer. Mrs. P. R. Rankin of Mount Gilead writes that she has another member to add to her large family. This is the Book Club of Biscoe with Mrs. W. C. Kanoy as president.

The Garner Woman's Club has recently complected a highway beautification project that bespeaks the energy and public spiritedness of its members. Under the leadership of Mrs. R. B. Hutchinson, 350 mimosa and crape myrtle trees have been planted on both sides of the highway, beginning at the western boundary line of Garner and extending two miles toward Raleigh.

Raleigh Sunday *News and Observer,* p. 13 (Society, p. 1)

23 APRIL 1933

FEDERATION CONVENTION PROGRAM FULL AND VARIED

Many of State's Best Thinkers and Speakers Will Appear On Conference Programs; Mrs. Ehringhaus To Honor Club Women With Tea at Executive Mansion; Other Social Affairs Planned

By Mrs. J. Henry Highsmith

With the final shaping of the three-day program of the annual convention of the State Federation of Women's Clubs, which meets in Raleigh Wednesday,

Thursday and Friday, May 3, 4 and 5, Mrs. J. M. Hobgood, president, expresses herself as being well pleased with the outlook and says she anticipates one of the largest and best conventions ever held in the State. The program, she says, is well balanced, comprised as it is of a variety of interests that will appeal to every club woman regardless of her tastes. The speakers are not to be surpassed, thinks Mrs. Hobgood, and their topics are timely and forward looking.

The General Federation of Women's Clubs will be represented by Mrs. Josephine J. Doggett, of Washington, director of General Headquarters. Mrs. Doggett will bring a message much in demand at this time on "Building Club Programs." Another speaker to bring a timely and important message is Albert Coates of Chapel Hill. He will outline the part that club women will be expected to play in carrying out the plans of the Institute of Government.

The speakers chosen for the breakfast and luncheon conference are among the best in the State, each being an expert in his subject. Dr. Frederick Koch, of the University of North Carolina, will be the principal speaker at the luncheon conference on Literature on Thursday at 1 o'clock in the new dining room of the Sir Walter Hotel. His subject will be "Folk Playmaking in North Carolina." Mrs. Eugene Reilley, chairman of Biblical Literature in the Federation, and Miss Jenny Coltrane, chairman of Radio, will be additional speakers. Mrs. B. F. Long, chairman of the Department of Literature will preside.

Dr. J. Henry Highsmith, director of Instructional Service of the State Department of Education, will be one of the speakers at the luncheon conference on Education to be held in the Manteo room of the Sir Walter Hotel on Thursday of convention week. Another speaker will be Mrs. Eva Edgerton Penland, chairman of Adult Illiteracy. Mrs. M. M. Stewart, chairman of Better English Week; Miss Margaret Elbert, chairman of Library Extension, and Mrs. J. G. Fearing, chairman of School Information, will report on their work.

At the breakfast conference on Gardens Friday morning, Mrs. Z. P. Metcalf and Miss Elizabeth Lawrence will be the speakers. At the conference on Music at the same hour, Miss Hattie Parrott and Mrs. J. S. Correll will be the speakers. Miss Isabel Busbee will preside over the conference on Gardens and Miss Jesse Moye over the conference on Music.

At the Art luncheon on Friday Ernest Seeman, consultant in personality at Duke University, will be the speaker. Mrs. J. J. Andoe will preside. At the Public Welfare luncheon at the same hour, Dr. Harold D. Meyer, of the University of North Carolina, will speak on the subject "Leisure and the Unemployed." Mrs. D. J. Thurston will speak on "The Welfare of the Child." Mrs. B. A. Hocutt will preside. Dr. Ernest Grove, of Chapel Hill, will be the principal speaker at the luncheon conference of the American Home on

Friday. His subject will be "Conserving the American Family." Mrs. J. N. Britt, chairman, will preside.

Mrs. Edward M. Land, chairman of the Junior Department of the General Federation, and J. J. Phoenix, superintendent of the Children's Home in Greensboro will address the Juniors at their luncheon on Friday at the Woman's Club. Mrs. D. F. Giles will preside.

Among the recreational and social features planned for the visiting club women will be a tea at the Governor's Mansion by courtesy of Mrs. J. C. B. Ehringhaus at 4 o'clock on Thursday afternoon. On Friday afternoon at 5 o'clock there will be a garden party at the home of Dr. and Mrs. E. C. Brooks, by courtesy of the State College Woman's Club. At 4 o'clock the same afternoon there will be a drive over the city and a tea at Carolina Pines Country Club by courtesy of the Raleigh Junior Club and the Carolina Pines Club. The climax of the social features as well as of the convention as a whole will be the Federation banquet on Friday evening. Music, creative dances and an original skit will be the entertaining features.

Raleigh Sunday *News and Observer*, p. 15 (Society, p. 1)

30 APRIL 1933

PROGRAM HIGHLIGHTS FOR FEDERATION CONVENTION

Dr. Douglas Freeman of Richmond, Virginia, To Be Chief Speaker at Thirty-First Annual Convention of State Federation of Women's Clubs; Governor Ehringhaus to Present Certificate of Attainment

By Mrs. J. Henry Highsmith

Dr. Douglas, Freeman, of Richmond, Va., scholar, orator and editor of the Richmond News-Leader, will be the chief speaker at the 31st annual convention of the State Federation of Women's Clubs to be held in Raleigh, Wednesday, Thursday and Friday. Dr. Freeman will address the convention Thursday evening in the Sir Walter ballroom when the program will deal with the fine arts—music, literature and art. He will be introduced by Mrs. E. L. McKee, of Sylva, North Carolina's first woman Senator.

The opening session of the convention Wednesday evening will be featured by the address of the president, Mrs. J. M. Hobgood, the address of welcome by Mrs. Palmer Jerman, the response by Mrs. R. H. Latham, the presentation of the Federation mascot, little Miss Mary Louis Jackson Cooper, and special music by the Meredith College Trio and the St. Cecilia Choral Club. Immediately following the exercises a reception will be held in the hotel dining room as a courtesy to all the club women from the Raleigh Woman's Club and the Sir Walter Hotel.

A feature of special interest at the Thursday morning session will be the presentation of more than 400 certificates of attainment to the night school pupils of the State who have been taught to read and write this year through the interest and assistance of club women. Governor J. C. B. Ehringhaus will deliver the certificates.

A courtesy which club women appreciate and take advantage of is the course of instruction in parliamentary law given free each morning at 9 o'clock in the assembly room. Miss Margaret L. Gibson, of Asheville, will this year be the instructor. The first session of the Club Institute of which Mrs. Eugene Reilley, of Charlotte, is chairman will be held Wednesday at 2:30 o'clock in the assembly room and will be given over to a conference on the theme: "Write It Right." Mrs. L. E. Covington, of Raleigh, teacher of journalism, will conduct the conference. All club women are invited to attend.

Mrs. Josephine Doggett, of Washington, D. C., director of research and club service of the General Federation, will address the Federation Friday morning on the subject "Program Building." Following her address will be the election of delegates to the general council meeting in Richmond May 22–26. During the same session will be the election of officers of the State Federation—a president, second and third vice-presidents, corresponding secretary and State director of the General Federation. The following new department chairmen are to be elected by the board of directors at the close of the convention Friday evening: Art, Literature, Education, American Home, Gardens, Civics, Music and Junior Membership.

Fifteen charming young women have been appointed to serve as pages. Mrs. Hobgood will have as her personal pages her nieces, Misses Rosalie and Rebekah Hassell of Charlotte, Miss Lula Belle Highsmith and Mrs. Cary Petty Cooper of Raleigh, Miss Frances Joyner of Farmville, and Miss Mary Margaret Giles of Peace Junior College. The Junior Woman's Club of Raleigh will furnish the following pages: Miss Helen Leigh Bailey, chief; Misses Nancy Rand, Arabella Cox, Davetta Levine and Mesdames Zach Bacon, Margaret York, Wilson; C. W. Norman, Sidney Smith and Sam Ruark.

The art exhibit held each year in connection with the convention promises to be unusually interesting. Already many entries have been made and ample space on the lower floor of the hotel, Davie entrance, has been procured, Mrs. J. J. Andoe, State chairman, anticipates one of the largest exhibits of arts and crafts ever displayed at convention. All artists of the different branches are invited to send specimens of their work. Prizes in art, poetry, short-story writing, plays; and in instrumental and vocal music compositions will be awarded Thursday evening following the address of Dr. Douglas Freeman. Special music will be a delightful part of the fine-arts program.

Raleigh Sunday *News and Observer,* p. 17 (Society, p. 1)

7 MAY 1933

CLUB WOMEN SEEK MATERNITY SAFETY FOR U. S. MOTHERS

"Make Motherhood Safe for Mothers" is New Slogan; Music Week Starts Today

By Mrs. J. Henry Highsmith

Mother's Day in North Carolina will have a new significance this year, as will be the case in many other states of the union. Whereas sentiment alone has characterized the observance of Mother's Day in past years, public opinion demands today that something more tangible be done to show appreciation of mother's love and mother's sacrifice, that sentiment be turned into action to save mothers.

"Make Motherhood Safe for Mothers" is the new slogan for Mother's Day, May 14. Club women in North Carolina and throughout the country have been called on to observe the day in its new meaning. Mrs. Grace Morrison Poole, president of the General Federation of Women's Clubs, and Julia K. Jaffrey, chairman of the department of public welfare of the Federation, have joined in a public statement calling for the co-operation of the women's clubs of the country in crystalizing public opinion and taking action on the vital need of improving maternity care. They say that too long has sentiment alone been the characteristic of Mother's Day and not until the public knows that at least half of the 16,000 annual deaths in maternity are preventable and ought to be prevented, will there be much hope of reducing America's maternity death rate to a point where it will stand comparison with other leading nations.

The call as issued came straight home to North Carolinians. Addressing the North Carolina Public Health Association in Raleigh a few weeks ago, Dr. John H. Hamilton, head of the bureau of vital statistics of the State Board of Health, said that 600 North Carolina mothers lost their lives in childbirth last year. This was a death rate, he said, of 8.5 per 1,000 live births or 30 per cent higher than for the nation as a whole. The maternity death rate in England is 4.2, in Sweden 3, and in Denmark, 2.5, he said, which shows Mother's Day is annually and almost religiously observed.

And yet an effort to save the state from its unenviable record of having so high a death rate of mothers met with instant defeat from the House of Representatives this spring when it voted down the bill to give control of 4,500 midwives to the State Board of Health. The bill sought only the regulation and education of midwives in better sanitary methods and nothing in condemnation.

While the Federation convention has come and gone, annual reports have been made and new officers chosen, the work of the Federation goes on unhampered by any of these changes. The picture memory contest for the public schools of the state will be held in Raleigh, Saturday, May 13, at the Hugh Morson High School. Miss Juanita McDougald of the state Department of Education, who is in charge of the contest, announces that registration begins at 10 o'clock, the contest at 11 o'clock, luncheon at the woman's club at 1 o'clock, a drive over the city at 2 o'clock and a party at the Executive Mansion by Mrs. J. C. B. Ehringhaus at 3.

More than a hundred children are expected to participate in the contest. A first prize of $15 is offered the representative of the school making the highest number of points. Other prizes include trips to Washington, framed copies of prints of famous pictures, copper etchings, pottery, and photographs of North Carolina beauty spots. Misses Mildred English and Georgia Kirkpatrick will conduct the contest and Mrs. R. L. McMillan and Mrs. J. C. Cox will be hostesses at lunch. Mrs. A. T. Allen will make the awards.

This week is being observed through the state and nation as national music week. The tenth annual observance of this week begins today and has for its purpose the awakening of the community to the importance of music as a factor in its life. Reaching the people with the message of music and aiming to elevate musical standards are the chief characteristics of music week programs. Miss Hattie Parrott of Raleigh is chairman of Music Week of the Federation and will be glad to furnish program suggestions to the club for the observance of this week.

Charlotte Sunday Observer, p. 17 (section 2, p. 3)

14 MAY 1933

THE NEW PERSONNEL OF FEDERATION NEXT YEAR

By Mrs. J. Henry Highsmith

Satisfied that definite progress in all phases of Federation work marked the recent convention of the the State Federation of Women's Clubs, the several hundred members attending the convention in Raleigh returned home inspired to undertake even greater things for another year.

Practically a new personnel will command the Federation's activities for the next two years. With Mrs. R. H. Latham of Winston-Salem as president and with her able and efficient corps of workers, including the members of her official family, a biennium of progress and constructive achievement is anticipated.

With her many years experience as an active member and officer of the Federation, more recently its treasurer and first vice-president, Mrs. Latham comes to the presidency not only well equipped for the work of the office but also with the love and admiration of the members of her organization. Service, efficiency and loyalty to Federation principles and interests characterize the members of the new board.

Members of the new official family are: Mrs. R. H. Latham, president; Mrs. J. N. Britt of Lumberton first vice-president; Mrs. Howard G. Etheridge of Asheville, second vice-president; Mrs. J. Wilbur Bunn of Raleigh, third vice-president; Mrs. Guy Masten of Winston-Salem, corresponding secretary; Mrs. J. M. Hobgood of Farmville, General Federation director.

Often referred to as the backbone of the Federation are the sixteen district presidents. Five of the sixteen had their elections of last fall confirmed at the convention meeting. These were Mrs. R. N. Barber of Waynesville, president of the first district; Mrs. Johnstone of Gastonia, president of the fourth district; Mrs. Hector Clark of Clarkton, president of the tenth district; Mrs. R. R. Cusick of Salemburg, president of the eleventh district and Mrs. J. M. O'Neal of Selma, president of the thirteenth district.

All work of the Federation is grouped under its ten departments and several standing committees. Heading each is a woman of training and experience. Six of the ten department chairmen newly elected were: Mrs. Andrew Jamieson of Oxford, chairman of Art; Mrs. J. J. Purdy of Oriental, chairman of American Home; Mrs. George Marshall of Mount Airy, Education; Mrs. John D. Robinson of Wallace, Gardens; Mrs. R. W. Green of Raleigh, Literature; Mrs. R. D. V. Jones of New Bern, Civics; and Mrs. D. F. Giles of Marion, Juniors. The chairman of Music has not yet been named. Mrs. E. L. McKee of Sylva will remain for another year as chairman of Citizenship and Mrs. B. A. Hocutt of Clayton will remain chairman of Public Welfare.

New Committee heads elected were Miss Gertrude Weil of Goldsboro, chairman of Finance; Mrs. C. G. Doak of Raleigh, chairman of International Relations; Mrs. E. M. Land of Statesville, chairman of Legislation. Mrs. W. J. Brogden of Durham will remain as chairman of the Sallie Southall Cotton Loan Fund and Miss Nellie Roberson of Chapel Hill, chairman of University Extension Service. The Junior Membership committee was changed to that of a department, and that of Safety to a division under the American Home department.

The 1934 annual convention will be held in Asheville at the George Vanderbilt Hotel. The 1933 fall council meeting will be held in New Bern Tuesday and Wednesday of the first week in October.

Mrs. R. L. Grumman, Chapel Hill, recording secretary of the Federation, is asking all club women who will have reports or other information for the 1933–34 Year Book to have this material to her by June 1. All new club officers or changes in club presidents made since the Federation should be sent to her immediately. Mrs. Grumman is asking the cooperation of all club women to make the new year book one of useful information and service with as few errors as possible.

Raleigh Sunday *News and Observer,* p. 15 (Society, p. 1)

21 May 1933

State Club Women Will Attend Council Meeting

**General Federation Council Meeting Opens In
Richmond Tomorrow**

By Mrs. J. Henry Highsmith

North Carolina club women will this week have their interest centered on the council meeting of the General Federation which meets in Richmond, Virginia, and which many are planning to attend during the four day sessions from Monday, May 22 through Thursday, May 25, with the following Friday as play day. An unusually large number of Carolina club women is expected to attend, especially in view of the fact that not in a long time will another meeting of the General Federation likely come so near. Attending by virtue of the office of chairmanship each holds in the general body will be Mrs. R. H. Latham, State president; Mrs. J. M. Hobgood, State director; Mrs. Palmer Jerman, trustee; Mrs. Edward M. Land, chairman of the department of juniors; Mrs. Thos. O'Berry, regional chairman of public welfare; Mrs. Park Mathews, divisional chairman of pre-school education, and Mrs. J. Henry Highsmith, division chairman of editorials of State federation magazines.

Representing the State Federation will be the seven delegates elected at the recent State convention in Raleigh. These are: Mrs. E. L. McKee of Sylva; Mrs. George E. Marshall of Mount Airy; Mrs. Thomas O'Berry of Goldsboro; Mrs. Eugene Davis of Statesville; Mrs. J. D. McCall of Charlotte; Mrs. Howard G. Etheridge of Asheville, and Miss Annie Perkins of Farmville.

Club women who do not attend the council meeting are asked to tune in on Richmond or New York, Wednesday morning, May 24 from 11:30 to 12:30, Eastern Standard Time, to hear the address of Mrs. Grace Morrison Poole whose subject will be "March of the General Federation." Mrs. Poole's address will be broadcast through the courtesy of the National Broadcasting Company which has arranged a nationwide hookup for this program. Following the address, each of the chairmen of the nine major departments will give highlights from her program. All club women are urged to remember the hour and listen in.

Among the many interesting speakers who will address the council meeting will be Miss Frances Perkins of Washington, Secretary of Labor; Mrs. Anna M. C. Tillinghast, Commissioner of Immigration for New England at the port of Boston and Angela Morgan, poet, author and lecturer. Mr. William Hard, internationally known newspaper and magazine writer and radio broadcaster, will speak on "The World Marches On."

"These United States," the keynote of the present administration and "Thrift," the thought around which the program of the meeting has been built, will be combined in the basic trends of the deliberations. Many workable and forward looking plans for meeting present day problems are expected to come out of the conferences and deliberations of these four days. Breakfasts, luncheons and dinners will be utilized for conferences and programs as well as for good fellowship.

Many social and recreational features have been planned. Friday has been designated as "Play Day," for which a special trip has been planned for everyone to go to Williamsburg, Yorktown and Jamestown. All delegates on this trip will be the guests of the Virginia Federation. Lunch will be served on the Palace Green in Williamsburg. On Tuesday afternoon following the session, a sight-seeing trip around Richmond will be made which will include historic shrines and the gardens of Mrs. Douglas Vanderhoof, Mrs. E. M. Crutchfield and Mrs. John Hays. On Thursday afternoon, Mrs. Alexander Weddell will open her home to visiting club women.

All sessions of the meeting will be held at the Mosque. The galleries of the Mosque will be open to the public for the four evening meetings. John Marshall Hotel will be official headquarters. The opening session will be held Monday night and is to be known as Virginia's Night. Governor John Garland Pollard, Mayor J. Fulmer Bright, Dr. Douglas Freeman and Mrs. L. J. Giles, president of the Virginia Federation, will make brief addresses. Governor Pollard will entertain members of the board of directors at tea at the Executive Mansion, Wednesday afternoon. The Colonial Dames of Richmond will keep open house for visiting Colonial Dames on Wednesday afternoon also.

Raleigh Sunday *News and Observer*, p. 22 (Society, p. 8)

10 SEPTEMBER 1933

AUSPICIOUS BEGINNING FOR STATE FEDERATION

President Announces Definite Constructive Program Of Club Year; New Program Leaflets and Federation Year Books Issues; Woman's Club Ready for Work Under Capable Group Of Officers

By Mrs. J. Henry Highsmith

The club year of 1933–34 of the State Federation of Women's Clubs is opening under auspicious circumstances. The governing body, though for the most part new in office, is composed of strong, capable women, each trained to service and acquainted with Federation ideals and standards. Probably at no time has it been felt that the affairs of the Federation were in better hands

The president, Mrs. R. H. Latham of Winston-Salem, realizing that the business of being a club woman was never so serious or important as it is today, has announced a program that challenges the cooperation and support of the club women through out the state. Included in her program is the wholehearted support of the National Recovery Administration, cooperation with agencies aimed at bettering the living conditions of people, and above all holding fast the lines that would conserve and increase cultural and character building processes. "To see that human welfare transcends every other agency in this readjusting process" is the first duty pointed out to club women by their president, Mrs. Latham.

Another factor presaging a busy and worthwhile club year is the high standard of club study that has been set in the series of program leaflets prepared and issued by the nine department chairmen in cooperation with Mrs. J. Wilbur Bunn of Raleigh, director of Departments. Copies of the program leaflets which contain suggestions and sources of material for club study sufficient for a year have been sent to local presidents to be used in supplementing their study programs.

Subjects covered under the American Home department, of which Mrs. J. J. Purdy of Oriental is chairman, are home-making, family relationships, child development, home education, safety, and rural cooperation. Under the department of literature with Mrs. R. W. Green of Raleigh, chairman, are program suggestions on life and literature of the South including programs on North Carolina literature; also creative writing, Biblical literature and radio service. Under the Garden department with Mrs. John D. Robinson chairman are practical gardening suggestions for every month in the year, also planting suggestions for highways.

Adult illiteracy, library extension, better English and school information are treated under the department of Education of which Mrs. George E. Marshall is chairman. Civics under the chairmanship of Mrs. R. D. V. Jones of New Bern contains practical program suggestions for community service and conservation. Art under Mrs. Andrew Jamieson of Oxford contains suggestions for the art appreciation contest, community fine arts festival, contest of North Carolina women's club artists, penny art fund and children's creative interests. Under the department of Music with Mrs. Charles G. Gulley of Cullowhee chairman are programs of American folk music, sacred music, favorite opera selections, famous marches, love ballads and waltzes, modern music and musicians and public school music. Under public welfare, Mrs. B. A. Hocutt, chairman, are programs on health, child welfare, Negro welfare, Indian welfare, institutional relations and on community gardening and club canning.

For the Juniors under the chairmanship of Mrs. D. F. Giles, there are suggestions for organizing new clubs, club rating sheet and various club programs, also suggested club activities.

The Federation year book which is the club worker's hand book and guide has been sent to all state officers, department and division chairmen, to heads of committees and to all club presidents. Editing and issuing the year book has been the summertime work of Mrs. R. M. Grumman of Chapel Hill, recording secretary of the Federation.

Mrs. J. Henry Highsmith of Raleigh, executive secretary and press chairman of the Federation, has returned from Europe where she spent ten weeks this summer visiting ten countries including England. She has resumed her duties at Federation Headquarters on the mezzanine floor of the Sir Walter Hotel and is again ready to serve the club women of the State.

Raleigh Sunday *News and Observer*, p. 9 (Society, p. 1)
Charlotte Sunday Observer, p. 16 (section 2, p. 4)

17 SEPTEMBER 1933

FALL COUNCIL MEET OF WOMEN'S CLUBS TO BE HELD AT NEW BERN OCTOBER 3–4

Dr. Malcolm McDermott of Duke University Chief Speaker Listed on Interesting Two-Day Program

By Mrs. J. Henry Highsmith

The fall council meeting of the State Federation of Women's Clubs will be held in New Bern October 3 and 4, with the Gaston Hotel as headquarters and the Woman's Club of New Bern as hostess. An interesting two-day program of business and pleasure has been prepared by Mrs. W. E. Whitehurst, president, who is in charge of local arrangements. Dr. Malcolm McDermott of Duke University will be the principal speaker,

Club women of the State will travel to New Bern with peculiar pleasure and interest to attend this council meeting of the Federation since it was in this historic town twenty years ago that many of the highlights of the Federation's history were enacted. The organization at that time was ten years old and was presided over by Mrs. R. R. Cotten.

Some of the important happenings that took place at the convention in New Bern in May 1913, to mention only a few, were: The Federation received its charter, thereby becoming legally incorporated; adopted its seal and motto—"The Union of All for the Good of All"; formed a board of trustees to handle its endowment fund which by this time had been increased to a goodly sum; celebrated the final passage of the bill that permitted women to serve the school boards of the state—its first legislative experience and victory; and last but not least established the Sallie Southall Cotten Loan Fund, the story of which is familiar to all North Carolina club women; Mrs. Cotten was also made honorary president of the Federation at this convention.

Another event that marked this convention was the memorable session on the theme, "The Legal Status of Women in North Carolina." Judge Walter

Clark, chief justice of the Supreme Court of North Carolina, a staunch friend of women and a defender of their rights, was the speaker. According to Mrs. Cotten, who tells the story in her interesting History of the North Carolina Federation of Women's Clubs, the stage was appropriately set, the hall packed with eager listeners and a tenseness of excitement possessed all who were in charge. On the platform with Judge Clark were Mrs. Cotten, Miss Edith Royster, Mrs. M. L. Stover, Mrs. Sol Weil and Miss May Hendren. The exercises opened with a rendition of the "Lost Chord," "the lost chord supposedly being the woman to whom so many of the fields of activity were legally closed."

Miss Royster introduced Judge Clark who gave an elaborate and illuminating address on the status of women, past, present and future. He pictured the past when women were chattels, dwelt on the present with woman's mental and social development and prophesied the future when women would be free and equal citizens of this commonwealth. In this speech and the lively discussion that followed were sown the seed that blossomed in the fight for woman's suffrage and ripened later in woman's enfranchisement. In conclusion the Angels Chorus was sung "supposedly," says Mrs. Cotten, "to represent the joy of angels when justice becomes supreme."

Mrs. Howard G. Etheridge of Asheville, chairman of districts, reports the federation of four new clubs. One is the Junior Woman's Civic Club of Asheville in the second district of which Mrs. George C. Osborne is acting president. The other three were federated by Mrs. P. R. Rankin, president of the fifth district. They are the Thursday Afternoon Club of Polkton with Mrs. S. R. Bolch, president, the Wise and Otherwise Club of Polkton with Miss Edna M. Flake, president, and the Woman's Club of Marshville, with Mrs. M. P. Blair, president. Miss Dorothy Jordan is president of the Junior Woman's Civic Club of Asheville.

Mrs. R. H. Latham, president, Mrs. Wilbur Bunn, Mrs. John D. Robinson and Mrs. J. Henry Highsmith attended the Get-Together Dinner of the Clayton's Woman's Club Wednesday evening, on which occasion Mrs. Latham was honor guest and speaker. Mrs. Charles G. Gulley of Cullowhee, chairman of music in the Federation, was present and sang two numbers. Mrs. Robinson, chairman of Gardens, spoke on "Making a Spring Garden."

Among the recent visitors to headquarters were Mrs. R. H. Latham, Mrs. B. A. Hocutt, Mrs. Jas. G. Fearing, Mrs. P. R. Rankin, Mrs. John B. Robinson, Mrs. Harvie Bonie, and Mr. Albert Coates.

Note: the council meeting was moved to Raleigh; see next article.

Charlotte Sunday Observer, p. 15 (section 2, p. 3)

24 SEPTEMBER 1933

FEDERATION COUNCIL MEET WILL BE HELD IN RALEIGH

By Mrs. J. Henry Highsmith

On account of the devastating storm which visited New Bern and Eastern North Carolina recently, completely wrecking the club building of the New Bern Woman's Club, the fall council meeting of the Federation will not be held in New Bern as previously announced, but instead will be held in Raleigh on Monday night and Tuesday, October 2 and 3, at the Sir Walter Hotel and the Woman's Club. This decision was reached by Mrs. R. H. Latham, president of the Federation, after communicating with Mrs. R. E. Whitehurst, president of the New Bern club, and learning the seriousness of the local situation. Only the business sessions of the council will be held in Raleigh and these will be confined as far as possible to one day, says Mrs. Latham.

According to the official council call issued Thursday, Mrs. Latham is calling a meeting of the board of trustees at Federation Headquarters at 8 o'clock on Monday evening, and immediately following a meeting of the finance committee at the same place.

The program for Tuesday will be held at the Woman's Club beginning at 10 o'clock with a meeting of the executive board. At 11 o'clock there will be two conferences, one for district presidents and one for department chairmen. Mrs. Howard G. Etheridge will preside over the district presidents and Mrs. Wilbur J. Bunn will preside over the department chairmen. Luncheon will be served at the club at 1 o'clock. At 2:30 the main business session will be held in the club auditorium.

October is the month of district meetings in the Federation. Following the council meeting in Raleigh Mrs. R. H. Latham and Mrs. Howard Etheridge will begin their itinerary of 16 district meetings which will take them as far west as Waynesville and as far east as Beaufort. They begin with Beaufort on Thursday, October 5. The following schedule of district meetings will be carried out:

Beaufort, Thursday, October 5, District No. 12.

Ayden, Friday, October 6, District No. 15.

Edenton, nearby school, Saturday, October 7, District No. 16.

Scotland Neck, Monday, October 9, District No. 14.

Smithfield, Tuesday, October 10, District No. 13.

Kenansville, Wednesday, October 11, District No. 11.

Wananish, Thursday, October 12, District No. 10.

Raeford, Friday, October 13, District No. 9.

Durham, Saturday, October 14, District No. 8.

Kernersville, Monday, October 23, District No. 6.
Madison, Tuesday, October 24, District No. 7.
Taylorsville, Wednesday, October 25, District No. 3.
Waxhaw, Thursday, October 26, District No. 5.
Kings Mountain, Friday, October 27, District No. 4.
Black Mountain, Saturday, October 28, District No. 2.
Waynesville, Monday, October 30, District No. 1.

Keen enthusiasm, says Mrs. Latham, is felt over the approaching visits that she and Mrs. Etheridge are to make to the districts. "I am looking forward with pleasure," she says, "to having this opportunity of knowing the club women of the State in their own homes and in their own communities. According to their letters everything is in readiness for us and fine meetings are anticipated."

Raleigh Sunday *News and Observer,* p. 9 (Society, p. 1)

1 OCTOBER 1933

CLUB WOMEN MUST WORK HARD TO KEEP WORLD PEACE, GENERAL PRESIDENT SAYS

Mrs. Grace Morrison Poole, Back From Trip Abroad, Says War Clouds Threatening In Europe

By Mrs. J. Henry Highsmith

Club women of North Carolina will be especially interested in the message of Mrs. Grace Morrison Poole, president of the General Federation of Women's Clubs, on returning recently from Europe, where she conducted the Federation's first World Friendship tour this summer.

"Club women," she says, "in every country of the world must work together for the preservation of peace, which is being violently threatened today by national politicians."

Mrs. Poole's party was composed of 45 club women, drawn from 14 states and the Island of Cuba. They were received at the American Embassies of the countries they visited and by women's clubs at London, Paris, Berlin, Dusseldorf, Vienna, Prague and Zurich.

"Everywhere the war clouds were apparent," Mrs. Poole stated. "Germany's determination to get back her place in the sun is so strong that if it can't be obtained one way, it will be another. The enthusiasm of the German youth for the Nazi movement is intensely alarming. France has—to use a slang term—the 'jitters' over Germany's undeclared intentions.

"Europe is jealous of the United States. The peoples of other countries may be friendly enough to us. But it is the politicians, the national leaders, who dislike our advantageous and isolated position and who feel that it is motivated by commercial selfishness. It seems almost impossible for them any longer to conceive of a nation as being unselfish, disinterested and humanitarian.

"Treaties and disarmament pacts lacking the co-operation of the United States will never prevent war among the countries of Europe. They are particularly ineffective without definite assurance from our government that she will consult with them in the event of war.

"Our absorption in our own economic problems must not blind us to the existence of an explosive super-nationalism that is taking possession of Europe, or to the difficulties of combating it. Club women throughout the world have a weapon in their hand against war. It is to arouse the mothers of the race to the necessity for immediate, concerted action in order to keep their sons and daughters from perishing in the most abominable slaughter the world has yet seen. The enlightened women of every nation dread another war. Let them, then, throw their united force against it. The government heads themselves admit that women can do more toward preventing other wars than any treaty or disarmament pact."

A major project of the State Federation for the club year 1933–34 is to be the building and carrying out of better club programs, the principle being that the better the program the club works by, the better the entries and results obtained. The purpose of the project which will be conducted in the form of a contest is to stimulate interest and initiative in making better club programs and in seeing that they are carried out. To this end the Federation is offering $30 in prizes. All federated clubs are eligible to enter the contest under one or two classifications: 1. Study clubs, book clubs, literature clubs, history clubs, music clubs, etc. 2. Departmental clubs—those having as many as three departments.

For the best program or year book in each of the two classes, a prize of $10 will be given. For the second best program or year book in each class a prize of $5 will be given. All year books entering the contest should be sent to Mrs. J. Henry Highsmith, Sir Walter Hotel, Raleigh, N. C., not later than January 1, 1934. Competent judges will pass on the merits of the programs submitted and announcements of the awards will be made.

Helps and suggestions for making programs may be obtained from the department chairman of the Federation, from the State Library Commission, Raleigh, from the department chairman of the General Federation, and from Mrs. Josephine Doggett, 1734 N. Street N. W., Washington, D. C. Material from local libraries should be used as much as possible.

> *Note:* Mrs. Poole's first World Friendship Tour was not related to Mrs. Highsmith's ten-week European journey of the same period.

Charlotte Sunday Observer, p. 17 (section 2, p. 5)

15 October 1933

Maternal Mortality To Be Studied By Women

By Mrs. J. Henry Highsmith

Club women of the State have had their attention called to two serious health problems existing in North Carolina today by two timely articles appearing in the October issue of the bulletin of the State Federation of Women's Clubs, which issue is just from the press. One article is on "Maternal Mortality in North Carolina" by Drs. John H. Hamilton and D. F. Milam of the State Board of Health and the other is on "Cancer and Its Prevention" by Dr. Ivan Proctor, of Raleigh. Since thousands of North Carolina women, particularly mothers, come to their untimely deaths by cancer, and thousands more by conditions met with in connection with childbirth, both causes of death being to a large extent preventable, it was the thought and hope of the writers in giving these facts to challenge the attention of club women and enlist their co-operation in controlling these diseases.

As shown by Dr. Hamilton and Dr. Milam, the death rate of mothers in this State from diseases and conditions incident to maternity is more than twice as high as that for communities where rates are considered good. They say: "Our rates of approximately 8.5 per 1,000 live births are 30 per cent greater than those of the United States registration area, which are approximately 6.5, as compared with the rate of 5.6 for Canada; 4.2 for England; 3.0 for Sweden, and 2.5 for Denmark."

They say further: "A condition which kills more than 600 citizens of North Carolina each year is important. This importance is accentuated if the citizens are in those age groups for which the State has completed its investment for their education and training. The major portion of this group are just entering upon a life of usefulness and productivity. Further emphasis is added by the fact that these individuals are killed in the act of creating new life—the most valuable service which can be rendered to the State or nation. This briefly and inadequately is a statement of the maternal mortality problem in North Carolina."

According to Drs. Hamilton and Milam, the need for a better understanding of the state's maternal mortality problem is apparent, and complete reporting of birth and death certificates is essential. They urge a wide dissemination of facts concerning proper maternity care and the creating of a strong public opinion that will not tolerate such conditions to exist, and that will soon do something to decrease the hazard which women must now undergo to bring new life into the world.

In the case of cancer, 1,117 women died from this disease in North Carolina in 1932. This gives the state a death rate of 70 for cancer alone for women, while the state's death rate from all diseases for women is only 8.8.

Dr. Proctor estimates that cancer is probably the greatest enemy of the human race, killing more than war and crippling twice as many as it kills. He says that there is no foundation for the belief that cancer is contagious and but little proof that it is hereditary. But he insists that prevention is the keynote to the treatment of cancer. Eradication of conditions that precede cancer, he says, is relatively easy and safe, and these conditions should be detected at routine annual and semi-annual examinations. "Cancer always begins in some local disease which is more or less of long standing, whether it be a growth, ulcer, injury, chronic irritation or infection."

That Mrs. Charles R. Whitaker of Lenoir, chairman of health of the Federation, is urging club women to cooperate with the state and county agencies for the control of cancer and the high death rate of mothers is hopeful that some definite accomplishments toward this end may be made by the club women this year.

Mrs. A. D. Folger, president of the Sixth District, reports federation of Walnut Cove Woman's Club with 16 members and four active departments. The president is Mrs. Paul Fulton and the treasurer, Mrs. Leak Lovin.

Miss Jenn Coltrane of Concord represented North Carolina at the third Annual Women's Conference in New York City sponsored by the New York Herald Tribune Thursday and Friday of last week. She will probably bring the club women of the state a message from the conference over radio from Station WBT Charlotte, on October 19.

Raleigh Sunday *News and Observer,* p. 9 (Society, p. 1)

22 OCTOBER 1933

CLUB WOMEN PLAN WORK FOR UNEMPLOYED TEACHERS

By Mrs. J. Henry Highsmith

Teaching adult illiterates has been a major interest of the club women of the state for many years. Through their efforts several hundred each year have had their lives opened up to blessings and pleasures they have never known before. They have been given "their chance" at last though to many of them it comes late in life and is shorn of its best possibilities.

In instructions recently issued to county and city superintendents of schools concerning the policies governing work-relief for needy, unemployed school teachers, Dr. J. Henry Highsmith, director of Adult Education for the State Department of Public Instruction, states: "Needy unemployed persons competent to teach adults to read and write English may be employed for this purpose. This refers to teaching those who are usually termed illiterates."

While Dr. Highsmith regrets that the adult illiterate work in the state is not to benefit greatly through the work-relief program that has been set up for needy teachers, he emphasizes the fact that primarily the program is aimed to give financial relief and not for educational purposes. He points out that its main function is "to provide employment for teachers, men and women, who are in dire need of financial assistance and who are regularly certificated with ample experience. Only persons certified by the State Emergency Relief Administration or its authorized agents as being entitled to work-relief may be employed as teachers. Teachers who are appointed will be investigated and selected by the county or city superintendent of public schools and the local director of Relief."

Vocational training may also be taught by work-relief teachers. The rulings governing this phase of the work are: "All unemployed adults who can benefit from vocational training and cannot obtain the training desired through the regular channels of such education shall be eligible to receive instructions from work-relief teachers. Such classes shall include persons in need of vocational rehabilitation as well as those who for other reasons are in need of vocational education to make them employable."

Further rulings regarding work-relief for teachers issued by Dr. Highsmith, all of which have the approval of Mrs. Thomas O'Berry, director of Relief, [specify that teachers] will receive forty cents per hour, the number of hours to be determined by the director of relief according to the needs of the applicant, the total wages not to exceed $12.00 a week for not more than thirty hours per week. Classes may be held during any hours of the day or evening. Facilities made available by schools, churches, clubs or other agencies may be used for this instruction. Following certification of teachers, work project applications must be approved by the State Relief Administration. Textbooks for use in adult classes may be borrowed from local school authorities. All students should purchase textbooks if possible. Books may be purchased from Federal Relief Funds for adult students who are relief cases and therefore unable to purchase the necessary books."

Better English Week will be observed in North Carolina the week of February 19–25. Miss Alice Laidlaw, of Raleigh, chairman of the Better English Committee of the Federation, says: "During this week schools, clubs and other organizations will be requested to emphasize the fact that the consistent use of correct and effective English is an instrument for individual enrichment and social progress." She advises that suggestions suitable for observing this week will be sent to the clubs and other interested groups and individuals early in January.

A new Junior Club recently organized and brought into the Federation is the Junior Woman's Club of Chadbourn. It is sponsored by the local senior club, the Maids and Matrons, and has for its president Miss Alice Lowe, and for its secretary Miss Nell Koons.

Raleigh Sunday *News and Observer*, p. 9 (Society, p. 1)

29 OCTOBER 1933

CLUB WOMEN WILL AID IN OBSERVANCE [OF] BOOK WEEK

By Mrs. J. Henry Highsmith

Describing North Carolina as a book-hungry State, with 62 per cent, or two out of three of its people, without books or other good reading matter, Mrs. R. W. Green of Raleigh, chairman of literature for the State Federation of Women's Clubs, is urging club women of the State during Book Week, November 12–18, to make available more children's books and put more children to reading in their respective communities. Practical suggestions offered by Mrs. Green, whose pen name is Charlotte Hilton Green, to woman's clubs, book clubs and individuals interested in relieving the low rate of the State as to the number of readers in communities where there is not [a library]; or a children's department in the town or city library, or add to the school library by buying new books, magazines and equipment.

"Growing up With Books" is the slogan to be used in observing Book Week in 1933. The movement started fifteen years ago with a call to observe Boys' Book week. This developed into Children's Book Week and today it is observed as a general Book Week recognizing the need of more reading facilities for young and old alike. Mrs. Green sees however that the children of the State are the greatest sufferers from the great economy program that has closed school libraries and cut them off from borrowing books from the State Library Commission, and it is in their behalf that she appeals for help. She says the children of the State are hungry for books, as are men and women with enforced leisure and nothing with which to employ or improve their minds.

"In facing the facts," says Mrs. Green, "which are not at all pleasant, we find in the 1930 census that North Carolina with twelve other Southern States occupy the lowest place in literacy. Forty-four of her counties have no library service and two out of three of her people have no books to read. Whereas recognized library standards require a minimum income of $1 per capita per year, North Carolina's income is 6 cents per capita per year."

Give books for prizes, suggests Mrs. Green, to bridge clubs and other organizations and groups offering prizes. Or what is better, she says, "If all the bridge clubs in the State would give all the money that would otherwise go for prizes to buying children's books during Book Week and these be gotten together, there would be the starting of a library or children's department in a local library."

Dr. Frank P. Graham, president of the University of North Carolina, has this to say as to the value of children's reading: "Something real happens when a great book and a human being get together. In the nexus of a great soul at work in a book and a great personality at work in the world is the focus of our civilization. History proves to us that great libraries are both the fruits and the roots of great civilizations. Close to the source of many events and movements is the fact that a boy and a book got together."

The Oxford Woman's Club will observe its twenty-fifth anniversary on November 1 with an all day meeting the program of which will be provided by the seven departments of the club. Features of the day will be the annual chrysanthemum show, a Granville County art exhibit, a noonday luncheon and an afternoon play, "The Dreamer of Dreams." Mrs. Andrew Jamieson, chairman of art in the Federation, is president of the Oxford club. On Friday night the literature department of the club will sponsor two plays to be given to the public. In addition to the play "The Maker of Dreams," by Oliphant Down, there will also be a presentation of Christopher Morley's "Thursday Evening." Both plays will be staged under the direction of Miss Grace Jean Sauls of Oxford, who for 15 years was connected with the School of Dramatic Art of Brenau College, Gainesville, Ga.

Miss Jenn Coltrane of Concord, chairman of radio, announces that a Federation Hour has been arranged for each week by both WBT Charlotte and WPTF Raleigh, and that the stations at Wilmington, Greensboro and Winston-Salem will give a series of programs as of last year. Mrs. J. C. Williams will be in charge of the Wilmington station, Mrs. J. J. Andoe of Greensboro, and Mrs. George Hemingway of Winston-Salem. Mrs. J. Henry Highsmith will again have charge of the Raleigh station and the hour of the broadcast will be at 3 o'clock each Thursday. Miss Coltrane will have charge of WBT and the hour is 1:30 Thursdays of each week.

Raleigh Sunday *News and Observer,* p. 9 (Society, p. 1)

5 NOVEMBER 1933

MAKE EFFORTS TO REDUCE DEATH RATE OF MOTHERS

By Mrs. J. Henry Highsmith

Believing the club women of North Carolina to be greatly concerned with conditions in the State that are said to be responsible for the great increase in the number of deaths of infants and mothers, ninety per cent of which could be prevented, Dr. G. M. Cooper, director of the Division of Maternity and Infancy of the State Board of Health, is calling on them for their co-operation and support in an effort to remedy the serious situation.

According to Dr. Cooper the problem centers largely around the ignorant and untrained midwife, and the harder the times become, the greater the problem grows. That 8,121 white women, 17,514 colored women and 404 Indian women were attended in maternity by midwives in 1932 shows the size of the problem. That twice this number of mothers did not have the services of a physician or nurse to instruct them in prenatal care presents another side of the problem.

Finding the services of midwives far below the point of safety and protection, some of them never having heard of the law that requires the dropping of silver nitrate solution into the eyes of new-born babies to prevent blindness, and having no equipment whatever, Dr. Cooper believes that the club women in any town or community can be of invaluable service in helping to provide the proper equipment for the midwives and thereby eliminating one of the greatest elements of danger in their service. He proposes with the aid of the nurses in his department to conduct institutes for midwives in counties having no health officer whose responsibility it would be to look after this work.

According to Dr. Cooper, this work is already well under way and accomplishing results. The past summer the nurses examined 1,108 midwives, giving them individual instructions and training. Of the 1,108 examined, only 224 met the minimum requirements; 403 had partial equipment and 454 had none whatever. The club women's best work would be to help equip the midwives of their community with such essentials as overdress, cap, and first aid materials.

An interesting example of co-operation cited by Dr. Cooper is that of Mrs. J. M. Pruden of Edenton, chairman of the local Red Cross Chapter. She with the members of her chapter working with the nurses last summer saw that every midwife in Chowan County had the proper equipment for her services. What Mrs. Pruden did for the safety and protection of the mothers in her county who were too poor to have the services of a physician, Dr. Cooper feels that other women can do for theirs.

In this connection, it is interesting to note that the State Federation of Florida last summer co-operated with the Florida State Board of Health in conducting institutes for midwives. Mrs. Meade A. Love, president, making the principal speech at the opening of the campaign and the club women providing the transportation of the midwives desiring to attend the institute.

It is regretted that the Federation hour previously announced for each Thursday afternoon over WPTF, Raleigh, has had to be indefinitely postponed on account of the station going on the NBC network from 10 to 5 o'clock, p. m. However, a General Federation broadcast has been announced for each Thursday afternoon at 5 o'clock. All club women are invited to tune in at that hour on Station WPTF, Raleigh.

Over Station WBT, Charlotte, Mrs. P. R. Rankin of Mt. Gilead, president of the Fifth District, will speak on the subject, "Parent Education in this New Day," the hour being from 1:30 to 1:45 on Thursday, November 9. On the 16th, the Charlotte Woman's Club will be responsible for the program at the same hour.

Many clubs are entering their year books and club programs in the Program Building Contest. Already there are signs that the contest is of

Statewide interest and that better programs are already being made. The contest does not close till January 1. All clubs are urged to have part by entering their program booklets.

Raleigh Sunday *News and Observer,* p. 9 (Society, p. 1)

12 NOVEMBER 1933

CLUB WOMEN ENCOURAGE NATIVE TALENT IN ART

By Mrs. J. Henry Highsmith

North Carolina is going to make a decided step forward in its study and appreciation of art this year if the plans and program prepared by Mrs. Andrew Jamieson of Oxford, state art chairman of the Federation of Women's Clubs, and her division chairmen go through. With the conviction that North Carolina art and artists should first be studied and appreciated and native talent be encouraged and supported, Mrs. Jamieson and her associates have prepared a comprehensive and practical program for the clubs of the state, the keynote of which is "Buy and Own a North Carolina Painting."

One of the ways devised by Mrs. Jamieson for stimulating art in the community is through holding a Community Fine Arts Festival. This is to be a bringing together on one day a representation of the best the community affords in every branch of the arts—music, painting, sculpture, drama, poetry, plays, handwork, needlework, pottery and porcelains. All local art work of any description should be given recognition. It is suggested that the program be held at some central, commodious place where a luncheon, dinner or tea might be served as a means of furnishing social contact. The morning hours according, to the suggestions, might be given over to viewing the exhibitions with competent persons to explain and interpret them, to be followed by a musical program. The luncheon hour would offer a fine setting for reading of poems, singing songs and for awarding prizes to successful contestants. The afternoon could well be used for a home-talent play as well as originals in musical composition.

Such an occasion as suggested above has recently been held in Oxford by the Oxford Woman's Club of which Mrs. Jamieson is president. The occasion was the celebration of the club's 25th anniversary. The program consisted of a county art and crafts exhibit, a chrysanthemum show, a midday luncheon and two home talent plays for the afternoon. Prizes are offered by the State and the General Federation to clubs and communities accomplishing most through a community fine-arts festival. Write to Mrs. Jamieson for further particulars.

Another means of encouraging art planned by Mrs. Jamieson is through the state-wide art contest for club members. Heretofore the art department of the Federation has sponsored an art exhibition at its annual convention in the Spring for all the artists of the state. But since the organization of the

North Carolina Professional Artists Club, which sponsors its own exhibits, the Federation art workers feel that their efforts should be given more to the art work of the clubs and individual club members. Consequently the art contest this year and the usual list of prizes will be held for club women.

Each Woman's Club in the state is urged to hold an exhibit sometime in advance of the State Convention in May—at least two weeks before the convention. From this contest or exhibit the four best works of art are to be chosen to be sent to the state convention. Paintings must be originals, not copies, and must be done without the aid of a teacher, and all contestants must be members of the State Federation.

The Penny Art Fund is still another plan adopted for aiding the interests of art in the state. The plan which is being used by most of the states and just this year adopted for North Carolina is that every club woman contributes a penny a year to a fund to be used by the state art chairman for purchasing American pieces of art to give as prizes to the clubs doing the most to spread the knowledge of art and beauty in their communities.

Through the Art Appreciation Contest conducted in the schools under the direction of Miss Juanita McDougald of Raleigh, the children of the state are given an opportunity to become acquainted with the world's best artists and their work. And through the division of Creative Interests, of which Mrs. J. J. Andoe of Greensboro is chairman, the mothers of the state are advised concerning the talents and "natural bents" of their children with a view of encouraging them to develop the creative abilities of their children, at the best stage of their development—their early youth.

Raleigh Sunday *News and Observer,* p. 9 (Society, p. 1)

19 NOVEMBER 1933

FEDERATION PRESIDENT VISITS CLUB DISTRICTS

Mrs. R. H. Latham, President Of North Carolina Federation Of Women's Clubs, Finds Fine Spirit And Growth Of Club Work; Accompanied On Tour By Mrs. Howard G. Etheridge, Chairman of Districts

By Mrs. J. Henry Highsmith

On finishing a trip of 2,000 miles attending sixteen district meetings and covering every section of the state from Beaufort to beyond the Blue-Ridge—Waynesville—Mrs. R. H. Latham, president of the State Federation of Women's Clubs, and Mrs. Howard G. Etheridge, chairman of district work, are enthusiastic in their praise of the fine club spirit and healthful growth of the clubs they found throughout the state. Mrs. Latham found to her delight that practically every club reported that it was cooperating with the NRA program which is being stressed as a major project of the Federation this year. Mrs. Etheridge was particularly pleased with the attendance at the district meetings, which with but two exceptions was larger than that of last year. Both Mrs. Etheridge and Mrs. Latham consider that the weather man was their good friend on this trip as not a drop of rain interfered with their program, which enabled them to see the whole of the state in the best of weather and in the most beautiful season of the year.

Mrs. Latham and her husband are making Chapel Hill their home this winter. Their address is 19 Hooper Lane, Chapel Hill.

Commenting on the major interests of the club women as gathered from their reports at the meetings, Mrs. Latham says: "First in the hearts of North Carolina club women is the Sallie Southall Cotten Loan Fund. Clubs reported almost 100 per cent as having made gifts to this fund, which shows that the education of our girls is of paramount consideration in clubdom. Schools came second in their affections. Realizing the lowered standards of education, the club women are trying in every possible way, even to the extent of supplementing the salaries of art and music teachers, to maintain an efficient system. They are also interested in parliamentary law, studying it in classes. They have dramatized Bible stories and have found these with other dramatic efforts helpful and entertaining. They are sponsoring flower shows and in many ways boosting the Garden Department. One club reported that two of their members walked five miles rather than to miss the club meeting when the family ear was not available.

Mrs. Etheridge noted that while welfare work was reported as a major activity by a majority of the clubs that the cultural subjects of art, music, literature and gardening, even by the rural clubs, were not being neglected. Neither Mrs. Latham nor Mrs. Etheridge was prepared to find so many attractive club houses, all paid for, and so much wholehearted, gracious hospitality as they met on this trip. They feel deeply in debt to all who were their hostesses and those who contributed to the comfort and pleasure of their trip.

Of particular importance to club women is the announcement of Col. Dodge, commanding officer of Oteen [Veterans Administration] Hospital, that all club women be urged not to send anything to the patients at Oteen but cigarettes and stamps. No use, says the officer, can be made of the fruit, candy, toys and articles sent to amuse the patients. These, he advises, should be sent to those who need them and can appreciate them. In consequence of this statement by the commanding officer at Oteen, who Mrs. Etheridge interviewed personally, and in view of the large number of "stockings sent to Oteen" reported each year, Mrs. Etheridge is writing the club women through their district presidents to confine their gifts and remembrances to the Oteen patients this Christmas to stamps and cigarettes.

Two new clubs have recently been organized and brought into the Federation family. These are the Woman's Club of Pinnacle with Mrs. J. C.

Killinger as president and Miss Etta Lee Clore as treasurer. The club will work through the departments of Public Welfare, Health and Gardens. The other is the Tea and Topics Club of Lillington, with Mrs. Joel G. Layton as president and Mrs. S. B. McKay as treasurer. The club has ten members and its study will be literary subjects.

The Winton Woman's Club, though organized for some time, has just recently come into the fold of the Federation. Its president is Miss Emma Riddick Parker and treasurer is Mrs. T. D. Northcutt. Its departments are Civics, American Home, Literature, Education and Gardens.

Raleigh Sunday *News and Observer*, p. 9 (Society, p. 1)

26 NOVEMBER 1933

CHILD PSYCHOLOGY EXPERTS TO GIVE LECTURE SERVICE

Many Experts In Child Personality Training Included In List Of Those Whose Lectures Are Available To Club Women Of The State; Project In Work Of Art Department Of The State Federation

By Mrs. J. Henry Highsmith

Announcement is made to the club women of the State of a lecture service on phases of child personality training that has been made available through the division of Children's Creative Interests, a subject under the Art Department of the Federation of which Mrs. J. J. Andoe of Greensboro is chairman. These services are now available to club women with their subjects given:

Dr. Donald K. Adams, Durham, "The Psychology of the Child"; Mrs. Edouard Albion, Pinehurst, "Fostering the Child's Imagination"; Miss Louel Collins, Winston-Salem, "Children's Books and Reading Problems"; Dr. Walter Cutter, Duke University, "Story Telling as a Fine Art"; Mrs. Gifford Davis, Durham, "Ideals of the Nursery School"; Dr. Ernest Groves, Chapel Hill, "Family and Marriage Adjustment in Relation to the Child's Development"; Gladys H. Groves, Chapel Hill, "Problems of Parents and Children"; C. Walton Johnson, Asheville, "Outdoor Life and the Child, the Prevention of Abnormal Personality"; Marion Y. Keith, M.D., Greensboro, "Physical Care as a Background for Creative Personality"; Mary B. Mason Durham, "Developing Rhythmic Expression"; James A. McLean, Raleigh, "Painting and the Plastic Arts"; Dr. Harold D. Meyer, Chapel Hill, "Child Welfare"; Miss Wally Reichenberg, Durham, "European Methods of Creative Education"; Dr. Joseph Rhyne, Duke University, "The Abnormal Child"; Dr. Frank Howard Richardson, Black Mountain, "Health and Growth of the Child"; Prof. Clyde P. Richman, Durham, "Tools and Manual Training Crafts"; Rev. Douglas L. Rights, Winston-Salem, "The Child and the Collecting Instinct"; Dr. Robert H. Wright, Greenville, "Furthering the Cause of Child Training"; Dr. John W. Carr, Duke University, and Ernest Seeman, Duke University, "Talent and Personal Aptitude."

Speaking of the work of this new division of the Federation, Mrs. Andoe says it has passed its experimental stage and is proving to meet a real need in helping parents to recognize and foster the "natural bents" of their children. Mrs. Andoe gives Ernest Seeman of Duke University credit for the idea as well as for much of the success of the division.

Miss Hattie Parrott of Raleigh announces that she will send to club women and teachers requesting it The Music Achievement Handbook and any information concerning the Music Memory Contest and the program for Music Achievement day. Write to her in care of State Education Department, Raleigh.

Under the direction of Mrs. J. C. Williams of Wilmington, an educational program is given once a week over the Wilmington radio station, on Friday mornings from 11:45 to 12 o'clock. Members of the North Carolina Sorosis assist Mrs. Williams in broadcasting.

At a book tea held recently by the Sorosis of Wilmington, more than one hundred books were received to be placed in the rural schools of the county. A similar tea held last year was the occasion for the city high school library receiving many valuable and much needed reference books.

Raleigh Sunday *News and Observer*, p. 9 (Society, p. 1)

10 DECEMBER 1933

CLUB WOMEN'S PRESIDENT URGES CAROLINA CHRISTMAS

Mrs. R. H. Latham, President Of State Federation, Says State Rich in Native Art Treasures And Urges Women To Buy Works of North Carolina Artists and Craftsmen For Gifts

By Mrs. J. Henry Highsmith

A recent journey through the State of North Carolina has convinced Mrs. R. H. Latham, President of the State Federation of Women's Club, that no woman need go outside the borders of her state to find Christmas presents of a highly artistic value, fine workmanship and of satisfactory service. Consequently, Mrs. Latham is making an appeal to all women of the state to make this a "Carolina Christmas" by buying Carolina-made gifts, products of her native sons and daughters.

Mrs. Latham's tour this fall of the sixteen districts of the state brought her in contact with the great variety of handicrafts and other various forms of art that are produced within her borders and made her wonder why North Carolinians would go elsewhere for objects of art and the various crafts when they have at home fine products, the work of native artists. She found scattered over the state men and women who are skilled in the various crafts, whose techniques and patterns, she says, have been handed down from forebears of other days and other lands. Their work is of a rich inheritance, conceived in good taste and executed in fine craftsmanship. Their products are both useful and beautiful making it a joy to own them.

In the realm of crafts, she points out, one finds at Penland articles of real beauty and value, the quality of which was recognized by the First Lady of the Land when she placed a substantial order for Christmas with these weavers. Here are found closely woven, smooth table linens, coverlets, bags, towels and runners. During their exhibit at the Century of Progress Exposition in Chicago this past summer, the popularity of their hand-woven smocks made it difficult to supply the demand. One finds also here pottery rich in color and unique in design, decorated tiles, balsam pillows, pudgy dogs made of genuine sheep skin, and quaint dolls made from the humble corn husk and appropriately named "Cornelius and Maizie Husk." Pewter in beautiful patterns is fashioned at Penland—plates, bowls, porringers, candle sticks, trays and platters. Much of this work is done too at Chapel Hill by George Bison, who is a true Carolina craftsman.

At Tryon beautiful toys are made whose fame has traveled far and wide. Brasstown is a unique farm colony whose happy motto, "I sing behind the plow," is felt in the gay abandon of the attractive animals carved from applewood. In addition there is the old time fire bellows, the hearth broom with quaintly carved handle, the marshmallow fork, candle sticks and other products of wrought-iron, Here too, is done a superior quality of weaving in wool.

Burnsville boasts a real son of the forge—Daniel Boone, fifth in descent from the original Daniel of the wandering foot. This 1933 Boone Model is content to stay in useful things of iron, which include attractive andirons, pokers and forks for the fireplace, candle sticks, lamp bases and ash stands, all wrought to the rhythm of song, the cooling process taking place at regular counts in the music.

In Greensboro the Stronghold Crafts show carving and weaving and at Jugtown is to be seen pottery with a national reputation.

The Allenstand Industries in Asheville display baskets of wonderful design and rugs which are works of art, as well as potterybearing the well known brands of Pisgah Forest, Hilton and Cole.

At Plumtree the Tarheel Mica Company makes lampshades of mica in tones of red, green, amber and pearl, which not only shed a soft light but are quite durable.

Mrs. Latham calls attention also to a special sale of pictures, works of the members of the North Carolina Professional Artists Club, which have been priced at unusually low prices and offered for sale during the exhibition now being held at the Sir Walter Hotel in Raleigh. Among the number now being offered for sale are etchings, landscapes in oil and water-colors, block prints, flower studies in oil and many decorative paintings, all marked at half price or less for this particular sale. The exhibit will continue through December 16.

Believing that women need a wider and more intimate knowledge of their state and local governments, Mrs. Latham is asking the club women of the state to listen in on the state-wide radio program set for Tuesday December 12th, at 1:30 o'clock, when further plans and purposes of the Institute of Government will be given. December 12th has been designated by Governor Ehringhaus as Institute of Government Day in North Carolina, and on that day a state-wide radio hook-up will enable every citizen of the state to become acquainted with the progress already made and further plans to be undertaken in the immediate future by those in charge of the work of the institute.

As a group of citizens particularly interested in better government, writes Mrs. Latham, the North Carolina Federation of Women's Clubs, is glad to join in this in every possible way to hasten the day of more efficient government in the state. She has asked all club presidents to notify their members of this radio program and to urge them to listen in.

Raleigh Sunday *News and Observer,* p. 11 (Society, p. 1)

17 DECEMBER 1933

FEDERATION MUSIC LEADER APPEALS FOR SCHOOL MUSIC

By Mrs. J. Henry Highsmith

"Let All the People Sing" this Christmas is the appeal of Mrs. Chas. G. Gulley of Cullowhee, chairman of Music of the State Federation of Women's Clubs. Mrs. Gulley says Christmas is the one season of the year that is largely dependent upon music for its true interpretation and for its most beautiful expression. Through music as through no other medium, she says, one catches a vision of the first Christmas morning and is permitted to join in the universal chorus of praise and thanksgiving. She urges more of the beautiful old hymns whose inspiration was the birth of a Babe, God's greatest gift to man. Sing more of the beautiful Christmas carols and folk songs of this and other countries, she advises, to catch the true spirit of Christmas.

Along with Mrs. Gulley's appeal to make this a singing Christmas, is expressed her concern for the music, or lack of it, in the schools of the State. She says it took only three years of the Depression to wipe out the efforts of the twenty years or more it took to get music placed in the schools. She deplores the fact that the subject is still regarded as a frill or non-essential, and that to find a school with a supervisor of music who is paid from public funds is a rarity.

Believing that the situation regarding music in the schools is not beyond recovery, Mrs. Gulley calls on the club women of the state to come to its rescue. She says: "I appeal to you fellow club women to lend your aid and encouragement in this crisis. Visit the schools of your town and find out the real situation as to music. Some of you are trained teachers. Could you not give a few hours a week to help where there is no music teacher? I have the satisfaction of doing this myself, and I speak from experience when I say that my efforts have probably yielded larger returns than any investment I have ever made. Interest your school in the State Music Appreciation Course and the Music Achievement Contest. Is there not some struggling musician in your town who needs the used sheet music of real value which you have packed in the attic of your home and forgotten? And the music magazine which you have discarded? Do the Sunday Schools of your town sing from Sunday to Sunday a type of so-called hymn which is cheap as to words and as to musical setting while the great masterpieces which breathe worship in every strain and syllable lie unused? Are you interested enough in music to turn aside from your busy life and try with kindliness to remedy these unfortunate situations?"

Recently, Mrs. E. E. Randolph of Raleigh, who is chairman of Public School Music in the Federation, also called on the club women of the state to do their utmost to keep music in the schools. She wrote: "Just now, more than ever in the past ten years, the children and teachers of the state need the assistance of club women to help keep music in the schools. Some definite preparation must be given the boys and girls of today through the schools to equip them for the leisure hours that will be theirs through the new deal that we are about to enter. I believe there is absolutely nothing that will take the place of music in the lives of school boys and girls to fill their leisure time, to give them balance, meet their emotional needs and afford them wholesome pleasure.

"The simplest and perhaps the most beneficial and attractive means of giving school children the opportunity to become acquainted with the field of music is through the State Music Appreciation and Music Achievement Contest. Write to Miss Hattie S. Parrott, State Department of Education, Raleigh, for a copy of the Music Appreciation and Music Achievement Contest handbook. It gives specific directions for conducting the courses and is free to those requesting it."

Working with Mrs. Gulley, Mrs. Randolph, and Miss Parrott in the department of music of the Federation are Mrs. Isaac G. Greer of Thomasville, chairman of music in Religious Education, Mrs. E. M. Boshart of Raleigh, chairman of Civic music, and Mrs. Arthur S. Kennickell, Jr., of Winston-Salem, chairman of the Music Production Fund. Miss Hattie Parrott is chairman of National Music week as well as Music Appreciation and Achievement.

Raleigh Sunday *News and Observer,* p. 11 (Society, p. 1)

24 DECEMBER 1933

SENDS CHRISTMAS MESSAGE TO CLUB WOMEN OF STATE

Mrs. R. H. Latham, President of State Federation of Women's Clubs, Sends Season's Greetings To Club Members; Urges Dedication of Efforts In New Year to Making Happier Homes and Better Communities

By Mrs. J. Henry Highsmith

Contained in the Christmas message which Mrs. R. H. Latham, president of the State Federation of Women's Clubs, is sending to the club women of North Carolina is the expressed hope that they will dedicate their efforts in the New Year to three objectives, namely, the making of happier homes, better communities and a warless world.

Mrs. Latham and her husband are moving to Asheville where they will make their home as Mr. Latham has been elected superintendent of the city schools. After January 1st, they will be at home at the Jefferson Apartments. Prior to going to Asheville, Mr. and Mrs. Latham were living in Chapel Hill where Mr. Latham was lecturing and studying at the University, and also at Duke University. Mrs. Latham says she anticipates a most pleasant and profitable year in the mountain city and will be ready to welcome all club members who will attend the State Federation convention in May. She says she already has been made to feel welcome and at home there in the midst of so many federated clubs. Asheville has the distinction of having 11 clubs members of the Federation.

Mrs. Latham's Christmas message to club women reads: "On this most important of all days, my good club friends, I am wishing you each and every one a good old-fashioned Christmas, one of peace and joy On this happy Sabbath—Christmas eve—I can visualize you resting from the rush and hurry incident to celebrating the world's greatest holiday, the birthday of our Lord. And while you rest I would have you think on this: If there had been no Christmas with its glad tidings of great joy, there would have been no Easter with its glorious promise of life eternal; there would have been no earthly life of a divine Savior, who though tempted in all things even as we are, left a message that comforts and sustains us.

"Christmas is the season of unselfishness, when every spark of selfishness through the Christmas spirit is turned into joy and service for others. Surely if there were no such day as Christmas, there would have to be some such occasion set aside for purging our lives annually of purely selfish interests. Christmas brings out the best in the human race and gives us confidence to hope for better things in the future.

"Occasionally, it may seem to us that we are literally indulging in an orgy of spending and giving, of needless generosity and thought and worry for others. Is it worth it? After the tinsel is cleared away, the glow of the candles gone and the berries faded on the shimmering green, when there's nothing left but the memory of happy voices, warm hearts and radiant smiles—a day of drawing closer the bonds of love and kinship—is it worth it? Indeed! Our souls have been reborn in the baptism of the Christmas spirit, the heart of which is to minister to rather than to be ministered unto.

"Let us as women, as mothers, and as preservers of the race take to ourselves the message which was proclaimed among the Judean hills on the first Christmas morning: 'Peace on earth good will to men,' and dedicate anew our efforts to three objectives—happier homes, better communities and a warless world, all of which were included in the plan given us by our self-sacrificing Savior."

Raleigh Sunday *News and Observer,* p. 9 (Society, p. 1)

31 DECEMBER 1933

CLUB WOMEN WILL HONOR MEMORY OF MRS. COTTEN

State Federation Will Present to General Organization Three Chairs for Use in Board Room When Directors Hold Mid-Winter Meeting

By Mrs. J. Henry Highsmith

As a memorial to Mrs. R. R. Cotten, known to most North Carolina club women as "Mother Cotten," the State Federation of Women's Clubs will present to the General Federation of Women's Clubs a presiding officer's table and a set of three officer's chairs to be used in the board room at General Federation Headquarters at Washington, D. C. The presentation will take place at headquarters on Wednesday morning, January 10th, at the annual mid-winter meeting of the board of directors of the General Federation.

At the 1930 State Federation convention held at Pinehurst a committee was appointed and authorized to select a fitting memorial to Mrs. Cotten to be placed at National Headquarters. The committee was composed of the state president, who was then Mrs. Edward M. Land; the state director, who was Mrs. Thomas O'Berry; and Mrs. Palmer Jerman, a member of the board of trustees of the General Federation. On becoming president Mrs. J. M. Hobgood succeeded Mrs. Land as a member of the committee, and likewise Mrs. Land succeeded Mrs. O'Berry. Consequently it fell to Mrs. Hobgood, Mrs. Land and Mrs. Jerman to select the memorial, which they will have the honor to present at the annual meeting next week.

In presenting this gift to National Headquarters in honor of her distinguished pioneer club woman, North Carolina is keeping step with other states who have honored their distinguished club leaders in similar ways. Today headquarters is attractively and appropriately furnished with gifts that have been sent by state federations and individual clubs in memory of their outstanding club women. North Carolina's gift of a table and three arm chairs of Victorian style, made of walnut and beautifully carved, the committee feels, is most appropriate and is a lovely tribute to Mrs. Cotten. On the table is an engraved copper plate bearing the inscription: "Presented to the General Federation of Women's Clubs by the North Carolina Federation of Women's Clubs in loving memory of Sallie Southall Cotten, 1846–1929, A Pioneer Club Woman."

Attending the board of directors meeting in Washington from January 9–13, in addition to Mrs. Hobgood, Mrs. Land and Mrs. Jerman, will be Mrs. R. H. Latham, of Asheville, president of the State Federation. They will all reach Washington on Monday, the 8th, to be ready for the preliminary meetings that take place on Tuesday. At the official board meeting, which will begin Wednesday morning, Mrs. Grace Morrison Poole will preside. "These United States" will be the theme of the meeting, but the new significance of the tremendous changes and developments that have taken place in "these United States" within the past nine months will be studied and emphasized.

Outstanding in interest will be the dinner given by the board Friday evening when Mrs. Franklin D. Roosevelt will be the honor guest speaker. At the Thursday evening meeting a prominent representative of the United States government will discuss the NRA in terms of industry, labor and the consumer. Dr. Frederic Howe will explain the workings of the A. A. A.—the Agricultural Adjustment Administration. Another speaker of special interest will be Count Rene de Harnoncourt, internationally known authority on art, who is soon to begin a series of broadcasts on art appreciation. This will be under the sponsorship of the division of art of the General Federation. Count Harnoncourt's address will be on Wednesday evening. At the Saturday morning meeting both sides of the proposed amendments to the Pure Food and Drugs Act will be explained by outside representatives.

In accordance with established custom a reception will be held at headquarters on Tuesday evening with club women from every State having as their guests their own Senators and Representatives and their wives. Other entertaining features planned for the visiting club women include a tea to be held at the Women's City Club with Mrs. Harvey W. Wiley as hostess, also a tea at the Chevy Chase Woman's Club and one at the historic Gadby's Tavern in Alexandria. Thursday afternoon will be left free for sightseeing.

Raleigh Sunday *News and Observer*, p. 9 (Society, p. 1)

1934

17 February — responding, with other notables, to the start of a two-year inquiry on state curriculum, tells press that her central wish is for the teaching of cultural subjects and temperance

4 March — as chair of women's group, promotes "Go to Church and Sunday School" campaign, to conclude on Easter Sunday

23 March — receives, with Dr. Highsmith (and Governor and Mrs. Ehring-haus, among others), at Raleigh Teachers' Association dinner and dance

26 March — addresses Apex Junior Woman's Club on "How the Junior Woman's Club Can Serve Its Community"

27 March — attends state meeting of League for Woman Voters at Woman's College, Greensboro; elected second vice president.

6 April — speaks briefly at State Music Achievement Contest elementary school music festival (grades 6 and 7) in Hill Hall, UNC, on "Music of Foreign Lands"

19 April — receives after RWC Literature Department tea honoring book clubs of Raleigh and Charlotte Hilton Green's new book *Birds of the South*

26 April — is patron, with Dr. Highsmith and dozens of others, including Governor and Mrs. Ehringhaus, of RWC revue "Pirate Gold"

27 April — attends steering committee of NC Conference for Social Service, as president of the League of Women Voters

1–4 May — attends 32nd annual NCFWC annual convention, Asheville

10 May — reports to RWC on NCFWC convention

16 May — takes second place in the Iris division, Raleigh Garden Club Spring Flower show, Sir Walter Hotel

22 May — assists at a "brilliant reception" at RWC for Ambassador and Mrs. Josephus Daniels

31 May — J. Henry Highsmith is conferred Doctor of Education degree at 100th Commencement of Wake Forest College, one of eleven honorary doctorates that day

1 June — addresses Wake County League of Woman Voters on her recent visit to the seat of the League of Nations at Geneva and the World Court at The Hague.

6 June — addresses Raleigh Garden Club on "The Use of Flowers on the Continent"

7 June — following last yearly meeting of RWC, attends memorial service for Dr. Delia Dixon-Carroll, charter member and former president, killed in an automobile accident

9 June — elected precinct representative to Wake County Democratic Convention

10 June — Eleanor Roosevelt speaks at Memorial Auditorium

6 July — hosts, at 832, a farewell tea for her friends Mrs. Palmer Jerman and Miss Flora Creech, being transferred to Greensboro with IRS offices; Mary Belle greets, Lula Belle and others serve; Jean says goodbyes

8 July — presides, as superintendent of Sunday School adult division, over farewell services for Miss Creech at Edenton Street

12 July — addresses annual Public Welfare Institute at UNC on child labor amendment

13 July — addresses a rally favoring school supplement allowing Raleigh city schools to run 9 months

30 July for a week — vacations at White Lake with Mary Belle, Lula Belle, Katherine, and Louise, as guests of Mr. and Mrs. Troy R. Herring of Roseboro

4 August — named to non-partisan committee to pass revised constitution for NC in November election

8 August — assists Lula Belle at a tea honoring a recent bride

11 August for a week — visits Mrs. Latham in Asheville

25–29 September — travels, with Mrs. Latham, to New York for Conference on Current Social Problems, a New York *Herald-Tribune* forum at the Waldorf-Astoria

4 October — addresses RWC on Conference on Current Problems; that evening addresses initial meeting of Zu Zammen Book Club at the RWC

7 October — carries civic club greetings to National Recognition Day for Sunday School teachers, a "mass meeting" in Hugh Morson auditorium

8 October — among civic leaders and clubs endorsing speech in Raleigh of Mrs. Sherman Barnes of the Woman's International League for Peace and Freedom, speaking against munitions

12 October — leads delegation of citizens from six cities to home of Senator Josiah W. Bailey, North Blount Street, to support fight against munitions manufacture, a project of the Women's International League for Peace and Freedom

16 October — leads discussion of the presentation on "China's New Day" at Twentieth Century Book Club, also honoring Mrs. J. S. Mitchener for her 50th anniversary

18 October — addresses RWC Literature Department on "Today's Trend in Southern Literature"

21 October — gives "inspirational address" to 52nd WCTU convention, jointly with United Dry Forces (and against repeal)

22–24 October — assists at Garden School presented by Raleigh Garden Club

26 October — presides, representing Wake County League of Women Voters, at address on child labor amendment by James E. Sidel of National Child Labor Committee, sponsored by a consortium of women's clubs

27 October — addresses Franklin County Federation of Home Demonstration Clubs, Mills, on "Legislation and Good Citizenship"

5 November — attends newly renamed North Carolina Legislative Council as it adopts legislative program for 1935 Legislature; re-elected as executive secretary

6 November — addresses Raleigh Council of Jewish Women on New York Conference

7 December — addresses Clinton Garden Club on "The Use of Flowers on the European Continent" repeating spring paper to Raleigh Garden Club

3 December — presides at meeting of Literature Department of RWC, reads poems by North Carolinians James Larkin Pearson and Zoe Kincaid Brockman

21 JANUARY 1934

CLUB WOMEN COOPERATE IN ADULT EDUCATION WORK

By Mrs. J. Henry Highsmith

Because of the interest and accomplishment of the club women of North Carolina in the field of adult education, when their services were for the most part voluntary and unremunerated, Dr. J. Henry Highsmith, director of the Division of Instructional Service of the State Department of Education, invites their co-operation in carrying out a state-wide program now when 900 emergency relief teachers may be employed at $50 a month from emergency relief funds to teach adults. While the ERE [Emergency Relief Education] program is first of all a relief program, says Dr. Highsmith, and only secondarily an educational program, great achievements educationally are possible and confidently expected, and club women can be of great assistance in stimulating and directing the teachers who shall be employed in this work. Their experience and training in teaching adult illiterates will be of incalculable value at this time.

According to Dr. Highsmith there are six projects included in the emergency relief in education program—rural education, vocational agriculture, vocational rehabilitation, literary classes, general adult education and nursery school education—but the last three are of particular interest to club women. Since there are 236,261 persons ten years of age and over who can neither read nor write, according to the 1920 U. S. Census for North Carolina, the literary classes provided for is a most timely and inviting field. Thousands of these illiterates, says Dr. Highsmith, can be taught to read and write within the next three months, and for the teachers as well as for the pupils it will mean a real opportunity of service and enlightenment, blessings for days to come.

The general adult education project of the ERE program offers well nigh unlimited opportunities to increase the training and education of adults, 16 years and over, who desire instruction along any worthwhile line. Activities in this field are limited, says Dr. Highsmith, only by the skill of the teachers and the intellectual desire and ability of the students.

Nursery School education is the feature that has been provided for children two to six years of age whose parents are on relief or are unemployed. The children may attend nursery school for six hours a day, five days a week, where such school can be organized. To conduct a nursery school successfully, it is necessary for the teacher whose salary is paid from ERE funds to have the hearty support of the CWA [Civil Works Administration] worker in securing equipment, and the local director of relief who furnishes food for the children.

The following rules are submitted by Dr. Highsmith as governing the employment and work of teachers in the ERE program:

"To be employed as an ERE teacher it is necessary for the applicant to be approved by the local director of relief as being eligible for relief and by the city or county superintendent and the State Department of Public Instruction as being capable of teaching.

"There are no positions to which teachers are assigned. They make their jobs. They organize and conduct their classes with such assistance as they are able to get. Classes may be held in schools, churches, club rooms, private homes and any other place approved by the school superintendent.

"Each class must be composed of ten members and may be taught morning, afternoon or night. The teacher must devote six hours per day five days a week, or 30 hours a week to the work—20 hours in actual class instruction and ten hours may be used for preparation.

"The teacher receives $12.50 per week or $50 a month. An amount equal to five per cent of the salary, but which does not come out of the salary, may be spent for instructional supplies.

"This ERE program does not duplicate, displace, nor interfere with the program of the public school."

Raleigh Sunday *News and Observer,* p. 9 (Society, p. 1)

11 February 1934

Nursery Schools Proving Practical And Popular

By Mrs. J. Henry Highsmith

A project of the ERE—Emergency Relief Education—program that seems to be meeting an acute need and proving a blessing to the communities in which they are established is the nursery school. At first this project was looked at askance because to conduct one successfully required a combination of efforts on the part of at least three federal agencies. The teacher even if she succeeded in organizing a class of ten children from two to six years of age whose parents were on relief or unemployed had to be paid from the ERE funds; she had to have the hearty support of the CWA worker in securing a place for her school and for proper equipment and also of the local director of relief in order to get food for the children.

But the plan works. Already more than 100 nursery schools have been organized in the state and there is a demand for more. They have not only been found practical in their operations but they are also serving a group that otherwise probably would not be reached. A picture of a nursery school operating in a mill village in the state is here given in a recent letter to the writer:

"I am taking the pleasure and privilege of writing you a little about the working plans of the nursery school here and to tell you how great we think it is. We have a large cotton mill here, a village of about 2,000 people, a large per cent being children. The mill village is about a half-mile from town where the children go to school. That leaves the little fellows under six with no entertainment of any sort. Most of the mothers work in the mills, so you can imagine what the children are like. I tell you this to make it clear just how much such a thing as a nursery school means to the children of a mill village.

"The school is being conducted by two local girls who are unemployed teachers. The Woman's Club house in the village is used for the building. A fence has been built around the grounds, sand piles have been made and as many conveniences as possible have been secured. Today I was invited to have lunch with the babies and I was thrilled beyond words to see the little awkward, wobbly, poorly dressed little fellows being taught to eat right, talk intelligibly and to play together. I had no idea that children of that class knew so little about these elemental things, not even how to play. It's a shame that their little legs are so thin, crooked and ungainly, their feet and hands so small and skinny. What a blessing it is to these few to be clean, well fed and taught, if nothing more, how to play and sing together!

"Won't you please urge your club women, church women and citizens interested in humanity to help make this service to the most unfortunate of all our people—little children of the poor and unemployed—permanent? If it could be made a part of the educational system of our great state what a blessing it would be! The good done would last as long as eternity."

Miss Nellie Roberson of Chapel Hill, chairman of University Extension Service, announces that two new programs suitable for women's clubs have been prepared and are now ready for use. One is Adventures in Reading, No. 6, edited by Mrs. Marjorie N. Bond of Chapel Hill, and the other is Everyday Science, edited by Dr. Carleton E. Preston, associate professor of science in the University. Miss Roberson will be glad to quote prices and give any other information regarding these or other courses offered by the University.

Raleigh Sunday *News and Observer,* p. 9 (Society, p. 1)

18 FEBRUARY 1934

JUNIOR WOMEN'S CLUBS TO COMPETE FOR STATE PRIZES

By Mrs. J. Henry Highsmith

Grass is not likely to grow this spring beneath the feet of North Carolina Junior Club members if they participate in all the contests and other club activities that have been provided for them by their State and General Federation chairmen. For the record they made two years ago in winning General Federation prizes—three in one year—they are now looked upon as being capable of winning any prize offered by either organization.

Consequently their proud state chairman, Mrs. D. F. Giles of Marion, is submitting to them and urging their hearty participation in four contests sponsored by the General Federation of Women's Clubs. She is also calling their attention to the fact that juniors are eligible to compete with the seniors for any of the prizes offered by the State Federation.

The four contests sponsored by the General Federation are:

Essay. The department of International Relations offers a prize of a silver cup for the best essay on "What Are the Most Powerful Influences Today Tending to Drive War Out of Civilization." The essay is to contain not more than 800 nor less than 500 words, and is to be sent to Mrs. Giles by April 15th. The prize to be held one year will be awarded at the council meeting in Hot Springs in May.

Song. A prize of $10 is offered for a suitable junior song. Words may be adapted to some popular air or the music may be original. Both words and music should be sent to Mrs. Giles by April 15th.

News Story. The department of Press and Publicity offers two prizes for the best news story on any subject pertinent to juniors. The first prize of $10 is offered for the best story that was accepted and published without editing in a newspaper with a state-wide circulation. Copy of article and printed story should be sent to Mrs. Giles by April 15. The second prize of $5 will be awarded to second best news story published. Prizes will be awarded at the Hot Springs meeting.

Quiz. The department of Fine Arts is offering a $25 prize to both senior and junior clubs who are winners in the contest: "Ask Me Another." Details of this contest will be given later.

Mrs. R. W. Green of Raleigh, chairman of the State Department of Literature, announces the following awards to be made this year at the annual state convention in Asheville May 2–5:

The Joseph P. Caldwell cup for the best short story.

The Sydney Lanier cup for the best one-net play.

The Separk cup for the most meritorious short poem.

The Albert L. Berry cup for the best narrative poem or metrical story.

An award is to be made for the best published newspaper or magazine article between May 1, 1933, and April 1, 1934. All entries for these contests must be in the hands of the chairman not later than April 1, 1934.

Mrs. Charles G. Gulley of Cullowhee, chairman of Music, announces that the Duncan cup will be awarded this year for the most meritorious original music composition, and that the Florence M. Cooper cup shall be awarded for the second best original music composition. These cups remain the property of the Federation and persons having won one twice shall not be eligible to compete a third time.

Raleigh Sunday *News and Observer,* p. 9 (Society, p. 1)

25 FEBRUARY 1934

WOMEN ASK FOR ACTION ON WORLD COURT ISSUE

Club Women Urged To Request Congress To Act On Issue This Session; Early Committee Hearing To Be Held To Determine Sentiment For Or Against United States' Entering World Court

By Mrs. J. Henry Highsmith

Among several important messages of interest to club women received recently from National Headquarters at Washington and from General Federation chairmen was one from Mrs. Grace Morrison Poole, president of the General Federation, and Mrs. Laura Waples McMullen, chairman of International Relations, advising that an important opportunity had arisen regarding the World Court and that immediate attention on the part of the clubs was essential. A committee hearing is soon to be held in Washington at which time all organizations favoring the entrance of the United States into the World Court will be heard. Mrs. Poole and Mrs. McMullen urge club women to get clubs, churches and other organizations in their communities to adopt resolutions asking that "the World Court issue be brought before the present session of Congress and that it be favorably acted upon." They request that these resolutions be sent to Mrs. Laura Waples McMullen, 668 Riverside, New York City, by February 27.

"Act quickly; this may be the straw that will win the entrance of the United States into the World Court," advises Mrs. McMullen. The following resolution is suggested: "Whereas option in our organization has never faltered in its devotion to the campaign to make the United States a member of the World Court, Resolved, that we urge that the World Court issue be brought before the present session of Congress and favorably acted upon." The name of the organization and its address should be given.

"Money Talks" is the title of a valuable booklet issued by Mrs. Annie Peaks Kenny, Dover-Foxcroft, Maine, chairman of the division of Family Finance, of the General Federation. In her plans to reach club women in every state with her program of financial education, Mrs. Kenny is offering "Money Talks" free to club women writing her for copies. Another booklet that should accompany it, "Sliding Scales of Income," costs five cents per copy. "Ten Thousand a Year" is another interesting leaflet to be had from Mrs. Kenny.

Plans for a Grace Morrison Poole birthday party to be held at the council meeting at Hot Springs, Arkansas, in May, are going forward under the chairmanship of Mrs. H. G. Reynolds of Paducah, Kentucky. The object is to augment the Foundation Fund of the General Federation. North Carolina club women have been given advance information about the plans of the party, the kind of cake and the ingredients of the "filling" by Mrs. J. M. Hobgood, state director, in a recent letter sent to club presidents. She is now asking for responses to what shall be North Carolina's share of the cake's filling.

Announcement is made that the General Federation of Women's Clubs will sponsor its second World Friendship tour next summer, the itinerary to include the West Indies, Panama Canal, California, Honolulu, Japan, China, and the Philippines. The party will sail from New York June 21, and return to Seattle September 4. It will be conducted by Mrs. Poole, who is a world traveller and lecturer on international questions. The first world friendship tour sponsored by the General Federation was taken last year to England and Europe. "The success of the first," says Mrs. Poole, "encouraged us to propose this second tour."

Mrs. Howard G. Etheridge of Asheville reports the federation of two new clubs: Quakey Book Club of Halifax with Mrs. F. H. Gregory, president, and Mrs. R. L. Applewhite, secretary and treasurer. The other is the Kannaheeta Club of Andrews, of which Mrs. Zez Conley is president and Mrs. L. B. Nichols is treasurer. There are fifteen members.

Raleigh Sunday *News and Observer,* p. 9 (Society, p. 1)

4 MARCH 1934

FINE RESPONSE TO BETTER CLUB PROGRAMS CONTEST

By Mrs. J. Henry Highsmith

In the first year contest of a two-year campaign sponsored by the State Federation of Women's Clubs in the interest of building better club programs, plans has been made to have judged the 30 club programs submitted in the contest. The judges who have been asked to serve are Miss Cornelia Love of Chapel Hill; Miss Annie Petty of Archdale, formerly with the State Library Commission at Raleigh; and Miss Juanita McDougall of Raleigh, who is with the State Department of Education. While the judging will take place within the next month, announcement of the prize-winning clubs and awarding of the $30 in prizes will not be made before the meeting of the State convention in Asheville in May.

Believing that better club programs make better clubs and give purpose and direction to club work, the Federation undertook last fall a two-year program building contest for the purpose of stimulating and interesting the clubs in building better club programs. The response to the first year's effort has been good, but from the experience and information gained through the contest recently closed, a much larger number of entries is anticipated for next year. Of the 30 clubs competing, 18 are departmental clubs and 12 are study clubs. For the best program or year-book for the club year 1933–1934 submitted by clubs of each of these two classes, a prize of $10 is offered. For the second best program or year book in each class, a prize of $3 is offered.

In building club programs embodying a year's work, five points have been emphasized: Having a definite purpose, unity of subject matter, educational and cultural value, originality, and conformity with Federation's ideals and objectives. Local needs are also taken into account. Style, shape and arrangement are left largely to the initiative of the makers.

The clubs submitting programs and year-books are: The Woman's Clubs of Biscoe, Aurora, Clayton, Canton, Elkin, Concord, Greensboro, Mount Airy, Rose Hill, Moyock, Oxford, Oriental, Raleigh, Salisbury, Taylorsville and Wallace; the Art Study Club of New Bern, Clarksville Literary Club, Scotland Neck; Colonial Literary Club, Asheville; Leaksville-Spray Hickory Club; Lincolnton Literature Department; Maid and Matrons Club, Chadbourn; North Carolina Sorosis, Wilmington; Norlina Literary Club; Research Club of Asheville; Research Club of Mt. Gilead; Ramblers Literary Club of Summerfield; Saluda Book Club, Sorosis of Charlotte; Sorosis of Winston-Salem; and the Worth While Club of Mount Gilead.

Mrs. W. J. Brogden of Durham, chairman of the Sallie Southall Cotten Loan Fund, is reminding clubs that their pledges to this fund are now due. She says that payment of loans to the 26 girls who are now in college through aid from this fund must soon be made, and that the pledges made by the clubs to this fund are counted on for the purpose. Mrs. Brogden commends most heartily the cooperation of club women in paying their pledges to the S. S. C. L. Fund promptly, which enables her to keep faith with the girls depending on her for help.

The West End Book Club makes the fourteenth club to be federated this club year. Mrs. W. F. Elliott is president of the club and Miss Mary Ritter is treasurer. Mrs. Howard Etheridge of Asheville writes that only one club has withdrawn this year and that only two have temporarily disbanded. She considers this a good report in view of the pressing financial situation that clubs and other organizations have been called on to face.

Raleigh Sunday *News and Observer*, p. 9 (Society, p. 1)

25 MARCH 1934

FEDERATION COUNCIL WILL CONVENE AT HOT SPRINGS
By Mrs. J. Henry Highsmith

Discussion of pertinent though highly controversial questions of today, such as birth control, equal rights for women, old age pensions and unemployment insurance will constitute a part of the program of the council meeting of the General Federation of Women's Clubs to be held in Hot Springs, Arkansas, May 21–26. Margaret Sanger, president of the National Committee on Federal Legislation for Birth Control, will speak for birth control while there will be a strong speaker against it. Both sides of the other three questions will also be given by speakers of national repute but not with the view that any action on any question will be taken at this time. The open discussions are for the information of the club women who will attend.

Mrs. Grace Morrison Poole, president of the General Federation, announces that the keynote of the council meeting will be: "Your old men shall dream dreams, your young men shall see visions" (Joel 2:28), having in mind that "without vision the people perish." Women and men of national prominence will be heard in a discussion of present day problems and their solution, and there will be reports of the work accomplished and of plans for future projects by the chairmen of the nine major departments of work.

"Club Women, What of the Future?" will be the subject of a symposium when each State Federation president will speak for two minutes on what she sees ahead in club work. Many attractive social and recreational features have been arranged by Mrs. W. F. Lake of Arkansas, chairman of arrangements. Hotel Arlington will be official headquarters and will house the sessions as well. In addition to General and State Federation officials, the president of every club directly federated with the General Federation is entitled to attend the council as a delegate and all club women are welcome as visitors.

An additional award in the State Music Achievement contest which is to be held at the University of North Carolina, Chapel Hill, Friday, April 6th— The Sarah Taylor Hassell Scholarship prize of $10 for the highest winner in the State Contest—is announced by Mrs. E. E. Randolph of Raleigh, chairman of Public School Music in the State Federation of Women's Clubs. This prize offered for the first time this year is given by Mrs. J. M. Hobgood of Farmville, former president of the Federation, in memory of her mother, the late Mrs. Sarah Taylor Hassell. It is offered with the view of aiding the young girl or boy winning the contest to develop further his musical talents.

Mrs. R. W. Green of Raleigh, chairman of Literature, reports many entries being made for the prizes offered by her department for creative writing. In addition to the Caldwell Cup for the best short story, the Lanier Cup for the best one-set play, the Separk Cup for the best short poem and the Berry Cup for the best narrative poem or metrical story, there will be an award for the best published newspaper or magazine article between May 1, 1933 and April 1, 1934. All entries must be in the hands of the chairman not later than April 1, 1934.

Mrs. P. R. Rankin of Mount Gilead, president of the 5th District, reports organizing and federating two new clubs—the Book Club of Troy with Mrs. A. L. Capel, president and Mrs. O. R. Denton, Jr., as treasurer, and the Woman's Club of Huntersville with Mrs. Fred Hastings as president and Mrs. Dwight Cross as treasurer. With these two clubs, Mrs. Rankin has five to her credit for this club year, and writes that she has prospects of one or two more before the club year closes, or probably before the state convention. To the district president federating the largest number of clubs during the year goes the Cooper gavel.

Raleigh Sunday *News and Observer,* p. 9 (Society, p. 1)

1 APRIL 1934

FEDERATION HEAD ISSUES STATE CONVENTION CALL

By Mrs. J. Henry Highsmith

In an official call which Mrs. R. H. Latham of Asheville, president of the State Federation of Women's Clubs, has just issued to all officers, department chairmen and heads of committees, and to local club presidents, it is noted that a program of noted speakers, entertaining features of various sorts and constructive business sessions await the members and visitors who will attend. The convention begins Wednesday, May 2 and continue through Friday, May 4. Plans for entertaining one of the largest crowds ever to attend a Federation convention are being made by the ten federated clubs of Asheville who will play host to the convention. While the George Vanderbilt Hotel will be official headquarters, the Battery Park and the Asheville Biltmore will assist in entertaining the visitors.

The opening session will be held in the ballroom of the George Vanderbilt Wednesday evening with special music, addresses and a reception by the hostess clubs as part of the program. Mrs. Latham will make her report as president at this time. A meeting of the executive board has been called for 10 o'clock Wednesday morning at the Asheville Country Club, where a luncheon will be served members of the board at 1 o'clock with the presidents of the local federated clubs as hostesses. At 3 o'clock the board of trustees will meet at the hotel and at the same hour a class in parliamentary procedure conducted by Miss Margaret L. Gibson will be held for the club presidents. At 4 o'clock an important meeting of the board directors will be held in the ballroom. Dinners for the past presidents, district presidents and department chairmen have been arranged for 6 o'clock.

Two delightful programs have been planned for the evening sessions of Thursday and Friday. Miss Clementine Douglas of the Spinning Wheel of Asheville will be the speaker for Fine Arts evening Thursday, at which time and on other occasions of the convention the arts and crafts of North Carolina will be featured. Miss Douglas will speak on the art of spinning and weaving. Other phases of the fine arts will be presented in the evening's program, special music in particular. At the Federation dinner on Friday evening Mrs. Grace Morrison Poole will be the honor guest and speaker. Special music and the awarding of the prizes offered by the departments of the Federation will be features of the dinner program.

An innovation that will be followed this year as an experiment will be leaving off all breakfast conferences and combining the luncheon conferences so as to have only two each day. On Thursday there will be a luncheon sponsored by the departments of arts. music and literature at which Mrs. Andrew Jamieson of Oxford will preside and Mr. Burnam Standish Colburn of Biltmore will be the principal speaker. At the same hour but at the Battery Park Hotel there will be a luncheon conference sponsored by the departments of gardens, civics and American Home. Mrs. R. D. V. Jones of New Bern will preside and Dr. Frank Howard Richardson of Black Mountain will be the speaker. In addition, Mrs. Proffitt of Asheville will give an illustrated lecture on gardens.

On Friday the departments of Public Welfare and American Citizenship will hold their luncheon conference on the roof garden of the Battery Park Hotel at which Mrs. B. A. Hocutt will preside and Mrs. Carl W. Illig of Massachusetts will be the speaker. At the same hour in the ballroom of the Battery Park there will be a luncheon for club presidents at which Mrs. Grace Morrison Poole will be the speaker. This conference is held at Mrs. Poole's request.

Raleigh Sunday *News and Observer,* p. 9 (Society, p. 1)

8 APRIL 1934

ART APPRECIATION TESTS WILL BE CONDUCTED SOON

By Mrs. J. Henry Highsmith

Preparatory to the State Art Appreciation Contest which will be held in Raleigh, Saturday, May 5, for the public school children of the State, there will be 16 district art contests held on Friday, April 28, at places designated by the district chairmen having the contest in charge.

The district contests will serve to select representatives to be sent to the State contest in May. One representative from each high school and each elementary school in a district may compete. The chairmen sponsoring the contests in the 16 Federation districts are:

Mrs. R. N. Barber, Waynesville; Mrs. George C. Osborne, West Asheville; Mrs. J. W. McIntosh, Lenoir; Mrs. Elizabeth Knox Hood, of Gastonia; Mrs. P. R. Rankin, Mount Gilead; Mrs. A. D. Folger, Dobson; Mrs. R. E. Labberton; Mrs. J. Guy Penny, Garner; Mrs. T. G. Monroe, Hamlet; Mrs. Glenn Strole, Chadbourn; Mrs. R. R. Cusick, Salemburg; Mrs. J. M. West, New Bern; Mrs. J. M. O'Neal, Selma; Mrs. Wade Dickens, Scotland Neck; Mrs. W. S. Carawan, Columbia; and Mrs. Arthur W. Greene, Ahoskie.

The committee members working with Miss Juanita McDougald, of the State Department of Education, in the interest of the State Art Contest are Miss Ida Potent of Meredith College, Miss Nannie Smith of Saint Mary's School and Mrs. R. L. McMillan, all of Raleigh, and Mrs. Andrew Jamieson of Oxford.

The first prize in the State contest is offered by the State Federation of Women's Clubs and will be awarded to the union schools—elementary and high—whose representative totals the highest number of points in the contest. The money, $25, is to be spent for art materials of permanent value for the schools.

Mrs. R. H. Latham of Asheville, president of the Federation, and Mrs. J. Henry Highsmith of Raleigh, executive secretary, attended the State Music Achievement Contest held Friday at Chapel Hill. Mrs. Latham awarded the Federation prize of $25 to the representative of the winning school. Mrs. J. M. Hobgood of Farmville, State Director in the Federation, also attended the contest and awarded the Sarah Taylor Hassell Scholarship prize of $10 which is given by Mrs. Hobgood in memory of her mother. The prize is offered to the young boy or girl winning the contest with the hope of encouraging the winner to pursue further his musical education.

Music Week in May.

Miss Hattie Parrott of Raleigh, chairman of National Music Week for the Federation, announces that the 11th National Music Week will be celebrated this year from May 6 to May 12. The objective to be aimed at during this week, she says, is to provide such musical activities in the community as will develop "A More Fruitful Use of Leisure Through Music." Music Week, she says, is expected to foster the use of music as a salutary form of recreation during the present emergency, thereby strengthening the general community morale. It is urged further by the committee that Music Week be utilised to secure support of local music activities, especially music education in the schools.

According to Mrs. J. D. McCall of Charlotte, treasurer of the Federation, the following clubs have paid in full their quota to the General Foundation Fund: Asheville Time and Tide Club, Chadbourn Maids and Matrons, Clayton Halcyon, Farmville Literary, Lexington Club of Twelve, Sylva Twentieth Century, Wilmington Sorosis, and the Woman's Clubs of Aurora, Ayden, Enfield, Garner, Kannapolis, Varina, Warrenton, Weldon, and Williamston. Many clubs that are near the top are expected to go over before making their reports at convention.

Raleigh Sunday *News and Observer*, p. 9 (Society, p. 1)
Charlotte Sunday Observer, p. 22 (section 2, p. 6)

15 April 1934

State Arts and Crafts To Feature Convention

By Mrs. J. Henry Highsmith

A particularly fitting feature of the approaching convention of the State Federation of Women's Clubs to be held at Asheville, Wednesday, Thursday and Friday May 2, 3, and 4, will be the place and emphasis given to North

Carolina arts and crafts. In the first place, the convention is being held in the heart of the Blue Ridge mountains where native skill and crafts have been preserved and in more recent years developed under expert training, so that today these have become widely recognized and worthwhile industries.

In the second place, this special recognition is in line with the slogan adopted for the club year by the president of the Federation, Mrs. R. H. Latham—"Our North Carolina."

Back in the fall, Mrs. Latham after traveling over the State and seeing the great variety of handiworks being made by its gifted citizens, called on the club women to make it a North Carolina Christmas by purchasing one or more objects of art, the works of North Carolina craftsmen, as Christmas presents.

In addition to an extensive exhibition of the works of the various arts and crafts in the vicinity of Asheville, there will be an address on Fine Arts Evening, Thursday, by Miss Clementine Douglas of Asheville, director and founder of "The Spinning Wheel." Her subject will be "Weaving Through the Ages," and it will be illustrated with objects of art gathered during her travels in many countries. "The Spinning Wheel" is the attractive social and work center established by Miss Douglas for the purpose of developing and marketing their wares end as a place for teaching and putting into practice wholesome social ideals. It is located about two miles from Asheville on the highway leading to Beaver Lake.

Another art project of interest in connection with the convention is the exhibit of art works by North Carolina club women. Mrs. Andrew Jamieson of Oxford, chairman of art, is anticipating a large number of club women co-operating to make this exhibit interesting and beneficial by sending one or more of their art productions to Asheville to be entered in the exhibit. She will be glad to give specific instruction to those desiring further information concerning the exhibit. The prizes offered this year are: For the best water color, the Margaret Nowell Graham sliver vase; for the best portrait, the Mrs. S. Clay Williams silver cup; for the best piece of sculpture, the Henry Dwire set of copper etchings; for the best essay on "Art in Precious Metals and as a Source of History," the Bernau silver cup. This offer is not limited to club women, therefore the cup will be awarded to any North Carolina woman writing the best essay on this subject,

According to Mrs. Jamieson, 18 clubs have joined the Penny Art Fund Club, and keen interest is being manifested in the Fine Arts Community Festival contest. Clubs are again advised that unless they are members of the Penny Art Fund Club they are not eligible to compete for the Penny Art Fund prize, which now amounts to more than $15. Reports can be made to Mrs. Jamieson as late as April 19.

Mrs. P. R. Rankin of Mount Gilead has organized and federated another club, a club of 12 members, in Troy with Mrs. J. E. Griffin as president and Mrs. Charles Brown as treasurer.

Raleigh Sunday News and Observer, p. 9 (Society, p. 1)

29 April 1934

Federation Convention Has Auspicious Setting

Asheville Will Entertain One Of Largest Delegations Of Club Women Ever To Attend A State Convention; Three-Day Meeting Opens Wednesday; Joint Discussion Of Constitution Will Be High Light

By Mrs. J. Henry Highsmith

With the finishing touches put to an already full and inviting three-day program, with a setting unsurpassed for natural beauty by any country in the world—Western North Carolina in May—and with ideal weather and the best roads of any state in the Union, the thirty-second annual convention of the State Federation of Women's Clubs convenes auspiciously in Asheville, Wednesday, and continues through Friday. Under such favorable and enticing circumstances Asheville is prepared to welcome and entertain one of the largest delegations of club women that ever attended a state convention.

The formal opening of the convention takes place Wednesday evening at 8 o'clock in the ballroom of the George Vanderbilt Hotel with the president, Mrs. R. H. Latham, presiding. Following the procession of the official family of the Federation and singing of the Clubwoman's Hymn, Rt. Rev. Robert E. Gribbon of Asheville will make the invocation. Salute to the flag will be led by Mrs. Sydney P. Cooper of Henderson. Following will be the presentation of the Federation mascot, Mary Louise Jackson Cooper, and the convention pages. Wickes Womboldt, mayor of Asheville, will extend welcome on the part of the city of Asheville, while Mrs. E. L. McKee of Sylva will extend a welcome on the part of Western North Carolina. Mrs. Palmer Jerman of Raleigh will make the response.

Greetings from the State Federation of Music Clubs will be given by Mrs. Eugene Davis; from the State Federation of Home Demonstration Clubs, by Mrs. Gordon Reid; from the State Congress of Parents and Teachers, by Mrs. J. L. Henderson; from the State Garden Clubs, by Mrs. Dameron Williams, and from the National Altrusa, by Mrs. Chase Going Woodhouse. Following the president's address by Mrs. Latham, there will be a reception held in the parlors of the hotel complimentary to the visiting club women and visitors as a courtesy of the federated clubs of Asheville.

The following members of the Junior Woman's Civic Club of Asheville will serve as convention pages: Miss Dorothy Jordan, chief page; Mrs. Craig

Hurst, Mrs. Thomas Huffines, Mrs. Ross Stribbling, Mrs. A. J. Coffey, Miss Helen Conroy, Mrs. DeVere Lentz, Mrs. W. T. Reade, Mrs. A. J. Garner, Mrs. W. B. Henderson and Mrs. Howard Covington. Serving as personal pages to the president will be the following members of the Junior Woman's Club of Winston-Salem: Mrs. Howard Grubbs, Miss Lois Strickland, Mrs. A. H. Doggett and Miss Mary Crutchfield. Mrs. Chas. G. Gulley will be leader for assembly singing and Mrs. Eugene Davis accompanist. Miss Margaret L. Gibson will serve as parliamentarian in addition to conducting the classes in parliamentary law each morning

Since the question whether or not the proposed revisions to the State Constitution will be adopted is to be settled at the polls next November, the joint discussion of this subject planned for Thursday evening will be one of the highlights of the convention. The public will be invited to this session. Senator Carpus Waynick of High Point and Raleigh will discuss the Constitution favoring the proposed changes, and Dennis G. Brummitt will present the opposition.

Rarely are lovelier recreational features planned for a convention than those awaiting the club women attending the Asheville meeting. The tea to be given at the Biltmore Country Club on Thursday afternoon, the drive through Biltmore Forest, the panoramic view from the clubhouse terrace will become cherished memories, as will be the visits to some of Asheville's loveliest gardens. A visit to Biltmore House, one of America's showplaces, which has been arranged by the committee will be a rare privilege, Every North Carolinian should see "this choice bit of the best of Europe that has found its way to America and to North Carolina."

Raleigh Sunday *News and Observer*, p. 9 (Society, p. 1)

13 MAY 1934

FEDERATION COUNCIL MEETS IN HOT SPRINGS MAY 21–26

North Carolina Will Be Well Represented At General Federation Council Meet; Club Women Reminded That Action, Not Sentiment Should Characterize Observance Of Mothers' Day

By Mrs. J. Henry Highsmith

The next high peak of interest to claim the attention of North Carolina club women is the council meeting of the General Federation that is to be held at Hot Springs, Arkansas, May 21–26. North Carolina will be represented at this meeting by Mrs. R. H. Latham of Asheville, president of the State Federation; by Mrs. J. M. Hobgood of Farmville, State director; Mrs. Edward M. Land of Statesville, general chairman of Juniors, and possibly by the seven delegates elected at the recent meeting of the State convention in Asheville. These were Mrs. E. L. McKee of Sylva; Mrs. Andrew Jamieson of Oxford;

Mrs. B. A. Hocutt of Clayton; Mrs. E. L. Layfield of Raleigh; Mrs. George Marshall of Mt. Airy; Miss Ethel Parker of Gatesville and Mrs. P. R. Rankin of Mount Gilead. Alternates were Mrs. Claude Morris of Salisbury; Mrs. Gilbert Morris; Mrs. J. J. Purdy; Mrs. Dale Thrash; Mrs. W. S. Johnstone and Mrs. Frank Lethco.

Of keen interest is the innovation in the council program which provides for discussion of some of the foremost topics of the day having special interest to women. Opposing viewpoints by distinguished men and women will be given on such subjects as birth control, equal rights for women, old age pensions and compulsory unemployment insurance.

Five resolutions will be offered at the council meeting. Two call for direct action on a current national problem and three direct intensive study of facts and issues involved in pending legislation. One resolution endorses the general principle and purpose of the Copeland Pure Food and Drugs Bill. Another firmly opposes the return of the saloon and recommends that temperance instruction be emphasized in our public school systems. Studies of unemployment insurance, old age pensions, equal rights amendment and of crime prevention and control measures are called for in resolutions.

Mothers Day.

Today is Mothers Day. It has been the custom to celebrate it with tender sentiment for living mothers and cherished memories for those who have passed on. But not until motherhood is made safer for mothers is sentiment alone fitting or sufficient for the proper observance of a day so filled with blessed memories and sacred associations. Particularly is this true in North Carolina where more than 600 mothers die each year from causes incident to childbirth, a large number of which deaths could have been prevented. That this number of deaths of mothers in North Carolina is larger than the average for the United States is a further reason why Mothers' Day should have a new meaning this year. Club women should resolve with public spirited men and women of other organizations—with their physicians and health officers, their pastors, educators and lawmakers to change conditions that render motherhood possibly the most dangerous profession that a woman can enter.

To create a public opinion that will demand better care of mothers is essential but not enough. Women must be educated as to what constitutes adequate maternal care and how to get it. The size of this task is comprehended from the statement of Dr. G. W. Cooper who says that the primary cause of North Carolina's high maternal death rate is probably the "prevalent notion that child-bearing is a natural process and that death from such a cause is but the will of God."

Ignorance and neglect and not the "will of God" are to be blamed for the high death rate of mothers in this and other states, and there is some comfort in the fact that this stigma is beginning to weigh heavily on the conscience of groups of men and women who have it in their power to remedy the situation.

Raleigh Sunday *News and Observer,* p. 9 (Society, p. 1)

20 MAY 1934

STATE FEDERATION PLANS JUNE CONFERENCE AT DUKE

Purpose of Meeting is to Provide Guidance in Planning Year's Work; Will Continue Two Days

By Mrs. J. Henry Highsmith

Raleigh, May 19.—A conference where club women may come together and under expert guidance work out their plans and programs for another club year has been planned by the State Federation of Women's Clubs in co-operation with Duke University. This conference is to be held this summer, June 11 and 12, at Duke University, the first two days of the second Institute of International Relations. Mrs. R. H. Latham, president of the State Federation, in making the announcement, says that it is the hope of her organization to make this summer conference for club workers an annual event, but with a more fully developed program and for a longer period of time for the conferences in the coming years.

An invitation to all club women to attend the sessions of the conference has been extended through their club presidents. Arrangements have been made with Duke University to entertain the visiting club women for the two days and one night on the University campus.

It will be the good fortune of club women attending the conference at Duke this summer to hear two of the outstanding speakers that have been secured for the International Relations Institute being held there at that time. These are Mrs. Franklin D. Roosevelt, who will speak on the evening of the eleventh, and Leyton Richards of Birmingham, England, who speaks on Tuesday the twelfth. Mr. Richard's subject will be, "The Individual's Relation to War." Other speakers on the institute program are Kirby Page, editor of "The World Tomorrow"; Grover Clark, national authority on "The Far Eastern Conflict"; Dudley D. Carroll of the University of North Carolina; Justin Miller of Duke law school; Calvin Hoover, famous student of European affairs; Devere Allen, well known editor and author; Fred Rippey, of Duke University; Paul Harris, Jr., of Washington D. C.

New officers and department chairmen elected at the recent convention of the Federation held in Asheville were: first vice president, Mrs. Andrew Jamieson, of Oxford; corresponding secretary, Mrs. B. F. Giles, of Marion; recording secretary, Mrs. J. C. Williams, Wilmington; treasurer, Mrs. J. D. McCall, Charlotte. The department chairmen elected were: Mrs. T. G. Monroe of Hamlet, public welfare; Mrs. A. D. Folger of Dobson, junior membership; and Mrs. Karl Bishopric, of Spray, American citizenship.

Charlotte Sunday Observer, p. 20 (section 2, p. 6)

23 SEPTEMBER 1934

STATE FEDERATION COUNCIL WILL MEET IN SALISBURY

By Mrs. J. Henry Highsmith

The fall council meeting of the State Federation of Women's Clubs will be held in Salisbury Tuesday and Wednesday, October 9 and 10. The Woman's Club of Salisbury will be hostess and the Yadkin Hotel, council headquarters.

The meeting will get under way Tuesday morning at 10:30 o'clock with an executive board meeting at the home of Mrs. Pritchard Carlton. This will be followed with a luncheon for the members of the board at Mrs. Carlton's home, a courtesy of the hostess club. In the afternoon at the Yadkin Hotel the board of trustees and the finance committee will meet and there will be conferences of the department chairmen and the district presidents. A dinner conference will be held at the hotel in the evening, featured by a prominent guest speaker. Wednesday morning's program will consist of a general business session, followed by a luncheon for council members at Catawba College, courtesy of the college.

Members of the council are the officers of the Federation, the chairmen of departments, chairmen of standing committees and district presidents. All past presidents of the Federation, chairmen of special committees and all division chairmen are invited to attend the meeting of the council as conference members.

Mrs. R. H. Latham, president, is urging club presidents also to attend the council meeting as conference members, believing that the meeting will be of special value to them in planning and directing their work.

In recent messages sent to the club women of the State by both Mrs. Latham and Mrs. Grace Morrison Poole, president of the General Federation, high notes of endeavor were sounded by both leaders. These messages went out last week in the Federation Year Book, together with program leaflets issued by the department chairmen. Mrs. Poole's message in part was:

"Last year was largely a year of experimentation. This year must be one of adaptation, and you, the club women of your beloved State, must be leaders in this difficult task. Let us never forget that homely proverb, 'The Lord helps him who helps himself.' There is little to choose between the fatal indifference to the public good of yesterday and the growing sentiment that the government can and will feed and clothe us without any effort on our part. Both ideas lead only to disaster. Let us work towards a tomorrow where every citizen of these United States may have the opportunity to make his own way, confident that if he does his part he will have protection against a tragic tomorrow."

Mrs. Latham laid emphasis on the importance of club women being informed on the social and political questions that are in the public mind today. These she mentioned as unemployment insurance, old age pensions, child labor amendment, equal rights amendment and birth control. She asks club women to study both forms of the State Constitution whether we vote on it this year or not, and that they actively support the legislative measures which have been endorsed by the Federation.

Mrs. Latham was a member of the North Carolina party, headed by the Governor, who went to Washington last week to appear before Secretary Harold L. Ickes in the interest of securing the entrance for the Great Smoky Mountain National Park for North Carolina. From Washington, Mrs. Latham will go to Charlottesville, Va., where she will visit before going to the National Current Problem Conference in New York, September 26 and 27. Mrs. Latham will be joined in Washington by Mrs. J. Henry Highsmith, who will also attend the New York convention.

Raleigh Sunday *News and Observer,* p. 9 (Society, p. 1)

28 OCTOBER 1934

CLUB WOMEN TO SUPPORT ADEQUATE SCHOOL PROGRAM

By Mrs. J. Henry Highsmith

The club women of North Carolina pledge to the new State Superintendent of Public Instruction, Clyde A. Erwin, their cooperation and support in working out a more adequate educational program for the children of the State. As they have worked faithfully with Dr. A. T. Allen in the recent past in an effort to determine and help develop a more timely and appropriate course of study for the public schools of the State, they will continue in their efforts to be of service in this and other phases of educational work.

Mrs. George E. Marshall of Mt. Airy, chairman of the department of Education in the Federation of Women's Clubs, believing that the club women have a worthwhile contribution to make in reshaping the educational program of the State, is calling on them to think through at least some of the problems and emergencies that are known to exist and to submit their conclusions in writing to her that all or a part may help to form the Club Woman's Educational Charter for North Carolina. In order to determine a satisfactory and worthy educational creed for club women, she is offering a prize of $5.00 to the club or clubwoman who sends in the best original statement as to what constitutes "the rightful heritage of the children, our children, the future makers of North Carolina."

Rules and regulations as well as further information concerning this contest may be had by writing either Mrs. Marshall at Mt. Airy or Miss

Juanita McDougald at the State Department of Education at Raleigh. The information will include a list of books and pamphlets which treat the subject matter and which are indispensable to intelligent and constructive work. The November issue of the North Carolina Club Woman will also give this information.

Announcement has been made that a service in memory of the late Dr. Elizabeth Delia Dixon Carroll, whose death occurred in Raleigh last May, will be held on Wednesday morning, October 31, in the Chapel of the Cross at Samarcand Manor, Eagle Springs. Dr. Carroll, a highly gifted and warm hearted club woman, was one of the founders of the Samarcand Home for Girls. She was a member of the board of directors of this institution from its beginning in 1917 till the day of her untimely death.

Amazing will describe but not adequately the many features of the three-day garden school sponsored last week at the Woman's Club in Raleigh by the local Garden Club. Amazing was the interest manifested by the several hundred who attended daily from towns far and near, to say nothing of the benefit and pleasure experienced by the members and other Raleigh people. Amazing was the variety of unique entertaining features having both social and educational values. Amazing was the variety of unique entertaining features having both social and educational values. Amazing was the beauty effected by the artistic blending and arranging of fall flowers, berries and foliage. Amazing was the high type of lecture and instructional service provided free for all; and most amazing was the conception of such a public-spirit service and the ease, efficiency and joy with which it was carried out. Congratulations to the Raleigh Garden Club for this fine example of social and civic betterment.

Among the many club women who attended the Raleigh Garden School were Mrs. John D. Robinson of Wallace, chairman of Gardens in the Federation; Mrs. J. J. Andoe of Greensboro, Mrs. H. B. Moore and Mrs. Wooten of Greenville; Mrs. Wade Dickens and Mrs. Leavitt of Scotland Neck and Mrs. Guy Penny of Garner.

Raleigh Sunday *News and Observer*, p. 9 (Society, p. 1)

11 NOVEMBER 1934

STATE LEGISLATIVE COUNCIL ADOPTS PROGRAM FOR YEAR

By Mrs. J. Henry Highsmith

Raleigh, Nov. 10.—Preparatory to the meeting of the 1935 Legislature, the State Legislative Council met in Raleigh recently and adopted a program of forward looking legislative measures. The one measure having the endorsement of the ten groups holding membership in the council was the ratification of the Child Labor amendment to the Federal Constitution.

Four other measures by unanimous consent were placed on the list that will be presented to the Legislature to be enacted into laws. These are:

1. To secure more modern limitations on the number of hours per day and week men and women may be employed. As the present law stands, North Carolina allows the longest work day—11 hours—of any state or country in the Western World where any restriction at all is attempted. The number of hours to be asked for was left to the judgment of the executive committee of the council.

2. To remove the poverty exemption clause in the present child labor law that would allow a boy over 14 and under 16, who is the sole support of himself or widowed mother, to work up to 11 hours per day and as much as 60 hours per week.

3. To require double compensation under the Workmen's Compensation act for children if injured while illegally employed.

4. To ask the state to assume full responsibility for enlargement and maintenance of the State Industrial School for Negro Girls at Efland.

Unemployment insurance was another measure receiving unanimous endorsement. The council pledged to the commission appointed by the governor to study and make recommendations to the Legislature concerning this subject, [and] its co-operation and support in any effort made to get an adequate unemployment insurance law. Likewise it voted to endorse and support the legislative platform submitted by the State Congress of Parents and Teachers. This included requests for an efficient eight months school term, reducing the teacher load by employing more teachers with as much as a 25 per cent increase in pay, change in the school curriculum to meet present social and economic needs, trained leadership, public health service for all school children, wise economy in government expenditure and a survey of the state's ability to meet its educational and social obligations.

Other measures having the approbation of the council for support were the principles of old age pensions, the retention of the Turlington act, improvement of elections laws, the enforcement of the state's bill board advertising laws and bills promoting highway beautification. The legislative programs of the Department of Education, the Department of Public Welfare and the Department of Health were unanimously endorsed. The educational program included consideration of the recommendations of the Governor's Commission on Negro Education; that of the Public Welfare asked for a reasonable program for mental defectives, including more adequate facilities for Caswell Training school and better provision for the Negro feebleminded.

The State Legislative Council was effected last summer, being the enlargement of the Legislative Council of North Carolina Women so as to include groups having men as members and sponsoring a social legislative program, such as the North Carolina Conference for Social Service and the State Congress of Parents and Teachers. The officers are Dr. E. McNeill Poteat, president; Miss Elsie Riddick, first vice president; Harold D. Meyer, second vice president; Mrs. Palmer Jerman, third vice president; Mrs. C. S. Hicks, secretary and Mrs. Charles G. Doak, treasurer. Mrs. J. Henry Highsmith was again elected secretary. Legislative headquarters will be at the Sir Walter Hotel. Plans are being made for a statewide committee to sponsor the Child Labor Amendment.

Charlotte Sunday Observer, p. 18 (section 2, p. 4)
Asheville Citizen-Times, p. 16 (section C, p. 2)

25 NOVEMBER 1934

SCENIC HIGHWAY PROJECT SUPPORTED BY CLUB WOMEN

By Mrs. J. Henry Highsmith

Club women are among the most enthusiastic of jubilant Western North Carolina citizens at this time over the recent decision of Secretary Harold L. Ickes to locate the great Park to Park Highway as well as an eastern entrance to the Great Smoky Mountains National Park in North Carolina. They see in the accomplishment of this wonderful project many of the possibilities only barely dreamed of heretofore in these mountain vastnesses rapidly coming to life. Their anticipation for this new day in the mountains of the State is perhaps all the more keen because of the emphasis stressed for the past two years by the Federation on the study of "Our North Carolina."

Mrs. R. H. Latham, president, chose this as the watch-word of her administration on taking office more than a year and half ago. In compliance with her suggestion, club women have studied North Carolina to know afresh its history, geography, people; its resources latent and developed, having both economic and social values, and the future needs and possibilities of a great commonwealth. That a new deal is at last coming to the people of the mountain district of the State is most gratifying to all its citizens.

"You should see the happy faces in and around Asheville since Secretary Ickes rendered his decision in favor of North Carolina," writes Mrs. Latham. "These mountaineers really believe in Santa Claus now. This is of course going to mean great things to this section of the state and indeed to the entire state. I hope it will help to unify the different sections—not West versus East or Piedmont versus both—but to make of North Carolina a bigger, better state."

Mrs. Latham was most active in helping to secure this scenic park way and park entrance for the state. She was a member of the North Carolina party which, headed by the Governor, went to Washington in September to present the state's claim to the proposed scenic highway. In addition, she has made talks and written letters to Washington urging the fairness of routing the way through North Carolina. That it is assured with innumerable benefits to be realized by all the states on the eastern seaboard is cause for great rejoicing on the part of many states.

More and more is the Institute of Government under the direction of Albert Coates of Chapel Hill proving its worth and reason to be. This fact was demonstrated in the recent session held for public officials in Raleigh. Attending was a large group of legislators, state, county and city office-holders and would-be office-holders two and four years hence, also numbers of club women and interested citizens, all seeking after better government. The separate sessions or schools devoted to the study of special problems found in today's government were found enlightening and helpful.

The address of Judge Florence Allen of the United States Circuit Court of Appeals of Ohio, was the high light of the institute. She captivated her large audience of men and women from all parts of the state at the beginning and held it while she presented the need for a more modern interpretation and application of the principles of government established by our forefathers. She plead for individual and collective thinking on the problems of government and highly commended Mr. Coates and the Institute of Government in North Carolina for its program to secure a more efficient and at the same time a more economical government in city, county and state units.

Raleigh Sunday *News and Observer*, p. 19 (Society, p. 1)
Charlotte Sunday Observer, p. 23 (section 2, p. 7)

9 DECEMBER 1934

MEETINGS IN RALEIGH SET FORWARD FINE ARTS IN STATE

By Mrs. J. Henry Highsmith

Raleigh, Dec. 8.—That the artistic and intellectual life of the state was perceptibly quickened and set pulsating to hopes of bigger and better achievements as a result of the three day meetings devoted to art, history, literature, poetry and folk-lore held in Raleigh last week was the expressed opinion of many who attended the meetings. It was the general feeling that the interest manifested in these meetings was more representative than usual of all the people of the state, and that the addresses, papers and reports were of an unusually high order. Reports revealed plans and projects now in the process of accomplishment which when finished will be dreams come true.

One of these is the obtainment of a State Art Museum. Mrs. Katherine Pendleton Arrington, president of the North Carolina Art Society, announced that the beautiful Cameron home in Raleigh could be secured for this purpose at a reasonable price. Arrangements for financing the loan and making available this one of the few remaining types of southern mansions, with its colonial architecture and magnificent oak grove, as a storehouse and center of art interests in the state are now under way. Dr. Frank Graham, president of the State Literary and Historical Association, announced that through the gift of a friend and the co-operation of the Carnegie Foundation an art museum was under construction at the State university. Dr. A. R. Newsome, secretary of the State Literary and Historical Association, reported that the project sponsored by his organization and the State Department of Conservation and Development of placing markers on the highways to denote the location of important historic spots was going forward satisfactorily.

But the high light or sensation of the series of meetings was the discovery by North Carolinians of their mountain poet, James Larkin Pearson, probably the state's most famous poet. He had already been discovered, it seems, by the peoples of other states, New Yorkers in particular, but it took Dr. Frank Graham, his ardent friend, to bring him down to Raleigh and introduce him to a select group of men and women, some of whom were his kith and kin and knew it not. The ovation given him after hearing his life-story and the reading of several of his poems, the most popular of which is entitled "Fifty Acres," showed that he had conquered. Figuratively speaking, the literati were at his feet and all were kindred spirits. This experience, he said, and the genial words of praise and appreciation of his new found friends would enable him to continue his quest for the soul poetry with the faith to win.

This somewhat belated discovery of Mr. Pearson by his own people makes one wonder if there are not others of his calling—poets, artists, craftsmen, writers and musicians—back in the coves, in the mills or down on the farms, that need only a good friend to bring them out, introduce them and have the creative fire kindle within their souls. At least it should make North Carolinians more alert to recognize, appreciate and encourage those of their own kind who have the gifts and the soul to create.

Among the club women of the state who attended the meetings were Miss Adelaide Fries, Winston-Salem; Mrs. Andrew Jamieson, Oxford; Mrs. C. J. Sawyer, Windsor; Mrs. J. J. Andoe, Greensboro; Mrs. P. R. Rankin, Mount Gilead; and Mrs. W. W. Parker of Lumberton.

At the recent meeting of the Sixth District held at Thomasville, Mrs. W. E. Tomlinson of Thomasville was elected district president to succeed Mrs. Clay Ring of Kernersville, who found she could not serve.

The recent death of Mrs. Gilmer S. Korner of Kernersville marks the passing of one of North Carolina's pioneer club women—one who loved and served the Federation well for a period of more than 30 years. Her faith and her example as evidenced in the work and love for the Woman's Club has been an inspiration to younger club women who will carry on after her.

Charlotte Sunday Observer, p. 24 (section 2, p. 8)

23 DECEMBER 1934

CLUB WOMEN ARE EXTENDED GREETINGS BY STATE HEAD
Card of Cheer is Also Issued by Mrs. Poole, President of General Federation of Women's Clubs

By Mrs. J. Henry Highsmith

Raleigh, Dec. 22.—Before leaving to spend the Christmas holidays in New Orleans and visiting friends in southern cities, Mrs. R. H. Latham, president of the State Federation of Women's Clubs, took time to send the club women of North Carolina a Christmas message. It is this:

> "God grant you happiness and mirth
> And best of friends around your hearth
> And the joys of Health,
>
> "And may you own the glorious things
> Which true contentment always brings
> And just enough Wealth.
>
> "And may you find along the way
> The Christmas spirit every day."

She also makes several suggestions for cheering and inspiriting the family at Christmas time. She says:

"Read aloud Dickens' 'Christmas Carol,' 'The Bird's Christmas Carol' by Kate Douglas Wiggin, and 'The Other Wise Man' by Van Dyke. Read again those stories of the Nativity to your children as you gather around the fireplace on Christmas Day.

"Join the choral clubs in singing carols around the community Christmas tree or at the doors of shut-ins.

"Share your homes with the lonely and the homeless on Christmas day.

"Let love and interest prompt your giving this year.

"Give glimpses of the Christmas customs in other lands to your children through books. Here are two: 'This Way to Christmas,' by Ruth Sawyer, and 'The Feast of Noel,' by Gertrude Crownfield.

"Pageants and tableaux in our churches and schools will give us a new wonder and meaning of Christmas.

"Co-operate with your ministers in emphasizing World Peace."

An interesting Christmas card from Mrs. Grace Morrison Poole, president of the General Federation of Women's Clubs, shows in symbolism that the General Federation Christmas tree this year will burn a candle for club members in twenty foreign countries. These are in addition to a galaxy of stars at the top of the tree representing the club groups of the United States. The foreign clubs remembered by Mrs. Poole this Christmas are in Peru, New Zealand, West Indies, Brazil, Argentina, Australia, Japan, China,

Africa, Egypt, Spain, France, England, Germany, Austria, Czechoslovakia, Uruguay, Mexico and Canada.

Mrs. Poole's Christmas message to all club women this year is: "I shall be thinking of you on December 25. And I shall be thinking of you in relation to children. To make every child happy on that day is the desire of every human being, but why do we stop with that day alone? If we should put as much effort into giving our children the right kind of a world in which to live as we do into giving them the happy Christmas, the millennium would come much faster than is now apparent. Let's think of that as we say each other and the world at large "Happy Christmas to You."

The writer takes this occasion to wish every reader of her column a very merry Christmas and happy New Year.

Charlotte Sunday Observer, p. 16 (section 2, p. 4)

30 DECEMBER 1934

CLUB WOMEN OF STATE ACTIVE FOR AMENDMENT

By Mrs. J. Henry Highsmith

To enlist the active support of North Carolina club women in behalf of the ratification of the Child Labor Amendment by the 1935 State Legislature is the purpose of a recent letter issued to club women by their president, Mrs. R. H. Latham of Asheville. She calls attention to the fact that both the State and General Federations of Women's Clubs had endorsed the Amendment and that the State Legislative Council, of which the Federation is a member, is conducting at this time a special campaign in behalf of its ratification.

Before listing certain facts which she would have club women consider in connection with the ratification of the Amendment, Mrs. Latham quotes the text which she says is generally misunderstood and misrepresented. The text is:

Section 1. The Congress shall have power to limit regulate and prohibit the labor of persons under eighteen years of age.

Section 2. The power of the several states is unimpaired by this article except that the operation of state laws shall be suspended to the extent necessary to give effect to legislation enacted by Congress.

In the opinion of Mrs. Latham, this is the acceptable year—psychologically, economically and humanely—when North Carolina by act of its Legislature should go on record as having ratified the Amendment. Its Legislature is one of 44 meeting in 1935, all of which will be called on to ratify the Amendment and thereby furnish the 16 more states needed to make the Amendment become effective. To date 20 states have ratified when 36 are needed.

The facts that Mrs. Latham would have club women consider concerning ratification are: Twenty-two national and twelve state organizations are supporting it. Twenty states have already ratified it while only 18 more are needed to make it a federal law. It will not prevent children from helping their parents at home or on the farm. It will prevent children under 18 years from being employed in dangerous occupations. It is aimed not against work for children but against the employment of children under 18 years at pitifully small wages when there are not jobs enough for adults; against depriving children of their rightful heritage of health, play and a chance for an education when there are idle men and women in need of work. The NRA codes which have taken children for the most part out of industry and demonstrated that a Federal child labor law can and will work effectively, are likely to expire in June, 1935, when the 100,000 children that are now protected will be left without safeguards to be swept back into employment, the result being a low wage level for all and a piling up of unemployment for adults.

The State organizations that are supporting the Amendment are: American Legion American, Legion Auxiliary, North Carolina Conference for Social Service, State Federation of Women's Clubs, State Federation of Business and Professional Women's Clubs, State League of Women Voters, State Nurses Association, State Federation of Labor, Western North Carolina Conference of the Methodist Church South, Women's Missionary Society of the N. C. Conference, Methodist Church South; Women's Auxiliary of the Protestant Episcopal Church, Diocese of North Carolina; State Branch of American Association of University Women, Woman's Christian Temperance Union, North Carolina Association of Jewish Women and North Carolina Association of Superintendents of Public Welfare.

Raleigh Sunday *News and Observer,* p. 17 (Society, p. 1)
Charlotte Sunday Observer, p. 22 (section 2, p. 8)

1935

3 January — addresses RWC on Legislative Council agenda of five measures proposed to 1935 Legislature; club endorses

15 January — addresses Twentieth Century Book Club on "The New Germany"

17 January — joins speaker's bureau supporting Child Labor Amendment

29 January — addresses Sir Walter Cabinet on legislative program of State Legislative Council

29 January — assists with local arrangements for visit of Helen Keller and Polly Thomson to Raleigh Memorial Auditorium

7 February — attends NCFWC board meeting in Raleigh; hosts Mrs. Latham and Mrs. Bishopric

18 February — attends, with Vara, International Relations Institute supper at the RWC

19 February — endorses council–manager plan of government for Raleigh "because it embodies scientific principles"; she and Vara are on advisory committee favoring

20 February — reports to Raleigh Garden Club on recommendations for new constitution

26 February — speaks in favor of council–manager plan over WPTF

4 April — chairs Literature Department RWC meeting to which all book clubs in Raleigh have been invited; tea following

5 April — elected second vice president, North Carolina League of Women Voters, at 14th annual convention, Chapel Hill

17 April — attends hearing of Senate Committee on Manufacturing, Labor and Commerce, speaking in favor of limiting working hours of women in industry to 48 hours per week; committee reports out without prejudice

26 April — speaks briefly at RWC Get-Together Dinner with husbands and friends

30 April — as part of Better Speech Week, judges, with Dr. Highsmith, an essay contest for Raleigh high school students

1 May — attends luncheon for Mrs. Josephus Daniels, home for a vacation from Mexico City

2 May — is unanimously endorsed by RWC for president, NCFWC (which doesn't happen for several more years)

7–10 May — attends for 33rd annual NCFWC convention, Elizabeth City

1935–36, 1936–37, 1937–38
Chair of Press and Publicity
General Federation of Women's Clubs

May — begins 3-year term as national publicity chair, GWFC in the administration of Mrs. Roberta Campbell Lawson, with the mission "Every person writing club publicity a trained person"

8 May — named chair, legislative committee, Murphey School PTA

25 June – 9 July — motor trip to New England and Canada with Vara and Mary Belle and Miss Elizabeth Aldred of Durham; returning via Portland, Boston, and New York, where Mary Belle remains to attend Columbia Sumer School for six weeks

late July — judges spoken essay contest of Cotton Growers Cooperative Association, on "What a Unified Program of Cooperative Purchasing and Marketing Can Mean to Farmers in North Carolina"

late July — vacations with Katherine and Louise at Herring Cottage, White Lake, returning 2 August

c. 4 August — attends Southern Writers' Conference at Blue Ridge

27 September — attends annual Get-Together Dinner of RWC; presents dedication of yearbook to Bessie Massey Layfield (Mrs. E. L. Layfield)

3 October — attends first RWC meeting of year, on libraries

22 October — death of her brother, Troy I. Herring, 52, in Reidsville after suffering a heart attack while visiting relatives; funeral 24 October in Roseboro

1 November — General Federation announces her appointment as chairman of Press and Publicity in a release carried by newspapers across the country

8 November — attends, as committee member, exhibition at RWC of paintings of Charles W. Ward of Trenton NJ and tea offered by Twentieth Century Book Club

6 JANUARY 1935

TWO WASHINGTON MEETINGS INTEREST WOMEN OF STATE

By Mrs. J. Henry Highsmith

Two meetings that will claim the attention of North Carolina club women this month take place in Washington D. C. One is the midwinter Board meeting of the General Federation of Women's Clubs and the other is the Tenth Anniversary Conference of the National Committee on the Cause and Cure of War. The General Board meeting will be held at National Headquarters January 16–19, and will be presided over by the president, Mrs. Grace Morrison Poole. The Cause and Cure of War conference will be held January 22–25 and will feature an address by its honorary chairman, Mrs. Carrie Chapman Catt, who will review the ten years' work of the women toward world peace.

Among North Carolina club women who will attend one or both of these conferences will be Mrs. R. H. Latham of Asheville, Mrs. J. M. Hobgood of Farmville, Mrs. Edward M. Land of Statesville, Miss Gertrude Weil of Goldsboro, Mrs. Karl Bishopric of Spray and Miss Courtney Sharpe of Lumberton.

Secretary of Labor, Frances Perkins; Secretary of Commerce, Daniel C. Roper; and Senator Gerald P. Nye of North Dakota are among the nationally known figures who will address the club women's board meeting. Other speakers will include a representative from the Department of Justice who will discuss the campaign on crime; a representative from the American Legion who will speak on the organization's bill that would conscript national resources; and Senator Nye will discuss pertinent issues arising from the investigation of the munitions inquiry. The government's housing program will be presented by Louis J. Alber and Dr. John W. Studebaker, U. S. Commissioner of Education, will speak on the education program that will be presented to Congress. Mrs. William Brown Meloney of New York and Mrs. Harvey W. Wiley of Washington will be other speakers.

Mrs. Franklin D. Roosevelt will honor members of the board with a tea at the White House, Wednesday afternoon of the meeting. Another social event will be a reception by Mrs. Eugene Meyer, vice-president of the Washington Post and a patron of the arts, at her home Thursday afternoon. The annual reception, always a highlight of Washington's social functions, given by the board with members of Congress and their wives as guests, will be held Tuesday evening at Headquarters. Mrs. A. N. Connett, Jr., president of the American Woman's Club of Paris, will be honored at an informal dinner at the Iron Gate Inn by the executive committee Thursday evening.

The principal speaker at the banquet of the Cause and Cure of War Conference will be Mrs. Franklin D. Roosevelt. The first lady's program will be devoted to a review of The World Today, followed by speakers who will interpret these events according to their influence for peace or war. The last day's sessions will be devoted to the National Marathon Roundtable. The speakers who are to go out to the regional conferences in ten cities will be presented and speeded on their way. The delegates also will be received at the White House.

Miss Gertrude Weil, who is a faithful attendant upon these meetings, says: "We should have a full North Carolina delegation at this year's Conference which promises to be better than usual if that is possible. Each State organization is entitled to two delegates and to two alternates. While there is a new and a wider spread interest in peace right now than ever before, perhaps, we should take advantage of these gains and strive to make them permanent. I sincerely hope a large number of women—young women—will attend this conference." Miss Weil will be glad to give further information concerning the Cause and Cure of War Conference to those who are contemplating attending. Write her at 20 Chestnut Street, Goldsboro.

Raleigh Sunday *News and Observer*, p. 17 (Society, p. 1)

13 January 1935

Asks Aid of Club Women in Fight Against Cancer

By Mrs. J. Henry Highsmith

Mrs. Chas. R. Whitaker of Lenoir, chairman of Health in the State Federation of Women's Clubs, is announcing that her division beginning this month will wage a fight against cancer. The slogan of the campaign, she says, is "Cancer Thrives on Ignorance. Fight It with Knowledge." She is calling on the club women of the State to cooperate in this fight that is of so great importance to women and reminds them that this request comes also from the department of health of the General Federation.

Mrs. Whitaker further announces that Dr. W. D. James of Hamlet has been secured to assist in the campaign and that he will give his services free in lecturing to the clubs. With his lectures he shows highly valued colored lantern slides which show the before and after treatment of cancer with radium and X-ray. Dr. James has already lectured to the club women of Hamlet, Bayboro, Mount Airy, Sanford, Whiteville, Hillsboro and Elizabethtown. He has engagements to address the clubs of New Bern and Swan Quarter in the near future. Mrs. Whitaker is asking club presidents and health chairmen of a community, county or district to get together and arrange for a series of lectures by Dr. James, which plan would reduce expenses and work to a great advantage to him. She advises writing him immediately as to available dates.

The program adopted for the campaign on cancer has already been printed in the program suggestions issued by the Department of Public Welfare, copies of which may be had by writing Mrs. Whitaker or Mrs. J. Henry Highsmith at Sir Walter Hotel, Raleigh. The program emphasizes certain important facts as: Cancer is not contagious, it is not inherited, it is not a bacterial disease, one third of all cancers are preventable and 80 per cent of all cancers that are accessible are curable if adequately treated when localized. Another important fact is that while tuberculosis has decreased over 65 per cent as the result of educational efforts, cancer has increased to over 53 per cent, which brings it into the second place as the cause of death. What has been done for tuberculosis, health experts assure can be done for cancer.

Mrs. Zach Lanier Whitaker of Oak Ridge writes a letter with such a timely and valuable suggestion to legislators and of special interest to hundreds of citizens of North Carolina concerned over the same source of horror, that we pass it on for the support it deserves:

"We women of Oak Ridge have been much concerned over a series of maddog outbreaks not only in our own community but through out the State. At the last meeting of our Woman's Club we discussed the problem and decided to urge our Representatives of the General Assembly to enact legislation that would cause all dogs to be vaccinated against rabies. We are asking them to devise a plan by which the serum to be furnished by the State might be administered upon payment of the tax. The tax tag attached to the dog's neck would show that the dog had been treated and this would protect him from extermination by the officers.

"We believe that if club women and other interested citizens of the State should urge this upon our legislators, rabies could be made as nearly extinct as smallpox. England and Canada have done this. Why not North Carolina and by this Legislature?

Among the several guests calling at headquarters this past week were two club presidents seeking plans and blue-prints for club homes. These were Mrs. W. P. Byrd of Lillington and Mrs. E. R. Anderson of Wendell. We take this to be a good sign that times are better. Mrs. C. C. Hilton of Greenville, the new editor of the Junior Page in the Clubwoman, was another caller. Mrs. Hilton has made her appearance in the January issue and has plans for having an interesting page each month from the Juniors.

Raleigh Sunday *News and Observer,* p. 19 (Society, p. 1)
Charlotte Sunday Observer, p. 18 (section 2, p. 4)

20 JANUARY 1935

CANCER CAMPAIGN GAINS FAVOR WITH CLUB WOMEN

Members of State Federation of Women's Clubs Cooperate in Cancer Educational Program

By Mrs. J. Henry Highsmith

Raleigh, Jan. 19.—Recent announcement of the cancer campaign which the health division of the State Federation of Women's Clubs is sponsoring has evoked interest from many sources. Club women are requesting literature and information and write to express their appreciation of the services of Dr. W. D. James of Hamlet, who is giving free lectures to the clubs on the subject of cancer and its prevention.

Dr. James's lecture appointments are made by writing to him at Hamlet as much in advance of the date as possible. It is both his idea and that of Mrs. Charles R. Whitaker's, state chairman of health of the Federation, to reach as nearly all the clubs in the Federation as possible with this cancer message. Slides showing the before and after treatments of cancer with X-ray, radium and surgery at the Hamlet hospital are shown with the lectures.

What North Carolina club women are attempting in the way of a cancer educational program has attracted the attention of the chairman of health in the General Federation, Mrs. Carl W. Illig of Onset, Mass. In congratulating Mrs. Whitaker on the successful start of the movement in her state, she adds that North Carolina is one of several states in the Union now engaged in a fight against cancer.

Miss Gertrude Weil of Goldsboro reports that North Carolina will have a fine representation at the Tenth Annual Conference on the Cause and Cure of War to be held in Washington next week. Representing the State Federation of Women's Clubs will be Mrs. R. H. Latham of Asheville, president; Mrs. Karl Bishopric of Spray; Mrs. J. G. Farrell of Spray; Mrs. Gibson Packer of Asheville and Miss Anne Courtney Sharpe of Lumberton. Representing the American Association of University Women will be Miss Katherine Allen of Meredith College, Raleigh. Representing the State League of Women Voters will be Mrs. C. W. Tillett, Jr., of Charlotte, president; Miss Harriett Elliot of Greensboro; Mrs. May Thompson Evans of Raleigh; Mrs. L. P. McMahon, Charlotte; Mrs. T. D. Williams, Mrs. A. C. Avery, Sr., and Mrs. John McRae of Charlotte. Miss Gertrude Weil will represent the National Women's Trade Union League.

Attending the winter board meeting of the General Federation of Women's Clubs in Washington this week at National Headquarters are Mrs. Latham, Mrs. Palmer Jerman and Mrs. Edward M. Land. Mrs. Latham writes that she will visit friends in Baltimore between the board meeting and the Cause and Cure of War conference, and that she will visit her aunt in Virginia for a night or two on her return trip.

Mrs. W. J. Brogden of Durham, chairman of the Sallie Southall Cotten Loan Fund, in writing to club presidents, says: "We shall never be satisfied until every club in the Federation contributes to the Sallie Southall Cotten Loan Fund every year. When that happens we can tell how much we can do for the girls of our state. The girls we are now aiding will soon be looking to us to keep them in school next year. What we shall be able to do depends on the response of the club women both in paying their pledges now and pledging again at our next convention. In addition to paying their pledges and sending their contributions promptly to the state treasurer, Mrs. J. D. McCall of Charlotte, Mrs. Brogden is asking the clubs to have at least one program on the Sallie Cotten Loan Fund to know what it is, what it has done and what it may do toward helping to educate the young girls of the state.

Charlotte Sunday Observer, p. 18 (section 2, p. 4)

24 JANUARY 1935

THE FARMER AND THE FEDERAL CHILD LABOR AMENDMENT

By Mrs. J. Henry Highsmith

One of the recommendations of Governor Ehringhaus to members of the General Assembly was ratification of the Federal Child Labor Amendment. In urging its ratification, he said:

"Child labor has already been outlawed under the NRA codes. The elimination of this social evil may be assured on exactly equal terms in all the states by adoption of the proposed Child Labor Amendment to the Federal Constitution. Such legislation is peculiarly of national scope and significance and I therefore recommend to you its adoption as in line with the progressive thought and trend of the times."

Farmers have been told that this Amendment is aimed at the work that children do on the farm, that boys and girls under 18 years of age will not be allowed to wash dishes, milk cows or work in the fields.

Nothing could be further from the truth. The Amendment would in no way affect the work children do for their parents. It would merely give Congress the right to regulate the "labor" of children, but the word labor has been construed by the courts to mean labor for hire, or gainful employment. It has never been held to include work done around the home or farm.

After all it is Congress who will determine the terms of any child labor law that is passed. Members of Congress are elected by the people the same as State legislators, and it is inconceivable that Congress would pass laws that nobody wants. Each State has far more power than this Amendment gives to Congress but no State has ever tried to regulate the work children do at home.

Some years ago the Farmer's State Rights League flooded the farm press with propaganda against the Amendment. This organization was found to exist only on paper and was not a farm organization at all, but a tool of the textile interests, long known as the exploiters of children. And similarly this year, a new organization called the National Committee for the Protection of the Child, Family, School and Home, is spreading the same propaganda. The organization is not concerned with protecting either children or the home, but merely with protecting industry.

Child labor means lowered wages. Even the presence in the labor market of a large group of low-paid children competing with adults, forces down adult wage rates and low wage scales meaning low purchasing power for farm products. If the 100.000 children taken out of industry by the codes are permitted to re-enter the labor market when the codes expire, wages will be depressed and sweat shops again will flourish. Therefore, it is to the economic interest of the farmer to see that this state ratifies the Amendment. He has nothing to lose but all to gain through its ratification.

Nashville (NC) *Graphic,* p. 2

3 FEBRUARY 1935

CLUB WOMEN TO SPONSOR BETTER SPEECH WEEK HERE

By Mrs. J. Henry Highsmith

For many years the State Federation of Women's Clubs has sponsored once each year, usually in February, a "Better Speech Week." This effort of the club women during these years to keep the English language as far as possible "pure and undefiled" and to raise the level of correct usage, which we are told is none too high in states of the South, has been rewarded with letters of approval and commendation from time to time, but for the most part from men. Whether men use better English as a rule and are therefore more sensitive to and appreciative of good speech habits is a question we will leave to Nell Battle Lewis to determine through her delightful column. However, these expressions of appreciation and good will have helped to keep this effort of speech improvement before the people.

"Better English Week" for 1935 is February 18 to 23. Mrs. C. Spears Hicks of Raleigh and Durham, chairman, in calling on clubs, schools and other educational groups to make the observance of this week of special value to the community, says:

"The proper observance of this week will do much toward making children, as well as grown-ups of your community, sensitive to incorrect speech, coarse and sloven usage, careless enunciation and to 'overworked' and abused words and phrases. At the same time it will create an appreciation of and desire for a more pleasing and expressive vocabulary, for correct pronunciation, for well chosen words and for pure and correct English. In short, the observance of Better Speech Week in the school, clubs and all educational groups of the community will tend to establish correct speech habits and cultivate the rare gift of using the English language adequately."

To encourage greater interest in and a wider observance of Better Speech Week, Mrs. Hicks is offering a prize of $5 to either the Junior or Senior Club that provides for the best observance of this week. Three judges will determine this from the reports that will be sent to Mrs. Hicks at her address, 115 North Dillard Street, Durham, by April 1.

Mrs. R. W. Green, of Raleigh, chairman of Literature in the Federation, announces that five cups will be offered by her department this year in the interest of original literary efforts. These are: Federation Poetry Cup, which takes the place of the Separk Cup withdrawn, for the best original poem; The Albert L. Berry Cup, for the most meritorious composition in poetry; The Joseph Pearson Caldwell Cup, for the best short story; The Feature Story Cup, offered by the Literature Department of the Federation for the best feature article published in a magazine or newspaper in or out of the State within May 1, 1934, and April 1, 1935; and the Lanier Club Cup for the best one-act play.

Mrs. Green explained that the Federation will retain the book rights to all manuscripts but that writers shall own the magazine rights to all their articles which will enable them to sell their products. She hopes that this ruling of the executive committee will encourage writers to send their best works to be entered in the Federation contest. In regard to plays, writers may retain the acting but not the book rights. All manuscripts must be sent to Mrs. Green, White Oak Road, Raleigh, on or before April 1.

A further boost to the cancer campaign, which continues to grow in interest and helpfulness, comes from Dr. W. D. James, of Hamlet, who says: "Please say to the club women that there will be no expense whatever with my visits to their clubs to lecture on cancer. I am glad to defray all expenses if I can only reach the women of the State with the timely message of cancer and its prevention."

Raleigh Sunday *News and Observer,* p. 17 (Society, p. 1)

10 February 1935

Club Women Convene in Elizabeth City in May

By Mrs. J. Henry Highsmith

Plans for making the 1933 Annual Convention of the State Federation of Women's Clubs to be held in Elizabeth City, May 7 to 10, an outstanding event were considered at the midwinter meeting of the Executive Board held Thursday at Federation Headquarters, Raleigh. The suggestion of the hostess club, the Woman's Club of Elizabeth City, of which Mrs. W. W. Stinemates is president, that the last day of the Convention be made a play day and given over to recreation and pleasure when the whole body of club women would motor over to Kitty Hawk, Nag's Head and Manteo for a day's pleasure was most enthusiastically received. This provision of affording delegates and club women from all parts of the State an opportunity to visit this unique and historic section of North Carolina was thought to be a happy climax to a busy convention week and one that the club women would be glad to accept.

Other interesting items considered by the board included speakers for the convention, department conferences, and revision of some of the department divisions. Attending the meeting were Mrs. R. H. Latham of Asheville, president; Mrs. Andrew Jamieson of Oxford, first vice-president; Mrs. Howard G. Etheridge of Asheville, second vice-president; Mrs. J. Wilbur Bunn of Raleigh, third vice-president; Mrs. J. C. Williams of Wilmington, recording secretary; Mrs. Karl Bishopric of Spray, chairman of American citizenship; Mrs. R. W. Green of Raleigh, chairman of literature; and Mrs. Guy Penny of Garner, chairman of juniors, and Mrs. J. Henry Highsmith, executive secretary.

It is of interest to North Carolina club women that their representatives who attended the recent conference on the Cause and Cure of War in Washington called in person on Senator Robert R. Reynolds to protest his statement—"The majority of intelligent people in North Carolina—98 per cent of the people as a whole—don't want foreign justice or to have anything to do with them foreigners." The group was headed by Mrs. Karl Bishopric of Spray and Miss Anne Courtney Sharpe of Lumberton, who is sponsor for the local junior club and president of the North Carolina Peace Action.

The Senator's statement, the club women claimed, was unfair and misrepresentative of North Carolina—her churches, schools, clubs and other Christian institutions that hold world cooperation and international understanding to be fundamental to both economic progress and world peace. They defended the point that only 2 per cent of the State citizens were international minded, believed in foreign justice and wanted friendly understanding and peaceful relationship with foreign nations.

Friends of the Federal Child Labor Amendment are advised to listen in on Radio Station WPTF Tuesday evening, Wednesday evening, and perhaps Thursday evening of this week from 6:45 to 7 o'clock for lectures by distinguished citizens on the amendment.

Raleigh Sunday *News and Observer,* p. 17 (Society, p. 1)

24 FEBRUARY 1935

CLUB WOMEN ENDORSE FEDERAL HOUSING ACT

By Mrs. J. Henry Highsmith

So much in keeping with the Federation's ideals of home and the standards of living are the ultimate aims of the Federal Housing Act, that Mrs. R. H. Latham, president of the State Federation of Women's Clubs, enthusiastically endorses the Federal Housing Program and bespeaks the cooperation of the club women of the State in behalf of its effective operation in their communities. Mrs. Latham believes that this governmental Act provides an unusual opportunity for all club women, particularly those working with the American Home department of their clubs, to achieve definite gain in improving housing conditions for all their people.

In a recent communication, she emphasized the fact that on account of the Depression and economic stress for the past four years, innumerable houses have fallen in such a sad state of disrepair that both family and community morals have been seriously affected. But she sees in the Federal Housing Program that offers a loan on an easy payment plan a safe and practical way by which home and property owners may repair their homes and thus overcome many of the evil hang-overs of the Depression. In consequence, she is urging all women, as guardians of the home, to stand in readiness to join forces with the FHA officials on their arrival in their community to put the act into effective operation. For further information interested persons are advised to write to Theodore Sumner, Federal Housing Administrator for North Carolina, Asheville, N. C.

Mrs. R. D. V. Jones of New Bern, chairman of Civics, calls attention to the fact that early Spring is the best season of the year for achieving satisfactory results from projects undertaken in the interest of civic improvements. It is none too early, she says, to make plans and organize for all sorts of community betterment work, such as clean up and paint up campaigns, tree plantings, cleaning and planting public parks, parkways and community plots, and not least in importance, beautifying town entrances. Mrs. Jones has made the beautifying of town entrances a special project of her department this year. To increase interest in this particular phase of civic work, she is offering a silver vase to the club that achieves the greatest success. If the town's entrance is marked on the highway by something definite as a gate, tree or town-marker, she suggests that this spot be landscaped for effective planting. In case there is no definite marker, her suggestion is that the highway be planted and beautified for at least a mile or two as it wends its way into the town.

Mrs. Jones' department is again offering the O'Berry cup for the outstanding civic achievement sponsored by any club exclusive of beautifying town entrances. She requests that kodak pictures be taken of all projects competing for these prizes, the pictures to show views of both before and after completion.

Unusual interest is being manifested in Better Speech Week, which is now being observed among women's clubs, schools and educational groups throughout the state. Mrs. C. Spears Hicks of Raleigh and Durham, chairman, says that the North Carolina Better Speech Program has attracted attention as far away as Seattle Washington, a request having come to her recently from that State for a copy of the North Carolina program. The Junior and Senior Woman's Clubs of Raleigh cooperated in sponsoring Better Speech Week in the schools, clubs and over the radio this past week. It has been observed that the Press of the State also has taken increased interest in the Better Speech Program.

Among recent callers at State Headquarters this week were Mrs. Karl Bishopric of Spray and Mrs. John D. Robinson of Wallace. Both Mrs. Bishopric and Mrs. Robinson were interested in arranging worthwhile and entertaining programs for their luncheon conferences at convention.

Raleigh Sunday *News and Observer,* p. 17 (Society, p. 1)

10 MARCH 1935

CLUB WOMEN STAND BACK OF STATE PARK PROJECT

By Mrs. J. Henry Highsmith

Club women are particularly gratified to know that efforts are being made to have the State take over and develop the Big Savannah in Pender County as a State park. Mrs. L. H. Mahler of Raleigh, legislative chairman of the State Garden Clubs, is actively promoting this project and expects soon to have a bill ready to present to the Legislature. The undertaking has the endorsement and support of the State Legislative Council and the 120 garden departments of the Federation of Women's Clubs.

Mrs. Mahler believes this unique area near Burgaw has unlimited possibilities for development into a park that will be prized for its natural beauty, its scientific interest, as well as for its tourist and recreational attractions. This area of around 2,000 acres is on the main highway from Goldsboro to Wilmington. Some of the reasons given as to why it is desirable as a State park are as follows:

The area is one of the finest examples of a distinctive Southern vegetation in the entire South. On it, acre for acre, grow more species of wild flowers and in greater abundance than in any other area in the Eastern United States. Flowers are present throughout eleven months of the year. Its open level character gives it the aspect of a prairie—a unique feature in the coastal plain. On it all of the land types of remarkable insectivorous plants grow in profusion, including the world renowned Venus Flytrap, the proposed State flower for North Carolina. Both the soil, which is of the mineral bog type, and the peculiar vegetation found thereon are of great scientific interest. Here occur numerous examples of the remarkable fire-repressed gum and magnolia tree which have a shrub like aspect even though they are from 50 to 100 years old.

Club women are also interested in the public hearing that will be given the Child Labor Amendment bill which was introduced in the House last week by Representative Ernest Gardner and referred to the Constitutional Amendments Committee. The hearing takes place Tuesday evening, March 12, at 8 o'clock in the Senate chamber. Many able men and women will speak for the bill. which has been endorsed by President Roosevelt, Governor Ehringhaus, seventeen State-wide organizations and 22 national organizations. Representative Tam Bowie is chairman of the committee.

Mrs. John D. Robinson of Wallace, chairman of Gardens of the Federation, calls attention to three interesting garden events in the near future: The Duke Iris Gardens containing 75,000 bulbs, 40,000 of which are iris, will soon be in bloom and will be worth, she says, a trip to Duke to see, though the full beauty of the garden will not be possible this the first year. The annual Dogwood Festival at Chapel Hill takes place April 26–28. A visit to the University at this time, she says, will be one not soon to be forgotten. National Garden Week will be observed April 14–20. The slogan for this week is more and better gardens for the home, community and the State.

Mrs. Robinson, accompanied by Mrs. Harvey Boney of Wallace, attended the Regional Conference on Government sponsored by the Women's Division in Richmond March 7 and 8. The institute is under the direction of Miss Harriett Elliott, assisted by Mrs. C. W. Tillett, both North Carolinians who are connected with the Democratic administration at Washington, D. C.

Mrs. Robinson is again announcing the Fannie Chase Staton silver goblet to the club that does most to beautify the homes of its members by plantings, the number to be determined by the percentage basis. Mrs. T. G. Monroe of Hamlet was a recent visitor to headquarters, coming in the interest of her public welfare program at convention.

Raleigh Sunday *News and Observer,* p. 19 (Society, p. 1)

17 MARCH 1935

CLUB WOMEN TO SUPPORT UNIFORM NARCOTICS LAW

By Mrs. J. Henry Highsmith

While club women have advocated for a number of years the enactment of Uniform Narcotics Laws, not until recently have North Carolina club women been made to realize that this State has insistent need for adequate legislation concerning the manufacture, sale and use of narcotic drugs. This fact was brought home to thinking citizens of the State recently when it was learned that a most dangerous habit-forming drug was being sold in the form of the Mexican, Reefer, or Marihuana cigarettes; and in certain places in the State was being distributed free to school children.

Another fact that emphasizes the need of North Carolina's adopting the Uniform Narcotic Law is that with Virginia, Maryland, South Carolina and Florida having enacted this form of legislation, North Carolina is left open to be the refuge of all the drug addicts, peddlers and other violators of the law. The State Board of Health is ready to have a narcotic bill introduced this Legislature which would have State and Federal cooperation in the control of all traffic in narcotic drugs. Ten states have already adopted the Uniform Narcotic Drug Law which was drafted by the National Conference of Commissioners on Uniform State Laws and endorsed by the American Bar Association, American Medical Association, National Drug Manufacturing

Association, the General and State Federations of Women's Clubs, the National Congress of Parents and Teachers and other nationwide groups.

Whatever fate the Child Labor Amendment bill may meet when it comes up for ratification in the House of Representatives Tuesday morning, it can be said that a fair, courteous and thoughtful hearing was granted it before the Committee on Constitutional Amendments Tuesday evening. Of the eleven members present five voted for and five against a favorable report, with the chairman, Representative Tam Bowie, breaking the tie making it 6 to 5 against. This entitled the bill to come to the floor on a minority report where it will be discussed and voted on. Friends of the amendment feel that the chances for its ratification are still good, much favorable sentiment having been expressed since the hearing.

Mrs. R. H. Latham of Asheville, president of the Federation, stopped by headquarters on both trips to and from Elizabeth City, where she shared honors with Mrs. Grace Morrison Poole, president of the General Federation, both guests of the Woman's Club. Mrs. Poole addressed the members of the club and special guests at a beautifully appointed luncheon on Tuesday. While in Elizabeth City, Mrs. Latham made final arrangements for the annual Convention of the Federation to be held there May 7–10.

The lectures of W. D. James of Hamlet on cancer and its prevention are gaining in favor and appreciation as he and his wife and helpers from his hospital continue to spread the message of hope and courage concerning cancer. He has recently completed a lecture tour to the eastern part of the State, visiting New Bern, Edenton, and other women's clubs. Prior to this trip he visited and lectured to clubs in the south central part of the State, including Lilesville.

Much interest is being manifested by women particularly in House Bill No. 19 introduced by Mr. Victor Bryant of Durham, which would amend the present divorce law to extend its benefits to the injured party only. The Community Club of Chapel Hill has petitioned the Civics Department of the Federation to use its influence in behalf of the Bryant Bill. The author is glad to have the support of women in behalf of his bill which will be discussed in the House this week.

Raleigh Sunday *News and Observer,* p. 19 (Society, p. 1)

31 MARCH 1935

WOMEN'S CLUBS TO GATHER IN ELIZABETH CITY IN MAY

By Mrs. J. Henry Highsmith

Tentative plans for the Annual State Convention of the State Federation of Women's Clubs to be held in Elizabeth City, May 7–10 inclusive, show several new and attractive features, one of which is the selection of an unusually large number of interesting speakers. Mrs. William Dick Sporborg of Port Chester, New York, will be the honored guest and speaker, addressing the Convention Thursday evening at the annual dinner. Miss Julia Jaffray of New York City, will speak on "Crime Control," probably at the Civics dinner held Wednesday evening preceding the Peace Panel.

"World Peace" has been taken as the theme of the Convention by Mrs. R. H. Latham, president, and a panel discussion on Peace with several prominent speakers taking part has been arranged for Wednesday evening. No breakfast conferences will be held this year and only two luncheon conferences. On Wednesday, there will be a Fine Arts Luncheon sponsored by the department of Art, Music and Literature. On Thursday will be the Home Luncheon sponsored by the department of American Home, Education and Gardens.

An interesting innovation is play day on Friday, when the Convention will motor down to Manteo and Fort Raleigh, where at the latter place the Dare County Country Club women will be hostesses to a fish fry. After visiting this historic spot and other points of interest on Roanoke Island, stops will be made returning at Nags Head and the Wright Memorial.

In addition to the Annual State Art Appreciation Contest to be held May 4th in the House of Representatives at Raleigh, there will be held the first creative state art contest for the pupils of the public schools of the State. Mrs. J. J. Andoe of Greensboro is chairman of the Creative activities of the Art Department of the Federation and Miss Juanita McDougald of Raleigh is chairman of the Art Appreciation Contests. Mrs. I. M. Meekins of Elizabeth City is chairman of Prizes for the contest and Mrs. C. J. Sawyer of Windsor is State Art chairman for the Federation.

This year the State Art Contest will include not only the appreciation phase but the creative phase also. Small cash prizes and ribbons will be offered for the best original pencil drawing, brush drawing, etching, wood carving, tempera painting, oil painting, pen and ink sketch, metal work, modeling in clay, textile design, sketch for room decoration, block print, and basketry.

A number of attractive prizes are to be awarded to the winners in the Appreciation contest. The Federation is offering a prize of $20.00 to the school whose team makes the highest number of points, and $5.00 to the school making the second highest number of points. Before the State Contest is held, there will be district contests held in the sixteen Federation Districts with a prominent club woman in charge. The district chairmen are:

Mrs. R. H. Barber, Waynesville; Mrs. John D. McRae, Asheville; Mrs. R. C. Linney, Taylorsville; Miss Knox Hood, Gastonia; Mrs. P. R. Rankin, Mt. Gilead; Mrs. W. S. S. Blackburn, Summerfield; Mrs. B. B. Mangum, Roxboro; Mrs. Joel B. Layton, Lillington; Mrs. Glen Stroll, Chadbourn; Miss Rena

Coles, Wilmington; Mrs. J. M. West, New Bern; Mrs. J. M. O'Neal, Selma; Miss Grace Jean Sails, Oxford; Mrs. J. Stuart Windt, Plymouth and Mrs. John McMullen, Elizabeth City.

Raleigh Sunday *News and Observer,* p. 9 (Society, p. 1)
Charlotte Sunday Observer, p. 22 (section 2, p. 6)

14 APRIL 1935

VARIED FOUR-DAY PROGRAM IS PLANNED FOR NORTH CAROLINA
CLUB WOMEN'S CONVENTION

**Annual Meeting To Be Held May 7–10 In Elizabeth City;
Officers To Be Named**

By Mrs. J. Henry Highsmith

In issuing the official call of the State Federation of Women's Clubs to its members regarding the 33rd annual convention of the Federation to be held in Elizabeth City, May 7–10, the president, Mrs. R. H. Latham of Asheville, outlines a four-day program of conferences, reports, speeches, entertainment and recreation. The Woman's Club of Elizabeth City and the Federated Clubs of the 16th district will be hostesses. The Virginia Dare Hotel of Elizabeth City will be headquarters, while the New Southern Hotel and the Duke Inn will assist in entertaining the convention.

The opening session will be Tuesday evening, May 7, in the ballroom of the Virginia Dare. Preliminary meetings of the executive board, the board of trustees and the board of directors will be held during the day. Dinner meetings will be held for the past presidents, the district presidents, the department chairmen and the pages. A reception, the courtesy of the Federated Clubs of the 16th district, will follow the opening session.

While there will be no breakfast conferences, two well-appointed luncheon conferences have been planned—the Fine Arts luncheon for Wednesday with the Music, Art and Literature departments participating, and the Home Luncheon conference on Thursday with American Home, Education and Garden departments participating. There will be a Civics dinner on Wednesday evening with the departments of American Citizenship, Civics and Public Welfare participating. Following the dinner, there will be an evening's program on "World Peace," the theme of the convention, with a number of the State's most able speakers on the program.

Many courtesies in the way of social entertainment and recreation have been planned by the local committees. Mrs. W. W. Stinemates, president of the local club, will entertain the members of the executive board at luncheon on Tuesday at the Woman's Club. Mrs. James G. Fearing will entertain the past presidents at dinner Tuesday evening. Mrs. Carroll Abbott will serve a buffet supper at her home Tuesday evening to the convention pages. The Elizabeth City Woman's Club will be hostess at a tea at the club Wednesday afternoon. Judge and Mrs. I. M. Meekins will be at home to the members of the convention Thursday afternoon. The Elizabeth City school children will give a spring pageant at the Federation dinner Thursday evening.

Of special interest will be the Fine Arts Festival on Wednesday afternoon when Francis Speight, North Carolina artist now living in Philadelphia, will be one of the speakers. Other North Carolina artists, musicians, poets and authors—winners in the Federation contests of former years—will be presented. The annual art exhibit held in the parish house of the Episcopal church will be reviewed at this time. The Garden Club of Elizabeth City will hold a flower show in connection with the art exhibit for the pleasure of the visiting club women.

The election of officers, always an interesting event of every convention, will be of special interest this year. The officers to be elected are president, second vice-president, third vice-president, corresponding secretary and General Federation director. Department chairmen to be elected are American Home, Art, Civics, Education, Gardens, Literature and Music. Nominations for the department chairmen should be sent to Mrs. D. F. Giles, of Marion, chairman of the nominating committee for the board of directors.

Club women will vote at the convention whether or not the North Carolina Federation will adopt the three-year plan of officeholding and conform to the plan of the General Federation or retain its present plan of two years.

Raleigh Sunday *News and Observer,* p. 9 (Society, p. 1)

21 APRIL 1935

CLUB WOMEN WILL FEATURE CONTROVERSIAL TOPICS ON NATIONAL CONVENTION PROGRAM

Many North Carolina Women To Attend General Federation Meeting

By Mrs. J. Henry Highsmith

If North Carolina club women are to keep step with their mother organization, the General Federation of Women's Clubs, they will soon be featuring such controversial subjects on their convention programs as birth control, universal fingerprinting, lynching, the foreign policy of the United States and present economic and political trends. These and other subjects of present day interest will be discussed and resolutions of endorsement voted on at the meeting of the Triennial Convention of the General Federation to be held in Detroit, June 4–12. Many North Carolina club women are expected to attend this convention that is anticipating an attendance of about 5,000. Mrs. Grace Morrison Poole, president, will preside at all the sessions.

Of the eight resolutions to be offered the one on birth control will call for endorsement of "the principle of Federal legislation for the dissemination of scientifically regulated birth control information." The anti-lynching resolution will declare the Federation's "unequivocal opposition to the practice of lynching, and will urge its member State conventions to apply such educational activities as will uphold laws prohibiting this iniquitous practice." Endorsement will be asked for the nation-wide campaign for universal fingerprinting as a protective measure for every citizen and resident of these United States. Another resolution will reiterate the Federation's endorsement of the adherence of the United States to the World Court. A Declaration of Democracy will be voiced in the resolution which opposes all forms of dictatorships, including Communism and Fascism, and recommends "an impartial study of the national and international factual problems which concern the welfare of our country."

Internationally known men and women will speak at the sessions and in the forums of the convention. Among these will be Miss Josephine Roche, Assistant Secretary of the Treasury of the United States; Dr. Glenn Frank, president of the University of Wisconsin; and Senator Thomas P. Gore of Oklahoma, the eloquent blind statesman. In the forum, Present Political Trends, the Democratic party will be represented by Miss Roche, who holds a key position in the administration, having general supervision of the operations of the United States Public Health Service, the activities of which affect the daily lives of 130,000,000 people. In a recent poll, Miss Roche was voted the nation's most prominent business woman.

Mrs. B. B. Mangum of Roxboro, president of the Eighth District of the Federation, announces that the art appreciation contest of the Eighth District will be held in Durham, Friday, April 26 at the Durham High School on the invitation of the art department of the Durham Woman's Club. Ten schools, she reports, have entered their pupils in this contest. These are from the counties of Person, Durham, Orange, Chatham and Wake. Registration for the contest begins at 10 o'clock, the contest at 11, lunch at 1 o'clock and a tour of Duke University at o'clock. This will include a visit to the University art galleries, the Chapel, and an organ and carillon recital. At 4 o'clock the Club will serve tea to the art contestants.

The Woman's Club of Greenville with the Junior Club cooperating has just concluded a two-day and night fine arts festival. Practically every phase of art, including painting, sculpture, fancy work, music, dancing, play writing and acting, was included in the program.

The Ahoskie Woman's Club has recently moved into its new quarters and is equipped to serve parties, the civic clubs and other organizations of the community needing a meeting place or catering services. The club has started a town library using the club for this purpose, and recently held a book tea for the benefit of the library. Mrs. J. Claxton Brett is president of the club and Mrs. W. H. Windle, secretary.

Raleigh Sunday *News and Observer,* p. 9 (Society, p. 1)

28 APRIL 1935

PROMINENT SPEAKERS APPEAR ON FEDERATION CONVENTION PROGRAM

Mrs. William Sporborg and Francis W. Speight
To Address Club Women

By Mrs. J. Henry Highsmith

Among the number of unusually interesting speakers to appear on the Convention program of the State Federation of Women's Clubs to be held in Elizabeth City, May 7–10, are Mrs. William Dick Sporborg of Port Chester, New York, and Francis Speight of North Carolina and Pennsylvania. Other outstanding speakers will be William Hunt and Phillips Russell of Chapel Hill, W. E. Bird of Cullowhee, Cora A. Harriss of Charlotte, Mrs. Bess Naylor Rosa of Woman's College, Greensboro, Albert Coates of Chapel Hill, Rev. T. A. Sykes of High Point, Rev. Joseph Fletcher of St. Mary's School, Raleigh, Clyde Erwin of Raleigh, Ann Courtney Sharpe of Lumberton, and others to be announced.

Mrs. Sporborg will be honor guest and speaker at the Federation Dinner Thursday evening. She is past president and director of the New York State Federation, is chairman of resolutions of the General Federation and is recording secretary of the Cause and Cure of War Conference. She is a dynamic and pleasing speaker.

Francis Speight, one of North Carolina's most distinguished artists, now instructor in the Pennsylvania Academy of Fine Arts, will speak at the Fine Arts Festival Wednesday afternoon on some timely art subject. Other topics to be discussed by the other speakers range all the way from a peaceful mountain ballad to a treatise on war and from a study of flowers, pictures and music to a study of local, State and national government. Crime prevention, better housing, parent education and public school curricula will also be subjects of discussion and study during the Convention.

The return of Francis Speight at this time to his State and community is looked forward to with particular interest. The following sketch of his achievements in the realm of art is apropos his coming: Francis W Speight was born near Windsor in 1896. He was educated in both the private and public schools of his community. He studied two years at Wake Forest College, meanwhile taking art lessons at Meredith College on Saturdays. While at Wake Forest he was cartoonist for Old Gold and Black. Later he became a pupil of the Corcoran School of Art and the Pennsylvania Academy of Fine Arts.

Almost from the beginning, the work of Mr. Speight received national recognition. He is the recipient of many awards of distinction. Among these are the Cresson Traveling Scholarships to Europe by the Pennsylvania Academy in 1923 and 1925; the Gold Medal Award at the Annual Exhibition of the Fellowship of the P. A. F. A in 1926; first prize for Landscape from the Society of Washington Artists in 1929; the Fellowship prize from the Annual Exhibition of American Painting in 1930, the First [Julius] Hallgarten Prize, National Academy of Design in 1930, the Kohnstamm Prize, Art Institute of Chicago in 1930; Landscape prize, Connecticut's Academy of Fine Arts in 1932.

His works have been exhibited in all recent major exhibitions in America, including the Carnegie International at Pittsburgh, the Century of Progress Exposition at Chicago, the exhibition of Contemporary American Paintings now being shown by the National Gallery of Canada; also in New Zealand and Australia. His works are represented in the permanent collections of the Metropolitan Museum of Art, New York City; Museum of Toronto; the Pennsylvania Academy of Fine Arts, and in many private collections. The Milch Galleries of New York are his dealers.

Club women interested in greater library facilities for the State should petition their Senators in the Legislature to restore the $3,460 which the Senate Appropriations Committee deducted from the amount voted by the House for the State Library Commission. Miss Marjorie Beal, secretary and director, says that this amount is needed to replace worn-out books and for the travel expenses of a field worker for assisting communities in establishing local libraries.

Raleigh Sunday *News and Observer,* p. 9 (Society, p. 1)

5 MAY 1935

STATE CLUB WOMEN GATHER IN ELIZABETH CITY TUESDAY

Timely Subjects Feature Four-day Program; Play-Day Planned

By Mrs. J. Henry Highsmith

With final touches put on the program of the thirty-third annual convention of the State Federation of Woman's Clubs, which meets Tuesday in Elizabeth City and continues through Friday, plans are complete for one of the largest and best conventions the Federation has ever held. The president, Mrs. R. H. Latham, of Asheville, who will preside at all business sessions, has put into the program features that will attract stimulate, and challenge the best thought and action of the club women in the State. Many new subjects for study and discussion have been introduced and many excellent speakers have accepted invitations to address sessions of the convention.

The fact that the convention is meeting for the first time in this northeast section of the State with all good roads leading direct to this friendly convention city and the further fact that every delegate and visiting club woman will be given on Friday the opportunity to visit two of North Carolina's firsts—birthplace of Virginia Dare, first white child born in America, and the Wright Memorial Monument, where the Wright Brothers flew the first airplane—promise an unusually large and interesting attendance.

Mrs. W. W. Stinemates, president of the hostess club, is general chairman of arrangements. She will be assisted by Mrs. Carroll Abbott, president of the Junior Club; Miss Nellie Boyce, Mrs. H. I. Glass, Mrs. Sprig Brentt, Mrs. Taylor, Miss Ethel Parker, Mrs. J. G. Fearing, Mrs. H. D. Walker, Mrs. I. M. Meekins, Mrs. Victor Fink, Miss Margaret Fearing, Mrs. S. W. Gregory, and Mrs. M. R. Griffin.

Mrs. J. D. McCall of Charlotte will serve as chairman of committee on credentials. Miss Margaret Lovell Gibson of Asheville will serve as parliamentarian, and will conduct three classes in parliamentary law—1 to 3 o'clock Tuesday afternoon and each morning at 8:30 o'clock. Mrs. Charles G. Gulley of Cullowhee will be leader for assembly singing and Mrs. Madge Taylor will be accompanist. Mrs. Charles G. Doak of Raleigh will be official reporter. Special music will feature each session of the convention, the following musicians taking part: Mesdames Margarette Love, J. W. Foreman, H. E. Nixon, W. P. Duff, I. M. Meekins, George Bell, J. P. Greenleaf, Victor Meekins, J. H. Cartwright, Clyde Liskey, Fentress Homer, T. P. Bennette, T. G. Shannonhouse, Misses Frances Singleton, Camilla Foreman. Alice Barrow, and Messrs H. C. Foreman. Larry Skinner, R. S. Denton, Roland Sawyer, S. G. Scott, Bobby Elliott; Miss Minnie Nash, accompanist. Mrs. L. E. Skinner will have charge of the Spring Pageant by the public school children on Thursday evening at Federation dinner.

The formal opening of the convention will be 8 o'clock Tuesday evening when the president, Mrs. Latham, will make her annual report and the district presidents and their pages will be presented by Mrs. Howard G. Etheridge. Mayor Jerome Flora will make the address of welcome, which will be responded to by Mrs. D. F. Giles of Marion and Mrs. C. C. Hilton of Greenville. The invocation will be said by Rev. H. I. Glass. Mrs. Sydney P. Cooper will give the salute to the flag. Miss Margaret Fearing, chief page, will introduce other convention pages who are the members of the Junior Club of Elizabeth City. They are Mrs. L. S. Blades, Jr., Mrs. W. A. Houtz, Mrs. J. B. McMullan, Miss Bertha Cooper, Mrs. W. W. Cohoon, Mrs. William Anderson, Mrs. Worth Gregory, Mrs. L. W. Topping, Mrs. F. F. Garrett and Mrs. Pierce Eves.

Personal pages to the president are: Mrs. John Meredith Jones of Edenton, Mrs. Lenoir Thomas Avery of Aberdeen, Mrs. Robert Easton Townsend, Norfolk, Va., and Miss Ruby Adams, Formosa, Va.

Two special programs promising unusual interest are the Fine Arts Festival for Wednesday afternoon, and the Peace Program for Wednesday evening. The Fine Arts Festival will feature addresses by Francis Speight on "The Appreciation of Art"; Phillips Russell on "Creative Writing and the Writer's Conference"; and Dean W. E. Bird on "Our Native Ballads." Several former Federation prize winners in music will be presented, who will give their musical compositions. These are Mrs. I. M. Meekins, Miss Alla Pearl Little, Mrs. Bessie Pfohl, Vera Roundtree, Pearl R. Blades, Gertrude Johnson, Dorothy Turlington Royall and Mrs. N. C. Cochran. On the Peace Program Rev. Joseph will discuss the "Munitions Industry" and Dean Elbert Russell of Duke University will speak on "Public Opinion for Peace or War." Miss Ann Courtney Sharpe, State president for Peace Action, will talk on the subject "What Can the Young Do About It?" An open discussion on World Peace will follow the addresses.

Dr. Grace Langdon of New York City and Washington, who is director of Educational Advisory Service in New York, and specialist in Emergency Nursery Schools of the FERA, will address the luncheon conference on Thursday on the subject of "Emergency in Education." Dr. Langdon, who is an instructor in the Child Development Institute, Teachers College, Columbia University, and member of the Board of Advisory Editors of Parents Magazine, is the author of the well-known book "Home Guidance for Young Children," and several pamphlets dealing with various phases of Child Care. While in North Carolina, Mr. Langdon will visit several of the E. R. E. Nursery Schools, in company with Mrs. M. G. Scarborough, State Supervisor of Nursery Schools and Parent Education.

Speakers for the Civic Dinner held Wednesday evening will be Albert Coates of Chapel Hill, who will speak on the "Working Plan of the Institute of Government" and Dr. Henry Jerome Langston of Virginia, whose subject will be "Neglected Phases of Maternal Health." Miss Cora A. Harris speaks at the Wednesday morning session on "Women's Part in the Federal Housing Program" and Mrs. Bess Rosa speaks at the Thursday morning session on "Personality Values in the Home." At the Junior Club luncheon held Thursday at the Woman's Club, Miss Ann Courtney Sharpe will speak on "The Junior Club Woman in a Growing World."

Featuring the Thursday afternoon session will be an address on "Gardening in North Carolina" by William Lanier Hunt, writer and lecturer of Chapel Hill. Mr. Hunt, Native North Carolinian, is a specialist in Southern Floriculture and civic beautification. He is the author of the recent U. N. C. Library Extension Bulletin, "The Southern Garden." His especial interest is native plants and their development, having made many valuable experiment's with southern plants, the iris test field being one example. He lectured monthly during the past winter to the Charleston Garden Club and is on the board of the National Lecture Council of State Garden Club Federations. He is vice president of the American Rock Garden Society and a member of the National Horticulture Society.

Climaxing three full days of the Convention will be the Annual Federation Dinner on Thursday evening, when Mrs. William Rick Sporborg will be honored guest and speaker. Her subject will be "Woman's Day Out." She will be introduced by Mrs. J. M. Hobgood. The annual Federation Awards will be presented by Mrs. Andrew Jamieson. Special music by local musicians and a spring pageant by local school children will be special attractions.

The following young ladies will serve as personal pages to the District Presidents at their exercises on Tuesday evening: Mary Ashworth Barber, Mrs. Junius Reister, Mrs. Wm. H. Kelley, Mrs. W. L. Robinson, Miss Catherine Rankin, Mrs. Walter Johnston, Miss Edna Sockwell, Mrs. Allen Griffin, Mrs. Wilbur R. Adams, Mrs. P. R. Floyd, Miss Anna Carr, Miss Dowena Lucas, Mrs. Nelson Ricks, Mrs. Randolph Teague, Miss Alma Sanderson and Mrs. Carroll Abbott.

Bringing greetings from their respective organizations will be Mrs. Brooks Tucker, Mrs. J. C. Correll, Mrs. Wesley Taylor, Mrs. T. W. Guthrie, Mrs. W. B. Aycock, Miss Mae Reynolds, Miss Anne McRae and Mrs. Henry Eley of Suffolk, Va.

Little Miss Mary Louise Cooper, Federation Mascot, will toast the Convention at the opening session Tuesday evening.

Raleigh Sunday *News and Observer,* p. 9 (Society p. 2)

1936

February 1936 – December 1938
Assistant Director of Health Education
North Carolina Board of Health

25 February — returns to State Board of Health as assistant director of Health Education, with emphasis on maternity and infant healthcare

7–10 April — attends 34th annual NCFWC convention, High Point

25 April — leaves for GFWC meeting in Miami; stops in Jacksonville FL to visit Lula Belle

27 April – 1 May — GFWC triennial council meeting in Miami; presents Publicity report

1–3 May — goes with Mrs. Latham and other clubwomen to Havana for the weekend

May — her monthly articles resume in *The Health Bulletin*

7 May — reports to RWC on Miami meeting

11 May — joins anti-war conference and peace demonstration of Emergency Peace Campaign, meeting at Edenton Street; speaks on "Pacific Alternates to Armed Conflict"

12–14 May — Attends annual convention of Virginia Federation, in Fredericksburg; addresses press luncheon

8 June — attends 84th Commencement at Duke (649 graduates); announces to Alumni Association that class of 1906 has pledged $5,000 for an endowed scholarship

18–19 June — attends Woman's Club institute at UNC, "Climbing Up the Golden Stairs of the Federation; offers a session for publicity personnel

26 September — speaks in Snow Hill on Board of Health's Maternity and Infancy program

22 October — co-hosts Duke Alumnae meeting at 604 North Blount Street; Dean Alice Baldwin and Miss Annie Crews are guests

18 November — addresses Kenly Woman's Club on "Death Rate of Mothers and Babies"

19 November — addresses Scotland Neck Woman's Club on "Why So Many Mothers and Babies Die Needlessly in North Carolina"

1 March 1936

Mrs. J. H. Highsmith Urges Training For Club Reporters

At the request of Mrs. Harvie Jordan, Georgia Federation chairman of press and publicity, Mrs. J. Henry Highsmith, of Raleigh. N. C, and General Federation chairman of this department, sends the following message to the clubwomen of Georgia:

"I am glad to send to you through Mrs. Harvie Jordan and your interesting club page in The Atlanta Constitution a message concerning the work of the press and publicity department of the General Federation. The chairman with the assistance of her able division chairmen—Mrs. Fred R. Lufkin, of Elgin, Ill; Mrs. J. Ralston Wells, of Daytona Beach, Fla., and Miss Jeanette Calkins, of Portland, Ore., have endeavored to formulate a program of publicity that will meet the needs of the clubs in all the states. We found the greatest need to be more and better trained writers of club news. The department's program, therefore, is set up to urge, encourage and help those who have not had training in the technique of writing for the newspapers to acquire it this year if possible.

"Training by one of the following methods is advised: 1. Courses in journalism offered by state universities and colleges—usually short courses in summer. 2. Press institutes or training schools sponsored by the state or district Federation, the state press chairman, large newspapers, or a local club or group. 3. By correspondence—with some extension department or correspondence school of journalism.

"We hope to enroll a large number of the 10,000 writers of club news in the country in one or more of these training courses this year, and before the triennium is out, to say that every writer of club publicity is a trained writer. We are asking state press chairmen, club reporters, editors of club publications, state, district and local club presidents to co-operate with us to achieve this goal. We are counting on Georgia to take her place in the vanguard of the procession and be one of the first states to report a 100 per cent trained personnel of club reporters."

Atlanta Sunday Constitution, p. 34 (section K, p. 5)

29 MARCH 1936

RECORDS SHOW '35 GOOD HEALTH YEAR

**There Were 1,407 Fewer Deaths Than in 1934,
Says State Health Board**

By Mrs. J. Henry Highsmith

Last year was not such a bad year from a health standpoint, according to the 1935 annual statistics of the State's sickness and death rates which have recently been compiled by the State Board of Health. The death statistics show that there were 1,407 fewer deaths in the State in 1935 than in 1934 and there were 190 more births. They show also that there were reductions in the number of deaths from nearly all the major diseases now reported to the State Board of Health, except from influenza and poliomyelitis or infantile paralysis. It will be recalled that North Carolina suffered from an epidemic of this disease last summer, which accounts for the higher rate recorded for infantile paralysis last year.

Possibly the most noteworthy decline in death rates last year—one that State health workers were rejoiced to see—was that of infant deaths under one year of age. The rate in one year fell more than 10 points—from 77.9 per 1,000 live births, an unusual high rate, to 67.2. This means that there are 838 more babies living in the State than would have been the case had the rate for 1934 obtained. There was also a saving of 82 mothers from causes or diseases incident to maternity. While this is a decided improvement in the care of mothers and babies, it is far from enough to bring the North Carolina death rate for babies down to the national average, which was 59.9 in 1934 the last available statistics.

The death rates for measles, whooping cough, scarlet fever and diphtheria showed marked declines in 1935, but those contagious diseases of children are variable depending largely on the degree of immunity that has been established by previous outbreaks, and so cannot be taken as indicative of true health conditions. But there are a number of decreased rates which [suggest that the] health of the people of the State is on the mend. We have reference particularly to cancer, tuberculosis, diabetes, pellagra and homicides. While these improvements are only slight, we hope they are the beginning of an upward and permanent turn for better health.

But the morbidity rate of a people is the true index of their health. Death statistics reveal only the last chapter, while a whole volume may not be able to tell the story of the mental and physical suffering that illness from some preventable disease may cause one. In other words, the amount of sickness and not the number of deaths is the gauge of a people's health.

The annual morbidity report of the State Board of Health in keeping with the death statistics shows a decrease in the number of cases reported in eight of the 13 more important reportable diseases, but six of these were children's diseases. On the other hand it shows either an increase in or a too large number of cases that people could, if they would, wipe out or reduce to a minimum—namely diphtheria, typhoid, pellagra, smallpox, ophthalmia neonatorum which often causes blindness in babies, whooping cough and rabies.

Dr. J. C. Knox, director of the Division of Epidemiology of the State Board of Health, in whose division the morbidity report was compiled, says there is evidence that all is not being done that could be done, and that people know how to do, to keep down disease and death. For instance, he says, we know that vaccination will prevent typhoid fever, diphtheria, rabies and smallpox, and will make whooping cough less serious; we know that a diet of milk, eggs, fresh fruits and vegetables and lean meat will prevent pellagra, and that a drop of a solution of silver nitrate put into the baby's eyes at birth by the physician or nurse will prevent blindness in babies. Yet, he asks, do we do these simple things?

A comparison of the State's morbidity or sickness rate with its death rate for 1935 gives the following answer:

Last year there were 1,720 deaths of diphtheria reported to the State Board of Health and 158 deaths; 671 cases of typhoid and para-typhoid and 80 deaths—an increase over the year before of 192 cases but one less death; smallpox, 24 cases, no deaths; pellagra, 732 cases with 387 deaths; ophthalmia neonatorum, 18 cases; rabies, five cases and five deaths; and whooping cough, 10,075 cases and 299 deaths.

It is readily seen that the people themselves are responsible for a large number of deaths from preventable diseases.

Raleigh Sunday *News and Observer,* p. 24 (Features, p. 2)

5 APRIL 1936

BLAMES LOVE OF PETS FOR RABIES PROBLEM

State Health Official Says Animals Bitten by Mad Dogs Should be Killed Whether Vaccinated or Not

By Mrs. J. Henry Highsmith

The old notion that rabies was more infectious in spring and summer than in any other part of the year seems to be without foundation except for the fact that there are more stray dogs to spread it in spring and summer, and children are more exposed to their attacks on account of being freer and more lightly clothed. But the disease is a perennial problem which costs the State thousands of dollars annually and its citizens fearful anxiety and suffering.

Something of the prevalence of this disease in the State today may be seen from this item: 211 animal heads were examined at the State Laboratory of Hygiene in the months of January and February this year and 104 of these were found positive. This average of 105 examinations a month is low when compared with the monthly average for all last year which was 174 and with a finding of a little less than 50 per cent positive. Five deaths were recorded from this disease last year as against none the year before.

Can Be Wiped Out.

But the significant thing about rabies is it could be exterminated altogether, as it already has been in several European countries, but for the fact it is protected and kept endemic by an impregnable wall of sentiment—false sentiment usually for the mongrel dog and the vagrant cat, these being the most frequent conveyors of the disease.

According to James W. Kellogg, assistant director of the State Laboratory of Hygiene, an authority on the subject of rabies, enough is known about the disease—about the nature of the germ which causes it, how it is conveyed from one animal to another and from animal to man, and how to give protection against the infection—to eradicate it altogether if people would apply the knowledge they possess. And yet there were 222 more persons treated for the disease last year than the year before, and five more deaths reported.

Kellogg believes enforcement of the State law which requires all dogs known to have been bitten by a mad dog to be killed, and the enactment of another law that would confine all dogs to the premises of the owner for a definite period of time, would be effective in the control of rabies. He says these methods coupled with the destruction of the stray or ownerless dog have been tried in several countries with striking results.

Disease Eradicated.

He says further:

"Rabies has been exterminated from Denmark, Norway, and Sweden for more than 30 years. Before the war it was unknown in Germany except along the borders, and in England there was no rabies for over 20 years until it was reintroduced by returning soldiers who brought back infected dogs from France. It has again been eradicated from England. In Australia there has never been a case of rabies, for that continent has always had a quarantine law for dogs. The enforcement of similar measures would entirely do away with rabies in the United States."

Kellogg believes that the law passed by the last Legislature providing for the State-wide vaccination of dogs should be a factor in the control of rabies, but he warns against putting too much dependence in that alone. He says that the practice of anti-rabic vaccination of a dog which has been bitten by a mad dog is not only a dangerous experiment but it is a vicious disregard of the State law. Dogs bitten by animals known to be rabid should be destroyed even if previously vaccinated.

Cites Danger.

In many cases, he says, the attempt to immunize a dog which already has been bit by a mad dog will result in the animal going mad before immunity can be established. In fact, a quarantine of at least six months would be necessary to free the dog from suspicion, he advises.

Commenting further on what he believes the best methods of control of rabies, Kellogg says: "There are arguments for universal vaccination of dogs, and from the standpoint of the individual owner it is desirable. However, the protection obtained is never absolute and re-vaccination is advisable at least every 12 months. In the light of present knowledge, such prophylactic measures in addition to the proper restriction of the liberty of the dog, would seem to be the best method of control of rabies."

Regarding what steps to take when one is bitten, Kellogg advises: "If the dog appears normal and there seems to be no reason to believe that he is mad, he should not be killed at once, but securely confined and observed for a period of 10 days or two weeks, to determine whether he was in the early stages of rabies at the time the person was bitten. If on the other hand the dog develops rabies within the period of observation, the patient still has time to take the treatment and ward off the disease. Except in cases of bites on the face or head, it is advisable to delay treatment until symptoms develop in the dog or until a definite diagnosis can be made. In such cases treatment may be started immediately and later discontinued if the animal proves not to be mad."

Charlotte Sunday Observer, p. 44 (section 4, p. 2)

12 April 1936

Hold Undernourishment Is Handicap to Schools

Health Authorities Stress Importance Of School Lunches

By Mrs. J. Henry Highsmith

The school lunch, like busses and good roads, has come to be regarded as a regular feature of school organization in the best school systems. It is now known that it is not a wise expenditure of school money to undertake to teach children who are hungry and undernourished; that it is a waste of time and money to attempt to build up a strong mind in a poor, emaciated body. School authorities are recognizing also that while their responsibility is to develop the child's mental faculties, the shortest way to do this is through a happy, contented mind and a sound, properly nourished body. Hence, providing the mid-day lunch becomes the school's responsibility as one of the modern facilities for advancing education, and is no longer left to the whim of the child or the convenience of the parents.

This subject of providing a hot midday lunch for school children is one that Dr. G. M. Cooper, assistant State health officer, finds to have a direct relation to the general health condition of the school children of the State. In the April number of the Health Bulletin just released, of which he is editor, he deplores the fact that while thousands of the State's children do have the benefit of well-prepared school lunches, thousands do not, and this latter group are rendered thereby more susceptible to infectious diseases. A discussion of this matter, he says, is considered trivial to many people today because it is assumed that almost every school community has some form of hot lunch made available to its pupils, whereas a large majority of the children in the State still carry their lunch to school and eat it on the schoolhouse ground.

Dr. Cooper keeps in close touch with the State's school children's needs through the work of eight public health nurses, who under the supervision of his department work with the schools in counties not having whole-time county health officers. A phase of the school lunch problem is revealed in the following report of one of the nurses which is typical of the many he receives:

"This week I have worked in Blank School. I think that they have a very nice school and a fine system throughout the school with the exception of a store in the building in which they sell so much candy. I can see now why they have so many children underweight and malnourished. I did my best to get them to sell fruit instead. The principal uses the argument that the children are going to buy candy anyhow and the school had just as well sell it and make the profit because if the school did not sell it the children would go to a store nearby and buy it anyhow. Then they would be subjected to the danger of being run over by cars as they crossed the road to the store. It seems to me that the chief motive is that there is more profit in selling candy, it is easier to handle, there is no loss in decay and no wastage in that respect."

Dr. Cooper believes that the practice of selling cheap candy, age-old cakes and soft drinks to school children at their lunch period, or allowing them to purchase these at the corner store, is largely responsible for a large number of children found underweight and malnourished in the schools today. He says allowing a child the chance to purchase with his nickel either candy, milk or soup is an injustice to the child. He will undoubtedly buy the candy. For the school system to be guilty of subjecting children to any such temptation, he says, is unfair to the parents and the child.

Dr. Cooper's interest in the health of school children is not of recent origin. It began about 35 years ago when he taught four years, the last at Halls High School in Sampson County, and began to observe what constituted the average noonday lunch of the school children of that community. He found the chief ingredients to be sweet potato biscuit and fat meat or sausage, brought to school in the buckets or baskets, as was the custom in all rural schools of that day. This, he concluded, was not a fit lunch for small children, even when freshly prepared, except in small quantities, and by the time it got cold and bogged up in the tin bucket, it was unfit for human consumption.

Being a man of positive and daring convictions he decided to do something about it. He became a physician, practiced among his own people and later was called to serve his county as health officer. His opportunity had come and he lost no time in helping to work out a cooperative plan whereby the parents and the school could come together and furnish a hot soup or other nourishing food to every member of the school. He saw three such cooperative plans go into effect in his county, which was 22 years ago. The same system is being used in the county today but more extensively and with good results.

But that was not the end of the hot school lunch interest. Later on, becoming director of the Medical Inspection of Schools Bureau of the State Board of Health, his first work was to agitate for a hot midday lunch for all the school children of the State. The movement that had a good start was given a terrible setback during the Depression and many children have suffered in consequence. But with better times returning and with an increasing appreciation of better health for school children, it is hoped that the hot school lunch will yet be made available for all of the State's school children.

Raleigh Sunday *News and Observer,* p. 31 (Features, p. 3)

19 APRIL 1936

CHILD HEALTH MAY DAY CAUSE

Security of Children Will Be Stressed in This Year's Observance
By Mrs. J. Henry Highsmith

Special emphasis is to be on the health and security of children in the observance of May Day – Child Health Day in North Carolina this year. Plans are now being made whereby State and local health officers, child welfare agencies and other groups concerned with child health and welfare will get together and adopt plans for promoting on this day the health and security program of the child that has recently been made available to the State, through cooperation with the Federal government. This plan is in keeping with suggestions issued by the Children's Bureau of the United States Department of Labor, which is sponsoring May Day observance this year and of which Miss Katherine F. Lenroot is chief.

In setting forth the purpose of this nation-wide observance of May Day, Miss Lenroot says it is to review in each State and community the social security program and other measures for promoting child health and welfare, and to make plans for their further development. Since Federal aid is now available, she says, for maternal and child health, for the care of crippled children, for extending child welfare services, and for aid to dependent children, and since plans have been submitted and approved for State cooperation, the next step is to put the plans into effect; to see that the children for whom the benefits are intended are reached. She says further that on each community rests the obligation to determine the needs of its mothers and children and to see that the provisions of this program are carried out.

Forming the May Day State Committee will be Dr. G. M. Cooper, director of the Maternal and Child Health Services; Mrs. W. T. Bost, director of Extension of Child Welfare Services; J. T. Barnes, in charge of the work in behalf of Crippled Children; and Miss Lily Mitchell, in charge of aiding dependent children in their homes. Mrs. J. Henry Highsmith has been named program chairman.

The announcement that this new and enlarged health program for mothers and babies and dependent children of North Carolina has been made possible through Federal, State and local co-operation, is not only good news for everyone, but it is especially heartening to public health officials who for years have been laboring to protect the lives of mothers and infants, but under great difficulties, the greatest being in adequate funds. Consequently, the State's death rates of infants and mothers have been shamefully high, particularly during the recent years of the Depression.

Another encouraging feature of the new program is that it is to be directed toward safeguarding the lives of mothers and children more particularly in the rural and neglected areas of the State. In recent years the rural infant mortality rate has been higher than the urban infant mortality rate, and the same is true of maternal deaths.

To reach the remote sections of the State with health information, and the knowledge of preventing diseases, particularly as measures affecting the health of mothers and babies before and after birth, and the welfare of children through adolescence is the objective of the new health program.

Raleigh Sunday *News and Observer,* p. 24 (Editorial, p. 2)

14 JUNE 1936

HIGH INFANT DEATH RATE LAID TO FALSE ECONOMY

Failure Of Expectant Mothers To Consult Physicians Caused Rise

By Mrs. J. Henry Highsmith

Just why the death rate of mothers and babies in this State rose in 1934 to an alarmingly high point, 6,072 babies dying before they were one year old, is a question for which doctors and public health workers have ever since been seeking the answer. The procedure by which all public health progress has been made is by knowing first the cause of the disease or unhealthful condition and then seeking to remedy or remove the cause.

It is interesting to note that a recent study of this question made in Durham and Durham County by students of Duke University under the direction of Dr. W. C. Davison, dean of the Medical School of Duke, found the causes to be the same as those given sometime ago by Dr. G. M. Cooper, director of Maternal and Child Health Service of the State Board of Health, namely, that mothers in order to meet the family needs made urgent by the Depression sought to economize by consulting no physician during the period before their baby was born, and by having the services of a midwife instead of a physician at the time of its birth.

This false economy, says Dr. Davison, was largely responsible for the increased death rate of mothers and infants in 1933 and '34, and the hangover of this notion as well as its practice is keeping the rates well up today. The Depression is over, he said, and the rates should now be restored to their pre-Depression level, if not lower.

The point of attack in this problem of saving maternal and infant lives, thinks Dr. Davison, is the mothers themselves. They must be made to know what constitutes safe prenatal care and the importance of having it regardless of the cost. They must be made to know that the safest protection to be had during the prenatal period is from placing themselves in the care of a physician and following his instruction.

Husbands as well as wives must be taught that an economy that deprives a woman of a physician's services at the most crucial time of her life is not only false, but it is costly and oftentimes deadly. Not until all women know, he says, especially new mothers, the compelling reasons for having the oversight of a physician not only at their baby's birth but during the period before will the maternal and baby death rate be materially reduced.

Primarily it is an educational problem in which all agencies must help. Local groups like the woman's club, the parent-teacher association and the church and the school can cooperate with the health forces to educate the mothers of the community to realize the risks they run when they fail to have the care of a physician.

Raleigh Sunday *News and Observer*, p. 33 (Features, p. 10)

5 JULY 1936

COMMON SENSE MAKES SUMMER COMFORTABLE

Light Clothing, Plenty Of Water, And Shade Suggested For Health

By Mrs. J. Henry Highsmith

Contrary to the opinion of most people something can be done about the weather, especially the very hot weather, to make it more endurable and ourselves more comfortable and healthful. Or rather we can do something about ourselves so that our relation to the hot weather is less direct and its effect on our minds and bodies less severe.

In the first place, direct exposure to the sun should be avoided as much as possible. Seek the shade. Walk on the shady side of the street. Work on the shady side of the house. Plan to have shade about the house through trees, vines and awnings. Use the cool, shady spots in the yard or on the lawn for an outdoor living room, or for serving suppers and cool drinks.

Don't expose the head to the sun's direct rays. Wear a hat, or better still carry an umbrella, if fashion has not relegated this sensible custom too far toward the rear. Wear light loose clothing—light in color and texture. For comfort in hot weather, nothing takes the place of bathing frequently and keeping the body free from dirt.

Eating and drinking decently are wise precautions. Too heavy dinners of meats and fatty foods should be replaced with dinners having more fruit and vegetable dishes and more appetizing cold plates, salads and desserts. Liberal amounts of cool—not ice-cold—water should be drunk daily that there may be sufficient water in the body for digesting the food and for replacing all that passes off through evaporation and perspiration.

Sunstroke is a hot weather disorder to be guarded against by careful hygienic living. According to Edward F. Hertung, writing in the June issue of Hygeia, sunstroke occurs only when a person is exposed to three climatic conditions at the same time—sunlight, highly humid atmosphere and a dearth of breeze. He says sunstroke is usually due to an interference with the evaporation of perspiration from the skin, an interference due to too little water in the body, or so much humidity that evaporation of perspiration does not take place, or to little or no breeze. Since the amount of humidity in the atmosphere is a factor over which there is yet no control, says the writer, drinking plenty of water and obtaining a breeze are important precautions against sunstroke. Fortunately breezes can be manufactured by fanning either by a hand fan or an electric fan.

Other precautions against sun stroke advised are using discretion against too much physical exertion in the sun whether it as work or play, hard manual labor or golf and tennis. Careful planning of all outdoor work in summer, and of jobs in and about the house so as to use the cooler parts of the day is advisable.

"The consumption of alcohol has a direct relationship to sunstroke," says the writer. "When a man is exposed to conditions which make sunstroke possible he is more susceptible to the disorder if he has taken alcohol in any form. There is no question about this matter. It has been mentioned in army reports from the tropics and elsewhere. In the Philippines our own government observed that sunstroke occurred rarely, even among newly arrived troops, unless alcohol was taken in some form or another."

An attack of sunstroke usually develops suddenly. The introductory symptoms, says the writer, may consist of general depression, headache, dizziness, nausea, abdominal pain, great thirst and perhaps convulsions. The victim becomes unconscious and his skin is hot, dry and flushed. His temperature is high and pulse rapid.

Immediate treatment is to remove the victim to a shady place, loosen the clothing, apply water and produce a breeze by fanning. Meanwhile call the doctor. Following an attack the patient should remain in bed 48 hours.

Raleigh Sunday *News and Observer,* p. 41 (Features, p. 11)

12 JULY 1936

HEALTH SERVICE ENTERS NEW ERA

Mothers and Babies In Out-of-Way Places Will Be Given Added Attention

SOCIAL SECURITY ACT MAKES WORK POSSIBLE

Efforts For 'Forgotten Mother and Child' Directed Toward Saving Lives and Promoting Welfare of Babies to School Age; Health Centers Planned

By Mrs. J. Henry Highsmith

What is looked upon as a new era in public health work already has begun in North Carolina. It certainly will be a new era for two groups of the State's citizens hitherto unreached and in some instances almost forgotten in the State's program for health work. These are the mothers and babies back on the farms, down on the coast, up in the hills and wherever isolation and depression have deprived them of medical attention and the State's free health services.

This new field of health work made possible through the Social Security Act and directed by the Children's Bureau in Washington is being administered in North Carolina by the State Board of Health. Dr. G. M. Cooper, director of the Division of Preventive Medicine, is in charge of that phase of the work having to do with maternal and child health, with efforts directed toward safeguarding the life of the mother and child before and after birth and toward promoting the health of babies through infancy to school age. The plan adopted by Dr. Cooper is to get into some of the counties having organized county health service and into some where there is no such service, and set up health centers at convenient places where mothers and their babies may be brought for health instruction and medical advice. Already, public health nurses are at work in Pasquotank, Perquimans, Chowan, Gates, Dare, Camden, Warren and Greene counties making the preliminary arrangements with local physicians and dentists for the establishment of health centers.

Regular Schedules.

The health centers or clinics will be conducted one day in the month throughout the year, always with a physician and one or two nurses in charge. Cooperating in this county and community project besides the physicians, dentists and health officials, will be local club women, parent-teacher groups, the county superintendent of public welfare, and public-spirited citizens interested in saving the lives of mothers and babies of the community. While no treatments will be given at the health centers, efforts to provide such service through the county welfare officers will be made.

This work of bringing mothers in the prenatal stage to a physician for advice and counsel is the means undertaken to reach that large group of mothers that are not in the habit, for economic or social reasons, of calling a doctor even at the birth of their babies—a factor that largely is responsible for the tremendous loss of infant and mother lives in this State. While the clinics largely are object lessons and their chief end is health education, they are looked on to change and improve many an old fogey notion and insanitary practice that now is in use in connection with the confinement of the indigent class of mothers. Getting mothers to consult a physician during their prenatal period now is recognized as the crux of the whole problem of lowering the maternal and infancy mortality rate, not only in North Carolina but wherever similar situations exist.

Another factor to be recognized as affecting the problem is the midwife, especially the dirty, ignorant and unskilled midwife. Consequently, a feature of the program is to hold training classes for midwives at central places in these counties. Health nurses not only instruct midwives in the essentials of maternal care and sanitation but issue certificates of efficiency to those deserving recognition for ability and effort.

Raleigh Sunday *News and Observer,* p. 23 (Amusements, p. 1)

MAY 1936

PRE-SCHOOL AGE MOST IMPORTANT HEALTH PERIOD

By Mrs. J. Henry Highsmith

That period in a child's life known as the pre-school age—from two to six years—is probably the most important he will ever have from a health standpoint. It is important because in this period the foundation is laid for his future health. Great physical and mental growth takes place and he makes those adjustments that are necessary to live in a socially complicated world. It is in this period when he forms physical, mental and emotional habits that are to determine largely the state of his future mental and body health, and whether or not he becomes a stable social asset as a citizen in his community.

The pre-school age is a period in which perplexing problems concerning their children's health confront parents. In passing from infancy to childhood many changes take place. A child completes his first set of teeth and starts building his second; he doubles his weight, also his height, and usually contracts some or all of the contagious children's diseases that are going the rounds in the community, such as measles, whooping cough, chickenpox, and the like. Instead of children in this period having the most watchful care and supervision regarding their physical development, they are frequently left to themselves and are dreadfully neglected. Bad habits are allowed to form with defects and abnormalities as the result, and minor troubles that could have been easily remedied are permitted to become serious.

The safest way for parents to supervise the growth and development of their children during this important period is to have them examined periodically by a doctor and a dentist, at least every six months. At such examinations little defects are often discovered which are easily corrected, but which if they be allowed to persist, become difficult to handle. Advice and directions are given at these examinations for preventing as well as for correcting unhealthy conditions.

Parents are learning that it is economy to go to a doctor to keep their children well, rather than go to him only to cure diseases that might have been prevented. They are no longer satisfied to have "puny," "sickly" children since they know that these are abnormal conditions frequently caused by some defect that is easily remedied. Nothing short of really healthy children should satisfy parents. The healthy child who has the best chance of growing into the healthy adult is the one who lives a regular life, has good health habits, eats well-planned meals at regular hours, gets plenty of sleep in fresh air, plays vigorously out of doors in the sunshine, and has good posture.

One specific duty of parents is to get their child ready to enter school for the first time, free of all defects and physical handicaps. A physical defect puts a child at a disadvantage with its schoolmates. Poor sight or hearing may make him seem dull in school and cause him to become discouraged and uninterested. The first step in getting him ready to take his place well equipped with other children is a thorough physical examination by a physician and a dentist in the spring or early summer. This will allow the summertime for correction of defects and for immunization against diphtheria, smallpox and typhoid.

Questions that parents should ask themselves before starting their six-year-old to school are: Does he see and hear well? are his teeth sound and well kept? are his nose and throat in a healthy condition? has he been gaining steadily in weight? has he been growing in height? are his eyes bright, cheeks red, muscles firm, posture erect? Has he been vaccinated against smallpox and immunized against diphtheria and typhoid? Has he good habits of eating, sleeping, exercise, bathing, elimination, self-control and obedience? If so, he is ready for school and the chances are he will not be a "repeater," not a liability to the State and community.

The Health Bulletin [North Carolina State Board of Health] 51/5 (May 1936), pp. 8–10

MAY 1936

GOOD HEALTH HABITS EASILY FORMED

By Mrs. J. Henry Highsmith

There is nothing that stands a person in good stead like good health habits formed early in youth. The secret of living to a ripe old age and meanwhile keeping vigorous and fit is usually found to be the observance of good health rules which have been practiced from youth up. So important are good health habits in keeping down sickness and in preventing those insidious diseases that steal upon man around middle age that the formation of health habits in children is considered a parent's first duty.

Psychology has recently given us many helpful hints and suggestions for helping a child to form wholesome habits. One is that the thing to be learned must be made as pleasing and attractive as possible. The more satisfaction there is in doing a thing the first time, the easier it is to do it the second and third.

Another is that the child should be taught as soon as he is able to comprehend it, what he is doing and why. An intelligent reason for doing a thing makes all the difference in the care, interest and application one gives to the task whether he be a child or an adult.

Praise is also essential. A little word of encouragement now and then not only relieves the process of monotony and fatigue but speeds up progress and leads to efficiency.

Of course there must be regularity for any degree of success. To insist on regularity is to give it importance and emphasize its value. It is a child's conviction as well as an adult's that a thing that is worth doing at all is worth doing well and regularly.

By way of applying these simple rules, take the process of teaching a child to form the habit of brushing his teeth at least twice daily. In the first place, he should have an attractive new brush, child's size, and a pleasant tasting paste, to start with. A frequent change of paste and style of brush will help to keep up interest. The use of a mirror will be of great aid. To know that he is keeping his teeth clean and free of germs in order to prevent their decay is the motive for his efforts. To be told that he is succeeding, that his teeth are being kept clean and free of disease germs, will redouble his interest and efforts, and to teach him the necessity of brushing his teeth regularly twice a day will not only cause him to form the habit readily but will make him satisfied with no other but a clean, healthful mouth.

Other health habits that children should be taught to form early in life are: eating regularly of the food served them without fuss or play; going to the toilet at regular intervals during the day; and going to sleep promptly when put to bed.

The Health Bulletin [North Carolina State Board of Health] 51/5 (May 1936), pp. 11–12

MAY 1936

MALARIA ON THE INCREASE

Observance of All Practical Methods of Mosquito Control Urged

By Mrs. J. Henry Highsmith

A disturbing note sounded at the Sanitarians School–Conference held at State College, February 18–21, was that malaria in North Carolina is on the increase. This was adjudged from the fact that deaths from malaria has risen from 50 in 1933 to 78 in 1934 and to 93 in 1935. The cause of this almost sudden rise has not yet been determined but the fact was sufficient to arouse keen interest among the sanitarians and to stimulate more determined efforts on their part to effect mosquito control.

While much is now known about the cause and spread of malaria—the anopheles mosquito—its control remains a difficult as well as a perennial problem. The mosquito and the house fly were said to be the two remaining insect pests that affect human health and happiness to any great extent for which no permanent and definite control has been found. However, enough is known about malaria control which if applied rigorously and persistently will greatly reduce the incidence as well as the severity of the disease.

In addition to cooperating in the program of malaria control that is sponsored by the State Board of Health, the observance of the more easy and yet practical methods of controlling malaria was urged by malaria experts attending the school. These were mentioned as ditching, draining, filling-in, straightening streams, oiling stagnant pools, covering dump heaps, screening houses and rain-barrels, keeping rain gutters open, stocking lily pools with fish and minnows, and spraying.

Pyrethrum sprays were recommended as being among the most effective, the ingredients to be had from local druggists. It was brought out also that this spray used in large quantities two hours in advance would repel mosquitoes at out-door gatherings such as barbecues, picnics and camping parties. A repellant recommended for home and personal use was composed of citronella, 1 oz.; camphor, 1 oz.; oil of cedar, ½ oz. For bites, the application of ordinary soap was suggested, also the external use of alcohol.

For effective screening against mosquitoes, an 18 or 20-inch mesh screen was advised, the regular 14 and 16-inch mesh used against flies having been found ineffective against mosquitoes. The treatment of malaria, it was emphasized, should always be under the direction of a physician.

The Health Bulletin [North Carolina State Board of Health] 51/5 (May 1936), pp. 12–13

June 1936

Taking Some of the Guess Work Out of Life

By Mrs. J. Henry Highsmith

No procedure has been found more beneficial for staying off disabling diseases and lifting loads of worry than the periodic physical health examination. It may not be the most generally popular means of preventing disease and illness, but it is one of the most effective and certainly inexpensive. Physicians and health workers look forward to the day when the physical health examinations will be the more generally practiced measure of maintaining personal health and efficiency, and incidentally of increasing the sum total of human happiness.

Twenty years ago a physical examination at regular intervals was especially advised as a means of staying off the ailments of old age—the degenerative diseases, mainly of the heart, arteries and kidneys. This was to avoid premature breakdowns and other dreaded conditions feared for old age. But more positive health and a greater degree of assurance is wanted today. One is not willing to wait till he feels old age creeping on to ascertain whether or not he is sound physically. He considers health too valuable an asset to take chances on losing it, especially when it is no more than a matter of neglect or delay.

Young people are taking this attitude toward health and are doing something about it. They make friends with their doctor, seek his counsel and relieve their minds of further worry. They are courageous. They want to know the facts about themselves so as to proceed intelligently with their plans, without running risks or depending on guess-work. That is the enlightened spirit of modern youth, and because of this intelligence and wholesome attitude the health, happiness and efficiency of tomorrow's citizens can be counted on to surpass that of today.

Another good health forecast for the future is that babies and young children are being taught to consider the doctor as their friend, as the guardian of their health. This friendly relationship will not only stand them in good stead while they are babies and young children, but it will be a comfort and protection in maturity and on through the years.

A close friendly relationship with one's family physician—choose one whom you can hold in the highest esteem, and consult regularly and confidently—is the more modern and sensible method of keeping one's self in fine shape physically. It is in keeping with the more intelligent health standards and practices of today. The good physician who is made to feel that he is held accountable for the health and efficiency of his patients, will study to know his patients thoroughly, so as to advise competently. The plan works advantageously to both parties.

The Health Bulletin [North Carolina State Board of Health] 51/6 (June 1936), pp. 10–11

JULY 1936

NEW HOPE FOUND FOR STUTTERERS

Baffling Old Disease Yields to Mental, Physical and Social Treatment

By Mrs. J. Henry Highsmith

Stuttering, which has been called a "pernicious living thorn in the flesh" and is one of the oldest diseases known, is not to remain one of the unconquered maladies that afflict mankind. It is now yielding to treatment as the conditions and environments causing it are understood, changed or removed.

Dr. James S. Greene, medical director for the National Hospital for Speech Disorders in New York City, has materially advanced the knowledge of the cause and cure of stuttering during the past seventeen years, in which his institution for the treatment of speech disorders has handled 15,000 cases of stuttering and in addition several thousands of other speech defectives.

Stutterers, he says, are not speech defectives as generally understood. They can all speak normally under certain conditions. Their intermittent spasmodic speech is not the result of some defective speech organism, but is conditioned by highly emotionalized states of mind. The adult stutterer usually gives a history of having been a nervous, fearful child, often living in a parental atmosphere surcharged with nervous tension. A nervous child living in a home with high-strung nervous parents, he says, is fertile soil for producing the stutterer-type of personality.

According to Dr. Greene, the treatment of stuttering has always been a baffling task because the basic problem of the stutterer has not been fully understood. But opinions emanating from different points of view and from different psychologists have now centered on the fact that stuttering is an emotional personality problem, and consequently, successful treatment must start from reshaping the patient's mental and emotional processes. This naturally is a complicated process calling for medical, psychologic, reeducational and social measures, and employing the group approach. The purpose is to reorganize the stutterer, and start him with a new chain of emotions and mental reactions.

An effective means of treatment employed by Dr. Greene is creating for his patients a special atmosphere in which informality, encouragement and sympathy hold sway, and in which there is calm and peace—perhaps the first mental and spiritual calm the patient has ever known. In such an atmosphere old habits of a nonsocial, egocentric, fearful individual are broken down, and symptoms which complement his stuttering speech respond to new and wholesome suggestions.

In this new environment, the patient emerges from his introverted shell and takes on a feeling of confidence and belief in himself. He sooner or later gets his first hold of confidence in his speech situation, and finds himself adjusted to a new environment of calm assurance and emotional control.

It is safe to conclude from the foregoing diagnosis and treatment that there is much parents can do to prevent stuttering. The environment of the nervous child, especially its home and family life, should be made as tranquil and normal as possible. Lack of emotional control seems to play an important part in producing stuttering; therefore control of the emotions and avoidance of excitable conditions are advised as measures against this old disease.

The Health Bulletin [North Carolina State Board of Health] 51/7 (July 1936), p. 6

JULY 1936

SLEEP AND HEALTH

By Mrs. J. Henry Highsmith

Since Thomas A. Edison upset the sleep health-chart by saying that up to his sixtieth year of life four hours of sleep a day sufficed him, and that sleep is a matter of habit to be controlled and even diminished by the power of the will, there has been much questioning as to what amount of sleep is necessary to maintain physical and mental health. There is no doubt but that Edison's example and his statement concerning sleep have been responsible for many persons getting insufficient sleep, even to the point of impairing their health. They fail to recognize in him the exception that makes the rule, and likewise fail to take into account their own mental and physiological constitution and needs.

Recent experiments with dogs to determine the value of sleep found that puppies can live two or three times as long without food as without sleep. It is stated that human beings can live only about two weeks without sleep, whereas they can live from fifteen to sixty days without food. In the loss of sleep the brain gets no rest, and only those who "can't sleep" know the agony of a mind and brain exhausted from lack of sleep.

Sufficient sleep for maintaining health depends on many factors, but most of all on the soundness and depth of the sleep. One authority on health and efficiency has said that five hours' sound sleep—a sleep in which you are "dead to the world"—is far more capable of restoring the body and mind to normal capacity for work than a ten-hour period of restlessness and tossing in bed, with an occasional nightmare.

Since sleep is for rest and for restoring used-up energy, it is safe to say that only when one rises thoroughly refreshed and invigorated from a night's sleep, eager to be up and doing, has he had enough. The amount will depend on the kind and intensity of his work, on his habits of living and eating, also on the amount of recreation and play he gets, as well as on his age. But for the average man 7 or 8 hours, and for the average woman 8 or 9 hours of sound sleep a day is considered the minimum for keeping the mind and the body up to their best functioning powers.

People who begrudge the time they must, perforce, spend in bed for sleep to "knit up the ravel'd sleave of care," should look well to their sleep habits. Shorter hours will be necessary if one falls asleep immediately on going to bed, and sleeps soundly in the early part of the night. But all too frequently people build up the wrong sleeping habits. They read after going to bed, take home work to be done at night, or keep late hours eating, drinking and seeking forms of entertainment or excitement. They insist on burning the candle at both ends, and consequently pay the price in inefficient labor, poor health and shattered nerves.

The Health Bulletin [North Carolina State Board of Health] 51/7 (July 1937), pp. 9–20

August 1936

Random Observations

By Mrs. J. Henry Highsmith

Harnett County Organizes for Health Protection.

Harnett County has recently taken the forward step of organizing a county health department. Dr. W. B. Hunter of Lillington is the health officer. When the new service which began June 12 is completely organized, the personnel will consist of one whole-time health officer, Dr. Hunter, two public health nurses, one sanitary officer, one clerk, and twenty weeks of a dental health program. Harnett makes the fifty-fifth county in the State to provide for a county-wide health service.

To Study the Effect of Housing on Health.

Just what effect poor, crowded housing conditions have on health is a subject that is attracting more than nation-wide attention. As a matter of fact, it is of such importance that the Health Section of the League of Nations is undertaking a study of this question, in which the American Public Health Association has been asked to co-operate. In compliance, a committee on the Hygiene of Housing has been appointed by the A. P. H. A., of which Dr. C. E. A. Winslow of Yale University is chairman and R. H. Britten of the U. S. Public Health Service is secretary.

Slum Clearance and Better Health.

Slum clearance is a civic and health project that several nations are undertaking as an economic recovery program. England seems to have led the way in this. Within the past four years about one million new houses have been built in England and Wales, about half of which were subsidized by the government. Recently a new slum-clearance project has been started by the English government which within five years is expected to demolish all officially condemned slums and do away with overcrowding. Whether there is any direct connection or not with the housing program, it is interesting to note that the infant mortality rate of England decreased from 65 per 1,000 in 1932 to 58.6 in 1934.

In line with the program and purpose of the Federal Housing Administration, many cities in America are undertaking slum clearance but in modified forms. A statement of slum conditions found recently in a central Pennsylvania city by A. J. Bohl, treasurer of the Pennsylvania Public Health Association, is interesting and is here given:

"In these slums exist about ninety per cent of the city's commercial prostitution. About the same percentage of the felonious assaults occur here, together with eighty per cent of the liquor law violations, and seventy-five per cent of the highway robberies and larcenies. Generally, ninety per cent of all the crime in the city is committed here or, if elsewhere, is committed by residents of these areas. From a health and sanitation standpoint, also, the picture is of the darkest hue."

Beware of Poison Ivy.

Poison ivy or poison oak may be an unpleasant aftermath of an otherwise pleasant vacation spent in the mountains or woods unless one is careful to avoid contact with these plants. Only one who is highly sensitive to plant poisoning and who has suffered the inconvenience as well as the pain of this infection knows how much better it is to avoid it altogether rather than run the risk of contacting it.

Poison ivy, poison oak and poison sumac grow in nearly every section of this State. They may be found near streams, ditches, and growing on or about fences. Each contains an acid secretion which is very poisonous to individuals who are susceptible. Consequently it is well to know these plants by sight, which should be one of the first steps toward getting ready for a vacation to be spent in the woods or mountains.

First and early treatment after contact has been made should be to bathe the affected parts in hot salt water, or hot soap and water, using a strong alkali soap. A brush should not be used as there is danger of breaking the skin and making the infection deeper. A strong solution of Epsom salts and water is also recommended. If the infection persists, see a doctor for further treatment.

Swimming Is Not Always Free From Danger.

Swimming is a sport not without its dangers, even to the so-called good swimmer. There are perils for the over-confident and unwary as there are for those just beginning to learn. Especially is this true for those who swim in rivers, creeks and ponds, where there is no supervision or means of rescue. It is in such places that drownings occur much more frequently than at the seashore, at supervised lake beaches or in municipal swimming pools.

Some of the more frequent perils met by the uncautious swimmer are from reckless diving—not knowing the depth of the water; from unsuspected step-offs, obstructions and currents—being unfamiliar with the bathing place; from over-exertion or staying in the water too long for one's strength; from fool-hardiness, especially on the part of young swimmers, and from cramps.

Cramps in the stomach are usually due to excessive eating or drinking or too much exertion without "cooling off" before going in. Cramps in the feet and legs are primarily due to the unaccustomed exercise that these members have been suddenly called on to do.

Two good rules for all persons going in bathing to remember, especially if bathing or swimming in rivers, creeks and ponds, are: first, never go into the water alone. Unforeseen mishaps may occur to the most accomplished swimmer. Second, consider all dark and muddy waters unsafe. Turbid or muddy water may hide sticks, stones, glass and tin cans which could cause serious injuries. It conceals its depth and does not allow quick recovery if one should go down in it. Such waters take many innocent victims in North Carolina every year.

The Health Bulletin [North Carolina State Board of Health] 51/8 (August 1936), pp. 11–12

DECEMBER 1936

WHY MOTHERS AND BABIES DIE NEEDLESSLY IN NORTH CAROLINA

By Mrs. J. Henry Highsmith
Assistant Director, Health Education
State Board of Health

The message I am bringing to you this month is by request. It is the story of why so many mothers and babies die needlessly in North Carolina, and what is being done by the State Board of Health and the Children's Bureau in Washington to remedy this situation.

A few years ago North Carolina prided itself on being called the "Baby State," not because it was the youngest, or the smallest, or gave promise of rapid growth and development, but because it produced the most babies per 100,000 of its population of any State in the Union. But North Carolina no longer takes pride in this appellation for the reason that it has lost this distinction to New Mexico, and the further significant fact that it has not been able to raise the babies that were born to its mothers. Now, the trend is upward again and we may be able to recapture our boastful "first." However, it is no distinction to have babies and not be able to raise them. It is a disgrace. North Carolina loses a shamefully large number of babies every year. In 1934 we lost 6,169 under one year of age, which was more than any other state per population except South Carolina, Georgia, New Mexico, and

Arizona. While times are better and our death rate is beginning to decline we are still losing between three and five hundred babies each month or about 5,000 a year, and between 40 and 50 mothers a month, or about 500 a year. Physicians say that between 75 and 85 per cent of these deaths are needless. In other words, they could have been prevented, since many of them were due mainly to neglect.

To determine the causes of the State's high death rate of mothers and babies in recent years has entailed much study and many investigations. Among those making studies of the situation were a group of Duke University students under the direction of Dr. W. C. Davison, members of the State Medical Society, and the Division of Preventive Medicine of the State Board of Health. Interesting were the causes found by each investigation, and strikingly similar. These were found for the most part to be the State's high birth rate, ignorance and indifference, poverty, isolation, and the use of midwives.

Naturally, it is to be expected that more deaths would follow a high birth rate than a lower one, especially if these babies were born to parents of small means, low incomes, amid crowded and poor living conditions and under circumstances which denied them even the minimum care that babies must have to survive.

But ignorance and indifference were found to be large contributing factors, especially that hopeless ignorance that refuses to know better and still holds to old notions and customs of a generation ago; that kind of ignorance that fosters superstitions, old-fogey notions, insanitary practices, and all the backward customs of thinking and living. It is a regrettable fact that superstitions and old wives' tales are responsible for the neglect, and perhaps the death, of many babies in this State today. Even some husbands and fathers are hiding behind these old-fogey notions, making them their excuse for not providing adequate care for their wives, when in that delicate period preceding the birth of their babies. They will tell you that birth is a natural process and needs no interference, not even from a doctor or a nurse, and that the services of a midwife, regardless of how unskilled, insanitary, and ignorant she may be, are all that are needed for the coming of the baby. Is it any wonder that mothers and babies die under such conditions as are found in nearly every section of this State?

Poverty, too, was found to be a contributing factor to the State's high death rate of babies and mothers. That false economy that is brought on by poverty and was increased by the recent Depression, made having the services of a physician to attend the pregnant mother and care for her baby at birth considered unnecessary, and in too many cases it was dispensed with altogether. Thus the habit of doing without a physician's services was more fully established. False economy of failing to have a physician has been responsible for not only a mother doing without proper food and proper care before the arrival of her baby, but also for paying for this neglect in prolonged illness and perhaps, invalidism, if not with her life.

Isolation, too, was found to be a cause, especially isolation that made accessibility to a doctor difficult and long delayed. Families back on the farm, down on the coast, and up in the hills—those far removed from centers of educational, religious, and social life—were found to have suffered greatly for the lack of general information and free health service that is to be had today. To reach these mothers never before served by the free agencies of the State is our privilege and task.

Another determining factor of great importance is the general use of midwives. It is estimated that one-eighth of the white mothers, and two-thirds of the colored have only the services of midwives at the birth of their babies. Some day, it may be the millennium, I predict that we will look back on this period when ignorant, unskilled insanitary midwives deliver one-third of the babies of the State, as a relic of the dark ages. As our civilization is constructed at present, perhaps there is a place and service for the midwife, but the ideal of our public health workers and all interested in the well-being of the race look forward to the time when every mother will have adequate care during the period of pregnancy and at the birth of her baby.

Thus we see our problem, and it is my privilege and pleasure to tell you something of the program that has been set up for the remedy of this situation in our State. Last August there was passed by Congress what has been called one of the greatest human documents ever enacted by a law-making body—"The Social Security Act," a phase of which was to make more secure the lives and health of mothers and babies throughout our great country.

To the Children's Bureau was given the responsibility of administering the section of the Social Security Act, providing Federal aid for maternal child health services, and to the North Carolina State Board of Health, under the direction of Dr. G. M. Cooper, has been given the responsibility of putting into operation this special health project in the State. By matching funds with the Federal Government the State Board of Health has been able to secure certain health services for mothers and children, particularly for those in rural or neglected areas, or in places of economic distress. The program set up by Dr. Cooper and his co-workers includes the organization of health centers in conveniently located places, and these to be served by local physicians, pediatricians, obstetricians, dentists, and one or more public health nurses. So far, these have been placed mostly in sections of the State where the maternal and baby death rates are among the highest. To these centers are invited needy and indigent mothers of the community who have been sought out by the public health nurses and urged to attend.

At the centers, which are held regularly each month, they are given a physical examination and are advised as to what constitutes proper care for themselves and their babies, both before and after birth. Valuable literature is put into their hands, with the instruction as to its best use and helpful meaning.

The centers or clinics are under the supervision of local doctors, which means that mothers attending these centers are brought face to face with their county or community physicians probably for the first times in their lives. Here they are enabled, also probably for the first time, to know and appreciate the services of a doctor. Furthermore, barriers of embarrassment due to false modesty and inexperience are broken down and the way is made easier for them to confer with a physician and have him administer to their personal needs. While a general physical examination is given, there are no provisions for treatment. Patients needing treatment are advised to go to their local or family doctor, and emergencies are handled through the county public welfare officer, or some other local agency.

Another phase of the center work is the instruction given to mothers regarding the feeding and care of their babies. They are advised to bring their babies regularly each month to the center, and the child's growth and development is carefully watched. While at the center, the babies are often given the immunizing treatment against diphtheria and smallpox. Dental needs of the mother and baby are also taken note of, as well as other phases of their general health. Thus the health center in any community becomes both a health and educational institution.

To date, nearly 100 health centers have been established in North Carolina in about 30 counties. Sixteen of these counties are without any organized health department or public health nursing service, while the others have this maternity and infancy work as a supplement to their regular health program. Already hundreds of mothers have been served at these clinics or centers and the darkest spot in the State's public health work is beginning to clear up.

But the baby problem in North Carolina will not be met and settled by this one program alone. It is too large and too involved to be met and handled so easily. However, every little bit is a decided help. Underlying it are all the social, economic, moral and health problems that affect a people. Dr. Cooper, who is familiar with the conditions that are largely responsible for the State's high death rate of mothers and babies, has repeatedly stated these to be: Lack of pre-natal and competent obstetrical service at child-birth; lack of knowledge on the part of mothers concerning themselves before their baby's birth, and concerning the care and needs of the baby after birth; lack of home comforts, and home and community sanitation, and lack of foresight or provision on the part of the husband or father for the arrival of another member of the family.

All of which is to say that poverty, ignorance, and indifference are playing too big a part in the background of the State's future citizens. And all of which shows that the science of eugenics must be made general and practical, and the problem of improving the race be made the concern of the State.

Primarily it is an educational problem in which all agencies must help. Local groups like the woman's club, the parent-teacher association, home demonstration clubs, the schools, and the church can cooperate with the health forces to educate the mothers of the community to realize the risks they run when they fail to have the care of a physician.

The Health Bulletin [North Carolina State Board of Health] 51/12 (December 1936), pp. 13–15

1937

2 January — named first vice president of NC State Legislative Council

7 January — attends inauguration of Governor Clyde R. Hoey

12 January — assists at reception for Mrs. Clyde R. Hoey and family at Hartness mansion on North Blount Street

13–16 January — attends board meeting of GFWC in Washington; receives, with president Mrs. Roberta Campbell Lawson, at "chief social event" of the meetings; "Mrs. Highsmith wore a gown of violet colored crepe"; does not stay in Washington for presidential inauguration on the 20th

19 January — presents panel "Safeguarding the Health of School Children" at Hugh Morson High School PTA

27 January — broadcasts on "Our State Wild Flower Reserve," WPTF Garden School of the Air, a project of the Raleigh Garden Club

3 February — addresses Pittsboro Woman's Club

11 February — addresses Fred A. Olds School PTA on "Helping the Child to Find Himself"

12 February — gives luncheon for Mrs. Hoey, Isabel Hoey, and Mrs. E. L. McKee, Sir Walter Hotel

c. 9 March — is appointed Girl Scout Troop mother, Troop 1, Hugh Morson High School

7–9 April—attends 35th annual NCFWC convention, Charlotte; speaks on publicity opening night

22 April — attends small luncheon for Mrs. Hoey at Sir Walter Hotel given by Mrs. O'Berry

26 April–1 May — attends GFWC national council meeting, Tulsa; pictured in *The Daily Oklahoman*

7 May — assists a tea in the Governor's Mansion given by Mrs. Hoey, honoring NC Garden Club 12th Annual Meeting

15 June — during a 30-minute radio broadcast in opposition to legalization of liquor in election of June 22, Mrs. Doak reads statement by Mrs. Highsmith

16 June — addresses NCFWC second annual Woman's Club Institute at UNC on health services for all counties

19 June — receives at a bridal tea on Hillsboro Street

18 September — attends a wedding in Clarkton (Bladen County)

September — takes in a lodger, Miss Ellen Ross of Clinton, student at St. Mary's School on Hillsboro Street

27–29 September — addresses NCFWC annual planning council meeting, Morganton, to propose cancer and high infant mortality as subjects to be undertaken

1 October — opens contest, until March 1, 1938, for best piece of club writing, nationwide; announcement carried in newspapers nationwide

12 October — presents program at Twentieth Century Book Club, topic not specified

November — her article on Marriage Laws (in the *Health Bulletin*) receives statewide coverage in the papers

20 November — addresses the Home Demonstration Club women of Robeson County, in Lumberton

JANUARY 1937

OUR IMMEDIATE TASK—TAKE THE TRAGEDY OUT OF CHILDBIRTH

By Mrs. J. Henry Highsmith

At the beginning of this new year one thing is clear: Tragedy should be taken out of childbirth. Motherhood, which is a woman's most fundamentally significant experience in life, should not entail the risk of death and invalidism that it does today for some classes of women. It should be made safe. It should be rid of fear, gloom and dread. Every woman should know wherein lies the means of safety concerning this, her most critical period.

It is the boast of science that it now knows how to combat death in connection with childbirth. Then, for the sake of the mothers who do the dying, and for the good of maintaining the nation, why not try to prevent the most tragic of all deaths, the death of mothers in childbirth?

More women die between the ages of fifteen and forty-five from diseases incident to pregnancy and childbirth than from any other cause, except perhaps tuberculosis, and this in the face of the fact that many of these deaths are preventable. In the United States, last year, more than 15,000 mothers lost their lives from causes incident to giving birth to their babies; in North Carolina more than 500.

But this deplorable situation does not have to remain so. Some communities have already demonstrated that the lives of mothers need not be sacrificed at childbirth. They have found that good medical care and an informed public that will seek that care, are the keys to the situation. In communities where doctors, nurses and civic leaders work together in providing good care for all who need it, surprisingly few have been the deaths of mothers at childbirth. On the other hand, where ignorance and indifference cause expectant mothers to delay seeking care until it is too late, and where there are no facilities for saving lives, such as trained obstetricians and nurses, and well equipped hospitals, mothers continue to die.

Fortunately, the year 1937 finds a fair beginning made in North Carolina in a permanent program to save the lives of mothers and babies. Already 110 communities in the State, in about 40 counties, are now engaged in maintaining health centers where pregnant mothers can come once a month and seek to learn what constitutes proper prenatal care. The centers are supervised by the public spirited physicians and obstetricians of the community and one or more public health nurses. Here the mothers are given a physical examination and are advised as to their physical needs and safe personal care.

Are the mothers being reached through these centers? During the month of October, when the work in most of the centers was just getting under way, 1236 mothers attended the clinics. The mothers are interested. Furthermore, they are cooperative and grateful for this service.

What is even more significant and encouraging, women are taking up this fight. Club women, parent-teacher groups and home demonstration clubs are becoming aroused and are asking their physicians, county commissioners, and others responsible for the welfare of their people to take steps to save the lives of the mothers of their community.

Club women especially are interested in an educational program that is intended to reach every woman in the State with the personal message that *"Early and Adequate Prenatal Care Will Greatly Reduce the Risks of Motherhood."* They believe that a better educated womanhood will soon come to demand better obstetrical care for all mothers, as well as more adequate nursing and hospital service.

In their program club women are urging on the part of every club:

1. To know the maternal death rate of its community for over a period of three years and to compare it with the State and national average.

2. To know how many of the maternal deaths were preventable. How many were due to lack of proper obstetrical care. How many due to negligence on the part of the mothers themselves or their families.

3. To know what prenatal health services are available to the mothers of the community.

4. To study the bearing of the economic conditions under which the mothers live upon the maternal death rate.

5. To cooperate with the State and county boards of health, local physicians and nurses, superintendents of public welfare, in reaching and caring for indigent pregnant mothers.

For mothers themselves the club woman's program stresses the following points:

1. Examination as early as possible during pregnancy by a competent physician.

2. Subsequent visits by expectant mothers at regular intervals to their physicians.

3. An aseptic delivery by a competent doctor.

4. Post partum examination immediately after delivery and about six weeks later.

5. Adequate post-natal care, including medical and nursing service, and treatment of post partum complications.

The Health Bulletin [North Carolina State Board of Health] 52/1 (January 1937), pp. 6–7

FEBRUARY 1937

ENDEMIC TYPHUS IN NORTH CAROLINA

Believed To Be Transmitted By Rat Flea

By Mrs. J. Henry Highsmith
State Board of Health

The appearance of thirty or more cases of typhus fever in North Carolina during 1936, resulting in three deaths, is cause for no great alarm; however, the severity and fatality of the disease are serious enough to warrant every precaution being made to prevent its spread. Especially is this true now since the question as to how this disease is carried from man to man, long a controversial matter, is believed to have been settled.

Typhus fever is associated in the minds of most Americans with the World War, armies, camps, and trenches. The body louse or "cootie," as the doughboys called it, was known to be the carrier. But the typhus that is found in North Carolina and other Southern states today is not the epidemic form which was so prevalent during the World War and which is still more or less common in many countries of Europe and other parts of the world. Neither is it the type that is associated with slums, filth, and squalor. It is a more benign type, less severe in its reactions and having a low fatality rate. The rate is usually about 5 per cent or one death in twenty cases. However, the fatality varies with age—less than 2 per cent under 45 years and about 30 per cent above 65 years. This disease found in many of the southeastern states is believed to have come from Mexico. In many respects it resembles "Tabardillo," the Mexican form of typhus.

Both the epidemic and endemic forms of typhus are said to be caused by the same germ, the only difference being a new host and a new means of transportation for the endemic type. It is well known that the epidemic typhus is borne from man to man by the body louse, and it is reasonably certain that the endemic type is borne from rat to man by the rat flea. The epidemic typhus is more deadly, shows a decided preference for cities, especially crowded slums, and prevails during the winter and spring. It is highly communicable. Endemic typhus shows a preference for rural communities and has its maximum incidence during the summer and fall. It does not spread as rapidly as the epidemic type and is less fatal.

In both forms, the disease is marked by a sudden onset with headache, dizziness, and a fever lasting usually about two weeks. There is always a rash, a most characteristic symptom, which appears about the fifth day and lasts from two to ten days.

According to the July–September report of the Health Section of the League of Nations, there are four types of typhus-like diseases in the United States, these not including the louse borne type. The endemic benign form known as Brill's Disease is one of the group, but it is not to be confused with the type found in the South. In recent years numerous studies have been made of this newer type of typhus fever in order to find its host and means of transmission. Kenneth F. Maxcy, past Assistant Surgeon of the United States Public Health Service, was the first to point out that all evidence was against louse transmission and to suggest that the reservoir might be the rat. This assumption was later verified by his co-workers, Dyer, Badger, Ceder, Rumreich, Workman, and Kemp. These workers are now agreed that the disease actually has its reservoir in rats and that it is transmitted from rat to rat and occasionally from rat to man by rat fleas.

The question then is, will endemic typhus, which is flea borne from rats to man, become in the future as widespread and devastating as epidemic typhus, louse borne from man to man, has been in the past? The answer to this question, it stands to reason, will depend on the control or lack of control of rats. To eradicate endemic typhus it will be necessary to eradicate rats.

A distressing note concerning typhus fever in the South is that it is on the increase. "Birmingham's Health," a bulletin published monthly by the Jefferson County Board of Health of Alabama, reports that the disease began to appear in South Alabama about 1921, and since that time there have been no less than 2,500 cases of the disease and 102 deaths. The Bulletin says:

"The highest incidence was in 1933 when 823 cases were reported. In the first nine months of 1936, 266 cases were reported of which eight occurred in Jefferson County. Thus the disease is apparently on the increase in this territory. While the majority of Alabama cases have been in rural areas, association with food handling establishments constitutes an important factor in urban cases.

"Negroes are relatively free from the infection, the attack rate being approximately one-tenth of that of the white population. Adults are more often attacked.

"The disquieting fact must be faced: typhus has secured a dangerous foothold in certain sections of this State and each year is spreading northward in increasing incidence. A broad program for the control and eradication of rats is, therefore, an immediate public health necessity."

The League of Nations Journal recently issued is also of the opinion that endemic typhus is on the increase in the United States. It says:

"It seems that murine typhus (rat borne) in man has been increasingly frequent in the United States. In Alabama, for instance, some 60 to 80 cases per year have been reported since Maxcy and Havens discovered it in 1922 through the Weil-Felix reaction. It was limited to the cities of the south and southeastern part of the State. In 1932 the number of cases rose to 237 (11 deaths) and in 1933 to 823 (35 deaths). The disease had spread to strictly rural areas without modifying either its mode of spread or its fatality (Baker, McAlpine & Gill, 1935). In Texas, 417 cases were reported in 1934 against 5 in 1922 (Bohls, 1935). A check in the increase was, however, obtained as a result of extensive rat-destruction campaigns in Texas, Alabama and Georgia."

The Health Bulletin [North Carolina State Board of Health] 52/2 (February 1937), pp. 14–16

APRIL 1937

MANY HEALTH RISKS INVOLVED IN MODERN BEAUTY PROCESSES

By Mrs. J. Henry Highsmith
Assistant Director, Health Education

Never before in history, except in the days of ancient Greece, perhaps, has there ever been so much attention given to physical beauty as there is today. Think of the millions of dollars invested in machinery devoted to one or two beauty processes only—to put the crimp in the hair for one race and to take it out for another! Think of other millions invested in the manufacture of beauty-producing goods and appliances, such as lotions, oils, grease, paints, paste, perfumes, and the various paraphernalia used for shaping the body, mainly for reducing it. Surely neither the Greeks nor the Romans, with all their arts and artifices employed in the quest for beauty, measured up to the American women of today. In true American style they surpass them all—the Egyptians who taught the use of paints, perfumes and oils, also the beauty treatment for the eyes and the painting of the finger nails; the Greeks who gave the world models of natural beauty of the human body; the Romans who perfected and carried to extreme, perhaps, the health baths, and all the other nations who have devised ways and means for making their women beautiful.

Neither the State Board of Health nor the writer has any quarrel with any one, man or woman, who wishes to improve his or her looks. On the other hand, we commend it. The point we wish to make in this connection is that too much emphasis is being placed on the artificial processes of beauty culture—on machines, manipulations, fads and fancies, and too little on knowing and maintaining the real basis of beauty, which is a healthful body.

Health workers throughout the country are agreed that if physical beauty and its counterpart, personal health, are to become lasting qualities in the life and character of the American people, women must be more rational. They must seek to know and apply daily the fundamental principles underlying health, beauty and character. Simply stated, these are correct eating habits, sufficient rest and sleep, outdoor exercise, regular and normal elimination, and, above all, control of the emotions.

In the first place, women must use common sense in meeting much of the high-pressure sales talk of today. They are said to be more credulous than men, of being easily duped, and of making it possible for charlatans and imposters to flourish throughout the country at their expense. I do not subscribe altogether to this accusation, but I do know that some women take little pains to know what it is they buy, whether their purchases be cosmetics, medicine, food or clothing. Oftentimes they purchase potent poisons in the name of medicine, such as headache remedies, cold cures, and sleeping tablets, not knowing that what may be a harmless remedy for one person may be a poison for another.

It is well known that a woman's pride as well as her purse are easily appealed to through her inordinate desire to follow fashion's decree. This has been evidenced in recent years in the craze for slimness. What crimes have been committed in its name! What a price women are paying for this one phase of beauty culture and fad or fashion! Who of us does not know of one or more persons who have become either mental or physical wrecks as a result of efforts to slenderize without medical supervision. In most cases these sad plights have been brought about by some one undertaking to reduce by hearsay methods or ill-advised diets, perhaps by fasting, doing without food for long periods, or eating only one or two meals a day, when they have been accustomed to three.

However, not all the desires on the part of women to reduce are mere whims. Some need to reduce for their health's sake as well as for fashion's sake. Obesity can be as much a menace to health as thinness. Overweight can put a strain on the heart, or predispose to diabetes or other organic diseases, as surely as underweight can predispose to tuberculosis, colds, pneumonia, and other respiratory diseases.

But what every woman should know is that there is a right way to reduce. When she feels the necessity or the urge, she should ask herself the question, not "how shall I do it?" but, first, "do I really need to reduce?" If her weight is normal for her age, sex, race, physique and bodily activity, she should make no attempt to change it. If, however, she insists on reducing, she should first have a careful medical examination in which racial and hereditary characteristics as well as the general state of her health are taken into account. She should proceed only under the direction of her physician. She should remember also that in any sane reducing system the procedure should be gradual, losing not more than one or two pounds a week. Anything more drastic than this is likely to weaken the system, predispose the body to disease and cause mental upsets.

Since prevention is the basis on which progress for the most part in public health work has been made, the wiser plan, it seems, would be to prevent the necessity for reducing. Overweight and obesity are almost always the direct result of dietary indiscretions, mainly overeating, therefore the correct procedure would be to diminish the intake of food, taking care, however, to eat nourishing foods in sufficient quantities to provide a maintenance diet.

The person who habitually eats more than the body requires for its energy needs will store up the excess in the form of fat. A low caloric diet consisting mainly of the protective foods such as milk and dairy products, fruits, eggs, green and yellow vegetables and whole wheat cereals, will supply vitamins and minerals in abundance and will protect the body against dietary inefficiencies.

There are several insurance companies, we are told, who, in order to combat the evils of stringent and ill advised dieting among their policyholders, have launched a campaign against drastic reducing diets and measures. To send home the lesson of the dangers involved in reducing too vigorously or without the advice of a physician, they have adopted two slogans: "Better be fat than dead," and "Diet and die." These are extreme slogans, we will admit, but insurance companies care to take no chances on such great and unnecessary risks as those involved in drastic dieting.

> *Note:* No articles are attributed to Mrs. Highsmith in May, June, or July. However the June article "About Virginia Dare and the Roanoke Island Celebration," which concerns the 350th anniversary of the Lost Colony (vol. 52, no. 6, pp. 4–6), may well be by her, as it reflects her particular interest in Virginia Dare and cites her acquaintance D. Bradford Fearing of Manteo.

The Health Bulletin [North Carolina State Board of Health] 52/4 (April 1937), pp. 12–13

AUGUST 1937

HEALTH WORK BECOMES LARGELY A PERSONAL RESPONSIBILITY

By Mrs. J. Henry Highsmith
Assistant Director of Health Education
State Board of Health

It is very evident today that a significant change has taken place on the public health front. Whereas the point of attack in public health work in years past has been centered largely on the fight against communicable or germ-borne diseases, it is now being directed toward combating serious personal ailments known as degenerative diseases. Health workers say and statistics prove that if the death rate is to be further reduced and health work strengthened at its weakest point, the degenerative diseases must be the next important object of attack, and personal interest and initiative must be appealed to as major factors in their control.

Communicable diseases can and are being brought under control through State and community programs, but heart and kidney diseases, high blood pressure, hardening of the arteries, and other conditions due to the breaking down of the organs of the body continue to take an ever increasing toll. The death rate from such causes is constantly on the increase.

What, then, is to be the remedy for their control and where is the place to begin? Directed and applied health education for everybody is recognized as the most effective remedy, and the public school is the starting place. We believe that effective personal health work must come through instruction and directed practice in the public schools, and through a coordinated health program sponsored jointly by the State Department of Education and the State Board of Health. We trust that the day is not far distant when such a program will be provided for the children of North Carolina.

Twenty-five years ago the main objective in the program to conserve the people's health was to keep down germs, those invisible forms of life responsible for the spread of many diseases. Well do we remember "Swat the Fly" campaigns, and the first efforts to secure safe milk and water supplies, the construction of effective sewer systems, the passage of laws for clean food, and other measures aimed at the protection of the people's health.

Back in 1914, which was the beginning of keeping records of the births and deaths in North Carolina, a large number of all deaths in the state were due to communicable diseases—such diseases as typhoid, diphtheria, whooping cough, measles, scarlet fever and smallpox. To be exact, from these six diseases in 1914 there were 1,660 deaths, whereas there were only 335 deaths from these same causes in 1935, and yet the State by this time had a much larger population. This was a reduction of 80 per cent, a magnificent achievement in public health work in twenty-one years.

Consider another picture, of six other conditions or diseases, namely, heart disease, kidney trouble, hardening of the arteries, high blood pressure, diabetes and cancer. In 1914 there were 5,511 deaths from these conditions in North Carolina. In 1935 there were 13,628, or an increase of more than 40 per cent. According to the mortality statistics for the nation these diseases have increased 54 per cent in the past 34 years, and this in spite of the progress which has been made by medical science in diagnosing, treating, and often preventing them altogether.

It is seen therefore that the public health problem of today is to get the individual man or woman intelligently interested in conserving his or her health, in adopting a regimen of living that will guard against the untimely breakdown of the vital organs and a wreck of the human system. While we believe that the most effective personal health work must come through the schools, there is much the adult man and woman can do to prolong their physical powers and insure their enjoyment of life for years to come. In the first place, each must determine what his own health problem is, what hinders him from enjoying health and efficiency 100%, and then he must set about to remedy it.

When it is known that faulty living habits are more often responsible for prematurely shortened lives than any other single factor, the correct procedure would be to consider first one's way of living. Perhaps overwork, with too many and too long hours given to one's job with no provision made for rest, recreation or play is YOUR health problem. Then why not plan to take a vacation, even if at your own expense? It will pay big returns in better health, efficiency, and a contented spirit. Oftentimes, the only obstacle standing in the way of a vacation is the planning for one. Why not plan now to get a much needed rest this summer? Every person who carries any responsibility year after year needs a change, a letting up of the tenseness and strain that the burden of responsibility puts upon the nerves, the brain and the heart. A wiser plan, however, would be to see that every day, rather than that every year, has a definite period of relaxation and rest. Overwork and working continuously under pressure are hazardous to health and long life.

Perhaps your personal health problem is not overwork but over-eating, or eating unwisely. Lack of interest in the proper selection and combination of foods, together with faulty eating habits, are the cause of most stomach ailments, and much personal ill health. Today one should be well informed as to the basic elements and values of food and should apply this knowledge to his every day living. In fact, it should be one's first business to see that his body, the human machine, is kept in good condition and that it continues to function properly.

Whatever one's health problem may be, he owes it to himself and his loved ones to set about with diligence and integrity to correct it. Especially should men and women of around fifty be on guard against the approach of physical disabilities connected with later life. Fortunately, modern medical science offers new hopes to the man and woman of fifty. They need not necessarily accept the possibility that they will have heart trouble, kidney disease or high blood pressure when they grow older. Physicians know that these diseases are no longer inevitable. They can be avoided altogether. The main requirement by way of checking and preventing them is to consult one's physician while he is yet well, before the onset of any disease, and to have a physical going-over and checking-up at regular intervals. There is nothing formidable about this. It is the only sensible way known to insure lengthening one's life and to make the maturing years happy and profitable.

We take pride and find consolation in the fact that science has materially lengthened the span of life, adding from 12 to 15 years to one's expectancy. But we forget that the gain has been made in the age bracket below 45, mainly in preventing infant deaths and in protecting the lives of children and young people. Thus far, little gain apparently has been made in the group above 50. The truth is, this age group through their disregard for health teaching and lack of interest in preserving their health at this valuable time of life are not only blocking a further extension to the average life span, but they are presenting a stubborn, major health problem.

We would not have you feel, however, that years and years alone are the chief end of living, or the specific objective of health work. To quote Dr. C. E. A. Winslow, professor of Public Health at Yale University, "Health is not freedom from disease; it involves personal well being and wholesome living." It is this positive note, that health is a means to a higher end, and not an end in itself, that I would emphasize.

There is a certain admiration and distinction today for those who live to a ripe old age, regardless of the kind of life they have lived. Their long years are sometimes made the subject of nation-wide publicity and they themselves are sought out by the curious public. We prefer quality to quantity even in the number of years permitted to us to live, fewer years filled with service for others, love of family and friends, peace of mind, and a zest for living, rather than many years of dull, drab existence with only self at the center.

Obviously, not much more can be done toward lengthening life, but infinite are the possibilities of enriching it and making it worth the living. The oncoming of age is no longer a drawback to the acquisition and practice of some of the finest virtues. Some persons, like good wines, get better as they grow older. That lovely mellowing that comes with the years can be noted in their characters as well as reflected in their faces. Irritability and impatience give place to a certain serenity and forbearance; selfishness gives way to charity, and unreasonableness to understanding and graciousness.

At no period of the world's history has old age been more generously considered or greatly favored. Old age pensions will relieve, it is hoped, to a great extent the anxiety and fear associated with growing old, for many people, and becoming dependent. Science has made it possible for aging mouths, ears and eyes to continue functioning sufficiently; the automobile affords travel, recreation, and relief from monotonous situations; while the radio and the motion picture bring the world's best drama, news, and even the Gospel to one's own fireside.

The wise person will, while he or she is yet on the sunny side of life, take thought for the years beyond his three score year mark. He will strive to keep not only physically fit, but mentally young. Dr. Charles H. Mayo recently questioned the wisdom of prolonging the human span when nothing is done to prolong the virility of the mind. "The mind," he said, "must be treated with the same rules of care and exercise as the body. New interests, continued education, and variety will keep the brain up to the pace set by the fine and durable bodies with which science now endows even the aged."

So, to quote Clarence W. Lieb in the April number of *Hygeia:* "We should cultivate our best abilities and develop the work and ideas in which we are most interested. The better the quality of the mental storage leading up to the meridian of life, the less we shall have to fear the onset of old age. The habit of stocking the mind with constructive philosophy, good music, poetry, facts and fiction will enable the aging person to draw on this accumulated knowledge, artistry and experience and become a wise counselor to the younger generation. Productive old age and the utilization of acquired knowledge and experience should be the aim of every human being. The mere attainment of old age is a worthless objective if linked up with this effort there is not a purposive struggle to conserve the spirit and mind of youth."

Since science and government are doing much to mitigate the ills that old age has always been heir to, is there not something we can do in our own lives to remove the clouds of fear and apprehension, and to make "growing old gracefully" more than a pleasant sounding phrase? Can we not resolve with Charlotte Perkins Gilman, who says:

> To keep my health!
> To do my work!
> To live!
> To see to it I grow and gain and give!
> Never to look behind me for an hour!
> To wait in weakness, and to walk in power;
> But always fronting onward to the light,
> Always and always facing toward the right.
> Robbed, starved, defeated, fallen, wide astray—
> On, with what strength I have!
> Back to the way!

Note: another reflection on old age appears in the December 1938 issue of *The Health Bulletin,* below. This 1937 piece may be the longest of her tenure at the Health Department.

Mrs. Highsmith probably also wrote the previous piece in the August 1937 issue, "Are Your Children Ready for School?" The content and stance are nearly identical to her "Back to School" bulletin of 18 August 1938.

The Health Bulletin [North Carolina State Board of Health] 52/8 (August 1937), pp. 6–9

SEPTEMBER 1937

SUGGESTIONS FOR THE LUNCH BOX

By Mrs. J. Henry Highsmith

Since it will not be practical for all of North Carolina's school children to have lunch at school this winter, it will be necessary for many of them to carry lunch from home. Following are a number of suggestions for properly preparing the lunch and making the food meet the health needs of the child:

1. Select the container, box, basket or pail that can be kept clean, and that will keep the food dry and free from insects, dust and dirt. It should permit the air to circulate through it freely, yet keep out flies and ants. The type of box equipped with a thermos bottle for taking hot soup or chocolate in winter and cold milk, orange and tomato juice in summer is desirable.

2. In general, every lunch should include a meat or its equivalent, bread, a fruit or vegetable, either fresh or cooked, a sweet and a beverage.

3. Sandwiches may compose the foundation for the lunch, but by no means should they always be the stereotyped bread and meat variety. Tasty sandwiches can be made of nuts and cream cheese, nuts and dates or raisins, jelly, peanut butter, chopped eggs, and many other wholesome combinations.

4. Lunches may be varied by substituting for the usual sandwich a salad, a dessert, or some semi-liquid food like custard or stewed fruit. These may be placed in small glass jars with tight fitting covers. Jars in which mayonnaise, peanut butter or jam are sold, make excellent containers for desserts.

5. Use wax paper for wrapping sandwiches and keeping the different kinds of food separate. Thus by the flavor of the foods not mixing, the lunch is made more attractive and more appetizing.

6. Paper napkins, paraffin covered paper cups, and cardboard spoons and forks—the kind used for picnics—are useful accessories for the lunch box.

Instead of enumerating typical menus, a list of foods suitable for lunch boxes is given below. Foods which go well together and provide proper balance are listed across the page, but other combinations may be made. A beverage, such as milk or cocoa, is taken for granted, and judgment is expected in making combinations. [Table in original:]

Bread and Meat
Chicken sandwich
Minced ham sandwich
Chopped egg sandwich
Jelly sandwich
Peanut butter sandwich
Chopped dates and nuts
Graham muffins—deviled egg
Corn bread—chopped bacon filling
Cheese sandwich

Fruit or Vegetable
Celery
Whole Tomato
Orange
Apple
Banana
Grapes
Pears
Peaches
Raw carrots

Dessert
Rice pudding
Tarts
Oatmeal crackers
Gingerbread
Fruit gelatine
Baked custard
Cookies
Chocolate pudding

or Sweet
Dates
Figs
Jelly or preserves
Sweet chocolate
Cocoanut
Raisins

Cheese used with nuts or fruits such as pineapple, dried apricots, peaches and apples offer a variety of appetizing and nourishing sandwiches. Lettuce used in making meat, egg and tomato sandwiches will add much to the tastiness and value of the lunch provided the lunch can be kept in a cool place until time to eat.

The Health Bulletin [North Carolina State Board of Health] 52/9 (September, 1937), pp. 7–9

September 1937

The School Lunch Problem

By Mrs. J. Henry Highsmith

Following a better understanding of the relation of diet to disease, of malnourishment to ill-health and inefficiency, more and more attention is being given to the food and eating habits of school children. No good school of today fails to consider the nutrition needs of its pupils. Too vital and too unmistakable has been found the relationship between failure in school, ill-health, backwardness and truancy, and a long, deep-seated hunger. Educators are beginning to ask what gain is there in trying repeatedly to teach the half-starved boy or girl whose mind and body no longer function normally, for lack of proper and sufficient food.

There's no denying the fact that providing proper food for children and supervising their eating habits is a problem, even if well managed, for the average home, to say nothing of what it becomes when taken to the school and made to apply to several hundred children. However, it is a problem which the schools are finding they cannot afford to overlook. The reason is, a well-fed, healthy, happy child is taught more easily. He learns more rapidly. He adjusts himself more readily to the school program and to community life. He is not a problem. On the other hand, a child suffering from hidden hunger is likely to be a diseased child, defective in some sense organ, or debilitated so as to be liable to infectious diseases. Furthermore, he is likely to be a misfit. If he fails to make his grade from year to year, he soon becomes discouraged, and drops out. At this stage, some children develop anti-social tendencies, and some few are later found with court records.

Many North Carolina schools are today faced with the school lunch problem. A check made last year of the annual reports of the 750 white high schools in the State showed that only 370 or a little over half operated school lunch rooms or cafeterias. Of the 370 cafeterias listed, 311 were classified as being operated by rural schools and 61 by city schools. It is interesting to note that the schools operated 189 or 51 per cent of the cafeterias, while the local Parent-Teacher Association sponsored 80, or 22 per cent, and the FERA 51, or 14 per cent. The Woman's Club, it was found, operated 9, while 30 or more were privately operated.

While no estimate has been made as to the number of elementary schools which provide cafeteria service, it is reasonable to believe that the percentage of these is no higher than that of the high schools. Consequently, for at least half of the school children of the state no provision for the noonday school lunch has been made.

The ideal plan is to have the school itself operate the lunch room or cafeteria where a hot, nourishing lunch can be served every school child who wants it, and especially those who need it, even though they cannot pay. A paid director should be in charge, and should have assistants who may be furnished by the NYA or WPA or they may be self-help students. The director or supervisor may be the Home Economics teacher, but in that case she should have a cook and adequate help, and not be expected to manage the cafeteria and keep up her class work at the same time. Neither should the pupils studying home economics be expected to do the work that is required daily in a lunch room or cafeteria.

Most city school systems have these provisions, and find that, due to the large number served daily, a lunch room can be operated on a self-paying basis with many decided benefits to the school. As desirable and beneficial as lunch rooms are for city schools, they are even more desirable for rural schools. Where the pupils have to leave home early and go long distances, a hot lunch is almost a necessity, if sufficient strength and energy are to be had for the work of the day.

One rural school of about 125 pupils and five teachers, at Colfax, North Carolina, has demonstrated that the school lunch problem can be met and solved satisfactorily and at little cost. The way this school managed it was to convert a former classroom into a lunch room by having the school carpenter build in a counter, several cabinets and a number of long tables and benches. A partition of screen wire separated the service area of the room from the space where the food was prepared. Equipment of dishes, knives, forks and spoons, and cooking utensils for serving thirty-six pupils at one time or an average of 75 daily, by having two lunch periods, was bought. The entire cost of providing the lunch room and its equipment was $250.00. In this school the home economics teacher supervised the buying, preparation and serving of the food, but under her was a paid cook and one or two NYA helpers, also several students who paid for their lunches by assisting with the serving. The principal, Mr. W. H. Cude, or the Home Economics teacher, Miss Martha Sample, will furnish further information on how the rural elementary-high school may successfully handle the school lunch problem.

If it is found impossible for a school management to provide a full hot lunch during the winter months of school, the next best thing is to serve a hot beverage to accompany the pupil's cold lunch brought from home. This can take the form of hot soups—vegetable or cream—hot cocoa, bouillon and milk. It takes little equipment for this service and can be served in the separate class rooms. In the warmer months, ice cream, cool drinks of fruit and vegetable juices, and in every case, milk, can take the place of hot beverages.

Many rural schools have found it practical to operate lunch rooms on a cooperative basis. The children furnish the fruits, vegetables and meats, and the school or some civic organization employs a cook or matron to prepare and serve the food. By the pupils helping with the work, they receive valuable training in addition to their noonday meal. Parent-Teacher Associations, Women's Clubs, civic organizations such as the Kiwanis, Rotary, Civitan and Lions Clubs, have all shown a willingness to help in such worthy enterprises.

Another reason why every up-to-date school should operate a lunch room is its educational value in the community. Here children learn proper food combinations and what constitutes a wholesome diet. They become acquainted with new dishes, new ways of preparing and serving food, food sanitation, and table manners. They form new tastes and learn to like new foods, all of which help to meet their food-health needs. These new ideas and practices find their way into their homes and soon their families are preparing and serving food a-la-school-cafeteria style, which is a great improvement on the style which prevails in the average rural home.

Better no cafeteria service, however, than to sell candy and package grocery store cakes as the principal items.

The Health Bulletin [North Carolina State Board of Health] 52/9 (September, 1937), pp. 8–11

SEPTEMBER 1937

THE RIGHT OF EVERY CHILD TO SEE

By Mrs. J. Henry Highsmith

Outstanding among human rights is the right to see. This God-given gift is often denied persons through no fault of their own. What is more thought-provoking, three-fourths of the blindness in this country could have been prevented. That is, 90,000 of the 120,000 blind persons in the United States need not have been blind.

A study of the causes of blindness reveals that accidents in industry cause about 100 persons to go totally blind each year. About 300,000 other persons suffer the loss or the serious impairment of sight in one eye.

Accidents involving fireworks, air rifles, jackknives, scissors, fishhooks and other playthings of children carelessly used are responsible for another large group, mostly of children, being made blind.

Heredity, especially where persons who are disposed to blindness marry and transmit the disposition to their children, is said to cause about one-fourth of all blindness.

Another cause, hideous in all its manifestations, is syphilis. At least 15 per cent of all loss of sight is attributable to syphilis, both congenital and acquired. Blindness from this source, however, can be entirely wiped out. Acquired syphilis can be accurately diagnosed in its early stages, and through long and intensive treatment can be arrested. Congenital syphilis can also be brought under control through systematic treatment.

Fortunately, the attack on this cause of blindness has already begun. There is now hope that blindness caused by syphilis will be brought under control as blindness from that other venereal disease has been. Fifty years ago, ophthalmia neonatorum, or "babies' sore eyes," caused by gonorrheal infection at the time of birth was the largest single cause of blindness in children. By requiring that a silver nitrate solution be instilled in the eyes of newborn babies, the rate of blindness from this disease has been reduced from 40 to 7.5 per cent.

Gabriel Farrell, Director of the Perkins Institution for the Blind, discussing the Right of Sight in July Hygeia, says:

"To bring about the possible eradication of congenital syphilis and the conservation of sight destroyed by it involves the full cooperation of doctors, the support of the press and the radio, and the active approval of an enlightened public. Medical authorities know that treatment of an infected pregnant woman started at about the fourth month will protect the child from the curse of congenital syphilis. If medical schools will make this routine the established practice in teaching, if all doctors will as a part of prenatal examination give blood tests followed by treatment where results indicate its need, and if prospective parents can be taught to demand this care, thousands of children can be saved from the ravages of this gruesome disease."

There are ten ways, summarized by Mr. Farrell, for safeguarding the right of sight to everyone. These are:

1. Drops of silver nitrate solution administered at birth of every child.
2. The eyes of all children regularly and periodically examined and tested.
3. Corrective glasses scientifically prescribed and treatments given as needed.
4. Sightsaving classes organized for school children having defective vision.
5. Children's sight safeguarded from accidents, especially from fireworks, air rifles, scissors, etc.
6. Campaigns for safety in industry, and explicit observance of rules by all workers.
7. Avoidance of marriage or at least of parenthood by persons with transmissible causes of blindness.
8. A blood test before marriage.
9. Blood tests as a routine part of prenatal care with treatment when necessary.
10. The support of every movement aiming to conserve sight as an inalienable right.

The Health Bulletin [North Carolina State Board of Health] 52/9 (September 1937), pp. 13–14

OCTOBER 1937

ECONOMY VERSUS THE SAFETY OF SCHOOL CHILDREN

By Mrs. J. Henry Highsmith

The great school disaster in New London, Texas, last March, startled the world. Schools, homes, communities and every agency responsible for the safety of children were shocked into the realization that deadly hazards may be lurking even in some of today's most modern and well equipped buildings. School officials all over the country resolved then to be more alert and to employ every precautionary measure in behalf of the safety of the children under their care. Six months have elapsed since the New London catastrophe, just about enough time for the country as a whole to forget the Texas tragedy, also their resolves to be more vigilant concerning the safety of school children. But should they be allowed to forget?

So complete was the destruction of the school building in Texas that it may never be definitely known what caused the disaster. But it is known that false economy and technical carelessness or ignorance were criminally involved. It was brought out in the testimonies given at the investigation that a cheaper heating system was installed in place of that originally specified, and that a more dangerous high pressure "wet" natural gas was substituted for a safer low pressure "dry" gas, because it was cheaper. Furthermore, no impartial engineer was called on to inspect the finished installation and report on its safety. Even the salesman who persuaded the school to buy his heating system was shocked at the recklessness with which they substituted the cheaper for the more expensive, but safer system, and insisted on the use of pressure reducing regulators which were adopted eventually, but which were insufficient for safety.

It is evident that the lessons for schools to learn from New London are many: That economy in planning and maintaining a school building has its danger points. That too often the practice of economy becomes an extravagant waste. That only expert and impartial service should be employed in planning and constructing a building, and in the installation of all scientific equipment. That frequent and careful inspection by technicians should be made regularly of the entire building and grounds. That janitorial service is not to be depended on for safety, neither is a salesman's talk.

Probably the most needed lesson for North Carolina to learn from the above tragedy is one also having to do with false economy. The danger involved may be nothing so sudden and spectacular as an explosion, but it is just as real. It is the diseases and unhealthful conditions that school children are subjected to through inadequate or no school sanitation, particularly the disposal of school sewage. A few years ago North Carolina had the disgraceful record of having no sewage facilities whatsoever for 1,009 schools, or an enrollment of 47,041 pupils. But a recent survey made of 93 counties shows that only about 114 schools with an enrollment of 4,091 pupils are without sewage disposal in any form.

This is a great improvement, but according to the survey, there are still 2,584 public schools in the state serving approximately a quarter of a million of school children which have no other means of sewage disposal than privies. This means they are without the sanitary facilities that running water would provide and in some cases it means that the water supply is still a questionable pump, well or spring. But what is probably a worse crime against sanitation, health and decency, and one most generally complained of to the State Board of Health, is an inadequate water supply in some of the larger schools, many of them having new and apparently finely constructed buildings, and purporting to have modern and efficient systems of plumbing. What they actually have is not enough water for effective drinking fountain purposes, for washing hands and for flushing toilets. The complaint has been made that the water is cut off between recesses or for several hours during the day. In consequence, children have to go with unwashed hands, and the unflushed toilets become unbearably indecent and insanitary. Improperly installed and cheap plumbing is often given as the excuse for such intolerable conditions.

Hence, economy at any cost, or carelessness and indifference are the prices being paid for filth, infection and disease. There have been no fewer than three outbreaks of venereal diseases among school children of the State due to insanitary toilets, and who knows how many intestinal disturbances, skin infections and communicable diseases have been contracted in such unsafe surroundings as theirs at school? Another complaint that may be laid to false economy, short sightedness or to both is the hazards involved in the lack of transportation facilities for some schools. In order to transport the pupils with an insufficient number of busses, it becomes necessary to make two trips each morning and afternoon. Those living furthest from school are required to be ready for the first trip not later than seven o'clock, necessitating their getting up at six. They return around five or six o'clock in the afternoon, having spent ten or twelve hours in getting to and from, and at school. The complaint against the excessively long school day is that it often means the pupils go without breakfast and sufficient rest, they are exposed to cold, and in making haste for the second trip, there is an increased element of danger.

Obviously, for the sake of economy, school children are made to suffer unnecessary hardships, and run risks dangerous to their health and their lives, and the school is made more ineffective in its service to the community. Economy may sometimes mean a saving, but often as here, it means inefficiency and waste.

The Health Bulletin [North Carolina State Board of Health] 52/10 (October 1937), pp. 9–10

OCTOBER 1937

WHAT ABOUT THE TEACHER'S HEALTH?

By Mrs. J. Henry Highsmith

Much is being said and done these days in the interest of the mental and physical health of school children, but less is being said and done about the health and physical fitness of the teacher. And yet there is a close and definite relation between the two. The state of the teacher's health, and of her mental and emotional well-being, largely determines those states in her pupils. The teacher's health, personality, general attitude and outlook on life are readily reflected in the attitude and conduct of her pupils. Their behavior patterns are largely of her making.

Teachers owe it to themselves, their profession and to the children put in their charge for eight or nine months of the year to keep themselves as mentally alert and physically well as possible.

The Health Bulletin [North Carolina State Board of Health] 52/10 (October 1937), p. 16

NOVEMBER 1937

SHALL NORTH CAROLINA HAVE SAFER MARRIAGE LAWS?

By Mrs. J. Henry Highsmith

North Carolina has practically no laws for safeguarding marriage and the beginning of the home. On the statute books are two laws, neither of which as it operates today is worth the effort to enforce it. This is the opinion of one registrar of deeds, who says that the present marriage law which requires the male applicant for a marriage license to sign an affidavit saying that he has no active tuberculosis or a venereal disease, and has not had for two years prior thereto, is totally ineffectual. This law is an alternative to a prior law which required a health certificate from the groom in order to obtain a marriage license. Neither law requires anything of the prospective bride— not even a written statement to the effect that she has no tuberculosis or a venereal disease in the active stage.

But has not the time come when North Carolina can and will take steps to protect its children from the ravages of venereal disease? It is estimated that there are 20,000 children under fifteen years of age in North Carolina today who have syphilis inherited from infected and neglectful parents. And yet this large number is not the whole story. Only about 43 percent of syphilitic babies live to reach ten years of age. Therefore, it is safe to say that at least 70,000 other babies were born syphilitic but died in infancy or early childhood.

When it is known that children inherit blindness, feeble-mindedness, insanity, susceptibility to disease and premature death from syphilitic parents, and when it is further known that 90 per cent of these tragedies could be prevented through an enforced law requiring a Wassermann test of both men and women before marriage and another law requiring the proper treatment of expectant mothers showing a positive blood test, does it not seem that public opinion would demand this protection for innocent, helpless childhood?

Fortunately, there is a growing sentiment today in behalf of these measures. A poll conducted recently by the American Institute of Public Opinion found that 92 per cent of those voting on the question, whether or not there should be premarital Wassermann tests, were in favor. Of all the votes cast in the Southern states, 94 per cent were favorable.

In connection with the campaign being waged against syphilis, a number of states have enacted laws requiring, as a prerequisite for the issuance of a marriage license, evidence of negative Wassermann or similar blood tests. Connecticut enacted such a law in 1935 and, contrary to many predictions, it works and works well. As evidence that it has popular support, about 10 per cent more laboratory examinations were made for prospective brides and bridegrooms during the first five months of 1937 than for the same period in 1936. Illinois passed a bill in the spring requiring compulsory health examinations for all couples applying for marriage license, which went into effect July 1, 1937. Michigan has a similar law that goes into effect October 29, 1937, and New Hampshire's law becomes effective October 1, 1938. New Jersey is preparing a bill patterned after the Connecticut law to be introduced in the 1938 New Jersey legislature.

North Carolina also will sponsor a marriage license law at the next session of the General Assembly, according to Dr. Carl V. Reynolds, Secretary of the State Board of Health and State Health Officer. He says a marriage law is a part of the State's program to control venereal disease, and that he will press the passage of the bill when the Legislature meets in 1939.

As evidence that such a law is needed, witness the number of cases of syphilis that are being reported daily to the State Board of Health—an average of 33 a day, 1,000 a month, or 12,000 a year. A fair estimate places the number of syphilitics in North Carolina at 300,000. Without restrictions for preventing the spread of the disease and proper means of treatment for those infected, this will mean that we will continue to have 100 new cases of infection every day, and the birth of ten new-born syphilitic babies every day.

> *Note:* This article, like the one on marijuana, was widely reprinted: a subsequent issue of *The Health Bulletin* suggests at least 50 in-full reuses and many extracts, some with added editorial comment.

The Health Bulletin [North Carolina State Board of Health] 52/11 (November 1937), pp. 11–12

DECEMBER 1937

DOING SOMETHING ABOUT OLD AGE

By Mrs. J. Henry Highsmith

Unlike the weather, something can be done about growing old. To be sure, much can be done to defer decrepit old age, and what is more important, rid it of its dread and terror.

It has been said we are living in an ageless era, when science, education, and public health work have pushed back the frontiers of old age till it is now difficult to determine where the age line—old age—begins. Yesterday one was old at forty and forty-five. Today one is not old at sixty-five and seventy. Old age has been conquered. People are learning how to live, how to keep well and enjoy life fully to the end.

As Exhibit A we present Judge Robert Winston, who ten years ago, at the age of sixty-five, reentered the University of North Carolina. He dubbed himself, in his writings, "a freshman at sixty-five." Turning at that point from the practice of law to further study and historical writing, he has to his credit today three great biographies, and his autobiography, "It's a Far Cry," his latest book. And now we are told that he is at work on his fifth book.

While Judge Winston is a busy man, lecturing occasionally in addition to his writing, he takes pains to play, to rest, and to visit his hosts of friends. Today, at seventy-five, he is hale and hearty, hard working and happy.

Science, in recent years, has come to the rescue of old age. One need not now grow old and helpless prematurely. By taking advantage of every benefit, every discovery and bit of progress that medical science has made in recent years in the interest of prolonging life, one may live to a ripe old age and find it profitable and pleasurable. However, no drug, elixir or quick and easy means has been found for deferring old age. The process is one of intelligent foresight and action on the part of the individual in regulating his living in accordance with health laws, and in taking advantage of what medical science has to offer. For instance, medical science has decreed that such degenerative conditions—those indicating a break-down of the body organs—as kidney trouble, heart disease, hardening of the arteries, high blood pressure, and diabetes, are not inevitable. They may be long deferred or prevented altogether. The oncoming of years does not necessarily mean the oncoming of disease.

The best procedure yet found for preventing the onset of degenerative diseases is the habit of going regularly to one's physician for a thorough physical examination, and following his suggestions closely. Oftentimes, simple measures like regulating one's diet, getting more sleep and rest, avoiding too strenuous exercise or labor, or ridding one's mind of fear or worry, are all that is needed to offset some tendency toward a serious disease.

Yet this takes courage and determination—courage to seek to know, through a physical examination, what one's health needs are, and determination to meet these needs. The simplest way is to choose a good physician and take his counsel.

Dental science has also made its contribution to the art of staving off old age. Skilled workmanship, discovery of new anesthetics, and new processes of making dentures and treating defects of the mouth, make it possible for one to have a comfortable, efficiently functioning mouth and teeth even in old age. This fact not only aids one's digestion and indirectly his health and longevity, but by improving his looks and keeping him young in appearance, it aids his mental processes and brightens his outlook on life.

By means of modern science, vision and hearing also may be preserved, and one's enjoyment of life extended beyond his three score and ten mark. Crutches and even canes, except those carried for style, are being relegated to the past as orthopedics straightens limbs and makes cripples to walk.

In addition to what medical science, dentistry, and other material aids can do to halt the infirmities of age, there's much the individual can do to make this period not the worst but the best of life—"the last of life for which the first was made." Among the more practical ways, we suggest:

1. Keeping abreast of the times by reading the daily papers and current periodicals, by means of the radio, motion pictures, by conversing with friends, and by travel. There never has been such easy, comfortable and profitable means of traveling as is afforded today. It is a delightful diversion, and one that old people should enjoy frequently.

2. Keeping up interest in community, state and national life, and participating in home and community interests, a person should not lose interest in all life about him just because he is not as young as he once was. He should be interested in local politics and government, elections, the church, schools, clubs, civic and social organizations and all activities undertaken for the good of the community.

3. Holding old friends and making new ones when the opportunity presents itself. There is no easier way to induce old age, loneliness and, worst of all, self-pity than by losing contact with friends and acquaintances. Drawing into one's shell should be deferred as long as possible.

4. Having some creative interest to turn to when the cares of home and family life are given up. Some people who are wise use this period for taking up some congenial work long deferred for want of time and leisure. Perhaps it was music, art, gardening, writing, or maybe it was collecting something with a peculiar fascination, or just a pet hobby. This is the time to follow after the desires of one's heart. The writer knows three women who turned to music for recreation and pleasure and who are now

making a contribution to the cultural life of their communities, one by directing a church choir, another by serving as a pianist at Sunday School, and another by directing children's entertainments. For finding congenial interests among congenial group members, we recommend, especially for women, active membership in the church and church school, in the Woman's Club, the Garden Club, book clubs, or even in a knitting club. For men we recommend, in addition to reading and maybe writing, such hobbies as growing flowers, vegetables, or raising chickens, pedigreed pigs or cows or some other congenial outdoor work. We would not omit playing golf for those who have the means. Men especially cannot afford to lead an idle, inactive life. The law with them is "do or die," especially if they have always been accustomed to a busy, active life.

5. Building up a philosophy that will recognize in life a divine plan, and the futility of man in rebelling against it. Such a philosophy will strengthen and sustain one in accepting the inevitable with resignation and cheerfulness. It will help him to make proper adjustments to his surroundings and changed conditions. To rebel, to complain, to become cynical and intolerant will convert what should be the glorious and peaceful sunset of life into an inglorious and tragic ending.

6. Finally, there is no solace or comfort for old age comparable to true religion, and an implicit trust in God.

The Health Bulletin [North Carolina State Board of Health] 52/12 (December 1937), pp. 7–9

1938

15 January — reports to Board of Directors of GFWC, in Washington, D. C., stressing "unprecedented goodwill" between Women's Clubs and the press of the country

19 January — addresses Lewis School PTA on "Sex Education in the Home"

11 February — speaks to a session of the State Public Welfare Institute for Negro Social Workers

3 March — is honored guest at RWC, extending greetings from GFWC

8 March — attends pre-convention luncheon of Raleigh Junior Woman's Club

10 March — Dr. Highsmith inaugurates Health Institutes for Public School Teachers in North Carolina, a series of 37 sessions statewide, "Better Heath for Better Living and Learning," concluding 28 April

18 March — attends luncheon for workers in the NC Women's Field Army for Control of Cancer, honoring national commander, Mrs. Marjorie B. Illig of New York

1–3 April — attends first annual Alumnae Weekend at Duke, as member of the program committee

9 April — comments to press on 11 April issue of *Life* magazine, which had published explicit stills from the documentary film "The Birth of a Baby"

27–29 April — attends 36th annual NCFWC convention, Wilmington; addresses opening session on her work as chair of Press and Publicity at CFW, "Why Tell the World?" later changed to "Modern Education Presents a Challenge to Club Women."

1 May — as State May Day Chairman, participates in Child Health Day

5 May — receives at a reception in Roseboro for her nephew Troy Marvin Herring and his bride, married 16 April

8–17 May — travels to Kansas City for triennial GFWC convention, the last of her term as national publicity chair; addresses press conference; Mrs. Latham elected national chairman of budget

18 May — UNC Extension announces a non-credit course in writing publicity for men's and women's organizations, ten lessons taught by Prof. Walter Spearman, attributed to Mrs. Highsmith

June — appointed to represent North Carolina on National Advisory Committee for Women's Participation in the New York World's Fair

July–August — participates in district gatherings sponsored by WPA on health education

2 August — speaks at Health Day, a WPA adult education course at East Carolina Teacher's College, which draws 80 students from 53 counties in eastern NC.

15 September — named to general Centennial Committee, Duke University

25 September — speaks at annual reunion of Isaiah Warren, Sr., Association, Westbrook High School, Sampson County, as great-great-granddaughter

29 September — attends luncheon meeting of Clinton Garden Club, with Mrs. Clyde R. Hoey as speaker

17 October — attends Raleigh chapter of Meredith College Alumnae Association, of which she is chairman of projects

18 October — co-hosts meeting of Wake County Duke Alumnae

c. 10 November — addresses Ahoskie Woman's Club

9–11 November — hosts Miss Alvis Long of Columbia SC, Peace College alumna and speaker for Armistice Day observances

29 November — addresses Twentieth Century Book Club on Robert Berkov's *Strong Man of China: Chiang Kai-Shek*

1 December — receives at reception for 300 following meeting of State Literary and Historical Association, featuring George Stevens, editor of the *Saturday Review*

8 December — attends Hugh Morson High School PTA annual banquet for teachers

13 December — addresses Lumberton Woman's Club on public welfare: "The Part Women's Clubs Play in the Health Needs of their Communities,"

27 December — attends silver wedding anniversary open house for Mr. and Mrs. Charles G. Doak

31 December — presides, as first vice president, over meeting of State Legislative Council to formulate program for forthcoming Legislature; elected president

FEBRUARY 1938

MARIHUANA

By Mrs. J. Henry Highsmith

Marihuana is a new world old world drug whose ancient history is black with crime and insanity. It was introduced only a few years ago into the border country of the United States by Mexican laborers. Today it is known to have spread to every state in the Union, and the number of marihuana addicts is now estimated to be more than 100,000, the majority of whom are of high school and college age.

Marihuana, or marijuana, is the Mexican name for the dried flowers and leaves of the commercial hemp plant, cannabis sativa. In Asia the plant is known as cannabis indica, or Indian hemp, and the narcotic derived from it is called hashish. The English word "assassin" is derived from the Arabic "hashishin," or "hemp eaters," an oriental religious and military society noted for its violence and crimes committed under the influence of hashish. Orientals long ago learned that hashish produced the proper mental and emotional state for committing crimes of the most heinous nature.

Marihuana circulates in the United States usually in the form of cigarettes under a variety of local names, such as reefers, greefas, mutahs, muggles, miggles, love weed, giggle weed, joy-smoke and the like. It is peddled out especially to high school boys and girls by vagabond dope peddlers. It is made alluring to youth by a whispered secret that it is a cigarette with a new thrill, a "real kick," with no harmful aftereffects. Its introduction into the United States was preceded by a whispering campaign which represented it as able to perform miracles, to produce great physical and mental strength, and to sharpen one's wits and social gifts.

In this country the effects of the drug are obtained almost entirely by smoking the dried leaves and flowers of the plant. It has been found being sold not only in high school and college communities, but across refreshment counters, in second rate dance halls, low amusement places, barbecue stands and some filling stations. Marihuana dens have been found in some of the larger cities, and many of these were visited by high school boys and girls in search of a new sensation.

The effect of the marihuana drug differs with the individual. No one can predict what the reaction in any case will be. On the immature brain of the young, it acts as an almost overpowering stimulant. Its continued use undoubtedly results in general instability, mental weakness and finally in insanity. "Floating" is the term given to marihuana intoxication. In this condition the person's ego becomes greatly magnified, and nothing appears impossible. All sense of time, place, conscience or consequence is lost. Marihuana victims suffer hallucinations which often take the form of a persecution complex, with violent murders, maybe of father, mother or best friend, as the result.

A. J. Anslinger, U. S. Commissioner of Narcotics, says: "Marihuana is contributing to an alarming wave of sex crimes. How many murders, suicides, robberies, criminal assaults, holdups, burglaries and maniacal insanity are caused each year by marihuana can only be conjectured. The sweeping march of its addiction has been so insidious that it thrives in numerous communities and is only found out by the commitment of a heinous crime."

That marihuana, or cannabis sativa, is a weed that grows wild throughout the country, that it is a habit-forming drug making dope addicts of thousands of men and women, and that the youth of the country has been chosen by the peddlers of this poison as their most fertile field, make it a problem of serious concern to every man and woman.

To bring the traffic in this drug under control, says Mr. Anslinger, means a job of unceasing watchfulness on the part of the police, parents, school officials, public health officials and all welfare workers. It means education through the schools, the home and the press. It means also cooperation on the part of all good citizens in securing the strict enforcement of State and Federal Narcotic Laws.

Fortunately, North Carolina has a State law for the control of marihuana, but not until last summer when Congressman R. L. Doughton introduced and secured the passage of a law by Congress did we have a Federal Law. One without the other was ineffective, while both, it is believed, will be able to curb the traffic in the marihuana drug.

> *Note:* Very widely reprinted in newspapers throughout the country. The Nashville reprint was introduced with a note on "the evils of the weed which when smoked makes perverts and demons out of its victims."

The Health Bulletin [North Carolina State Board of Health] 53/2 (February 1938), pp. 14–15

Nashville (NC) *Graphic,* 10 February 1938, p. 6

MARCH 1938

TREATMENT VERSUS PREVENTION

By Mrs. J. Henry Highsmith

Recently there was dedicated in Jersey City a county tuberculosis hospital of skyscraper proportions. It is twenty-five stories high, approximately 300 feet, and was built at a cost of $3,000,000, secured from the WPA. When it is furnished and equipped at a cost of $750,000 more, it will have a capacity for between 500 and 600 tuberculosis patients, and it will be the finest county-owned tuberculosis hospital in the country. Into it will go every modern facility that is available to any hospital. There will be in addition to the most up-to-date clinical, diagnostic and treatment facilities such features as an auditorium for lectures and entertainment of the patients, a swimming pool, a Roman Catholic chapel with stained glass windows, bronze and marble trimmed halls, a modern dental department and an ear, nose and throat division.

In the erection of this institution, according to the dedication issue of the Jersey Journal, the mayor of the city "has advanced a step nearer his ambition to give the residents of Jersey City and Hudson County one of the finest and most complete medical centers in the new world."

We quote again from one of the dedicatory speeches recorded in the Jersey Journal: "This magnificent new hospital unit, one of the finest and best equipped of its kind in the country, is surely a splendid addition to Jersey City's great Medical Center of which we are all so proud. No more humane work could be done, or is being done, than caring for the thousands who fall victim to what is commonly called the 'white plague,' and this new building, with its staff of doctors and nurses, is destined to bring still further renown to the already famous names of Jersey City and Hudson County, for the work achieved here in the tuberculosis field."

Could it be that in this modern, grand way that the mayor of Jersey City has chosen to meet the tuberculosis needs of his people, every feature of which is fine, that one of the most modern and effective measures has been disregarded? What about preventing tuberculosis and saving the 600 young lives from falling victims to the Great White Plague, making their treatment unnecessary? Nothing was said in any of the speeches or reports carried in the 36 page dedication issue of the Jersey Journal concerning any program of prevention, such as better housing, more and better food, better living conditions, shorter work hours, adequate pay, safe and sanitary conditions in which to work as well as to live, more recreational facilities and a better all round chance to avoid the misfortune of becoming an invalid with tuberculosis. Hudson County may be carrying on an adequate preventive program of this kind. If so, well and good. The point we wish to make is that adequate hospitalization is only one of the essentials in a well-balanced tuberculosis control program.

Treatment of the victims of the Great White Plague is humane, but more humane, more compassionate, more rational, and more economical is it to prevent boys and girls, men and women, from becoming White Plague victims.

There may be a place and a need now in Jersey City's health program for a great skyscraper tuberculosis hospital, but let us hope that it will not be ever thus, and that its policy will be to serve more as part of the fence on top of the cliff rather than as the ambulance down in the valley.

The Health Bulletin [North Carolina State Board of Health] 53/3 (March 1938), p. 7

APRIL 1938

BEST HEALTH SECURITY IS HOME SANITATION

By Mrs. J. Henry Highsmith
Assistant Director of Health Education

Security is the watchword of today. More people than at any other time perhaps are seeking some means of security against the uncertainties of life, against danger, diseases, disaster, and the forces over which they have no control. It is said that more money is being spent in this country at the present time to purchase some of the various forms represented as security than has ever been known before. These forms include every form of insurance from life to lightning rods. There's no doubt but the confused and threatening times in which we are living as well as the paralyzing fears of the recent Depression have been a factor in making people security-conscious. It's an ill wind that blows nobody good.

Another and perhaps a better form of security is that being promoted through the Better Homes in America movement, whose state chairman is Miss Pauline Smith of State College, Home Beautification Specialist, with the State Home Demonstration work. This organization holds that the modern home must provide safety, security and satisfaction if it is to meet the supreme needs of the occupants. Miss Smith, who is a beauty specialist for homes and communities, puts sanitation down as the ground work for such home needs as beauty, health, happiness, and security. She hopes, and so do we, that during Better Homes Week, which is to be observed from April 24–30, many home-owners in North Carolina will lay the foundation for safeguarding health by seeing that their homes and surroundings are sanitarily safe.

Sanitation is another word for cleanliness, particularly as it affects health. To apply it effectively in the home requires an understanding of what constitutes scientific cleanliness—that state in which there are no harmful bacteria, no filth and no carriers of filth.

Are You a Clean Housekeeper?

Some housewives take pride in calling themselves good housekeepers, when in many instances if their kitchens and pantries were inspected and scored as the law requires those of hotels, cafes and other public eating places in the State, they would collapse with shock at the score given their homes. The law has the right to close up shop for those who do not comply with the sanitary regulations adopted by the State Board of Health for the protection of the public who eat away from home. But the law does not go into the home and show up conditions as to where, what and how the family eats or where it sleeps, nor could it close it up, if it were found an unsafe place for the family to eat and sleep. The health and safety of the household must thrive or perish according to the housewife's good judgment, scientific information concerning health and sanitation, as well as her knowledge of foods and their proper care and preparation.

Perhaps housewives would like to know what a government inspector looks for in examining a hotel or other public eating place. As to the kitchen and pantry, it must be screened against flies, be well lighted and ventilated, and protected against roaches, mice, ants and other vermin. The cooking utensils must be cleaned thoroughly after each usage and kept clean. Dishes must be washed with hot water and soap and allowed to drain dry. No hand drying is allowed. Many of the better eating places use dishwashing machines which not only wash but sterilize by the use of steam or scalding all eating utensils. The refrigerator must be kept clean and free from all odors and rancid food. It must keep the proper degree of lowered temperature that is sufficient to preserve food and prevent food-poisoning. Food must be stored, handled and prepared without coming in contact with insanitary objects. The milk and water supply must be known to be the best. All garbage must be placed in covered metal bins, and all possible measures must be taken to keep down flies and mosquitoes. Furthermore, all food handlers, including cooks, waiters and waitresses, must hold a certificate from a reputable physician showing that they are free from syphilis, gonorrhea, tuberculosis and other communicable diseases, and that they are not typhoid carriers. The cook and all kitchen help must wear white caps, coats and aprons, and maintain a state of cleanliness about the entire kitchen. Housekeepers may make their own scores by comparing their practices and methods with these state standards.

Flies a Problem in Sanitation.

Flies make filth doubly dangerous. By the peculiar structure of their six feet and hairy body they are capable of carrying millions of bacteria from the foulest place to the cleanest, be that from the garbage can, privy, cuspidor, or stable to the choicest food on the dinner table. Furthermore, through their proboscis they suck up liquid filth and shortly afterwards deposit it as excreta wherever they happen to be, most likely on the hands and face, or food, of the baby. If the filth contains the causative germs of human disease, and much of it does, the unfortunate individual may become ill and suffer and never suspect the innocent looking house fly.

Practically all authorities are agreed that flies carry the germs of such diseases as typhoid fever, summer diarrhea, tuberculosis, intestinal diseases of infants, cholera, abscesses, trachoma and pink eye, and as disease carriers and one of man's greatest enemies, they should be exterminated.

Fly control then becomes the first step in home sanitation and home safety. Flies are ravenous feeders and cannot live long without food. They feed on and breed in filth. Therefore, cleanliness will deprive them of both food and breeding places.

The best method yet found for combating flies is to destroy their breeding places. Flies breed in horse manure by preference, but may breed in manure from the cow stable, chicken house, or pig-pen. In fact, they breed in any moist, decaying animal or vegetable matter. If manure be removed and scattered on the farm at least twice a week in summer or be not allowed to accumulate, flies cannot breed in it. Other means of controlling flies about the home are keeping garbage cans tightly covered at all times, burning all rubbish and decaying matter about the premises, making privies fly tight, making all food inaccessible to flies, screening all doors and windows, and remembering that flies will pass up a clean home for a dirty one.

The Health Bulletin [North Carolina State Board of Health] 53/4 (April 1938), pp. 8–10

APRIL 1938

IF SHOE TONGUES COULD TALK

By Mrs. J. Henry Highsmith

Assistant Director of Health Education

Some one has said that if shoe tongues could talk they would literally scream at what goes on in some women's shoes. Men's are more sensible. These tongues likely would cry out in protest against the pain and discomfort that the enclosed feet are made to suffer, while the wearer manages to keep silent and smile, and Spartan like endure the agony.

If shoe tongues could talk they would probably explain many unaccountable aches and pains which women suffer, as well as premature wrinkles and drawn faces. Part of their story would deal undoubtedly with frayed nerves, irritable dispositions, undue fatigue and rheumatic joints.

Naturally the question is asked, Why do women do it? Fashion no longer decrees that high heels, pointed toes and narrow soles be worn, or else be out of style and out of date. As a matter of fact, fashion is more kind to women's feet today than it has been in many a season. One can wear high heels or low, wide soles or narrow, soft or hard-grained leather, oxfords or pumps, sandals, sneakers, or most any variety, and yet be in style. Of course the time and place are to be considered but nevertheless comfort and style can be had in most modern footwear.

But to be fair to many women who are suffering today from foot deformities, it might be said that much of the mischief was done in other years, perhaps when shoe styles were not as sensible as they are today or when they themselves were not as sensible, and, what is more to the point, these defects and deformities have never been corrected. How much better it would have been then to have sought proper treatment and had all bunions, corns, callouses, fallen arches or ill-shaped bones and muscles properly adjusted.

Restoring a mistreated and ill-shaped foot is not an easy process. It takes time and patience, and in some cases requires the services of an orthopedic surgeon. All of which emphasizes the fact that foot evils are more easily prevented than corrected, and that no sane person should let a stupid fad, fashion or shoe ruin her feet, jeopardize her health and mar much of the enjoyment of her life. In the light of the modern woman's intelligence and training a continuation of this barbaric treatment of one's feet should be no longer tolerated.

Not only health and efficiency demand better foot care, but beauty also. Beauty specialists say that if more attention were given to the feet, and if more cream were rubbed on the feet at night instead of on the face, the results would be far more satisfactory.

Neglect is at the bottom of most foot troubles. Sore, burning feet as well as corns, bunions and callouses could be largely prevented through the daily practice of foot-hygiene rules. These include such simple but essential processes as cleanliness, care of nails, care of skin and the selection of proper stockings and shoes.

Cleanliness requires, if not a daily foot bath with plenty of soap and water, one at least three times a week. Through the bath, accumulations of dead skin and tissue worn out through pressure, are softened and removed, and the blood is kept in circulation through all parts of the foot, thus preventing the formation of tender spots, corns and callouses. Persons having very tender feet might find relief through the daily application of rubbing alcohol which toughens the skin. Those having dry, thick skin should apply some form of grease such as lanolin.

The nails should be cut often and with care. This is best done after the bath when the nails are soft, the feet clean, and when there is less danger of infection if the skin should be damaged. In case of an injury to the skin in trimming the nails, apply a mild antiseptic. The nails should be cut straight across with the corners left intact to prevent ingrowing nails.

The selection of shoes and stockings is most important. Shoes should be large enough for the foot to expand when walking. They should fit at every point and be comfortable to the feet. Note that the lining is smooth. If heel pads are needed to prevent slipping, wear them, but under no circumstances wear shoes with run-down or one-sided heels. Have heels built up often and save not only the shape of the shoe but the comfort of the foot and the looks of the wearer.

Stockings should be long enough but not too long. They should be washed often for their own good and for that of the wearer. A good plan is to change shoes and stockings often, not to wear one pair every day as long as they last. More care given to the feet will mean fewer corns and bunions and less frayed nerves and irritation.

The Health Bulletin [North Carolina State Board of Health] 53/4 (April 1938), pp. 10–11

JUNE 1938

CHILD HEALTH DAY OBSERVED IN NORTH CAROLINA

By Mrs. J. Henry Highsmith
State May Day Chairman

Through a state-wide observance of Child Health Day in North Carolina this year, we have reason to believe that children have benefitted in innumerable ways and that many permanent advances have been made in child health services. While it is too early and probably impossible to have complete reports of the May Day activities entered into in the interest of children's health, we have sufficient returns to warrant our feeling that definite gains have been made and that children have made progress on the road to health.

Through the cooperation of the State Department of Public Instruction we were able to reach a large number of the 900,000 school children in the State with specially prepared May Day programs featuring health in songs, recitations, plays, contests, pageants and festivals. Who can estimate the potential health values derived from these children and their teachers taking part in the observance and magnifying the importance of personal health? Will it mean nothing to the six-year-old Tommies who committed to memory and declaimed:

> I'll fill my chest, and breathe my best
> And stand up on my toes
> Then down again and up again
> The way a see-saw goes.
>
> I'll watch my chin, and hold it in.
> I'll hold my head up high.
> And just you wait; I'll grow up straight
> Or know the reason why?

Or will the hundreds of groups of boys and girls who repeated together the following health pledge fail to get a new concept of their body and their responsibility for keeping it and making it serve its highest purposes?

> My body is the temple of my soul!
> Therefore:
>
> I will keep my body clean within and without. I will breathe pure air and I will live in the sunlight. I will do no act that might endanger the health of others. I will try to learn and practice the rules of healthy living. I will work, rest and play at the right time and in the right way, that my mind may be strong, my body healthy and that I may lead a useful life and be an honor to my parents, to my friends and to my country.

More than eight thousand copies of a May Day – Child Health Day program, prepared by the Education Department of the State Board of

Health, were placed either in the hands of teachers or sent to them by mail. Included were three health plays: "The Health Wedding," suitable for grades from one to four; "A Fellow's Best Friends," suitable for boys in grades five, six and seven; and "A Lesson From the Past," suitable for Junior or High School grades.

The lesson taught in the "Health Wedding," which is an adaptation of the Tom Thumb wedding, is that good health and happiness are ideal states of the home and are maintained and supported by the whole family of foods and certain other health factors. Mr. Good Health marries Miss Happiness. He has as attendants his friends and associates of the vegetable family. Mr. Bean is his best man, Messrs. Corn, Peas and Okra are his groomsmen, and Messrs. Radish, Beet, Celery and Parsnip are the ushers. Miss Happiness has as her maid of honor, Miss Lemon, and her matron of honor, Mrs. Orange. Her bridesmaids are Misses Pineapple, Peach, Grapefruit, Pear, Banana, and Tangerine. Flower girls are little Misses Strawberry, Apricot, Cherry and Plum. Tommy Tomato is the ring bearer. He carries an onion ring on a carrot, and Peter Pepper bears the bride's train. Mr. Cauliflower is the announcer, Miss Rhubarb the soloist, and Mr. Pumpkin plays the organ. Invited guests are other members of the fruit, vegetable and cereal kingdoms. Specially invited guests, who are announced on entering and are shown prominent seats in the audience are Dr. and Mrs. Milk, Mrs. Egg, Captain and Mrs. Steak, Colonel and Mrs. Fish, and several members of the Green family—Misses Lettuce, Spinach and Cabbage. Their lowly but most dependable neighbors, too, are there, Mr. and Mrs. Potato and Mr. and Mrs. Squash. Madame Sunshine, the bride's godmother, is present to give her blessing, while the Rev. A. C. D. Vitamin joins together Good Health and Happiness into the ideal state of home and family life.

The importance of a daily diet of well prepared foods, consisting of plenty of vegetables, fruits, cereals, milk, eggs and meat, is brought home to the members of the audience in the lesson of the play and through the words of admonition of the officiating clergyman.

Surely, school children who saw "A Fellow's Best Friends" cannot soon forget the transformation that took place in Tommy Atwood after he was administered to by the good health fairies. Tommy was a neglected youth, undernourished and suffering from several physical defects. Since he was a worthy lad, the good health fairies visited him by night, took him in hand and through applied health rules and personal hygiene principles, wrought in him a marvelous change.

In "A Lesson From the Past" the sad truth is dramatized that diphtheria is still a most treacherous disease of childhood unless protection is had through immunization. The father of the young child is finally led to see that delay and indifference lead to tragedy. He becomes convinced that modern medical science in the discovery of toxoid is able to safeguard children from diphtheria and save parents from tragic suffering.

Through the cooperative efforts of county health officers and public health nurses, we believe, child health needs have been served where needs are greatest and service means most—in aiding needy expectant mothers.

What is more fundamental than helping a baby to get a good start from birth? The work that is being done in the 130 maternity and infancy centers in the State, serving over 10,000 mothers and their babies, is doing even more. It is helping mothers, many of them, to understand for the first time the essentials of prenatal care that are necessary to safeguard their own lives and that of their babies. The need for promoting this particular phase of public health work has been consistently urged by the State May Day Committee.

Another child health need that has been emphasized in May Day programs concerns the crippled child. Since the establishment of the Crippled Children's Service under the supervision of the State Board of Health, 11,935 crippled children have been located and treated. This number is sixty per cent of all the estimated crippled children in the State. Eighteen orthopedic clinics are now in operation which served last year 8,000 crippled children.

Through the press and the radio, surely the public has been made to feel that the health and welfare of little children is the first concern of the people, and that a community, county or state that fails to provide health protection for its children fails seriously.

The Health Bulletin [North Carolina State Board of Health] 53/6 (June 1938), pp. 14–15

JULY 1938

RECREATION A COMMUNITY RESPONSIBILITY

Play Now Seen As Preventive of Unwholesome Mental and Social States

By Mrs. J. Henry Highsmith
Assistant Director, Health Education
State Board of Health

No town of any size or consequence today thinks of being without lighted streets, sewers, a police force and numerous other means for protecting the life and health of its people. In the near future, we have reason to believe, no progressive town will be without playgrounds, parks and recreation centers for its people, and will provide these in the same spirit and understanding as it now provides sanitation, food inspection and modern health safeguards.

There is being created today a new concept regarding play, recreation and leisure which is quite different from that which dominated the country, especially the rural sections, in its struggle period at the end of the nineteenth century and the beginning of the twentieth. Then the whole rhythm of life was attuned to work. Play was considered evil or to no purpose; when it could not be repressed, it was tolerated. Work was glorified. Leisure to most people meant idleness, and idleness meant loafing on the job. Everything worth while was then supposed to be achieved through hard work. Hence leisure became almost synonymous with laziness, and laziness became the opprobrium that marked a person for life.

There are many of us, no doubt, who feel that we were cheated in those days through those erroneous ideas and evils of unbalanced thinking. Under the driving power that it was a disgrace to be idle unless it was for a few hours on Saturday afternoon, few dared brave public opinion and engage in leisure time activities on week days. Recreation for recreation's sake, unless it was taken on Sundays or in the sense of recuperation, was laughed out of court. Who knows but that the ever mounting death rate from heart diseases and other worn out conditions of the body that we have today, as well as the ever increasing number of nervous and mental breakdowns, are not in some way due to that regimen of living that failed to recognize the place that play and recreation have in maintaining health and sanity and in developing personality and character?

In terms of modern thinking, recreation serves as the spare tire that enables one to get where he is going. It prevents the complete breakdown that otherwise would waylay him on his journey. What is more to the point, it is insurance taken out in youth against premature and disabling states of the mind and body, such as extreme nervousness, melancholia, introspection and unstable mental and emotional states. Dr. Charles Loomis Dana, Professor of Nervous Diseases at the Cornell Medical School, says: "When young folks are taught the worth and ways of recreation, they are taking out insurance against nervous disorders, and in middle age, when they come to collect, they will find themselves reimbursed a hundredfold." Dr. Pearce Bailey, a leading authority on neurology and psychiatry, says: "Non medical agencies, such as boy's clubs, boy and girl scouts, settlement agencies and playgrounds promise most in the line of prevention of nervous disorders."

That it is a community's responsibility to provide safe and adequate places for its children to play is no longer questioned. Municipalities and metropolitan centers which have invested time and money in programs and facilities for their peoples' play and recreation have found a more happy and contented people, with more pride in their homes and personal appearance; fewer domestic troubles, less tendency to visit cheap shows and places of bad influence; more regard for the amenities of life, and what naturally follows, sounder minds in sounder bodies. Some of these programs and facilities which are within the reach of even rural communities, and are the right of every normal boy and girl, are supervised playgrounds and swimming pools, ball parks, free tennis courts, recreational parks, picnic grounds, boys and girls camps, play streets, band concerts and opportunities for social gatherings of all groups. In winter community centers for leisure time activities such as reading, music and indoor games should not be overlooked.

The curative value of play has been recognized for some time in the treatment of patients suffering from mental and nervous upsets, also of physically handicapped children. But isn't it time to recognize its place as a preventive of such states and conditions, and work to secure: "For every child a community which recognizes and plans for his needs, protects him against physical dangers, moral hazards, and disease; provides him with safe and wholesome places for play and recreation, and makes provision for his cultural and social needs?"

The Health Bulletin [North Carolina State Board of Health] 53/7 (July 1938), pp. 15–16

AUGUST 1938

SAVING BABIES FROM SYPHILIS

Three States Pass Laws Requiring Blood Test of all Prospective Mothers

By Mrs. J. Henry Highsmith
Assistant Director, Health Education
State Board of Health

As a result of breaking the "age-old conspiracy of silence" surrounding syphilis, States, counties and towns are now able to get legislative action for the prevention and control of syphilis which a few years ago would have been impossible. In view of the fact that public opinion is aroused concerning this terrible old disease, and science is ready with specific remedies and means for its prevention, now is the time for every State and community to go after its venereal disease problem and bring it under control. Never before have conditions been so favorable. Never before have the public health agencies interested in stamping out this killing disease had the support of the press, the radio and an informed people. Surely this is the time to pass legislation and adopt measures for saving diseased, defective babies, invalid wives and mothers and decrepit insane men and women.

Three States have recently enacted legislation for saving their babies from syphilis. These are New York, New Jersey and Rhode Island. The act requires that all prospective mothers be given a blood test as part of the routine prenatal examination that every expectant mother should have. Through this law New York considers it will be able to save approximately 13,000 babies annually. Each year in New York State, according to the State and City Health Departments, almost 4,000 babies are born syphilitic and 9,000 more are born dead because of syphilis in the mother.

This advanced step in the syphilis control program is based on the most important factor yet discovered by medical science in regard to the treatment of syphilis: that congenital syphilis can be prevented in more than 90 per cent of the cases if the expectant mother who is found to have syphilis is treated by the fifth month of pregnancy. Under the law all persons licensed to attend women in pregnancy must administer or cause to have administered a standard serological test for syphilis, and must indicate on the birth or stillbirth certificate the fact that the test was made, and when it was made, or give reason why it was not made. However, the law does not require that the results of such tests be indicated on the birth certificate.

Providing a prenatal blood test is one of the minimal legal measures urged by Surgeon General Parran in any State or city program for syphilis control. Another is a pre-marital law, which requires a health certificate from a physician showing that both the contracting parties to marriage have submitted to a standard laboratory blood test for syphilis and that in the opinion of such physician the person is not infected or is not in the stage to communicate it to others. Nine States have recently passed pre-marital laws against syphilis, and many other States are planning to seek such legislation when their law-making bodies next assemble. States having recently enacted marriage laws against syphilis are Connecticut, New Hampshire, Illinois, Michigan, Wisconsin, Kentucky, New Jersey, Rhode Island and New York.

North Carolina has neither a prenatal nor a pre-marital law against syphilis. And yet syphilis is being reported to the State Board of Health in increasing numbers weekly. Whereas an average of 236 cases were reported weekly during 1937, for the first six months of 1938, an average of 342 cases have been reported each week. For the first half of this year, 8,205 cases were reported, against 5,751 cases for the same time last year. This means, unless measures are instituted against it, that more babies will die a premature death, more will be born syphilitic, defective in mind and body, and that insanity and the long list of disabling diseases due to syphilis will continue to take their toll. Last year there were reported 3,160 stillbirths in North Carolina, a large number of which deaths were due to syphilis. This number does not include a much larger number of babies who died at birth or during the first month of life, nor to the tragic group doomed to live as syphilitics.

If New York proposes annually to save 13,000 babies made up of every nationality on earth, should it take North Carolina long to decide whether or not her babies are worth saving?

The Health Bulletin [North Carolina State Board of Health] 53/8 (August 1938), pp. 4–5

18 AUGUST 1938

GET YOUR CHILDREN READY FOR SCHOOL

**Health Director Stresses Importance of Physical Fitness
to School Children**

[attributed in first paragraph]

The importance of getting children "ready"' for school was emphasized by
Mrs. J. Henry Highsmith, assistant director of health education, State Board
of Health, when she declared:

"In a few weeks nearly 900,000 children will be trekking back to school
in North Carolina. This should be a thrilling picture—boys and girls aglow
with health, full of energy and the happy spirit of care-free youth marching
back to take up their books. But will it be? Will these boys and girls be
found ready for school after a summer's vacation? Will they be mentally
and physically alert, handicapped by no defect or disease, eager to be back
at their desks, or will they be found marching back listless, tired, anemic,
dreading the tasks ahead?

"This will depend largely on their physical fitness, or whether or not
their vacations have been restful, pleasant and invigorating, and whether or
not their bodies have been checked over and put in good condition.

"Last spring thousands of children went through the pre-school clinics
and were examined physically to determine whether or not they were in
shape to enter school this fall. Their parents were advised as to the conditions
found and were urged to have any and all defects remedied by school time.
These were the beginners. They will likely be the best group in school from
a health point of view, this fall, that is, if their parents took seriously the
findings of the clinic examination and made the corrections as advised.

"A group that will probably be less prepared will be the boys and girls
who have not had a school examination recently and whose parents have
not taken the pains to have them looked over by a dentist or physician. They
may be returning, but in what condition? They may be swallowing poison
every day from diseased tonsils, decayed and abscessed teeth, gum boils, or
they may be anemic, underweight, overweight or on the borderline of some
disease.

"Parents can do no better day's work than to take their child to the
dentist and to the doctor before he starts to school to see whether or not
he is in fine shape for the school job ahead. Not to do so will not be merely
an oversight; it will be neglect, carelessness, failure, which are too often
rewarded with sorrow and regret.

"Fortunately, a few days remain in which this much needed work can be
done. In fact, it is important enough to do at any time even after school has
begun. The child who starts out on a new school year with all physical defects

corrected, with good teeth, a healthful mouth, good vision and hearing, proper weight and vaccinated against diphtheria, typhoid and smallpox will be less likely to contract colds, scarlet fever and other communicable diseases and more likely to find pleasure in his work as well as ease in making his grades."

Nashville (NC) *Graphic,* p. 1
Raleigh *News and Observer,* p. 14 (partial, in "Views and Observations")
Chatham Record, Pittsboro, 25 August 1938, p. 3

SEPTEMBER 1938

SCHOOL JANITOR BECOMES IMPORTANT HEALTH FACTOR

Health and Safety of Pupils and Teachers Dependent on Efficient Janitorial Service

By Mrs. J. Henry Highsmith
Assistant Director, Health Education
State Board of Health

The place of the school janitor of other days has changed from one of minor importance which usually implied sweeping floors, removing ashes and firing a stove or furnace, to one of increasing importance. Modern school buildings require the services of janitor-engineers who have considerable technical knowledge about the operation of the mechanical equipment of a school plant, who have an understanding of the scientific principles employed in sanitation, disease prevention and general safety, and who have good moral habits, good judgment, fine cooperative attitudes and school loyalty. The janitor of today must be engineer-sanitarian-diplomat and general manager. He must be chosen with care, next to that of the principal, as upon the efficiency of his services depend the safety, health, comfort and general welfare of the inmates of the building.

In the school health program, the janitor comes next to the teacher in promoting health conditions and enabling health teachings to be put into practice. If he is trained to know what constitutes cleanliness, how diseases are spread, and what are some of the practical, common-sense methods of keeping down dirt and disease, his services are found invaluable in maintaining healthful surroundings and making possible more efficient work on the part of the pupils.

As to the efficiency of the janitorial service in the schools of this State, there seems to be a question. Recently we noted in a national school journal that North Carolina was highly commended for its foresighted policy of conducting a training school for janitors and for requiring of every applicant for janitor positions a health certificate from a reputable physician. About the same time we heard a number of complaints from teachers and principals to the effect that the practice of health rules and hygiene instruction in school is difficult if not impossible on account of poor janitor service.

Our interest in health work in the schools, particularly at this time when the State Board of Health and the State Department of Education are cooperating to get established in the schools a better correlated program of health education, has led us to investigate the status of janitorial service in the public schools, especially as it affects health conditions. Now that this progressive health program is about to be launched, with teachers, principals and superintendents all willing to cooperate, we would by no means have the janitor's service become the lion in the path of progress.

We might say here that the criticisms or complaints coming to our attention have fallen under one of five heads, as follows:

1. Janitor service inefficient, and often a menace as a possible spreader of filth and disease germs.

2. Janitor, untrained, knows nothing of the principles of cleanliness and school sanitation.

3. Janitor unable to read and write, and hence incapable of reading and understanding the reasons for doing certain things; therefore, he leaves many important things undone.

4. Janitor gives only part-time service to school. Says he's paid around $40 per month and must seek outside work to earn a living wage.

5. Janitor's supplies, such as soap, towels, toilet paper, brooms, brushes and cleansing materials (not fumigants) wholly inadequate for maintaining cleanliness. Sufficient water for hand-washing purposes not allowed in many instances.

Through a visit to the State School Commission, whose duty among other things is to "set the standards for operating the public schools" of the State and jointly with the State Board of Education to fix the salary schedules for all its employees, we learned that training for janitors is furnished free, but not made available to all, that a comparatively small number apply for this short course of instruction each year. The school for white janitors was held for one week this summer as usual at State College, Raleigh, with sixty janitors attending. The one for colored was held at A. & T. College, Greensboro, with fifty attending. The instruction for the most part had to do with the care and keeping of school property, boilers, furnaces, floors, walls, toilets, grounds, etc., and only incidentally with the health and safety of the pupils and teachers. The student-janitors were given little technical or scientific information concerning filth as a carrier of disease, cleanliness and its relation to health, methods of disease prevention and essential measures of safety as such.

We found that janitors are underpaid for the work they are supposed to do, the maximum monthly wage paid by the Commission for janitorial service being $52.80. It was explained, however, that wherever a janitor deserves more pay the local school board is expected to supplement the State wage. A similar explanation was given to the complaint that janitorial supplies are frequently inadequate. Ability to read and write is not one of the general qualifications listed for a janitor, but he "must be able-bodied and of average intelligence, a man of high moral character, sober, honest and have a good reputation," and yet is paid $30, $40 or $50 per month, not over $52.80 at most, from the State School funds.

The State law requires of janitors, as of teachers and school superintendents, a health certificate which shall be filed in the office of the superintendent each year, and which shall certify "that the said person has not an open or active infectious state of tuberculosis or other contagious disease." But the enforcement of this law is left to the superintendent or school board employing the janitor. It is the opinion of one member of the School Commission that many superintendents do demand health certificates while a larger number do not.

From the foregoing it is apparent that if the schools are to be made and kept safe and sanitary and provide the conditions under which pupils and teachers can do their best work, there should be:

1. Better trained janitors employed, and higher standards or qualifications set up and met.

2. More adequate provision made by the State and local school units for training the janitors now in service, which training should include the principles of hygiene and sanitation.

3. An increased wage scale that will attract more capable workers.

4. Increased funds sought through the Legislature, that there may be sufficient supplies and facilities for teaching children the simplest health habits, and safeguarding the lives of nearly 900,000 future men and women.

The Health Bulletin [North Carolina State Board of Health] 53/9 (September 1938), pp. 13–15

OCTOBER 1938

MORE INTELLIGENCE NEEDED AS TO WHAT TO EAT

Many Illnesses Due to Improper Use of Foods

By Mrs. J. Henry Highsmith

The automobile has been used many times to illustrate some pertinent truth about the human body. Again we make use of it, this time to call attention to the fact that by the same methods by which many lives are being saved—through a more intelligent use of the automobile—-the same results could be achieved with respect to the human machine. As long as nothing more was required of automobile drivers but to learn "to turn on the gas, start the engine with clutch in neutral, and release the brake," just so long we had horrible accidents and mounting death lists. But since training schools for drivers have been instituted in many of the more progressive States, North Carolina being one of these (thanks to the WPA for starting the movement), there is beginning to show a decided decline in the total number of serious automobile accidents and deaths. In addition to the saving of lives, this program prolongs the use of cars and increases the profit and pleasure to be had from them.

Intelligent use makes the difference. Intelligent treatment and foresight applied to the human machine, the stomach and digestive system, would likewise save lives, as well as much unnecessary wear and tear on the machinery, and many premature breakdowns due to abuses and wrong treatment of the stomach. Particularly is this true in regard to food. The time was when we knew little about the chemistry and nutritional properties of food, but today we not only have this knowledge, but have it in simple and understandable terms, which even beginners may use to order their lives more successfully, with health and efficiency theirs in the end.

That 30 per cent or more of all American school children are estimated to be undernourished is evidence of the widespread ignorance and carelessness concerning the preparation and use of foods. That Duke Hospital finds four out of five of its charity patients suffering from nutritional defects or digestive diseases is another evidence of the great general need of more and more education regarding food and its relation to health.

This truth is further impressed on us by public health nurses, case workers and teachers in the adult educational program of the State, who go directly into the homes of the sick and the indigent and see for themselves the part that ignorance of food purposes are playing in the restricted lives of the people. It is no wonder to them, they say, that the little ones are pale, anemic and underweight, and the older ones are rheumatic and constantly ailing from some sort of stomach trouble. That they have maintained existence at all on their accustomed diet is a marvel to them.

Meeting the Problem.

That the problem is an educational one and must be met by all the educational agencies of the State and community must be fully recognized. The field heretofore has been left mainly to the efforts of the Home Demonstration agents, the State Board of Health and a limited number of home economics teachers in the schools. The area is too large and the problem too deep-seated and complicated to be met by these existing agencies. Such an educational task can be met only through a coordinated plan in which the various official and non-official agencies of the community may and do participate. Supplementing the work of the State Health Department, the Home

Demonstration agents, and the schools must be a more intensified general program including the press, radio, public talks, demonstrations, exhibits at fairs and conventions, study classes and nutritional surveys. Such a program necessarily must be developed slowly and on a long-time basis, as the dietary habits of a people are slow to change. But no longer should child life be wasted and adult usefulness be cut off on account of discrepancies in diet due to ignorance and indifference.

The Health Bulletin [North Carolina State Board of Health] 53/10 (October 1938), pp. 11–12

2 OCTOBER 1938

HUMAN LIVES ARE IN DANGER

North Carolinians Urged to Be Doubly Careful as Hunting Season Opens

By Mrs. J. Henry Highsmith
Assistant Director, Health Education
State Board of Health

Already, the hunting season is taking its annual toll of deaths, not of wild animals only, but of men—and not a few children. Newspapers have begun to publish accounts of fatal accidents from the proverbial unloaded gun, as hunters take down their weapons to clean and shine them in anticipation this fall of stalking a covey of quail, a deer, a bear or maybe just an old field rabbit.

According to government statistics, about 1,000 persons are killed annually in this country in connection with the sport of hunting, and nearly three times as many are fatally wounded in firearm accidents generally. In North Carolina, the average number of accidental deaths each year by firearms is about 100, but just how many of these are due to accidents in connection with the hunting season is not known.

A recent study made by a large insurance company of a certain number of deaths occurring on the hunt, found that the greatest number of these were from wounds accidentally self inflicted.

Accidental Falls.

These usually were from such causes as slipping, stumbling or falling while carrying a loaded gun, or climbing over, under or through a fence, crossing a ditch or becoming entangled in briars, vines or shrubbery thereby causing the gun to discharge accidentally, or when entering or leaving an automobile or boat with the gun not locked in the "safe" position. The safest procedure is to unload the gun or break the breech.

Accidental shooting by a hunting companion was responsible for the next highest number, or 36 per cent, of the tragedies. Two or more hunting together should always keep in line or certainly in sight of each other.

The next largest number of deaths of hunters were caused by persons in parties other than their own who fired hurriedly at objects disturbing the underbrush or moving indistinctly at a distance without first determining the object or cause of movement.

But these deaths of hunters are not all the tragedies occasioned by the hunt. Hundreds more are met annually by hunters' firearms of persons who know nothing perhaps of the sport of tracking the fields, swamps and woods in search of wild life to shoot.

Careless Handling.

Many sad deaths are met in and about the home, when guns are being cleaned, especially in the presence of children; when they are left carelessly around the house, perhaps leaning against a tree or "hid" behind the door, or when there's shooting at random for the purpose of displaying skill, or in the name of practice. Parents and sportsmen should keep their guns under lock and key away from children—and children should be taught never to point even toy guns or pistols at others. It is a bad habit and may lend to tragedy from an "unloaded" gun in later years.

It is evident that carelessness plays a part too big and tragic in each year's hunting season—a part that should not be allowed to continue without protest. Fortunately several states are waking up, and are attempting to curb the carelessness with which so many hunters are accustomed to handle their guns. Some few states have enacted laws that give authority to revoke one's license for a long period or permanently when carelessness is shown, while others make it mandatory in certain cases to bring a charge of manslaughter for wanton carelessness.

In North Carolina there are no limiting laws except for the protection of birds and animals. And yet each year hunters' guns kill many men and children, and sometimes women, accidentally of course but nevertheless as dead as if killed intentionally.

[*News and Observer* version (which begins at "It is evident") continues:]

There's not even a statute for holding accountable a person who playfully or in that bravado spirit which is made all the more daring and dangerous perhaps by one or two drinks, orders another to hold up his hands, that he may snap at him his "unloaded" gun, too often and too late found loaded and fatal.

While establishing more game refuges and making possible more of the "hunter's paradise" in the State, there should be a program of education supported by legislation in the interest of protecting innocent people against the carelessness with which too many hunters are accustomed to handle their guns.

Charlotte Sunday Observer, p. 52 (section 4, p. 2)
Raleigh Sunday *News and Observer*, p. 6 (partial, in "Views and Observations")

DECEMBER 1938

ONLY ONE RECIPE FOR LIVING TO A RIPE OLD AGE

By Mrs. J. Henry Highsmith

Recipes for longevity are as eagerly sought after as buried treasures. Both intrigue the imagination in the hope of finding a short-cut or easy way of living, with success the assured end. But a long life recipe is usually like many a cake recipe—a failure in new or inexperienced hands. The secret of one person's long and happy life may not, and usually is not, the secret of another's. One's personality factor plays a large and determining part in all prescribed rules for a long life.

However, most all worthwhile rules or recipes for living a long life have one foundation—moderation. Many variations of this basic rule are often given as the one way of attaining longevity, e. g., "don't worry," "nine hours' sleep," "never overeat," "hard work," "drink plenty of water," "avoid excesses," etc. All of these points are essential, but they are not inclusive. It is quite true that excessive indulgence in even the best things of life are detrimental to health and cause many degenerative diseases and untimely deaths, but there are as many positive elements as negative elements in all good recipes.

Someone has given the following as an all-round, safe formula for living out one's three-score-and-ten years, and then some: Hard work, but work that is congenial and worthwhile; good food, varied and simple; happy home and family life; some leisure for recreation and riding a hobby; temperance in all things; a few close friends; an aim in life; and faith in God. We would add that health like beauty must be desired, cultivated and prized beyond measure. One must work out a regimen all his own, adapted to his needs and in keeping with his tastes and ambitions. Furthermore, he must have the courage to follow it through.

My grandmother, who lived to be one hundred and two years old and had remarkable use of all her faculties to the day of her death—she could read without glasses, hear well, and remember easily names and faces— was frequently asked by what rules she had lived to such a good old age. Her usual modest reply was: "Live right, my son." Her life was altogether exemplary of this brief but comprehensive bit of advice.

We who lived with her and knew her daily habits and commonsense way of meeting life, observed that there were certain practices to which many of her happy years could have been attributed. Temperance could be said to be her chief virtue. She more than any other person I have ever known was temperate in all things—work, rest, play, food and fun. She worked hard, but she knew when to rest. She enjoyed a good meal, but she never overate. When she was fifty years old, she found she suffered with indigestion if she ate a regular evening meal. Forthwith, she decided to eat nothing at night except fruit occasionally, a glass of milk or something light, and it was often said of her that for fifty-two years she did without supper. She found time for all things without hurry and hustle. She never worried excessively, and yet her interests were varied and extensive. Young people were her joy and delight.

Furthermore, God was real to her. Religion was vital. She attended services at her church regularly, even on the Sunday a week before her death.

Needless to say, that the commonsense practices and wholesome philosophy of this centenarian which enabled her to live far more than the usual allotment of years and meanwhile retain an uncommon use of body and mind—at no time helpless or an invalid, but enjoying life to the end— can be recommended to all who would live long and enjoy life to the end.

> (Mrs. Highsmith has omitted the most important item in Longevity— Ancestors.—Editor)

> *Note:* the grandmother she describes is Elizabeth Ann McPhail, Mrs. Joseph Herring (1812–1913), her paternal grandmother. So far as I know this is the only written description of her. I do remember, I think, my grandmother talking about *her* grandmother hiding the silver from Sherman's troops— who indeed passed right through Herring Township.

DECEMBER 1938

INDIFFERENCE AND INERTIA SLOW UP TUBERCULOSIS CONTROL PROGRAM

By Mrs. J. Henry Highsmith

Undoubtedly one of the greatest drawbacks in the fight to control tuberculosis is the illusion or wrong impression that the battle has practically been won, and tuberculosis is no longer a major health problem in this State. This general misconception in the lay mind is probably responsible for more indifference and inertia with respect to the problem of tuberculosis than any other one thing. To be more specific, there is a general impression in this State that the two State sanatoria and the nine county or district sanatoria are quite able to serve all the tuberculous sick of the State who need institutional treatment, and are doing this in an adequate way, while the Woman's Club, church societies, the Rotary, Kiwanis or other civic organizations are looking after those not yet admitted to a sanatorium for care and treatment.

The facts in the case may not even now produce that enthusiasm and interest that characterized the tuberculosis campaigns of two or three decades ago, but they should at least convince one that tuberculosis is still a major disease problem, and that too many people are dying annually, especially for what medical science knows about curing and preventing the disease, and that while the fight drags on endlessly and human life is being wasted needlessly and tragically.

Is there cause for complacent indifference when tuberculosis killed 1,912 people in North Carolina last year, and 2,104 the year before, and when there are now at least 20,000 persons sick and disabled with the white plague? Will men and women continue to rest on their laurels of years ago while tuberculosis remains the greatest killer of boys and girls between fifteen and twenty years, and of young women between the ages of twenty and forty years?

To consider tuberculosis from an economic point of view, there is no other disease that cripples the money-earning period of life and makes for permanent dependency as does tuberculosis. It is more closely associated with poverty than any other disease, as it both produces and is produced by poverty. Keen interest is felt in a National plan to attack the problem from this angle by providing better homes, more and better food, more adequate pay, shorter work hours and hospital treatment for all who need it, regardless of ability to pay. Such a program will naturally be expensive at first, but it is directed at the roots of much of the problem and probably will not cost in the end as much as building and maintaining more sanatoria and hospitals and providing a more efficient and larger staff of nurses and doctors.

Another human interest fact connected with tuberculosis is that with reference to "contacts"—persons who have been closely associated with an open case of tuberculosis during childhood, whether they were aware of it or not. Such persons are far more likely to develop the disease later than those who have not been so exposed. An adult in the home with an open case of tuberculosis, and without proper control, is capable of infecting an entire family. The fact that tuberculosis is more prevalent among Negroes than among Whites, and the further fact that they are closely associated with white people as cooks, nurses, cleaners, butlers, janitors and chauffeurs, make the "contact" problem a serious one, particularly in the South. Control measures among the colored people are woefully inadequate. Poor living conditions, especially the huddling together of large families in one or two-room huts, keep up constant exposure, a high sickness rate and an unusually high death rate.

The Health Bulletin [North Carolina State Board of Health] 53/12 (December 1938), pp. 13–15

1939–1945

1939–41, 1941–43
President, North Carolina State Legislative Council

5 January — addresses luncheon of RWC Welfare Department

10 January — as president Legislative Council, addresses first meeting of Sir Walter Cabinet on legislative agenda

11 January — visit to Raleigh of Frances Perkins, US Secretary of Labor, including conference with women leaders, address to joint session of Legislature, luncheon with Mrs. Hoey at the Governor's Mansion

21 January — attends luncheon at Sir Walter Hotel for Kate Burr Johnson, now of Trenton NJ

31 January — attends meeting of Sir Walter Cabinet with Lt. Governor Wilkins P. Horton

February — named to governing committee of GFWC Department of Press and Publicity for 1939–41

14 February — attends, with Dr. Highsmith, buffet supper for State Senator and Mrs. Gordon Gray of Winston-Salem, given at the Hartness mansion on North Blount Street; among the guests are Governor and Mrs. Hoey

15 February — assists in introductions when Raleigh PTA Council hosts Mrs. J. K. Pettingill, president of national umbrella organization, Carolina Hotel; also facilitates group discussion after day of presentations at Statewide Conference on Better Care for Mothers and Babies

17–19 April — attends 37th annual NCFWC convention, Raleigh; but cancels address, "Social and Health Laws Recently Enacted," owing to illness; paper is read by Mrs. Doak

27–28 May — hosts Alice Baldwin, Dean of Women at Duke, at her home mid-June — the Herrings and Highsmiths are visited by Pauline and her husband James Sloo

15–16 July — hosts Gladys (Mrs. Troy Herring) and Pauline and Jim Sloo at 832; Louise is at Girl Scout camp at Crabtree Recreational Park; Lula Belle returns from a house party at Lake Lure

20–30 July — vacations, with Katherine, Louise, and Vara, at Fearing Cottage, Nag's Head, and attends 100th presentation of *The Lost Colony*

August — visits New York World's Fair with Dr. Highsmith and Lula Belle, Katherine, and Louise

14 August — attends, with other members of Health Department, Harnett County "Baby Party" in Erwin, celebrating births and improvement in infancy and maternity

October — attends installation of Rho chapter, Beta Sigma Phi, of which she is sponsor, at Sir Walter Hotel

25 October — addresses October meeting of Lewis School PTA on "Our Children's Health"

11–12 November — Katherine weekends at 832; Mary Belle comes from Rockingham to weekend with Vara and Jean

15 November — addresses Asheboro Woman's Club on "Conserving Democracy for the Youth of Tomorrow"

16 November — receives, in the "second receiving line," after a large Episcopal wedding of Clinton relatives (Ellen Ramah Ross and Clarence Ervin, Jr.)

22 November — hosts Duke University Club at 832

30 November — Katherine home for Thanksgiving, with two students from Duke

c. 6–10 December — hosts a New Bern guest in Raleigh to attend State Art Society and State Literary and Historical Association meetings.

23 December — Katherine and Lula Belle (of Saint Augustine, Florida) arrive for Christmas

24 December — receives, in the dining room of the Governor's Mansion, at Governor and Mrs. Hoey's Christmas Eve reception

1940

2 January — attends buffet supper of Rho Chapter, Beta Sigma Phi

20–21 January — Dean Alice Baldwin weekends with the Highsmiths

17 January — addresses Boylan Heights PTA meeting

4–17 March — travels, with Vara and others, to New Orleans for Methodist Church Missionary Council meeting; en route they visit Bellingrath Gardens and Mobile Azalea Trail in Alabama and, returning, the gardens of Natchez, Mississippi

28–30 March — attends, as president of the State Legislative Council, national Legislative Council on State Government, Willard Hotel, Washington

26–27 April — assists at Raleigh Garden Club Annual Spring Flower Show

30 April — attends Beta Sigma Phi Founders' Day banquet at Sir Walter Hotel

1–3 May — attends 38th annual NCFWC convention, Greensboro; speaks 2 May on responsibility of women in government

c. 1 May — attends reception given by Mrs. William Preston Few of Duke University honoring Mrs. Clyde R. Hoey and Miss Isabel Hoey (the governor's wife and daughter); after luncheon Mrs. Few and her guests accompany Mary Duke Biddle through a tour of her gardens

10 May — named to executive board of North Carolina Commission on Interracial Cooperation

c. 23–25 May — visited by Mrs. Troy Herring and son, Troy III

25 June — co-hosts bridal reception at 832 for Mrs. Grant Bolmer, president of Rho chapter, Beta Sigma Phi

1 July 1940 — speaks at "Keep America Out of War" meeting at Wake County Courthouse, followed by raucous debate and personal attack

11 July — entertains at a luncheon at 832 for Mrs. Clyde R. Hoey and Mrs. William Preston Few, assisted by Vara and Louise

17 August — assists Lula Belle at a bridal luncheon at 832 honoring her cousin, Julia Lee Highsmith of Durham; among guests are Katherine and Mrs. John Henry Highsmith, Jr. (Aunt Eva)

27 August — receives at debutante tea offered by Katherine for two other debutantes; assisted by Lula Belle, Louise, and Mary Belle, among others

30 August — joins advisory council on merit examinations for public welfare workers

6 September — debut of Katherine, escorted by her cousin Geddie Herring, at the North Carolina Debutante Ball

c. 1 October — is named to administrative committee of Olivia Raney Library

7 October — speaks on WPTF on home and school working together, part of Childhood and Youth Week sponsored by NC Conference of the Methodist Church

16 October — addresses North Carolina State Nurses Association convention in Winston-Salem on pending legislation

24 October — addresses Get-Together Banquet of Raleigh B&PWC on "Voting Intelligently"

28 October — attends bridge tournament of the Duke University Alumnae at the Woman's Club, hosting a table

c. 30 October — attends, with Vara and Jean, Paul Green's new play *The Highland Call* in Fayetteville

1 November — receives at an event welcoming Miss Clyde Smith, new librarian of Olivia Raney Library

22 November — receives at a Beta Sigma Phi event on Lassiter's Mill Road

Christmas season — serves on speakers bureau for 1940 Christmas Seals drive in Wake County

3 December — presides at meeting of State Legislative Council in advance of the 1941 Legislature; is re-elected president

7 December — represents Legislative Council at public hearings on proposed wage-hour law by Commission on Fair Labor Standards

17 December — pours for Mrs. Clyde R. Hoey at a Governor's Mansion tea for Peace College faculty and students

18 December — State Legislative Council announces its 10-point agenda for 1941 Legislature

25 December — Dr. and Mrs. Highsmith attend Christmas night open house of Mr. and Mrs. Claude F. Gaddy

1941

Third vice president, NCFWC
(in charge of programs)

8 January — attends NCFWC Executive Board meeting, Raleigh

7 January — attends meeting of Rho Chapter, Beta Sigma Phi

14 January — attends first meeting of Sir Walter Cabinet to outline legislative program

14 January — addresses supper meeting of Smithfield B&PWC

28 January — hosts Twentieth Century Book Club; Mrs. Earl Brian new member; her guests are Mrs. W. H. Herring, Mrs. Mollie Harrell, Miss Mary Shotwell, and Miss Vara Herring

2 February — nominates Mamie Latham for GFWC treasurer

13 February — co-hosts, with Mrs. R. N. Simms at Simms home on Wake

Forest Road, coffee for first lady, Mrs. J. Melville Broughton, and Mrs. B. B. Everett, president of Sir Walter Cabinet

17 February — attends opening of Wake County Mental Hygiene Clinic, sponsored by circles at Edenton Street, among others; she is a member of the board

20 February — attends 22nd annual conference of North Carolina Commission on Interracial Corporation

14 March — attends state executive committee of American Society for the Control of Cancer

15–30 April — joins statewide Cancer Control Drive, via Woman's Field Army for Control of Cancer

2 May — hosts luncheon at 832 for Miss Ann Simms and Miss Nancy Cox, brides elect

7–9 May — attends 39th annual NCFWC convention, Winston-Salem; elected third vice president; she is mentioned with Mrs. P. R. Rankin of Mount Gilead as a candidate for president

19–24 May — attends Golden Jubilee triennial of GFWC in Atlantic City; presents Mamie Latham for treasurer; appears in Golden Guard episode of the pageant, "The Long Path"

28 May — attends luncheon given by Mrs. Broughton at Governor's Mansion for Mrs. R. L. Harris, wife of the Lieutenant Governor

11 June — hosts "The Woman's Digest" on WPTF, focusing on national defense

1941–42, 1942–43
President, Raleigh Woman's Club

11 June — inauguration day: 1:00 is entertained at luncheon by Mrs. Doak; 3:30 is installed as president RNC, succeeding Mrs. Charles G. Doak; Mrs. Harold Glascock had been elected but resigned because of illness; executive board has chosen Mrs. Highsmith

18 June — offers, at Raleigh Civic Council Meeting on Defense and Civil Defense to host social gatherings at RWC for men in uniform

5 July — pours punch at Salter–Browne society wedding

10 July — calls RWC board meeting concerning use of clubhouse for young ladies being bussed to Fort Bragg on Friday evenings

8 July — attends conference of NC Committee on Nutrition focused on national defense and postwar plans

18 July — calls for women to search their homes for aluminum to donate in drive 21–29

23 July — at a luncheon of Raleigh Civic Council (of civic clubs), endorses aluminum reclamation, suggests Council provide farmers' center in Raleigh

27–28 July — her silhouette is featured in *News and Observer*'s summer quiz on Raleigh celebrities

5 August — serves with Dr. Highsmith and other notables as patron of dance at NC State, 9:00 p. m. until midnight, for British officers and sailors quartered in Crabtree Creek Park (now William B. Umstead State Park)

29–30 September — attends NCFWC Council–Institute in Raleigh

3 October — attends annual Get-Together Dinner at RWC on theme "Women in Defense"

8 October — raises flag at RWC, following directive from GFWC; unfurls and "pays tribute" to the flag

10 October — attends, at residence of Mrs. R. N. Simms, regent, a meeting of Bloomsbury Chapter, Daughters of the American Revolution; speaker is Dean Alice M. Baldwin of Duke

22 October — attends Eighth District meeting in Fuquay Springs; then attends, and receives at, a tea honoring her house-guests including Mrs. P. R. Rankin, NCFWC president

28 October — signs, with other Raleigh notables in the Committee to Defend America by Aiding the Allies, petition supporting bill to allow merchant ships to carry arms

4 November — attends a planning meeting for welcome home party for Ambassador and Mrs. Josephus Daniels, returning from ambassadorship in Mexico

11 November — presides at executive board meeting, RWC

16 November — attends welcome event for Ambassador and Mrs. Daniels, stationed in Mexico City for 8 years, Memorial Auditorium

23 November — Katherine returns to Duke after Thanksgiving with her parents; attends Carolina–Virginia football game in Chapel Hill, presumably with her husband-to-be

4 December — attends 15th annual meeting of State Art Society

7 December — Japan bombs Pearl Harbor; the following day, US enters World War II

10 December — attends dinner party given by Mrs. Charles Doak for visiting noted author and artist Hope Summerell Chamberlain, former president of RWC

24–25 December — accommodates a soldier for Christmas

28 December — attends, with Dr. Highsmith, small dinner at the Governor's Mansion with Governor and Mrs. J. Melville Broughton

1942

3 January — heads receiving line at reception for Mrs. Josephus Daniels, Mrs. Palmer Jerman, and Miss Flora Creech; also in line are Ambassador Daniels and Governor and Mrs. J. Melville Broughton; assisting are Lula Belle, Katherine, Louise, and many friends

8 January — pours tea after RWC meeting with E. A. Wayne, executive secretary of the NC Bankers Association

9 January — on behalf of Wake County Defense Savings program, meets with school principals and superintendents

12 January — serves as patron, with Dr. Highsmith, of 3rd annual Institute of Religion of the United Church: "Building for Tomorrow"

14 January — presides at RWC meeting featuring Dr. Jane McKimmon: "What Home-Makers Owe to Their Country in a Time like This"

15 January — attends board meeting of NCFWC, in Raleigh

19 January — supports March of Dimes, National Foundation for Infantile Paralysis, Wake County

21 January — announces "Victory Book Committee" at RWC to collect books for soldiers in army camps

23–26 January — attends GFWC board meeting and defense forum, Washington, including tea with Mrs. Roosevelt at the White House

8 February — pours at tea following a RWC lecture by Gordon Dunthorne, English expert on old fruit and flower prints

16 February — honored for her previous work by Hugh Morson High School PTA

24 February — addresses B&PWC on "What Is Woman's Place in National Defense?"

13 March — visits Women's Prison, Raleigh, at the invitation of Prison Director

18 March — serves as hostess for "Woman's Club Day" at Taylor's department store, basically a fashion show

April — promotes cancer control drive in various venues

17 April — chairs advisory committee for address by noted national newscaster H. V. Kaltenborn at Memorial Auditorium, with introduction by Josephus Daniels and music by the State College band; sits on platform

21–25 April — attends 40th annual NCFWC convention, Asheville; speaks over station WWNC

28 April — attends morale-building revue "You Can Defend America" which she has seen in Asheville; promotes in press; sponsors post-event reception at RWC with Governor and Mrs. Broughton and the mayor; impromptu program concludes with song "Yo-Ho to the Broughtons"

4–9 May — pledge drive, War Stamps and Bonds Defense Savings for North Carolina

15 May — new gasoline restrictions become effective, limiting travel to conferences

20–21 — chairs women's activities for Rotary District 189 convention

10 June — entertains RWC board and guests at luncheon preceding last RWC meeting of year, on cancer control

11–12 June — attends house party and NCFWC board meeting at home of president, Mrs. P. R. Rankin, in Mount Gilead

25 June — is elected vice chairman, Raleigh Civic Council

14 July — attends, as committee member, a "Win The War" rally at Memorial Auditorium

31 July — attends luncheon for Mrs. Eddie Rickenbacker, representing Aircraft Warning Service of Air Force, to secure volunteers

28 August — assists Katherine in a luncheon at 832 for new Duke students, using the Duke plates now in the possession of DKH

29 August — is appointed to advisory board for State War Savings Staff for NCFWC

29–30 September — briefly addresses NCFWC Council–Institute: "Win-the-War Through Efficient Service on the Home Front"

2 October — attends RWC Get-Together Dinner; speaker is Raphael Lemkin, Polish statesman and diplomat former attorney-general of Poland

5 October — Mrs. Bost receives degree of Doctor of Laws at Woman's College, Greensboro

7 October — attends War Savings meeting for Wake and Durham counties

14 October — Katherine, a senior, named to Dean's List at Duke, where she is a member of Delta Gamma, YWCA, and Music Study Club

15 October — at first meeting of RWC, Mrs. Jerman's resolution to support her as president of NCFWC is passed unanimously

21 October — welcomes NC Nurses Association 40th annual meeting

28 October — receives with Mrs. J. Melville Broughton at tea in the Governor's Mansion for NC Nurses Association

30 October — attends Eighth District meeting in Wendell; Mrs. Jerman's resolution again endorsed unanimously

10–11 November — Katherine weekends with her parents

13 November — attends, as a member of the Raleigh committee, North Carolina Symphony season opening, Benjamin Swalin, conductor, at Duke Woman's College Auditorium (now Alice Baldwin Auditorium)

17 November — attends Wake County Duke Alumni Association dinner; recognized as past president of Alumnae

18 November — attends Beta Sigma Phi reception at Sir Walter Hotel

19 November — substituting for Mrs. Rankin, addresses Sorosis of Wilmington: "Today's Upheaval, Woman's Opportunity"

22–25 November — has high profile in events surrounding National War Bond Week

25 November — as part of Women at War Week, hosts tea for every mother in Wake County with a son in service

27 November — presides at her last meeting of the State Legislative Council, retiring after seven years

29 November — gives dinner for NCFWC officials visiting Raleigh

Christmas — Katherine (from Duke) and Lula Belle (who teaches in St. Augustine FL) holiday with their parents and Louise; Mollie Harrell holidays with her children in Greensboro; Mary Belle holidays with Vara and Jean; Jane Herring [Dr. Wooten] concludes Duke Medical School, soon to report to Massachusetts General for short internship.

1943

10 January — laudatory biographical article by noted Charlotte journalist Mrs. J. A. Yarbrough appears in the *Sunday Observer*

20 January — State Legislative Council meeting; Dr. Ellen Winston is new president

22 January — meets with executive board, NCFWC; resolution favors $100,000 legislative appropriation for care and treatment of indigent persons suffering from cancer

27 January — as vice chair, presides at Raleigh Civic Council meeting to discuss food shortage

30–31 January — Katherine weekends with her parents, to attend the Tally–Self wedding; Dr. and Mrs. Highsmith help receive at the large reception at RWC

2 March — Charlotte Woman's Club endorses her candidacy for NCFWC state president

9 March — attends "Dutch supper" at S&W following Mrs. Karl Bishopric's radio broadcast over WPTF concerning Women in the War Savings Program

12 March — addresses annual meeting of the Clinton Study Cub

18 March — meets with State Legislative Council: of nine measures, six passed, one was tabled, two failed

21 April — is honored by RWC 1941–42 and 1942–43 executive boards on the occasion of the end of her term of office

23 April — Katherine's engagement to William Kern Holoman, United States Army, is announced by her parents; she weekends at 832

27–29 April — attends 41st annual NCFWC convention, High Point; is elected president 29 April without opposition

1943–44, 1944–45
President, North Carolina Federation
of Women's Clubs (NCFWC)

7 May — witnesses launch of the SS Sallie S. Cotton at North Carolina Shipbuilding Yard in Wilmington

12 May — is honored at a reception at RWC with Mrs. Micou Browne, new president of Juniors

24 May — attends luncheon of War Savings Women's Division, with movie star Constance Bennett

30 May — issues call for equipment for Red Cross camp and hospital services

22 May — Katherine graduates from Duke with Bachelor of Arts degree

9 June — last RWC meeting of her presidency and 1942–43 year; succeeded by Mrs. R. M. Cornick

22 June — wedding of Katherine Herring Highsmith to W. Kern Holoman at Edenton Street; Louis and Lula Belle are attendants; reception at RWC

26 June — leaves for Swampscott, Mass., for seven-day meeting of GFWC council

16 August — Office of Price Administration and Department of Home Economics, Woman's College, release a publication "Forum Subjects and Discussion Outlines on How We Can Keep Prices Down: Our Wartime Job," in which she had a part

September — Miss Renette Ross of Hamlet, a new faculty member at Barbee School on Blount Street, takes lodging at 832

15–17 September — attends annual Council–Institute of NCFWC, headlined on Thursday evening by Nell Battle Lewis of Smith College, noted Raleigh writer, on "Post War Planning for Peace"

21 September — yearbook of Twentieth Century Book Club is dedicated to her and to Mrs. J. S. Mitchener, her corresponding secretary

2 October — attends RWC Get-Together Dinner, where she is serenaded by a quartet singing "Let Me Call You Sweetheart"

2–3 October — Katherine and Kern visit from New Brunswick, New Jersey; Louise weekends from Woman's College

5–29 October — visits all sixteen Woman's Club districts, from Waxhaw to Leaksville-Spray, and from Moyock to Sylva: District 10, Wagram, 5 October; District 9, Hamlet, 6 October; District 5, Waxhaw, 7 October; District 4, Rutherfordton, 8 October; District 1, Sylva, 11 October; District 2, Asheville, 12 October; District 3, West Jefferson, 13 October; District 6, Elkin, 14 October; District 7, Leaksville, 15 October; District 14, Norlina, 20 October; District 15, Greensboro, 21 October; District 16, Moyock, 22 October; District 12, New Bern, 26 October; District 11, Burgaw, 27 October; District 13, Smithfield, 28 October; District 8, Raleigh, 29 October; overnights and weekends along the way with Mrs. E. M. Land, Statesville; Mrs. R. H. Latham, Asheville; Mrs. E. L. McKee, Sylva; Mrs. McLaughlin, Yadkinville; Mrs. Karl Bishopric, Spray; Mrs. C. W. Beasley, Colerain; Mrs. E. P. Brown Murfreesboro; the Foreman family, Elizabeth City

16–19 October — home for a few days

23–24 October — festive weekend in Elizabeth City with friends, including luncheon on 23 October with Mrs. Leigh Sheep, then visit to Consolidated-Vulltee Aircraft Corp. plant, and tea; dinner parties Saturday and Sunday night

29 October — home to Raleigh

21 November — GFWC president Mrs. John L. Whitehurst calls for discussion and vote on ERA by 1 December

23 November — participates in luncheon meeting called by Dr. Winston to study ERA; vote postponed until 30 November

16–17 November — attends New York *Herald-Tribune* forum

1 December — extends deadline for study and vote on proposed ERA

1 December — receives at State Art Gallery, State Library Building, after meeting of NC State Art Society; 2 December is elected to Board of Directors

Christmas holidays — Katherine and Kern visit from Rutgers, in New Brunswick, New Jersey; also Louise, from Woman's College, Greensboro, and Lula Belle, teaching at State School for the Deaf, Trenton

1944

1 January — joins other prominent North Carolinians in promoting war bonds and stamps

4 January — Katherine and Louise assist their mother in hosting Twentieth Century Book Club; among the special guests are Mrs. J. Melville Broughton, Mollie Harrell, Mary Herring, and Vara

19–21 January — visits Charlotte to plan convention; honored at multiple luncheons and dinners

21 January — honored at a banquet of Mooresville Woman's Club

27 January — presides at executive board meeting, NFCFW

1 February — presents a paper, "India Without Fable," at Twentieth Century Book Club

2 February — attends meeting of Associated Women of the North Carolina Farm Bureau Federation (est. 1942) and proposes slogan "Education, Legislation and Beautification"

6 February — in Sunday papers comments favorably on Legal Aid for Poor and on price control, having distributed "Community Price List" leaflet to clubwomen

6 February — attends Goldsboro funeral of Mrs. Thomas O'Berry, née Annie Land, former president of NCFWC and Depression-era administrator, North Carolina Emergency Relief Commission

8 February — repeats her paper on India to Cosmos Book Club of Raleigh

13 February — at a conference of State Library Commission lobbies for increased state funding for public libraries

1 March — brings greetings of NCFWC to joint dinner meeting of Daughters of the American Colonies, Daughters of Colonial Wars, and Daughters of 1812

4–5 March — Katherine and Kern visit their parents in Raleigh before Kern, who "has recently finished training at Rutgers University," is shipped to Europe; Louise visits from Greensboro; "Mrs. Holoman will make her home with her parents for a short while"

9 March — addresses Rockingham Civic Club on joining the Federation; overnights in Mount Gilead as guest of Mrs. P. R. Rankin

15 March — addresses clubs in Faison

14 April — attends, as guest of honor with Mrs. Charles G. Doak, luncheon and meeting of the Community Club, Carolina Inn, Chapel Hill

4–6 April — during planning visit to Charlotte, addresses a Woman's Club luncheon; on 5 April visits Kannapolis Woman's Cub; several other social affairs offered during her stay

20 April — departs Raleigh for Chicago

21–22 April — represents Dr. Winston and State Legislative Council at convention of National Council on State Legislation; speaks Friday evening on "Marriage and Divorce"

24 April — travels Chicago to St. Louis

24–29 April — attends GFWC convention, St. Louis

16–19 May — attends and presides at 42nd annual NCFWC convention, Charlotte; Eddie Rickenbacker, WW I flying ace and founder of Eastern Air Lines, is principal speaker

summer — Louise at home; Lula Belle comes from Trenton for two weeks in late June

June — summer polio epidemic sweeps through western North Carolina, continues through summer; quarantines on 15-year-olds and below begin to be lifted in September

1 June — attends Goldsboro Woman's Club with Mrs. Doak

12 June – 8 July — leads Fifth War Loan drive, with Mrs. P. R. Rankin; NCFWC goal is $3 million in bonds sold

1 July — receives at tea given by Louise and Katherine at 832 for bride-elect Miss Lorraine Glenn of Durham (engaged to son of Mrs. R. N. Simms); assisting are Lula Belle, Mary Belle, and Mollie Harrell

23 July — appointed by North Carolina Planning Board to Health and Welfare Unit for post-war planning

20–22 September — presides over Council–Institute, attracting over 100, simultaneous with Home Demonstration Club council and State Nurses Association meeting

26 September – 3 November — visits all 16 Woman's Clubs districts (for the second time), with topic "Leadership in the Post-War Period" and text "The future belongs to children, but the children belong to God": District 9, Sanford, 26 September; District 7, Asheboro, 27 September; District 5, Mt. Gilead, 28 September; District 4, Boiling Springs, 29 September; District 1, Waynesville, 2 October; District 2, Asheville, 4 October; District 3, Morganton, 5 October; District 5, Walkerton, 6 October; [interval; resumes 24 October]; District 14, Oxford, 24 October; District 16, Gatesville, 25 October; District 15, Ayden, 26 October; District 12, Morehead City, 27 October; District 11, Wilmington, 31 October; District 10, Pembroke 1 November; District 13,

Kenly, 2 November; District 8, Cary, 3 November

7–9 October — weekends at home

10 October — attends, with Mrs. Jerman, meeting of State Planning Board at Chapel Hill on public health

12 October — departs for New York

14–18 October — attends GFWC board meeting in New York and *Herald-Tribune* Forum, New York; entertains Governor and Mrs. Broughton at dinner at the Waldorf-Astoria; he addresses the Forum

28 October — associates with capital campaign for Guilford College in Greensboro

8 November — receives after RWC meeting devoted to polio, speaker from Warm Springs Foundation in Georgia; an iron lung and photographs of polio cases from 1935 and 1944 epidemics on display

18 November — attends convention of North Carolina Press Women (Margaret Harper of Southport, president), concluding with tea at the Governor's Mansion

21 November — receives following a program of "Living Pictures" at RWC

28 November — attends, with Dr. Winston, southeastern meeting in Clinton of the Public Welfare Association

6 December — receives, with Governor Broughton and others, at a reception following meeting of the State Art Society; 7 December is elected (with Governor Broughton) to board of directors

10 December — outlines her plan for prevention of juvenile crime and delinquency post-war, the beginning of her Youth Conservation Program for North Carolina

12 December — with Vara, hosts coffee hour at 604 North Blount Street honoring wives of Methodist ministers, assisted by Jean, Katherine, Mary Herring, Mollie Harrell, Blanche Brian, and others

16 December — attends joint meeting of educational associations including PTAs and NCEA to adopt five-point plan for 1945 Legislature

late December — intercedes with Governor Broughton on behalf of a 15-year-old scheduled for execution by electric chair

Christmas season — state chair, 1944 Christmas Seals

1945

16 January — travels to Charlotte for regional meeting of Women's Interests section, Board of Public Relations War Department

21 January — writes, during Infantile Paralysis campaign, in support of statewide health plan expanding two-year medical school at UNC into four-years plus teaching hospital, as well as a hospital and medical care program for entire state

24 January — assists Vara and Eugenia at tea, 604 North Blount Street, honoring Gladys Herring of Roseboro and Mrs. Joseph Beaman of Greensboro, visiting the city

4 February — opposes new "easy" divorce laws introduced in Legislature

11 February — calls clubs to hold special meeting in February to consider, analyze, and express opinion on Dumbarton Oaks proposals

4 March — joins appeal for recruits to hospital companies, Women's Army Corps, with goal of 105 enlistees by March 20

11 March — supports Experimental Forests for the South program in forest management

12 March — attends Eleanor Roosevelt address at Memorial Auditorium to Institute of Religion, United Church

13 March — executive board of NCFWC called to consider governance if no convention can be held

18 March — supports clothing drive for needy and liberated countries of the world, sponsored by GFWC; signs, with many notables, letter in support of state hospital and medical care program, to reach the state Senate on the 19th (passed, with amendments)

19–23 March — visits Henderson, Mount Olive, and Faison clubs

21 March — named to North Carolina Division of the Field Army of the American Cancer Society for 1945

1 April — telegrams support, to Secretary of State Stettinius, for Commission of Human Rights and Fundamental Freedoms at UN organizational meetings upcoming in San Francisco

3 April — attends symposium The Consumer in Wartime, held at UNC by Office of Price Administration

11 April — introduces Prof. Edward J. Woodhouse, professor of political science at UNC, to speak on to RWC on Dumbarton Oaks peace conference, etc.

15 May — reports to North Carolina Tuberculosis Association on 1944 Christmas Seals: total sales $272,461.75, up $74,351.62 over 1943

22 May — leads mission study class of Wesleyan Service Guild at Edenton Street on "The American Indian"

26 May — addresses Louisburg College Alumnae-Alumni on "Youth and the World of Tomorrow"

20 May — begins to receive reports from consultants sent by GFWC to San Francisco Conference on the United Nations

28 May — entertains her board at pre-convention meeting; she presents gifts to each member of the board

29–30 May — in lieu of 43rd annual NCFWC convention, expanded board meeting in Raleigh; principal speaker is Judge Anna M. Kross of NYC; among the pages are Mrs. Kern Holoman and Miss Louise Highsmith; Mrs. Karl Bishopric of Spray elected to succeed her; concludes her presidency

c. 15–22 July — vacations at Wrightsville Beach with Katherine and Mollie Harrell; Louise returns to Raleigh after summer course at Davidson College

3 August — attends luncheon meeting of Women's Economic Council, NC Branch, of which she is chairman

1945–1950
Founding Chair, Youth Conservation Committee
North Carolina Federation of Women's Clubs

5–6 September — attends autumn council meeting of NCFWC; preceded on 4 September by Youth Conservation Committee; leads, on 6 September, Youth Conservation symposium

10 September — leads Beta Sigma Phi discussion of all phases of happiness

18 September — her 65th birthday observed at Twentieth Century Book Club meeting at Hartness mansion on North Blount Street; first lady Mrs. R. Gregg Cherry is a guest

7 October — greets at a tea given at 832 by Mollie Harrell for B&PWC, Eugenia and Katherine assisting

5 October — addresses Sanford Women's Club on Youth Conservation

11 October — addresses Hamlet Women's Club on Youth Conservation

15 October — attends planning committee for Youth Conservation Institute on 29–30 October

23 October — addresses 12-state meeting, in Durham, of American Cancer Society: "The Role of Women's Civic Groups"

27 October – 2 November — attends *Herald-Tribune* Forum, New York

13 November — addresses 35 new members of RWC: "The National Federation"

20 November — attends dinner meeting of Raleigh B&PWC

28 November – 1 December — attends GFWC board meeting in Washington
to review special postwar programs; 30 November spent entirely on Youth
Conservation Committee chaired by Judge Anna M. Kross; tea at White
House with Mrs. Truman

12 December — receives, alongside Governor and Mrs. Cherry, former
Governor and Mrs. Broughton and other notables, at reception following
19th annual meeting of North Carolina State Art Society

16 December — joint Mrs. Bost and others in commending a Pediatric Study
and Survey underway

FEBRUARY 1939

CITIZENS' GROUPS PROVE HELPFUL IN SAVING LIVES OF MOTHERS AND BABIES

By Mrs. J. Henry Highsmith
Assistant Director, Health Education

That lay groups are becoming interested in the problem of making motherhood
and babyhood safe in their communities, and are doing something about
it, indicates that real progress is now being made in this important field
of health work. It means that the public attitude is changing in regard to
whose responsibility it is to prevent mothers losing their lives at childbirth
and babies dying the first few days or weeks of life. We are encouraged to
think that the people now realize that while the doctors, nurses, hospitals
and clinics still have the major responsibility for saving mothers and babies,
that the people themselves are not without their share of the responsibility;
that the job requires both the lay and professional groups working hand-in-
glove together. One group working alone has not been able to improve the
situation to any great extent, but all working together have proved that the
job can be done surprisingly well.

One of these citizens' groups whose activities are particularly noteworthy
is the Maternity Welfare Committee of Pinebluff. Under the chairmanship
of Mrs. Walter MacNeille, this committee, composed of eighteen or twenty
energetic, kind-hearted women of the village community, supports the
maternity and infancy work of Moore County in numerous ways. In addition
to raising a sum of from three to five hundred dollars annually to be used
in purchasing food, clothes, medicine and doctor's care for the neediest
patients, they look up and transport needy patients to the hospital and
clinics, they follow up and investigate referred cases, assist at local clinics
and provide work for men and women who are able to repay for some service
rendered them or their families. Funds are raised through donations of
cash, donations of articles to sell or material to be converted into clothes,
layettes or bassinets; through the Good-will Shop which sells secondhand
articles from clothes, furs and jewelry to andirons and pokers; and through
commissions on the sale of certain articles and services.

A special activity of this committee is sewing, making garments for the poor. The members meet one afternoon each week at the home of the chairman, who has converted her sleeping porch into a well-equipped sewing room. Here they make layettes and bassinets with all their fittings for the needy. The group made eighty-five bassinets last year, whose cost and that of their fittings averaged $5.00 each. The services and cooperative efforts of this fine group of citizens is beyond calculation in its relation to reducing the sickness and suffering of mothers and babies in Moore County.

Another citizens' group that has pointed the way of service, especially for younger women, is the Junior Guild of Rocky Mount. This group of fine, intelligent young matrons and girls responded to the call of the city health officer for volunteer work and funds in behalf of the indigent mothers and needy babies of Rocky Mount. Forty or more enlisted for service and organized themselves into the Junior Guild, an organization patterned along the lines of Junior Leagues of larger cities. They took for their objective the challenge to reduce infant mortality in their community. A plan was adopted whereby each underprivileged baby was made the responsibility of two of the members, who were required to visit the child once a week, provide cod liver oil, milk, clothing, or other supplies which the family could not afford for the baby, and furnish transportation for the mother and child to the maternity and infancy center on the days it was held. The Guild has had under its care throughout the year between forty and fifty babies, and incidentally, their mothers. The babies' health and welfare are supervised through infancy and early childhood and often through the preschool years. The members work in close cooperation with the physicians, city health department, the public welfare workers and other local agencies.

A recent visit by the writer to the Junior Guild headquarters found the members busy and enthusiastic about what they were able to do and contemplated doing in the future. They admitted that they had less time for bridge, parties and movies, but that they found a satisfaction in service which more than repaid them.

The Ahoskie Woman's Club illustrates what a club or similar organization can do to meet a local need. Two years ago this group of earnest women sponsored the establishment of a Maternity and Infancy Center in the town of Ahoskie, where indigent mothers come and get medical advice for themselves and their babies free. The center which they have provided and equipped is on the ground-floor, is easily reached, and has separate waiting rooms for white and colored patients, a private examining room, physician's private office, nurses' room and toilets. The county health officer and one or more nurses have charge. The center serves thirty or forty needy mothers and as many babies twice a month. One of the local citizens said, in speaking of what the center has meant to the community, "I can't say all that it has meant, but I would hate to think of the suffering mothers and babies we would have without it."

Health Bulletin [North Carolina State Board of Health] 54/2 (February 1939), pp. 6–8

APRIL 1939

AN ANALYTICAL STUDY OF THE RECENT MATERNITY AND INFANCY CONFERENCE

By Mrs. J. Henry Highsmith
Assistant Director of Health Education

Every one is agreed, we think, that the recent conference on "Better Care for Mothers and Babies," held in Raleigh, was a great success. But was it? Judging from the thought-provoking speeches, papers and discussions given, the valuable suggestions and timely remedies offered, as well as the rapt attention of the large and representative audience, it was a tremendous success. But whether six months from now it will be classed as just another conference or remembered as the beginning of a new and better day for mothers and babies in North Carolina remains to be seen. It will depend largely on whether or not health officers, physicians, nurses, clubwomen and citizens of whatever classification took home with them a conviction and probably a pattern by which to start work on their local problems of providing better care for mothers and babies.

Purpose of Conference.

The purpose of the conference was to bring together representatives of the State's official, medical, professional and citizens' groups and lay before them the facts underlying one of the State's most urgent health problems—how to save the large number of mothers and babies who die needlessly every year from causes or conditions incident to childbirth—with a view of impressing them with a sense of their responsibility in bringing about a solution to their problem.

A number of very revealing facts were brought out in the discussions of the conference. One was that North Carolina has a baby death rate that is altogether too high—66 per 1,000 live births in 1937 and almost 68 in 1938, as against 54 for the Nation. This means that North Carolina now loses about 1,000 babies every year more than she would lose if she had as low rate as the average for all the States. The State has nearly 80,000 babies born alive each year—about two-thirds white and one-third colored—but more than 5,000 of these babies die annually. Only six States have a higher infant death rate than North Carolina; these are Arizona, Colorado, New Mexico, South Carolina, Texas and Virginia; Louisiana reports the same rate as North Carolina.

Deaths Among Very Young.

A significant fact brought out in connection with the State's high infant death rate was that large numbers of babies die when only one day or one week old.

In 1937, 1,233 babies died the first day of life, and 2,124 during the first week of life. This means to a great extent that this large number of 3,357 babies were denied their first rights—to be born well and to be given every chance to live. Usually it means that their mothers either neglected themselves during pregnancy or were unable to get the medical and nursing care before and at birth that a baby requires to be born well and get a good start in life.

Another disconcerting fact brought out in the conference was that a North Carolina mother is more than twice as likely to die in pregnancy or childbirth as a mother in Connecticut, or a baby born in North Carolina has only about one-half the chances for living to its first birthday that a baby in New Jersey has.

It is now known that doctors and nurses alone cannot cope with the problem. It is too deep-seated, involving inheritances, conditions and customs that only the schools, churches, clinics, hospitals and all the State and professional agencies working together can reach. As has been pointed out before and reemphasized in the conference, there is one source of power that has not yet been harnessed in behalf of better care for mothers and babies, and yet this is the most natural and logical of all—the woman-power of the State. High health authorities have repeatedly said that when women themselves become interested and demand better care for mothers and babies, then and not until then will they get it. This challenge was forcefully presented to the women attending the conference by Dr. Bayard Carter, of Duke Hospital. He made the statement that women must go after this problem in the same spirit and zeal with which they worked in their missionary societies in other days. "Go and tell," he said, carried the Gospel of salvation to the heathen with results that have astonished believers and transformed nations. "Go and tell" mothers, he said, in ignorant, benighted families, isolated and poverty-ridden homes that they or their babies need not die at childbirth, must be the method employed if tragic mother and baby deaths are to be stopped. Half-hearted measures and efforts, he declared, will never do it. In conclusion, he said with dramatic force, "We now know what do, and for God's sake, let's get out and do it."

The Health Bulletin [North Carolina State Board of Health] 54/4 (April 1939), pp. 3–4

2 FEBRUARY 1941

NOMINATION OF MRS. R. H. LATHAM FOR TREASURER, GENERAL FEDERATION OF WOMEN'S CLUBS, 1941–1944

Cited by Susan Iden

The North Carolina Federation of Women's Clubs presents Mrs. Rowland Hill Latham of Asheville for treasurer of the General Federation of Women's Clubs 1941–1944.

In presenting Mrs. Rowland Hill Latham for treasurer of the General Federation of Women's Clubs for 1941–1944, North Carolina honors one of her best-loved women, affectionately known throughout the State as Mamie Latham.

Although born, reared and educated at the University of Virginia, her married life has been spent in North Carolina and her loyalty to her adopted State is deep and unquestioned.

From young womanhood Mrs. Latham has believed in women's organizations and she early found in club work an outlet for this interest. In the North Carolina Federation she has served as district president, treasurer, finance chairman, first vice-president, president and director.

Her interest in national questions extends beyond the boundaries of her State to include membership on the executive committee of the Southeastern Council on International Relations and Governor Hoey's State Council of National Defense. Membership on local boards of Girl Scouts, Y.W.C.A., Child Welfare and Adult Education Council and the Woman's Club expresses her interest in community problems.

Mrs. Latham has given eight years of service to the General Federation as Dean of State Directors, Contact Chairman, Program Chairman, Chairman of Credentials, Chairman of the Committee on Calendar Reform, and of the Golden Jubilee Flower Committee. During the present administration she has served as chairman of the Budget and the experience and knowledge of the General Federation's financial status gained in this position definitely fit her for the office of Treasurer.

No story of Mamie Latham would be complete without a glimpse into her attractive new home in Asheville where her versatility as wife, home-maker, hostess, and public-spirited citizen is revealed. Here one soon learns that friendship and selfless service are as everlasting a part of the home as the mountains that surround it.

Raleigh Sunday *News and Observer,* p. 19 (Society, p. 1)

1 JUNE 1941

FEDERATION OF WOMEN'S CLUBS TO KEYNOTE NATIONAL DEFENSE

By Mrs. J. Henry Highsmith

The Golden Jubilee celebration of the General Federation of Women's Clubs held at Atlantic City was all that the most enthusiastic club woman could have dreamed that it would be. Pageants, parades, processions, orchestras, bands, choruses, historical reviews, addresses, forums, receptions, dinners and banquets marked the five-day celebration of the 50th anniversary of the founding of the General Federation of Women's Clubs.

The celebration was pitched on a grand scale. The convention was held in the Atlantic City auditorium, "the largest auditorium in the world." The attendance was by far the largest that has ever been seen at a Federation convention. A national Golden Jubilee chorus of near a thousand voices gave an evening of song, assisted by grand opera stars and directed by the inimitable Gena Branscombe of New York. Hundreds of pioneer clubwomen from every state in the Union, attired in costumes of former days—the gay nineties, and the sad sixties, the covered wagon and goldrush days, contrasted with the more affluent city styles—staged one of the most thrilling and impressive ceremonies ever sponsored by the Federation as they marched in on the opening night, each following her state flag and escorted by one of her state juniors. Thousands witnessed the colorful and picturesque rolling chair parade, a feature of the Junior Night program that was staged in the arena of the auditorium. This spectacle was participated in by the Juniors of the 48 states and the District of Columbia and was followed by America's most celebrated radio forum, "Town Meeting of the Air," presided over by George V. Denny, Jr., president, and brought from New York to Atlantic City to give its regular weekly program for the benefit of visiting clubwomen.

North Carolina was represented by her delegates in many places and parts of the convention. On the official board was Mrs. R. H. Latham as chairman of the budget, later elected treasurer of the General Federation without opposition. Miss Margaret Gibson, Carolina's Clubwoman, in a costume of earlier days marched in the procession on Pioneer Night. Mrs. J. Henry Highsmith as a past chairman of the Federation took part in the Golden Guard episode of the pageant, "The Long Path." Mrs. E. E. Randolph, Mrs. William John Hayes and Mrs. Charles W. Parker sang in the Golden Jubilee chorus. Mrs. R. C. Boyce was "Miss North Carolina," who rode in the flower-bedecked rolling chair in the Junior parade, carrying blossoms of dogwood, the State flower. She was escorted by three other Juniors, Mrs. Beverly Milloway, Mrs. Micou Browne, and Mrs. Charles E. Brady, also by Mrs. Karl Bishopric, Mrs. P. R. Rankin and Mrs. John D. Robinson. Mrs. Robinson served as teller in the election. Mrs. Rankin, as president and director for North Carolina, attended the post-convention meeting of the board of directors. Other North Carolina delegates were: Mrs. C. W. Beasley, Mrs. E. W. Griffin, Mrs. Charles L. Haywood, Mrs. George Leftwich and Mrs. Blanton of Kinston.

A breakfast was given by Mrs. P. R. Rankin to the North Carolina delegates in honor of Mrs. Latham, North Carolina's nominee for treasurer. The breakfast was served in the North Carolina candidate's headquarters in the Dennis Hotel, of which Mrs. Robinson was in charge.

Another social occasion which the North Carolina delegates were privileged to attend as special guests was a reception given by Mrs. Harold V. Mulligan, honoring George V. Denny, president of the Town Meeting of the Air, and Mrs. Denny. Mr. Denny is a North Carolinian. Mrs. Denny is a Virginian but a loyal alumna of St. Mary's School, Raleigh.

A peak of interest of the convention was the election of officers for the next three years. All candidates were unopposed except three for second vice-president. In the first election Mrs. H. B. Ritchie of Georgia was eliminated and in the second run-off Mrs. J. Blair Buck of Virginia defeated Mrs. R. I. C. Prout of Michigan for second vice-president. The other officers are: President, Mrs. John L. Whitehurst of Baltimore; first vice-president, Mrs. LaFell Dickinson of New Hampshire; recording secretary, Mrs. A. L. Blackstone of Wisconsin; and treasurer, Mrs. R. H. Latham of North Carolina.

Another high peak of interest was adoption of the resolutions. Those adopted put the women on record as favoring giving whatever aid is necessary to help Britain win the war; favoring also the national defense program, the United Service Organization's efforts to provide recreation for soldiers, improvement of forestry service, better housing, fire precautions in homes, control of fireworks, cooperation with public health authorities in campaigns against heart disease, cancer, pneumonia, tuberculosis, influenza and syphilis, universal finger printing and the establishing of "Women of the Americas Day" on the first Saturday in May each year. The delegates failed to endorse suffrage for the District of Columbia, despite many pleas by its residents.

The Convention voted after much discussion to increase the annual dues of the General Federation from 10 to 15 cents a member with the understanding that additional funds be used to promote national defense. Furthermore it voted to change the status of Junior club women from that of a department to that of an extension division. The Juniors were divided as to whether this meant promotion or demotion. However, they won a long coveted point in that the convention voted to name a Junior as head of the Junior Division. Another change favored by the Juniors was the elimination of all age limits regarding Junior membership.

North Carolina received honorable mention for the amount of its birthday gift to the general fund. This was more than $3,000. Mrs. P. R. Rankin was chairman of the State Birthday committee.

Texas extended an invitation to hold the 1942 Council meeting at Austin. Indiana also invited the Federation to hold its next meeting at Indianapolis. The decision will be made by the executive board.

Mrs. John L. Whitehurst of Baltimore announced that National Defense will be the keynote of her administration.

Raleigh Sunday *News and Observer*, p. 25

24 FEBRUARY 1942

WHAT IS WOMAN'S PLACE IN NATIONAL DEFENSE?

**Excerpts from Address to Raleigh Business and
Professional Woman's Club**

"Some may think that there is something wrong, that we do not have our orders," said Mrs. J. Henry Highsmith, president of the Raleigh Woman's

Club as she spoke at the Tuesday evening meeting of the Raleigh Business and Professional Woman's Club at the Tally-Ho Inn. Her topic was "What is Woman's Place in National Defense?"

"We know that in the beginning there was a woman's program set up under the authority of the General Federation of Women's Clubs," Mrs. Highsmith said. "When Civilian Defense was set up, under the direction of Mayor Fiorello La Guardia, he did not want to separate the men's and the women's work. Mrs. Roosevelt thought that maybe she could smooth the troubled waters by working through a recreational program, but the storm in Congress killed the program. Now La Guardia has resigned; Mrs. Roosevelt has resigned; and a new setup is being worked out under the direction of James M. Landis and Jonathan Daniels. What are Mr. Landis and Mr. Daniels going to do about the program for women? In today's paper, Mr. Daniels' work was explained to be training for officers' service, but the article does not say that he will enroll women.

"To me one of the finest suggestions by Mrs. Roosevelt was that whatever you are doing, do it better than you ever did it before," said Mrs. Highsmith. "And then, when the President said to keep the physical, mental and spiritual standard of the family up to the highest state possible, he got down to the most vital part of national defense—the home. The next big general order is to keep the physical, mental and moral standards of the community up.

"While I was in Washington," the speaker stated, "the most important topic of conversation and the most stress was laid on saving for war material. Mrs. Roosevelt quoted in her column recently, attributing its source to Calvin Coolidge: 'Eat it up, wear it out, make it do, do without.'

"The next order," Mrs. Highsmith declared, "is to buy defense stamps and bonds. If the women own 95 per cent (or very near that amount) of all the money, it is up to us to buy bonds and stamps, and it is one of the finest investments.

"The next thing we have to do is produce," she said. "Produce or make it possible for someone else to produce, and this is not to be an 11-month job, but a 12-month job."

Mrs. Highsmith declared that the job of keeping up morale, "the fighting spirit," is the job of every woman.

Raleigh *News and Observer,* 27 February, p. 10

1946–1966

— ⬭⬤⬮ —

1946

late January — Louise home from Woman's College for a few days

24 January — cancels speaking engagement with Kinston Woman's Club owing to weather

25 January — presides at Youth Conservation Conference sponsored by NCFWC, which adopts nine-point action program

3 February — death of Mrs. Palmer Jerman of Raleigh, former RWC and NCFWC president and close personal friend; Mrs. Bost, Mrs. Doak, and Mrs. Highsmith arrange the RWC memorial service on 3 March

19 February — honored, with 14 others, at ceremony for past presidents of Hugh Morson PTA

9–10 March — Louise weekends at 832

27 April — introduces guests at wedding reception at RWC for Mrs. Doak's daughter, Eleanor

5 May — Youth Conservation Sunday observed as start of National Family Week

7 May — addresses Cary Woman's Club on "Youth Conservation"

14 May — attends Louise's senior recital at Woman's College and co-hosts reception following

29–31 May — attends 44th annual NCFWC convention, Greensboro

14–15 June attends National Council on State Legislation in Madison, as regional vice president

10 July — receives and pours at meeting of Rho Chapter, Beta Sigma Phi; Louise sings

late July — Highsmith family at White Lake for two weeks, also Mary Belle

14 August — assists Katherine at a coffee hour for 40 at 832 for a recent bride; also assisting are Louise, Mary Belle, and Mollie Harrell

21–22 August — attends NCFWC Council–Institute on Building the Peace; leads post-conference discussion of NCFWC four-point program for the year

6 September — speaks briefly on Youth Conservation to the District 8 meeting, Cary

13 September — named to new statewide community planning committee of NC State Planning Board

14–15 September — Louise weekends at 832

20 September — hosts, with Katherine, luncheon at 832 for bride-elect Jane Herring (Dr. Jane Wooten), a cousin

21 September — attends wedding of Jane Herring to Kenneth Wooten at Edenton Street

28–30 October — attends *Herald-Tribune* forum, New York; her report incorporated in Mrs. Doak's *News and Observer* article on Sunday, 10 November

14–15 November — attends second annual Youth Conservation Institute at RWC, brings official greeting to Thursday session

17 November — addresses Hugh Morson PTA on Youth Conservation

1947

5 March — speaks against state amendment removing eligibility of women for jury duty; has "men" replaced with with "persons"

13 March — addresses Elizabeth City Woman's Club on Youth Conservation

26 March — addresses Wendell Woman's Club on "The Basic Needs of All Youth"

29–30 March — Louise weekends at 832 from her job as public school music teacher and church choir director in Winston-Salem

March — member of committee supporting City Council – City Manager Form of Government on referendum of 18 March

31 March — attends showing of *Seeds of Destiny,* a 1946 War Department film on nations devastated by war

3 April — pursuant to the film, attends organization meeting for drive 20–27 April for food, clothing, medical supplies, games, kitchen utensils, and money

4 April — addresses Greensboro Woman's Club, then goes to Winston-Salem to spend Easter with Louise

23 April — drives to Columbia SC where she joins Miss Alves Long and motors on to Charleston for South Carolina Federation meeting; speaks on Youth Conservation

4 May — Youth Conservation Sunday / Christian Home Day, starting Christian Family Week

21–23 May — attends 45th annual NCFWC convention, Wrightsville

20 June — with Dr. Highsmith, hosts farewell reception at 832 for a Public Instruction librarian, Mrs. Clarence D. Douglas, moving to Raleigh Public Schools; assisted by Katherine and Kern, Lula Belle, and Mary Belle among others.

6 August — visits Mrs. Latham in Asheville

21 August — with Louise, accompanies Dr. Highsmith to Southern Educators Conference in Natural Bridge VA

8 September — birth of first grandchild, Dallas Kern Holoman

10–11 September — attends NCFWC Council–Institute in Raleigh: "Where We Stand Today"; leads Wednesday session on Youth Conservation

16 September — attends District 8 meeting, Cary; later speaks to RWC Art Department on "Increased Interest in Art in North Carolina Schools"; Youth Conservation remains one of two overall objectives of GFWC for 1947–48, alongside world peace

3 October — pours at a tea for 200 Beta Sigma Phi members from 30 chapters in NC and SC

18–25 October — attends *Herald-Tribune* Forum, New York

3–5 November — attends North Carolina Recreation Conference in Durham; addresses session on "Using Community Resources for Recreation"

11 November — addresses new members of RWC, noting that "the General Federation of Women's Clubs is the largest organized group of women in the world"

12 November — participates in organizing NC World Peace Forum based in Chapel Hill; is named to advisory committee

20 November — attends, as honored guest, Raleigh meeting of Garden Club of North Carolina

23 November — entertains rushees of Rho Chapter, Beta Sigma Phi

24 November — named eastern regional women chairman, Angier B. Duke Scholarships

9 December — greets and pins at initiation of Rho Chapter, Beta Sigma Phi

Christmas — Louise holidays with her parents

1948

5 January — Louise returns to Winston-Salem

c. 8 January — addresses Two Arts Club of Rose Hill, which subsequently federates as a Woman's Club

18 January — cosigns testimonial letter on Josephus Daniels (d. 15 January) with Mrs. Bost and Mrs. Doak, published in the *News and Observer*.

12–14 March — visits Lula Belle and Louise in Winston-Salem

5–8 May — attends National Conference on Family Life at the White House, representing the GFWC; meets Rev. T. Marvin Vick, eventual pastor of Edenton Street

4 June — assists Mr. and Mrs. Kern Holoman, at their home on West Park Drive, at a breakfast for bridal couple W. T. Martin, Jr., and Frances McKay

8–10 June — attends 46th annual NCFWC convention, Hendersonville; reports for Youth Conservation Committee, followed by address of Rev. T. Marvin Vick

2 July — co-hosts, with Katherine and Louise, tea at 832 for four brides-elect, assisted by Vara, Eugenia, Pauline, Mary Belle, Mollie Harrell, Dr. Ellen Winston, and others

1 October — hosts luncheon for Mrs. J. A. Gupton, president of GFWC, at the Reinlyn House; followed by RWC Get-Together Dinner that same evening

1949

5 January — addresses YWCA Public Affairs Forum on "How Can Women Influence Legislation?"

12 January — moderates a panel, "Strengthening Family Life," at RWC, with participants including Rev. T. Marvin Vick and Dr. Ellen Winston

17 January — speaks, as Youth Conservation chairman, to Hamlet Woman's Club

23 January — pours at a come-and-sit tea given by Rho Chapter, Beta Sigma Phi

28 January — receives at home of Mrs. Doak honoring first lady Mrs. W. Kerr Scott and Mrs. Forrest H. Shuford, wife of the Commissioner of Labor; Mrs. Dallas Holoman (Aunt Bessie Gray) also receives

17 February — introduces speaker at meeting of Wake County Alumnae of Duke University chapter

24 February — assists Vara and Pauline at Frances E. Willard Memorial tea for Raleigh WCTU at their home on Blount Street

9 March — attends funeral of Mrs. James M. Hobgood, former NCFWC president, in Greenville

19–21 April — attends 47th annual NCFWC convention, Goldsboro; oversees workshop 21 April of Youth Conservation Committee (on "Build a Better Community" program cosponsored with Kroger Co.)

25–30 April — attends GFWC convention in Miami, focused largely on Youth Conservation; 28 April gives address "Knowing the Need"

5 May — pours punch at RWC tea honoring Raleigh book clubs

6 May — attends luncheon for Mrs. W. Kerr Scott given by Mrs. Guy Ross of Clinton; Gladys Herring (Mrs. Troy) and Pauline, also Clintonians, at table.

10 May — pours coffee at reception given by Annie Crews for Mrs. K. W. Parham, returning to Raleigh; Mrs. Troy Herring also receives; Eugenia, Vara, Pauline, and Mrs. Henry Herring assist

11 May — attends, in Elizabeth City, dedication of portrait of Mrs. James Greene Fearing, founder of the club there

20 May — is elected to advisory committee of State Legislative Council

24 June — receives at bridal event for Louise, given by Mollie Harrell at the RWC; greeters include the bride's sisters and prospective sisters-in-law, and all her Herring aunts

8 July — stands with Louise to receive at an afternoon tea; Katherine assists

9 July — assists at coffee for Louise and another bride-elect

13 July — attends steak supper for Louise and Louis at the Flythe cabin on Knox Road; extended family present

16 July — attends luncheon for Louise given by family friend Flora Creech

19 July — attends three parties for Louise

20 July — attends two parties for Louise including luncheon given by Mesdames Dallas Holoman, Dallas Holoman, Jr., Chreston Holoman, and Boyce Holoman

22 July — Louise hosts her bridesmaids at 832 Wake Forest Road; wedding rehearsal at 8:00 pm; cake cutting at 9:00 given by Vara, Pauline, Jean, and Mary Belle

23 July — wedding breakfast at the Wilkerson home; wedding, at 5:00 pm, Edenton Street Methodist Church, of Louise and Louis Wilkerson; reception offered by Dr. and Mrs. J. Henry Highsmith at the RWC

6 August — Louise and Louis Wilkerson, returned from their wedding trip to New York, at home with the bride's parents; they subsequently move to Richmond for Louis's medical training

14 August — visits Mrs. Latham in Asheville

15–16 September — attends NCFWC Council–Institute in Raleigh: "Building a Better Community" and Youth Conservation late September — hosts Miss Alves Long of Columbia SC, noted clubwoman and international relations specialist, on a speaking tour

29 September — attends event for librarian of Olivia Raney Library

3–4 October — hosts president and vice president of NCFWC in conjunction with Eighth District meeting in Wendell

18 October — birth of grandson, Richard Highsmith Holoman

late November — as Youth Conservation Committee chair, releases message to club presidents on better health for public school children

1950

January — participates in a drive to raise $200K for a new YWCA

22 January — birth of granddaughter, Louise Highsmith Wilkerson

31 January — at Twentieth Century Book Club reviews William Vogt's *Road to Survival,* influential 1948 environmentalist tract

18 February — hosts, with Louise, bridal luncheon for Miss Hillman Thomas

23 March — serves on nominating committee for first North Carolina Distinguished Services Awards for Women, to be presented by Chi Omega sorority at UNC on 5 April

April — elected to a three-year term on board of directors of NC Conference for Social Service during 37th annual meeting; presents Youth Conservation report

18–20 April — attends 48th annual NCFWC convention, Raleigh; hosts past presidents at Reinlyn House after opening ceremonies at Edenton Street; attends large reception at RWC clubhouse, where other guests include Dr. Annie Louise Wilkerson and Mrs. Chreston Holoman (Aunt Luna), who played cocktail music at the piano

19 April — announces support of Frank P. Graham for U. S. Senate

20 April — attends tea for NCFWC given by Governor and Mrs. Kerr Scott at the Governor's Mansion; receives in the ballroom with other trustees and past presidents; others receiving and assisting include Dr. Annie Louise Wilkerson and Mrs. Kern Holoman; earlier in the day elected trustee of NCFWC to fill the unexpired term of Adelaide Fries, a position she retains for most of the rest of her life

May — widely cited in paid advertisements as a supporter of Frank Graham for U. S. Senate in a complicated election where Graham narrowly loses, in the primary, to Willis Smith.

11 May — among the hostesses greeting Democratic Convention delegates in the Graham room

24 May — attends luncheon of Olivia Raney Library Board honoring a departing staff member

29 May – 3 June — attends, as trustee, GFWC convention in Boston, with Mrs. R. N. Simms; speaks on Youth Conservation

26 June — Dr. Highsmith gives his granddaughter, Lula Marion Highsmith, in marriage, Green Cove Springs, Florida; earlier in the day, Lula Belle entertains at the wedding party with cake cutting

5 July — attends, as trustee, executive council meeting of NCFWC at UNC, Chapel Hill

August — visits friends in West Jefferson, Morganton, and Asheville; views *Unto These Hills*

13–15 September — speaks twice at council meeting of NCFWC in Raleigh, including summarizing a panel forum from the Youth Conservation movement; among the pages is Mrs. Kern Holoman

29 September — helps receive Judge (later Justice) Susie Sharp at Get-Together Dinner

1 October — Louise Wilkerson, of Richmond, weekends at 832

5 October — describes, with Mrs. Simms and Mrs. Bost, the state's Children's Charter to be taken to the White House Conference, at a Public Affairs Forum at the YWCA.

12 October — attends inauguration of Gordon Gray as president of the consolidated University of North Carolina

24 October — attends, as chair of Raleigh and Wake County UN Day committee, United Nations Day celebration on the Wake County Courthouse lawn; introduces keynote speaker, R. Mayne Albright, sometime Democratic candidate for governor

4 November — attends trustees meeting of NCFWC in Statesville, home of Mrs. E. M. Land

23 November — announced as member of Committee of One Thousand to secure a single building for State Museum of Natural History, State Art Gallery, Hall of History, and State Archives

3 December — attends Mid-Century White House Conference on Children and Youth, one of 39 delegates from NC, as chairman of the Youth Conservation Committee and member of state steering committee

December — after NCFWC acquires the large house at 1509 Hillsboro Street (for $4,000), joins Mrs. Bost, Mrs. Bunn, and Mrs. Cusick in readying the place, during the Christmas season, to be State Headquarters

1951

January — Mrs. R. H. Latham moves from Asheville to Raleigh to become hostess at Federation Headquarters

8 January — addresses Wake County Chapter of Duke Alumnae on the White House Conference

10 February — gives tea at her home for Mrs. Latham and Mrs. Ed M. Anderson, president; receiving line includes Mrs. E. M. Land, Mrs. Josephus Daniels, Mrs. Kate Burr Johnson, and other Woman's Club notables; greeters are her daughters Katherine and Louise; Dr. Winston receives

21 February — advocates at Legislature committee hearing against repeal of world government resolutions

early March — visits Louise and Louis in Richmond

15 March — dedication of State Headquarters at 1509 Hillsboro Street; receives with others, including Mrs. W. Kerr Scott, at two receptions

23 March — attends presentation of United Nations flag by Sub-Junior Clubs at 1509 Hillsboro

11 April — reports to RWC on the work of the legislative committee

24–27 April — attends 49th annual NCFWC convention, Charlotte, with Mrs. Bunn, Mrs. Latham, and Mrs. Leslie B. Evans; they pause in Statesville for dinner at Entre Nous Club; Mrs. Bunn of Raleigh elected president; Mrs. Highsmith re-elected for five-year terms as trustee

25 April — attends past presidents dinner at home of Mrs. Charles C. Hook

30 May — attends coffee given by Mrs. Josephus Daniels for her executive boards.

3 June — Mollie Harrell entertains at a luncheon for bride-elect Lula Belle at Colonial Pines

5 June — attends dinner at Woman's Club given by Mary and Henry Herring and Kenneth and Jane Wooten for Lula Belle and O. N. Rich

6 June — attends two events for Lula Belle: coffee for 50 given by Vara at 604 North Blount Street, and informal party given by Mrs. Gordon Riddick

7 June — attends luncheon for Lula Belle, given by Mrs. Simms, and bridge and canasta party that night by Mr. and Mrs. Howard Satterfield

10 June — wedding, at 832 Wake Forest Road, of Lula Belle Highsmith and O. N. Rich

26 June — assists at party for 200 given by Mr. and Mrs. Simms honoring their children and others

5 October — attends RWC Get-Together Dinner

c. 18 October — attends final payment and mortgage retirement ceremony for Headquarters building

c. 20 October — attends *Herald-Tribune* Forum, New York

8 November — offers invocation at RWC event focused on UNESCO

27 November — guest speaker at B&PWC meeting at S&W cafeteria on "Legislation"

6 December — Weldon's Thursday Afternoon Club devotes a biographical sketch of her in their "Outstanding Women of North Carolina" series

6 December — greets guests at meeting of North Carolina Society for Preservation of Antiquities, meeting at the Woman's Club; principal speaker is Kermit A. Hunter, author of *Unto These Hills*

1952

8–9 March — Louise and Louis visit from Richmond

19 March — offers invocation at RWC meeting where Hollis Edens, president of Duke University, is speaker

1 April — speaks, tracing the woman's club movement, at Lanier Book Club meeting in the home of Mrs. Dallas Holoman, Jr. (Aunt Bessie Gray)

23–25 April — attends 50th annual convention of NCFWC in Winston-Salem; she continues as a trustee

6 May — gives program at Twentieth Century Book Club

14 May — reports to RWC on recent convention in Winston-Salem, presenting local winners with their awards and honors

6–13 July — vacations in Gatlinburg TN and Fontana Dam with Dr. Highsmith, Mary Belle, and Mollie Harrell

18 July — attends NCFWC trustee meeting in Statesville at home of its chair, Mrs. E. M. Land

3 October — attends annual Get-Together Dinner at RWC

16 October — hosts Wake County Duke Alumnae at her home

21 October — birth of granddaughter, Carol Farthing Wilkerson

6 November — speaks to new members of RWC (now numbering 761) on the early years

13 November — joins Mrs. Bunn, Mrs. Land, and other trustees in launching a $50,000 Endowment Fund for the humanities program of the Federation

20 November — named to council of North Carolina Family Life Conference at its fifth annual meeting in Charlotte

1953

13 January — greets, with Dr. Highsmith, guests at reception for Governor and Mrs. William B. Umstead and Lt. Gov. and Mrs. Luther H. Hodges; governor misses event due to heart attack sustained just after taking office

29 January — pours at RWC executive board coffee hour for Sir Walter Cabinet

6–8 May — attends 51st annual NCFWC convention at Wrightsville Beach

8 May — death of J. Henry Highsmith, while she is at the convention

15–22 August — hosts, with Louise Wilkerson, the Kern Holoman family at White Lake

5 November — birth of grandson, Henry Highsmith Rich

16 November — elected to a four-year term on Board of Directors of State Legislative Council

1954

22–23 January — attends Mid-Winter Council meeting of NCFWC, as a trustee; hosts Mary Shotwell and other out-of-town delegates at her home

22 April — assists at reception of Mrs. William B. Umstead for the Wake County Alumnae of Duke University, at the Governor's Mansion

28–30 April — attends 52nd annual NCFWC convention, Asheville; is pictured with Mrs. Bost, Mrs. Latham, and Mrs. Land on front page of the Society section of *The Asheville Citizen,* 29 April

19 May — gives invocation at joint luncheon of RWC and Junior WC; her daughter Katherine, Mrs. Kern Holoman, is Junior president

22 September — gives invocation at District Meeting of NCFWC held at RWC

1 October 1954 — Golden Anniversary of the RWC; Katherine portrays her mother in a costume pageant, pictured in the *News and Observer* on 3 October

4 November — attends Sixth Annual Virginia Woman's Forum on the theme "Woman's Place in a Changing World"

9 November 1954 — gives invocation at New Members luncheon, RWC

1955

13 January — greets at NCFWC reception for Mrs. Luther H. Hodges, wife of the new governor

25 January — attends and greets at Sir Walter Cabinet meeting and reception

26–28 April — may have attended 53rd annual NCFWC convention, Greensboro

24–27 May — attends, with Mrs. Bunn, 64th GFWC convention in Philadelphia, returning via Richmond

30 July — greets at a tea for Anne Ray Moore, noted health education worker departing for a year in Burma

1956

19 January — hosts Wake County Chapter of Duke Alumnae

18 February — birth of grandson, Louis Reams Wilkerson, Jr.

24–26 April — attends 54th annual NCFWC convention, Winston-Salem; elected to another term as trustee

April — suffers first stroke

1957

13 March — past presidents of Raleigh Woman's Club receive Sir Walter Cabinet

2–3 April — attends 55th annual NCFWC convention, High Point; Katherine represents Raleigh Junior Woman's Club

14 October 1957 — birth of grandson, Christopher Louis Holoman

1958

15–27 April — attends 56th annual NCFWC convention, Charlotte

26 August — tends registry for debutante coffee for Miss Ginny Simms at home of Mrs. Simms on Wake Forest Road

1959

25 September — attends Get-Together Dinner at RWC

1960

26 January — birth of granddaughter, Martha Herring Wilkerson

5–7 April — attends 58th annual NCFWC convention, Raleigh; pours at reception 7 April given by first lady Mrs. Luther Hodges at the Governor's Mansion

10 May — attends first meeting of the Sesquicentennial Committee, Edenton Street Methodist Church, in the Joseph G. Brown Chapel

28 October — birth of grandson, David William Holoman

1961

January — at Mayview Convalescent Home recovering from a broken hip

31 March — death of stepson John Henry Highsmith in Green Cove Springs, Florida

15 July — attends last Pullen Park, Raleigh, meeting of Littleton College Memorial Association, with Pauline and Eugenia

September — returns home from Mayview to 832 Wake Forest Road

1962

16–18 May — attends 60th anniversary NCFWC convention, Winston-Salem; honored as past president

2 July — death of sister Vara Herring, in Raleigh

14 July — attends Littleton College Memorial Association annual meeting at North Carolina Wesleyan College, Rocky Mount, with Mary Belle, Eugenia, and Pauline; includes memorial service for Vara

11 September — attends annual Get-Together of RWC, "the most elegant affair the club has ever had;" is seated at table for past presidents and honorary life members, noting that she has "been confined because of illness in recent years"

6 November — hosts her Twentieth Century Book Club at home of Mrs. Louis Wilkerson, 2301 Dixie Trail

7 November — attends retirement party for Mrs. Latham at Carolina Country Club

23 December — recalls Christmas in Sampson County for *News and Observer* feature

1963

18 January — attends farewell dinner for Dr. Ellen Winston, departing for Washington to become U. S. Commissioner of Welfare

22 February — helps receive and serve at a tea, Woman's Club headquarters

4 April — attends lunch for nominees of Mother of the Year award, Sir Walter Hotel; both she and "Miss Annie" Wilkerson, Louise's mother-in-law, were nominees, and Louise sang ("Climb Every Mountain" and "Through the Years") for them

12 June — honored with other past presidents of RWC at end-of-year buffet

4 December — attends Heritage Tea at RWC, acting as hostess in Exhibit Room

1964

3 March — rides in a procession of antique cars, headed by a calliope, from Cameron Village to the Memorial Auditorium, to open first annual RWC antique show

March — endorses Dan K. Moore for governor; is added to his state advisory committee

1965

1966

2 October — death in Raleigh; funeral on 5 October at Edenton Street Methodist Church; burial at Montlawn Cemetery beside Dr. Highsmith

18 JANUARY 1948

WOMEN LEADERS PAY TRIBUTE TO DANIELS

Express Appreciation for Service to Causes "Dear to Women"

Without commission to speak for any group or any organization, we, who worked with Mr. Daniels for so many years in the advocacy of causes dear to the hearts of women—temperance, the protection of the home, education, suffrage and world peace—desire to express our appreciation of his great character and services.

Mr. Daniels had an innate reverence for womanhood, stimulated by having had a remarkable mother and a great and noble wife, to whom he was the devoted son and the ideal husband. How much of his democratic spirit came out of his own home—a truly great democratic one—his own life and that of Mrs. Daniels bear witness.

The capacity of women for useful service in other spheres than the home and church, Mr. Daniels recognized. He gave financial aid and opened the columns of his newspaper to women in their efforts to advance any worthy cause which they espoused.

Not the least of his contributions was becoming the courageous protagonist of equal suffrage, seeing in the miscalled "woman's movement" a worldwide and age-old aspiration of men and women to extend democracy. From the first Mr. Daniels was an ardent champion of women's rights, and when he lived in Washington as Secretary of the Navy, he and Mrs. Daniels became active leaders in the national suffrage movement. He was always disappointed that women did not enter the political field in larger numbers, and whenever he spoke to a group of women he urged their greater participation in politics and government, believing that they had a peculiar contribution to make in these fields. He was as much at home in a woman's club meeting or a gathering of church women as he was at a meeting of a men's club, or a political party convention.

The people of a sorrowing state and nation know that in the passing of Josephus Daniels a leader has gone. Our gratitude is immeasurable that Providence gave him to our State and permitted him for so long to lead its people with his uplifted standards in high endeavor toward righteous goals. His influence and spirit will continue a guiding hand for generations to come, and the memory of his useful and beautiful life will remain a benediction.

>   MRS. W. T. BOST
>   MRS. CHARLES G. DOAK
>   MRS. J. HENRY HIGHSMITH

Raleigh Sunday *News and Observer*, p. 24 (Society, p. 2)

27 NOVEMBER 1949

CLUBS STIMULATE INTEREST IN CHILD HEALTH

[Letter to clubwomen quoted in "Federation News"]

By Mrs. Charles G. Doak

"The Youth Conservation Committee of the State Federation of Women's Clubs firmly believes that this year women's clubs should put forth special efforts to secure better health for all North Carolina children through the public schools," according to the chairman of that committee, Mrs. J. Henry Highsmith of Raleigh, in a special message to club presidents last week.

"Why this year? And why through the public schools?" Mrs. Highsmith asks and she gives as the answer, "Because North Carolina has more money allotted to the schools for health services this year than ever before, and because, unless the school health program is made to reach and serve more adequately a far greater number of children than heretofore, the appropriation may be withdrawn at the end of these two years. No other State has such a program to be put in effect through its boards of Health and Education working together."

Mrs. Highsmith called the attention of club women to the fact that the 1949 General Assembly appropriated $550,000 to be used by the State Board of Education for an expanded school health program. Further, that this amount was estimated on a basis of 50 cents per pupil, plus $1,000 for each county. In addition, the State Board of Health has put aside a sum equivalent to 40 cents per pupil for school health services to the amount of 90 cents per child. These funds may be used for employing a health educator, for school nursing service, medical and dental examinations of school children, correction of defects, purchasing supplies and equipment, and for in-service training of teachers to teach health.

No one is happier over this opportunity that has come to provide better health for the State's children than is Mrs. Highsmith and the other members of the Youth Conservation Committee of the Federation.

Community Questionnaire.

Before World War II had ended the General Federation of Women's Clubs and the State Federations were making plans for a nationwide youth conservation movement. Mrs. Highsmith, at the close of her administration as president of the North Carolina Federation, took the chairmanship of the Youth Conservation Committee. The first work of the committee was to prepare a questionnaire to be used by women's clubs in making a survey of community resources for serving youth. This four-page questionnaire, which was to receive high praise from the General Federation and trained social workers, names as the basic needs of youth adequate health, education—both general and vocational—recreation, religion, remunerative employment, and happiness and security in the home.

In submitting the questionnaire to the clubs, Mrs. Highsmith made it plain that the State Federation, nor any of its clubs, would undertake to become youth-serving agencies, but their function would be to create interest and stimulate thinking and action toward securing for all North Carolina children more of the opportunities that would enable them to become useful and intelligent American citizens.

Governor's Conference.

When the questionnaires had come pouring in, the Governor of the State, R. Gregg Cherry, called a conference for January 25, 1946, of representatives of all youth serving agencies which was held at the Raleigh Woman's Club.

The findings of that conference named as basic needs of children those listed in the questionnaire. The State Committee on Services for Children and Youth was designated as the responsible agency for planning a state-wide program for the conservation of youth. The whole State has now become youth conscious and there is hardly a community in which there is not some effective work being done in behalf of youth.

"We do not claim credit for awakening all of this interest in our State in youth conservation," Mrs. Highsmith says, "but we are aware of the fine contribution women's clubs have made to it, and we are very proud of the many projects they have undertaken in their communities, such as scout work, nurseries, playgrounds, recreation centers, etc. in all of which youth themselves are encouraged to take part and are given responsibility."

"To see that every school child gets the equivalent in health services of his 90 cents now available is the big important work for club women to undertake in their communities at this time," Mrs. Highsmith wrote the club women.

Raleigh Sunday *News and Observer,* p. 34 (Society, p. 10)

NOTES FOR INTRODUCTION

(KMHH = Kate M. Herring Highsmith)

The Misses Herring

"We had a large family": Joan Brock, "Raleigh Residents Recall Past Christmases," Raleigh Sunday *News and Observer,* 23 December 1962, p. 46 (section 4, p. 10).

"My grandmother, who lived to be one hundred and two": KMHH, "Only One Recipe for Living to a Ripe Old Age," *The Health Bulletin* 53/12 (December 1938), pp. 13–14.

"For the past several months had declined rapidly": Wilmington *Morning Star,* 27 May 1898, p. 2, citing Clinton *Democrat.*

"My mamma takes your paper": Lucy Herring, *North Carolina Christian Advocate,* 23 March 1904, p. 6.

"Spacious and beautiful home": *North Carolina Christian Advocate,* 7 March 1912, p. 15.

"She leaves a family of bright children." Clinton *News Dispatch,* 1 February 1912, p. 2.

"Such a scene of beauty": "Delightful Barge Party," Raleigh *News and Observer,* 16 August 1908, p. 14

"Misses Herring at Home": Raleigh *News and Observer,* 12 July 1913, p. 4.

"As a photograph shows": see online album accompanying this book.

Writing for Health and Working for Victory

"During her year and a half": *Louisburg Echoes* vol. 2, no. 5 (5 January 1910), p. 1; online at newspapers.digitalnc.org.

"She has developed into a very bright newspaper woman": *North Carolina Christian Advocate,* 12 January 1911, p. 3, citing Durham *Sun.*

"Miss Kate M. Herring, the very talented and accomplished editor": *The Farmer and Mechanic* (Raleigh), 28 November 1911, p. 7.

"Joined their sister" in Raleigh: "Misses Herring to Make Home Here," Raleigh *News and Observer,* 15 August 1916, p. 6.

"Dr. and Mrs. Harold Glascock": Raleigh *News and Observer,* 23 May 1915, p. 6.

"Miss Herring was greatly pleased": *Greensboro Daily News,* 21 August 1917, pp. 1, 4.

"Miss Herring is a trained newspaper woman": Raleigh *News and Observer,* 27 January 1918, p. 5.

"She will write various newspaper copy": Winston-Salem *Journal,* 3 February 1918, p. 2.

"Recently several very complimentary editorials": "Miss Herring to Write for Papers," Winston-Salem *Journal,* 5 February 1918, p. 3.

"The other was editing *War Savings News*": Francis Henry Fries, *History of War*

Savings Campaign of 1918 in North Carolina (Winston-Salem, 1919), p. 23; online at docsouth.unc.edu.

"Every family a fighting family": Raleigh *News and Observer,* 28 June 1918, p. 8; also among others, Morganton *News-Herald,* 20 June; *Monroe Journal,* 21 June; *Salisbury Evening Post,* 24 June.

"The blackest counties are the richest counties": *South Atlantic Quarterly,* vol. 19, no. 1 (1 January 1919) p. 40; online at haithitrust.org.

"The work has been notable throughout the state": "State Headquarters of Big Movement Here Will Be Closed Soon," *Winston-Salem Journal,* 28 December 1918, p. 8.

"Ready, with a wider experience as a journalist": W. S. Rankin, "To North Carolina Newspaper Men," 5 January 1919; printed in, e. g., *Wilmington Morning Star,* 7 January 1919, p. 4.

"The work of Miss Herring was a conspicuous success": *Concord Times* (Concord NC), 6 January 1919, p. 4.

"She seems to be especially talented": *Oxford Public Ledger* (Oxford NC), 14 January 1919, p. 5.

"She has been again conscripted": "Again Under Confiscation," *Charlotte Observer,* 24 January 1919, p. 6.

"Crowded off the program": H. Galt Braxton, "Editors Will Tell World They Favor Leagues of Nations," *Daily Free Press* (Kinston NC), 2 August 1919, p. 1.

"Four Big Nights!": *Greensboro Patriot,* 2 October 1919, p. 7.

"The business and professional men and women of Maryland": "Maryland Society Completes Organization," *The Social Hygiene Bulletin* (New York), vol. 7, no. 2 (February 1920), p. 11; online at Google Books.

"You know I enjoyed that": "Prominent Men at Trinity Exercises," Durham *Morning Herald,* 30 March 1920, p. 12.

Leaving Baltimore: *Trinity Alumni Register,* no. 7, no. 1 (April 1921), p. 67.

"Miss Herring and Mr. Highsmith have a wide circle of friends": "Miss Herring and Mr. Highsmith to Marry," Raleigh *News and Observer,* 12 May 1921, p. 5.

Mrs. J. Henry Highsmith of 832 Wake Forest Road

"Two Distinguished Sampsonians to Wed": *Sampson Democrat,* 26 May 1921, p. 2.

Joe "went away on June 15 and helped marry off Rufe": *Sampson Democrat,* 7 July 1921, p. 3.

"Her dress was grey canton crepe": "Highsmith-Herring," Raleigh *News and Observer,* 1 July 1921, p. 7.

"Both these distinguished people are native Sampsonians": *Sampson Democrat,* 7 July 1921, p. 3.

"One of the most picturesque to be found in any land": "Picturesque Western North Carolina," 64 four selected views on postcards, no. 24: Mountain Meadows Inn, Special Collections, Ramsey Library, UNC Asheville; online at toto.lib.unca.edu.

"In the northern part of the city": Raleigh *News and Observer,* 31 July 1923, p. 16.

"No work I have ever done was so rewarding": Mrs. Earl Brian, "Here's a Woman Devoted to N. C.," *Raleigh Times,* 4 January 1960, p. 12.

"Young man, preferred": Raleigh *News and Observer,* 12 January 1930, p. 22.

Writing for Women

"A splendid portrait of the bride": "Raleigh Bride of the Season, Mrs. John Henry Highsmith, Jr.," Raleigh *News and Observer,* 30 November 1929, p. 6.

"Annie Bost is retiring": Meredith Council, "Farewell Dinner at Woman's Club For Dr. Winston," Raleigh *News and Observer,* 21 January 1963, p. 7.

"One of the important leaders of our time": Ellen Black Winston, interviewed by Annette Smith, 2 December 1974, Southern Oral History Program Collection interview G-0064; online at docsouth.unc.edu.

"One of the world's great movements in adult education": Marie A. McBride, "McKimmon, Jane Simpson," from Dictionary of North Carolina Biography, ed. William S. Powell (6 vols.: Chapel Hill 1979–96); online at ncpedia.org.

"A long cherished dream of a Bulletin": Sallie Southall Cotten, *History of the North Carolina Federation of Women's Clubs, 1901–1925* (Raleigh, 1925), p. 201; online at docsouth.unc.edu.

"For every child, protection": KMHH, "Council Will Present Measures to Assembly," Raleigh *News and Observer,* 18 December 1932, p. 13 (Society, p. 1).

Eleven "laws of right": "Addresses Study Class," Raleigh *News and Observer,* 4 December 1929, p. 6.

"The PTA should accept the challenge": "Wiley School Group Holds Monthly Meet," Raleigh *News and Observer,* 11 November 1932, p. 2.

"Not so, barked Dr. Delia Dixon-Carroll": KMHH, "No Sinister Motives Behind Club Women's Request for Survey of Women in Industry," Raleigh *News and Observer,* 28 February 1926, p. 13 (Society, p. 1).

"Not to be carried out": KMHH, "Mrs. Kate Burr Johnson's Work Endorsed" (subheading), Raleigh *News and Observer,* 17 October 1926, p. 10.

"The people of North Carolina will demand it": R. E. Williams, "Thinks People of State to Demand Proposed Survey," Raleigh *News and Observer,* 20 July 1926, p. 1.

"Little Miss Katherine Highsmith": Raleigh *News and Observer,* 8 August 1926, p. 13 (Society, p. 2).

"Needy unemployed persons": KMHH, "Club Women Plan for Unemployed Teachers," Raleigh *News and Observer,* 22 October 1933, p. 9 (Society, p. 1).

"We will give as we have never given before": Mrs. J. M. Hobgood to clubwomen, cited in Raleigh *News and Observer,* 18 October 1931, p. 9 (Society, p. 1).

"'I would that we Club Women": Mrs. John F. Sippel, New Year's message to GFWC, cited in *Charlotte Sunday Observer,* 18 January 1931, p. 19 (section 2, p. 5).

"Mrs. Highsmith, who is one of the nine women in the United States to be chosen": "To Be Honored by Woman's Club" (with photograph), Raleigh *News and Observer,* 2 March 1938, p. 8.

President and Past President

"When we can take tragedy out of the deaths": "Better Babies Conference Held," Raleigh *News and Observer,* 16 February 1939, p. 10.

"My purposes shall be to promote ... the American Way of Life": Dorothy Coble, "National Defense Theme Getting Hold on Nation," Raleigh *News and Observer,* 28 September 1941, p. 21 (Society, p. 1).

"Clubwomen throughout the nation": Mrs. Charles G. Doak, "Defense Chairman Issues Call For Sweaters For Service Men, Raleigh *News and Observer,* 14 December 1941, p. 28 (Society, p. 4).

"Mrs. Highsmith insists that she will make no campaign": Mrs. Charles G. Doak, "Charles Lee Smith Gift Announced by Federation," Raleigh *News and Observer,* 8 November 1942 p. 21 (Society, p. 3).

"She is widely known and greatly beloved": Mrs. Charles E. Platt, "Activities of Clubwomen," *Charlotte News,* 1 May 1943, p. 15 (section B, p. 3).

"Only Mrs. J. Henry Highsmith of Raleigh": Mrs. Charles G. Doak, "State Club-women Sell Bonds For Equipment for Regiments," Raleigh *News and Observer,* 9 May 1943, p. 18 (Society, p. 2).

"Trained, experience, efficient, wise": *The Clubwoman,* May–June 1943, cover.

"Mrs. Highsmith is a charming person": Lucy M. Cobb in the *Raleigh Times,* cited by *The Clubwoman,* May–June 1943, p. 5.

"No greater opportunity for world service has ever come to women": KMHH, "Message from New President," *The North Carolina Clubwoman,* May–June 1943, p. 4.

"The fearless spirit, indomitable faith, and will-to-do": Ibid.

"One of the main projects of her administration": "Mrs. J. Henry Highsmith Is Speaker At District Meeting In Gatesville," Raleigh *News and Observer,* 2 November 1944, p. 7.

Mrs. Highsmith "works steadily for adoption of the equal rights amendment": Mrs. Charles G. Doak, "Federation Joins State Groups To Forward Good Health Program," Raleigh *News and Observer,* 22 December 1946, p. 26 (Society, p. 6).

"My message to the clubwomen": Mrs. Charles G. Doak, "Federated Club Women Urges to Accelerate War Services," Raleigh *News and Observer*, 11 June 1944, p. 18 (Society, p. 2).

"Women should be interested in politics": "Mrs. J. Henry Highsmith Is Speaker At District Meeting In Gatesville," Raleigh *News and Observer*, 2 November 1944, p. 7.

"The State's most precious resource": Mrs. Charles G. Doak, "Youth Conservation Leaders Hold State-Wide Conference," Raleigh *News and Observer*, 17 January 1946, p. 25 (Society, p. 5).

"White People, Wake Up": 1950 Senate campaign flyer, signed "Know the Truth Committee," in Allard K. Lowenstein Papers (no. 4340), Southern Historical Collection, UNC-Chapel Hill; online at ncpedia.org.

"I recognize in [Frank P. Graham] the qualities of Christian leadership and character": Raleigh *News and Observer*, 24 May 1950, p. 7 (among others).

"Stand on world government": "Traditional Design Topic of Club Program," Raleigh *News and Observer*, 12 April 1951, p. 14.

"Since his young manhood": *Charlotte Observer*, 11 May 1953, p. 18.

Kate Herring Highsmith as Writer

"The best part of the work she did": "Women We Know," *Raleigh Times*, c. 15 May 1950.

"Her best work has been in popularizing the department": "The Mirror," *The State Journal* (Raleigh), 1 February 1918, p. 7.

"What is food for flies is poison for man," "Eat vegetables": "Editorial Brevities," *The Health Bulletin* 30/1 (April 1915), p. 3.

"Moral, physical and economic ravages:" "Maryland Society Completes Organization," *The Social Hygiene Bulletin* (New York), vol. 7, no. 2 (February 1920), p. 11; online at Google Books.

CPSIA information can be obtained
at www.ICGtesting.com
Printed in the USA
BVHW071431181120
593625BV00008B/559